An Ethnographic Study of Traditional Money

A Definition of Money and Descriptions of Traditional Money

CHARLES J. OPITZ

First Impressions Printing, Inc.
1847 SW 27th Avenue
Ocala, Florida 34474

 For information, address Charles J. Opitz, c/o First Impressions Printing, 1847 S.W. 27th Avenue, Ocala, Florida 34474. 352-237-6141

Library of Congress Cataloging Card Number:
ISBN 1-887930-11-6

A pamphlet is separately available from the author or your book seller which gives the current value for many of the items described.

Introduction

This is the only recent book to attempt to list most forms of traditional money (primitive money and odd & curious money) and describe how the items were used and valued by the people who used them.

I explore the definition of money as defined by economists, economic anthropologists and others. Many writers define money in many different and, in some cases, contradictory ways. I also attempt to define money in a more liberal way than most others.

Pictures of many of the items are included with a ruler to show their approximate size.

Many traditional money items continue to be used along with modern money. These items are, in many cases, used to purchase wives or fulfill other traditional obligations that cannot be fulfilled with modern money.

In the past in the United States these items were called odd & curious money. In Europe they are called primitive money. In Australia and among the native peoples they are called traditional money. No one term accurately describes all these items. I personally feel the term "traditional money" more accurately describes the majority of the items. It is also a more friendly term, and few people think of themselves (or are they) primitive or odd. Because a people use something different from what we use, they are not odd or primitive. Some of the money described is more complex than our money.

I have studied and collected traditional money for more than 42 years. Much information has been obtained by visiting many of the areas where much traditional money is still being used. I have visited the following areas: Papua New Guinea, Trobriand Islands, Solomon Islands, Thailand, China, Japan, India, Egypt, Turkey, Morocco, Ghana, Hong Kong, Irian Jaya, Bali, Sumba Island, Flores Island, Timor Island, Sulawesi, Sumatra, Ivory Coast, Macao, as well as Europe (many countries), Canada, Mexico and Russia. In many cases the natives gave me much information about traditional money currently being used at the time of the visit and other items that had been used in prior times. I was able to purchase many of the items described to me by the natives.

All of the pictures following the bead section are from some of my trips to visit and see first-hand the people actually having and using the traditional money items. Except where noted, all pictures were taken by the author and are of items in the author's collection.

Because much of the information came from only one source, and in many cases there are conflicting facts and opinions, some of the information is subject to error. Please excuse any errors. I would be grateful for any corrections or additional information you might have on any of the items listed or of other items that should have been listed.

Since I have given summary information on most of the items, I have attempted to give my source for that information, and that source should be consulted for additional in-depth information on the subject for those of you who want to study an item in more detail. I have tried to give only summary information on each subject because to give detailed information would have expanded this book to thousands of pages, resulting in an impossible book to read.

Acknowledgments

I am especially thankful to my late mother, Frieda, and my late father, Charles, for their encouragement and appreciation of my numismatic hobbies and all the numismatic items they bought me in my youth.

I wish to thank the late Gale Highsmith and the late Richard Rosholm for kindling my interest in traditional money (odd & curious money) in 1958.

For suggesting and encouraging me in 1975 to write a book on traditional money, I am indebted to Ken Bressett, retired Education Director and past President of the American Numismatic Association.

I am thankful for the use of photographs by Ken Bressett, Thomas Lautz and Radford Stearns. I also want to thank William & Rita Rosenblum, Scott Semans & Georgé Fisher for reviewing this manuscript for errors and omissions and allowing me to use information from some of his pamphlets and price lists.

Thanks to the following people for providing information used in this book: Colin Barron, Betty (a native on Solomon Islands), Rolf & Ilse Braun, Ken Bressett, Colin Bruce, Dr. Jack Crawford, George Fisher, Krause Publications, Daniel Howard III, Kurt Koschatzky, Bob Reis, and Deborah Waite.

I also want to thank Mike Annis for his help in obtaining many specimens for my collection and providing information on them.

For the use of their extensive numismatic library and their encouragement, I owe a special thanks to Nancy and John Wilson.

For her support and encouragement, I wish to thank my wife, Karen.

I owe a special thanks to the staff of First Impressions Printing, Inc. for working so hard to complete this book, for their craftsmanship and caring.

Unless stated, all items pictured are from the collection of the author and were photographed by him.

Definition of Money

Money has been defined and described by many people in many ways. There is no official or generally agreed-upon definition. Merriam Webster's Collegiate Dictionary defines money as "something generally accepted as a medium of exchange, a measure of value, or a means of payment. Officially coined or stamped metal currency, paper money." Webster defines legal tender as " money that is legally valid for the payment of debts and that must be accepted for that purpose when offered." The majority of definitions of money may be classed in two main categories: those which regard money as a commodity and those which regard it as an abstract unit. The former category of definitions is based on the function of money as a medium of exchange. Most monetary theorists deliberately confine their definition to a single aspect or very few aspects of money in order to emphasize those aspects in accordance with their favorite theories. They adapt their definition to their preconceived theory. Menger is its most prominent proponent and considers money and medium of exchange to be virtually synonymous. This definition excludes all non-commercial means of payments. (Einzig p. 321)

Alfred Marshall defined money as "those media of exchange, which pass freely from hand to hand, even among persons who are strangers to one another, and thus transfer the command of amounts of general purchasing power, which are set out in clear type on their faces." His definition was very restrictive and generally reflected modern cash and ignored primitive money and historical societies. Only since the late 19th century did the definition of money cover the inconvertible paper currency that came to be widely accepted.

John Maynard Keynes felt that only the function of money is decisive and the material substance is no longer important. A broader definition is made by Edwin Kemmerer when he defined money as "a medium of exchange which is commonly accepted in payment for goods and services without reference to the character or credit of the person who offers it." Raymond B. Kent defines money even more broadly when he says "money is anything which is commonly used and generally accepted as a medium of exchange or as a standard of value."

One class of definitions holds money as an object which confers on its holder general purchasing power. Lock states: Money represents a pledge whereby men were assured of obtaining valuable things equal to those with which they parted. This definition excludes much money in primitive communities where the right of holders of money may not make indiscriminate purchases and to require sellers to accept payment in it does not exist in law or in practice.

Some theorists feel that to be money it must be accepted by tale. Ellis states: Money exists when amongst primitive peoples tradition attaches a symbolic meaning to certain objects so that they are merely counted out in payment. On the other hand, objects such as tobacco, cattle, corn, etc., cannot properly be called money because their relative value was determined by weighing and measuring, and they were not passed by tale. This definition is unduly restrictive because it rules out all commodity-currencies and even metals changing hands by weight - especially if they were assayed every time they changed hands - which for many centuries played an important monetary part in Western Asia and most parts of Europe.

John Stuart Mill states: Money is the medium through which the incomes of the different members of the community are distributed to them and the measure by which they estimate their possessions.

Paul Einzig states "The study of primitive money is not a mere matter of economics. It embraces the study of mankind from its remote past right to the present day. It is the study of the evolution of civilization from its earliest beginnings." Einzig considered almost everything that has ever been prominently mentioned as money as such. He based this permissive view on an attitude of scholarly tolerance, arguing that any narrow conception of primitive money would unduly restrict the scope of the subject. Einzig states "Primitive religion provides a strong motive for barter before the development of private property or division of labor. The innumerable variety of temporary or permanent taboos imposed on the groups is apt to lead to the exchange of the products affected against products which the tribesmen are entitled to consume. Totemism leads to exchanges between the various totemic groups." Some monetary theorists feel money has both primary and secondary function. Generally the primary functions are a means of exchange and a measure of value. The secondary functions include a store of value, and a standard of deferred payment. The economist Paul Einzig has strongly recommended that monetary economists take much more interest in examining primitive money to compensate for their previous neglect and our understanding of modern money would be significantly improved as a result. Einzig suggested the following as a definition of primitive money. "It is a unit or object conforming to a reasonable degree to some standard of uniformity, which is employed for reckoning or for making a large proportion of the payments customary in the community concerned, and which is accepted in payment largely with the intention of employing it for making payments." Einzig further defines primitive money as follows:

1. If an object or an abstract unit serves as a unit of account to facilitate barter, it may be regarded as money but the system cannot be considered to be a monetary economy. It is described sometimes as "money-barter."

2. It is necessary to draw a distinction between a favorite medium of barter (an object which figures frequently in barter transactions and is readily accepted for non-monetary uses by most if not all people in a community) and primitive money. The former is accepted for direct consumption, while the latter is accepted in order that it should be used in exchange for other goods and services.

3. Through the simultaneous use of several kinds of primitive monies does not necessarily disqualify any one of them from being regarded as a money, if the multiplicity of objects used at the time in exchanges reduces the scope of each one of them beyond a certain limit none of them can be regarded as being anything but a medium of barter.

4. Though changes in the choice of primitive currencies used in a primitive community are apt to be more frequent than in a modern community, if they are so frequent that the monetary use of the objects in question cannot be depended upon at all they must be considered as media of barter.

5. Though the use of a medium of exchange in primitive communities is not necessarily as general as in modern communities, if it is accepted in payment for one or two kinds of goods and services only, it must be considered as a medium of barter. In this respect, however, we must bear in mind that the total number of categories of goods or services to be paid for in a primitive community is itself apt to be very small.

6. Foodstuffs or other objects of small value given as small change cannot be regarded as money unless they are accepted with the definite object of making payments with them.

7. Means of non-commercial payments may be considered as money under the broad definition adopted by the author. If, however, their sole use is the ceremonial exchange of units against each other without any direct or indirect economic objective, they cannot be considered as money.

A.C. Pigou states that "a pound sterling is not a thing at all. It is open to the government to proclaim at any time that a coin or paper note or any other thing they might decide is equivalent sterling. Indeed the pound sterling has changed considerably over the years both in value and in form.

Malinowski stated that primitive societies probably adopt money mainly as a result of contact with highly advanced, money-using civilizations.

Aristotle said that "Services, not goods, make up wealth in many archaic societies. They are formed by slaves, servants and retainers. But to make a human being disposed to serve as an outcome of their status is an aim of political (as against economic) power." Aristotle did not like the idea of respectable citizens making profit by the simple buying and selling. He felt that only low-class persons made a profit by buying and selling. He did not believe in commercial trade which is where money is used much of the time.

Dalton states, "Primitive money-stuff does not have that bundle of related uses which in our economy is conferred on dollars by market integration and by the use of dollars in both commercial and non-commercial transactions." He also states,"There are no words in English enabling us to label the usage of such objects precisely: they have been called social money, special-purpose money, non-commercial money, valuables reserved for status purposes, and rationing devices controlling access to status positions. It is far better, I believe, to avoid entirely calling this subset of valuables 'money' or 'currency' of any sort, because the familiar word money is so inextricably associated with ordinary commercial or market purchases. The primitive objects are regarded as valuables to be used in special ways only; they are necessary means of reciprocal payment in social relationships (marriage), to prevent group hostility and warfare (bloodwealth payments), to elevate one's political position (potlatch, moka), and to restore peaceful relationships between persons and groups disrupted by conflict (compensation for adultery, payments to allies who have lost men on our behalf in warfare)."

One source of ambiguity in the literature is the quest for a single all purpose definition of money... To concentrate attention on what all monies have in common is to discard those clues - how monies differ - which are surface expressions of different social and economic organizations. Money traits differ where socioeconomic organization differs. To concentrate attention on money traits independently of underlying organization leads writers to use the traits of Western money as a model of the real thing.

– George Dalton, *Primitive Money*

Rupert J. Ederer defines money as "anything which is in general use in a given community as a medium of exchange and/or a unit of reckoning." The definition covers both modern money and primitive money. Ederer describes modes of exchange as:

(1) Exchange of gifts.
(2) Silent barter.
(3) Open barter with fixed exchange ratios.
(4) Open barter with bargaining.
(5) Open barter with a general unit of reckoning.
(6) Open barter with a favorite medium of barter.
(7) Officially controlled distribution.

Dalton states, "Primitive money performs some of the functions of our own money, but rarely all; the conditions under which supplies are forthcoming are usually different; primitive money is used in some ways ours is not; our money is impersonal and commercial, while primitive money frequently has pedigree and personality, sacred uses, or moral and emotional connotations. Our government authorities control the quantity of money, but rarely is this so in primitive economies."

Max Weber divides primitive money into four general categories:

(1) Objects of personal adornment like shells
(2) Utility money like grain, cattle and slaves
(3) Clothing money like furs and skins
(4) Token money like game counters and bits of fur as used in Russia.

"If a small metal disk is issued by a *du jour* government for the purpose of acting as a medium of exchange for its citizens and others buying or selling within its territorial boundaries, it is termed "money." This definition would exclude all rebel pieces, siege pieces, coinage issued by unsuccessful claimants to a throne." according to Haynes. Is the 1804 silver dollar money? It was not made by a government and it was not made to circulate as money. (World Coins, February, 1970 p. 126)

Melitz feels that money need not serve significantly as a store of value. During the hyperinflation between September 1920 and July 1923, the value of German currency declined more than 50 percent per month, certainly not a good store of value. Money goods need not be units of account. They must consist of tradeable assets. A medium of exchange must be a means of payment, but a means of payment need not be a medium of exchange. Postage stamps, gambling chips and food coupons are all means of payment, but not money. He feels that we may easily question whether any traditional monetary function except that of medium of exchange plays any role as a tool of the definition of money. Melitz feels that only use as a medium of exchange is sufficient for money. He would not say, however, that only a medium of exchange may be considered as money. Like ordinary stores of value, media of exchange clearly are more effective if they are convertible at a low cost and if they can be held without major risk of a heavy fall in value. An essential guide to an understanding of early means of payment are the basic primitive examples: the tribute, the bride price and the "blood price." He also felt that money consists of all goods that are held in significant measure in order to economize on transaction costs in the activity of trading a variety of other types of goods. The demand for the cowry shell — one of the principal monies in all human history — often has stemmed exclusively from a desire for ornamentation, especially in parts of Oceania. In many parts of the world, few items have served as money. These areas are: the Australian aborigines, the Maori of New Zealand, the Hawaiian primitives, Latin America and the Andaman Islanders in the Bay of Bengal. Different societies consider payments for different services differently. Some societies have very few services that need to be compensated, while other societies have many such services. The Kapauku Papuans have some services that we in the Western civilization do not pay for. The Kapauku must reimburse his foster father for rearing him by special payment delivered to the foster parents during the tapa ceremony. He also has to pay the warrior who avenged the death of one of his relatives. He must also give blood money for a killed enemy if peace is being negotiated.

Davies also states that money is anything that is widely used for making payments and accounting for debts and credits. Money is so useful and performs so many functions that it always attracts substitutes and the nature of money is such that a clear distinction is impossible to uphold for any length of time according to Davies p. 26. Davies gives the functions of money as follows:

Specific functions-
1. Unit of account (abstract)
2. Common measure of value (abstract)
3. Medium of exchange (concrete)
4. Means of payment (concrete)
5. Standard of deferred payments (abstract)
6. Store of value (concrete)

General functions -
7. Liquid asset
8. Framework of the market allocation system (prices)
9. A causative factor in the economy
10. Controller of the economy

Karl Polanyi states that "Modern societies have impersonal all-purpose monies while primitive economies have limited or special-purpose monies. He feels that "the money function of a standard of value or a unit of account is more difficult to handle. A standard of value is an abstract unit that serves as a numeraire for calculating wealth, while a unit of account is an abstract unit that serves as a numeraire for calculating exchange values." In certain cattle-raising societies, many transactions are carried out in terms of cattle without cattle being a part of the exchange. Some primitive money might have the limitation of not fulfilling all of the commercial functions of a modern money. Another limitation of primitive money can be that it is used as a medium of exchange for only a small number of goods and not all goods as is modern money. This means that much primitive money is not a universal media of exchange. Many kinds of primitive money do not have some of the normal characteristics of universal money like: utility and value, portability, indestructibility, homogeneity, divisibility, stability of value, and cognizability. Most primitive money has some, but not all of these characteristics. "

Pryor states, " From Aristotle onward, money has been defined as something fulfilling a number of functions, such as: a medium of exchange, a store of value, a unit of account or a standard of value, and a standard and means of deferred payments. Difficulties arise in using such lists of functions in determining the existence of money in a particular society because the functions are overlapping. In addition, although in advanced capitalist economies one particular thing might serve all of these functions, in most primitive economies these functions are divided among a series of different things and not embodied exclusively in any single one." Pryor also feels that all of the commercial functions of a modern money may not be fulfilled by a primitive money. Further, he states, " The medium of exchange in many primitive economies is used to obtain only a small subset of the goods that are produced; some goods may not enter into exchange at all, while other goods may belong to an exchange sphere that is different from that of the medium of exchange under consideration."

Pryer states that "A widely used distinction by anthropologists differentiates between commercial money (a medium of exchange) and noncommercial money (sometimes designated as a "means of payment"). Noncommercial money is a standardized stuff which is employed in a variety of social transactions such as marriage payments, for taxes or tribute, in sacrifices, in other religious ceremonies, in festive gifts, in blood money, in fines, in peace offerings, in funerals, in other ceremonial purposes, in payment for skilled or sacred labor, and in ornaments and prestige tokens. Wampum was a noncommercial money to the Iroquois Indians of New York prior to the coming of the white settlers. When the settlers came they used wampum as a commercial money. Although livestock appears to be a popular noncommercial money, it is seldom used as a commercial money. Many advanced societies have different kinds of money for internal and external use. In the United States the trade dollar was made solely for foreign use and was not legal tender. Sometimes money has a limited use, such as during a military occupation. Our military certificates are an example of a limited currency. In 1942 the United States issued regular-looking currency with blue serial numbers and a yellow Treasury seal for use by our troops in North Africa. It was planned that if our troops were captured, the money would be declared worthless, and the enemy would not have our money to spend. The bills are still legal tender today. Because they look different, most people would not accept them as money even though they are legal lender. Do they fit the definition of money?

There is ethnographic evidence that many primitive people consider money to have magic qualities. Some also use linguistic evidence which shows that money has strong religious connotations like the whale teeth (tambu) of Fiji, which mean 'sacred'.

Most writers imply that societies at higher stages of economic development are more likely to have money than those at lower levels. Both Quiggin and Einzig feel that the single most important use of noncommercial monies is in marriage transactions and that all other single purposes are considerably less important. Einzig states, "There are some monies which only measure value very approximately in accordance with the undeveloped sense of value of their users. There are other currencies which constitute a highly accurate standard. Many currencies were chosen because their material is valuable; others were entirely worthless and derived their value solely from the monetary use to which they were put. There are some monies which constitute obvious units of a high degree of uniformity and which have only to be counted when passing from hand to hand. In other words, they pass by tale. There are others which have to be weighed, or measured, and the quality of which has to be assayed or tested on every occasion when used in payment. The extent to which primitive money possesses the monetary qualities which the modern economist considers indispensable varies with extreme limits."

Most economists feel that if an item is not money, it is a barter item. It seems probable that when items became money out of barter they did so not because barter had become intolerable through an increase in the commercial turnover, but because more people found it convenient to use the same intermediate item in their transactions. (Einzig p. 354) It is difficult to determine when an item changed from a favorite barter item to a form of money. There appears to be much gray area between the two terms. These items were probably a staple item of export, a generally desired article of ornament or consumption, or a standard of deferred payment often demanded by debtors. Non-commercial requirements may also lead some items to become money. Items may be used for bride money, pay blood money, for religious sacrifices, or for fines or tribute. He also stated, " It is justifiable and indeed necessary to include among primitive currencies any object that fulfills to a reasonable degree, either the function of a medium or exchange or that of a standard of value, standard of deferred payment or means of unilateral payments."

Some people take a very narrow view of what is money and what is really only a barter item or just a valuable item. I am more interested in defining odd and curious money (primitive money) in terms of collectors of the subject and consequently what items should be included in their collections rather than some abstract monetary theory and how it relates to economics.

Generally most economists feel that money has certain characteristics that are required to be met before an item can be considered as money. The United States government states that all coins and money issued by the U.S. government are by law to be legal tender and money, except trade dollars, which were demonetized, and possibly gold coins which were recalled by the government in 1933.

Under the definitions stated above and the position of the U.S. government, how do such items as 1/2 cent coins, three cent coins, half-dimes, 20 cent coins, Eisenhower dollars, $1,000 denomination paper money, and fractional currency meet the definitions of money? I feel that items do not need to meet all the characteristics to be considered as money. Only when we look at United States money in detail do we see that even it does not to fit some of the requirements listed in prior paragraphs.

Try to use an Eisenhower dollar or a large size piece of paper money to buy something. Few people will accept a $1,000 bill or $500 bill or in some cases even a $100 bill. Does this mean these items are not money? The United States government says they are money. I believe that the definition of money needs much gray area with no hard and fast rules meant to be required of all money. It just needs to meet the majority of these characteristics.

Coin collectors will pay from one cent to hundreds of dollars for a 1909-S VDB one cent coin. Does this limit the items that are considered money because most definitions require a fixed value? All U.S. money does not have the same value to all - ask any coin collector. The fact that a coin collector places a higher value on a coin than many other people does not mean the coin is not money or legal tender. Are gambling tokens in Las Vegas money? They would certainly be accepted over large-size U.S. paper money. I feel that the period in time must be considered carefully. The German mark was used as money in Germany before and during World War II. The same mark was not money after the war. Because it is not currently money does not mean it was not money.

Who accepts the money is also very important as the definition of money includes the acceptability of money. The French franc is money in France, but try to use it in the United States. It is money to the French people - not Americans.

In summary the definition of money is different to most experts on the subject. There does not seem to be any universal agreement as to what money is. As shown above many expects have differing views on the definition of money. When we look at United States legal tender most definitions of money would exclude many legal tender items.

Items to be considered as money should have the majority but may not have all of the below characteristics to be considered as money. These basic characteristics are:

1. **Media of exchange**
2. **Standard value**
3. **Store of value**
4. **General acceptability**

Items should be considered from all aspects of use and general characteristics.

TRADITIONAL MONEY EXAMPLES

Abaquaro

Abalone (Haliotis) Shell

Abrus Precatoriuos

ABAQUARO

Solomon Islands

This shell disk armband was made with strips of disks set at alternating 45-degree angles. The shell beads are white, black and red. The same technique was used for bracelets, belts, anklets and necklaces. They were usually worn by men at feasts and weddings. They are an example of the finest shell disk money from Malaita. The workmanship is extremely precise and the quality of the shell beads is very good. A piece like this one is on display in the Solomon Islands National Bank Museum of traditional money from the Islands. They describe it as money. My informant in the Solomons, Betty, said it was used as money for bride price and exchange. The shells are always worn in pairs at major feasts. (See Dubin p. 240)

ABALONE (HALIOTIS) SHELL

California Pacific Coast

The shell was a barter item and is rectangular in shape. In the middle of the19th century the shells were worth $1 each. In New Mexico they were 2″ to 10″. At the turn of the century, Indians valued the shell at $6, which was equal to the value of a horse. (See Taxay p. 71-74)

Maidu Indians, California

Abalone shell flat beads with holes at one or both ends were used as money, and worth $1 per bead. Per Curley Mitchell.

ABOGWARO

Solomon Islands

Bracelets of shell money were worn on the upper arms with the shell beads woven in a colored pattern with the shells offset. This is the finest-quality shell article made.

ABRUS PRECATORIUS *Southern Nigeria and the Cameroons*

Small red black-spotted peas called *damba, rati* seeds and "cat eye or crab's eye" are 1/4″ in diameter. One hundred peas were worth one penny. At one time their importance rivaled that of the cowry shell. All the seeds had basically the same weight; 48 were the weight of one mitkal. At one time the abrus precatorius had the same value as a cowry. I believe the peas are poisonous so they should not be put into the mouth. Keep away from children. (See Quiggin p.83)

ABUTA - See *Mauwai*

ADZE - See Axe Money

AES GRAVE

Roman Empire, middle to late third century B.C.

The unit was one as. Bronze cast pieces originally represented one Roman pound of bronze in barter but varied in weight and size. The large pieces were not well accepted and soon replaced by smaller coins. It was a convenient medium of barter rather than a true coinage. A cavalry officer was allowed 10,000 asses by paying a horse and 2,000 asses per year for feeding the horse. A slave could buy his freedom for 10,000 asses. Various types were used in and around Rome. The most common and popular pieces show the prow of a ship on the reverse. The "heavy" Janus-Mercury series were the earliest *aes grave* pieces and it is believed they were made from 289 B.C. to 245 B.C. There are many other series of *aes grave.*

Aes Grave

AES RUDE

Central Italy, to the late fourth century B.C.

Irregular lumps of bronze served as bullion or trade items prior to introduction of coined money. In 450 B.C. one ox was worth 1000 asses. One ox was 100 lbs. of bronze. One sheep was worth 10 asses. Various weights and sizes of raw metal without any stamp or mark of value from 8 grams to over 300 grams.

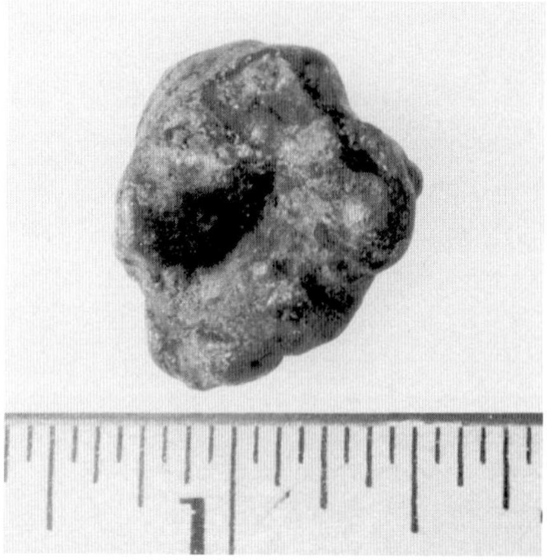

Aes Rude

AES SIGNATUM

Roman Republic of Central Italy, late fourth to early third century B.C.

They were cast bronze ingots with designs on both faces. They were not a proper coinage but were regarded as currency or exchanged as bullion. Often they were found broken into fragments representing subdivisions of weight. There are many designs, sizes and weights.

Aes Signatum - Courtesy of Radford Stearns

Aes Signatum

AGATE BELT MONEY - See Belt Money

AGGRY BEADS - See Beads

AGUT - See Flying Fox Teeth

ALAS - See Turtle Shell

ALMONDS

India, 16th and 17th century

Bitter almonds were used as small change (too bitter to eat). Thirty-two to 40 almonds were worth a pice, the smallest coin at the time. They were called Baden.

Aluminum Foil Money

Amber Beads

In 1669 36 Baden were equal to one Paisa, a small copper coin. (See Einzig p. 310 to 311) (See Quiggin p. 192)

ALUMINUM FOIL MONEY

Germany, 1919-1922 Inflation period following World War I

Part of the Notgeld series of unusual forms of money for collectors or for limited use in various cities. These notes were printed on aluminum foil. 3″ x 4 3/4″

AMBER BEADS

There are many imitations of amber and copal. Many are plastic, and many are difficult to detect. True amber will charge a natural fabric if it is rubbed against the material. True amber will chip if a pin is jabbed near or in the perforation, plastics will not. True amber will give a pine-like smell when rubbed in the palm of your hand although some plastics also will. It is best to try several tests on the material because plastic can duplicate some of the properties of amber but not all the properties. Amber has a hardness of 2-3 and a specific gravity of 1.05 to 1.09. Softening occurs at about 50 degrees centigrade and melts at 250-350 degrees. See Beads, amber.

Egypt, Russia, New Zealand

This amber does not look as good as true amber, even though it is actual amber. Beads containing embedded insects were more valuable. Amber is a completely fossilized resin that must be at least 2 million years old. It is mined on the Baltic Sea and on the shores of the Dominican Republic. All other amber is ethnic from Morocco, Ghana, Gambia, Ethiopia, etc. Copal is a resin in semi-fossilized state and is thousands of years old. It is found in Zanzibar, off the coast of Tanzania. It is also found in New Zealand, Brazil and Malaysia. Ambroid is pressed amber and is formed by compressing small pieces of amber together. (See Schulman p.11)

African West Coast, Morocco, Mali

As recently as 30 years ago amber beads were used in bride purchases in Mali, Upper Volta. One large bead was worth four cows. It is still used in some areas. Many imitations exist. Imitation amber is also used in beads.

AM FAT - See Shell Money - Tanga

AMOLE - See Salt Money

ANCHOR CURRENCY - See *Zong* and *Mandjong*

ANDANA

Solomon Islands

An associated form of poata shell ring which is notched but not sufficiently so as to be termed *mbarake*. See Poata (See Miller p. 292)

ANGOT - See Flying Fox Teeth

ANIMAL MONEY

Bamoon Area of Cameroon, Africa

This brass frog was made by the lost wax method. The frog shape was made out of wax and covered with clay. When dry, the clay was heated to allow the wax to melt and run out. Molten brass was then poured into this mold, allowed to harden and then broken. An exact replica of the frog shape resulted, no two being alike. Some question if it was used as money. This same method was used to produce Ashanti gold weights. 4″ length.

Perak & Selangor - *gambar*

18th century

These figures were made of tin in the shape of a tortoise, elephant, crocodile, cockerel, grasshopper, fish or goat. They weighed from 50 grams to 1100 grams. See Singh p.189-195

ANKLET MONEY - See Ring Money

ANT NOSE - See Ghost's Head Money

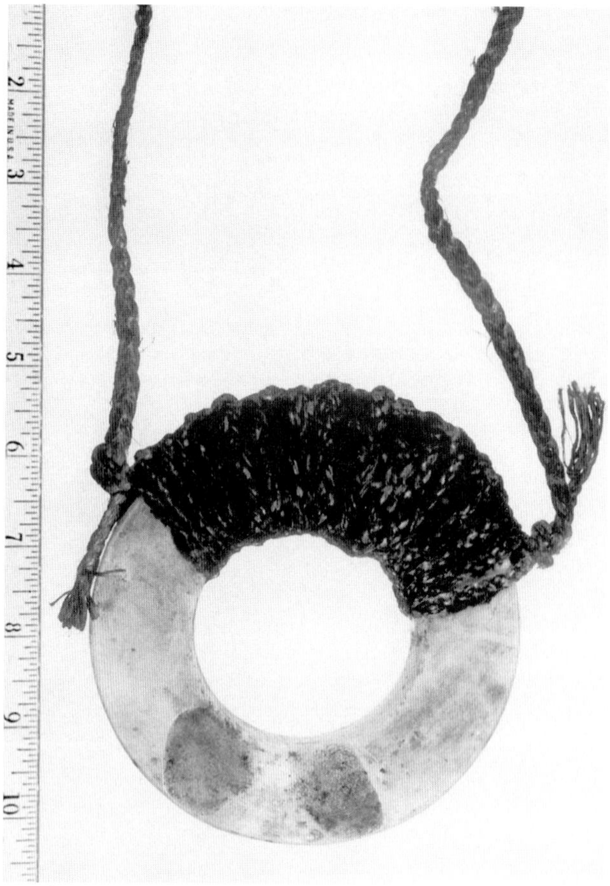

Andana

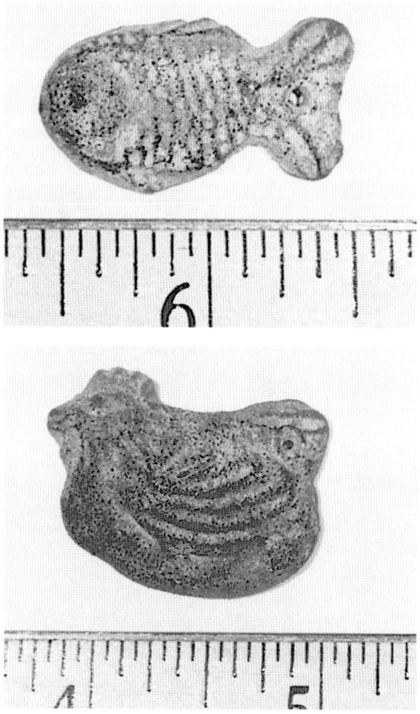

Gambar

Animal Money

Antimony Lump - Top View

Antimony Lump - Side View

ANTIMONY LUMPS

Siam

Lumps of iron or antimony metal 1/2″ to 1 1/4″ diameter. All are current fantasy pieces.

APRONS - BEADED

Irian Jaya

Because of the rarity and power of beads, these aprons were worn at some ritual ceremonies and also used in bride price. (See Taylor p. 277)

APUTA - See Mauwai

ARAGONITE - See Stone Money

ARANGIT

New Ireland

It is the most common shell money in the central part of New Ireland. It has a reddish brown color and was worth 50 to 75 cents per fathom. (See Lewis p. 20-21)

ARECA NUTS

New Britain

The nuts are wild and fairly abundant. The interior population traded these nuts with coastal peoples for coconuts, pieces of glass bottles, matches and loincloths.

ARINGIT

New Ireland

This shell string is called diwarra on Duke of York, tambu on New Britain and aringit on New Ireland. (See George Brown p. 294)

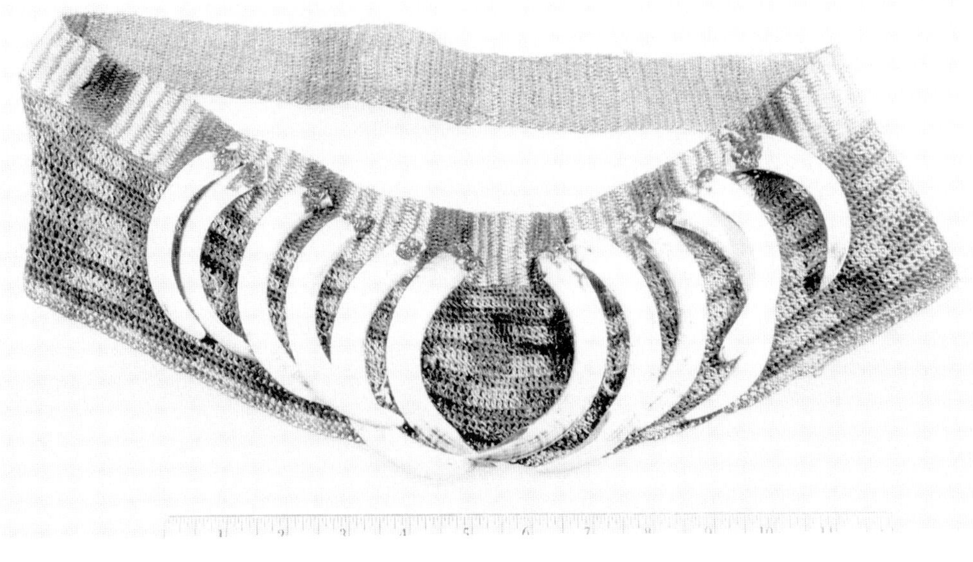

Beaded Apron

ARMBAND MONEY

Malaita, Solomon Islands

This shell disk armband was made of the finest-quality disks in red, black and white. The beads are woven at 45-degree angles and used as money. See *ABAQUARO* p. 11

ARM RING MONEY

New Ireland

Shell arm rings made of *Tridacna* shell were made on Tanga as well as on the small islands of Seleo and Angel in Berlin Harbor. A ring would purchase 500 to 1,000 pounds of sago meal. A fine ring would buy a wife or one or two large pigs. The finest pieces, called *angfat,* would buy even more. (See Lewis p.10-11)

Papua New Guinea

In the southeast, arm rings were made of conus shell and were one of the most valued native possessions. Some were made of three or four pieces of shell fastened together. The rings were the chief valuable among the Arapesh in the Sepik River area. They were made of *Tridacna* shell and varied in size from 3 or 4 inches in diameter to 8 to 10 inches. These large rings were very highly prized and even specially named. They were all imported. (See Lewis p.13) (See Mead, The Mountain Arapesh)

ARROW MONEY

Papua New Guinea

Wood arrows with hardened wood tips or with cassowary or possum bone tips were used in male initiation ceremonies. The arrows were a valued item and possibly could have been used as a limited form of money.

Torres Island

Arrows were used as money and also served as weapons. See Needle Money, Spear Money

ARROWHEAD MONEY

Africa, Tanzania and Environs

Iron arrowhead on small shaft spear. 7" in length.

Bororo Tribe, Brazil

Many different kinds. Karaja Indians also used arrows as payment in intertribal trade.

China, 1000 B.C. to 500 B.C.

Bronze arrow points were probably used as a medium of exchange in China at some period of their existence due

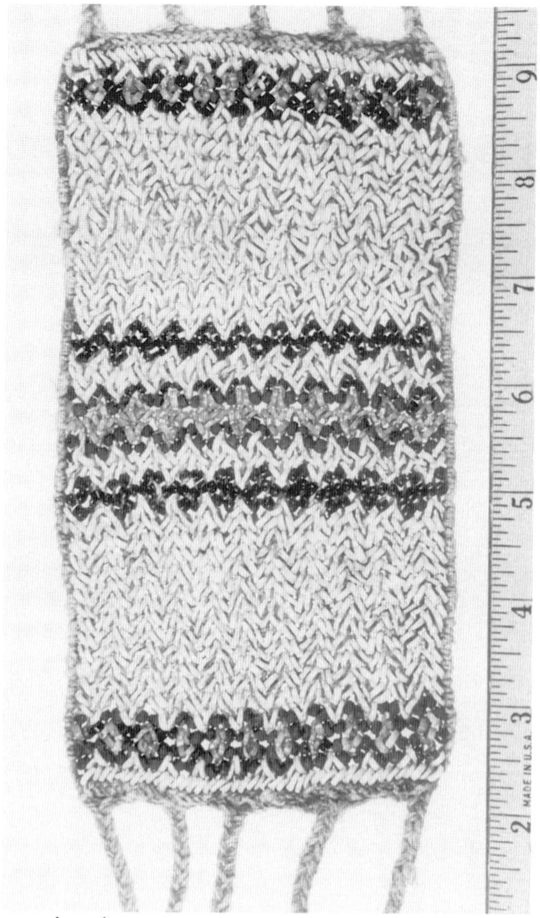

Armband Money

Arrowhead Money - Africa

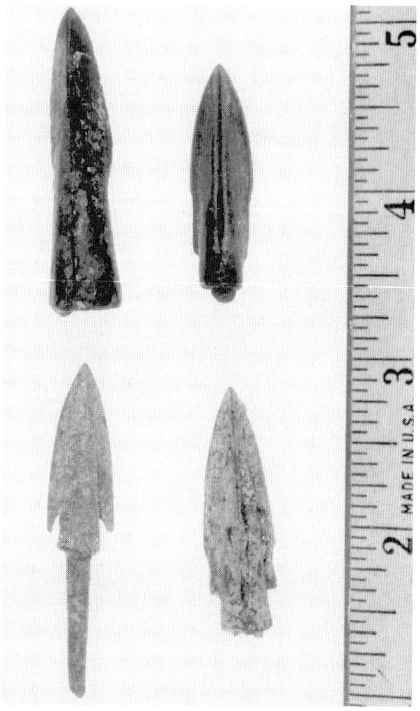

Arrowhead Money - China

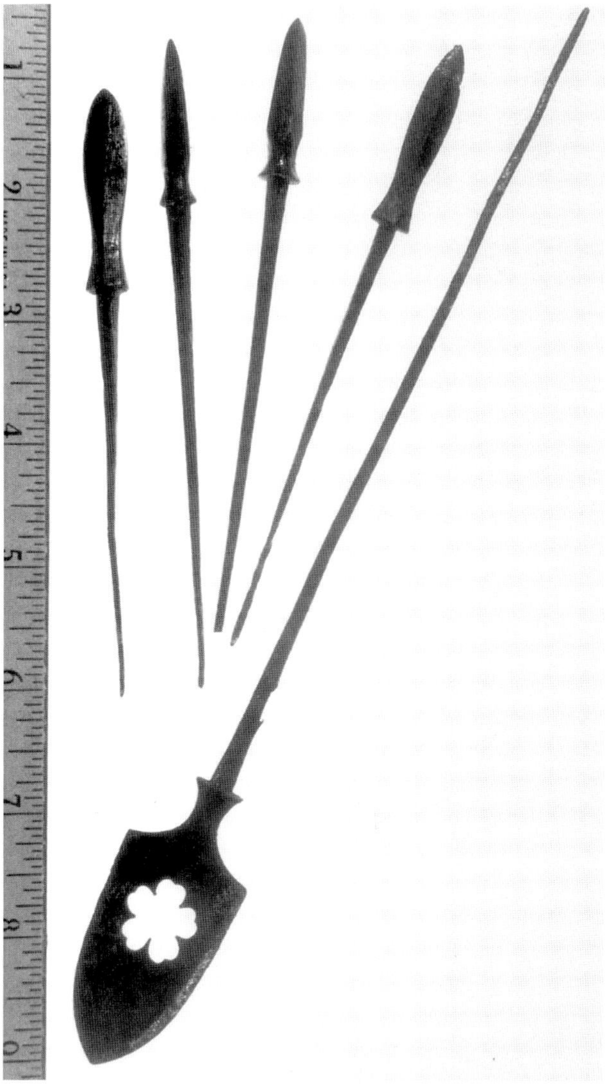

Arrowhead Money - Korea

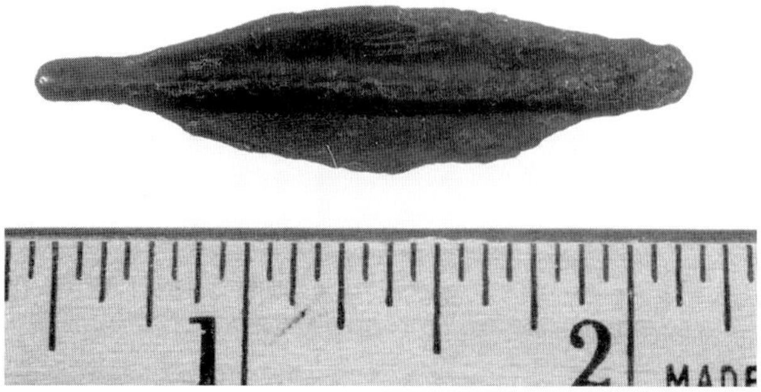

Arrowhead Money - Thrace

to their metal value and small size, according to Ramsden p. 20. Most are very small; the large pieces are very rare. There are many different types, as shown. (Ramsden p 20-22)

Japan, Prehistoric Period

Small arrowheads of agate and semi-precious stones were too precious to use as weapons. (See Einzig p. 197)

Korea, 1400s

Money in the shape of an arrowhead had letters inscribed on the shank. The arrowhead was intended for use as coin during peace and a weapon during war. They were exchangeable for four pieces of paper money but were not accepted by the people.

Russia, Neolithic Period

Flint, beautifully finished. The use as money was based on finding large numbers of beautifully finished arrowheads in hoards. (See Einzig p. 278)

Thrace, Black Sea

6th or 5th centuries BC

They are sometimes called arrows or leaves and are made of bronze. Large hoards have recently been found. They could have been a unit of exchange or a way to quantify the amount of bronze.

ASHANTI WEIGHTS - See Weights

AUMAK - See Bamboo- Papua New Guinea

AXE MONEY

Africa

Many tribes used axes as money.

Africa, Lele tribe

The Lele of central Zaire used this ceremonial axe to show the importance of the person carrying the axe. The wood handle has engraved characteristic Lele designs at the blade end. Originally the lower edge of the blade had a raffia binding to protect the carrier's shoulder. (See Ballarini p. 94-95)

Africa, Luba/Nsapo tribe

The forged iron blade is attached to a wood handle covered with lizard skin. The ceremonial adze was used to show social rank and wealth. (See Ballarini p.94)

Africa, Nigeria

The non-functional iron two headed axe was used in brideprice in a village near Obomasso, Nigeria.

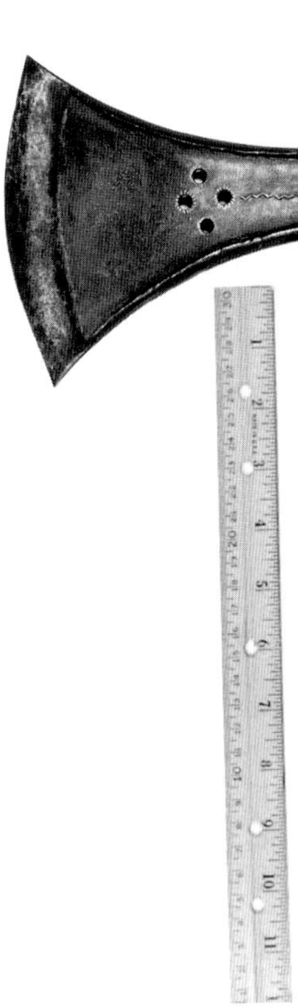

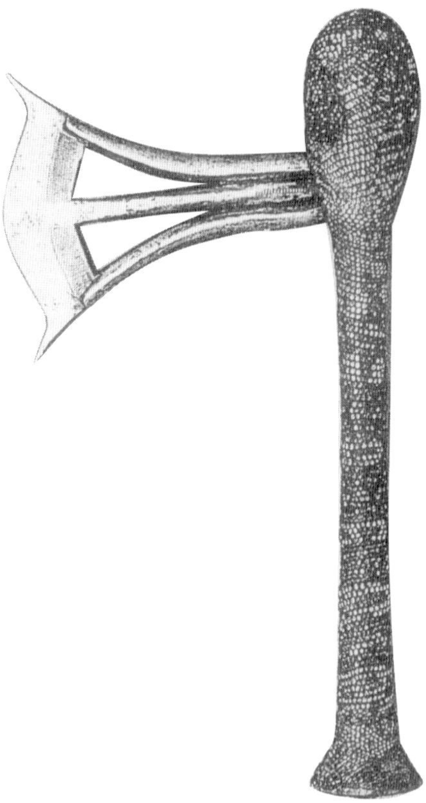

Axe Money - Africa

Axe Money - Africa, Lele Tribe

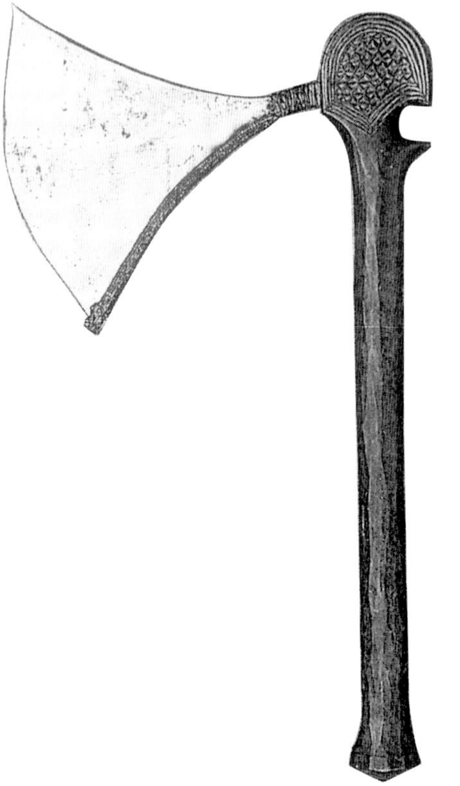

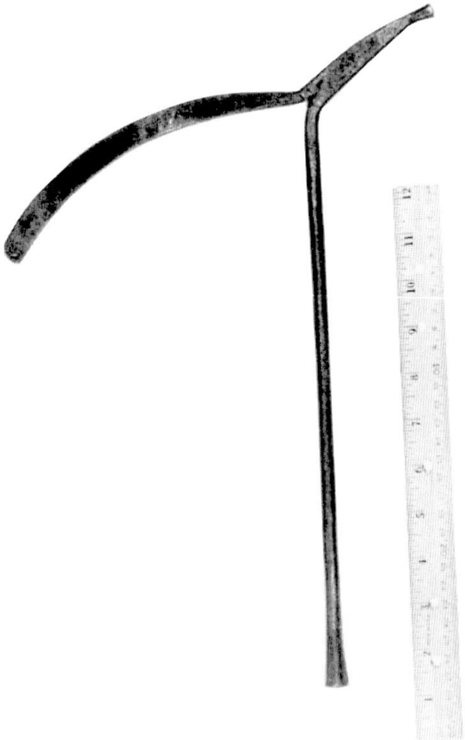

Axe Money - Africa, Luba/Nsapo Tribe

Axe Money - Nigeria

Axe Money - Africa, Songe-Luba Region

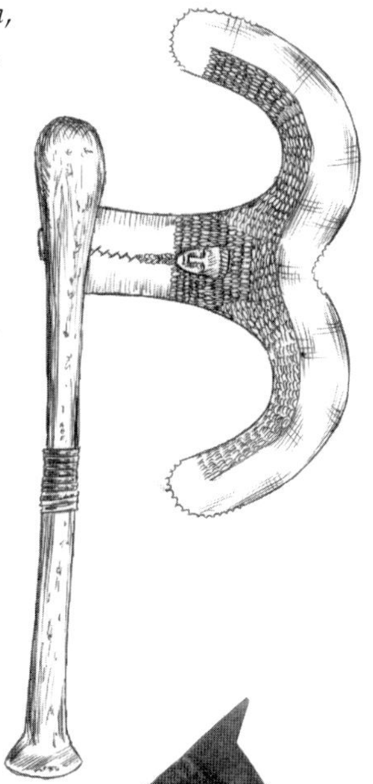

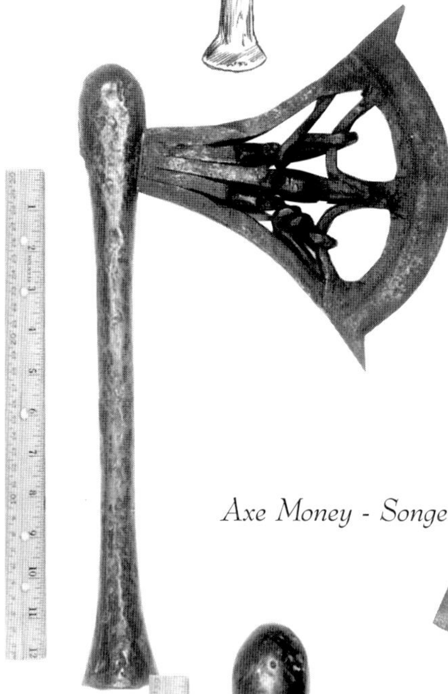

Axe Money - Songe-Luba Region

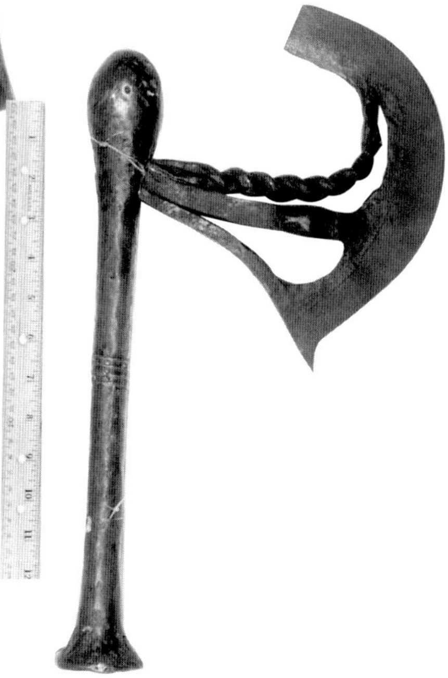

Africa, Songe-Luba region, Sapo-Sapo

These axes have a splayed blade and some have flanges or decoration on the blade in the form of a copper plug with cut-outs of various designs. Some have a copper cover on the handle. These axes are sometimes called Kasai types because they were from the Kasai River area. A few blades are made completely out of copper. Many of the axes have an open-worked copper design of a "handa" - a cross-shaped ancient means of payment - in the middle of the blade. Some of the axes resemble the Zappozap axe. (See Widstrand p. 50-53) (Zirngibl p. 124-130) (Fischer p. 160-168)

Cape York Peninsula, Australia

Stone axes were valued at 12 spears and were made with sting ray spines for the tips. These spears were traded with people 400 miles to the south by the aborigines. The southern people quarried the stone and made the stone axes there. At that location a stone axe was worth one spear. The Yir Yoront group had no stone in their area, so they traded with a series of tribes through many other tribes to obtain stone from a quarry 400 miles away. One sting ray barbed spear was worth one stone axe 150 miles from the Yir Yoront. Later, steel axes replaced these stone axes.

Canada

Metal axe head on wood handle used as money in the Wahashee Georgian Bay, District of Canada. 15" (See Mosher p. 62)

China

Hollow copper axe sometimes inscribed with a numeral. (Per Scott Semans.)

Ireland, Bronze Age

Bronze celts with a socket and a small metal loop near the entrance to the socket. The sides have chevron decoration. It is assumed they were used as money or at least in trade. (See Ridgeway, An Irish Decorated, Socketed Bronze Axe, #84.)

Irian Jaya

Used by Asmat tribe and worth a small amount of salt or a medium quantity of meat. In 1962 the quarry at Yalime produced three different kinds of stone to make axes. The most valuable was a greenish stone, the second most valuable was a bluish stone and the least valuable was a black flint. All were used in bride price, however. Even as late as 1981, they were still used in bride price. It took about three months to sharpen an axe. (See Muller p. 128)

Irian Jaya

Dani tribe. Dark Stone (deep green or black) axe blades used as traditional bride price. The blades were made prior to 1900 and had smooth surfaces. The Dani obtain their adzes from the Nogolo Basin quarry through the Grand Valley to their area. Adzes also come from the Star Mountain region and follow a regular trade network. The only difference between the axe blade and the adze is shape. The axe blade is asymmetrical along the long axis, but the cutting edge tends to be straight or S-curved. The adze, however, is symmetrical vertically and the cutting edge is crescent-formed when looked at from the cutting edge. The adze haft is T-shaped, while the axe's haft is a straight piece of wood with a hole near one end in which the stone axe fits. 2 1/2" x 5 1/2".

Irian Jaya

Used in Lake Sentani area. Speckled stone, smooth highly polished surface in beautiful greens and blues. Used for bride price. Second type called *"ormu stones"* also used in Lake Sentani, not in Ormu. Worth only 2/3 value of Sentani stone. Worth 80 baskets of sago. During the making of the stone it is believed that the stone must be constantly "rested" because if not, they would break. Therefore, each stone can be worked on for only a short period each day. As a result it takes a year to make a good axe head. 2 1/2" x 5 1/2"

New Zealand

The Maori used nephrite adzes as payment for ceding land titles to others, funeral practices, compensation for crimes and for the performances of rituals. (See Weiner, Inalienable Possessions p. 58.)

Normandy, c. 1000 B.C.

Socketed bronze axe from the late Bronze Age. These were trade items made to resemble an ancient barter axe and were found along the northern coast of France in large numbers. (See Quiggin p. 276)

Papua New Guinea

Smooth stone axes secured from the east were, along with adzes, the most important trade items. They were worth one cooking pot. An adze mounted on a ceremonial handle was worth a young pig or dog or a string of shell disks. (See Saville p. 162.) Many tribes traded axes to get them from the quarries to the final user. In some areas they were traded for pigs or bundles of salt. Many axes came from the quarries to the west in present-day Irian Jaya. As these blades moved east, they were used by the tribes along the way. Therefore, the further east they went, the smaller they became. (See Schuurkamp.) Another popular piece was the stone disk with a hole in the center through which a stick was

Axe Money - Songe-Luba Region

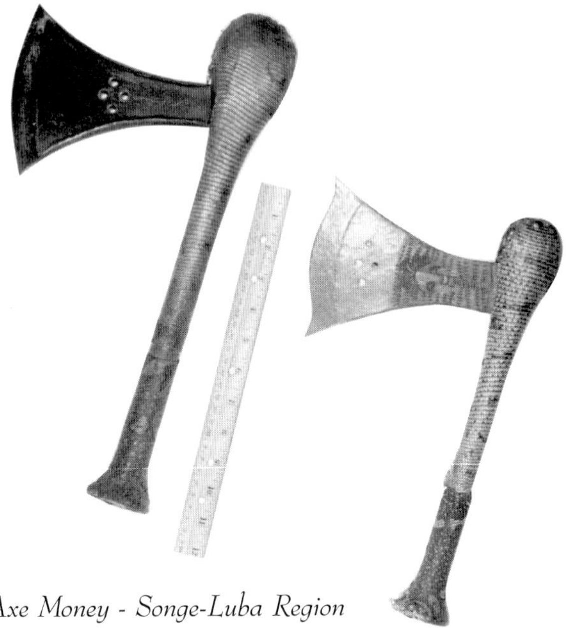

Axe Money - Songe-Luba Region

Stone Axe Head - Irian Jaya

placed to form a club. The Min of the Star Mountains, as well as the Kukukuku tribe, used them as weapons and as money. The stone disk was not fastened on the pole but was loose with a cord of plaited fiber wound around one end. When the user swung the club, the stone disk would fly to the end of the pole. This added to the force of the blow. Of course, the woven piece at the end kept the disk from flying off. A few stone disks actually were star-shaped, but they are rare. The Duna people got all their axe blades by trade, and the average male had two blades, which lasted from 10 to 20 years each.

The modern steel axe was used as a form of money by both the Europeans and the natives who obtained them. The steel axes were able to reduce the time the men spent on cutting from 80 percent of their time to 50 percent of their time. It also takes one hour of sharpening for every three to four hours of chopping. The axes moved at a distance of about 10 miles per year from the location where the axes were made to where the natives use them. Metal azes were an important trade item as well as a working tool that greatly reduced the men's labor. In the 1950s a native would have to pay 12 shillings (about 12 days of work for Europeans) to buy a steel axe from a trade store. It was estimated that a steel axe would last for 12 years in New Guinea. The wood handle would be replaced each year. There are only a few quarries in Papua New Guinea and Irian Jaya, so stone was traded from these quarries to most parts of Papua New Guinea. Axe types were Jimi Valley, Kafetu, Ganz-Tsenga, Abiamp, Dom and Yari. (See Hughes, New Guinea Stone Age Trade.)

Papua New Guinea, Bismarck Mountains

The stone axe was one of the principal measures of value along with the pig and kina shell, during the 1940s.

Papua New Guinea, Chimbu area

Stone axes were entirely replaced by steel axes by the middle 1950s. The steel axe also was, once for a short time, a form of money. It was valued at two or three pigs for one steel axe. As more steel axes came into the area a medium-size pig equaled the value of a steel axe. (See Nilles p. 13)

Papua New Guinea, Kundiawa

Polished green stone mounted in rough rattan bindings. The stone was a chert of volcanic origin. This working axe comes from the Kuli area. The Kuli people bring the axes to the Mount Hagen area to trade for salt gotten from the Enga people. Most of the Enga blades came from the Tuman quarry in the Western Highlands. They were used as a form of wealth and bride price. In general, stone axes were rarer, smaller in size and less highly polished away from the highland factories,

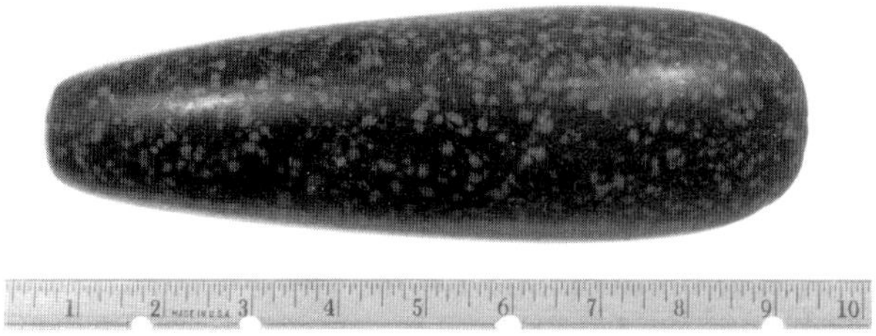

Stone Axe Head - Irian Jaya - Lake Sentani Area

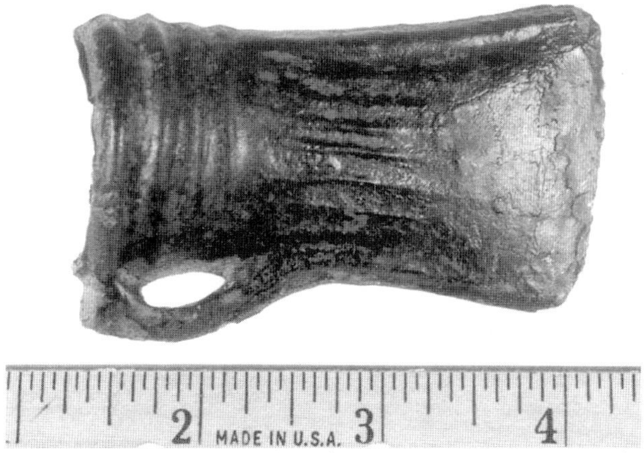

Socketed Bronze Head - Normandy

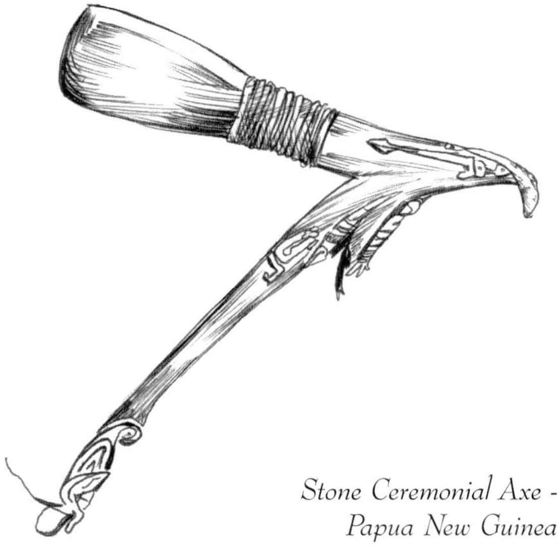

Stone Ceremonial Axe - Papua New Guinea

according to Hughes p. 134. 8"-15" length. (See Rogers p.120) (See Gitlow p.71)

Hand polished green stone axe. It takes two to three months to make one stone aze. 6" to 14". Same as above - axe head only.

Papua New Guinea, Motu tribe, Port Moresby area

Part of annual Hiri expedition. Stones were traded for adzes, which were then traded for sago. 24" length.

Papua New Guinea, Mt. Hagen

It was a thin light green stone axe in a finely decorated and patterned rattan handle. The stone was a chert of volcanic origin. It was used as a form of wealth and bride price. They now come from Enga and Chimbu Provinces instead of Mt. Hagen. Length of the haft and axe is 20". There are three kinds of axes: (1) The rough working light axe, used to cut firewood and trees and as a fighting weapon at close quarters, called *di*; (2) the bride price axe, called *gaima* or *kundun* depending on the color; and (3) the ceremonial axe called *di kurugu*, with a flint head called *rui*. The *rui* is about 5 inches wide at the sharp end, 2 1/2 inches wide at the shaft and about 10 inches long. The ceremonial axe called *di kurugu* is the type known as the Hagen axe. It shows the best workmanship. The stones come from only two quarries. One of the quarries was on the Ganz River, a tributary of the Jimi River. The other was on a spur above the Wagi River. The stones were selected and rough-chipped at the quarry. Then the blank was taken back to the village and polished. A sandstone block and water were all that was used to polish the axe head. The blank was rough chipped in about 30 minutes, while it took about three days to polish the axe head. The bride price axe is much larger than the other axes and was probably never used for cutting. The Jimi people traded the axes for cowry shells. The axes were then traded to others who then further traded the axes until the axes arrived at their final destination. The payment for a bride consisted primarily of axes, with three or four being bride-price-type axes and the remaining axes being the ceremonial axe type. The ceremonial axe was the standard of value. The bride price axe is long and very thin. Only the ordinary axe was not used for these purposes. There was a constant trade between axes, cowry shells, green snail shells, gold lip shells, orchid fiber bands, pigs, salt and Bird of Paradise plumes. When steel came to the area, it only replaced the ordinary axe and not the ceremonial axe or the bride price axe. The largest and most prized axes were carried in beautifully carved wood holders. Stone adzes made by the Wain and Naba people were traded to the Komba area for pigs and *tambu* shells. The

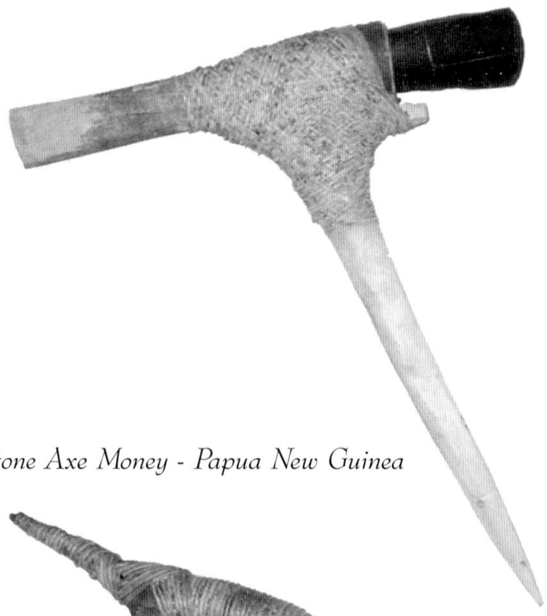

Stone Axe Money - Papua New Guinea

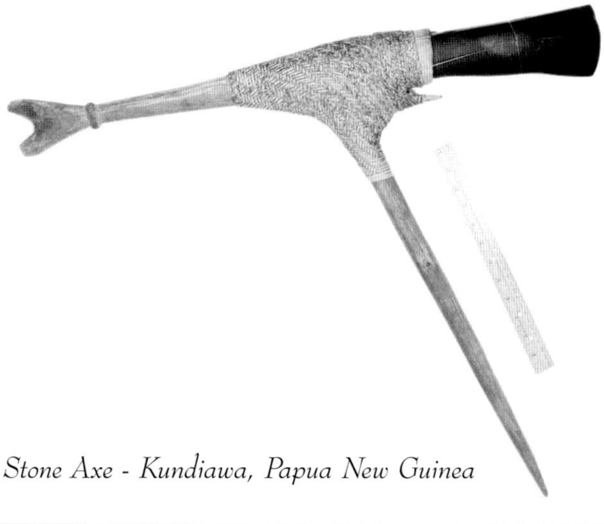

Stone Axe - Kundiawa, Papua New Guinea

Stone Axe, Mt Hagen, Papua New Guinea

Hagen axes came from the Jimi and Koronigl Valleys. At present, soft-stone versions of the Hagen axe are made for sale to tourists. They use medium gray stone called *koban* and a stronger grey-green stone called *ilipol*. The Kandangei used seven or eight different types of stone axes. The older men could tell the difference between them and therefore the quarry the stone came from. The axes were traded from one area to another. (See Healey p. 196.) Ceremonial axes were stored and exchanged but rarely used or carried except in warfare and dancing. An adze has the edge of the blade at a right angle to the handle. (See Gitlow p. 77-78) (See Vial)

Papua New Guinea

Steel axes were introduced by Europeans when they arrived. They were considered a valuable shortly after contact but lost that status as more steel axes were introduced. At present they are merely tools and are not considered valuables.

Stone Axes, Papua New Guinea

Solomon Islands

In the 1880s stone axes were used. Charles Woodford, an explorer, said he purchased 60 or 70 stone axes for one piece of tobacco each.

South America and Mexico

In general, the axes were made to a uniform range of sizes, forms and weights. The axes were not working axes, as they were not of a size and strength that they could be used for most purposes for which an axe would be used. Many of the axes also had blunted edges. Some axes were bundled, and most varieties were found in graves in large numbers. None of the axes show any sign of wear. If they had been used, certainly some would show some signs of use. These circumstances would tend to indicate that the axes would have more of the requirements for money than for a utilitarian weapon. Bundling was done only with the smaller pieces and it was done primarily in standard units of 20 pieces (or in one case of five pieces and 10 pieces). Arsenic was used in all axes and its content by weight varied from .1 percent to 6.5 percent. Most of the pieces in the Mexican area were in the range .1 percent to 10 percent. In the Ecuadorian area it was .5% to 2.0%. Smelting of arsenic-bearing copper ore caused the arsenic content and not some process of adding arsenic to the material later.

(The number designations and information come from Axe-Monies and Their Relatives by Dorothy Hosler, Heather Lechtman, and Olaf Holm)

Axe Money - Peru

Ecuador

They are found in the central and south coast of Ecuador. The heavy axes were made by casting the metal and then hammering and annealing the blank into the finished axe. One writer said that the axes were used as bridewealth by the people of the Quito area. The family of the bride would receive two axes in the bride exchange. The axe circulated as wealth in the Ecuadorian region prior to the Spanish invasion.

Axe Money - Equador - Cast

Mexico

Thin, stylized copper axe or hoe blades. Also called *tajaderas* and now *coas*. There are two basic shapes: One is a T-shaped form with down-curving arms, and the second is chisel-shaped with flaring at the end instead of the curved arm, which is also much thinner. They are found in Oaxaca, Guerrero, Puebla, Morelos, the Valley of Mexico and the Maya area. Originally they were only of high value if brightly polished. In 1548, the new pieces were valued at 1 1/4 Spanish reales each. If worn, they were refused and were sold to be melted at 10 to a Spanish reale. T-shaped aze was worth 250 cocoa beans. Before the Conquest a single axe would purchase eighty slaves but later depreciated to 2.5 slaves per axe. Now called *coas,* they come in many shapes and sizes. 1 1/2" to 7" in length. (See Sigler p. 30) (See Taxay p. 44-46)

Axe Head - Mexico - Coas

Mexico

These axes were introduced to West Mexico from Ecuador. The first type started in about 800 A.D. and continued to about 1200 A.D. The second type started shortly after the first type stopped and lasted until the Spanish invasion. Types 1a through 5c: Almost all Ecuadorian axes have linear grooving of the surfaces, while the Mexican types do not. All Mexican axes have raised flanges along the shank edges except for the West Mexican type, 1a, which is too thin to have such treatment. These axes are very common artifacts in Mesoamerica. They contain a large amount of arsenic. It is very likely that the mushroom-shaped axe was used for tribute and exchange and also was in a religious context.

Mexican Axe

Type 1a and 1b. Type 1a is most common, and type 1b is so small that the shoulder of the axe is not pronounced and therefore appears to be a triangle. They are normally found stacked and in packets. Type 2 is less common, as is type 3a. All these pieces are thin with edge ridges on the handles. The small axes are too small for ridges, but the edges are thickened to have greater strength. Copper-arsenic bronze is the material they are all made from. The arsenic strengthens the copper and changes its color to a pale pink, and if the arsenic present is 7 percent or higher the copper alloy looks silvery-white. The Manteno-Huancavilca and Milagro-Quevedo people, who are believed to have produced and used these axes, lived from about 800 A.D. to 1500 A.D. The pieces are

North Andrean Axe Money

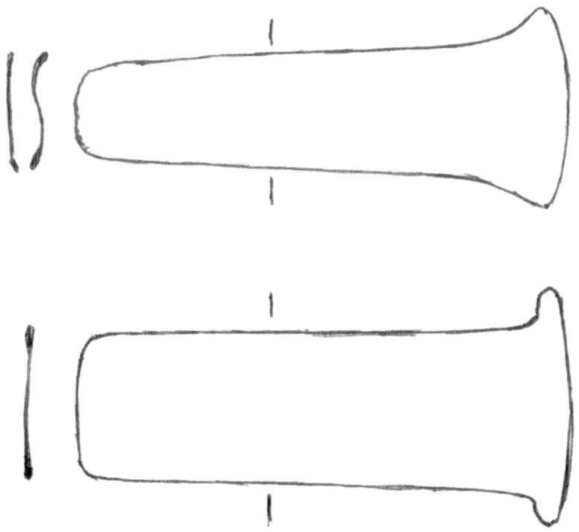

Type 1A & 1B

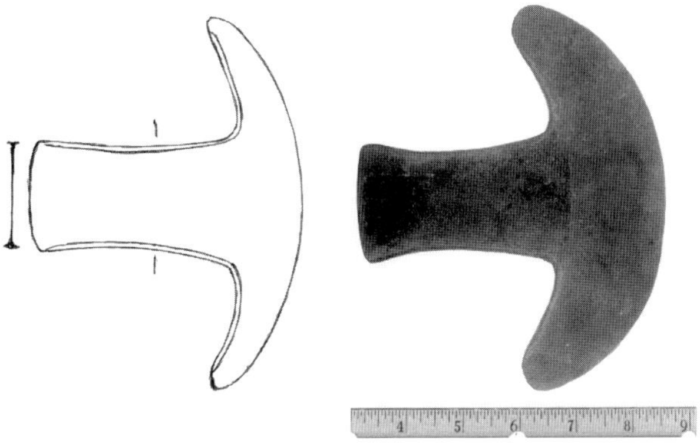

Type 2A & 2B

Type 3A

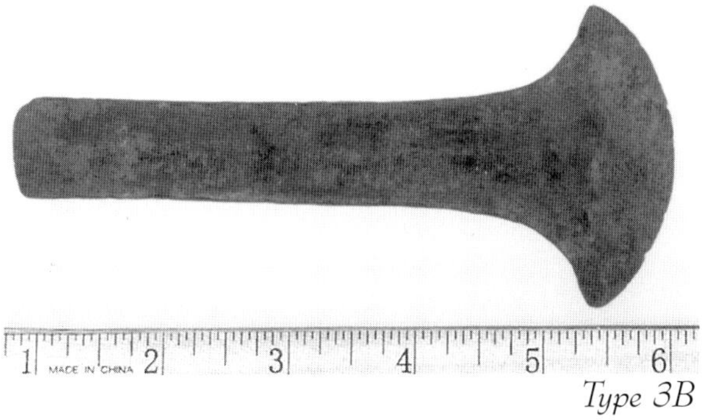

Type 3B

Type 4A

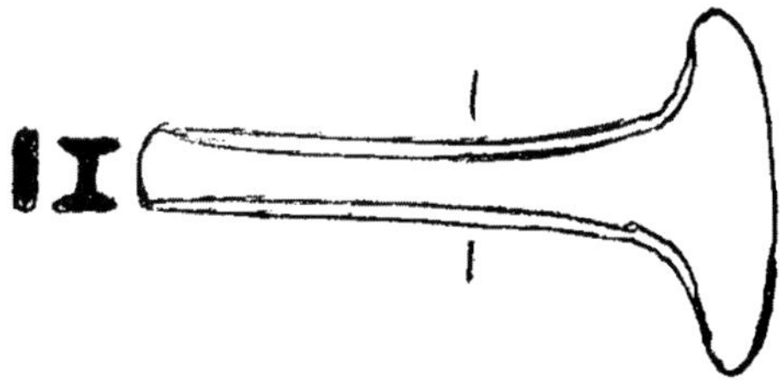

Type 4B

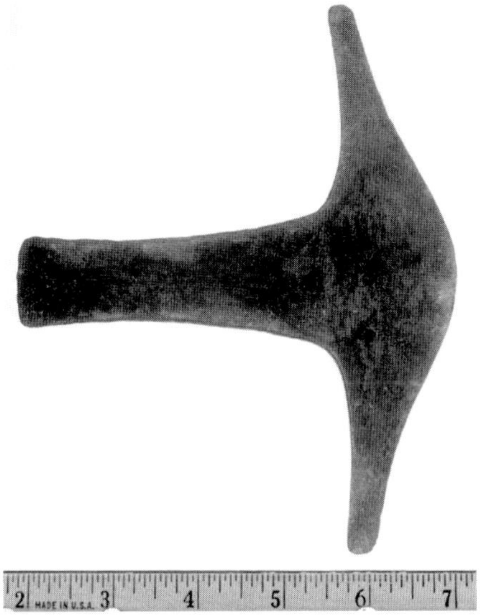

Type 5A

Type 5B

all from single or multiple graves. They were all near human remains. The tiny axes were found in packets of 20 or more.

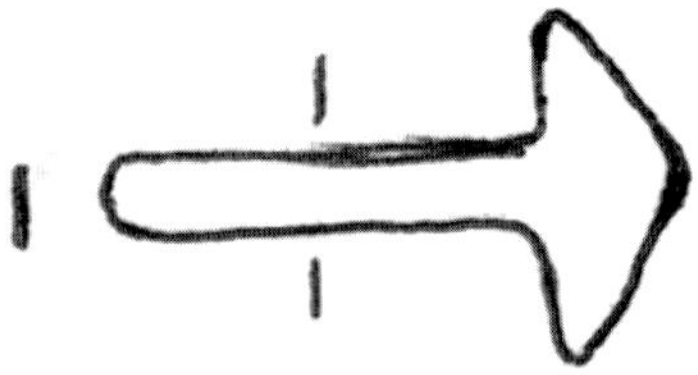

Type 5C

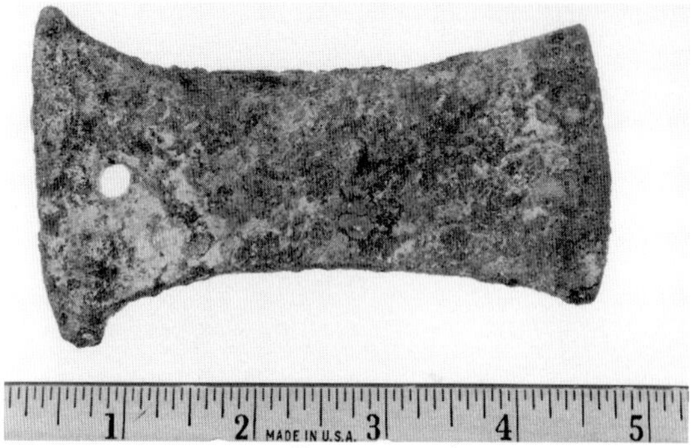

Axe Money - Micellaneous Shape

Naipe

In Peru a type of axe called the *naipe* was used as money. Shimada believes the *naipes* were a form of primitive money. It comes from the Lambayeque Valley complex and is most closely related to the Ecuadorian axe money. The *naipes* are sometime found in packets of up to 500 pieces. They date to the middle to late Middle Sican (900 A.D. - 1100 A.D.) All are the same basic shape. Some have a raised oval area in the center of the *naipe,* while others have a convex bulging on the two long edges. Most naipes were found in burials. The number of *naipes* in a tomb was related to the status of the person. The higher the status, the larger the number of *naipes* in the tomb. They were made of copper-arsenic bronze with a high arsenic content. The high arsenic content would have given the piece a pale pink color. No miniatures are known to exist. Some experts feel that the *naipes* were not money because of their limited geographic area and the fact that they were found with agricultural implements made of the same basic material. The *naipes* could have been some form of tribute or burial goods with strong ritual connotations.

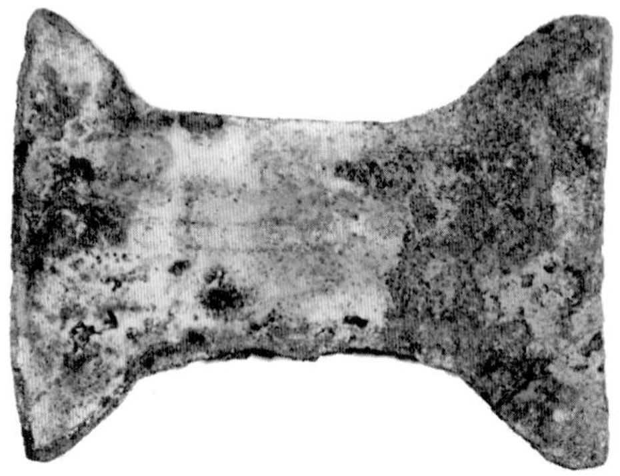

Naipe

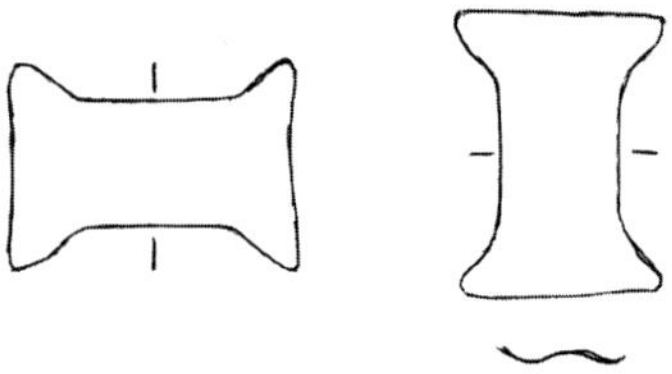

Feathers

The feather was used in the Andes in Peru. There are two types of feathers. One has the socketed end formed by turning over the two edges of metal and the second type has a spatulate end. They are said to be thin copper sheet used as headdress ornaments.The feathers are made from copper arsenic.

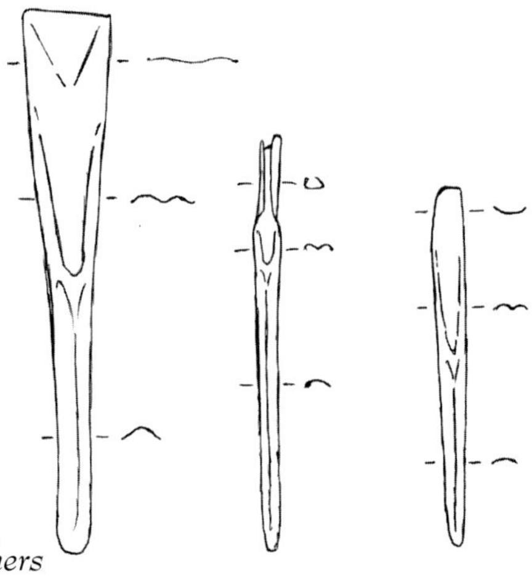

Feathers

Hides

This piece is made from thin copper-arsenic bronze plate with a raised edge flange around the entire piece. It is different from the other Equadorian axes. It is quite rare; less than 10 are known to exist.

Insignias

Made from thin copper-arsenic bronze plate with a raised edge flange around most of what normally would be the cutting area of the insignia, if it were an adze. Larger and possibly had more value than the normal axes.

Llamitas

These copper-tin objects are llama-like in shape, and many have one to three holes at the top for possibly attaching to clothing or being worn as a pendant. There are several other items that are very similar in general shape. Since they are found in graves, it has been speculated that they might also have been used as money. There is no good evidence to prove that, however.

Trobriand Islands, until 1910

Stone ceremonial axe blades called *beku* were used in ceremonial exchanges, bride price and other important purchases as well as in *kula*. See *Beku.*

Trobriand Islands

Stone for the blades (*benam*) of such axes was quarried on Murua and traded to Kiriwina, one of the Trobriand Islands, where it was polished and hafted. The carving of the haft was also carried out in Kiriwina. The finished axes were prized items used for bride-price and gift exchanges. (See Newton)

United States

Trade stone axes of heavy construction by American Indians were used as a medium of exchange.

Axes made from steel with touchmarks were used in trade. A French pipe-tomahawk with a bronze bit was used as a medium of exchange.

See Beku, Dao, Fang Axe, Munshi Axehead, Throwing knives, Zappozap.

AXEHEAD - See Munshi Axe Head

BABYLONIAN CLAY TABLET - See Clay Tablet

BAG MONEY - See *Grivna, Bilum*

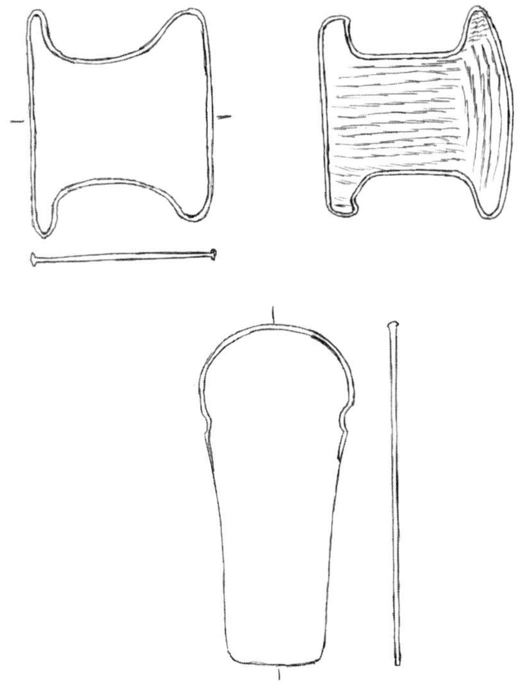

Hides - Top, Insignia - Bottom

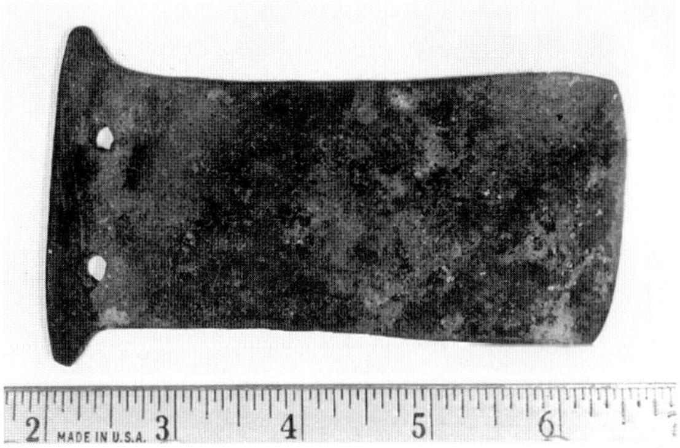

Axe Money - Looks Similar To Hide

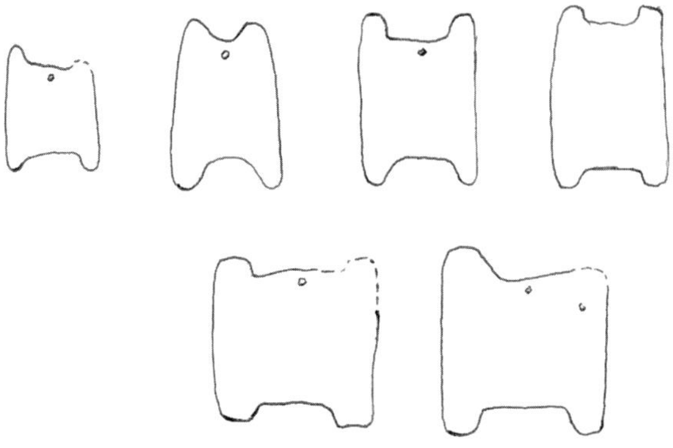

Llamitas

Steel Axe Head - United States

BAGI SHELL MONEY

Papua New Guinea

Bagi were also called "soulava" or "sounava" and now are called "vaygu'a". It was one of the main items used in Kula.

This shell necklace was made of red sapi-sapi shells (mainly made of *Chama Imbricata* or *Pacifica*) with a pendant made from the interior of the helmet shell. From the lip of the wide end of pendant hang edge to edge shell strings of sapi-sapi with a cut piece of pearl shell at the end. It was traded from Rossel Island to the Trobriand Islands. *Bagi* were used in payment for bride price, pigs, canoes, etc. These necklaces are a major Kula valuable traded in clockwise direction from island to island. The terms *soulava* and *bagi* describe different items in different places and at different times, but generally we call them all *soulava* or *bagi*. Sometimes it is said that more valuable pieces are called one name or the other. I have used *bagi* as a general term to describe all necklaces of the *bagi* and *soulava* type. The *bagi* consists of four parts: head, abdomen, ear and tail. The head is currently always a cowry, the abdomen and ear are the red shell disks and are marked by two white shell disks. The tail is the pearl shell. The best *bagi* have decorations suspended from the tail. The whole decoration is called *dauyoyo* and the cowry is called *surasura*. The sapi sapi shells are attached to a pendant made from the interior of a helmet shell, with black banana seeds and beads strung end to end as tassels with ovula ovuna shells at the end. The other ends are attached to the edges of the helmet shell. The sapi-sapi shells are now made only on Sudest and Rossel Island and some surrounding islands. Some are considered so valuable they are worn only on very festive days and have a name and history of their own. They are used for payments of bride price, canoes, pigs, mortuary commitments and land access. The shells (Chama) are collected in Yela (Rossel Island) and Vanatinai (Sudest Island) and are made into disks there. Some informants have said that in early times, *bagi* were from Sinaketa. The men do most of the shell-diving, but the women are expert bagi makers. Each bagi has a name, and they are ranked into three classes. The best *bagi* have very thin shell disks and smooth edges from much handling and travel around the Kula ring. The older *bagi* from the time of Malinowski had helmet shells instead of the modern gold-lipped oyster or pearl shell. *Bagi* are ranked from lower to higher as follows: Bagitorobwa, Taituyanabwa, Bagisam, Bagiyeru, Bagidou and Bagiriku. The criteria are age, history, color and size of the disks. The best color disks are salmon-red, with brown-red and dark red being lower in value. A high ranking shell string will look as thin as a fine fishing line and feel like oil. Only women wore the *bagi*.

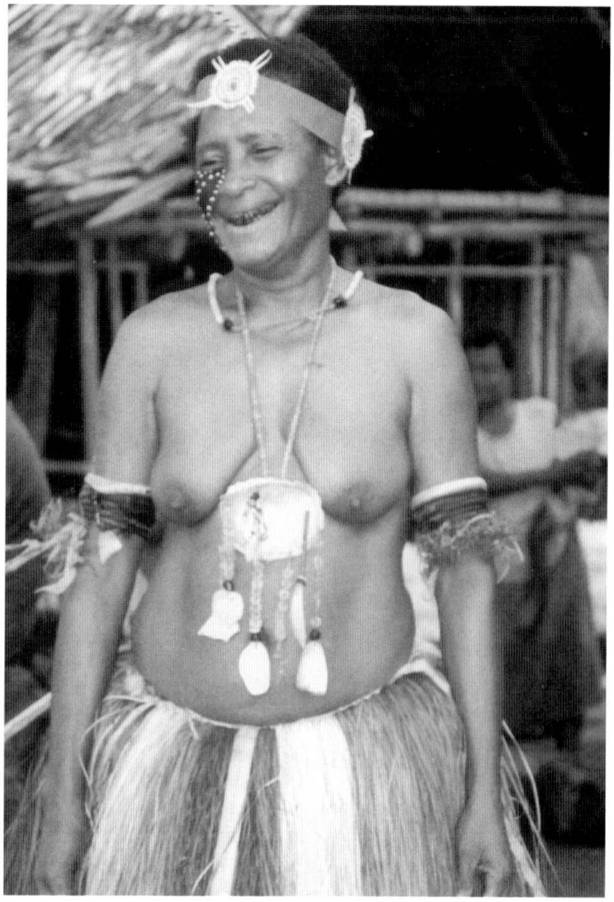

Trobriander Wearing A Bagi

Bagi

Bailer Shell Money

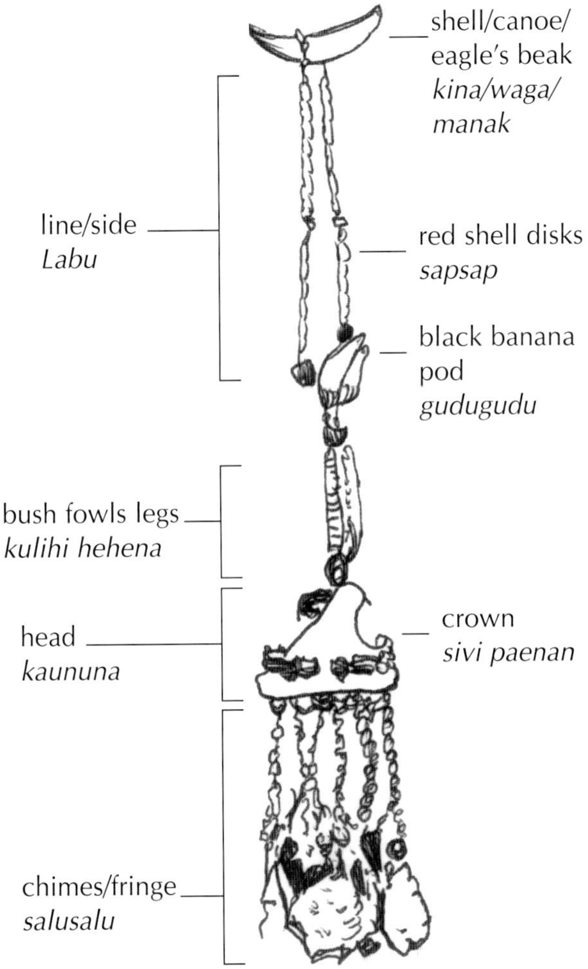

Bagi Necklace With Names

In the Trobriand Islands production of bagi stopped in the 1930s. The production continued on Rossel Island after World War II and increased during the 1870s and 1980s. Most were exported through the Catholic Mission. In the 1990s a European in the Trobriands is having the necklaces made in the Trobriands with shells imported from Rossel Island. (See Akin p. 146.) See Melo Shell. See Kula.

BAILER SHELL MONEY

New Guinea

Melo or Bailer or moon shell (*Cymbium*) were used as a breast ornament, decoration on the head, chest or penis. It was normally holed to be worn close to the body. They were also called *gam* among the Wola of Southern Highlands. Twenty bailer shells, also called *alup*, would purchase a canoe among the Badu people. In the Mount Hagen area, bailer shells were used as a part of bride price. A bride price could be ten pigs and five bailer shells. The amount and kind of item will vary. They were always considered scarcer than kina shells. The bailer shell was worth a pig or a kina shell. In about 1934, in the highlands one large bailer shell was worth 2 pigs. (See Quiggin p. 175)

BAKHIA

Santa Isabel, Solomon Islands

This highly prized breast ornament was used as money. It was also called *buksea*. It consists of a shell ring with native fiber woven around about one third of the ring and native fiber attached to the end of the woven part to form a necklace hung around the neck. The ring was made from the *tridacna* shell. The best old ones were made from fossil shell with a yellow streak on part of the shell (from the hinge). *Bakhia* were worn only by chiefs and were considered to be very valuable. This money was used in the olden days for purchasing land or food and solving problems between tribes or families. (Per. comm. Betty) (See Waite p. 153)

BAKONGA - See legband, Africa, Ekonda.

BALA

Solomon Islands

Bala is the name of all turtle shell ornaments such as earrings, nose pendants, fish hooks, shell money dividers, *dala* and *dafi* overlays, and beads. See each item for more information.

BALL - See Musket Ball, Quartz Balls, Rubber

BALUBA CROSS - See Cross, Katanga

Bakhia

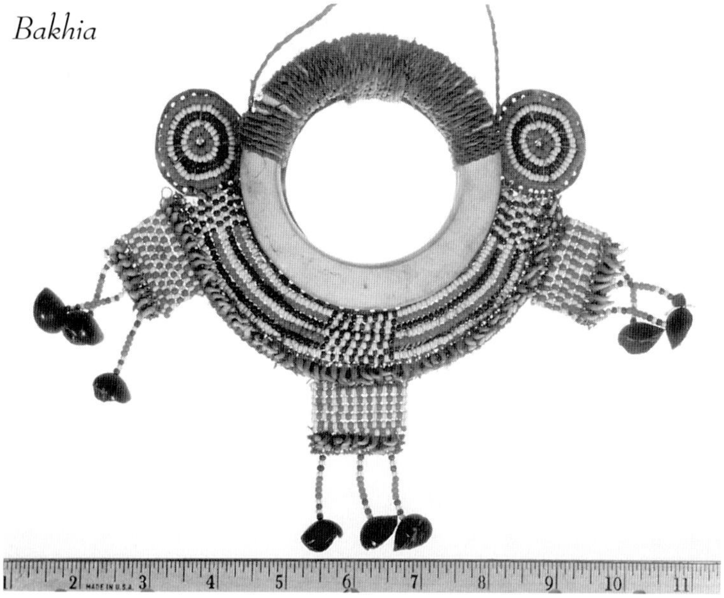

Bala

Bala Beads

Bamboo Money

Bamboo Money

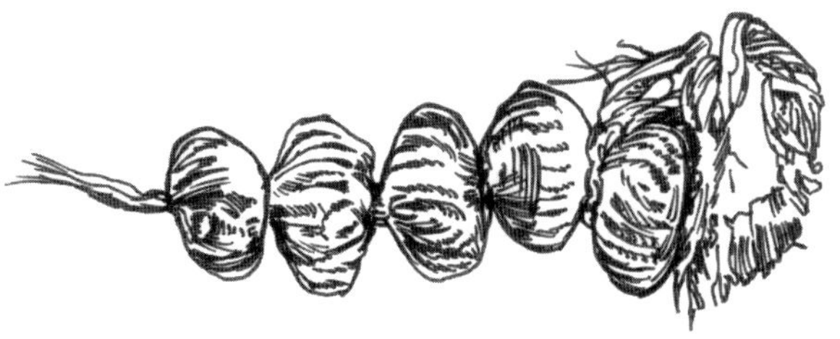

Banana Seed Money

BAMBOO MONEY

China, Japan. 1735 to mid-1900s

Some tally sticks made of bamboo were used by merchants as money. Many bamboo tokens were the equivalent of "good-for's" in the U.S. Many are denominated, such as "5 cents" or "1,000 cash" and others were good for tea, drinks, meals, haircuts, etc. For example, actual tally sticks were used in the manner of a boss giving a talley for each bag of goods a laborer loaded into a vehicle, then at day's end the laborer turned the sticks, or tallies, in for wages. Worth from 1/5 to 1/10 cent each. (See Tally sticks.)

Papua New Guinea

Parallel bamboo sticks were worn as a breastpiece. Each stick represented the value of seven to 10 *kina* or "things" and was presented with the expectation they would be repaid in a future ceremony. 4" wide sticks. (See Omak)

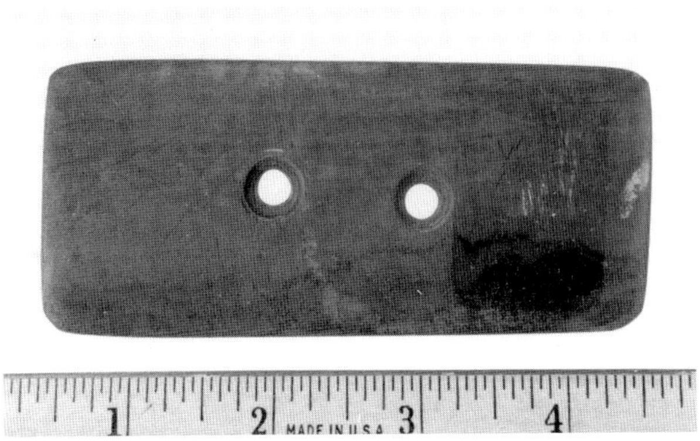

Banner Stone

BANGALA EXECUTION KNIFE - See Execution Knife - Bangala

BAGE - See Salt Money, Abyssinia, Ethiopia

BANANA SEED MONEY

Uganda, Africa

Many kinds of seed strings, including banana seeds were used as ornaments and to some extent as currency. (See Kula.) (See Quiggin p. 100)

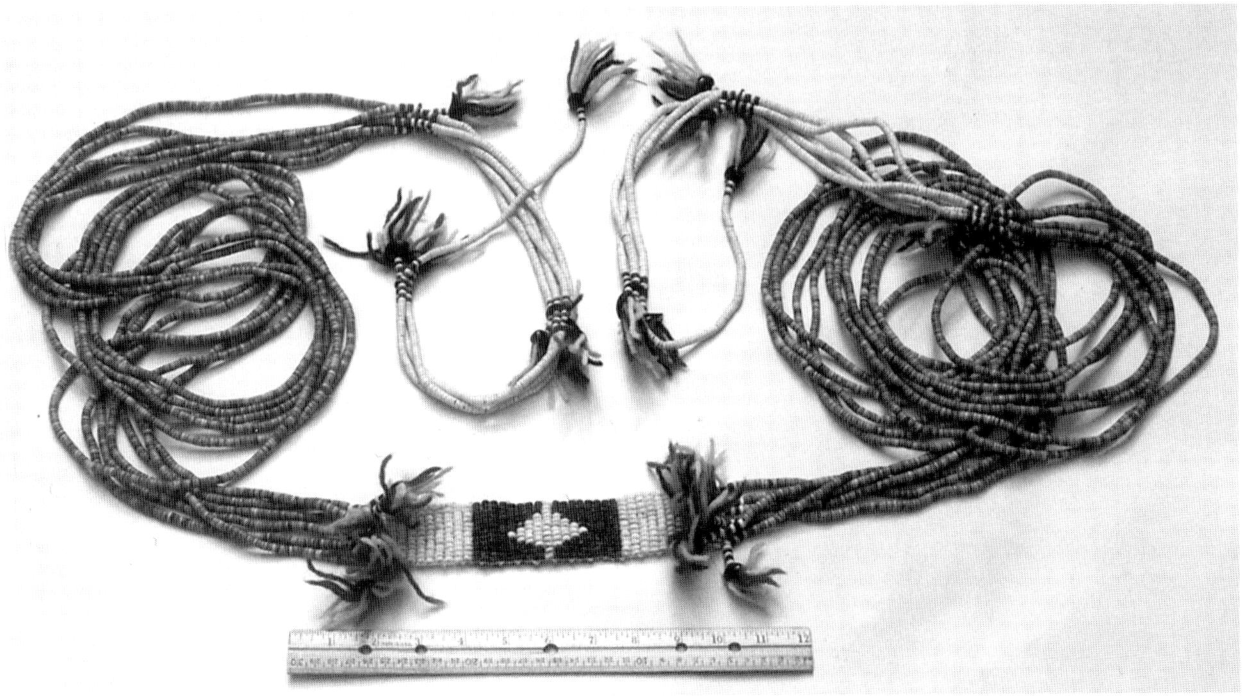

Bani'au

BANGALA SPEARHEAD MONEY

See Spearhead Money - Bangala

BANI'AU

Malaita Island, Solomon Islands

Similar to the tafuli'ae, except the bani'au contains six strings of shell beads that are each six arm lengths long. It is made of small coneshell beads called *Mamamala iavai*, which are enhanced with red beads. The Kwara'ae call it red money, and it is considered the southern type. It is used by the Kwaio people. It was used for bride price like tafuli'ae. (See Burt)

BANNER STONE

America

The American Indians made and used banner stones. These were flat stones, some of which have holes in them. Some believe the stones could have been used as money, but no concrete evidence exists to support this belief.

BA'O - See Porpoise teeth

BAR MONEY - See Bar Money, Bean Money, Calabar, Chogin, Lat, Mukuba wa matwi, Mint Bars, Onganda, Purr-Purr, Rod Money.

Africa Lomami (Mbole), Zaire

This U-shaped bronze ingot bar was used as currency. Many had five ridges on the outside edge. (See Ballarini p. 117.)

Africa

Copper bars of various shapes and sizes were used in Africa as money for an extensive period of time. In the 1880s 11 copper bars would purchase one pound of ivory in the Congo. (See Herbert p. 161.) The Bornu currency was called the *rotl* which was one pound of copper. Iron bars 39 inches long, 1 3/4" wide and 3/8" thick were used as money in the 1700s. Eight bars of iron were worth one pound of large amber stones, and five bars of iron were worth 100 carnelian beads. A slave was worth 130 bars of iron. One bar was worth five English pounds.

England

Early Iron Age

Iron bars are thought to have been used as a form of currency. Six different weights of bars have been found. (See Quiggen p.112.)

Mbole Tribe Bar Money

Annam Silver Bar Money

Annam Silver Bar Money

Annam Banana Bar

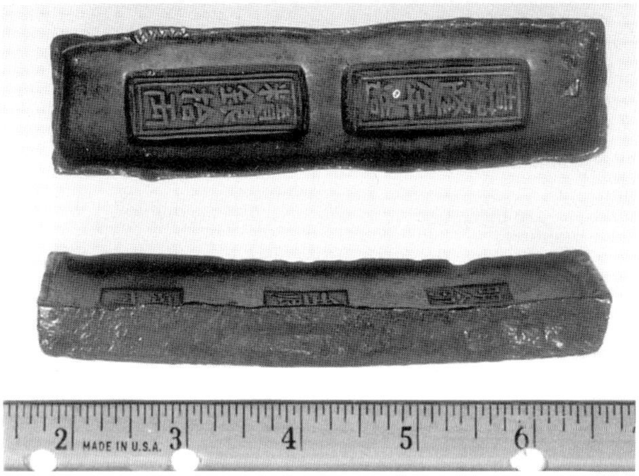

Annam Banana Bar - Stamps

Annam Banana Bar - No Stamps

Vietnam (Annam) 1802 - 1883

Thick rectangular silver bars inscribed with denomination, ruler's name and sometimes date and province were used as money. Sizes range from one tien (c. 3.85 gm) to 100 lang (c. 3830 gm).

Curved "banana" bars of 10 lang denomination were used as bride price. Also called *Ngern* or *Ngan* (money) *Rung* (feeding trough) and *Hang*. Old pieces have markings on the top surface. Modern bullion pieces have marks on ends and sides.

Silver

Denomination	Weight	Dates
1 Tien	3.8-4.2 grams	1820-1841
1 1/2 Tien	5-5.2 grams	1848-1883
2 Tien	6.8-8 grams	1820-1883
3 Tien	10.2-11.6 grams	1820-1883
4 Tien	15-15.5 grams	1820-1883
5 Tien	19-19.2 grams	1841-1883
1 Lang	37-38.69 grams	1802-1883
5 Lang	181-191 grams	1820-1847
10 Lang	385 grams	1841-1883
20 Lang to 100 Lang bars all rare		
1/2 Quan	Unknown	1848-1883
7/10 Quan	3.5 grams	1848-1883
1 Quan	5-5.28 grams	1848-1883
1 1/2 Quan	7.5-8 grams	1848-1883
2 Quan	10.3-10.5	1848-1883
2 1/2 Quan	13-13.5 grams	1848-1883
3 Quan	15.4-16.2 grams	1848-1883

Gold Bars

Were issued in denominations of one, two, three, four and five tien as well as one, 10, 30, 40, 50 and 100 Lang. All rare.

Curved "banana bar" silver,

The bars are valued at 10 Tael and have Chinese and occasionally Thai characters stamped on the sides and ends and occasionally on the top. They are also called *hang* and are a distinctly Vietnamese type of official sycee. They are also called *Ngern Rong* or *Ngan Rong* and were made from the early 1800s reportedly through World War II. They originated as tax ingots and were later used as bullion bars. There are many different types and styles. (See Semans p. 6)

10 Lang (old)	382-385 grams	1820-1841
10 Lang (bullion)	380-385 grams	late 19th cent.

Vietnamese Official Bars

Part of Vietnam's regular currency. Approximately one ounce silver bars with a stamp on top in various shapes.

Gold wafer

It is an extremely thin gold piece 1 3/8" x 3 3/4". The wafer was used by people fleeing Vietnam after the war and as a form of trade and money. The pieces had been used prior to that time as a store of wealth and in barter.

Indonesia, Java, early 19th century

Copper "bonks." Small copper bars dated and inscribed with denominations in stuivers. (See Krause)

Japan, 1772 - 1868

Isshu gin	1829-1869	One shu silver	1.89-2.63 grams
Nisshu gin	1772-1859	Two shu silver	7.53-13.62 grams
Ichibu gin	1837-1869	One bu silver	8.63-8.66 grams
Isshu kin	1824-1832	One shu gold	1.39 grams
Nisshu kin	1824-1869	Two shu gold	.75-1.62 grams
Ichibu kin	1819-1867	One bu gold	.82-3.27 grams
Nibu kin	1818-1869	Two bu gold	3.0-6.56 grams

Go Momme 1765-1772

Five momme, silver, 19 grams. The momme is a small weight. (See Krause & Mishler.) Counterfeits are common.

Various other oval and odd-shaped pieces exist in gold, silver and copper from central Japan and the provinces. Many are fantasies. In Japan they are usually called "plate" money, as in "*gimban*", meaning silver plate, (not plated).

Nigeria, 16th century

Iron bars traded to the natives by European merchants were originally used as tools and later used in the original form as money. A male slave was worth 13 bars, and a female slave was worth 10 bars. (See Johansson p. 36-37)

Nigeria

Brass U shaped bar. See *Okpoho Okuk*

BARAFE

Malaita Island, Solomon Islands

Shell disks were woven into shell money material. Native made string was used, and the barafe was used in bride price along with porpoise teeth on the northern part of Malaita Island. They were worn by males of the Tobita tribe in Northern Malaita. They were worn around the neck during pre-raiding ceremonies. If the raid was successful, the piece would be worn during the celebration. If the man who had worn it in the first ceremony was killed, the piece was put in a very sacred place. (Per. comm. Betty)

Vietnam Gold Wafer

Japan Gold 2 Bu

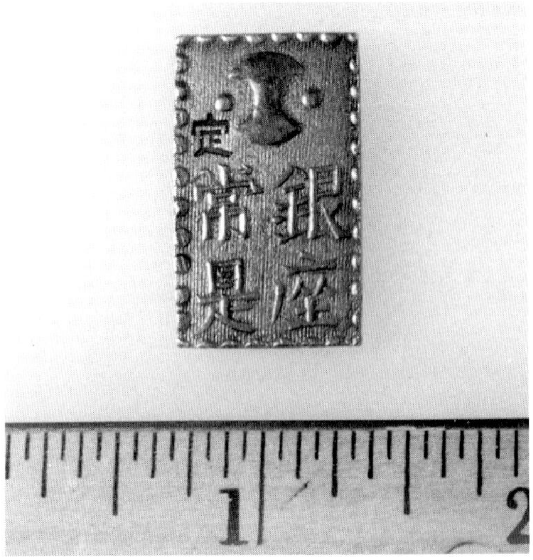

Japan Silver 2 Shu

Indonesia Bonk

Go Momme

BARAVA

Solomon Islands

A very old shell piece with seven carved people standing on a ring made from one piece of flat shell. It was used as money by the chiefs. 5 3/4" x 11 3/4" 3/8" (Per. comm. Betty)

BARI

Bari or more properly *bari-kira* are strings of white medium-sized cowry shells. The string is about three feet long and forms a part of bride price. (See cowry shells)

BARK CLOTH

Solomon Islands

Pieces of bark cloth were used as money and in bride price. They were also used as ceremonial gifts, as ritual offerings to gods and ancestors, and as wearing apparel. Bark cloth was sometimes used to pay for the making of a canoe. It took about three days to make bark cloth. It was made in Isabel, San Cristoval and Ulawa in the Eastern Solomon Islands. Many different designs were used, and the cloth is still being made today. This bark cloth served as clothing, wrapping and even as money. The Santa Cruz people use black soot and turmeric for the bright yellow color to create traditional designs. Isabel Island produced tapa with pale blue decoration made with a leaf dye. (See Tapa Cloth)

Barava

Uganda

Small pieces were manufactured exclusively for use as money. See Wiechhoff p. 34.

BARLEY

Grain Currency

BARRAS - See cross, I-shaped.

BARU'ILAA

Malaita, Solomon Islands

Six porpoise teeth pierced in a line in the nose. See Porpoise teeth

BASKET

Murik Tribe, Papua New Guinea

Reed baskets were made by the women and traded on the coast and with the islands. The baskets were of a variety of sizes and designs made for different purposes. The baskets were valued because they were strong and durable. A small basket called a *sakai suun,* about 14 inches square, was used for trading to the middle Schouten Islands for tobacco. Its value was one bark sheath of tobacco. Larger baskets were made to trade with the islands directly off shore, and they were used to haul firewood, coconuts and

Bark Cloth

Bat Bone Belt

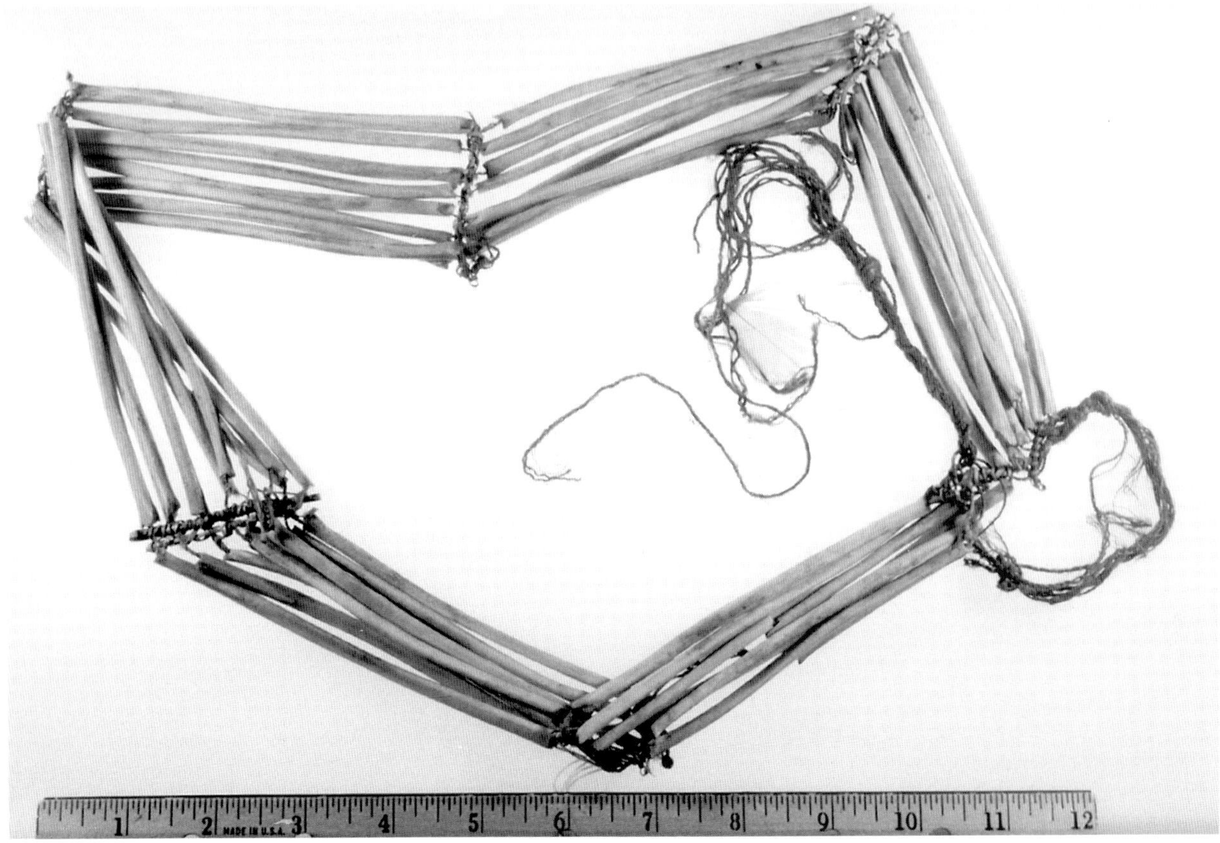

Bat Hoe Money

garden produce. The baskets are not made to look especially beautiful and were traded for the amount of canarium nuts they would hold. A very large basket of about one square meter, called *nimbrey-suun*, or pig basket was valued at one pig. (See Barlow p. 95)

BASI - *See Kula.*

BASIN

Gold Coast, Africa, 1400's - 1700's

Brass barber's basins were extremely valuable as a form of money, particularly for bride price payments. In the 1400's one would purchase a slave and her child. Other kinds of basins like urinals, chamber pots, kettles, cauldrons and shaving bowls were also used. At Elmina in that period, Herbert said 37 percent of the Portuguese trade was in manillas and basins. From 1529 to 1531, 9,000 vessels and 216,700 manillas were used. In the 1600s there was a report of these basins being worth one pound of gold, which represented 12 years of labor by a gold-digger. They were also called neptunes, which were used to make salt by evaporating sea-water. Neptunes ranged in size from less than one foot in diameter to more than three feet in diameter. They were described as small plates of brass and were exchanged for 5 kg. of rubber. (See Herbert p.126) (See Guyer p. 80-81)

BAT BONE BELT

Irian Jaya

The bones of bats were made into belts and worn by the natives. They were a valued item and it is thought they were a limited form of money.

BAT HOE MONEY

Nigeria

The hill pagens at Gayum village used this hoe as bride price and money. A small hoard has been found recently. (See Johansson p. 38) See Hoe - Nigeria

BAT TEETH

New Ireland

Strings of projecting bats' teeth are found on a cord. They were used for buying nets and weapons. They are also called *agut* or *angut.* (See Quiggin p. 128)

BATA

Malaita Province, Solomon Islands

This is the name of shell money in general. Kinds of *bata* are: red, the most valuable; orange, white and black, the least valuable. It was used as bride price among the Kwaio. It was also used in mortuary payments. They produced the white *bata* themselves from cone shells, but they obtained the red shell beads by trade. The standard denomination was a *lousu'u,* which was a length from a man's fingertips to above his elbow.

BATAFALU

Auki Island, Solomon Islands

It is similar to the tafuliae in that it has ten strings. Each string is nine feet long instead of the standard fathom. It was valued at eight pounds and was rare as only a few were made. (See Bartle p. 382)

BATAULIULI

Auki Island, Solomon Islands

A six-foot string of roughly chipped and drilled unpolished white shell disks was called *batulliuli.* It was worth five shillings and was made in Auki Island.

BATU CLOTH

Sulawesi, Indonesia

It is a long narrow cloth worn as a headdress at funerals and used in trade in Sulawesi.

BAUXITE BEADS - *See Beads*

BEADS

See Borjookes, Jacket, Kudatama, Ostrich Egg Shell Beads, Turquoise, Wooden Bead Money

Abo beads. Africa - See Bauxite beads.

Adjagba beads. Africa

A yellow Ghanaian powder glass bead similar to the bodom and Akosu beads. It has blue and red strips. It was used among the Krobo and was highly prized. It is the best known Krobo bead. It is a long bead with slightly spiral longitudinal strips. The beads are worn by girls who have reached puberty as they travel to another village to look for a husband. They show the potential husband the status of the girl's family. (See Francis, West African Powder Glass Beads p. 96.) (See Francis, Beads & People 2) (See Liu p.22)

Adjagba Bead

Agate. Africa

These beads were made in Idar-Oberstein in Germany of agates from Brazil. They also used carnelian from Brazil which was actually chalcedony that was soaked in an acid bath which had iron dissolved in it for several weeks. The stone absorbed some of the iron and was then heated to turn it red. Idar-Oberstein was better at producing strong colors than India, so it can be assumed that most of the very strong colored beads came from Germany. India also produced large quantities of agates with the center of the mines being in Ratanpur. These agates were traded in great numbers to East Africa. From 1820 to 1980 100 million beads were exported to Africa, especially to Mali, Togo and Gambia. Beads were also shipped to Europe and the Americas. Until 1966 all holes were made with bow drills. Many companies made the beads in Germany, with W. Constantin Wild and Co. being one of the more important companies particularly after it took over Julius Hirsch and Co. The beads were made in many shapes, including balls, cylinders, circular pendants, rinds, drops, angular pendants, lion claws, round olives and angular olives. In Mali they were sometimes worn by the Peul women with gold jewelry. The black and white dyed agate beads were used in Sudan as money. The triangular tanfouk pendants, also called talismen, were used by the Songhai of southern Mali and western Niger. The Berber and Tuareg also used the triangular *tanfouk* pendants as money and used them as pendants and earrings as well. (See Liu p.15)

Agate and carnelian beads were made and traded to many parts of the world from as early as 3000 B.C. The beads were traded to Sumeria as early as 2000 B.C. and in the 18th and 19th centuries traded to Africa. The Kalinga used agate beads, which they valued very highly. One of the larger beads was worth one carabao. (See Liu p. 16-18)

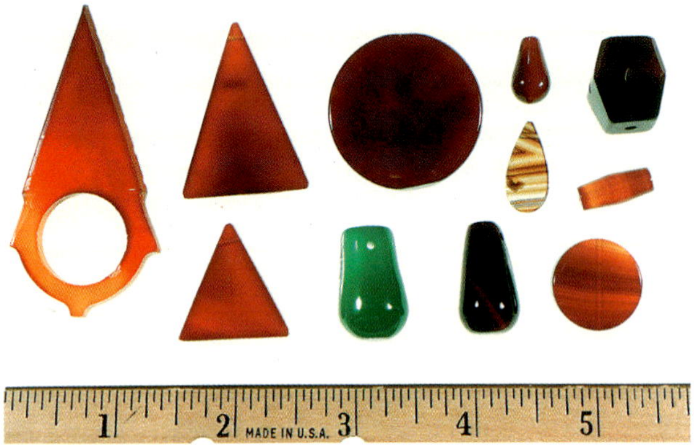

Idar-Oberstein Agate Beads

Milleflore (Aggry) Beads

Milleflore (Aggry) Beads

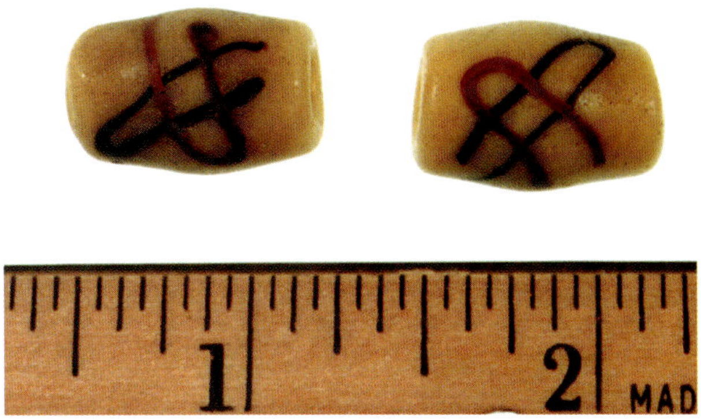

Akosu Beads

Alley Bead

Ambassador Beads

Amber Beads

Aggrey beads, Africa

These dichroic glass beads appeared sky-blue if looked at and sea-green if you looked through the bead. They were found east of the Gold Coast in what is now Nigeria. They were associated with water and were called "blue coral". Many thought the beads were created by a supernatural power. The original aggrey bead is a mystery, and its origin is not known. It was used as early as the 17th century. A new hypothesis feels they were silicate glass slag from a local iron ore smelting operation. The Europeans of the 15th and 17th century did not recognize the material the beads were made from. They did think it had been obtained from mining. Many feel the beads have some association with coral. Coral had been a valuable item and was traded for slaves and pepper in the 1600s. (See Van Landewijk p. 89) Chevrons, millefiories and others have been called aggrey beads. We are not certain exactly what the original aggrey beads were. Imitation aggrey beads were reworked in Ghana from European beads and are known as Koli beads, according to Francis, Beads & People 2. (See Liu p.15-17)

Aggry beads. Africa

Other aggries are made with inlaid glass in various designs.They are called millefiore (a thousand flowers). A warm core of glass was rolled over small pieces of colored glass, picking up the pieces of glass to form intricate, colorful designs. The long beads are worth more than the short beads. The large "elbow" beads are most valuable.

Akosu beads, Africa

Powder glass yellow beads with trailed decoration were used by the Ewe kings. They are similar to bodom beads but have different designs and do not have a dark core. The presence of gold flakes in the body of the beads determines if it is a genuine old bead. A modern one has none. Many have stripes or an eye symbol. (See Francis p.106)

Alley beads, striped, Africa

These beads look much like marbles with colored glass in a clear sphere. They were used in Togo and Nigeria and came from Europe. (See Liu p.48)

Ambassador beads. Africa

The Ndebele called them ambassador beads because the shamans wore them when they went into the hills to ask advice from the great god of the Matabele. The beads were also worn by the chiefs who met David Livingstone, the British missionary, in 1855 at Victoria Falls. (See Dubin p. 149)

Amber bead. Africa

Amber is fossilized tree resin. Imitations in copal, glass, plastic and other materials are hard to detect. Basically, no one test will prove the material to be amber. A series of several tests will do it. Amber will scratch with a knife, and glass will not. Amber is light compared with glass and many plastics. Both amber and copal will burn, but copal burns more vigorously. Both give off a pleasant piney smell. Amber is also fluorescent. Amber will produce static electricity by rubbing it against wool or silk. It will then pick up tiny bits of torn paper or hairs. The specific gravity of amber is 1.05 to 1.095 with water being 1.0. The Berbers have used amber beads for many centuries. The beads were used in Mauritania, Morocco, and Sudan. Prior to 1728, large stones were valued at eight bars of iron per pound of amber. After 1728 the value went to 1/2 bar per stone. Also see copal beads.

Amber Beads

Anahida beads. Indonesia

Small red brown beads, terra-cotta color, used mostly by the common people as money.

Asante beads. Africa

See Francis Beads & People plate 4.

Ban Chiang, Thailand. Dating back to the period from 500 B.C. to 200 B.C.

The Thais believe the beads were made locally, but this has not been proven. The beads are distinctive wound monochromes in translucent green and blue oblates, truncated bicones and very long cylinders. They also have a greasy appearance. (See Francis, beads and the Bead Trade in Southeast Asia p. 21) (See Liu p.84) (See Dubin p. 229)

Ban Chiang

Ban Chiang

Bauxite. Africa

Reddish brown beads also called Abo by the Hause traders of Chad and Niger. They are stone beads made from aluminum ore with the reddish color coming from traces of iron. They were worn in girdles by the women. Some women wore up to nine strings. In the 1940s one string was worth about 1s 6d sterling. 3/8″ to 3/4″ diameter

Bauxite Beads

Begger beads. India

Round and rectangular carved red agate beads were used in trade.

Bird beads. Indonesia

Probably made no later than the 7th century in East Asia or locally. They are dark blue glass with a design in white of either a bird with outstretched wings or a chicken (rare). The beads also have a sunburst on them also in white. The beads are quite rare, and modern fakes are currently being made. The genuine beads are an opaque dark blue, nearly black, with a rough texture and a large perforation. The rays of the star are thin, while many of the copies have thick rays in comparison. (See Adhyatman p.138)

Bodom beads. Africa

All bodom beads are predominately yellow and often have a dark gray or black inner core. Most of the old genuine ones have gold flecks in the core. They were used in Ghana from as early as the 16th century. They were reserved for the elite in Asante society. They were usually worn by chiefs or others of rank and reflected wealth and dignity. Some experts believed the beads were made in Europe while some experts feel they could have been of African manufacture. Legend has it they came from the ground and if buried they will reproduce. There are several styles, but most have the general characteristics described above. Imitation bodom beads. Africa (See Francis Beads & People 2. plate 4a) (See Liu p.20-21) (See Dubin p. 123)

Brass beads. Africa Munshi Tribe, Nigeria

The bead is a ball with a ring attached, all made from brass. The beads were used to buy slaves. (See Dubin p.146)

Bride price beads. Indonesia

Bung. Philippines

Cast bronze, silver or gold beads used as pendants made by the Ifugao of northern Luzon, Philippines. They date back 2,000 to 3,000 years and were originally worn as earrings. (See Francis p. 98)

Cards of sample beads. Africa Many of the bead producing companies made up cards with sample beads on them. In the 1930s, sample cards from J.F. Sick & Co. were used in Ghana. (Venetian sample cards with a Laughing Girl trademark in the upper left corner rubber stamped on.) They were from Italy in the 1930s. French cards were also made in the 1930s. The Gablonz (Jablonec) firm made cards in the late 1920s and showed they were made in Czechoslovakia. Some cards today have notations made on them showing what the beads were used for. Some have dates and the location of manufacture. (See Francis, West African Perspective The Size Of The Bead Trade p. 98-100) (See Dubin p.108-111)

Carnelian. Africa

It is the heart of the red agate stone. In 16th century Nigerian kings wore them and presented them to important visitors. They are used in Upper Volta for trade at present. The quality and color help to determine their value. The red color can be produced by heating the

Bird Bead

Bodom Bead - Old Genuine

Bodom Beads - Modern

Brass Beads

stones. Many of the carnelian and agate beads came from India where they were made from local stone. In Senegal after 1718, 100 carnelian beads were valued at 5 bars of iron. These beads were always expensive and in the early 18th century cost more than $2.00 each in Europe. (See Liu p. 38-41)

Chevron beads, Africa

They were first invented by the Venetians in about 1300 A.D. and later manufactured by the Dutch. They were also called star or rosetta beads. The earliest chevrons were seven layer beads, with the first and third layers from the core being transparent light blue-green, and were made from 1480 to 1600. This colorless or eventually white glass was considerably easier to make than the red and blue glass. In the early 1600s glass makers and their equipment were smuggled into Amsterdam, Holland, where they started making chevrons for The Dutch East Indies Company. The beads had facets ground on the ends. Most had 12 points and the colors were blue, red and white. In the early 17th century, other color combinations and patterns were made. These later chevrons had rounded ends instead of faceted ends as the earlier bead. Beads made after the 1500s all had less than seven layers, and their ends were round. Dutch copies of these Venetian chevrons were made later. Some of these copies are very large. At one time the beads were worth up to four times their weight in gold. Among the Ashanti, a thief who stole even one chevron bead was obligated to pay the owner seven slaves in restitution. Natives believed the beads came from the ground. The beads also could have been made in Egypt or Mesopotamia. Beads were formed of layers of glass — deep blue on the outside, opaque brick red under that, then a layer of transparent pale green. These layers were separated by thin layers of opaque white glass. The glass was forced into a tapered mold with corrugated sides thus producing points on the outer surface. When the bead was ground at the ends the inner layers show as chevrons. The beads have from two to eight layers and a variety of points with 12 being the most common. They were called chevrons as well as Bakim-Mutum by the traders. Chevron beads have been found in Egypt, Indonesia, Canada and Florida (in small quantities). The chevron has many different designs due to the grinding down of the chevron cane at various points to give different appearances. In the 1800s the Venetians produced large numbers of chevrons in a great variety of colors, sizes, shapes, layers and points. Most were from four to six layers. The red chevron was probably produced in the early 1900s by the Venetians. In Mauritania (West Africa) the chevron is a very valuable asset and is used in dowries at the present time. The broken beads are recycled into other beads and

Indonesian Bride Price Beads - Modern

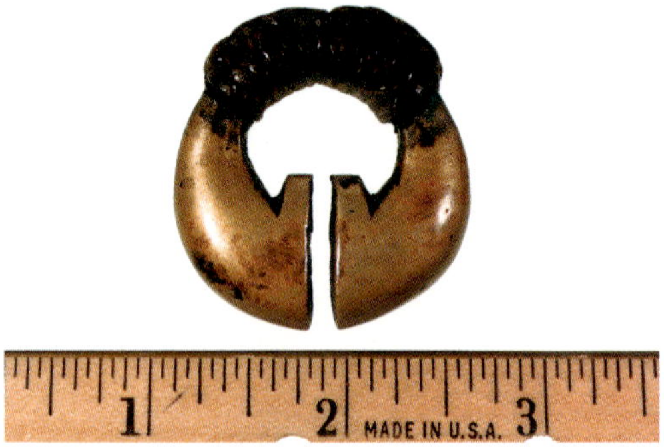

Bung

Bung - Left Bronze Right Gold

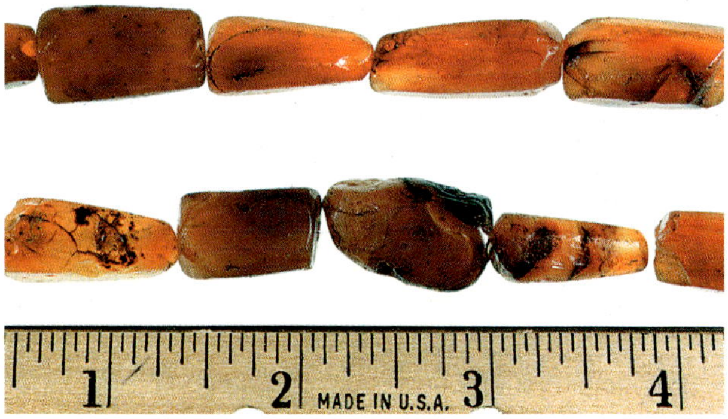

Carnelian Beads

Seven Layer Chevron Bead

Seven Layer Chevron Beads - Small Beads

Chevron Bead

Chevron Beads

pendants due to their high value. Only a few of the early chevrons have been found in Indonesia. (Adhyatman p. 87) Many imitations were probably made in Czechoslovakia. In the Cameroons, chevrons were called *perla rosetta* and had three different shapes. One shape was cylindrical with white lines running the length of the bead. The second shape was a barrel shape with white lines running most of the length of the bead, and the third shape was the same barrel shape with two white zigzag lines circling each bead near the ends. (See Harter p. 11) Jamey Allen (Chevron-Star-Rosetta Beads) said the beads are made in four operations. 1) forming of the core layer of the gather that surrounds a bubble of air; 2) layering the gather with additional glass (casing); 3) molding the gather; and 4) drawing the gather. Steps 2 and 3 could be repeated. In the process of molding, the two-layered gather was inserted into a star-shaped mold. The seven-layer was started with a double-layered gather of green and white glass, while the six-layer was made with only white glass. The white layers are usually thin and serve to outline the colored layers. Many modern imitations have been made, and most are impossible to detect without much scientific evaluation. (See Dubin p.116-117)

Chevron beads. Indonesia

The earliest chevrons were seven-layer beads with the first and third layers from the core being transparent light green. They were made from 1480 to 1600 AD. They were ground into facets on the ends. Most have 12 points, and the colors are blue, red and white. In the early 17th century, other color combinations and patterns were made. Beads made later had less than seven layers, and their ends were round. Dutch copies of the Venetian chevrons were made in the late 19th or early 20th century. Many of the beads found in Indonesia are the old beads with seven layers made before the 1600s. Some of these copies are very large. There are many imitation chevron beads. Kalimantan (Borneo)

Chevron beads. United States

Faceted chevrons were used during the 16th century, with the tumbled chevrons being used after 1600. They are found in Florida and other Southern states. They were found in the Parkin Mound in Arkansas; Chattanooga, Tennessee; and Weeki Wachee Springs, Florida. They were one of the earliest beads traded in America. Some of the chevrons found in Florida are believed to have arrived with the DeSoto expeditions of 1539. They are all seven layer chevrons.

Chief beads. United States

Small blue beads traded in lengths of a fathom were called "tia commochuck." They were used by the Lewis & Clark expedition in 1804. The beads are believed to be light blue opaque wound round beads similar to the padre beads of the Southwest. They came from China through Russian traders. It is also possible that they were what we know as "Russian beads" or may have been any blue beads of any size. These blue beads along with white beads (second best), were the only items the Indians wanted to trade. (See Francis, Ornament, #8, 1984.)

Clay beads. Africa

Small clay beads from Mali were originally said to be ancient beads that were dug up near the old trading center of Jenne'. So many beads are now available that we now do not believe the story about their origin. The larger beads are really spindle whorls. (See Francis p. 111)

Comb beads. Africa. - See feather beads.

Conus shell disc ornament beads. Africa

It was called *kibangwa* or "*vibangwa*" and the plural was "*vibangwa*". In East Africa they were introduced by the Arab traders and were used both as whole disks or half disks as a form of money. Two *vibangwa* were the price of a slave. Some of the whole disks were decorated and pierced and woven into women's hair as ornaments. The half disks were cut in a triangular shape. They were used over a wide area, including Tanganyika, Kenya, Uganda, the Congo, North and South Rhodesia, Nyasaland, Ethiopia, Ruanda-Urundi and Portuguese East Africa. In the 1870s the British destroyed the disks and half disks. They then introduced porcelain copies from Bohemia (Czechoslovakia) with serial numbers on them. Later the Bohemians made glass copies of the quarter disks (triangles) which were traded to the natives and used as money. The glass copies were made in several colors, including red, green and yellow. Copies also were made in bone and ivory. In 1926 one disc was worth 40 shillings, and in former times they were bought with an elephant tusk. In 1853 David Livingstone received a necklace containing a conus shell disc (*kibangwa*) and he was told that it was highly prized and that two would buy a slave or five would buy an elephant tusk. (See Francis p. 109) (See Harding p. 52) (See Liu p.34)

Copal beads. Africa

Copal is the semi-fossilized resin of an extinct tree that has been buried and pressed for as long as 20,000 years. It is found primarily in coastal Zanzibar and Mozambique. Its color ranges from golden yellow to deep red or warm brown. It is opaque or partially transparent. It was used in bride price by the Fulani tribe in Mali and Upper Volta. One large bead was worth four cows, while a smaller bead was worth only two cows. Imitation copal beads were made in Jablonec from

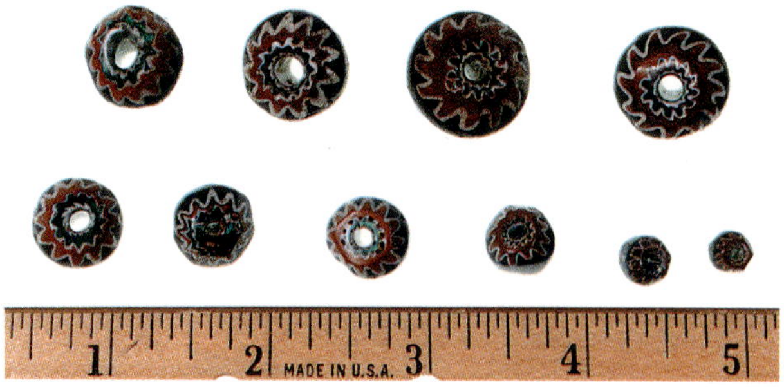

Seven Layer Chevron Beads

16th Century Seven Layer Chevrons

Clay Beads

Conus Shell Glass Beads

butter-yellow glass and, more recently, plastic or resin imitations. (See Liu p. 36, 131) See Amber beads.

Coral Beads - Africa

Coral. Africa

Coral comes from the ocean and is a structure produced by colonies of animals called polyps. They primarily consist of lime which is extracted from the sea water. Precious red coral (*Corallium rubrum*) comes from the Mediterranean Sea and was used from Roman times to present. Coral has been used in India, China, Mexico and many other areas. Another major type of coral is horny coral. It is made of a keratin-like substance. Both black coral and golden coral are types of horny coral. (See Francis, 20 Easy Steps To Identifying Most Beads In Most Collections p. 4) In Nigeria, coral beads were imported in fifteen different sizes and were popular with the women. The regalia of the king of Benin was made almost entirely of coral beads. The beads (*nkalari* or *aka*) were introduced by the Portuguese in the early 1500s. They were always expensive and would cost five to 10 pounds per kilogram. (See Opper, Diakhite: A Study Of The Beads From An 18th-19th Century Burial Site in Senegal, West Africa, p. 7. Also see Tibet, coral beads. (See Liu p. 36, 131)

Coral Beads - Nepal

Coral beads. Indonesia

Red coral (*Corallium rubrum*) has been used since early times in beads that were associated with the prevention of ailments of the blood. The beads were treasured as heirlooms in Nusa Tenggara, Sumatra and Kalimantan.

Coral Beads - Tibet

Coral bead. Nepal, Tibet

Since the 13th century, when Marco Polo first reported coral beads were used as money, they have served that purpose. Red coral beads were highly valued by the people and functioned as currency in the general area of Tibet. These included the people of Nepal. The best coral was imported from Italy and was reserved for the wealthy, as observed by Marco Polo in the 13th century. The oxblood-colored beads are expensive, and in Tibet a necklace of these old beads, 1 1/2" in diameter sold, for $740 per 11.5 grams. (See Dubin p. 209-210)

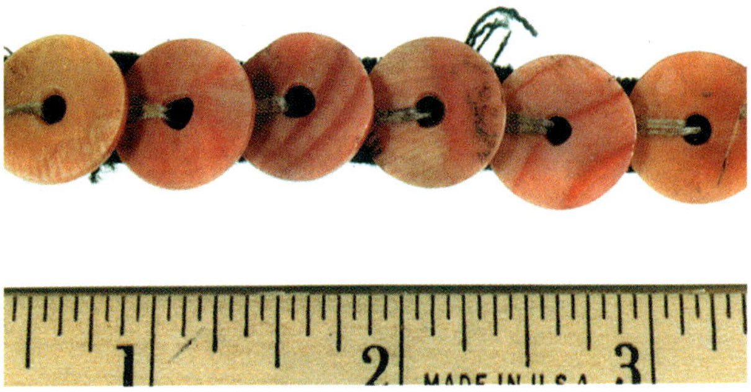

Coral Beads - Throbriand Islands

Coral bead. Trobriand Islands

Coral beads were strung in many forms and used as money. They were included in items used in the Kula ring. They were considered very valuable.

Coral simulation beads. Africa

Some coral-simulation beads were made from powder glass, others were made of glass and some were plastic imitations. Czech-molded glass imitations even were worn by rich women.

Coral beads were worn with silver necklaces in Yemen. The beads were used by women during their marriage ceremony and while receiving guests after giving birth. The large silver beads are called *jauz* the silver pendant is called heikal and the cone shaped ends are called mismar. Liu p. 24, 131

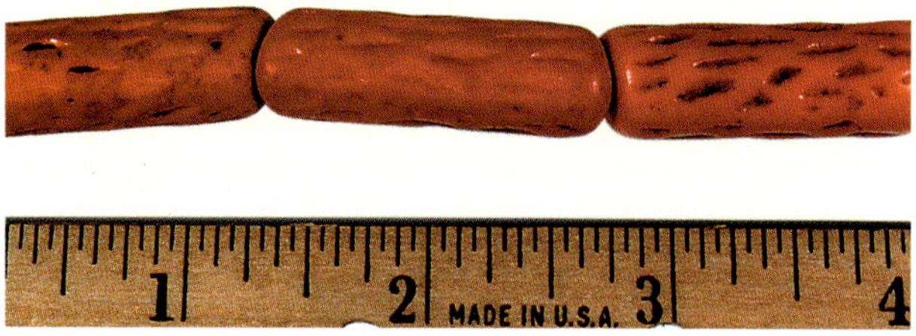

Coral Simulation Beads

Cornaline d'Aleppo beads. Africa

A compound wound bead made of two layers, The outer layer is red, and the inner core is white, yellow, green, blue, brown or pink. They are also known by the name of *rikiki*. They came from Venice.

Cornaline d'Aleppo beads. Indonesia

A compound wound bead made of two layers, the outer layer is red and the inner layer is white, yellow or pink. They were valuable, and copies were probably made in China.

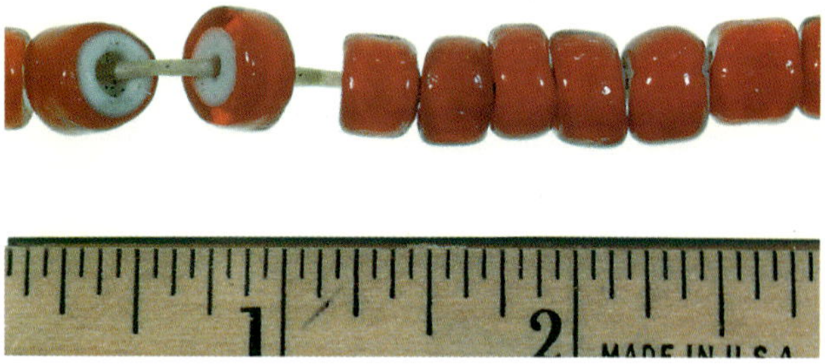

Cornaline D'Aleppo White Center Beads

Cornaline d'Aleppo beads. Guatemala

It has a white or slightly pinkish center and is considered by some as the "Spanish trading bead." (See Johnson p. 19)

Cornaline d'Aleppo beads. North America

This Venetian glass bead was found widely distributed over the North American continent and was known as the "Hudson's Bay bead." The beads were valued at 50 cents a pound, which was the value of one "made beaver" (a skin which had been dried and made ready for shipment to a tannery), the standard of value between the traders and the Indians. In actual trade with the Indians, six beads were the exchange value of one "made beaver" in one trading post. The values varied by area and time, as well as if the beads were being bought by the trader or sold to the Indians.

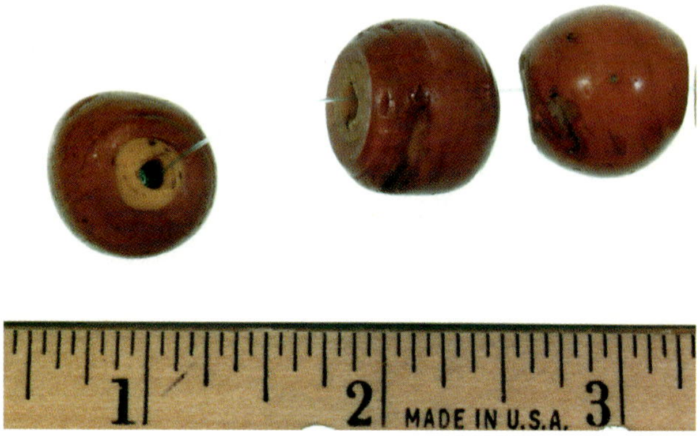

Cornaline D'Aleppo Yellow Center Beads

Copper beads. Africa

The beads are strung many times on leather pieces.

Crumb beads. Africa

The beads were rolled in bits of glass while they were still soft and then allowed to cool. They were probably made in Hebron.

Dau beads.

See Pagadua necklace.

Dogon beads. Africa

These beads are mostly white, light blue or dark blue and get their name from a people living in Mali. They were used as dowry wealth. See Dutch beads.

Copper Beads

Donkey beads. Iran, 1700s to present

Donkey beads are earthen trade beads covered with

blue glaze and strung on a leather thong and tied to animals for protection against the Evil Eye. To make donkey beads, local stones were ground up and mixed with clay and frit, then roughly formed into beads and packed with copper (for coloring) and soda and fired. They were used as small change. 1″ diameter. (See Moore)

Donut beads. Africa

Made in Bohemia or Bavaria for use in parts of West Africa in the beginning of the 20th centur of transparent blue, green, amber or clear glass. They were worn only by chiefs or dignitaries.

Dutch beads. Africa

The beads were made in Amsterdam beginning around 1575 by winding molten glass around a metal rod. They were translucent blue and white. Today they are found in the Mali region inhabited by the Dogon. They were used as bride price and in religious ceremonies. See Dogon beads.

Crumb Beads

Donkey Beads

Dogon Beads

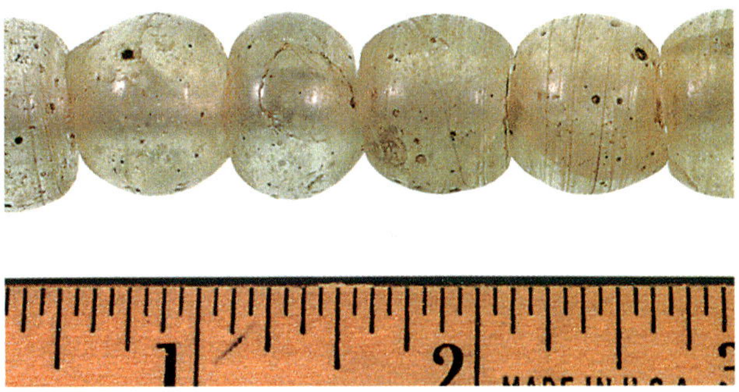

Dutch Beads

Dutch Beads

dZi beads. Tibet

Their origin, method of manufacture and even their definition are hotly debated. The dZi bead is a dark brown and white or black and white bead of etched or treated agate with a wide range of patterns. There are basically three types of dZi beads, according to Beck: type 1) white design on natural stone background; type 2) black design on whitened background; and type 3) the pure dZi beads are of type 2. To be considered pure, Ebbinghouse (p. 23) says the bead must have a desirable pattern, with good shape and color and shiny surface, and a lack of major flaws. There are regional preferences, so the beads have different importance depending on the area. Etched agate beads with pentagonal cells on a type 1 bead are called Indian dZi beads (not pure dZi beads) by the Tibetans (according to Ebbinghouse p. 24). They are found in the ground, so Tibetans cannot conceive of them being man-made. It was thought the beads adorned the gods, who discarded them when they became blemished, and this explains why they are seldom found in perfect condition. The beads are only found in the Himalayas. They never occur in Nepal, but they do occur in Bhutan and Ladakh. Deep colors and a smooth shiny surface as well as a higher number of eyes increases their value. The nine-eyed dZi bead is especially prized because the number nine is considered important. Chinese texts mention dZi beads as early as the 7th century A.D. They were revered and highly valued in Tibet. The most valuable have white circles, called eyes, on them surrounded with white angular lines. There are between two and nine eyes on a bead. Other beads have white lines around the beads in a banded form. These beads are of lesser value and called "*chung dZi*", which means "less important dZi". Other beads mainly have only random white angular lines. Some dZi beads look like buttons and are called tabular dZi beads. Tibetans feel that if you sell a valuable dZi bead you could become sick or may even die soon. Because the beads are magic, they have the power to protect the wearer from catastrophe. The use of dZi beads as money is not confirmed. However, Peter Francis (Bead Report XX) suggests that the *Do Tzi* was a unit of money in Tibet worth 13-15 pounds. The dZi possibly might have first become popular in Tibet around 1920-30 and received its name from the value put on it. This is a theory he feels might explain some facts about the beads. (See Liu p.80-83) (See Dubin p. 216-217)

Empress beads - *See seed beads.*

Ebony and silver beads. Africa. It is believed that these beads were used along with many other beads as a form of wealth, money and decoration. They are all called "trade beads."

Dzi Bead, Upper Right; Chung Dzi Bead, Lower Right; Tabular Dzi Bead, Lower Left Bead

Ebony And Silver Beads

Eye Beads

Face Bead

Face Beads - India

False Chevron Beads

Fancy Beads

Fancy Beads

Eye beads. Africa

Roman-style eye beads have been used at least as far back as 300 B.C. having crossed the Sahara and been found at Djenne, Mail.

Face beads. Africa

Baule tribe glass beads were made and used in 1875. They are named face beads because the three circles inside a larger circle resemble a face.

Face beads, modern, manufactured in India

False Chevron beads. Batanes Island Province, Sarawak, Malaysia, Bali and Taiwan

This bead is a wound imitation decorated with wavy lines. They are probably Chinese beads made in the 16th century. (See Francis, Beads and the Bead Trade in Southeast Asia p. 16)

Fancy beads. Africa

Venetian-made glass beads with much decoration on them are called fancy beads. Many were used in Africa and other parts of the world as trade beads. They were used as money in much of Africa as late as the 1930s. Some were used as early as the 1700s.

Feather beads. Africa

They are mainly found in Mobi in northern Nigeria near the Cameroon border and in Mali. They were exported to Ethiopia in large numbers. They are also known as comb beads.

Feather Beads

Feather Beads

Fiance beads. Egypt
A type of ceramic with a quartz sand body and a colored glaze. Made to simulate the stones used by the wealthy. Used in ancient times and found in the ancient burials of ancient Egypt. (See Liu p. 106-109)

Flush eye beads. Africa.
They are early European trade beads used in Ghana, West Africa.

French Ambassador beads. Africa
Mainly found in Mali.

Freshwater pearls. United States
The prehistoric cultures in the Midwest river valleys used the pearls for necklaces and armlets. It is believed they were considered wealth and possibly were used as money.

Garnet beads. United States
Hand made garnet beads were used as money in Wisconsin. (Per Gale Highsmith.)

Ghost beads. Africa
Glass beads made in 1931 in Czechoslovakia.

Glass beads. Africa
Among the Xhosa, glass trade beads were a recognized unit of currency, and the beads necessary to make a Xhosa woman's headdress were worth several head of cattle in the early 1800s. As more beads became available, the value of the beads fell. (See Blauer p. 31)

Glass Seed Beads. United States
Until the mid-20th century, seed beads were traded to most Indian tribes in the United States for use on clothing and many other decorations. They are smaller than pony beads and are used more frequently.

The first industrial enterprise established in the United States was a glass factory in 1607 near Jamestown. A second factory was established in 1622.

Gold-glass beads. Malaysia, Indonesia area
The beads were probably made in Egypt by inserting a gold foil-covered tube into a larger tube which protects the foil. False gold-glass beads have an amber-colored outer tube and the inner tube has no foil. See pango beads. (See Francis, Beads and the Bead Trade in Southeast Asia p. 17)

Gooseberry beads. Africa
These clear beads with white stripes are early European trade beads used in Ghana, West Africa. See tosi beads.

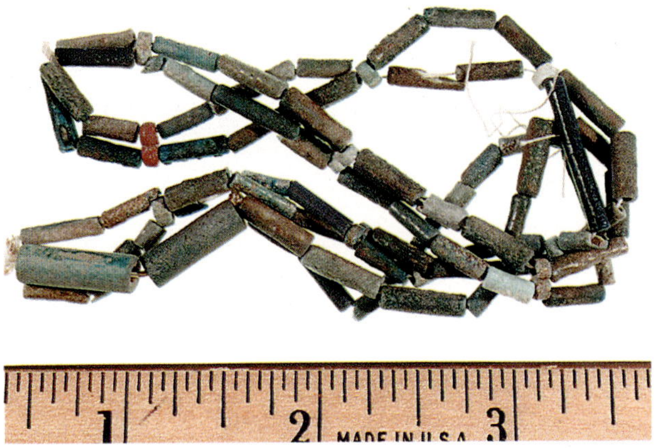

Fiance Beads

Freshwater Pearls

Garnet Beads

Ghost Beads

Glass Seed Beads

Hebron Glass Beads

Hippo Beads

"Hubbell" Beads

Granite beads. Africa

Most of these beads come from Mali, with the largest ones from the Dogon and the smaller beads from the vicinity of Djenne. There are also European imitations of these beads. (See Liu, Granitic Beads And Their Simulations p.12)

Harish beads. Africa

They are used in eastern Sudan and are small yellow furnace-wound beads. (See Francis, West African Perspective The Early Bead Trade p. 98-101)

Hebron manufactured green, yellow and sometimes blue and black beads. Africa

From some time after the twelfth century until the 1880s the salts of the Dead Sea were used as their alkali. After that they were only made from melted-down broken bottles and were a simpler bead. The old-type beads were used in the Sudan, where they were locally called mongur and used by the women. By the 1830s the natives no longer valued the beads. Hausa traders bought them up at low prices and took them home to Kano, Nigeria, and ground them flat and beveled them. Now they sell them in Sudan to the descendants of the original owners as Kano beads for high prices. The beads were not made in Kano. It was only a trader's term.

Hippo beads. Africa

The beads were not made from real hippo teeth, but were *Arca grandosa* or *A. senilis* shell pendants from Singapore strung into necklaces. Glass imitations are also known. The imitations are more rare than the original shell beads. The beads were once used to purchase cattle and other items. They were most frequently used in Nigeria and the Ivory Coast. Much of their value came from the many hours used to polish them with a wet sand mixture. (See Liu p. 31)

"Hubbell" beads. United States - Southwest

The beads were made in Czechoslovakia after the First World War and were in widespread use by 1926. They mainly imitated the Indians' valuable turquoise. They would pawn the turquoise and wear the glass "Hubbell" beads.

Hudson Bay Company traded beads for animal skins with the Indians. Canada

Six green or yellow beads the size of a pea were worth one beaver skin. Three larger light blue beads had the same value. A large light blue opaque bead was worth two "made beavers." Deep blue faceted beads were in great demand and had a high value. They were also called Russian trade beads. Sometimes white hearts were also known as Hudson Bay beads. (See Erikson p.47) (See Liu p. 168-169)

Indo-Pacific or trade wind beads. Pacific Ocean area

The beads were made in Funan, which was the first state in Southeast Asia. The beads were produced at various times and in many locations, including Sumatra. The beads were used over a large area of Indonesia, including Flores, Sumba, Timor and others. They were used as bride price and were handed down from father to son. The reddish-brown beads used in this area probably came from Srivijaya 800 or more years ago. (Francis p. 95).

Trade Wind Beads

Indo-Pacific beads

The beads have been made and traded for more than 2000 years, and (Francis p. 14) calls them the greatest trade item of all time. They were made in southern India and Sri Lanka as well as four other countries. They were first called trade-wind beads. The beads are small drawn monochrome glass beads in red-brown, yellow, turquoise, green and blackish blue. They were manufactured from 250 B.C. until 1300 A.D. There are some striped glass beads that are also called Indo-Pacific beads. Some are black with red and gray stripes, and others are green with yellow stripes. (See Dubin p.184)(See Pacific-Ocean area)

Indo-Pacific Beads

Interlocking beads. Africa

The beads were Czech, made mostly by the Prosser technique. Most are made of plastic and in the 20th century. Used in Africa in trade and jewelry. (See Francis, Beads & People 2.)

Interlocking Beads

Jade beads. Mexico

They were considered more precious than gold and were used as early as 200 A.D. Jade was imported from Guatemala, worked by the Mayan craftsmen and used as a medium of exchange. The jade was apple-colored or emerald green and also found in gray to blue green. The beads were used throughout southern Mexico and Central America. See Chalchihuitl (See Liu p. 144-145)

Jade Beads - Mexico

Jade beads. New Caledonia

Gabbroid amphibolite beads, sometimes labeled as jade or nephrite, were called *mejir* and are often included in money collections. The large green beads which are irregular in shape are of unknown origin. (See Quiggin p. 171-172)

Jadeite beads

Crudely cut, made of low-grade jade. Used for larger transactions. (See Moore)

Jade Beads - Mexico

Jalla beads. Nigeria

Antique Venetian clear or frosty glass beads were used in trade.

Jasper beads. Africa

These stone beads were used by the chiefs and were very valuable. See Lantana beads.

Jatim beads. Indonesia

Jatim is an abbreviation of Jawa Timor (east Java). These beads have only a thin coating of canes over a monochrome core. Jatim beads were mistakenly called *Majapahit* beads, which is a term introduced by dealers trying to make an item popular. These beads never came from the *Majapahit* sites. The exact period of manufacture is not known with certainty but could have started in either 300 A.D. or 600 A.D. and lasted to 900 A.D. Currently most types of ancient beads from this area are being reproduced for sale to both tourists and bead collectors. Some of the imitations are very poor, and others are very good, so be careful. (See Liu p.90-91)

Jalla Beads

Jasper Beads

Jatim Beads

Kano beads. Africa

Hebron-made beads used in Nigeria. See Hebron beads.

Kibangwa beads. Africa

See conus-shell disk beads.

Kiffa beads, Africa

These beads were made from polychrome powder glass in Mauritania, possibly in the towns of Kiffa, Oualata or Mederdra. Powdered glass was applied with saliva with the use of a needle to indigenous and European bead matrices. Many times the base was green bottle glass. They were imitations of ancient beads and in some cases milleflori beads. Only about three beads could be made in a day. This was called the wet-form process. They are found in six shapes: triangular, spherical, cylindrical, conical, hemispheric and lozenge. The triangular shape is the most popular shape, and they are either blue with white spots, solid red or fully decorated with many lines in many colors. The unit was three beads. The spherical beads, cylindrical and hemispheric beads were all multicolored with many lines on them. The lozenge-shaped beads come in three color combinations: solid red, all blue with white lines on the top only and red, white, yellow and black with lines. The older blue beads have two shades of blue, while the newer beads have only one shade of blue. (See Liu p.9,19)

King beads. Africa

Used from 1850 - 1930. They were highly prized bicone beads. They were worn by kings, but it must be remembered that in Ghana, a village chief was called a king. The women of Togo and the Benin Republic still use them in necklaces and bracelets in voodoo ceremonies.

Kings burial beads, Dogon Tribe, Africa

Stone beads were used in Mali in trade and as money.

Koli beads. Africa

Short blue Czech tube beads were heated in Ghana and became Koli beads. Also called cooked beads. Made by cooking in a pot with vegetable matter and then ground on their ends and other surfaces to form an opaque color. The stretch marks on the beads are bubbles bursting close to the surface. (Francis, Markets and the Alteration of Beads in West Africa, p.97.) (See Francis p. 105)

Krobo beads. Africa

The Ghanaian bead makers made these powder beads as copies of Venetian beads with trailed or milleflori decorations. Some of the beads were also made from coarsely crushed old glass beads. Experts disagree on the age of these beads with one expert feeling that the beads

Kiffa Beads

Kiffa Beads

Kiffa Beads

King Beads

King Beads

King Beads

Koli Beads

Krobo Beads

date to the 16th century and another feeling that they were only slightly more than 100 years old. The best known Krobo bead is the adjagba. See *adjagba* and *bodom beads*.

Lankan beads.

See pipe beads.

Lantana beads. Africa

In Old Oyo, the ancient capital of the Yoruba people, red jasper was used to make beads which were mostly long and either cylindrical, barrel-shaped or biconical and highly valued. The beads were hand-made with a man being able to make only a few beads per day. Production ended in the 1930s. (See Francis p. 108) O'Hear states the beads were made from jasper, banded agates or chalcedony which was quarried close to the Niger River at Litingo, Kirashi, Nigeria. Many of the beads were probably traded to Benin. The Emir and other chiefs received the beads as a form of access payment from those seeking favors or services. The beads were made in Ilorin, Nigeria, until as late as 1912. Chiefs would pay 10 pounds for a chain from the neck to the knees. They were used extensively by the important chiefs and other people. In the Festival of Corals, the beads actually used were red jasper, not coral. The beads (lantana) were also used to exchange for slaves. After 1922, the value, use and interest in the beads declined. The production also declined at that time. By 1929, glass copies of lantana were flooding the market. (See O'Hear)

Let beads. Indonesia

Dark blue beads found in Dayak necklaces and in Sarawak. Highly valued. (Adhyatman p.72)

Let beads. Kalimantan (Borneo)

The Kelabit use a dark blue (near black and a green are also known) barrel-shaped bead with flat ends. Let is the word used for valued beads. They were worn by both men and women, and 40 were worth a water buffalo. It is believed that because of their high lead content, many of the beads were made by Chinese living in Banten, Java, around 1600. They were traded to Borneo to obtain diamonds and gold. (See Francis, Heirlooms Of The Hills, p. 9)

Lewis & Clark beads. Africa

Found mainly in Mali.

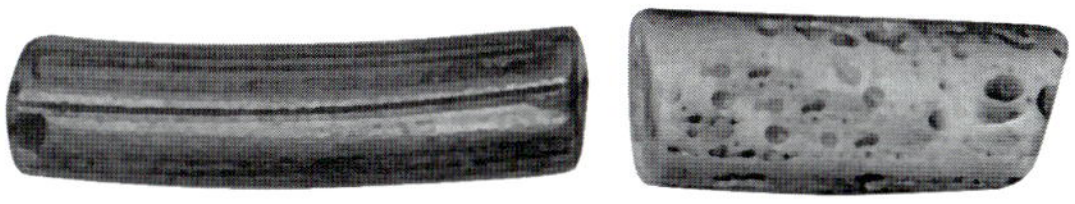
Koli Beads

Lukut Sekala bead. Sarawak

This is the most valuable bead of the Kayan of Sarawak and at one time was worth a male slave. It is reported there are only five now on Sarawak. It is a small black or dark blue lamp-wound bead with flattened ends and four rosettes in white, amber and yellow on the sides and one at each end. The bead was probably Venetian. It is currently worth about $4,000. (See Francis, Heirlooms Of The Hills p. 10)

Lun Bawang beads. Sarawak

The beads were used in making bead caps and were a medium of exchange. A cherry-sized yellow bead used in a bead cap was valued at 40 liters of unhusked rice. Fifty long thin orange beads or ten strands of yellow belt beads were worth one buffalo. An entire bead cap, called a pata, was worth about five buffaloes. A bead cap consists of six to eight strands of beads but can have as many as 11 strands. There are more than 20 kinds of beads used by the Lun Bawang. They range from the long thin orange beads, called *bau tulang buror* to yellow spherical beads called *bau alet.* Fake chevron beads with black zigzag bands as well as Amsterdam chevrons were also used. There are also long faceted carnelian beads (*aki*), black beads (*alet sukur*), black beads with white dots (*let sukur*), large red spherical beads (*alet sia*), gold-decorated beads (*rebuyong amas*) and many others. The origin of most of the beads is not known. After World War II the people changed their way of life from traditional to a more modern lifestyle and the use of beads as money stopped. (See Munan, Beads 5:45-60)

Macca beads.

First invented by Lorenzo Graziati in Venice in 1860. Drawn beads with hexagonal sections according to Francis (Beads at the Crossroads of Continents, p. 297).

Magnesite beads. Southwest United States

It took about 800 regular shell beads to equal one magnesite bead, which was the Pomo's high-value currency. These magnesite beads called po, pol, or fol were made by baking raw nodules of magnesite in a fire and then shaping and drilling the piece to form a bead. The magnesite, which was dull grayish-white, turned beautiful shades of orange which polished up well. Magnesite beads were also used by the Yuki, Wintun, Kuhlanapo, Habenapo, Miwok and Maidu.

Marble beads. Africa & Thailand

(See Liu p.48) - See Alley beads

Lantana Beads

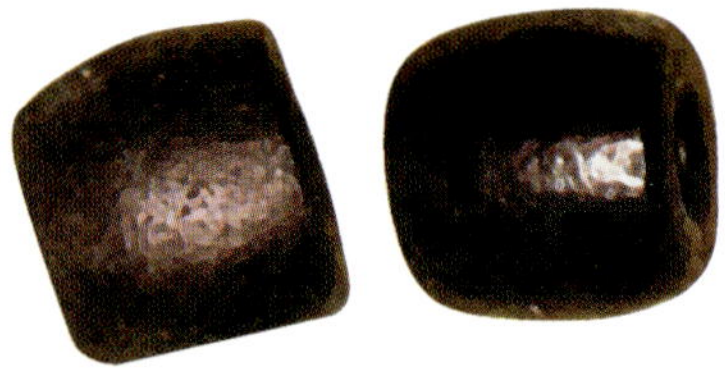

Let Beads

Lewis & Clark Beads

Magnisite Beads - Two On Left Are Heated One On Right Is Raw

Marble Beads

Melon Beads

Melon Beads. Irian Jaya

The beads were made as early as the 16th century and traded through Indonesia until they reached Irian Jaya. They are also called melon beads. The beads were an important part of bride price. It was thought that they came from bead trees grown in the East. On Lake Santani the beads were necessary for marriage. Stone axes and glass bracelets also were used in the bride price. They also were used in compensation, to settle disputes and for ceremonial objects. Copies are currently being made. (See Liu p. 92) (See Taylor p. 276)

Melon Beads. Papua New Guinea

The beads were used in the West Sepik river area. The beads were the same style as those used in Irian Jaya. (See Liu p. 92)

Millefiori beads. Africa

It is now believed that the millefiori bead did not become popular until the late 19th century or early 20th century. The beads were made in Murano, Italy. The name millefiori is an Italian word meaning "a thousand flowers." The beads are made in a two-step process. The mosaic cane is made and broken into thin slices, applied to a wound glass core. It is heated and can be pressed when hot to distort the canes to give many different looks. (See Dubin p.111-112)

Millefiori beads. Indonesia

These Venetian beads were used in trade from the 1830s until the 20th century.

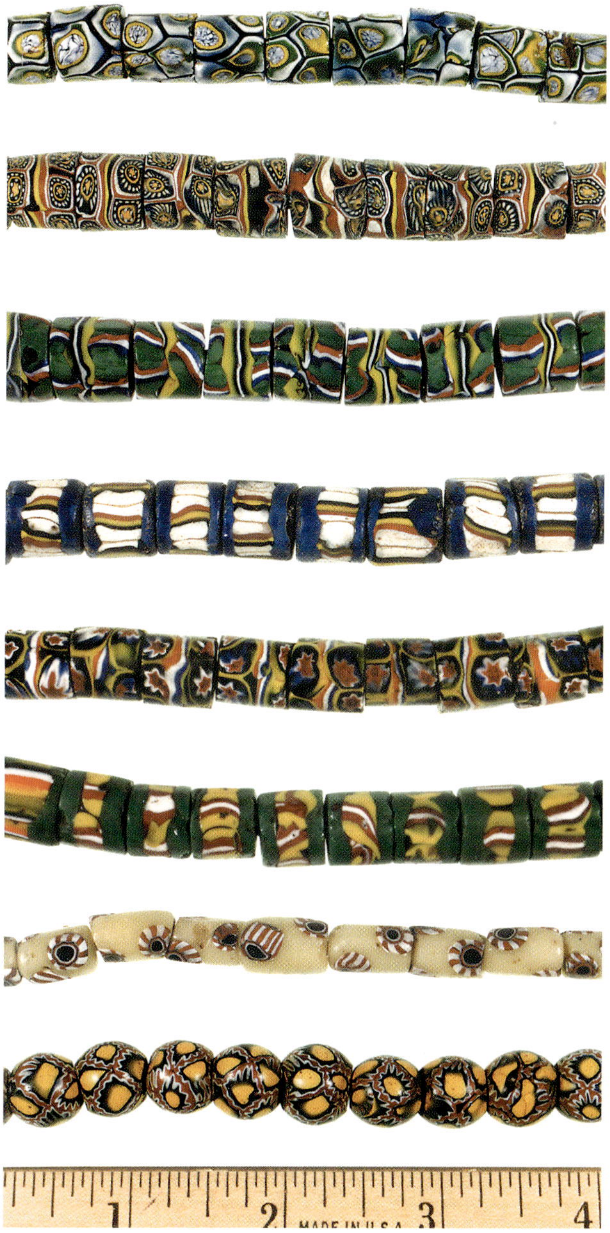

Mileflìori Beads

Ming beads

White glass Venetian wound bead with blue trail-decorated squiggles. The Kalinga value this bead as equal in value to a small pig. They regarded the bead as a porcelain bead from Syria. It is said they were each worth two water buffaloes in Luplupa. (See Francis, Heirlooms Of The Hills,p. 6) (See Liu p. 87)

Morfia beads. Egypt

It is a Fustat fused-rod bead made in Egypt around 900 A.D. or earlier. It is a mosaic and millefiori bead that is a very coveted ancient Islamic bead in Mauritania. The motifs on these beads are copied on the Kiffa beads in Mauritania.

Mutiraja beads. Indonesia Raja means king.

The royal families of the Eastern Lesser Sundas Islands use a small wound coil bead. Commoners cannot even touch these beads. They were traded by the Chinese for sandalwood and were used exclusively by the royal class. In bride purchase the beads are usually given to the groom by the bride's family, and the groom's family gives horses, water buffaloes and gold. These beads are at least 800 years old and are Chinese coil beads, which are seldom sold to outsiders. They are very expensive, and there are copies available that are almost impossible for the outsider to distinguish from the original. The natives use both new and old beads, but only the old beads have a very high value. (See Francis, Heirlooms Of The Hills, p. 12)

Mutisalah. Indonesia

The term does not refer to a particular bead but to all beads in the heirloom system on Timor, Flores, Sumba, Roti, Aru and other islands in the area. They are Indo-Pacific beads that are drawn. The brick red beads are called *mutibata*. Although they are all called *mutisalah* the red ones are also called *mutitanah* or earth beads. They are the beads of the commoners and are not expensive and are used by a man to give to his bride. The orange beads are called *mutibata* or brick beads. They are also beads of commoners but are more rare and valuable than the brick red beads. (See Francis, Mutisalah, p. 104)

Nana beads.

See pipe beads.

Nfwaya beads. Cameroon, Africa

These blue beads were reserved for chiefs and were used to purchase slaves at the rate of 100 beads (three necklaces) per slave.

Nila beads. Mauritania

Ancient small blue glass beads. (See Opper, Powdered-Glass Beads And Bead Trade In Mauritania)

Nueva Cadiz beads. Africa

The beads are named after the South American beads that look very similar to this African bead. (See Liu p. 28)

Milefliori Beads

Mutiraja Beads

Nueva Cadiz - Africa

Nueva Cadiz beads. North & South America

These beads date from the establishment of the town of Nueva Cadiz in 1498 and the abandonment of the town in 1545 following a natural disaster. The beads were not common after 1560. The town was located on an island off the coast of Venezuela. They are compound drawn beads without the star pattern of the chevrons. They have a square shape, and in some cases the square was twisted along the length. Most all have three layers with the outer layer being blue, from translucent to deep ultramarine. Some have stripes in each of the four outer flat surfaces running the length of the bead. The true Nueva Cadiz beads come only from South America around the time of the Spanish explorers. They were also used in the southeastern part of the United States. By about 1560 the large Nueva Cadiz styles dropped out. There are also red Nueva Cadiz style beads found in the northeastern part of the United States in Lancaster, PA, and upper New York. Similar beads called by the same name are now used in Africa. They look similar but are not nearly as old. Jargstorf suggests the beads may be of Dutch manufacture.

Ostrich eggshell beads. Africa

Turkana tribe members use the beads to make necklaces. These necklaces have been made in East Africa since at least 7000 B.C. In north Africa they have been used since 10,000 B.C. The beads were sometimes soaked in water before drilling. A man could make one necklace of beads per day.

Ox Eye beads.

See White heart beads.

Padre beads and anteater teeth. Thailand

In Thailand padre beads of many colors were strung with other items like these anteater teeth in necklaces.

Padre Beads. United States - Southwest

These small glass beads, about 3/8 inch in diameter, were also called chief beads. The beads were made in China and traveled to the their destination via the Philippines and were traded by the Spanish and later the Russians. In 1900 the Pima Indians would trade a good horse for 30 satiny sky-blue "padre" beads, according to Scottsdale Indian trader Dick Le Roy. The U. S. Army paid six pounds of these beads among other items as ransom for Olive Oatman. Some call any blue wound bead a padre bead, but that term should be reserved for beads of Chinese origin prior to the 1850s. (See Francis p. 114)

Mutislalah Beads

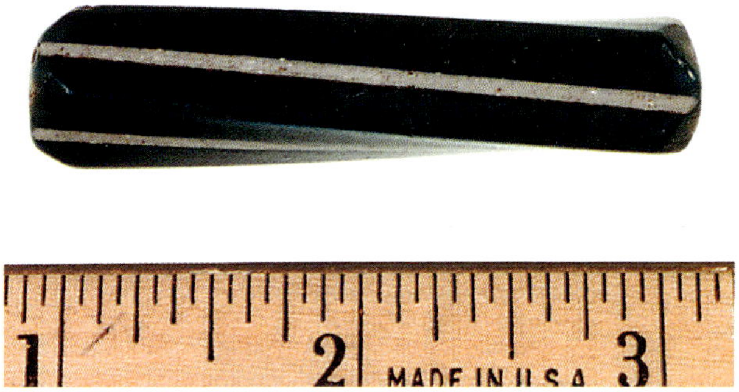

Nueva Cadiz - South America

Nueva Cadiz - South America

Pagadua necklace. Papua New Guinea, Kapauku tribe

In 1955, necklaces consisting of many kinds of glass beads were also considered money. (Pospisil p. 304) The Europeans introduced a cylindrical or spherical light blue glass bead called *dau*, which was money, and 30 of them were worth one *dege bomoje* cowry.

Pang-o beads. Philippine Islands

The Ifugao tribe valued one of these beads at one water buffalo or $250. It was their most valuable bead. It is a glass cylinder with a bright golden hue. It is a wound bead made with two layers of glass and a gold foil on the innermost layer. (See Francis, Ifugao Heirloom Beads, p. 113)

Peking glass beads. Indonesia

These monochrome beads with bubbly glass, large perforations and uneven shapes with small peaks of glass at the ends were used in Sarawak in the 14th to 16th centuries and are also found in Kalimantan (Borneo). Very few, if any, of these beads were ever made in Peking (Beijing). Peking beads were used in many parts of the world, including the Americas, via the Spanish Galleon trade. The Philippines used Chinese beads from a very early time. They were also used in Mexico, Alaska and various parts of Southeast Asia. (See Francis, Peking Glass Beads)

Pelangi beads. Indonesia

They were made around 900 A.D. Their decoration appears to be a series of swirls.

Pipe beads. Cameroons, Africa

Also known as *tomenda* or *fa* beads, they are drawn, undecorated tubular glass beads in blue or red. In 1850, the blue beads, called *nana*, were worth one-half their weight in gold dust. The beads had to be the smaller beads, and no substitutes would do. It is believed they were actually substitutes for earlier bluish-coral beads made in Benin and traded through West Africa.(Harter p. 6) The red tubular beads were called *lankan* and appear to be imitations of red coral. (See Harter p. 8)

Polychrome beads. Africa

They are Venetian-made glass beads.

Polychrome beads. United States

The Sioux, Blackfeet, Crow and Wallawalla used them in trade. They were made in Venice and had highly sophisticated and delicate designs of leaves and flowers. (See Liu p.28)

Ostrich Eggshell Beads

Padre Beads

Pang-O Beads

Pound Beads

Prayer Beads

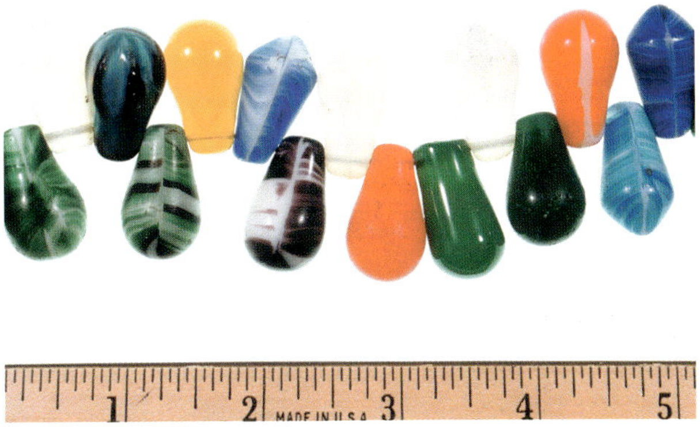

Prosser Beads

Prosser Beads

Pumtek Beads - Bottom - Genuine Old Beads
Top - Modern Made After 1926

Pony beads. United States - Midwest

In about 1675, the French traders introduced small beads called pony beads because they were transported by traders on ponies.

Pony beads. United States - Southwest

Small glass beads from 1/8 to 1/10 inch in diameter. They were used in the early 1800s and gradually replaced the traditional porcupine-quill work previously used. They are similar to seed beads but larger.

Porcelain beads. Africa

Drawn white glass beads.

Pot beads.

See sand cast beads

Pound beads. Africa

Tutsi Women from Rwanda wore necklaces of many strings of these beads. The number of strings denotes wealth. The most popular colors were black, white, dark blue and red. Also see seed beads.

Powder beads.

See sandcast beads

Prayer beads. Tibet

They were made from human bones with semi-precious bits of stone embedded. (See Dubin p. 78-81)

Priest beads.

See sandcast beads

Prosser beads. Africa

The beads are named after Richard and Thomas Prosser who patented a machine to make buttons in 1840 and 1841, which was improved by Jean-Felix Bapterosses in the next few decades, according to Francis, Beads & People 2. A powdered material is put into the machine, which exerted intense pressure on the material and turned it into a bead. Most Prosser beads have a thin, often hidden, seam and pitted areas on one end. (See Francis 20 Easy Steps To Identifying Most Beads In Most Collections, p. 17) (See Liu P. 32-33)

Pumtek beads. Burma

These beads were made from opalized (fossilized) palm wood around 1,000 to 1,500 years ago by the Pyu of Wadi. Since 1926, imitations have been made from fossilized (but not opalized) wood with finer grain. The beads are dark brown with white lines. They were valued among the Chin of Myanmar (Burma) and were called buried thunderbolts.They had a high exchange rate and are included in the obligatory payments that precede marriage. The fossilized hardwood used to make the modern beads is called *Dipteracarpoxylon burmensus*, while the opalized fossilized wood is called *Borassus flabellifer* wood. The opalized palmwood can be chipped in any direction, while the regular fossilized hardwood splits along only one plane. Around 1900, some villagers in Payagyi found pumtek beads in ruins, and they started selling them to the Chin. By 1926 they could find no more Pumtek beads, so they started to make imitations using the common petrified wood found around Payagyi. They used a white mixture of lime, soda and borax for the white part, several other chemicals to form the dark part and baked the resulting beads. The prices of these imitations were less because the Chin recognized them as imitations. (See Francis, Pumtek Beads, p. 104-105 See Liu p. 83)

Roman beads. Africa

No Roman beads should be found south of Algeria. Most of the Roman beads claimed from this southern area are actually early Islamic beads.)See Francis, Beads & People 2.) (See Dubin p.60-61)

Rose bead.

See White heart beads.

"Russian" trade beads. Alaska

They are short bugle or cane-type drawn beads with multiple facets. There were 18, 21 or 24 facets. The many colors are transparent blue, deep transparent green or amber, a translucent white and occasionally ruby red and lavender. Probably made in Bohemia (Czechoslovakia), shipped to Belgium, repackaged and shipped to China, and traded to Russian companies that used the beads to trade for furs. Some feel that the beads may have come from the Hudson Bay Company or John Jacob Astor, the owner of the American Fur Company.

The Indians of the Northwest Coast also valued a blue bead they called a "chief bead." This kind of bead was also traded in Africa. There it was called the ambassador bead because its purpose was to obtain the goodwill of the gods. (See Harris, The Russian Bead)

Russian blue bead. United States - Northwest

The Indians of the Columbia River valued the faceted and smooth blue beads and would trade furs for them. Six to eight beads were worth a beaver or three martins.

Sandcast beads

Parts of East and West Africa have been making beads with this method for more than 1,000 years, and in Ghana this method has been used since the 1600s. Scrap glass bottles were crushed very fine and then the powder was put into clay molds in the center of which a stem of the cassava plant was placed to form the hole of

Roman Beads

"Russian" Trade Beads

"Russian" Trade Beads

"Russian" Trade Beads

Sandcast Beads

Sandcast Beads

Silver Beads

Skunk Beads

the bead. It was then placed in an oven for about an hour. The designs of the beads depend on the colors of the glass and how the powdered glass was put in the mold. Clear glass produced white, green beer bottles produced green, sulfur added to clear glass produced yellow and washing blue added to clear glass produced blue. Some of the beads have decorations added or are polished. Priest beads are larger sandcast beads that have vertical stripes or layered bands of color. Many are beige, brown, gray, blue or green. Other beads are also made from powdered glass including *adjagba, akosu, bodom, kiffa* and *krobo* beads. (See Francis p. 105)

Seed beads.

Africa. Small drawn glass beads, also called empress beads, were used in bunches of five or six strings in different lengths. Four or five bunches weighed one pound. The Xhosa society used glass beads as a money equivalent, or rather as a cattle equivalent. In 1825 a series of fairs was established at Fort Wilshire along the banks of the Keiskamma River, where large quantities of ivory were traded for glass beads and other items. Later the value of the beads decreased to the point that by 1870 they were no longer a money item. In the Cameroons they were called *futomtcha* and many variations exist that are called this name. In the 1800s, one teaspoon of these beads was one full day's work. Also see pound beads.

Seed beads. Cameroons

These glass beads were of Venetian or Czechoslovakian manufacture and were used as a medium of exchange in the slave trade and traded for valuables. (See Northern p. 21)

Shell beads. Solomon Islands

Made on Malaita Island. A man gave many strings of shell beads as a bride-price. A bead lender became a leader in the community.

Small shell or stone beads were sewn jackets.

See jackets.

Shell beads. United States - California Coast

Pomo Indians were major suppliers of shell bead valuables to all of central California. Only specialists who inherited the privilege could make the actual beads. Many taboos had to be observed by the specialists. In 1900 a string consisted of 200 beads. A deer was worth six strings. A domestic bow taking eight to 10 days to make was worth 12 1/2 strings. Beads were made of clamshell. It also took about 800 regular beads to equal one of their magnesite beads which were their highest value currency. These magnesite beads, called *po, pol,* or *fol,* were made by baking raw nodules of magnesite in a fire and then shaping and drilling the piece to form a bead. The magnesite, which was dull grayish-white, turned beautiful shades of orange when heated and then polished up well. The beads were used as blood debt and in exchanges between families of the bride and groom.

Shell beads. United States - Midwest

Rolled tubular or rounded beads made from native copper from Lake Superior were traded several hundred miles away as early as 3000 B.C.

Shell beads. United States - Zuni Tribe

Beads with a purplish tinge made from the *Olivella biplicata* were used as a form of money with the traders paying two or three dollars for a string of 24 inches. The beads were about 1/16 inch in diameter. (See Orchard p. 27)

Silver beads. Ethiopia

Hollow old silver beads made in two halves and soldered together. Many have the sign of the Jewish bead maker. (See Liu p.132-135)

Skunk beads. Africa

Black Venetian glass or plastic beads with polka dots are called skunk beads. They were used in trade thoroughout Africa.

Snake bone beads

Africa Colorful zigzag glass beads which fit tightly together. They were probably made in Czechoslovakia in a mold and are also called interlocked beads. They imitate snake bones. (See Francis p. 24)

So-so beads

Africa A translucent yellow bead from Ghana that was subjected to heating. (See Francis, Beads & People 2 , p.4.)

Spondylus beads. Ecuador

Maya spondylus beads from 1500 A.D. Red shell beads were made of the spondylus shell and were believed to have been used as a medium of exchange. (See Hedges, July 1970) (See Dubin p.256-258)

Spondylus beads. Guatemala

Beads made from the thorny oyster were introduced as a medium of exchange by the Spaniards. (See Johnson p. 18)

Spondylus beads. Peru

The Inca culture from about 1100 A.D. used spondylus shell beads which were traded from Ecuador.

Snake Bone Beads

Spondylus Beads - Ecuador

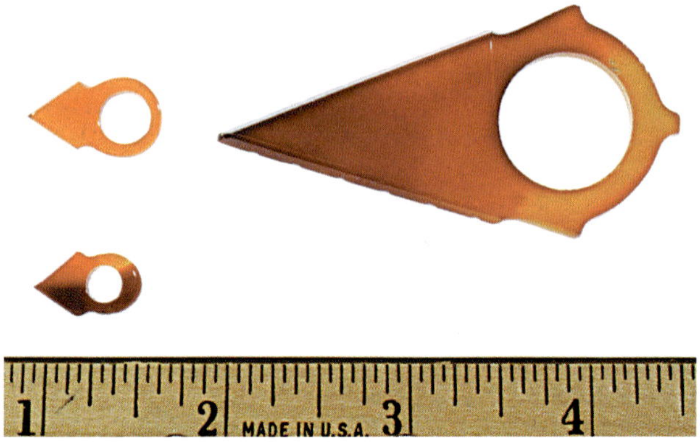

Talhakimt Pendant

Tictactoe Beads

Turquoise - South America

Turquoise - Tibet

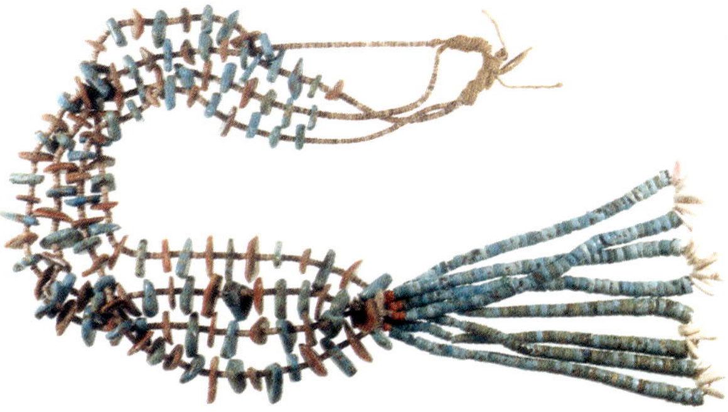

Turquoise Pawn

Udoud Beads - Courtesy Thomas Lautz

Stone beads. Indonesia

Semi-precious stone beads made of onyx, banded agate and carnelian probably came from India. A soft green stone was also used. The beads were at times decorated with soda, which leaves a smooth white line. This was done as early as 2600 B.C. and was known to the Assyrians, Persians and medieval Thais. Some were made in India. To obtain a dark line the area forming the line was soaked in sugar water and heated. It is felt this technique was also used to make the dZi beads from Tibet. (See Dubin p. 229)

Striped beads. Africa

The Africans requested striped beads as early as the 17th century. In 1603 it was reported in West Africa that only a light blue bead with up to three white stripes was wanted. Later the beads were made by the Venetians and Germans. (Jargstorf p. 72)

Talhakimt pendants. Africa

Agate triangular pendants with a hole at the wide end came from Idar-Oberstein and were similar to pieces collected in Dafur, Sudan, in the 1930s. Some are also Czech molded glass pieces and others are from India made from carnelian. The Czech pieces can be identified by the duller matte surface, while the Idar-Oberstein pieces are shiny and have good craftsmanship. The Indian pieces are shiny, but the workmanship is not nearly as good and they contain many nicks on the edges. There are also red plastic pieces that are worn by the Berber women in necklaces and are European in manufacture. (See Liu, India, Idar-Oberstein And Czechoslovakia Imitators And Competitors)

Telsum beads. Africa

These beads are actually small silver boxes that can be strung on a cord and were used in Ethiopia. Their use as money is still in question.

Tictactoe beads. Africa

A decorated wound-glass bead made and used in the 1800s for trade in West Africa as money.

Tosi beads. Cameroons, Africa

These beads are colorless or transparent pink decorated with thin white lines running the length of the beads. They look like gooseberry beads. Only the chiefs and dignitaries authorized by the chief could wear them and then only during public events. One stand of the beads was worth one wife or two slaves. Twenty beads was the price of one male slave. (See Harter, p. 10)

Trade-wind beads

Now called Indo-Pacific beads. See Indo-Pacific beads.

Turquoise. South America

Small turquoise beads were believed to have been used as money hundreds of years ago.

Turquoise. Tibet

Beads made of turquoise were used as a barter currency in Tibet for hundreds of years. Even the poorest Tibetan owned some turquoise beads. Nyinba women used turquoise in their headdresses. They most valued turquoise that shows a flawless, sky-blue color without matrix. (See Liu p. 82-83)

Turquoise beads. United States - Southwest. Hopi and Zuni Indians.

They were a store of wealth. An Indian pawns his turquoise jewelry to grow wool and other crops. When the crops are sold, the man reclaims his pawned jewelry and invests the balance in additional turquoise jewelry. (See Erikson p. 111) (See Dubin p.260-261)

Udoud beads. Palau Islands

The group of islands had 6,000 Palauans in 1946. The major island is Babeldaob, which was also the source of the majority of the Yap Island stone money. Udoud is the generic name for bead money on Palau. Palau's monetary system was one of the most highly developed and complex in the world. It consists of clear glass, pottery and polychrome beads as well as crescent bar gorgets. They are used in purchases as well as gifts for weddings, births, funerals and house building. The origin is not known, but there is speculation that they ultimately came from somewhere in Asia. Many legends tell of people taken to strange lands where the beads are common and even a swimming island that dispenses the money. The system was already operating in 1789.

There are three kinds of men's money.

The first kind appears to be a ceramic, #6 in hardness (Mohs Hardness Scale), orange luster waxy. Specific gravity 2.6. The origin of the beads is not known and is clouded in legend and mystery. Some pieces of Palau money are known to exist on Yap Island also. It is believed that some of the beads were brought to Palau by the Yapese when they went there for the stone money used on Yap Island. The system of values of the money is very difficult to understand, even for the Palauans. The shape, size, color and material all help to determine their value. The beads occur in two colors: red, called *mungau* and yellow called *barrak*. Kubary said that genuine *barrak* is a very hard, sulfur yellow substance with faint conchoidal cracks. The pores, when filled with

Vaseline Beads

Venetian Beads

Venetian Beads

Venetian Beads

Venetian Beads

Venetian Beads

Wood Beads

Zen Beads

dirt, give the surface a finely spotted appearance. They have a faint luster and often cracks and fissures. Most of the large pieces of money belong to this type. *Barrak* is more highly valued than *mungau*. There are different grades of both colors and a type which seems to be a mixture of the two. Below this value is a second yellow variety, called *mres*. There are two varieties which had a medium commercial value in early days. They only occur in the smallest denominations and are thin perforated disks. The red *mungau* occurs in several varieties. Many of the pieces are made from several colors of different materials and have veining, fissures, very fine pores and even what appears to be organic material in them.

The *orokommel* variety has red *mungau* and yellow *barrak* with the fissures in the material filled with black and occasionally purple or sap green.

The *ngarremek* variety has even amounts of red and yellow.

The *idik* variety has a brown hued true *mungau*. These all have the general name of *bakal* and most are from one to three inches long with a gradual curvature to the flat surfaces. All are perforated to be placed in a necklace.

Small round beads, disks and double cones made from *barrak* and **mungau** were equal to a *"mor a kaymo"* which is the lowest value any piece could have. Kubary named and described 14 of them, and it is believed that many more exist.

Bakals have proper names. The larger pieces were the most valuable and became famous. The most valuable type of bead was *ba'al* and it was traditionally owned by upper-rank families and never used in ordinary economic transactions.

The second kind of men's money is called beads. There are two classes and one sub-class. One main class is called *kalebukub*. This class was made of a vitreous compound that resembles porcelain and has a hole molded into it for suspension. Most were mottled or had patterns of white wings embedded in a blue, green or other colored matrix. Kubary said there were 25 varieties of *kalebukub* at his time. The other class was called *kluk*. To the non-expert the two classes look very much alike. The kluk was less valuable than the *kalebukub*. There were between 16 and 26 kinds of *kluks* according to Kubary. The general design consists of parallel, oblique or concentric veins. This *kluk* is the standard value for Palau money with a value of 100. At the present time it is worth $100 or 1,000 to 2,000 pounds of taro. The sub-class was called *adolobok* and was a porcelain bead. It is actually a slice of either a *kalebukub* or a *kluk*. The standard value was the *kluk* and it was an opaque polychrome bead used in many daily transactions. In 1948 a *kluk* was worth about 100 dollars. In German times a *kluk* was worth 100 marks. All are very rare and valuable. Many of the beads were buried with their owners or were lost when the beads were hid by their owners in times of danger.

The third class of men's money is made of glass and is called *kaldoyok*. This class has depreciated so much in value that it is really not considered money at present. The glass is old and imperfect and either tinted green or faint yellow. They are of a variety of shapes, from pear shaped to spherical and elliptical. *Kaldoyok* beads have many different surfaces.

In the 1880s, Kubary said a ranking *kalebukub* was valued at $60, while the best *adolobok* was worth $7.50. The best *kluk* was worth $12.50, and the best glass *kaldoyok* were worth only $2.50. The *kluk* was the unit of measure and, it was equated to American or Japanese money. The money collected in fines was the only source of income for the chiefs. The people also were required to make certain expenditures in their social life which were in native money. The money was used, for example, to get married, at the time of death and also at births. The money was essential to prestige and political influence. The money was acquired by earning it or through social custom. Just prior to the birth of a child, a ceremony was performed at which the father's family gives one *kluk* to the wife's family. At present, $5 to $30 can be given instead. If a child was named for a person, that person felt very honored and gave the father a present such as a turtle or a piece of money called a *kldait*. Fees were also paid for tattooing and to become an apprentice. Prior to the German administration, one village furnished another village a group of young women for a specified fee. They served as mistresses in the men's house. Payments were also made for adultery and for the return of an angered wife. Money was also paid for divorce and for prestige and succession ceremonies. Other times payments were made were: death of a spouse, inheritance, dances, building a men's house and war. In later years Palauan bead money was not in demand by the young men of the island and therefore its value in dollars was hard to equate. It was also hard to value because one bead cannot be replaced by another bead if the one was lost or broken. The money does not circulate freely because the Palauans do not feel competent to judge the value of the money and therefore get the advice of an expert before accepting a piece. In many cases the owners of the money do not actually possess the money, but instead it is held by certain family representatives for the owner. One money expert recited the names of 282 types of money totaling 2,947 pieces. Of this total, 73 types numbering 630 pieces are not used at the present time. There are no new pieces coming into the system, as all are of foreign manufacture and are antique. Only the oldest male in a group of matrilineal lineage mates can hold his own money and will also hold the money of his siblings and sister's children. A man also provides the money to pay for the bride of his son. Many other payments are required to be made for such things as a payment to the mother's brother of his daughter-in-law when she becomes pregnant, as well as a payment when a marriage is ended for any reason. Much of the value of a piece is dependent on its history. To obtain a more valuable piece you must pay more than its value in smaller pieces. This means that they are not exchangeable up and down at the same rate. Someone has said that Palauan money is more like our jewels than our money because the value goes up faster than the proportionate size like a two carat diamond is worth more than two one carat diamonds. Also some diamonds like the Hope diamond are worth more than another diamond of comparable size and color and flaws. It is believed that the opaque glass crescents are segments of glass bracelets identical to those found in ancient burial sites in the southern Philippines. It is suspected that the Palauan beads actually came from Yap and had been used to pay for food, canoe sailing and later for permission to quarry Yap stone money on Palau. Palauans do not like to show outsiders their money. (See Barnett) (See Ritzenthaler, he lists a complete inventory of the kinds and number of pieces)

Vaseline beads. Africa

The yellowish-green color is from uranium salts. These Czech bicone beads were molded and then the facets were ground onto them. They were used in Ghana and first appeared on the market in 1880. It is probable the name was attached in the 1970s when the beads came to the United States in large numbers.

Venetian beads. Africa

White heart, also known as rose bead and ox eye. Africa, North and Central America, Thailand, Burma.

They were originally made in Europe.

Wood beads. Nigeria

The beads were carved and decorated and used as small change. The most common were small wooden beads made by the turners of Upper Egypt, which were bought up chiefly by the Bedouin and other peasants. 3/8″ diameter. (See Francis, Beadmaking In Islam: The African Trade And The Rise Of Hebron, p. 18)

Zen beads. Tibet

The glass beads were also used in Nepal and made by The Sick Company in the 1920s.

Photos taken by the author on his trips to the Pacific.

Above: Melawei Village, Papua New Guinea - The native is carrying a drum with a reptile skin head and shell armbands and necklace. Notice the bird of paradise feathers in his head. Taken in 1973.

Upper left: In the Wahgi Valley, Papua New Guinea, this girl is prepared for a ceremony with bird of paradise feathers. Through her nose she has king of saxony feathers. Taken in 1973.

Lower left: This native from the Chimbu tribe, Papua New Guinea, is wearing two kina shells around his neck and broken kina shells hanging from his belt. His head band includes nassa shells on native fiber. Through his septum he is wearing a kina shell sliver and cone shell disk with a notch for his septum. Taken in 1973.

Above: This celebration in Papua New Guinea shows many of the bride price items used. The women have beads and kina shells around their necks. Most have bird of paradise feather head pieces. Taken in 1973.

Right: These women from Papua New Guinea show many items used as money. The woman on the right has a cassowary feather head piece. The woman in the center has a headband covered with nassa shells hanging from her neck. She also has a boar tusk necklace and a hearband made of lilly root (yellow) and green beetles in the lilly root weaving. The tan piece on her chest is a cuscus fur. The woman on the left has a nassa covered bark headband. Taken in 1973.

Above: In Andagalimp Village on the Sepik River in Papua New Guinea, the two natives are wearing paradise feather headdresses. Both are wearing an omak. The native on the left is holding a drum. Taken in 1973.

Upper Left: A shell money necklace and mask purchased by the author was carried by a native from Kandangei Village on the Sepik River in Papua New Guinea. Taken in 1973.

Lower Left: Papua New Guinea used dog teeth and kina shells as money. This girl is wearing a dog tooth necklace on a kina shell. She has a cuscus fur down her chest. She wears a headband made of lily root holding green beetles. This necklace was also used has money. Taken in 1973.

Right: In Papua New Guinea the Andagalimp people display a moka (man on left). The moka has a kina shell on an ochre covered board. The man on the right has a omak on his chest. it is a series of parallel bamboo sticks which represent a certain amount of goods that are owed to him. All three men have bird of paradise feather headdresses. Taken in 1973.

Below: The author is purchasing a boar tusk and cowry shell necklace from a native of Kubkain Village on the Sepik River in Papua New Guinea. The native is wearing a kina shell from his neck and a shell nosepiece in his nose. on his head he is wearing a cassowary feather nead piece and a headband covered with nassa shells. Both pieces were used as money. Taken in 1973.

Upper left: Trobriand islander making clam shell rings. Taken in 1995.

Lower left: The author on Sumba, Indonesia, wearing lodi around his neck with ikat cloth in the background. Taken in 1996.

Upper right: The Moon of Pejing (the largest moko drum) is located in a temple on the Island of Bali. Taken in 1994.

Lower right: In Tenganan Vvillage on Bali, Indonesia, double ikat cloth was made and used as money and wealth. this is a woman weaving double ikat cloth. Both the weft and warp are dyed prior to weaving into cloth. Taken in 1996.

Top: A closeup of the Moon of Pejeng in the temple. It is nine feet long. It is believed to have been made of bronze in 300 bc during the bronze age in Indonesia. Taken in 1994.

Center: Trobriand islanders scrapping banana leaves to make bundles - a form of money. Taken in 1995.

Bottom: This tomb is located on Sumba Island, Indonesia. Notice the mamuli on the right side and the taka on the left side. Both items were used as money and appeared on many other tombs on the island. Taken in 1996.

Upper left: The woman is holding mamuli on the island of Sumba, Idonesia. This mamuli was used in bride price. Taken in 1996.

Lower left: these brass rings were used as money on the island of Sumba, Indonesia. They were considered extremely valuable. Taken in 1996.

Above: A doga is worn by a native on the Trobriand islands. This doga is a modern piece made with a shell ring instead of a deformed boar tusk. Taken in 1995.

Top: These skirts were used as women's money on Kaileuna island in the Trobriand Islands. They were used in the Sagali ceremony among other uses. Taken in 1995.

Lower left: On the Trobriand Islands the kula ring uses kula canoes to travel between the islands to trade valuables such as mwali and soulava (bagi). This kula canoe has a decorated splash board. Yaken in 1995.

Lower right: This mwali is held by our guide on an island in the Trobriand Islands. This was the finest piece I saw on the island. Taken in 1995.

Bean Money

Bear Teeth

1705 Original Russian Beard Money - Courtesy Of Charles Stearns

BEAN MONEY

Japan, 1601-1865, Mameitagin.

Their weight ranges from under 2 grams to more than 10 grams of silver or billion. Most have designs or punch marks on a rough surface. They were originally used as bullion or to make up the casting weight differences of cho gin. One side has a God of Plenty with a legend to the left. There are many varieties issued during the Keicho, Genroku, Genbun, Bunsei, Tempo and Ansei periods. (See Krause & Mishler)

BEARSKIN

Quebec, Canada.

The skin became legal tender in 1673. (See Taxay p. 145)

BEAR TEETH

Alaska, British Columbia.

Polar bear teeth were a highly prized medium of exchange. (See Schulman & Gibbs p. 10)

BEARD MONEY

Russia, 1698-1725

In 1698 Peter the Great, Tsar of all the Russians, issued a decree that forbade beards and traditional dress. Later that same year a second order was passed allowing the people to retain their beards and Oriental clothing if they paid a tax for the privilege. Late in 1698 Peter ordered 50,000 tokens to be struck from red copper. Only one pattern is known. In 1705 a second issue was struck and put into circulation. They were within the tolerances of the contemporary half kopek. At the time of Peter's death, a third issue was in production. It was square, and all but a few of the 2600 struck were melted down in 1728. At that time the tax was 50 rubles per year per person. While the piece is not odd & curious money, some collectors include it in their collections because of its unique use.

BEAVER PENDANT

North America

Flat molded pendants in the outline shape of a beaver with a hole near the head were used in trade with the Indians by traders. Most pendants were silver, but copper pieces were also used. They represented "one made beaver" and became the Hudson Bay Company's standard of value for trading in the northwest. There are many modern copies.

BEAVER SKIN

North America

Trade item in Colonial America, Alaska and Canada. The beaver skin, or "made beaver", was a popular unit of measure and item of trade. In 1626 a trader received 10 beaver skins for a piece of cloth, two hatchets and some beads. (Francis p. 26) The Dutch paid two fathoms of white wampum and one fathom of black wampum for a beaver. A good bearskin was also worth one beaver. In 1655 a beaver was worth nine Dutch guilders. In 1670 one beaver was worth a fathom of tobacco, a quarter pound of powder, six knives or a few blue beads. The Indians of the Southern Plains valued a beaver at two good otters, 10 to 12 raccoons or four or five wild-cats. In 1703 in Massachusetts, one beaver skin was worth any of following: two yards of cotton, six knives, six combs, one shirt, two small axes, two small hoes, six fathoms of tobacco, two pints of powder, 40 biscuits, 10 lbs. of pork or one pint of shot. (Weeden p. 401) Other furs were also valued in terms of beaver. One beaver was worth any of the following: one otter skin, one bear skin, two foxes, two woodchucks, four martins, eight minks, four raccoons or one moose hide. (Weeden p. 402)

The main unit of account of the Hudson's Bay Company was the "made beaver". It had an established value that most other items were valued by. It was to represent the value of a prime beaver pelt. The trading of furs by the Indians to the Hudson's Bay Company was a very complicated affair. There was a very formal, complex ceremony that lasted several days. First there were gift-exchange ceremonies. These ceremonies were to formally establish new friendships or renew old ones. The Indians came as a group in canoes. The head of the post then met with the Indian leaders, and speeches were given by both sides. They basically welcomed each other and told what they had to trade. The post then gave the Indian leaders many gifts. In some instances the Indians then got liquor and drank for a couple of days. The peace pipe was then smoked. The trading then started through the window in the wall. No Indians were allowed in the factory or warehouse while the trading was being done. This was to prevent stealing. The Indians thought there was nothing wrong with taking things they wanted because the traders could not use all the goods they had. Indians considered hoarding to be anti-social behavior. The method of trading and the use of the "made beaver" as a unit of account changed over the years. The values of trade items as well as furs also changed over the years. A 4 1/2 ft. gun went from 10 "made beavers" in 1700 to 14 in 1760. In 1700 two wolverine skins were worth one "made beaver", while in 1760 one skin was worth two "made beavers". In 1700 eight knives were worth one "made beaver" and in 1760 only four knives were worth one "made beaver". From 1774 to 1784, the Legislature of the State of Franklin (now part of Tennessee) by law set the salary of the County Clerk at 300 beaver skins per annum. Generally the value of the "made beaver" went down over time. In

Beaver Pendant

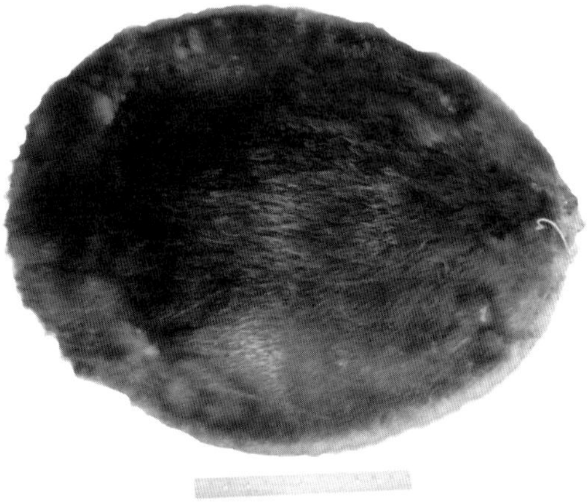

Beaver Skin

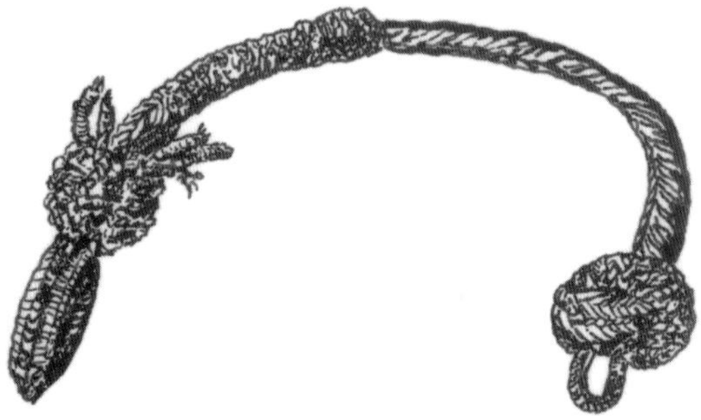

Becket

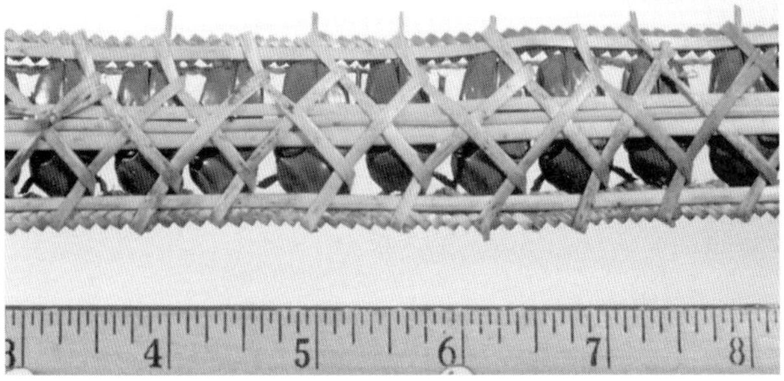

Beetle Head Band Money

the early eighteenth century one beaver was worth one bear skin, four martin skins, four seal skins, one shirt, two pints of powder, one pint of shot or two yards of cotton. (See trade silver) (See Taxey p.94)

BECKET
New Caledonia

Fur from the fruit-eating bat, Pteropus, was highly valued in New Caledonia and used for decorating weapons and also for making the *becket,* which served as currency and a spear-thrower. The bats were caught in nets or knocked down with sling-stones or sticks. The hair was pulled out and spread evenly between fine banana fibers and twisted into a furry cord. The cord was then dyed and woven into the becket or other items. (See Quiggen p. 168-169.)

BEEF
Massachusetts, Carolinas, New Jersey, Pennsylvania, 1690

Beef and other commodities were used as currency. (See Taxay p. 145-146)

BEER
England, 19th century

Beer was used as part of payment of wages in some coal mines. (See Mosher p. 41)

BEESWAX - See Wax

BEETLE MONEY
See Scarab

Ecuador, Peru, Brazil, Papua New Guinea

Dried iridescent beetles were used in South America.

Papua New Guinea.

Iridescent green beetles carapaces (*mormi*) were woven into headbands of golden cane lattice for use in the Asaro, Wahgi and Jimi regions. Headbands were a trading material and a minor form of money. Whole beetles or parts of beetles were used in headbands. (See Schulman & Gibbs p. 11) (O'Hanlon p.15)

BEETLE LEG MONEY
San Matthias Island

Brilliant peacock blue joints from the leg of a beetle which is a member of the *Buprestidae* family of beetles were strung on stiff fiber or softer two ply twine. A fathom equaled a mark or a chicken. (See Quiggin p. 130-131)

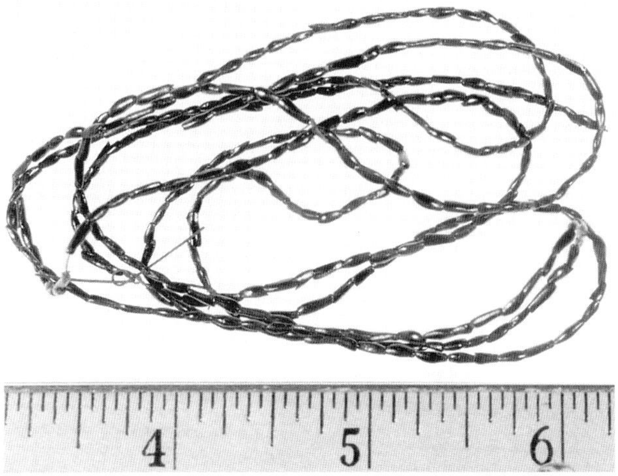

Beetle Leg Money

Beku

Bell Cash - China

BEKU
Trobriand Islands

The large green flecked stone ceremonial axe blade was used in bride price and for canoe purchase. It was also used by white traders, to purchase pearls, for performance of sorcery, payment for gaining allies in war, payment for killing someone and performance of magic spells. The stone was quarried on Muyua Island and Woodlark Island to the southwest of the Trobriands, and large pieces were brought to Kiriwina where specialists polished the finished blade. The biggest blades were very thin and well polished over the entire blade. The rarest *beku* axes had handles of a very distinctive style. They were then considered a very important valuable in the Kula ring. The blades were also used to form alliances in fights as well as arranging a battleground in another area so your village and gardens would not be damaged. They were used as *kaributu* gifts. In Kiriwina they were male valuables. *Beku* were individually owned and inherited by men. The blades are not being manufactured at present, but they still are being used to some extent. A man that had five *beku* was considered wealthy. *Beku* is considered an exchange object only on Kiriwina. In 1970 the blades were small, not used much and few in number. During exchange the blades were inserted into wooden handles, which were only props. On Sudest Island greenstone axe blades were called *tobotobo*. Long thin dark green axeblades were called *Giarova*. There are many other names for various axeblades used in the many islands. Each seems to have its own common size, shape and color, but most seem to have at least some green in them. Traders used them to purchase pearls from the natives. They were called *benam* in Tubetube.
See Kula.

BEALONG - See *Gambar*

BELA - See earrings, Flores, Indonesia

BELL - See Buffalo Bells, Deogonta, Hawkbell

BELL CASH
China, before 400 B.C.

Small bronze bells called Zhong Qian or bell money. Many experts do not consider these bells a currency, but they are included in many collections as barter items. Many different styles and sizes.

BELL- COPPER
Mexico

Copper bells were used by the Maya as money. Although abundant, silver was highly valued, but it did not serve

Bell Cash - China

Bell- Copper - Mexico

Bell- Copper - Mexico

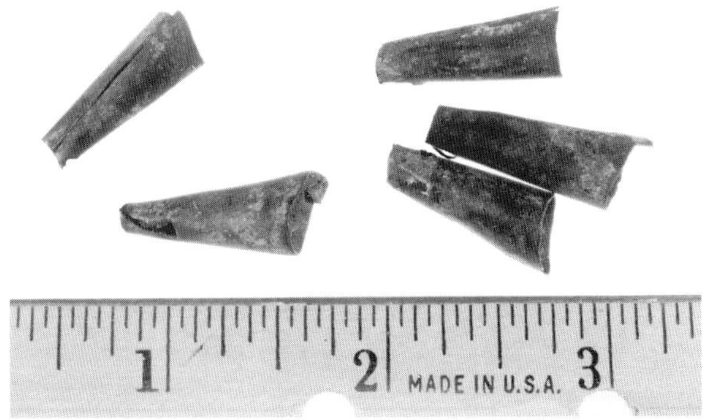

Bell- Copper - Mexico

as money. Bells were valued according to size. 3/4" (See Taxay p. 41)

Bell-Iron

BELL-IRON

Africa, Congo

They are found singly or in pairs connected by a rigid piece of curved iron and are called *ngke*. They have no tongues but were beaten with rubber-headed sticks. One hundred bells would purchase a slave. Five bells would buy a pot of palm oil. They were also used in ceremonies and, in a few cases, wars were fought over particular bells. They were used as a form of currency around the Ubangi bend in the late nineteenth century. The bells were also used as an insignia of leadership in African societies from as early as 1000 C.E. The bells were also used as tools of communication, instruments for conveying important messages. (See Kriger p. 141) (See Quiggin p. 75)

BELL

North America

From the 1500s bells made of copper and silver were used in trading. Many were made in two parts like buttons. (See Hamilton p. 128)

BELT MONEY

Berber Area - Africa Berber Tribe

A leather belt covered with agate stones set in brass bezels and made hundreds of years ago was used as money. (See Schulman p. 33)

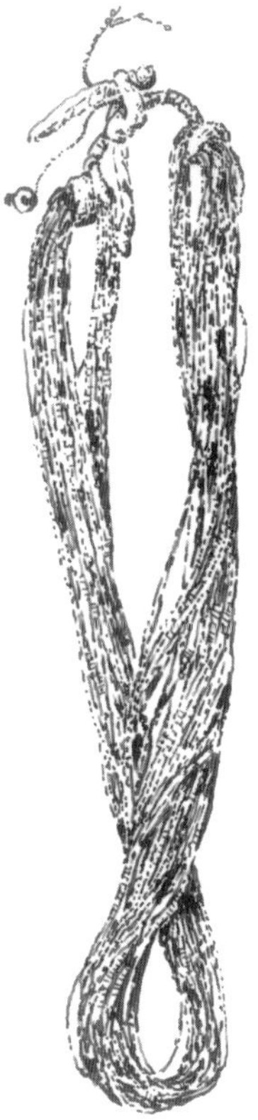

Matty Island Belt

Matty Island

A girdle in the form of a hank of soft black cord was very rare and expensive and was said to be worth five pounds. "The individual cord was a soft two-ply foundation bound spirally with fine blackened coconut fiber and was wound tightly to make a cord of only one millimeter in thickness. The spirals are parallel and look like black beads. (See Quiggin p. 133 - 134)

Berber Belt Money

BELT PENDANT MONEY

Africa, Namibia

Ivory decorated ornamental belt pendant. A husband presents his wife with one or more on their wedding day depending on how much livestock he owns. (See Borel p. 100)

BENAM - See Beku

BERBER AGATE BELT MONEY - See Belt Money - Berber

BETEL NUTS

Island of Palau, Papua New Guinea, Solomon Islands, Indonesia

Betel nuts and leaves served as small change and also were chewed as a stimulant. Lime and ginger was also used with the betel nuts. The nuts stain their teeth red and black, and the lime can cause cancer.

BIKIE

Southern Cameroon, Africa

Iron small spearheads without barbs were used as money to purchase food, livestock, barkcloth, pay fines, and in bride price. Plural for *ekie*. During the German colonial period they had an accepted rate of exchange. The Bene *bikie* were also called mimboss. In the Bene area, 20 spearheads were the price of a bride. They ceased to function as money in the 1920s. At one time a bride price consisted of 10,000 *bikie*. (See Guyer, The Iron Currencies of Southern Cameroon.) (See Kriger p. 108-109.)

Ntumu Bikie

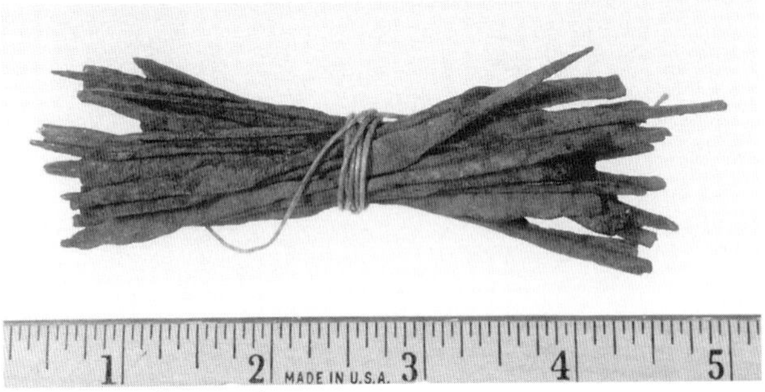

Bena Mimbas (Bikie)

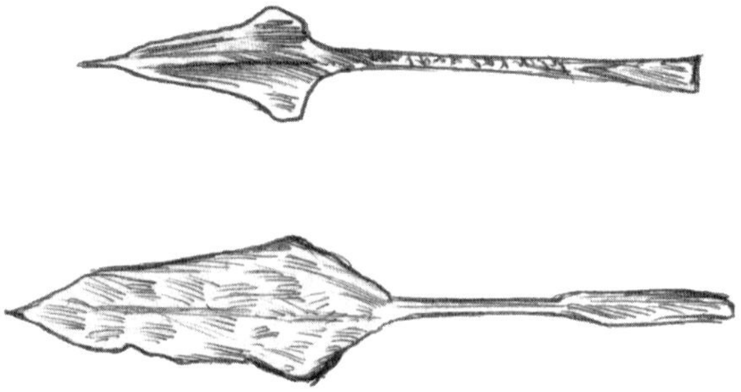

Iten'Ge (Bikie)

BILABA

A complex exchange system of central Africa.

BILL- HOOK - See Knife Money

BILUM (NET OR STRING BAG)

Papua New Guinea

These woven net bags were commonly used throughout all of Papua New Guinea. They are used by women to carry everything from sweet potatoes to babies. They are manufactured only on the mainland with the best ones coming from the interior. The Melpa tribe use new *bilums* as a dowry. They are made by her parents, sisters and brother's wives to give to her new sisters-in-law. In the Wosera area the *bilum* is a large portion of bride wealth payments. This *bilum* is a special kind that is much larger and made with a tighter weave and better workmanship using natural fibers and decorated in color. Among the Telefol the net bags along with 26 other different items made up the bride price. *Bilums* are also used in complex exchanges from strengthening friendships to a form of flirting. The kind, style and quality of the *bilum* all denote something. The complex tricolored bags take up to one year to make and have up to 48 strings being woven simultaneously. The bags also have a value in ritual exchanges of a traditional wealth item. To the Dani in Irian Jaya, *bilum* bags are one of the main exchange items. They were used as money. Tribes added decorations to the *bilum* to identify their tribe. In Abelam the tricolored *bilum* can be carried only by men who have attained certain stages in male initiation. The *bilum* is also used to denote political authority. *Bilums*

Bride Price Bilum

decorated with white cowry shells are used in the Murik Lakes area to identify a chief. There are many different types of *bilums*. Some are as small as a finger-sized amulet *bilum* to an exceptionally large and strong men's *bilum*. The most common type is the all purpose, large, open-looped, wide women's *bilum*. There are special purpose *bilums* like the *bilum* used to store a baby's umbilical cord until the baby has grown strong, at which time it is buried. Another type covered with wild fowl feathers is used in a male's first initiation. Some bilums are sacred. There are a large number of types of weaving with some having large holes, while other styles have a very tight weave. The looping can be an open spaced loop, strengthened loop, traditional loop or a chain loop. Decorations are used on the *bilums* with some kinds of decorations being wild pig's tails, bird feathers and cowries. Presently, extruded nylon thread is used to make the cheapest everyday *bilums*. The nylon thread is called *bilum* twine. It takes about 5.5 yards of twine to make an average size men's *bilum* and from 80 to 100 hours. Four *bilum* bags were worth one large pot. A *bilum* would last about three years in Papua New Guinea. In the 1960s the average bride price for an uneducated 18 year old was one pig, five *bilums*, 10 saucepans, 10 plates, one string of pig's tusks, one string of dog's teeth, 112 pounds of rice, 72 pounds of sugar, two bows, 72 loaves of bread and 36 tins of beef, all worth $117.20. The men use a *bilum* covered with feathers which they wear across their shoulders in public. The *bilum* is made by women just like they make all the other *bilums*, but the men will add the feathers. The *bilums* still are a valuable item. (See MacKenzie)

Bride Price Bilum

Feather Bilum

Feather Bilum

Old Net Bilum

BIPANE

Irian Jaya

Large curved shell nose stick. Used by the Asmat tribe to give them courage and to strike terror into the heart of the enemy. Possibly used as a money substitute. (See Traditional Money Association newsletter, Vol. 12 Number 2, Money of Men Who Eat Men, Col. Davidson.)

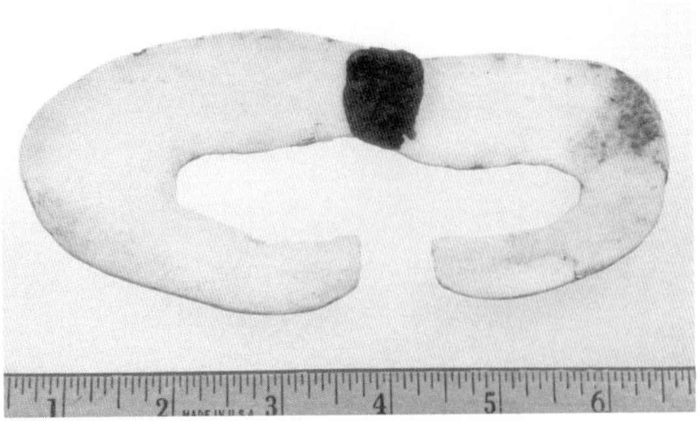

Bipane

BIRD OF PARADISE MONEY

Papua New Guinea

Both the feathers as well as the whole bird of paradise were used in bride price as well as in other transactions. While in Papua New Guinea, in 1973, I saw these feathers worn by the natives in headdresses and through their nose. They told me that the feathers were used as money and in bride price. The birds are on the endangered species list. Thirty-eight of the known forty-two species of bird of paradise live in New Guinea. The cream colored plumes of the majestic Lessor Bird of Paradise (*Paradisaea minor*) were used in many parts of Papua New Guinea as money and also as decoration. In the Min area they are now valued at U.S. $20 to $40. (See Schuurkam p.164) The Wola people prefer the light blue King of Saxony plumes, but if these are in short supply they will use the orange Raggiana bird of paradise. In the Wahgi valley the use of the Black Sicklebill and Lesser Bird of Paradise increased after 1933. By 1990 it was being sold for 40 - 100 kina per feather. The *Stephanie's Astrapia* was worth 6 - 5- kina each. (Sillitoe p. 98) In Papua New Guinea a white person cannot own bird of paradise feathers, only the natives can own them.

Bird Of Paradise Money

BIROK

New Ireland

Birok is the most elaborate and valuable form of shell money (pig money in Pidgin-English). It was used to pay for pigs, usually in connection with important ceremonies where pigs were killed. The identifying trait for *birok* is that the shells are strung edge to edge in long strands. Most *birok* are made up of several sections. The first section consists of a string of various kinds of shells about six or more feet long. Then there is a short section of shell money with a small woven rattan square strung diagonally on the string in the center. This is attached to a double string of shell disks strung edge to edge that is from 230 to 800 cm. long. Four large dog's teeth are attached on each side of those strings. Attached to those two strings are usually eight strings of shell disks strung edge to edge from 300 to 900 cm. long and with pig's tails or pieces of shells or both. Most specimens have some or all of the above parts. It is believed that each was worth one pig. (See Lewis p.24 - 26)

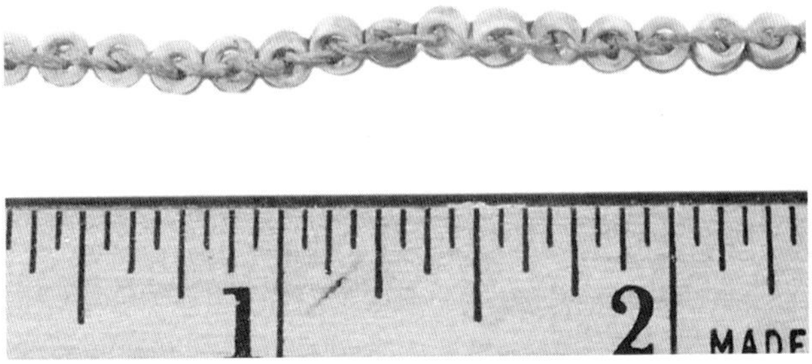

Birok

Birok

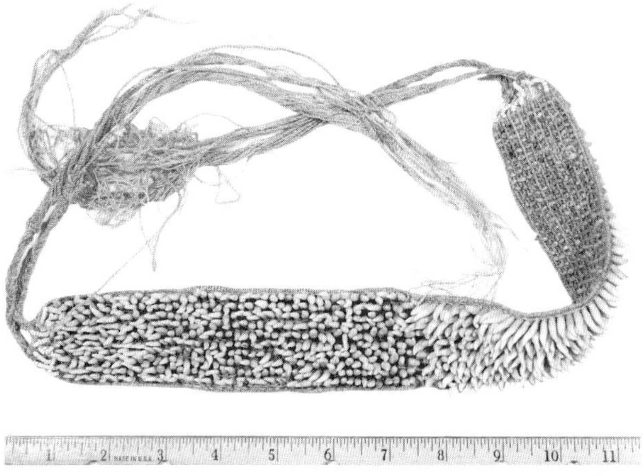

Biru

Chilkat Blanket

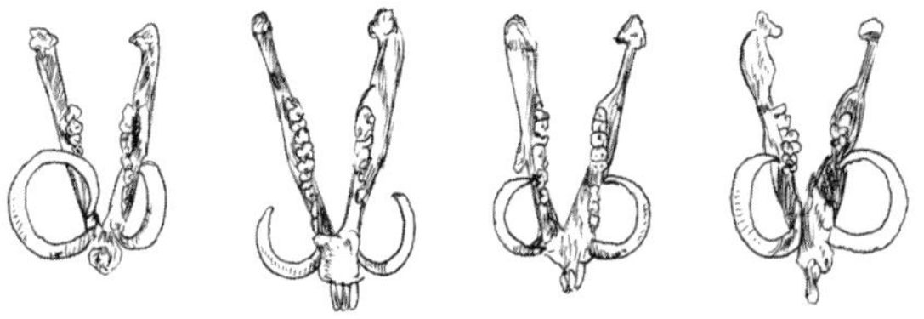

Boar Jaws Showing Full Circle Tusks

Boar Tusk With Pig Teeth (Sauad)

BIRU

Malaita, Solomon Islands

Neck bands and head bands made of porpoise teeth used as money are called *biru*. See Porpoise teeth

BIRUAN

Beroan, Beroana, North Solomon Islands Province

White is the most common color, and purple is the most valuable of these conus shell strings. Some disks are brown or bluish-white. They were used on Buke and in northern Bougainville and were imported from Careret Island. (See Quiggin p. 161) (See Lewis p.31)

BITCHIE - See Mandjong

BLADE - See Obsidian

BLANKET MONEY

Hudson Bay, Canada

The white wool blanket with blue bars at the ends originally obtained from the Hudson's Bay Company for $7.50 a pair was the unit of value. The value steadily declined until a single blanket was worth only 50 cents. White and red woolen blanket worth about 50 cents. Dark blue blankets were also used. The Hudson's Bay blanket was distinguished by points or marks on the edge, woven into the texture. The four point was the best and the one point was the poorest. In 1880 a 2 1/2 point blanket was worth $1.50. This was the standard unit and everything was valued in this unit including other point blankets. (Hodge p. 448) Blankets replaced furs and wampum as the monetary unit of account and served as a standard of deferred payments. Loans were made in blankets with interest charged at 100 percent per year. It was also used in potlatch, a system of competitive giving. When a potlatch was held, blankets and larger gifts like copper shields were given away or destroyed. It was expected that at a later date, all gifts would be returned with interest. Between 1849 and 1850, Hudson's Bay Company purchased 200 square miles of land from tribes in Vancouver Island for 950 blankets. In 1831 in Buffalo, a plant was set up to manufacture the Mackinaw blanket for trade with the Indians. In the 19th century the tribes that refused to wear modern dress wore these blankets and were called "blanket Indians." (See Taxay p. 96-99) See Potlatch.

Hudson Bay, Canada

Chilkat blankets were a store of wealth and could possibly have been a limited form of money. Chilkat blankets were of highest value in the potlatch. They had a crest of the owner on them. The blankets were produced by the Tlingit tribe and were the most original ceremonial robe. They were made of the wool of the mountain goat. The weaving of this type of blanket was originated by the Tsimshian and taken to the Tlingit. The men provided the mountain goat wool as well as the cedar bark, frame and painted pattern board. The women did the weaving. Three goat skins were used to make one blanket. Cedar bark was gathered in long strips in the springtime of the year. Only the inner bark was used. It was first dried, and when actually used to make the blanket it was boiled in water for up to two days to remove the sap. It was washed and left soaking in the water until it was pliable. Then it was shredded to separate the fibers, which were made into a continuous strand and covered with loose wool. It was again twisted so that the cedar bark core was covered in a layer of wool. The various parts of the wool were dyed different colors by the use of natural dyes. The black dye came from a long process of heating the bark in various combinations of old strong urine and copper. The yellow dye came from tree moss. Greenish-blue and yellow-green were obtained from a complicated process using urine, copper, and tree moss. By the late 19th century, commercial dyes from trade stores were used instead of the natural dyes. When the blanket was woven, the design was taken exactly as it appeared on a painted pattern board. The color scheme on all the blankets was the same even though the pattern changed. The field was a natural white of the goat, and the figure was outlined in black bands with the parts filled in with yellow and blue. An experienced weaver could produce a blanket in five or six months. The blankets were used in ceremonies and dances, and the wealthy used them as ceremonial robes. They were given to the most honored guests at a potlatch, and in some cases they were cut into two or three strips and given away. These strips were especially valuable as they could later be combined and made into dance aprons, caps or leggings. The strips were always divided evenly at a potlatch, while the whole blankets were given to the recipients as the host designated. Some blankets had strips of fur such as mink or otter attached to the upper border. Some older blankets were rectangular and did not have the cedar bark mixed with the wool. Some authorities think the classic Chilkat robe was a 19th century development from 18th century blankets. A Chilkat blanket was worth two black fox furs. Four blankets would also purchase a slave.

Woolen blankets were used by the Indians as a store of wealth and also as a unit of value and form of money after the Indians came in contact with Europeans. One report in 1859 announced the conversion from furs to blankets. Some tribes like the Kwakiutl may have made the conversion even earlier. Cheap white wool blankets were used among the Kwakiutl as money and valued at

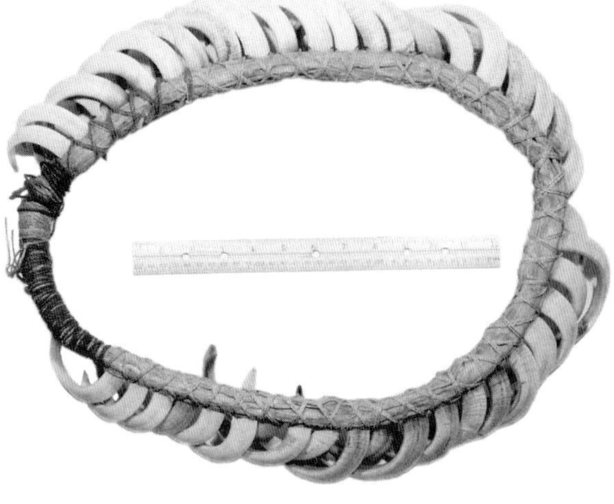

Boar Tusk Necklace

Boar Tusk Necklace With Cowry Shells

Boar Jaw

Trobriand Island Boar With Tusk

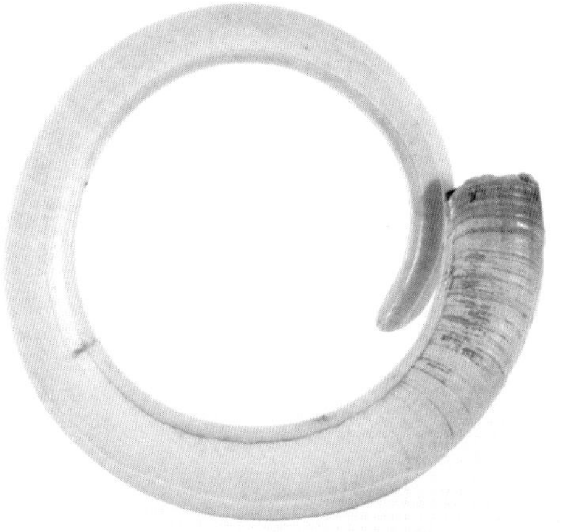

Full Circle Boar Tusk

Bokona

50 cents each. A double blanket was worth three single ones. Taxay writes that between 1849 and 1850, Hudson's Bay Company purchased 200 square miles of land for 950 blankets. Two blankets would purchase a gun, and twelve blankets would purchase a sea-otter skin. The Hudson's Bay trade blanket at one time was priced at 50 cents for a single blanket and $1.50 for a double blanket. In 1888 a new blanket had a price of $2.50 for a double but was worth only $1.50 in trade. Therefore no new blankets were entering the trade because of this difference in value. Money gradually took the place of the blanket. Blankets were used extensively in the potlatch. Some were covered with large pearl buttons. In the modern potlatch, Pendleton Company blankets are used. The blankets used for potlatching were never used for economic purposes or to keep warm. In 1859 a bear or land otter fur was worth one blanket. A beaver fur was worth two blankets. Lynx and fox furs were three blankets each, and a mink was 30 blankets.

Tibet, 19th century

Blankets made in Tibet were important in village barter. They became important in the 1870s when the British made a concentrated effort to open up and exploit the Tibetan market, according to Myers p. 29.

BLOOM OF IRON

Africa

Blooms of iron had served in bridewealth payments in precolonial times, according to Kriger p. 198-199.

BOAR TUSK

Papua New Guinea and Vanuatu (formerly New Hebrides Islands)

The upper canines of the boar are knocked out leaving the lower tusks to grow without being worn down by contact with the upper tusks. In New Hebrides only the live animal can be considered as money. There are more than 23 names given to various grades of pigs according to their development and the size and shape of their tusks. The pigs are never killed except for feasts or as part of a special ceremony. In Papua New Guinea the entire pig as well as the tusk was money. The tusks were used in large necklaces consisting of 50 or more tusks. The necklaces and individual tusks were used to purchase land and also as bride price, blood money, ranso, and admission to men's clubs and secret societies. In Kitava they were used in the doga and at one time the doga was a circulating valuable in kula like the *mwali*. The *doga* were then traded out of kula and are now scarce on the island. They had a theoretical value of about $7 in 1970 on the island, although none were sold at that price. The Tami Islanders consider the boar tusk an indispensable item of bride price. Presently five pairs of tusks along with other goods are the current bride price. The Tami Islanders traded their wood bowls for these boar tusks. A boar tusk pendant was worth two large bowls and one small bowl. In past times a large pair of tusks was worth a dozen bowls. In many areas, curved boar's tusks were the prerogative of the aristocracy alone. If a commoner received a curved boar's tusk, he had to pass it on to a member of the aristocracy. At present time the tusks are not considered money as in the past. Now they are used only to validate their position of leadership.

Imitation boar tusks were made from the giant clam shell (*Tridacna*). The village of Singor on the eastern Rai Coast was the main place of manufacture of imitation boar tusks. At one time a pair of average quality genuine tusks was worth one to two pounds. In 1935 a one-circle boar's tusk was worth 10 to 15 pounds sterling. A two circle tusk was worth 30 to 50 pounds sterling, and a three circle tusk was worth more than 150 pounds sterling. (See pigs for value of entire pig.) (see Pig Teeth)

New Hebrides - See Deacon p. 193

Papua New Guinea

Boar's tusks were a part of bride price along with dog's teeth and pigs. (See Hogbin, 1963 p. 120)

Torres Straits

Artificially deformed boars' tusks were worn with two pigs' teeth as a pendant at the conclusion of initiation ceremonies by important men. They were highly valued. Imitation tusks were made from the giant clam (*Tridacna*) and used in place of the actual boar's tusk. (See Haddon Vol. 4 p. 50-51)

Vanuatu

The most valuable pigs were those with the best-developed tusks, not the largest. In 1984, chiefs set the price of a live, full-circle tusker at VT 18,000. They also assigned the value of VT 16,000 on a dried, intact skull of a full-circle tusker. This confirms that the value is in the tusks, not the pig. (Rodman p. 160) It took seven to eight years for a boar to grow full-circle tusks. A double-circle tusk was extremely valuable and rare. The pigs and tusks were very important in all native life. They were used to gain entrance to graded societies.

Vitiaz Strait

A pair of boar's tusks were worth a dog's tooth headband or one dog or one pig. The tusks were always valuable and were hung in the clubhouse as trophies. They were valued along with pots, shell money, bowls and dog-teeth strings. (See Harding p. 139)

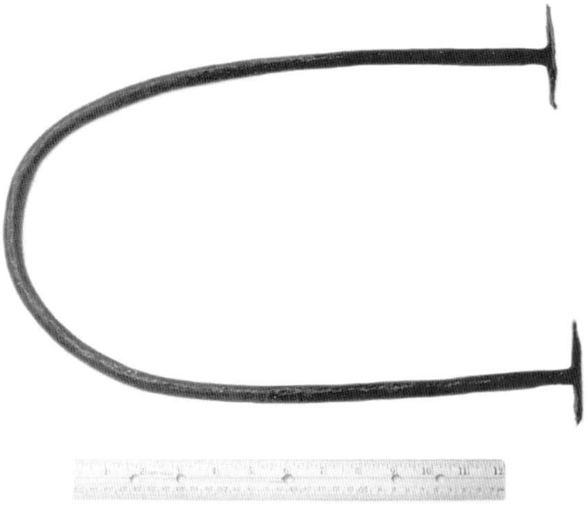

Boloko

Borjookes

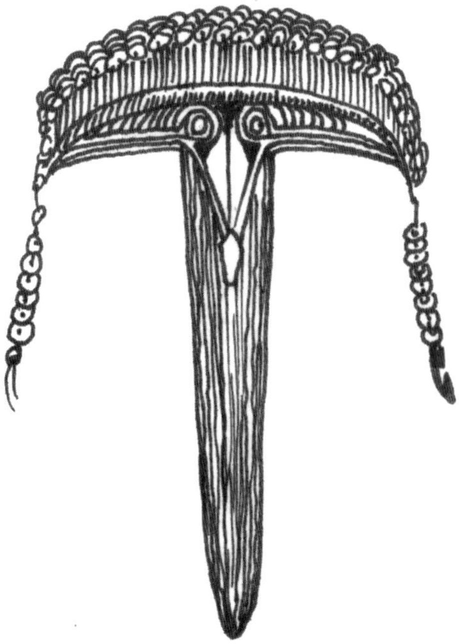

Bosu

Bosu

Bottle

BOAT - See Sycee

BOAT MONEY - See Lat

BOKONA

Africa

The general name of the currency pieces used was *bokona*. There were four pieces that were shaped differently and had different values. The *nkwa* had a value of 1/2, the *bokona* had a value of one, the *lingeme* had a value of two and *munseia* had a value of four. The pieces served as money until 1940, and the one *bokona* was worth five Belgiam francs. A common unit was ten *bokona*. (Information from Kurt Koschatzky.)

BOLOKO

Zaire, Songo-Meno / Nkutsbu / Ndengese

The *boloko* was worth 10 big *Kundja* or one or more male goats It was a U-shaped copper bar with splayed feet, and 10 *boloko* were worth a wife. *Boloko* were made by the Nkutsbu people from copper. They were also called *konga* or *kunga* by the Basonge. Two *boloko* would buy a male slave and three a female slave. In 1950 they were worth 50 Belgian francs. (See Ballarini p. 110) (see Quiggin p. 67-68) One *boloko* weighing 800 to 1,100 g. was worth ten units of *kundja* blades weighing about the same weight. *Boloko* come in several sizes. (See Kriger p. 89)

BOMPATA

Lake Mayi Ndombe, Africa

The knife is very light and thin. The knife circulated as a currency blade in the late 19th and early 20th century. The blade could be made easily by many of the less skilled blacksmiths. Therefore it was not a particularly coveted object of prestige among the wealthiest men in society. See Kriger p. 212

BONE MONEY - See ivory money.

BOOKMARK MONEY - See Hansatsu.

BORJOOKES

Ethiopia

The glass beads were made from old bottles and were used to pay porters on safari. Twelve beads were a day's wages for a porter.

BOSU

Papua New Guinea, to 20th century

Lime spatulas are made of whale bone, bone, wood or turtleshell and often are decorated with sapi sapi shells. They are used to take lime, which is used in betel chewing, from a container and put it into the mouth. They are used as *korotomna* gifts in the Kula cycle, as well as in other important purchases and in bride price. Also called *potuma*. (See Kula.)

BOTHA A YAR - See Yar Nu Au

BOTTLES

British Guiana and British Honduras, 1840s

Traders in British Guiana used empty bottles as currency during a chaotic period. During the same period of time British Honduras used bottles as currency among the retail traders. (See Taxay p. 59)

Korea, 1331

Shaped like a bottle made of silver alloyed with copper and weighed one pound. It was worth 100 pieces of linen.

See Gin Currency, Liquor money

BOW MONEY

Papua New Guinea

Bows and arrows were important in trade. The items were traded from one tribe to another. Palm wood was used in the best bows.

BOWLS - See Pots

Siassi Island, Papua New Guinea

These hand carved wood bowls were decorated with animal, fish and geometric designs. They were exchanged for food, pigs, dogs and bride price. One large bowl was worth one dog or one pig. They were traded throughout the area and used in the kula.

Abor, Near Tibetan border

Currency bowls of Chinese manufacture were worth about 30 pounds each and decorated inside with the conch, fish and the eight Buddhist; the exterior is decorated with four small lugs and wings. They were called *DANKI* and were used more for ceremonial presentation than as money. (See Quiggin p. 208)

Solomon Island

Wood bowls were used in ceremonial transactions and also in economic transactions including bride price exchanges. Many had inlaid shell and were ornately carved and painted black. The bowls are still being made for the tourist market. Some bowls were sacrificial and were used for sacrificing food to the gods while others were used only as money.

Wood Bowl - Siassi Island

Wood Bowl - Solomon Islands

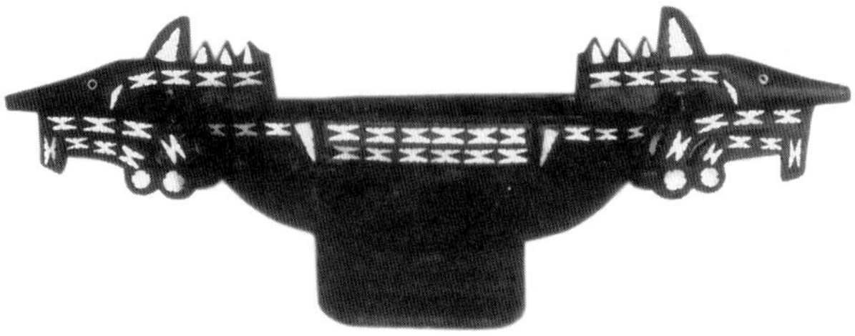

Wood Bowl - Solomon Islands

Brooch

BRACELET - See K'a K'im, Manilla, Ring Money

BRAMBLES -See Tingle-Dangle money

BRASS RING MONEY - See Ring money

Africa

Small brass rings resembling beads were strung on leather strips. A string was worth a male slave. See Beads - brass.

BRASS BEAD - See Bead - Brass

BRASS FROG MONEY - See Animal Money

BRICK TEA - See Tea Money

BRIDE PRICE

It is sometimes written bride-price. It is better called bride wealth because it is really not a purchase but compensation to her clan for the loss of her services. The custom also ensures the good treatment of the wife for if she runs away, her husband has lost his outlay. If there are children, he has no hope of getting the payment back. The money paid can be large. Since the 1930s the bridewealth values have increased, and their composition has also changed. In the 1960s and 1970s the number of pigs and cash increased, while the number of shells and steel tools decreased. (See Healey p. 153) In the Port Moresby area recently the price can run as high as 13,000 Kina. Since most young men do not have that kind of money, it becomes a clan venture. The whole thing is really a vast exchange system where wealth circulates and alliances are built up. It is a way to climb the prestige ladder.

Bubi Currancy

BRIDGE MONEY - CHINA

See Tingle Dangle Money

BRONZE DRUM - See Moko

BROOCH

American Indian

In 1769, women wore silver brooches which were used as money among the Oneida. They were worth one shilling each. Their value varied with their size. Most women had some brooches. (See Karklins p. 74, Figure 52)

BU MONEY - See PU money.

BUAYA - See Gambar

BUBI CURRENCY

Africa

Strings of shell disks called *dongo* made from the *Achatina* shell were plaited into broad flat plaits called *jibbu* and they were used as currency. A nice piece could be nearly a yard long and four inches wide. When these shell strings were made into bunches of six about as long as a forearm they were called *quiranda* or *kirana* and were worth 1,000 to 4,000 reis. (See Quiggin p. 49-50)

BUBU THROWING KNIFE - See Throwing Knife - *Bubu*

BUFFALO

Borneo and Annam

In Borneo the price of buffaloes remained constant, but interest on a loaned buffalo was many times the price of a calf. In Annam a buffalo was worth a small gong, two lances, 100 strings of cash or a bar of silver. A rhinoceros horn was worth eight buffaloes; a male slave, five to seven buffaloes and a large pair of elephant tusks, or six buffaloes.

BUFFALO BELL

Borneo

A bell was worth about 75 cents and weighed an average of 300 grams. A round metal ball or stone was inserted during manufacture for use instead of a clapper.

BUJI, Liberia

They date back more than 200 years and are the ancestors of the common kissi penny.

BULLET MONEY

Siam, (Thailand) 1237-1886

.900 to .950 fine silver, a few in gold or base metal. All signs and marks are die stamped except one which is engraved. Molten silver is poured into a wooden form and shaped into an elliptical bar. Then two shallow parallel crosscuts are made in the bar, and it is hammered into a nearly round shape. Stamps are made by hand by resting the bullet in the hollow of an elephant's leg bone and striking using a punch. There are commemorative, presentation and private bullets. Bullet money was demonetized on October 28, 1904. They were allowed to be exchanged for flat coins until October 26, 1905. This date was extended to July 24, 1908. The bullet money had lasted for more than 600 years.

Gold and silver "bullet coins have been a medium of exchange since midevil times. Interesting enoughis the fact that a 1 Bahht bullet made of gold will weigh the same as a 1 baht bullet in silver. The reason for this is that the Baht originally was a weight not a denomination. It was a coinage weight only until the time of the RamaVii, (1925-1935) and now it is a weight and also a denomination (as far as standard weight coins are concerned). Usually 1 gold baht was equal to 16 silver Baht on an exchange basis.

Bullet Weights

BAHT 15.40	1/2 BAHT 7.70	1/4 BAHT 3.85
1/8 BAHT 1.92	1/16 BAHT 0.96	1/32 BAHT 0.48
1/64 BAHT 0.24		

Chopmarks exist on bullet coins as they do on many other coins that have traveled on their way through the Orient. One must be careful not to mistake a money changers chopmark for the regular dynastic marks one the bullet. Some chopmarks are rather simple in design while others appear to be elaborate.

Buffalo Bell

Buffalo Bell

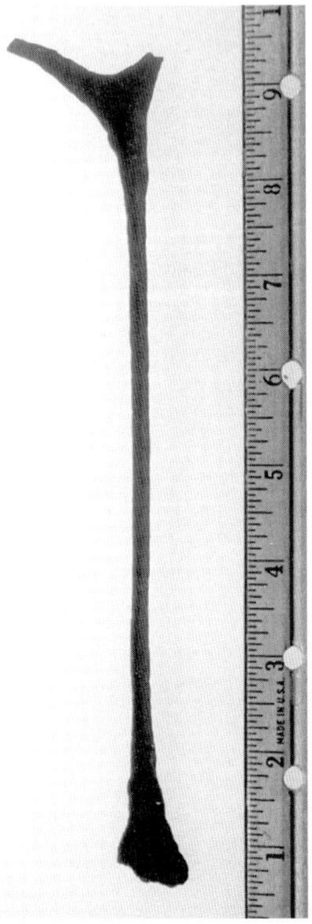

Buji

Chakra

RAMA I

Tri Unalom

RAMA II
Krut

RAMA III

Krut Sio Prasat Dok Mai

RAMA III

Bai Matum Ruang Puang Arrow Head Chaleo

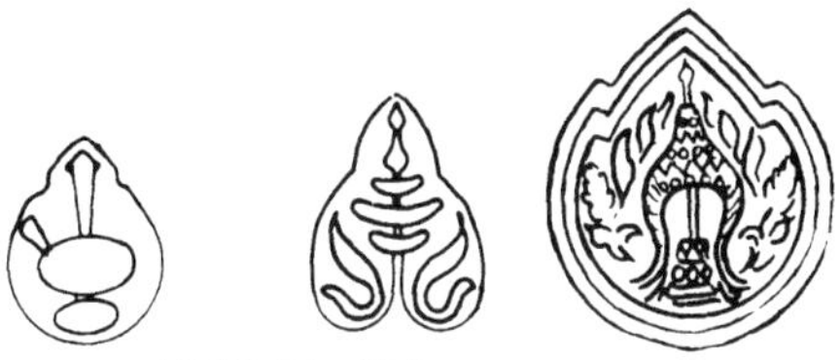

RAMA IV

P'ra Tao Mongkut

RAMA V

P'ra Kieo 1876 Cho Rampeuy 1880

These dynastic marks and listing of bullets is courtesy of Catalog of World Coins 1801-1900, Krause Publications, Standard, 1996
Phone (715) 445-2214

DYNASTIC MARKS

Chakra

The Chakra, symbol of the god Vishnu, is the mark of the Bangkok Dynasty. It varies slightly in design between issues, being very ornate on ceremonial issues.

RAMA I reigned 1782-1809

The trident, the symbol of the Hindu God, Shiva, was used as the first mark of Rama I. The *unalom* is an ornamented conch shell, used as the second mark of Rama I.

RAMA II 1809-1824

A facing *Krut,* half man-half bird, used as the mark of Rama II.

RAMA III 1824-1851

The *Krut* was used as the first mark of Rama III. The *Prasat* was the palace used as the second mark of Rama III. The *Dok Mai* was a flower used as the third mark of Rama III. The *Bai Matum* is a bale-fruit tree used as the fourth mark of Rama III, The *Ruang Puang* is a beehive used as the fifth mark of Rama III. It is very similar to *Dok Mai,* having only one dot below the point used as the sixth mark of Rama III. The *Chaleo* is a symbol of varied meanings. In this instance it is believed to represent a charm to ward off evil spirits, found as the seventh mark of Rama III.

RAMA IV 1851-1868

P'ra Tao Mongkut

The *P'ra Tao,* or royal water pot, was used as the first mark of Rama IV. The Royal Siamese Crown was used as the second mark of Rama IV.

RAMA V 1868-1910

P'ra Kieo (1876) Cho Rampeuy (1880)

The Royal Coronet worn on the top knot of the Royal Princess on ceremonial occasions. First used on the occasion of the funeral of Princess Charoenkamol Suksawadi, who died in 1874. The Thai flower was on a ceremonial issue along with an ornate crown of two vessels in memory of Somdet Pira Deb Sirindhra, the mother of Rama V, and commemorating his age, dated CS 1242.

Silver Pot Duang (Bullet coins)

1/128 BAHT
.12 grams, silver

Rama IV *P'ra Tao*

ATT (1/64 BAHT)
.24 grams, silver

Rama IV *P'ra Tao*

SIO (pai) (1/32 baht)
.48 grams, silver

Rama I *Tri*
Rama I *Unalom*
Rama III *Prasat*
Rama III *Dok Mai*
Rama III *Bai Matum*
Rama III *Ruang Puang*
Rama III Arrow Head
Rama IV *P'ra Tao*

SIK (1/16 baht)
.96 grams, silver

Rama I *Tri*
Rama I *Unalom*
Rama II *Krut*
Rama III *Prasat*
Rama III *Dok Mai*
Rama III *Bai Matum*
Rama III *Ruang Puang*
Rama III Arrow Head
Rama IV *P'ra Tao*
Rama IV *Mongkut*

FUANG (1/8 baht)
1.92 grams, silver

Rama I *Tri*
Rama I *Unalom*
Rama II *Krut*
Rama III *Prasat*
Rama III *Praset & Unalom*
Rama III *Prasat & Krut*
Rama III *Dok Mai*
Rama III *Bai Matum*
Rama III *Ruang Puang*
Rama III Arrow Head
Rama IV *P'ra Tao*
Rama IV *Mongkut*

SALU'NG (1/4 baht)
3.85 grams, silver

Rama I *Tri*
Rama I *Unalom*
Rama II *Krut*
Rama III *Prasat*
Rama III *Dok Mai*
Rama III *Bai Matum*
Rama III *Ruang Puang*
Rama III Arrow Head
Rama IV *P'ra Tao*
Rama IV *Mongkut*

2 SALU'NG (1/2 baht)
7.70 grams, silver

Rama I *Tri*
Rama I *Unalom*
Rama II *Krut*
Rama III Chaled
Rama III *Prasat*
Rama III *Dok Mai*
Rama III *Bai Matum*
Rama IV *Mongkut*
Rama IV *Mongkut & Prasat*

BAHT
15.40 grams, silver

Rama I **Tri**
Rama I *Unalom*
Rama II Krut
Rama III *Chaleo*
Rama III *Prasat*
Rama III *Dok Mai*
Rama III *Bai Matum*
Rama IV *P'ra Tao*
Rama IV *Mongkut*
Rama IV *Mongkut & Prasat*
Death of Princess Charoenkamol Suksawadi
Rama V *P'ra Kieo*

1 1/2 BAHT
23.10 grams, silver

Rama III *Prasat*

2 BAHT
grams, silver

Rama I *Unalom*
Rama II *Krut*
Rama III *Prasat*
c/m: 8 dots in *Chakra*
Rama IV *Mongkut*
c/m: 6 blades in *Chakra*
Rama IV *Mongkut*
c/m: 8 blades in *Chakra*, elaborate design
Rama IV *Mongkut*
Somdet P'ra Deb Sirindhra
Rama V *Cho Rampeuy*

2 1/2 BAHT
38.50 grams, silver

Rama III *Krut*

TAMLUNG (4 baht)
61.60 grams, silver

c/m: 8 dots in Chakra
Rama IV *Mongkut*
c/m: 7 dots in Chakra
Rama IV *Mongkut*
Cremation of Somdet P'ra Deb Sirindra
Rama V *Cho Rampeuy*

4 1/2 BAHT
silver

Rama III *Krut Sio*

8 BAHT
123.20 grams, silver

Rama III *Krut Sio*

2 1/2 TAMLUNG (10 baht)
154.00 grams, silver

Cremation of Somdet P'ra Deb Sirindra
Rama V *Cho Rampeuy*

5 TAMLUNG (20 baht)
308.00 grams, silver

Cremation of Somdet P'ra Deb Sirindra
Rama V *Cho Rampeuy*

10 TAMLUNG (40 baht)
616.00 grams, silver

Cremation of Somdet P'ra Deb Sirindra
Rama V *Cho Rampeuy*

20 TAMLUNG (80 baht)
1185.00 - 1232.00 grams, silver

Chakra-wheel engraved turning counterclockwise
Rama I *Mongkut*
Chakra-wheel engraved turning clockwise
Rama IV *Mongkut*
Cremation of Somdet P'ra Deb Sirindra
Rama V *Cho Rampeuy*

Silver Bullet Money 20 BAHT

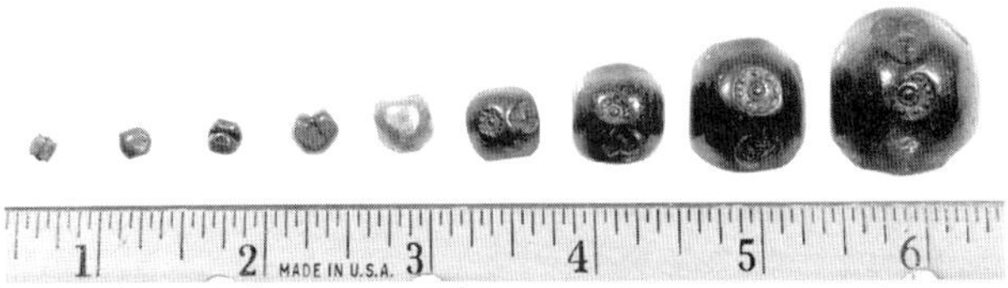

Silver Bullet Money (l to r):1/64, 1/32, 1/16, 1/8, 1/4, 1/2, 1, 2, 4

Gold Pot Duang (Bullet coins)

1/32 GOLD BAHT
.48 grams, gold

Rama IV *P'ra Tao*
Rama IV *Mongkut*

1/16 GOLD BAHT
.96 grams, gold

Rama III *Prasat*
Rama IV *P'ra Tao*
Rama IV *Mongkut*

1/8 GOLD BAHT
1.96 grams, gold

Rama III *Prasat*
Rama IV *Dok Mai*
Rama III *Bai Natum*
Rama IV *Pira Tao*

1/4 GOLD BAHT
3.85 grams, gold

Rama IV *P'ra Tao*
Rama IV *Mongkut*

1/2 GOLD BAHT
7.70 grams, gold

Rama III *Dok Mai*
Rama IV *Mongkut*

1 GOLD BAHT
15.40 grams, gold

Rama III *Prasat*
Rama IV *Mongkut*

1 1/2 GOLD BAHT (Mct Kanoon)
23.10 grams, gold
Rama IV *Mongkut*
Note: Ends are not hammered to form bullet, known as the jackfruit seed coin.

2 GOLD BAHT
30.80 grams, gold

Rama IV *Mongkut*

4 GOLD BAHT
61.60 grams, gold

Rama IV *Mongkut*

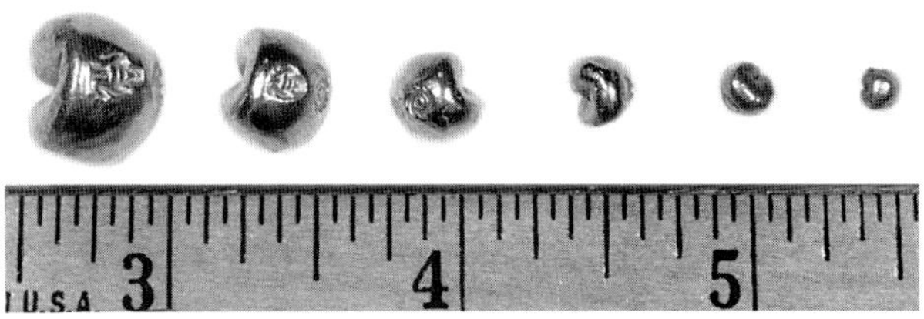

Gold Bullet Money (l to r):One Baht, 1/2 Baht, 1/4 Baht, 1/8 Baht, 1/16 Baht

Commemorative bullets

Some of the above bullets are special-type and multiple mark bullets. The *Krut Sio* for the cremation of Rama II and *Prinyit Unalom* are two commemorative bullet series.

Other forms:

Kidney-shaped elephant series

Thailand, Kingdom of Sukothai, 1250-1350

Three Baht and five Baht, Base metal and copper-nickel. Most are fakes. (See Mitchiner p.332)

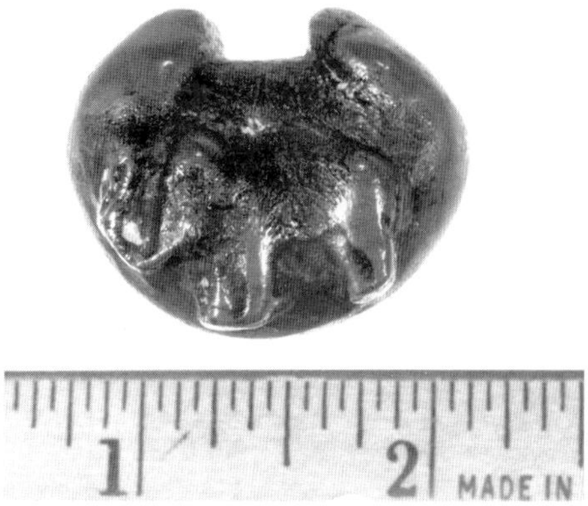

Kidney-Shaped Elephant Series

Base metal bullet-style types

Thailand, Kingdom of Sukothai, 1250-1350,

Bullet shape with flat top and two flat feet bearing stamps, zinc-lead. Most are fakes. (See Mitchiner p. 333)

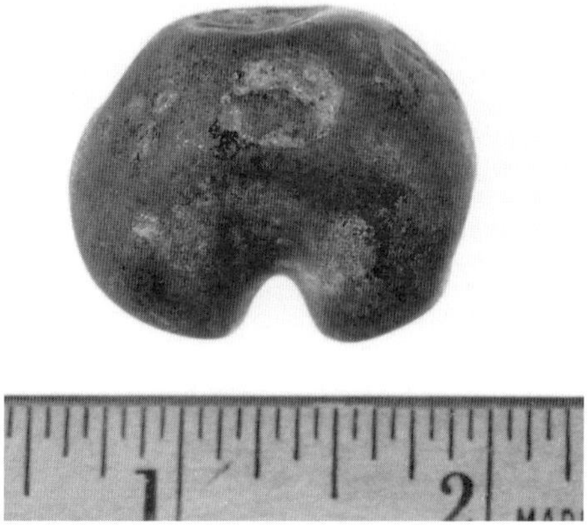

Base Metal Bullet-Style

Bullet money with loop.

Semans p. 7, feels the loops were added to the pieces at the mint or palace for easier attachment of a cloth or paper "floater".

Bullet shape with flat top and two pointed feet bearing stamps, zinc-lead, one Baht (15.3 grams) to four Baht (61.2 grams). Most are fakes. (See Mitchiner p.334-335)

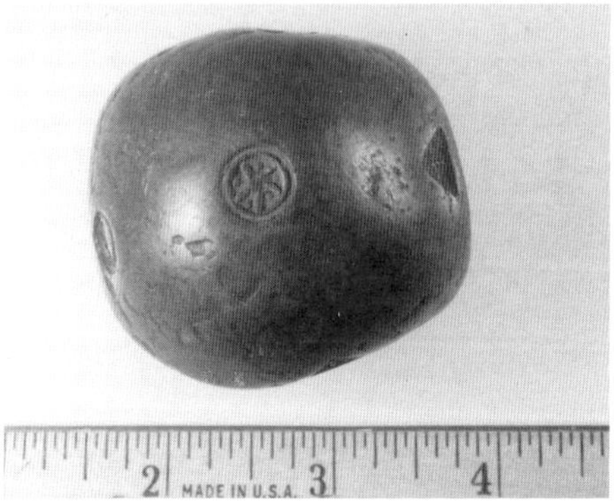

Base Metal Bullet-Style

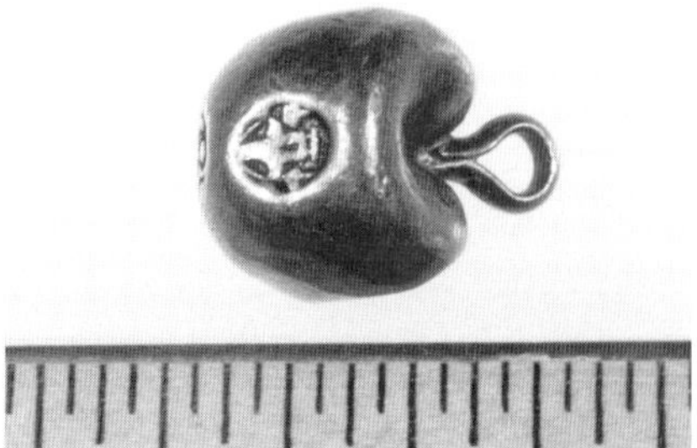

Bullet Money With Loop

Private bullets

Semans relates that he has heard some Hill Tribes were reluctant to accept the changeover to flat coins and continued to make bullets for their own use. Another explanation is the Wats made them as talismans. There are many styles and weights with many different stamps.

See Cartridge Money, Musket Balls

BUNDLES

Kiriwina Island, Trobriand Islands

Banana leaves are scraped, etched with a design, dried and bound into bundles by women in the villages. The bundles are used as money in a mortuary ceremony called a *sagali*. They distribute thousands of bundles worth hundreds of dollars to people who gave things of value to the deceased during their lifetime. The *sagali* is normally held five months after burial, and it marks the end of the major mourning period. During the ceremony $500 to $1,000 worth of bundles and skirts, as well as other items, are distributed. Bundles also form a limited currency. The price for one bundle, cut, rolled and tied on the beach, was one porpoise tooth. Five bundles were worth one stick of tobacco or 1.3 cents in 1976. The newly made bundles are called *yawovau*, and the old or dirty bundles are called *yapagatu* or *yabwabogwa*. They all have slightly different values. The women also make bundles to sell to other women who need them for a death. In 1971 a pig was worth 1,800 bundles. Only the women make and use bundles as money. Every person who in some way was associated with the dead person and a member of another lineage is given bundles. Sometimes skirts are also used instead of bundles. The woman who stands as the leader of the distribution is the "wealth" woman of the day because she has been able to collect more skirts and bundles than anyone else. A woman who shaves her hair in mourning for the dead will be given 10 to 15 bundles. Then other women give her five to 10 more. Important women and men receive many more bundles than younger people and people with little economic strength. An important person might receive 1,000 bundles and 10 or more skirts. There are 17 categories of mourning services which may receive payments. If they do not have bundles or skirts, cloth from a trade store is substituted. (See Weiner) See Kula.

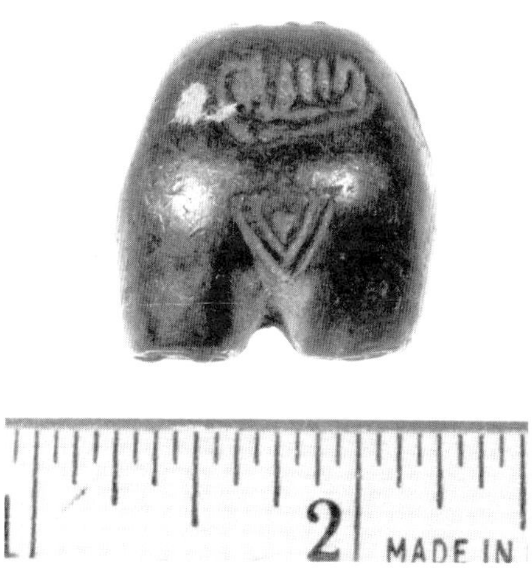

Bullet With Two Feet

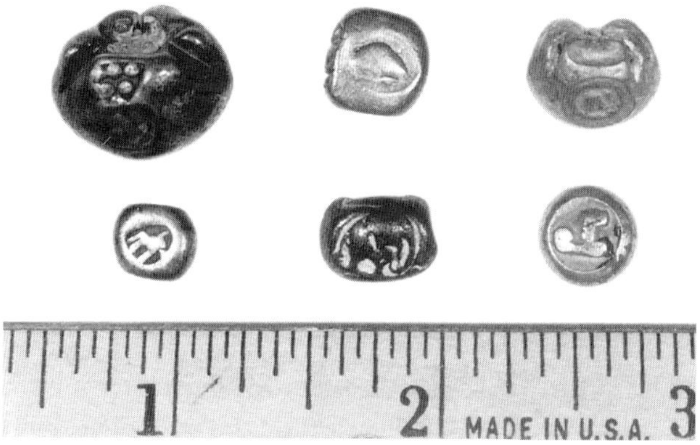

Private Issue Bullet Money

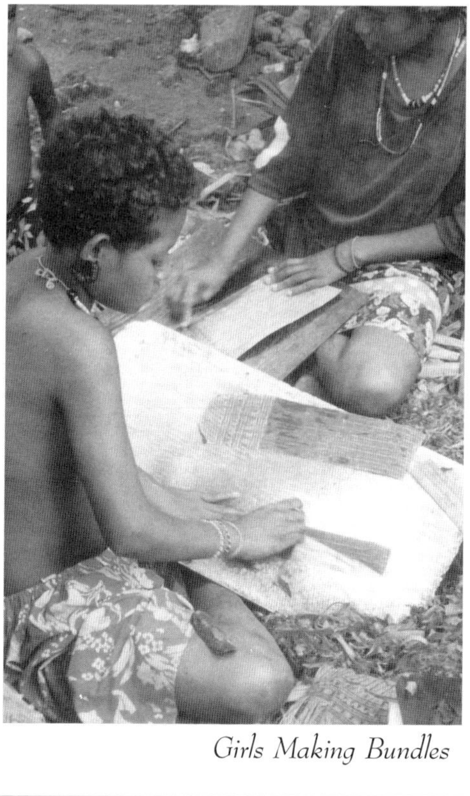
Girls Making Bundles

Bundles

BURIAL MONEY

China, as early as 200 B.C. to present

From August 18 to September 15, the Chinese offer gifts to appease the wandering ghosts. The gifts that they burn are paper replicas of miniature cars, boats, furniture, houses and also funeral money like banknotes, coins and gold bars.

The *gui* (in modern *pinyin*) or *kuei* (in old Wade-Giles system) or ghosts, are those who died alone, unloved and unremembered, or those who were not given a proper funeral to send them on to the world of the dead. They live indefinitely in purgatory except for one month each year when they are free to roam the earth. This time is the *Yue Lan*, or Hungry Ghost Festival. The festival climaxes in a series of celebrations that can last from a couple of days to up to a week, depending on the area. Temporary temples and altars are set up for worshipers to come and pray and burn incense sticks and huge coils of incense. Taoist priests and Buddhist monks carry out rituals and chant liturgies. Paper offerings of clothing and money are burnt. Monks and priests aboard colorfully decorated boats will circle the harbor to take offerings to the ghosts who died at sea. They also scatter rice on the water and launch paper boats filled with paper gifts. On the eve of the last day of the festival, lamps are lit outside the temple to make passing souls aware that they will receive offerings on the following day. On the last day a huge bonfire is lit to burn the offerings that were on display. The goddess of Mercy, Guanyin, gave the first party for the hungry ghosts, according to legend. Also according to legend, it ended in disaster when the ghosts became unruly. The next year she asked the god of the Underworld, Daih Su, to attend to keep order and make sure the ghosts behaved.

Of special interest to me was the funeral or ghost money. There are many different kinds. I personally obtained more than 30 different pieces. Most are bank notes of many sizes. They are for the most part from the Bank of Hell. The notes range in size from 2 1/4" x 4 1/2" to 5 1/4" x 10". They range from one color to four color process. Denominations range up to one billion. In recent years they also make paper copies of The Bank of Hell bank books, as well as checks and credit cards. Foil copies of gold coins such as Canadian Maple Leaf bullion coins are also used. A Chinese person I met told me how as a child she was shown how to take a special piece of paper with some gold foil on it and fold it into the shape of a sycee. She then burned it in the Hungry Ghost Festival. This festival is also held on the Island of Taiwan. There the employees of companies get together to burn funeral or ghost money as well as follow some of the other practices.

Burial Money

Burial Money

Burlap Money

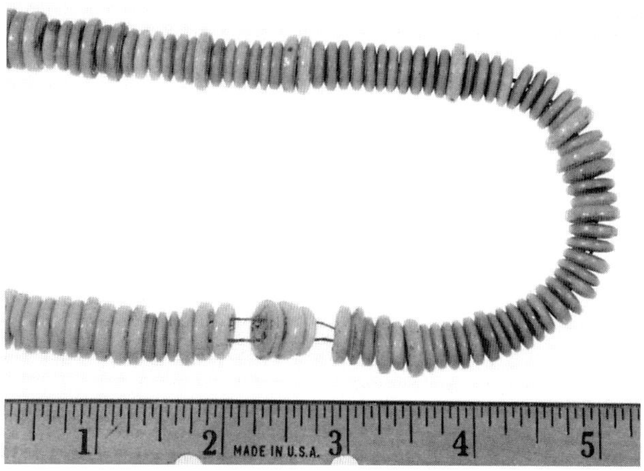

Button Money

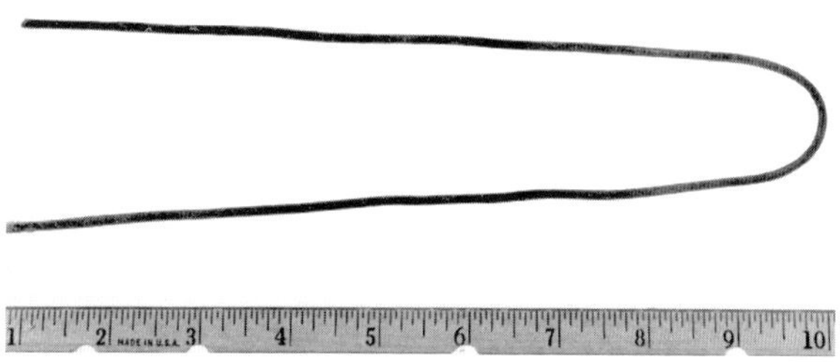

Calabar Bar

BURLAP MONEY
Germany, 1919-1922 Inflation period following World War I

Part of the Notgeld series of unusual forms of money for collectors or for limited use as money in the various cities. The notes were printed on pieces of burlap. 3″ x 4-3/4″.

BURNED MONEY - See burial money

BUSHMAN'S BEADS - See Ostrich Egg Shell Beads

BUTTER
Norway, 1300s

The unit of measure was a basket of butter. Ten baskets of butter were worth a horse or three cows. (See Einzig p. 275)

BUTTONS
Alaska

Many kinds of pearl buttons were used as money. Large pearl buttons with a brass shank had the highest value and were worth one martin skin. Small buttons were sewn on garments or kept on strings for circulation. Russian fur buyers would take the buttons off their coats to use as money to obtain skins from the Indians.

Papua New Guinea

Modern buttons were used as decorations as well as substitutes for nassa shell valuables. It is probable that they were used in trade. Cards of shirt buttons were used in bride price in 1937 in the Kundiawa area.

BWANA
North Pentecost

Finely made mats were worth about 5s. and 100 would purchase a boar. (See Quiggin p. 132)

CACAO - See Cocoa Bean Money

CAKE - See Salt Money, Soap Cakes, Tukula

CALABAR BAR
Nigeria, 17th century to 20th century

The brass rod was one yard long and was bent in half to form a U-shape. It weighed 1 1/2 pounds. It was imported from England and was worth 2 1/2 d. to 6 d. In the early 1600s, 23 rods would purchase a male slave. In 1698, it took 38 bars to purchase a male slave. Six iron knives were worth one bar. In 1856 one bar was worth one shilling. By the late 1800s they were replaced by the iron bar with one iron bar worth four copper bars. By 1907 rods were no longer in use, but the concept of the bar remained as a unit of reckoning. They were used by the Efiks of Old Calabar. Also called *okpoho okuk.*

CAMELS
British and Italian Somaliland

Camels were a principle store of value as well as a form of money. Blood money for a man killed was 100 she-camels and 50 for a woman killed. A bruise was worth three or four camels. Camels were used for large purchases. (See Einzig p. 125)

Northern Africa

The Tuareg use camels as bride price. The bride price of a wife may vary from one young camel to seven camels. In some tribes the price can be 10 to 20 camels. The bride's family is expected to provide a dowry, which many times is valued at more than the bride price paid by the groom's family. At the low end, 25 to 30 goats can be substituted for the one young camel.

CAMPHOR - Sudan and Borneo

CAMWOOD -See Tukula

CANDY

Many kinds of candy were used in Europe during World War II and in Italy during the 1970s.

CANNON MONEY

Borneo (Brunei) - 19th century to beginning of 20th century

Bronze, brass, copper, iron and other metals were used to make the cannons. They were used in Brunei, Sabah and Sarawak. The cannons were used for trading purposes, barter of goods, payment of fines, and in wedding and engagement ceremonies. The cannons were fired during weddings, births of children and visits of important people. Many were melted during World War II. Besides the usual cannon shape they were also shaped into dragons, buffaloes or crocodiles or had decorations of these animals on them. The making of cannons started at the beginning of the 16th century. There are three kinds of Brunei cannons: 1) *Bedil.* The most numerous (at least 95 percent) and also most important. 2) *Mariam.* Only a few are known. They are heavy built short and squat with a rounded large *knob* instead of a cylinder or tube found on the *Bedil.* They are probably not of Brunei manufacture. 3) *Boom.* Only two are known to exist. It is something between the traditional *Bedil* and the big *Mariam.* The barrel looks like long strips of palm leaves. The back has the *Mariam* -style knob with two decorated bands of outstanding leaves. They were all made for one wealthy man in Brunei in about 1880 A.D.There are four types of *Bedil.* 1a) Bedil Gargabus - has a big round mouth. There can be some decoration, but not necessarily . This is the oldest type of *Bedil* in Brunei. 1b) *Bedil Naga* - Dragon, crocodile or other designs with the mouth flared open. 1c) Completely smooth barrel and no decoration. 1d) *Bedil Lapis* - made from a mixture of minerals and can include any of the previous forms which are pure brass. They could also be made of iron. The minerals give a different color and texture to the cannon. Miniatures were also used. They are somewhere around 11 inches long. An interesting one is shaped like a buffalo with the barrel coming out between the horns or out the rear. There are also twin barreled cannons. The cannon were used in war; for signaling or warning; for royal occasions like births, coronations, weddings, circumcisions or other special occasions; conferring titles or awards; and during cerebrations such as weddings. (See Shariffuddin)

Cannon Money

Cannon Money

Irian Jaya

Antique cannon called *lela* were the most treasured components of bride price in the Fakfak area of Irian Jaya. The cannons were usually of Portuguese origin, and many are 300 to 400 years old. (See Muller p. 104)

CANOE MONEY - See Kula; See Lat ; See Potlatch.

Canoe Prow Stop Board

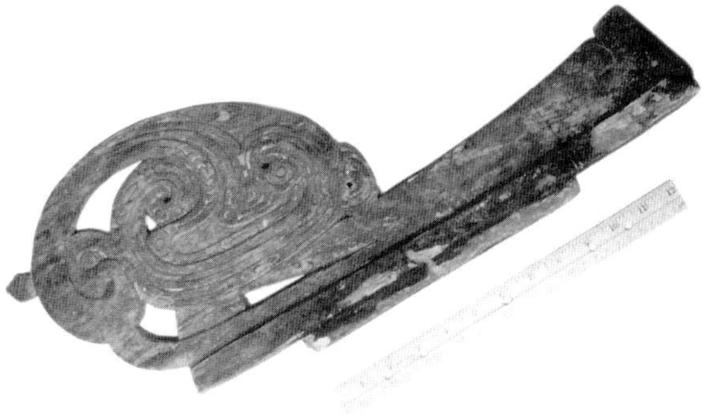

Canoe Prow

Carapace Money

Cardboard Coins

CANOE PROW

Trobriand Islands

The wood canoe prow was used as money and a valuable item.

CANVAS MONEY

Germany, 1919-1922. Inflation period following World War I.

Part of the "Notgeld" series of unusual forms of money for the collector or for limited use as money in various cities. The notes were printed on canvas. 3" x 4-3/4"

CARABAO

Philippines

Along with pigs and rice, carabao were a supplementary media of exchange used in acquiring and determining the value of land. (See Herskovits p.186)

CARAPACE MONEY

China

These items were either miniature representations of shields or horse trappings in imitation of the larger originals, according to Ramsden p. 24. The tops are, in most cases, ornamented with the underside usually having double parallel bars from one edge to the other over the concave area. (See Ramsden p. 24-25)

CARD MONEY - See Playing Card Money

CARDBOARD COINS

There are many hundreds of different kinds of round cardboard and paper disks used as coins by many countries. Below are just a few.

Algeria, Bougie Setif, 1916

Square cardboard scrip issued.

Chile, 1891

Many private issues were made by private businesses in the city of Lquique, including a 20-centavos piece.

Leyden, Holland, 1574

See Prayer Book Money

France, World War I

Many pieces were made because of the copper shortage. Around 1919, a five-centimes piece was issued by a printer at St. Etinenne. In 1918, a 10-centimes piece was made in Ax-les-Thermes.

Germany, World War I

France, Germany, World War II

Issued by Bank of Lille in Lille, France. Tokens issued by prison camps in Germany.

Mexico, 1915

Five centavos pieces were made during the Mexican Revolution.

CARGO CULT

The first cargo cult sprang up in Fiji in 1885. In 1932, a similar one sprang up in the Solomon Islands. In Papua New Guinea there have been more than 50 cargo cults. Other areas have also had them. The New Hebrides had seven, Fiji had four, the Solomon Islands had four and New Caledonia had two.

The natives believed that an accident, a death or a bad harvest were all due to spirits or to sorcery. They then had to track down the offender and avenge the victim. Cargo cults have existed since "contact" in the last century. The cults have multiplied since World War II. Natives felt that no person could possibly acquire all the goods that the airplanes brought for them. They felt that these goods came from spirits. They thought if they imitated the white man and did away with their native traditions, the goods would be delivered to them instead. In some instances the natives stopped gardening, killed off their pigs and waited for the appointed day. When nothing happened, the leader explained that the whites discovered some stronger magic that overcame the natives magic, and the whole process started again.

In the 1960s, the President Johnson cult started. A leader decided that if the natives raised $1,000 and used it to purchase President Johnson, he would then send all the goods to them. Even when the cultists were taken to Australia and shown that goods came from factories where people worked, they were not convinced. It seems that going from the Stone Age to modern society in one or two generations is too hard. The only materials the natives knew were stone, wood and vegetable fibers. Then white men came and brought astonishing new objects made from materials that the natives knew were not natural such as steel knives, plastic combs, radios and refrigerators. These objects must not be of human origin. The white people do not make the items. The items arrive by ship or airplane. The white men tell the natives to work hard so they can also obtain these items. The natives soon realize that as hard as they can work, they can never get as much cargo as the white men. The natives also notice the white men do not do as they say because the white men do not work. They only shuffle papers. The natives then decide that there must be some other secret the white men have to obtain the cargo. The natives then erect imitation radio aerials and talk on tin-can radios and dress up in identical clothing to the white men, hoping they have now found the magic for obtaining the cargo.

In 1940 in Tanna, New Hebrides, a typical cargo cult developed. It was started by a man named John Frum. He spoke to the headmen of the villages and told them if they would ignore the missionaries, spend all their money and quit the mission schools and mission churches, the natives would find the magic to obtain the cargo. When the officials found out about the cult they arrested some of the leaders and jailed them on another island. This failed to stop the cult. The cult continued for more than 19 years, and many of the people still believed that John Frum would come with all the cargo the natives wanted. When one of the natives was asked why, after 19 years of waiting, they still expected John to bring the cargo, the native replied that the white men had waited 2,000 years for the coming of Christ and he still had not come, and therefore he could wait more than 19 years for John Frum to come. (See Attenborough p.110)

CARIBOU SKIN MONEY

Southern Alaska, 1885

Tlingit tribe. A slave was worth 15-20 skins, an otter skin was worth five-six caribou skins and a good canoe was worth 10-15 skins. (See Taxay p. 92)

CARTONES

Mexico, Mexican Revolution (circa 1914-17)

They are made of thick cardboard in small rectangular shapes with low denominations. Most are common. Not generally considered primitive money.

CARTRIDGE MONEY

Ethiopia, 1800s to 1930s

Both loaded and spent cartridges were used as money. The unit of measure was four cartridges, which was worth a cake of salt. Four cakes of salt were worth a Maria Theresa dollar. In the old days, travelers frequently came upon warriors armed with spears but carrying bags of cartridges from the popular *Gras* rifle. The empty cartridges were valued at 28 to 32 to the dollar. Cartridges that were new with the paper band intact were worth 1/10 dollar each. The rates varied in different parts of the country and at different time periods. In 1908, in an effort to promote the use of coins

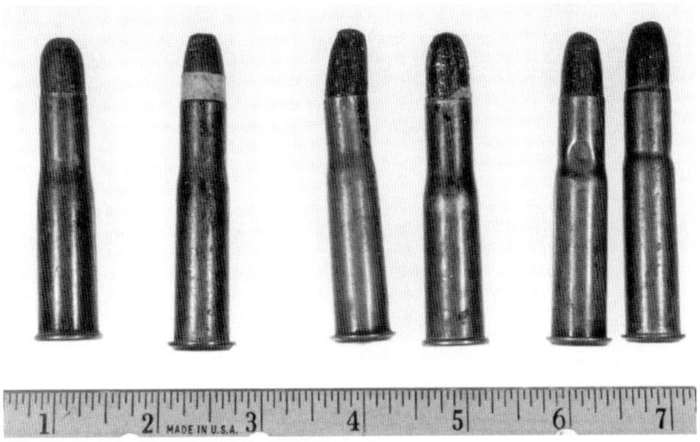

Cartridge Money

Cartones

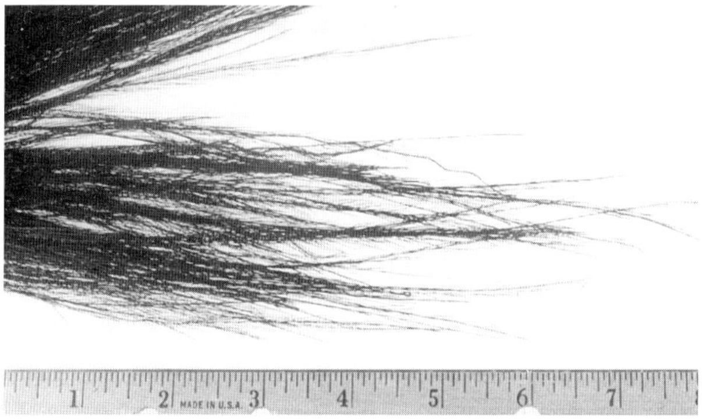

Cassowary Feather

as money instead of cartridges, a fine of $1 per cartridge was decreed if anyone was caught using the cartridges as money. In 1919 an embargo of arms to Ethiopia was declared by the European powers. This lead to an increase in the value of the cartridges. In the 1920s the cartridges were worth six to the dollar. The empty cartridges could always be refilled. At the beginning of World War I, cartridges were the most popular form of money, even more popular than salt. (See Gill, p.14)

CASH

China, Japan, Annam, Korea

The square-hole, cast, cash coins are the longest unbroken series of coins. They were first made in China in the 3rd century B.C. and ended in 1912. They are not odd & curious money, but some collectors include them in their collections. See Money Sword, Money Tree

CASSOWARY BONE - See Dagger Money

CASSOWARY FEATHER

Papua New Guinea

The cassowary is a large flightless bird similar to the emu and the ostrich. It is a powerful, swift runner and has a reputation for being aggressive and unruly. It grows to six feet tall and weighs up to 120 pounds. It can easily kill a full-grown person. The feathers are used to make headdresses and masks. It was used in bride price and in moka gifts. Sometimes the entire bird was used as money and was worth $400 to $500. In 1975 a bride price was three cassowary birds, one cow, 25 kina shells and $1,040 in cash. The Mae people in recent years have set up a trade in cassowaries where they buy the birds from the Maramuni people for $40 to $60 each and sell them to the Mendi and Tambul people for $150 to $200 each. There are several species of cassowary. In the Maring region there is the Dwarf Cassowary (*Casuarius bennetti*), known to the Maring people as *kombli* or *yongge*. In the Ramu and lower Simbai Valleys there is the larger Single-wattled cassowary (*C. unappendiculatus*). There are two kinds of cassowary head-dresses. The *koi kundil* is a cone of black cassowary feathers stuck or bound to a frame that has been filled with burrs. It indicates the wearer is giving away a set of 10 shells and it is worn only for a shell *moka*. The second is the *koi kngal* which consists of brown cassowary feathers woven into a small cap about three inches in diameter with feathers sticking out on the entire outside surface.

Torres Straits

Cassowary feathers were traded to a large extent in this area.

CAT EYE - See Abrus Precatorius

CATLINITE - See Peace Pipe

CATTLE

Many countries and areas such as Russia, South America, Africa, Ireland, Mongolia and Germany, used cattle at various times in history for money and as a unit of measure. In India the compensation for a man murdered, insulted or wounded was 100 cows. Bride price was also 100 cows. In the 12th century in Scotland, a serf was worth 10 cows. In Ireland a slave was worth three cows, and a clan chief was worth 180 cows.

Africa. The Nuer of southern Sudan

Cattle were used in bride price and also to communicate with ghosts and spirits. The cattle were owned by the groom's family and were given to the bride's family, including brothers, grandparents and relatives, who share in receiving the bride price.

Siberia

Among the Kirgiz, a Turkish tribe in southwestern Siberia, cattle were used in bride price with as many as 81 head of cattle being the price of a bride.

CELT

Europe

CH'ING BRIDGE - See Tingle Dangle Money

CHAINS

Ndao, Roti, Savu, Indonesia

Delicate gold chains were important male goods given to the bride's family during the Sumba wedding ceremonies.

CHABILI - See dao.

CHALCHIHUITL - See Jade Money

CHAMOIS MONEY

Germany, 1919-1922. Inflation period following World War I.

Part of the "Notgeld" series of unusual forms of money for collectors or for limited use in various cities. The notes were printed on chamois.

Celt

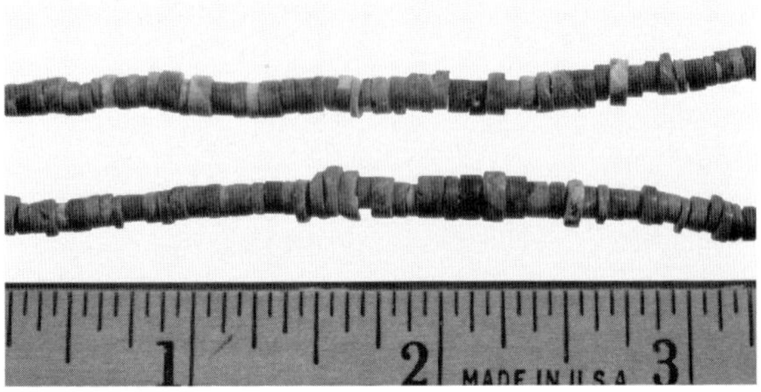

Chaquira

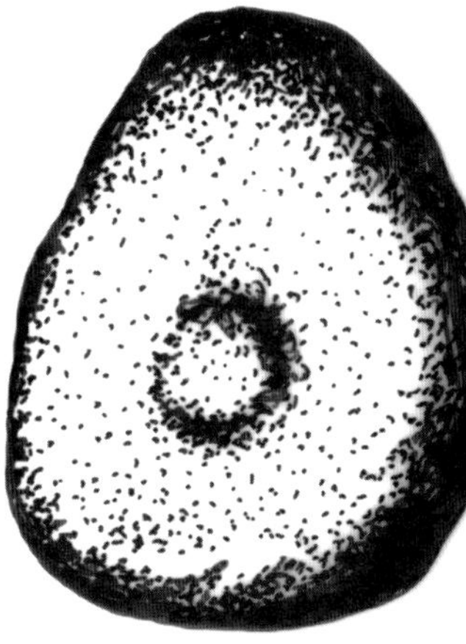

Cheese Money

Cheetem

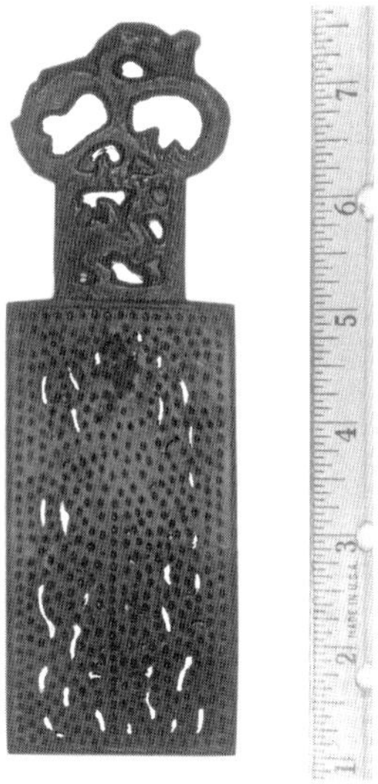

Chestnut Burr

Cho Gin

Choclate Disk Money

Chop Marked Coins

CHAQUIRA

Ecuador, 3000 B.C. and later to the 1500's A.D.

Tiny white-orange and reddish-orange beads made from *Spondylus* shell were very valuable and are believed to have been used as money. The shell was obtained on long-distance voyages made on balsa wood rafts going from Mexico to southcentral Peru. Experts believe that the beads were probably used as money, but no concrete proof is available. The beads were found in tombs. (See Hanson p.78-80)

CHEESE MONEY

Russia, World War I

Compressed cakes of cheese stamped by local government officials were used as money. (See Mosher p. 37)

CHEETEM

Nigeria

Captain Cheetem popularized the use of nine to 13 strands of fine copper wire as a form of money. *Cheetem* were valued at 1/8 d. in 1800s and 1/3 d. in 1920. (See Johansson p. 43-44 & Quiggin p. 88)

CHESTNUT BURR

China

They are also called Knotted Dragon big coins. Some experts think these pieces could possibly have been used as a medium of exchange. (See Coole P.112)

CHEVRON AGGRIES - See Beads

CH'I TAO - See Knife Money

CHICKEN - See Egg Money

CHIEM GIM - See Money Sword

CH'ING MONEY - See Tingle - Dangle Money

CHO GIN

Japan, 1601-1865

Large round-end bars of cast silver or billon ingot pieces are called *cho gin*. They were a more convenient form of storage than an actual trading unit. The silver content varied: Keicho (1601-1695) is 72 percent, Genroku (1695-1706) is 65 percent, Hoei (1706-1712) is 20 percent-51 percent, Kyoho (1714-1736) is 80 percent, Gembun (1736-1818) is 46 percent, Bunseil (1820-1837) is 36 percent, Tempo *cho gin* (1837-1858) is 26.1 percent, and Anseil *cho gin* (1859-1865) is 13.5 percent. There are several varieties. Numerous private issues closely resemble the official issues of *cho gin* and *momeita gin*. Many counterfeits exist. (See Mitchiner p. 587 and Krause)

CHOCOLATE DISK MONEY

Mexico, Area Around Campeche, 1930s

Round disks of chocolate were used as money. (See Mosher p. 38)

CHOP MARKED COINS

Many individuals placed chop marks on coins from many countries. Most were made in the Orient. The chop many times indicates value or purity. They are not odd & curious money, but are included in many collections.

CHUNG CH'IEN - See Bell Cash

C'IENG - See k'a kim.

CICADA MONEY

China

This piece is similar to the shield money in that the back has the same bar across the concave piece. It also appears possible it could be attached to articles of clothing. Its use as money has not been established. It could be a burial object. (See Ramsden p. 33-34)

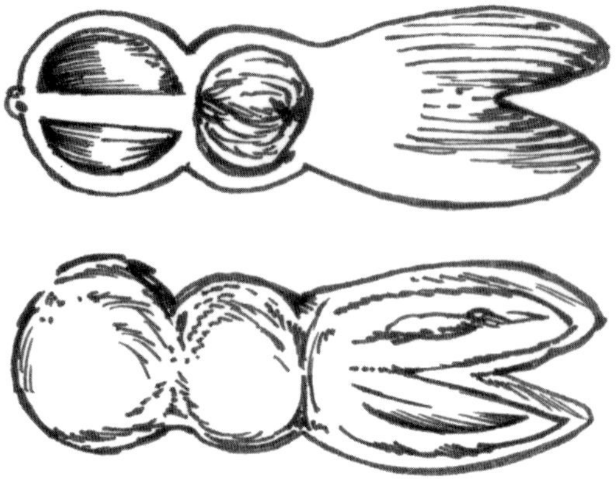

Cicada Money

CIGARETTES

Europe, Southeast Asia and South Pacific, during and following World War II

Packages of cigarettes were used for purchases, and as a store of value. Prices were quoted in cigarettes. In Germany during 1947, 25 cartons of cigarettes would purchase a Leica camera. In Vienna an apartment would rent for two packs of cigarettes per month. After World War II, during the war of independence in Indonesia, cigarettes were currency, and newspaper ads listed prices in cigarettes.

Cigarettes

CINNABAR

Ancient China

In Lingnan gold silver and cinnabar were used as a media of exchange. (See Wicks p. 49)

CLAM SHELL ARMBANDS

Papua New Guinea

Along the Sepik River, clamshell armbands were used as money as well as decoration. They were called *dubalin*. Glass and plastic imitations were also made and traded.

Clam Shell Armband - Glass

CLAMSHELL MONEY

United States, 1930s

During the Depression of the 1930s, in the United States, depression currency was made and used by various cities and some businesses. One of the most unusual currencies

Clamshell Money

was the clamshell money made and used in California. In Crescent City, the Chamber of Commerce, as well as the Cleanatorium, the Odorless Cleaners, the Electric Sho, and the Public Utilities Office made clam-shell money. Some of the shells had the information on pieces of paper that were pasted on the inside of the shell. Other shells had the information inked directly on the outside of the shell. The redemption was for six months after their issue. They were locally circulated and used only while the banks were closed. All shells presented for redemption were redeemed. Pismo Beach also used clamshell money. The following 11 places of business and the Chamber of Commerce made clamshell money: Beach Camp, Beach Store, California Market, Chamber of Commerce, Harter Drug Company, Henderson's Drug Store, Hi-Way Cigar Store, Leiter's Pharmacy, Phillip's Associated Service Station, Pomeroy Electric, Restwell Cabins and Wolverton Sign Company. All these shells had the information written directly on the shells with India ink in red and yellow with black being the principal color. All genuine clam shell money is very rare.

CLAW MONEY - See Magatama

CLAY COINS - See Porcelain Money

CLAY TABLET

Babylonia and Sumeria

3000 B.C. to 2000 B.C.

Clay tablets were used to record economic, legal and administrative information. Some were used as a form of promissory note. They were part of a highly developed credit system. Many of the tablets were bills for the sale of goods and services. They were not a true circulating money but had some of the features of money.

CLOAKS

New Zealand

The Maori used cloaks as payment for ceding land titles to others, compensation for crimes, funeral practices and for performances of rituals. (See Weiner, Inalienable Possessions p.58)

CLOTH MONEY

Cloth was used by many countries of the world as currency, as a substitute for paper, and as an exchange item. In many areas the women were the principal producers and users of it.

Africa.

Cloth was used as a unit of exchange and the units were called pieces or goods. A slave was worth 30 pieces; six pounds of muskets, 1/2 piece; barrel of brandy, one piece; five pounds of gunpowder, one piece; 20 pounds of iron, one piece. (See Payne A-36)

Africa. Baule tribe

The Baule used cloth in long-distance trade and as a form of currency. They grew the cotton, the women spun it into thread and dyed it indigo, and then the men did the weaving and sewing. The women controlled the cloth. (See Etienne p. 221)

Africa, Benin

Blue cotton cloth with four alternate white and blue stripes was called Benin cloth and was worth an elephant tusk weighing more than 100 pounds. (See Roth p. 141)

Africa, Congo

Units of 30 small mats sewed together were called nta and were used as money. They were also used to pay fines, compensations and marriage payments. A nta was worth only one franc. The average bride price was 100 nta. See Quiggin p. 58

Africa, Ethiopia, 1800's

American gray sheeting from the United States was used as money and called American or *Abudjedid.* Ethiopian-made cotton cloth was also used as a trade item. A piece four yards by four yards was worth one dollar. In some parts of Ethiopia, raw cotton was also used as money, according to Giday. Long strips of cloth eight to 11 yards long and 2/3 to 1 1/2 yards wide were worth one dollar each, according to Pankhurst p. 7. Another kind of cloth, called *ferghi,* which was 21 meters long and 80 centimeters wide was worth $2. As late as 1902, more than 5 percent of the government's revenue was in cloth. In many parts of Ethiopia, cloth was used in bride-price. See Gill p.10.

Africa, Ivory Coast

A locally produced cloth called *quaqua* was used as money, according to Herbert p. 136.

Africa, Lake Chad area

Narrow strips of cloth were used as money and were called *gubkas.* They were wound around the head and brought under the nose by the Kanemboos. See Spring p. 45.

Africa, Lele tribe - See Zaire

Africa, Mali

The Kano used *turkedi* cloth in the salt trade with the Moors. Six cloths were worth nine slabs of salt. (See Eyo, p.56) (Quiggin p. 59)

Clay Tablet

Africa, Mali

In some areas in Mali a faravel was used as money. A *faravel* was a narrow strip of cotton worth 300 shells. See Quiggin p. 59.

Africa, Manchester cotton print

The standard unit of cloth was a 10 yard bundle which was worth six shillings in Calabar.

Africa, Nigeria

Gabaga, from Borno. A white strip of cotton cloth was used as money worth eight cowries in 1858. (See Eyo p.56)

Africa, Nigeria

Six to eight yard pieces of cloth known as Dutch *hollandais* (wax print from Holland) were used as a part of marriage payments. (See Guyer p. 146)

Nigeria, Africa.

Langtang cloth. Strips were woven and rolled and were used in marriage payments until the 1940s. One roll was worth 6,000 cowries.

Africa, Nigeria, Rawanyi.

The Deba Habe tribe in Tere district used woven cloth as money (See Eyo, p.56)

Africa, Nigeria, Tel.

The Angas of the Plateau used woven cloth as money. In 1929 the cloth was worth four shillings or 16 iron bars (taji). See Eyo, p.56

Raffia Cloth

Africa, Nigeria, Leppol.

The Fulani people used cloth as money. (See Eyo, p.56)

Africa, Nigeria

Ten rolls of thread were equal to a strip of cloth called *kuntu*. Ten strips of the cloth were equal to a gown called *bul* and a gown was worth five brass bracelets in 1931. (See Quiggin p. 85)

Africa, Nigeria

Jioji cloth from Madras, India ,is still used as a store of value and is also used for funeral payments. Locally woven cloth called *abada* and very expensive *akwete* cloth were also used. (See Guyer p. 146-147)

Africa, Nigeria, Tiv tribe

A type of large white cloth known as *tugudu* was used as money until recently. One iron bar was worth one *tugudu* cloth. Formerly a bull was worth five *tugudu*, and a cow was worth 10 *tugudu*. Brass rods were also used as a unit of account with other items used in payment. (See Bohannan p. 62)

Africa, Toko.

The Kaltungo people used woven cloth as money. (See Eyo, p.56)

Africa, Wolof tribe. Gambia & Senegal.

In the nineteenth century and prior, the Wolof people used cloth as money and made the cloth from locally grown cotton. It was woven on a typical narrow West African loom in strips about five inches wide and 70 inches long. The strings were sometimes colored with indigo and occasionally with tie-dye techniques. They served in both economic exchange and ceremonial exchange. Several strips were sewed together to make a skirt or loincloth called a *pagn* or *pagne* by the English and French or *malan* by the Wolof. A boy had to pay the ruler of the area 16 strips of cloth to be circumcised. A man needed to pay his bride's family 480 strips of cloth. A plain white strip was the main medium of exchange with dyed cloth being more valuable but not used much as a medium of exchange. A 14-year-old female slave was worth 320 strips of cloth, a horse was worth 800 strips, a cow was worth 240 strips and a hoe was four strips. (See Ames)

Africa, Zaire. Lele tribe of the Kasai region of the Congo, Kuba kingdom

Raffia or *raphia* cloth (also called *madiba*) was made by the men of the Lele tribe from the raffia palm (*Raphia vinifera*). Young boys strip the fibrous leaves, and women prepare the fibers for weaving. Only the men do the actual weaving. The red color comes from a redwood called *tukula*. It took one day to make two to three lengths of cloth. Only new, unused cloth was used as money. Bride price was very complicated, and the amount could vary depending on who was married and if there were or existing ties with the village the girl was from. Toward the end of the 19th century the number of lengths of cloth increased from as low as nine or 12 lengths to many times this quantity. A common bride price was 50 lengths to the father and 40 lengths to the mother. Initiation into societies ranged from 20 to 100 lengths of cloth. The chiefs were paid tribute in cloth. Adultery was fined 100 lengths of cloth. A slave was also worth 100 lengths of raffia. Two lengths were needed to make a skirt which lasted about four months in use. The cloth was also traded for shells and salt in the south. It was used for both export and internal trade. Some of the substitutes for *raffia* cloth, such as iron bells, copper bars and slaves, are no longer used. At present, goats, camwood and money are used. Ten lengths (one bundle) of *raffia* was worth one axe, 90 to 100 lengths of *raffia* were worth a slave (ended in the 1930s), one male goat was worth 18 to 20 lengths of *raffia*, one female goat was worth 40 lengths of *raffia* and a three-foot piece of camwood was worth 20 lengths of *raffia*. *Raffia* was also used in ceremonial payments. When a man reached adulthood, he would give 20 lengths to his father so he would not be ashamed to ask his father to help raise the marriage price. A man would also give his wife 20 lengths of *raffia* on the delivery of each of her children. If he didn't, she could repudiate the marriage. Whenever anything was bought from a skilled specialist outside the buyer's close kinship group, *raffia* was used for the exchange. When *raffia* was valued in Belgian Congo francs, the *raffia* was undervalued, and therefore very little was exchanged. In 1924, a franc was worth two lengths of raffia cloth. Europeans accepted *raffia* cloth for taxes. In 1949, it took five francs to exchange for one length of *raffia*. By 1953, it was 10 francs. Even at that price it did not reflect its true value. The market price could not prevail because offering anything other than the official rate was disapproved of. This created a shortage of *raffia*. One hundred cloths were worth the rights to a woman. Since women were scarce, the *raffia* also kept its high value. *Raffia* was used as payment for various kinds of status payments, such as cult entrance fees, blood money, bride price and fines. A roll of cloth was fixed at 12 pieces. A *iboka* (plur: *maboka)* was a unit of *raffia* cloth equal to nine or 10 cloths, a *mihei* was worth 20 *raffia* cloths and a *lutuku* was worth 90 to 100 cloths. Among the Bushong tribe, a strip of *raffia* with 320 cowry shells sewn on it was the standard unit of money and was valued at 400 cowries. Most Kuba

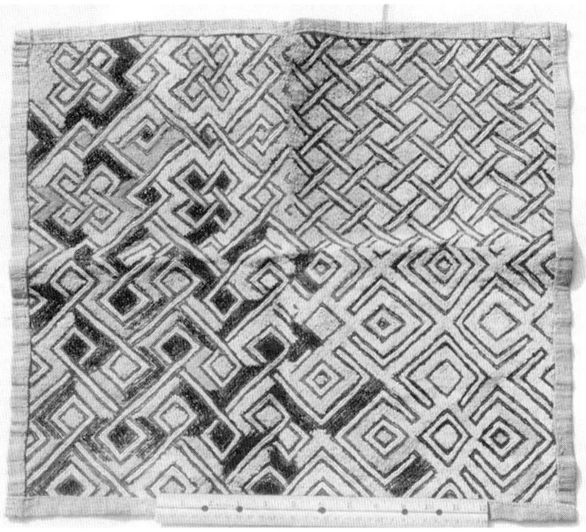

Raffia Cloth

China Cloth Money

textiles now consist of single, fringed, square *raffia* panels, embroidered with an all-plush surface, and they now lack the stitched lines that formerly alternated with the plush areas. They are still highly prized items which are used as gifts in marriage. Women's decorated skirts serve as compensation in legal settlements like adultery and divorce. The skirts are not freely sold but provide a standard of value. Douglas calls *raffia* a coupon and not primitive money. Part of the reason she felt that way was because there was no market at the official rate of 10 francs per cloth, and there was also no black market at a higher rate. She therefore felt that the cloth did not perform an effective monetary role. I define primitive money more liberally, and therefore I consider it as primitive money. In the Bolobo district there was a kind of *raffia* cloth called *moketu*. The Tio made large cloths by sewing together squares that were 38 centimeters by 38 centemeters. The Mpama made rectangles 46 by 60 centimeters. (See Harms p. 62-63) (See Douglas) See bark cloth.

Africa, Zaire

Bunches of *raphia* fiber were the unit of value used as money. The fibers were called *mbadi* or *mbari* and were used to make *raphia* cloth. The bundles were also a part of bride price until 1930. (See Quiggin p. 56)

German Cloth Money

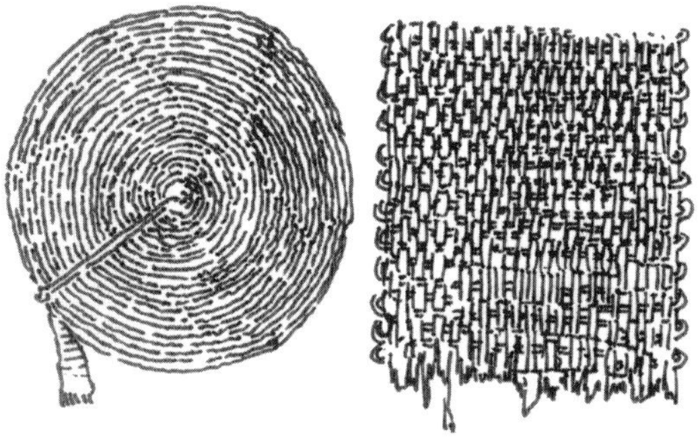

Nigeria Cloth Money

Indonesian Cloth Money - Ikat

Cambodia, 10th & 11th centuries

Cloth was used for the majority of purchases of land and slaves and was probably used for the purchase of many other items. A form of hemp cloth was also used with 100 pieces being the price of a good slave. (See Wicks p. 195.)

China, 1933

Communist issue by Szechuan-Shensi Provincial Soviet Workers and Farmers Bank. 100 cash. White cotton cloth. There are 28 different types in four different areas.

Germany, 1915 - 1922

Notgeld issue, one mark.

Iceland. Ancient times

Wadmal, a cloth spun from the fleece of sheep was used as money. (See Quiggin p. 284)

Indonesia

In the early period of European contact, cloth of various kinds was used. Prior to World War II the people of Kokas exchanged cloth for young slaves. There are many kinds of cloth and each kind has its own name. Some are: *Po* - a form of bark cloth with a limited life, *Po Bajm* (the reserved cloth) - an important part of marriage exchange, *Mon* - in marriage exchange a *Mon* cloth was expected from the bride-takers "for her belly", *Chafach* - formerly used in trade, but have gradually been removed from circulation, *Oan safe* - used in marriage exchange; *Sarim* - used in all sorts of exchanges, Oan kek - obtained in exchange for captured slaves, preferably children; *Topa* - included in all major items of exchange, and printed factory cloth was considered a substitute for it; *Pokek* - a red cloth used as a payment for slave children. *Ulos cloth* is used in bride price. During a traditional marriage ceremony, the father wraps a gift of *ulos* cloth around the newly married couple. The *ulos* was woven cotton made from locally grown cotton and dyed with natural dyes. It is also called *ikat* for the method of weaving. *Ragidup* cloth was the highest status cloth and was given by the bride's father to the groom's mother. Cloth was given for fines for sexual transgressions as well as for exchanges of the life cycle. There were traditionally 20 occasions of exchange. There were also many varieties of the major exchange cloth types which were traded over a large area. *Ikat* was used in dowry and also for bride price in some of the outer islands like Lembata. Many of the islands including Sumba, Flores, Timor and Bali produced many kinds of *ikat* cloth. On Sumba only the payment of bridewealth, like *ikat*, incorporated a wife and offspring into the husband's clan. (See Ikat.) (See Taylor p. 207) Beaded *tempan* textiles may have been part of the gift exchange of Lampung aristocrats.

Trobriand Islands Tapa

Solomon Islands Wood Club

Kabadir

The Kaltungo people in Bauchi State used cloth as bride-price. One *kabadir* was worth five hoes. (See Eyo, p.56)

Korea, 1445

Cloth was adopted as a medium of exchange due to the serious monetary problems at the time. (See Brown, Delmer, p. 27.)

Malay Peninsula

Lengths of cloth were used as a medium of exchange and measure of value. (See Wicks p. 241.)

Mexico, Aztec

A small cape was valued at 100 cacao beans, while another was 80 beans and a third type was 65 beans. A slave was valued at between 30 and 40 large capes, depending on how well the slave danced and how clean his body was. Only high quality cotton cloth was valued at these prices. (See Hedges, July, 1970)

Nepal

Women make cloth for bride price.

Papua New Guinea

Woven cloth called Mle. Used to buy wives, pay taxes, and debts. Often embroidered.

Trobriand Islands.

Many islands produced a form of tapa cloth and used it as a trade item. See Tapa Cloth

CLOVES

Brazil, 1712

Cloves were used to pay the salaries of troops, and the cloves were declared an official currency. (See Taxay p. 58)

Moluccas, 1820

Cloves were used as currency. (See Temple)

CLUBS

New Guinea

Stone headed clubs with wood sticks for the handles were used as a form of wealth and possibly as money. These two clubs were made in pre-contact times. There are many different shapes with many styles of binding. Haddon pictures over 100 different styles of clubs.

Solomon Islands

Various kinds and shapes of clubs were used in the Solomons and had a high value, but it has not been determined if they were actually a medium of exchange.

COAL MONEY

Kimmeridge, England 3rd century A.D.

Round flat discs of jet (coal) believed to be lathe-turned waste from jewelry and ornament production. They are thought to have been used as token money on the basis of burial finds. Two types. 1 3/8″ x 3/8″

New Guinea Stone Clubs

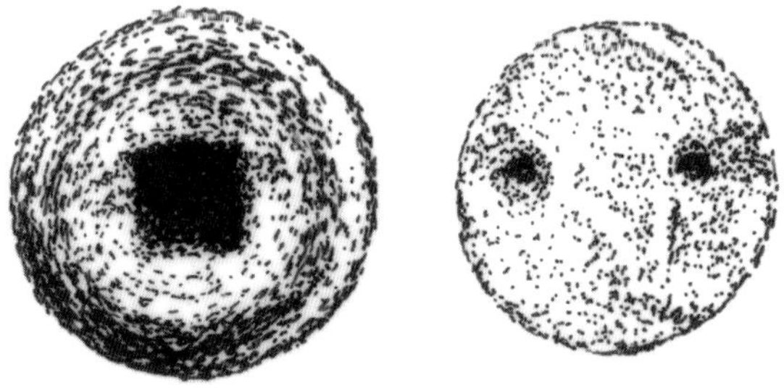

Coal Money

Coal Money - Germany

Germany
1922, Inflation period following World War I
These coal coins were made of compressed, soft brown coal which was baked hard. They were struck in 100, 500 and 1000-mark denominations by the C. Conradty firm for Rothenbach on the Pegnitz, near Nuremburg. All pieces have a hand scratched serial number on them. It is known that 2,500 serially numbered 100-mark pieces were made along with 2,499 serially numbered pieces of the 500 mark denomination and 3,500 serially numbered 1,000-mark pieces. It is unknown how many pieces without numbers were made. Pieces were also made in Lank and Lauter.

COAS - See Axe Money

COCK - See Crocodile Money, Gambar

COCOA BEAN MONEY

Mexico, Parts of Central America, ancient times to recent times

The beans were also called cacao and are the product of a small tree, "*Theobroma cacao,*" native to northern South America and much of Central America. The pods are oval and range in color from yellow to brown and deep red. Up to 50 individual beans grow inside a pod. This is not the common cocoa tree, but a particular kind of cacao-tree which had more beans per pod, according to Del Mar. The beans are removed from the pod and piled in heaps for fermenting, after which they are dried and further processed. The production and use of the beans was tightly controlled by the merchants and nobles. The beans were used as a medium of exchange, but the measure of value tended to be a piece of cotton fabric called a *quachtli*. The *quachtli* was worth 100 cocoa beans or 450 hours of work. Cocoa got its value because it was used to make a ritual drink used by warriors and aristocrats. The beans were also used to purchase slaves.

Cocoa beans were kept in bags of 24,000. The *Tzontle* contained 400 beans. At times the bean was debased by the removal of cocoa and the substitution of clay. Worthless beans could be detected by their weight.

At one time 100 beans was the price of a slave. In 1527, by Spanish decree, the beans were also used by measure, and the seal of the municipality where the exchange took place was put on the unit. In 1555, a Spanish real was worth 140 beans by Viceregal order. In 1590, one Escudo was worth 1,600 beans. Montezuma consumed great quantities of cocoa, and it was popular throughout Mesoamerica. The bean was used as money as late as 1875 in Nicaragua and as late as the early 1900s in Guatemala and remoter areas of southern

Cocoa Bean Money

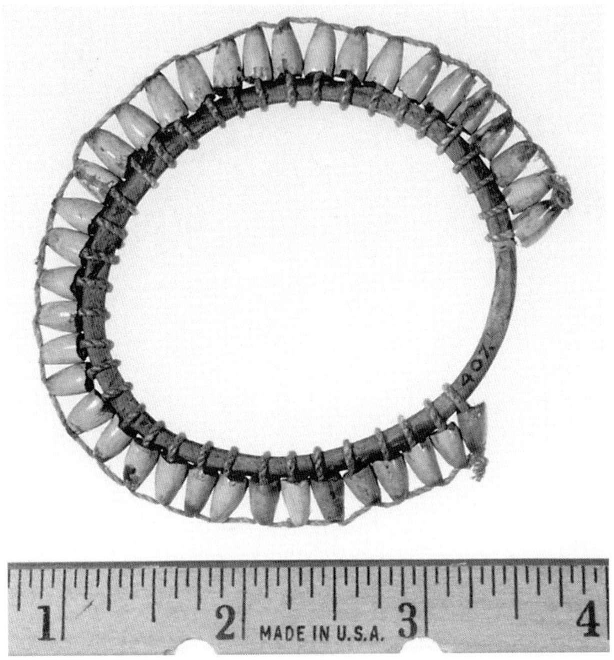

Coix Seed Money

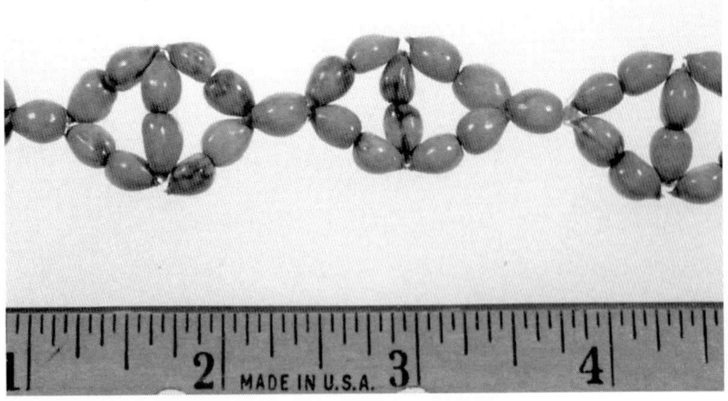

Coix Seed Money

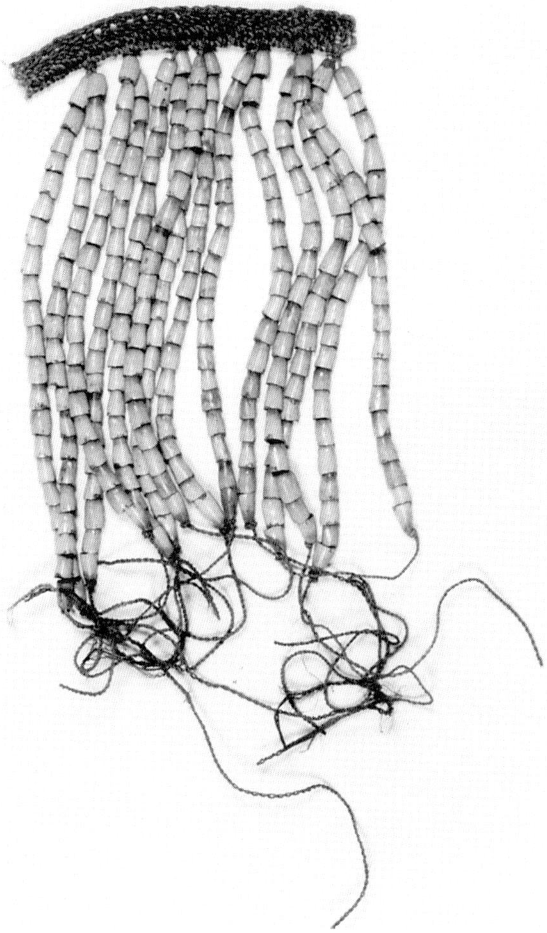

Coix Seed Money

Mexico. (As late as 1940 the Chorti-speaking Indians of Guatemala used cacao beans in formal gift making and as money.) (See Hedges)

COCONUTS

Nicobar Islands, up to World War II

The main food and item for export in the Nocobar Islands was coconuts. All items were valued in coconuts, 65 to 500 coconuts were worth one rupee; 100,000 were worth 25 ships; 35,000 were worth one large racing canoe. (See Quiggin p. 200) See Sinnet

Solomon Islands

1800s

Traders were always willing to purchase coconuts and would advance trade goods for future coconuts. In 1878 a musket was worth 2,000 coconuts, while 25 sticks of tobacco (1 lb.) were worth 600 coconuts. In 1893 the same 25 sticks of tobacco were worth 125 coconuts. (See Bennett p. 81.) In 1882 on the beach an axe was worth 100 coconuts, while in the interior 300-400 coconuts would be the price. (See Bennett p. 87.)

Trobriand Islands

The natives of Sinaketa acted as intermediaries between the natives of Dobu and Kuboma. A limepot or two pieces of betel was worth 12 coconuts. An armlet or two bunches of sago was worth eight coconuts.
(See Herskovitz p. 200)

COCONUT DISK - See Sek, Tekaroro

COCONUT FIBER - See Belt Money

COCOS KEELING MONEY - See ivory money

CODFISH

Newfoundland Coast, 19th century

In the Regulation of Fisheries document for Terra Nuova issued in 1825, fish were the official money to pay wages and other obligations.

COFFEE BEAN MONEY

Sumatra

Coffee beans were used as currency.

Persian Gulf Area

Until recently, coffee beans were used as small change.

France, early months after World War II

Coffee beans served as one of the many kinds of money.

COIL CURRENCY - See mitako

COIX SEED MONEY

Santa Cruz

The seeds were used in tassels and attached to red feather coil money on Santa Cruz. Many times the seeds are cut in half and strung. They are gray and oblong. This same seed was used in many of the surrounding areas for decoration and as money. In Papua New Guinea these seeds were used in mourning ceremonies.

Papua New Guinea

Strings of *coix* seed were used in trade. Whole and half.

COLLAR MONEY

A machicolated collar made of bronze by the Bateke people near Leopoldville. Quiggin (p.76) said it is doubtful that the collar was used as currency.

COMB MONEY

China

This item seems to be nothing more than a grater, and there is no proof it was used as money, according to Ramsden p. 33. It is included in many money collections however.

COMPRESSED COAL

See Coal Money

CONCH SHELL MONEY

Burma, Naga tribe

The whole shell was used as money until recently. Beads made from the columella of the conch shell were also used as money. In 1840, a pig was worth two conches, a cow was worth 10 to 12 conches, and a goat was worth two conches. In 1926, the conch had dropped in value to five rupees. Round convex disks of shell 40mm to 70mm in diameter were used as were triangular pieces. (Gabriel p. 40)

Thailand, Northern Provinces,

8th and 9th century

The conch shell was inscribed with Hindu and Buddhist markings. The colloquial expression to "shell out" comes from the time shells were used as a medium of exchange.

CONE SHELL

Africa

The basal whorl of the *Conus* was used as currency in 1850 among the Manyema to the west of Lake Tanganyika. The whorls or ground down disks were used over a large area and figured largely in ceremonial presentations and bride price and only rarely as currency. The larger *imperialis* species were imported from the Moluccas in the East Indies. In 1899, two would buy a slave, and five were worth an ivory tusk weighing 10 pounds. (See Quiggin p. 50)

CONUS SHELL - See *Biruan, Dibidibi, Mauwai, Som, To-Uba, Wauri*

CONUS SHELL ARMBANDS - See Mwali

CONUS SHELL DISK MONEY - See Beads Conus shell

Papua New Guinea

Ends of conus shells were knocked off and a hole was drilled. The shell disks were then attached to a cord or a woven belt and used as a form of money. In the village

Collar Money

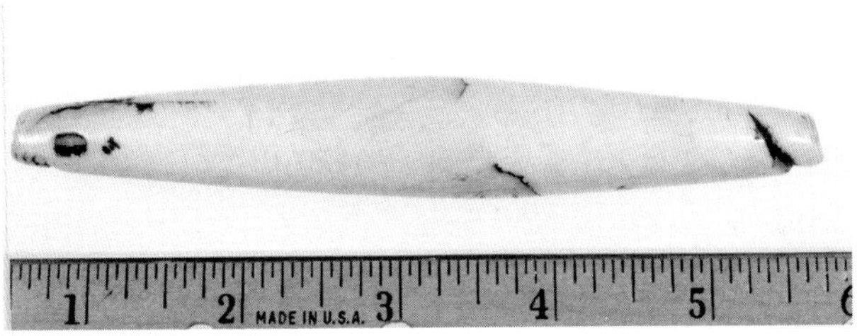

Conch Shell Bead Money

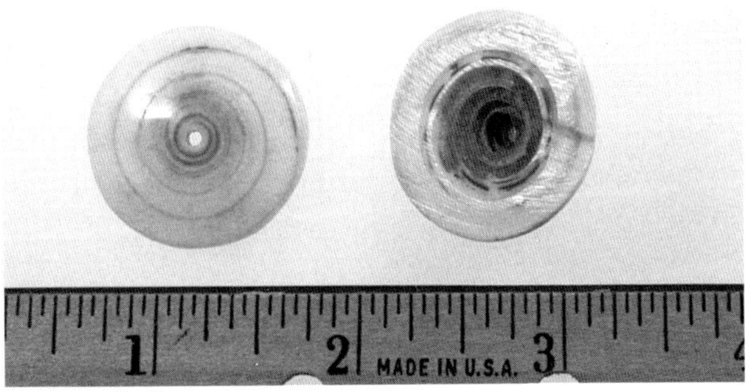

Cone Shell

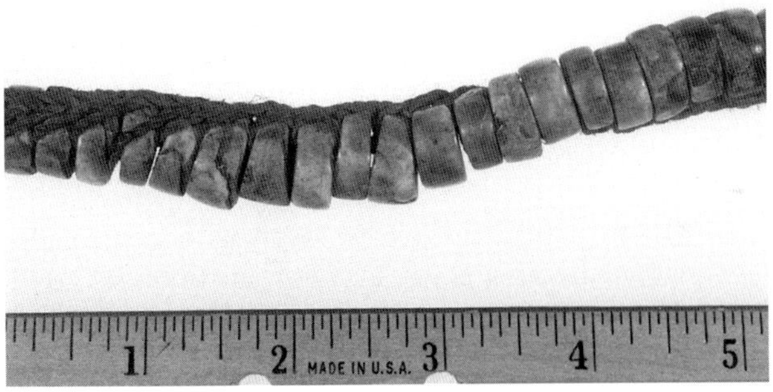

Conus Shell Bead Necklace

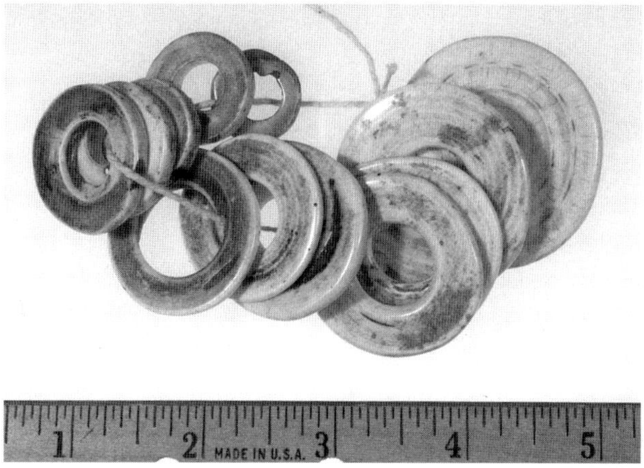

Conus Shell Tips

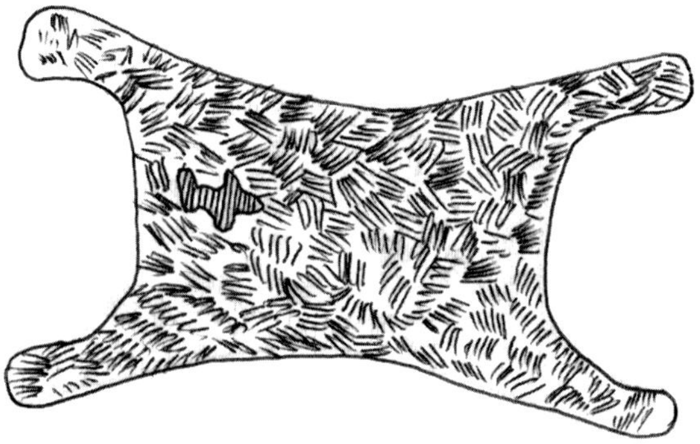

Bronze Talent, Mycenae

of Kandangei, on the Sepik River, I found this very rare form of money. 1″ to 2″ diameter, 36″ length.

CONUS SHELL NECKLACES

Papua New Guinea

Beads of shell strung on a cord and held by fiber along the edge of the beads instead of in the center of the bead. Melawea Village on the Sepik River used large quantities of these shell necklaces as money. Other villages on the Sepik also used these shell necklaces as money.

CONUS SHELL RINGS - See rings.

CONUS SHELL TIPS

Indonesia

Conus shell disks were used as money many years ago.

COON SKIN MONEY - See Raccoon Skin Money

COPPER

Europe

Copper ingots were used as a form of money in the Bronze age in the area of Cyprus and Crete going as far west as Sardina and the mainland of Greece. (See Quiggin p. 272-273)

United States

Nuggets of almost pure copper were found along Lake Superior and in a few other areas. The nuggets were often used in trade between native tribes and were formed into tubular hair pipes, beads, knives and axes.

COPPERS - See Shield Money

COPRA

Ontong Java

Ripe coconuts that have was their husks removed are called copra. The nuts were sold to Europeans and Americans, and the copra is then dried over an open flame and exported. The oil was extracted to make soap, candles and butter substitutes. The pulp became cattle feed. Copra served as currency with five sticks of tobacco worth 100 copra. A bolt of calico was worth about 1,000 copra, depending on the quality of the copra. (See Hogbin p. 267)

CORAL MONEY

The precious red coral (*Corallium rubrum*) lives primarily in the Mediterranean Sea. It is actually the support structure that is built by many small marine creatures. Of all the hundreds of kinds of coral, this one was mainly used in beads and carving and was considered a form of money or a store of wealth in many areas. It was imitated in many materials such as glass and plastic. Plastic will melt if a hot pin is touched to it, while real coral will not. Real coral will easily be scratched by glass, while glass imitation coral will not. Less valuable lighter corals will occasionally be dyed darker red to increase their value. If acetone is applied to the coral, it will show that dye has been used.

Tibet

Small beads in necklace form were used by the Dalai Lama to pay for his escape to India in 1959.

CORN

China

The ancient Chinese used a grain simular to corn as currency. The Book of Chow says, "The duty of the county officer is to gather grain both from open fields and from suburban lands with a view to cover the national expenditures." The use of corn as a medium of exchange was quite prevalent in normal years, but in times of national calamity, metallic coins were introduced to take its place. (See Waung p. 530)

United States, Quebec, Canada, Colonial times

Massachusetts made corn legal tender in 1631. Connecticut made Indian corn legal tender at the value of two shillings per bushel in 1642. (See Taxay p. 145-146)

CORN

Norway

Corn was used as money and was even deposited in banks, lent and borrowed. (See Jevon p. 25.) See Maize

COTTON

Barbados, 1631-1640 (See Taxay p. 145-146)

Burma, 1824 (See Temple p. 105)

COWRY SHELLS

Shells have a unique beauty that man, through the ages, has found hard to resist. Shells could be used as found or modified to fit the particular needs of the individual. The most common shell used throughout the ages has undoubtedly been the cowry. It is a shelled marine gastropod mollusk of the *Cypoea moneta* variety of the *Cypraidae* family. There are two general types of cowries used as money. The large orange or tiger cowry (*Cypraea aurora, C. tigris*) is one type and the money or ring cowry is the other. The main type of cowry used in trade was the money cowry called *Cypraea Moneta* and the ring-cowry called *C. Annulus*. Both are pearly white, occasionally bearing light bands of purple or yellow down each side. Sizes range from one half inch to more than one and one quarter inches. The large orange or tiger cowry (*Cypraea aurora, C. tigris*) was used as money mainly on Fiji.

The money cowry called *Cypraea Moneta* and ring cowry called *C. Annulus* are two of the approximately 200 recognized species of cowry. The name cowry is derived from the Hindi and Urdu "*kauri* and the Sanskrit "*kaparda*," but the varied names in different countries have often led to confusion. The early French name for cowry was *porcelaine*. Most came from the Maldive Islands in the Indian Ocean. The gastropod is slimy and somewhat dark in color. It eats algae, polyps, some corals and animal detritus with its ribbon-like tongue. Only when the animal dies and decays does the attractive shell appear.

The shells have many of the ideal properties of money. They are portable, durable, recognizable and divisible. Also they are not easily counterfeited. Their use as ornaments also increase their appeal as a form of money. They were the most widelspread form of money in world commerce.

The shells were used in most parts of the world from the seventh millennium B.C. in China to as late as World War II. As early as the 10th century, travelers have described the use of cowry shells as money in Ceylon (Maldive Islands). They were controlled by the royal monopoly. It is known that as early as the 13th century, shiploads of cowries were traded between Ceylon and Bengal in exchange for rice or other items. Other cowries were found in the Sulu Islands southwest of the Philippines in present-day Indonesia (especially from Bima near Makassar, Borneo, and coastal Sumatra), and the Ryukyu Islands near Japan.

The fortunes of nations rose and fell on the trade and use of cowry shells. The value of the shells has varied from unbelievably high, such as two cowries for a woman in parts of Africa in the 1500s to no value in other places. Cowries are also known by other names, such as cat's eyes, *bonges, zimbis, cowrie and dewarras.*

They were used in most parts of Africa, in the Hawaiian Islands in the 19th century, in New Caledonia, in Gilbert and Ellice Islands, in New Hebrides, in India and in New Guinea. They were also used for decoration and religious ritual in Europe and North America. They were used as sacred objects by the Ojibwa and Menomini Indians.

The cowries are collected by one of three methods. The first was to place branches in the shallows for a few months. During this time the cowries would attache themselves to the wood and leaves. The second and most popular method was to wade into the sea at low tide and detach the cowries from the stones with a short stick. This was done only twice a month. It was done on the 13th, 14th, and 15th, and also on the 27th, 28th, 29th and 30th. The great tidal changes take place on these days. A man could sometimes gather as many as 12,000 shells in a single day. This was a *kotta* of cowries, weighing about 25 to 30 lbs. A third method of "bait and line" is questionable. The shells were processed by digging a pit in the sand and burying the shells in the pit for two or three years (it could have been much less time). The mollusk decayed, and the shells retained their shine.

They were intimately connected to the slave trade. In the 14th century the traveler Ibu Battuta saw cowries used as money in the Mali Empire. It is possible they were used as early as the 11th century. They were used there before the age of European participation in the trade. They were also found in use in the Gulf of Guinea near Benin in 1480. At about that time the shells were worth 350 times

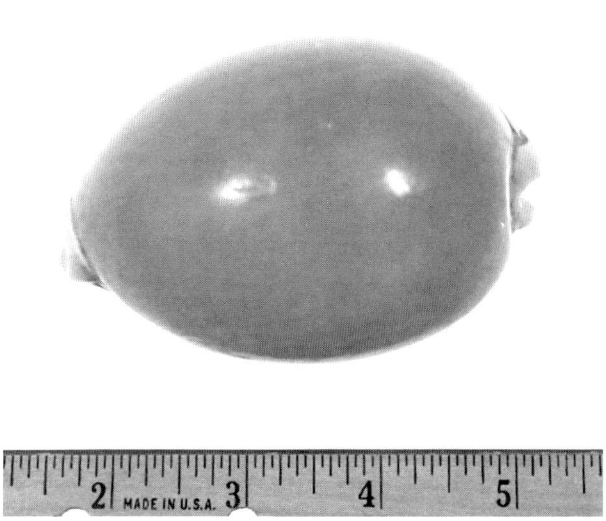

Golden Cowry Shell

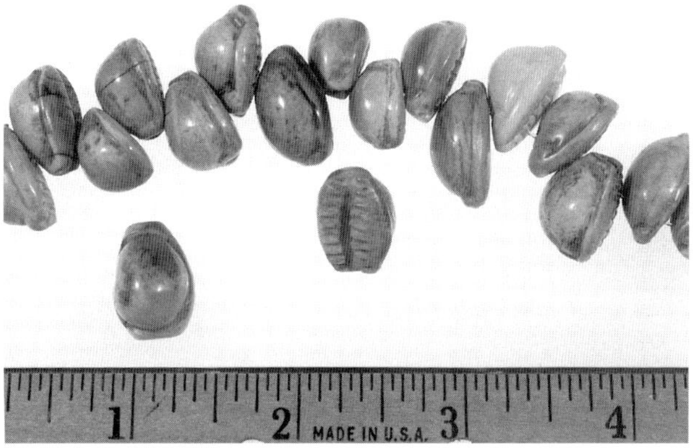

Carved Ivory Cowry Shells

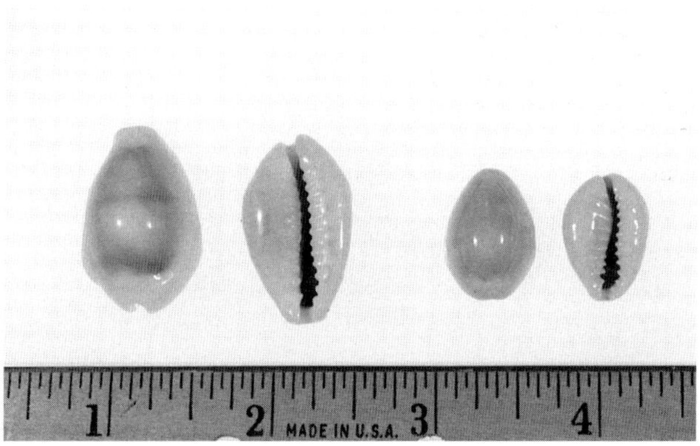

Money Cowry *Ring Cowry*

as much in West Africa as they were in the Maldives. The European trade in cowries started in the late 1400s. In the 1500s the Portuguese discovered they could obtain the cowries in the Maldives and transport them to Africa by ship instead of the trans-Saharan land route. They could be used also as ballast, which would normally be stones, sand or old iron that would not earn any revenue. They could still carry other revenue-earning cargo. They also attempted to colonize the Maldives to further increase their profits by controlling the trade. By 1522 the cowrie had become as important as *manillas* in Portuguese trade with Benin. Like almost all shell shipments by the Europeans as late as the 19th century, they were carried by ships around the Cape of Good Hope. A series of people was given grants of monopoly trading privileges by the Portuguese. They were allowed to trade in cowries without paying a fee. Profits made by the Portuguese were in the area of 300 to 500 percent. These ended in the mid 1600s and the Dutch and English started to compete for the trade at that time.

In 1642 the Dutch started to trade in cowries. The V.O.C. (Vereenigde Oost-Indische Compagnie) was chartered in 1602 and was granted a monopoly of Dutch trade east of the Cape of Good Hope and west of Cape Horn. The first purchases were probably made from the Portuguese at Goa and Cochin, in Bengal and Ceylon. By the 1660s the English were complaining of a Dutch monopoly in cowrie trade. It does not appear to have been a fact, however. The Dutch were paying 2 1/2 rupees for a *kotta* of 12,000 cowries and raised that price in several stages reaching more than five rupees in 1740. The Dutch did, however, capture the European part of the trade from the Portuguese. They announced in the 1720s that they wanted to purchase 500,000 pounds of shells per year. The actual figures were always below their projections. The price increased from 1.5 rix-dollars per *kotta* of 12,000 in 1697 to 3.0 in 1795. The Dutch were usually low in price, but at times they protected the area with their navy. After 1770 the monopoly power was broken. The years of 1785 to 1790, however, were great ones for the Dutch. After those years it collapsed.

The English purchased most of their cowries from Balasore, a little city in Orissa 60 miles from the mouth of the Hooghly River on the northwest side of the Bay of Bengal. It had a suitable anchorage, and the surrounding area grew rice for trade. The cowry trade in the later half of the 17th century went from the Maldives to Balasore and other Indian ports, then to Europe, primarily London, where the East India Company and other dealers sold them to traders in the African trade. The other stream went from the Maldives to Ceylon to the Netherlands, where the V.O.C. sent them to traders headed for West Africa. With the capture of Ceylon in

1796, the English were alone in the trade until the abolition of the "legitimate" slave trade in 1807. Most of the shells first went to Europe before going to West Africa. It would seem that a lot of traveling could be avoided if they were dropped off before going to Europe. This was not done because the spices were much more valuable and they were demanded in Europe, not West Africa. Also the shells were at the lowest level of stacked cargo and therefore would require removing all the other cargo to get to them. The prevailing winds and currents along the coast also meant it would be much harder to sail. The ports in West Africa also would not permit the larger ships to unload easily. They were two to four times larger than the usual slave ships. The shells would also be cleaned, repackaged and auctioned in Europe before shipment to West Africa. The cleaning raised the price for which the shells sold to the traders. The centers of the commerce were Amsterdam and London. This developed a healthy trade in Europe. The prices fluctuated widely due to changes in supply and demand and the successful effort to monopolize the trade. Between 1674 and 1720 the price varied from 3.35 pounds per cwt. to over 14 pounds per cwt.

The early West African cowry zone expanded geographically during the 17th and 18th centuries from what it was in the 16th century. The early zone included the middle Niger and a coastal enclave around Benin. They did not circulate in modern Senegal, the Gambia, Guinea-Bissau, Sierra Leone or Liberia.

The French also were involved in the cowry trade from about 1688 to the late 1700s.Their target was 300,000 pounds per year. In some years it was probably achieved. Their influence was not nearly as great as the Dutch or English. From 1700 to 1800 the English imported about 11,000,000 pounds of shells, while the Dutch imported about 14,900,000 pounds of shells. Between 1851 and 1869 just five German and French companies supplied more than 14,000,000 shells. They reached West Africa from Zanzibar and were *annulus.* The *annulus* did not replace the *moneta* of the Maldives but were used along side each other. This tremendous increase in shells did result in a great inflation in the value of the shells. From 1850 to 1895 the value decreased to only a little more than a tenth of their former value.The result was that a cargo of shells would be consumed by the cost of the human carriers within two or three weeks of travel. Consequently shells could not be transported great distances inland because of their low value. The last significant direct shipment of cowries was in 1891. By the beginning of the 20th century the cost of transporting the shells was more than the shells were worth. In 1904 Nigeria prohibited the import of cowry shells. In 1911 all taxes were collected in coin instead of cowries.

After 1807 the cowry trade almost stopped because slavery was abolished by the English. In 1820 palm oil replaced slaving as the export from Africa. It was used in lamps of homes and factories and many other uses. The cowry boon was on. From 1800 to 1850 13,800,000 pounds of cowries were exported to West Africa. In 1845, *annulus* from the east coast of Africa came to be accepted along with *moneta*. The cost of the shells and the freight were less (distance was shorter). The shells were larger, and therefore fewer shells could be transported in the same space.

In 1680 a slave was worth 25 pounds of cowries. In the 1860s a slave was also valued at one bar of salt or one or two cows or four pounds sterling. In 1716 a slave was worth 136 pounds of cowries, 16 guns, seven rolls of tobacco or 150 pounds of gunpowder. A few years earlier the same slave was worth only 100 pounds of cowries, 12 guns, five rolls of tobacco or 15 pounds of gunpowder. By the 1770s the price of a slave rose to 400 pounds of cowries. This was about 160,000 to 176,000 cowries per slave. By the 1830s cowries were used primarily for the purchase of palm oil and other trade items. The internal use in Africa of slaves for their own internal use continued long after England and America abolished the use of slaves. As late as the 1890s slaves were traded in Ghana for cowries. In the 1880s a slave was valued at 120,000 to 140,000 cowries. At the same time cowries were counted by different standards. It was very confusing, but 80 (Bambara rate) cowries could be counted as 100. At some places and times, 100 cowries were actually only 60 cowries (Mandingo rate).

In Africa the shells were inconvertible: neither the North African merchants nor the Europeans who brought them would take them back. They could be accurately traded by weight, by volume or by counting. About 400 to the pound. They are almost impossible to counterfeit. The smaller shells from the Maldive Islands were prefered because they were more easily transported. The smaller shells came from the warmer waters. They have varied in value from 10 cowries for a cow in Sudan in the 16th century to 400,000 cowries for a gold dinar in the Maldive Islands. In the late 1500s "two shells would buy a woman" in Uganda. They were counted and valued in many different units. In the bazaars of Male a "*kotta*" was 12,000 shells, worth one rupee and in the Maldives worth one larin, the silver wire of high purity bent in the shape of a Y or fishhook used as money. A hundred shells were called "*siya,*" 700 were called "*fal,*"and 100,000 were called "*bosta*". In 1747 in Christiansborg, 16,000 cowries were worth one ounce of gold. In Bornu in the 1840s, a "*rotl*" consisted of 32 shells worth four strips of cloth. In Bambara (Mali: West Africa) in 1790, food for a man and a horse for one day would cost 100

Top (left to right): Lead, Lead, Lead, Bronze Bottom: Wood, Clay, Stone, Shell

Top (left to right): Jade, Copper Covered With Gold, Copper; Bottom: Bronze, Stone, Shell

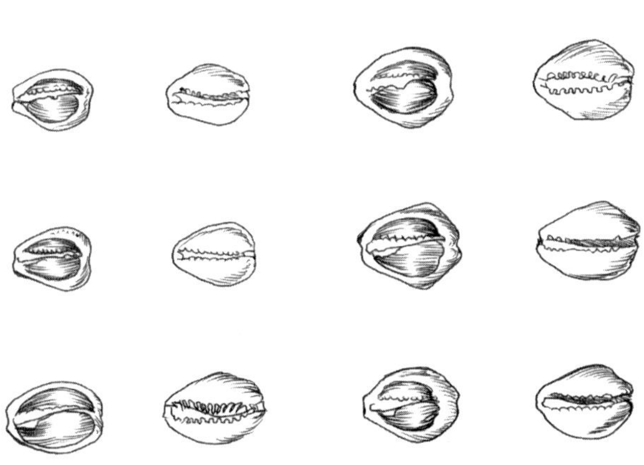

Cowry Shell Types: Kawane , Dege Bomofe, Buna Bomofe, Epaa Mege, Bodija, Tuanika Mege (Counterfeit); Label Top Left To Lower Right

cowries.They were used alongside the Maria Theresa dollar and were the official money. In the 1860s, 120-130 *rotl* were worth one Maria Theresa dollar. A "head" consisted of 1,000 cowries. Ten bunches were worth one head. five strings of 40 cowries were worth one bunch. A bag contained 10 to 12 heads. In the Niger, different kinds of strings with different numbers were used. In many cases the relationships of cowries to each other could not be calculated as the relationships were not logical. For example, in 1849, 120 shells were worth three pence, but 25,000 shells was not worth the equivalent of 2.6 pounds sterling. In 1850, in Congo, Central Africa, one chicken was worth 10 cowry and brideprice was 30 cowries. By the 1890s on the lower Niger the cowry was simply a unit of account without being a medium of exchange. Generally the value of cowries fell in Africa as greater numbers were imported. By the 1850s, when the first year's poll tax came into being, the dumping on the market of 40 million shells collected from the tax caused the value to decrease by 25 percent. Inflation continued after that. In the 1860s a slave was also valued at one bar of salt, one or two cows, or four pounds sterling. In Nigeria bride prices increased from 36,000 cowries in 1939 to 720,000 cowries in 1949.

In 1890, a horse was worth 70,000 cowries in Upper Volta. In 1896, 4,000 cowries were only worth one mark in German Togoland. In 1908 the Royal Niger Company refused to recognize cowries as a valid money. In 1907 in the Congo, Cental Africa, bride price was now 3,500 cowries. The governments first prohibited their import then refused to accept them for tax payment and finally provided large supplies of low-denomination coins. The shells vanished from the markets in the 1930s.

Along the Slave Coast in Africa, large storage houses completely decorated on the outside with cowry shells were used by the wealthy to house their shells.

The slave trade in Africa was transacted in cowries. In 1520, a slave sold for seven cabres (goats) valued at 6,370 cowries weighing 16 pounds. A slave went from 10,000-31,000 cowries in 1680 to 40,000-50,000 cowries in 1710. By the 1770s, the price was 160,000 to 176,000.

Imitation cowry shells were made of bone, stone, bronze, white stone, lead, hard black stone, jade, silver, crystal, terra cotta, gilded bronze and gold. The most common imitation was stone, then bone, clay with shell being rare. Realistic cowry imitations in metal are very rare. They were usually bronze but may be lead. As early as the 3rd century they were used in the Malay Peninsula and Borneo. Substitutes of ivory, bone, lead and stone were also used.

Burma

In Burma in the fifth century and as late as the 13th century, the time of Marco Polo, cowries were used as money.

China

It has been suggested that China and Japan were possibly the first countries that used cowries as tokens of value and a media of exchange. The North Chinese name for cowry is *bei* (*pei*), the Canton name is *puei* and the Korean name is *p'ae*. This *bei* (*pei*) character was part of more than 100 signs in the Emperor's national dictionary, which shows the importance of cowries in trade and commerce at that time. Cowries are found in Stone Age deposits in parts of China. Many imitations were made in mother-of-pearl, horn, stone, bone, copper, bronze, lead, ceramics, ivory and gold-leafed bronze; most were used as money.

The pre-Chinese population of China used cowry shells as a medium of exchange. They were used as early as the 24th century B.C. Cowry shells were used for small payments, while tortoise shells were used for large payments. Evidence indicates that in the 14th century B.C., cowry shells were used as a medium of exchange. By 221 B.C. the first emperor of China forbade the use of cowry shells, but by 10 A.D. the usurper emperor, Wang, briefly returned to their use. He utilized five different varieties of shells as monetary units. The smallest sizes were not used as money, but a pair of the largest were valued as equal to 216 ordinary cowries. Around 600 B.C., metallic cowries were used as money. They combined the cowry shell money with the advantages of using metals.

The ghost-face money, also known as ant-and-nose money, are "cowry exchange coins" and have been dated to the 6th or 7th century B.C. They are also known as "metallic cowries". As late as the 14th century cowries were still being used to pay taxes. The story goes that these coins were placed in nostrils of cadavers to keep ants out. (The ancient Chinese had no magnifying glasses to see what an ant's nose looked like.) See Ghost-head money. Their use in China was slowed by the lack of supply instead of the abundance of supply as in Africa and most of the world.

At one time cowries were used in Borneo for small money. They were found on some of the coasts of Borneo. Large quantities were exported to China, where they were exchanged for large jars that were highly valued by the Dyaks of Borneo. The Chinese then used the cowries for money. In China from as early as 1523 B.C., the cowry shell served as currency. It was also used later and was used to pay tribute to the emperor. (See Wicks p. 28.) The cowries were two or three inches long and were bone white with purple maculations and were collected in the south. They were required for certain tax purposes and possibly were used as a significant store of wealth.

India

In India the four cowry unit called *gandaka* was used as money during the 6th century. (See Wicks p. 74.)

Thailand used cowry shells as an important monetary item as well as a general standard of value until the latter part of the 19th century.

It is claimed that in the 16th-century India, cowry shells were used in Bengal as money. They were put in baskets or parcels of 12,000 shells, and merchants from all over India took them to Bengal for use as money. While the Chinese pierced the cowries and put them on strings, in India perforated shells were considered worthless.

Irian Jaya

In 1938 an expedition to Irian Jaya was able to trade 22 pounds of sweet potatoes for just one cowry shell while in 1962 one cowry shell was worth only one or two potatoes. (See Muller p. 128)

The Moni people of Irian Jaya are well known for their knowledge of cowry shells and have graded the shells and given values to each grade and sub grade. The *sae* is worth about $.50, with the *munga* worth $10 to $20, the *kubawi* worth $40 to $75, *indo lagupa* worth $50 to $100, hondo worth $200 to $1,500 and the *indo* worth $250 to $2,500. Within the class the value is determined by color, number of bumps and the style in which the back was cut off. (See Muller p. 132)

Papua New Guinea, Mount Hagen

Cowry shells were attached to ropes and used as money in the early period of first contact in the 1930s and 1940s. Later they lost so much value due to excess supply that they became worthless as money and bride price. In the 1930s tiger cowries (*Cypraea tigris*) and Arabian cowries (*Cypraea arabica*) were also valued according to Hughes p. 56.

Papua New Guinea, Kapauku tribe

According to Pospisil (p.301) there are two main categories: *meekaa mega*, the people's cowries, and *tuanikaa mege*, the white men's cowries. The old Kapauku cowries are two categories: *kawane* - a low value shell and *wei mege* - a precious shell. Popisil (p. 302-304) describes four *meekaa mege*: 1) *Kawane* - a smooth, elliptical cowry shell worth two to three glass beads in 1955 depending on the size. 2) *Bomoje* - the most common old cowry shell with two subtypes. The *dege bomoje*, which is yellowish-white, was worth 30 glass beads in 1955 the second subtype is *buna bomoje*, which is darker in color and worth 40 glass beads. 3) *Epaa mege* - This cowry is worth 60 glass beads and is a large cowry of the *wei mege* category. Similar to *bomoje*, but larger. 4) *Bodija* - the highest Kapauku denomination and is larger than the *epaa mege*. Its shape is the same as the *bomoje* and was worth 300 to 400 glass beads. The *Tuanikaa mege* is white man's cowry. They were worth three glass beads in 1955.

All the precious cowries are made by first making an incision with a flint knife on the top close to one end. The top part is split away using a bone awl, then the whole shell is neatly polished with a whetstone until it is highly polished and has luster.

Necklaces of the small white cowry-like shell (*Nassariidae, Nassarius*) consist of two strings which pass through the two perforations in each shell. The necklace is called *dedege woja*. It is the length of a man's arm and is worth 30 glass beads. Pospisil describes them as being used in bride price. The longer necklaces he says are six feet and worth 90 glass beads. In 1955, necklaces consisting of many kinds of glass beads were also considered money. (Pospisil p. 304) The Europeans introduced a cylindrical or spherical light blue glass bead called *dau* which was money, and 30 of them were worth one *dege bomoje* cowry. In 1955 an iron axe was worth five *dege bomoje* cowry, a 200-pound male pig was worth 20 *dege bomoje*, a kemo of salt (four 1/2 pounds) was worth one *dege bomoje* cowry, a large house was worth five *dege bomoje*, a bilum was worth one *dege bomoje* cowry and a good canoe was worth two *dege bomoje* cowry. (Pospisil p. 305-306)

Papua New Guinea, Wola people

Formerly, cowry shells were used as money and were used in three ways of presentation. The most common was to secure them on a vine to make a necklace. One kind of necklace called *taenjel enjat* had fewer shells because the shells were spaced out with their hole facing outward. The other kind of necklace was called *taenjel togo*, and the shells were packed more closely . The Kutubu people used a plaited rope with shells sewn along one side, also called *taenjel togo*. (See Sillitoe p. 148-149)

Russia

In Russia, cowries were found in excavations in northwest Russia and down along the Volga river. It appears they were used during the 12th and 13th centuries. Records suggest the cowries came from Riga on the Baltic Sea.

West New Guinea

The cowries were used loose and counted. They were also sometimes sewn into ropes of from two to nine feet with a nine foot rope being worth a kina shell and used to purchase a wife or pigs. The two-foot rope was the standard unit of value. In Papua New Guinea, the Adzera people of the Markham Valley used a *dangangtang*. It contained between 20 and 40 or more egg cowries (*Ovula ovum L.*) attached in two parallel lines around the circumference of a circular core made of coconut bast and bush rope or cane, called *uwap*. A single egg cowry is called *rarup* in Adzera. It was used as an important part of bride price. Ten or more *dangangtang*, a pig and bundles of spears were the bride price before World War II. The *wela* was also used in Papua New Guinea in the Morobe Province by the Mumeng. It is similar to the dangangtang but with only eight egg cowries attached and the central core decorated with *nassa* shells to make four quarters colored alternately blue and red. It was used as bride price.

The white egg-cowry (*Ovula voum L.*) was highly prized in the eastern highlands where it was called *gam* shell and was replaced by the large pearl oyster (gold lip or kina) in the western highlands. It was the unit of highest value at one time. A man would work one whole month in construction for just one egg-cowry. Later this shell was unacceptable for major purchases. (See Hughes)
Until recently they were used in Papua New Guinea, New Caledonia, Hawaii (Sandwich Islands), North America, India, and the Maldive Islands. In the Mount Hagen area of Papua New Guinea, nine feet of cowries sewn on a cord normally could pay for a bride, but much higher prices could be demanded as there was no set price. There the shells were called *tinale* or *tingala*. The shells were of such high value that items in daily use seldom would cost more than one shell. In 1924 in New Guinea, five cowry shells would get you a small pig. At that time a bride would cost a string of cowries the length of the girl's father's or the groom's outstretched arms. In one area a single cowry was worth many axes or knives. Ten cowries were considered a fortune.

As the interior opened to exploration in the 1930s the value of cowries fell dramatically. In New Guinea new shells were sometimes artifically aged to look like old specimens which were snowy white in color. In some areas only old shells had any value. The new or young ones were not even accepted as a present. The old shells were an important component in bride price. They were also used to pay for garden labor and medical assistance. During WW II the Japanese troops distributed many cowry shells and "thus endangered the economic and financial stability of the district."

In America we have found no evidence that cowries were used as money.

In Fiji orange cowries were used along with whales' teeth (*tambua*) as a very valuable item and both border on the use of money depending on your definition of money. The orange cowry was usually worn on the chest. One orange cowry was worth many whale's teeth, and the whale's teeth were carved to represent the shells. The orange cowries are one of the rarest shells in the world. (See Gitlow p.75)

COWRY SHELL BAND - See Yerak

CRAB'S EYE - See Abrus Precatorius

CRESCENT - RIDGED

Africa, Congo

Roughly cast brass ridged semi-circle crescents were used as a bullion-based money. They appear to be related to the legbands of the Mongo according to Scott Semans.

CROCODILE MONEY

Malaya, 17th and 18th century

The tin figures were also called *Buaya* and were worth 2-1/2 cents. The figures are in the shape of the elephant, tortoise, mantis and cock and were used as weights as well as money. (See Quiggin p. 254-255) Rare.

CROSS, KATANGA

Africa, Katanga region, 1100s and later

The St. Andrew's cross shape was made of copper by pouring the molten copper into molds made in the sand. In later years tin was added to the copper to form a variety of bronze which was shinier and more accepted than pure copper. They were also called Baluba crosses for the name of the tribe of people who smelted the copper in the Katanga region. At one time they were also called *handa*. (See *Handa*). One cross was worth 10 kilos of flour, five - six fowls, three or four kilos of rubber, or six axes. Ten crosses were worth one gun. A bride price consisted of 14 large crosses, one she-goat, one flintlock gun, and one female slave. A male slave would cost three - five crosses in 1907. A female slave would cost five - 10 crosses. The Ndembu paid 24 crosses for a rifle, 100 crosses for an elephant tusk and 150 crosses for a slave. The crosses varied considerably in value. The copper in these crosses was African and very red in color. The crosses were made at least from the middle of the 18th century to as late as the 1920s. In the 19th century they were used for payment of tribute by the Kingdom of Kazembe to the Lunda of the Mwant Yau, or by the Samba to the Luba. (Heusch p.136) They served

Crescent - Ridged

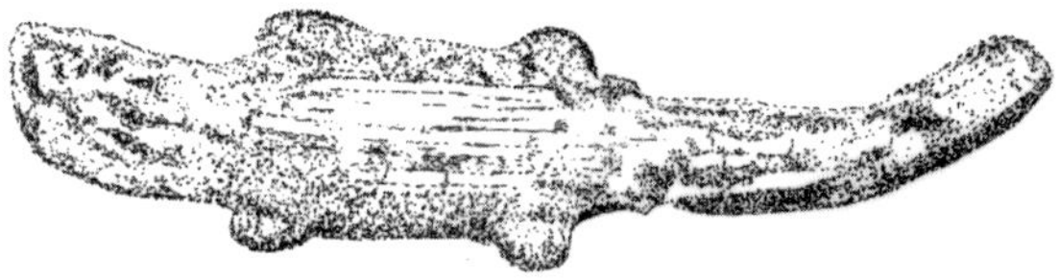

Crocodile Money

Cross - Katanga

Cross - Katanga

Cross - "H" Shaped

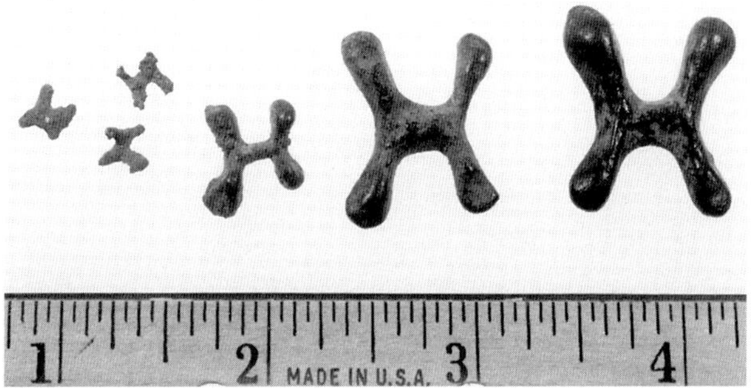

Cross - "H" Shaped

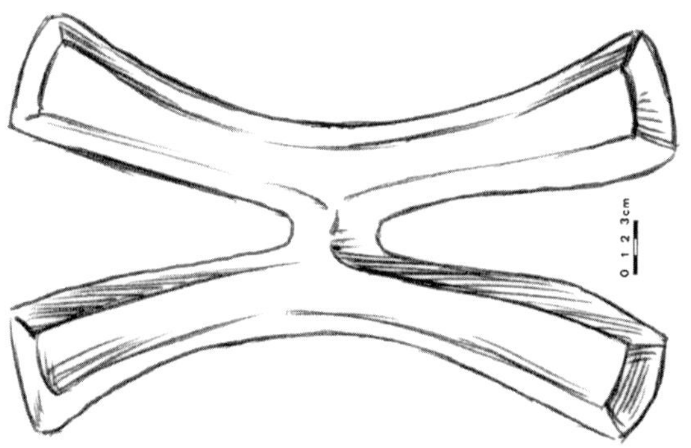

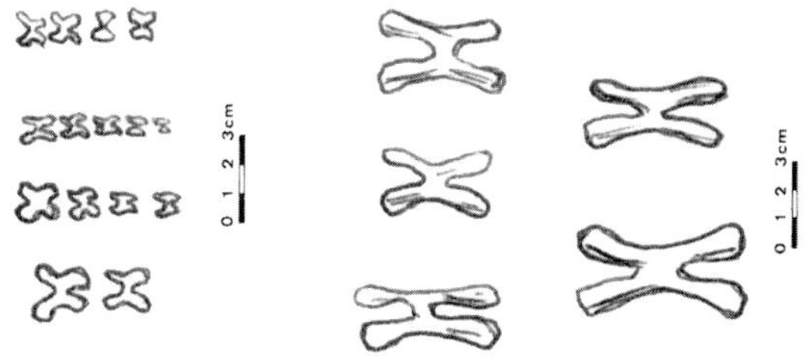

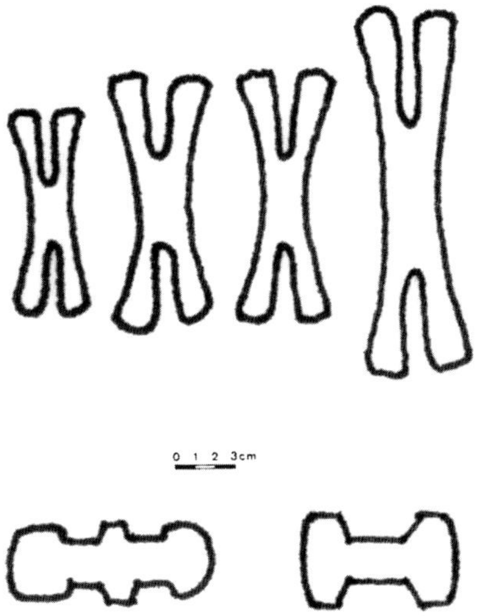

Cross - "H" Shaped

as medium of exchange, regalia, currency, raw material, insignia and emblem simultaneously. (See Payne A-1 and Sigler p. 17) (See Heusch p. 136-143)

CROSS - "H" SHAPED

Africa, Zimbabwe, 13th to the 17th centuries

The "H" shaped cross was used as money before the Katanga Cross was made. Prior to the 14th century the HX, HIH and HI crosses were used. The HX crosses have a narrow cross piece and were made in two sizes with the smallest found in Upemba basin in the 3.5 to 7-cm long range. The largest were found in Ruashi and were 36 cm long. The HIH crosses have an elongated cross-piece and range in size from 8 cm to 20 cm in length. The HI cross looks more like an I with the ends pulled in. The cross section of the H is almost as thin at the H is long. Some of the other HI crosses look more like rectangles than H crosses. The dates on these crosses (bars) have not been determined. From the 13th to the 17th centuries in the south (Zaire, Zambia, Zimbabwe and Mozambique) HXR crosses were used. These crosses have an intermediate shapes between an X and H. They are about 12 inches long, have a cross-section of a trapezoid and were found in large numbers in Zimbabwe. They were referred to as currency at their time of use. From the 13th to the 17th centuries, the HH and HX crosses were used in the Upemba basin. The HH crosses fall into two sizes. The smallest size is generally quite small, weighing on average .6 grams each and were used in the 16th or 17th centuries. The second size averages seven to nine grams and were used in the 13th to 15th centuries. By the late 1800s they became too numerous, lost all value and were replaced with beads as a currency. (See Heusch p. 138-142)

CROSS - I & DOUBLE T SHAPED

Africa, Zamba, 18th to 20th centuries

Copper bars weighing some 30 to 50 kilos were cast, it is believed, from the 18th century to the time of Livingstone. The straight bars with a triangular cross section and T-shaped ends are very rare and were found in Zambia. They are believed to have been made in the 18th century. The bars were important in long-distance trade as far away as India. It is believed the double T-shaped bars were produced from the beginning of the 19th century to 1903. They are also very rare. They are called coppers with ears. (See Heusch p. 135-138.)

Cross - Double T shaped

CROSS - SILVER

Africa, Ethiopia

The silver crosses were worn for more than 1,600 years they served as a valuable and were used in trade. There are many styles, and each was named for the town or province it came from. Each one was made from a Maria Theresa dollar or was cast by the lost wax method. (See Fisher, Africa Adorned.)

CRYSTAL

Virgin Islands, Mid-19th century

Carib and Arkwak Tribes.

The crystal was made in the form of beads and was family property and not individually owned. They are not considered money by many experts.

CUBS - GOLD

China 600 B.C.

It is believed that the first true coins from China were gold cubs cut from sheets of gold. (Cubs are known and partially uncut sheets are also known.) Rare.

CUNEIFORM - See Clay Tablets

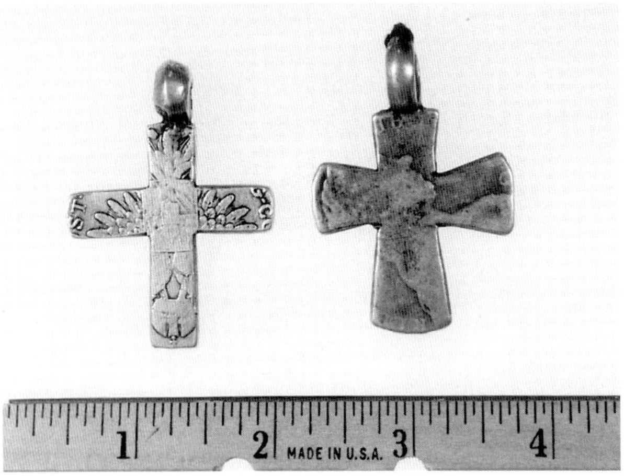

Cross made from Maria Theresa Dollar

Cross - Silver

Cubs - Gold

CUSCUS TEETH

Solomon Island, Papua New Guinea

The teeth are from a small opossum-like creature. The teeth are smaller than dog teeth and flat along the sides. A string of 100 cuscus teeth was worth a canoe. They were called *Paiou* by the Habi of Buka Island, North Solomons.

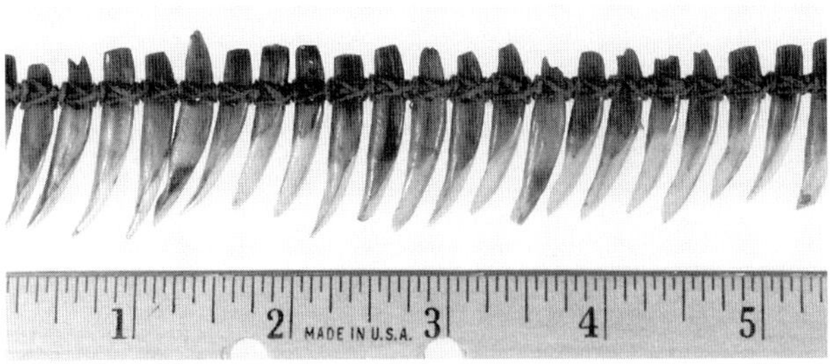

Cuscus Teeth

CYPRAEA MONETA - See Cowry Shell Money

DAFI

Malaita Island, Solomon Islands

This pearl shell gorget, with a turtle-shell frigate bird decoration attached to the upper center was used as a form of decoration and on Malaita Island.

DAGGER MONEY

Papua New Guinea, Irian Jaya

Cassowary and sometimes human bones were used to make daggers. Incised decorations were sometimes added to the handle. See Kris

Dafi

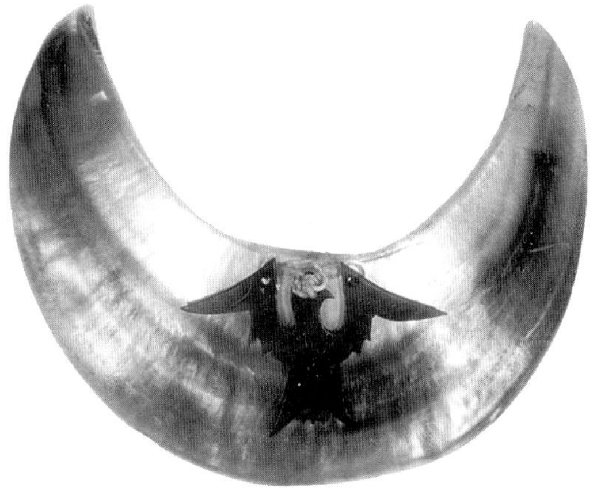

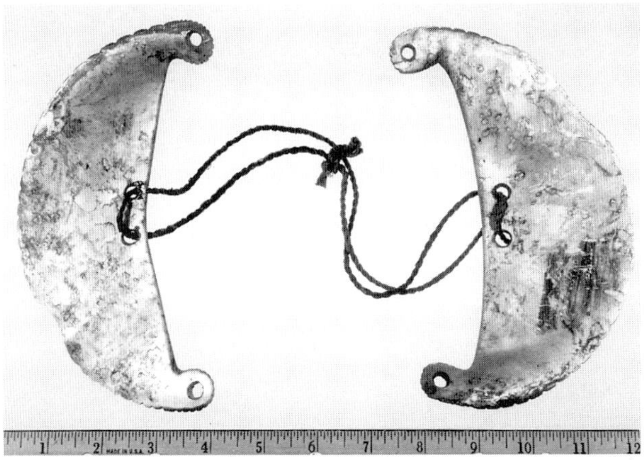

Dafi

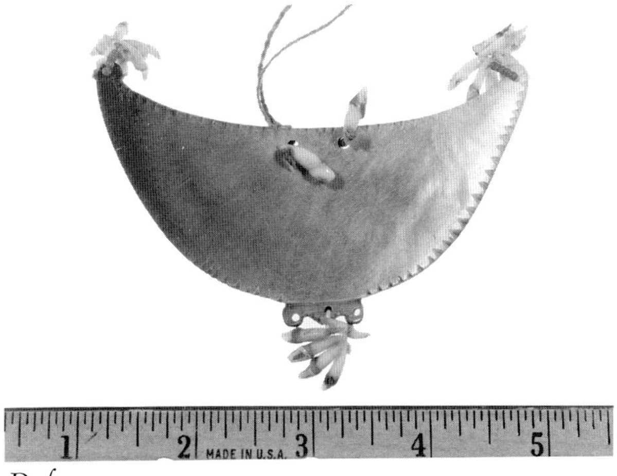

Dafi

DALA

Solomon Islands

A Western Solomon Islands word for *kapkap*. See kapkap.

DANGANGTANG

Papua New Guinea

This strange pendant was used by the Adzera people of the Markham Valley. It contains between 20 and 40 or more egg cowries (*Ovula ovum L.*) attached in two parallel lines around the circumference of a circular core made of coconut husk and bush rope or cane, called *uwap*. The *uwap* consists of two circular mats of coiled bush rope or cane between which cloth is sandwiched. A single egg cowry is called *'rarup'* in Adzera. It was used as an important part of bride price. Ten or more *dangangtang*, a pig and bundles of spears were the bride price before World War II. *Dangangtang* are not now used in bride price. (See Barron, Colin, TMA Nov 1989.) (See Wela)

DANKI - See Bowls

DAO

Assam

A form of axe. It was originally used as an ordinary working tool which later became money. It was given to medicine men to avert illness. A miniature dao was called a *chabili*. (See Quiggin p. 204)

DAP

Another name for ndap. (See ndap)

DAPI

Burma

The Konyaks used a large gong as a form of money. They also used a set of three smaller gongs. The value depended on the size and tone. (See Quiggin p. 207)

DAVE ALAVA

Malaita, Solomon Islands

A round disk of shell with a rim of black putty-nut around the edge of the shell was used as money. It was suspended from a string of shell money and worn around the neck. (See Russell)

DAVERI

Sudest Island

It is a shell currency identical to the lower-valued *ndap* found on Rossel Island. It is a small orange colored shell-piece which is two to three inches long. They are used as valuables and exchanged at memorial feasts on

Dagger Money with Dried Flap of Skin and Fur

Daggar Money

Dangangtang

Sudest and now also East Calvados Islands. (See Leach p. 487) See Kula.

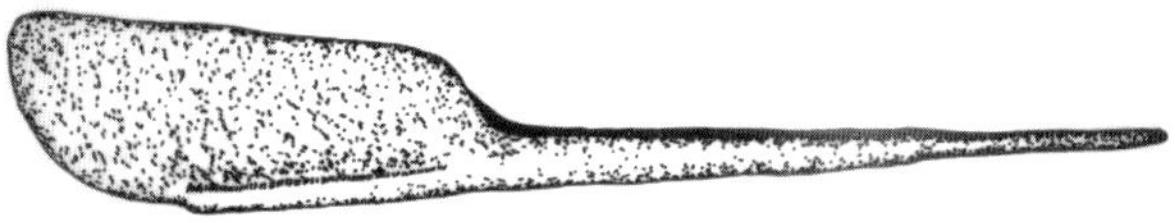

Dao

DE

Irian Jaya

Ancient glass beads and glass rings are called *de* and also *ho*. They were used as far away as Vanimo in the West Sepik Province. The rings were valued at 500 kina each, and the beads started at two kina each, depending on their color. Usually 300 beads are on a string. Natti of Vanimo tells how the rings came to be owned by men. "In the beginning, all was only mist and cloud with no firm ground or seas as we know the world now. Then there came walking through the mist a great being whose hair was the storm clouds, whose eyes were the lightning and whose smile was the sunshine. He came down carried by the foaming clouds. Where his feet were, there formed firm ground and beaches and mountains. Then slowly about him the mists dissolved and became the waters of the sea. Then on the beach between the seas and the land he created man. And he gave the men enough rings for all time. These first men were very big, and they wore rings on their fingers and toes. They tied the rings with vines from the trees and hung them around their ankles like shells are hung today for the sing-sings. Ahdai also made the blue beads. He made many more of these than he had made rings. Seeing that the men were lonely, he gave all these to them saying: For two of the rings you may buy the head of a woman. For two of the smaller beads you will buy her breasts, and with a larger bead you will buy her future labor pains when she will bring forth children so that you will no longer pass your days in loneliness. Then Ahdai turned his back on his labors and floated away on a cloud. As he disappeared from the earth, the sun followed him, and it was the first rainy season of the world. When it was over, there were many men upon earth and women too. Ahdai brought back the sunshine once again, and the people held a big sing-sing, but no one of today remembers it. To this day the men of the tribe must buy their wives with two rings, two small beads, and one large bead as taught us by Ahdai in the beginning." (See Traditional Money Association newsletters.)

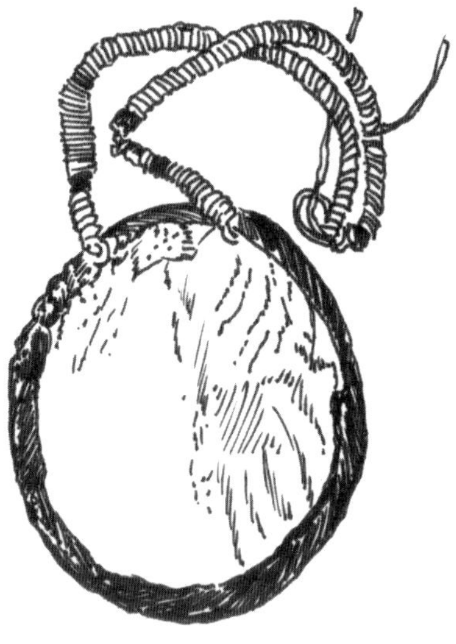

Dave Alava

DEDEGE NECKLACE MONEY - See nassa shell, Papua New Guinea, Kapauku tribe

DEER SKIN MONEY

State of Franklin (now part of Tennessee), late 1700s

Daniel Webster in an 1838 speech on currency, said the Legislature of Franklin set the salary of the Governor at 1,000 deer skins per year and the salary of the Chief Justice at 500 deer skins per year.

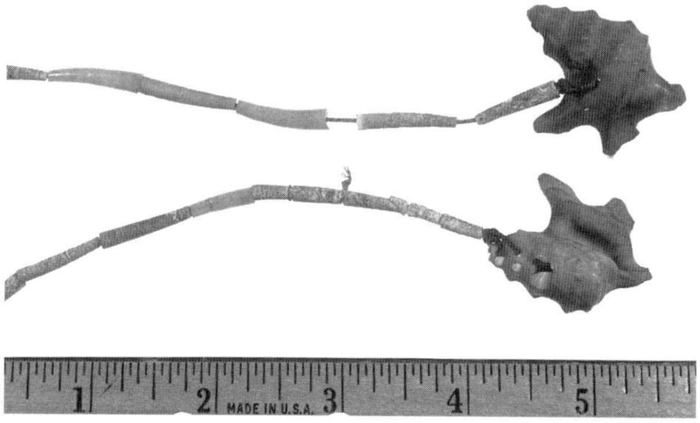

Dentalium Shell Money

Dentalium Shell Money

DENTALIUM SHELL MONEY

California and north to Alaska

Larger shells were considered more valuable than smaller shells. The shells varied in length from one inch to three inches. When used as money, the shells were wrapped spirally with narrow strips of snakeskin or fish skin, or sometimes a short section of snakeskin was wrapped over the entire shell. Sometimes a small tuft of red feathers from a woodpecker's crest was added to one end. In other cases the shells were incised with designs. Prices varied from $ 0.25 to $5; smaller shells were not considered money. Value was determined by how many shells it took to make a string of standard length (27 1/2"). Yurok valued a house at three 12-shell strings, a bride from a wealthy family at 10 strings of various sizes and a fine for adultery at five strings. They tried to have all of the shells on a string of the same size. The *Kergerpitl* shell was 2 1/2 inches long, and it took only 11 shells to make a string worth $50. The *Tsepupitl* shell was 1 1/2 inches, and it took 15 shells to make a string worth $2.50. Twelve shell strings were worth $20, 13 shell strings were worth $10, and 14 shell strings were worth $5. By 1920 the value of these strings was cut in half. A slave was worth one or two twelve-shell strings. A house was worth three twelve-shell strings. An obsidian or flint blade was worth 2 to 10 12-shell strings. Bride price from a wealthy family was 10 strings of shells of various numbers of shells. The Tolowa used 10 shells to a string. A longer string was more valuable. The Nootka of Vancouver Island, the Nuu-chah-nulth and also probably the Makah were the people who collected the shells. They devised complicated dredges to collect the *dentalia* from depths of 20 to 30 feet. They ate the meat and traded the shells to their southern neighbors. The farther from the source, the more valuable the shells were. The marriage price for a woman among the Shasta Indians in California was 15 or 20 large dentallium shells, 10 to 15 strings of disc-shaped beads, and 20 or 30 woodpecker scalps. Each shell was approximately 2" long. The shells were some of the wealth items used to proclaim rank and uphold prestige. The Yakima used dentalium-shell-decorated bridal headdresses in bride price. The headdresses were decorated in some cases with imported blue beads and Chinese cash coins. The Inuit used earrings decorated with dentalium shells and glass trade beads as decoration and in monetary uses. The Yurok valued one dentalium shell as worth a woman's cap full of tobacco.

DEOGANTA

Tibet

The metal bell with a handle was decorated and was used as money and in bride price. A bride price consisted of a deoganta bell, three oxen and six sheep.

Deoganta

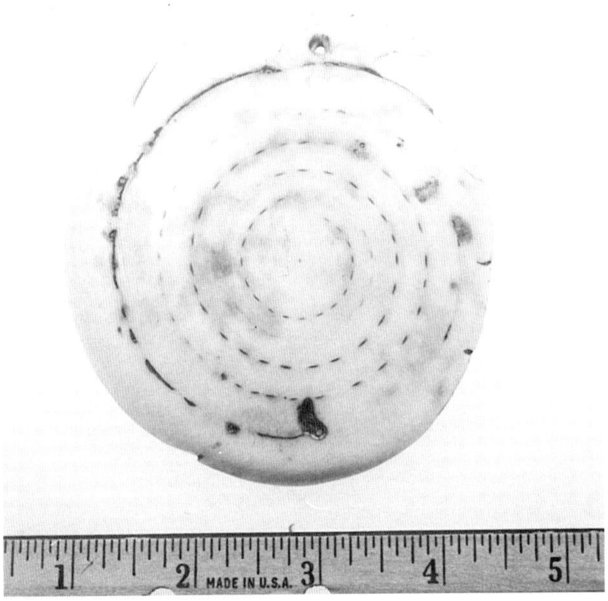

Dibidibi

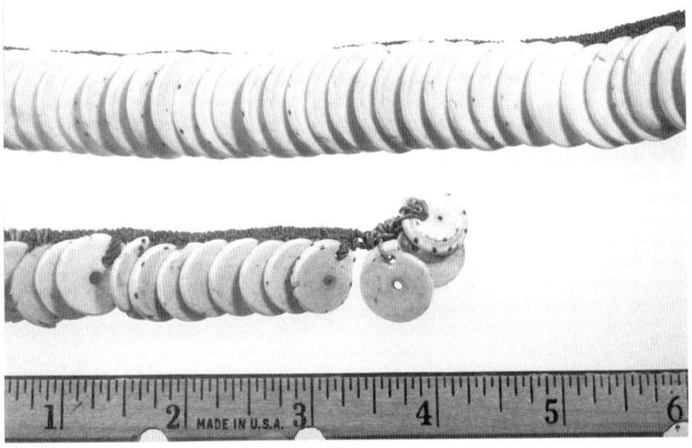

Dibidibi

Dice

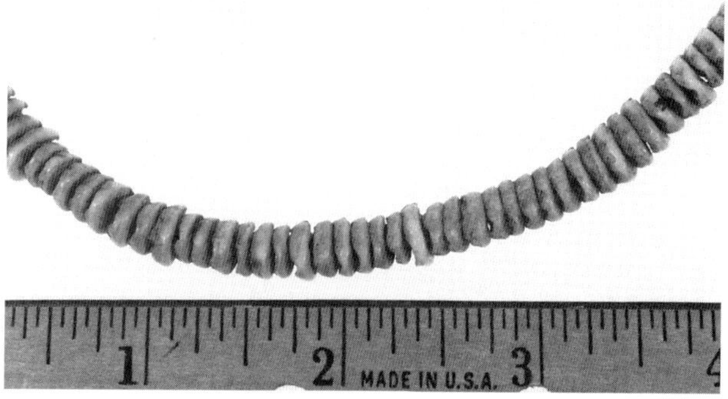
Diwarra

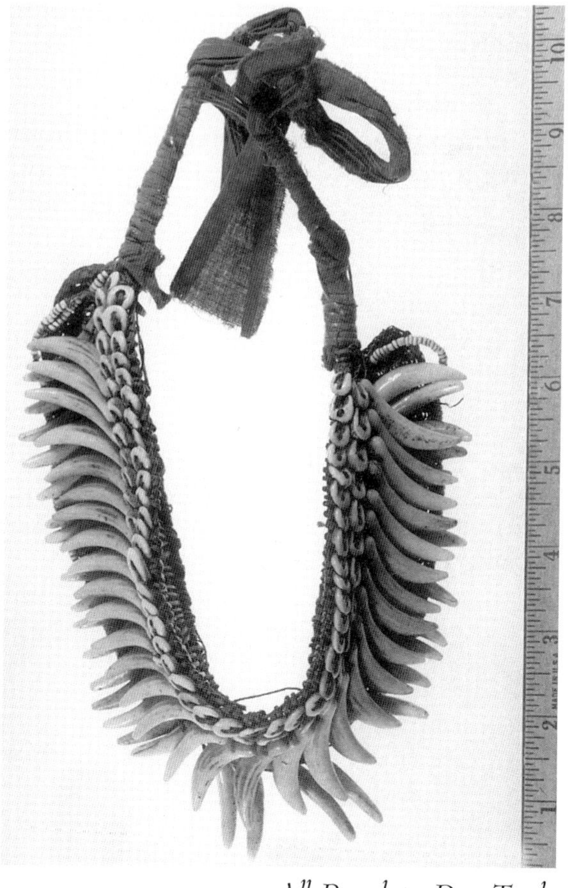
All Porcelain Dog Teeth

A bell was also worth about two year's work. In cash it was worth 6 d. to 1 pound 4 shillings. (See Payne A-7)

DIBANDA

Congo

A bar of salt weighing about 6 1/2 pounds was used as money in the Katanga region. (See Herskovits p. 214)

DIBIDIBI

Torres Straits

Circular shell disks from the top of the cone shell were used as money. They are also called *wauri* (*Conus litteratus var. millepunctatus*). The shell disk has a hole the near edge for stringing and was used in bride price. Ten to 12 were worth a canoe, a dugong harpoon or a wife. The canoes were normally paid for in three annual payments of three *dibidibi* or goods of equal value. The largest is about 3 3/4" in diameter. The finest *dibidibi* come from Tutu and other islands to the east. (See Quiggin p. 180-183)

DICE

Cameroons and Northern Gabon, South Africa

The dice were made from the Elma tree nut. The outside of the nut was ground and polished smooth. Various objects or scenes such as faces, shields, birds, nut, or animals were carved on them. The dice were used in the 19th century in a popular gambling game. The German authorities in the area considered the game dangerous to the natives. The gamblers many times lost their wives, children and houses in the game. To eliminate the game they used hanging as punishment for the artists who created the dice. Some believe they were used as money, but there is no proof at present. (See Burford, "Traditional Money Association Newsletter Vol. 2 Number 2.")

DISK - IRON - See Quartz Disk, To-Uba, Tyere

DIWARRA

New Ireland, Duke of York Islands

The *Nassa Camelus* or the *Nassa immersa* shell is collected from mangrove swamps from the north coast of New Britain, known as Nakanai. In that area the shells have no value except for trade and to ornament large spears. The shells are then buried for a year to improve their color. Then they are stuck in a cavity of a coconut shell, and the back is broken off so they can be threaded on a stiff strip of rattan. The two or three foot lengths of rattan are joined by splitting the ends and inserting the end of one piece into the end of another piece. A fathom consists of 300 to 400 shells. This is a true money used to buy everything and used in the same manner as our money. A wife was worth 100 to 150 fathoms. True *diwarra* must have the shells evenly spread and not touching each other. This *diwarra* was then made into large coils of from 50 to 200 fathoms, which were called *loloi*. The rings were rarely broken up except for mortuary purposes. They were also used in secret societies both as initiation fees and as fines for non-members. A stick of tobacco was worth one fathom of *diwarra*. Later the value changed to two sticks of tobacco for one fathom of *diwarra*. *Diwarra* was also loaned out with interest at a standard 10 percent. It was then used to pay initiation fees or for bride price. A fathom of *diwarra* was worth two yards of calico 100 years ago. A spade or axe was worth one to three fathoms of *diwarra*. (See Quiggin p. 160) Called *Tambu* on New Britain and *aringit* on New Ireland. See *Nassa* Shell Money

DJIMBU

Africa

These small shells were used as currency over a wide part of Africa. A female slave was at one time worth 15,000 to 20,000 shells. An iron hoe blade was worth 300 *djimbu*, and a goat was worth 800 djimbu. In Kolokoto 100 *djimbu* was worth four to six cents. In other areas and during other times, the value differed considerably. Twelve ounces of salt were also worth 300 djimbu.

DOBA

Trobriand Islands

The finest banana leaf skirt, See Skirt.

DOG TEETH MONEY

Papua New Guinea, Admiralty Islands, Guadalcanal, San Cristobal, Manus Province

Four teeth were the unit of measure. Only the canine teeth and the teeth immediately behind the canines were used as money. They were also used in bride price. The teeth were holed and strung into necklaces and used on headdresses. The Germans made a porcelain imitation for use by traders. At one time a string of dog teeth was worth from $5 to $100, depending on the number and condition of the teeth. Dog teeth were not used as money after 1960 in the Chimbu area. The Mafula used dog teeth to pay for pigs and other ornaments. The cost of a pig at one time was a chain of dog teeth that equaled the length of the pig from the nose to the base of the tail.

Admiralty Islands

A dog's tooth was worth 10 taro roots, 10 coconuts or 40 betel nuts in 1929. Mead wrote that the value of every object sold or exchanged could be expressed in terms of dog's teeth. A lime gourd was worth two teeth, and a lime spatula was worth five or six teeth. One hundred teeth were worth $5 or one pig. (See Einzig) (See Sigler p.20)

Guadalcanal

A number of dog's teeth and porpoise teeth plus 40 strings of *ndovu* shell money was the fine for seducing a single girl. This fine also reduced her bride price.

Manus Province

Dog teeth were used in most large exchanges. A single exchange could include as many as 10,000 dog teeth. A boy and girl are betrothed at an early age, at which time the boy's relatives give a large amount of dog teeth and shell money to the girl's relatives. The exchange is repeated at marriage and at their silver wedding anniversary. (See Einzig p. 77) In 1908 a string of shell disks had the same value as one dog's tooth. After 1912 the value of the teeth declined because Europeans started to import dog teeth from China and Turkey. Originally the teeth were taken only after ceremonies were performed on the dog to raise its spiritual level. The teeth were taken only after the dog died a natural death. It was not killed to obtain the teeth. Only dog teeth and shell disks would be used in affinal exchanges. Other items could not be substituted for them. The value of the teeth increased with age, just as it did for the shell disks. The Titan trading expeditions followed well established trading routes and traded a series of products in an established succession. First coconuts were traded for pottery, which at the next trade stop was traded for wooden bowls and at the end of the expedition was traded for dog teeth, shell disks and other items. (Gustafsson p. 55)

Papua New Guinea

Dog tooth ornaments were considered valuables and were used as money. At present they are no longer used as money or in trade, but are still considered valuables. The Min people from the Star Mountains in the past exchanged a string of dog teeth for bundles of tobacco, and today a string is valued at the equivalent of $100 in U.S. currency. The upper-Simbai Kalam made the finest dog-tooth necklaces, which were traded to the Kundagai for stone axes, pigs, cowry and nassa shells. (See Healey p. 184)

Porcelain imitation tooth

Traders had porcelain teeth made so as to have something to trade with the natives when genuine dog teeth were not available or were too costly. In some

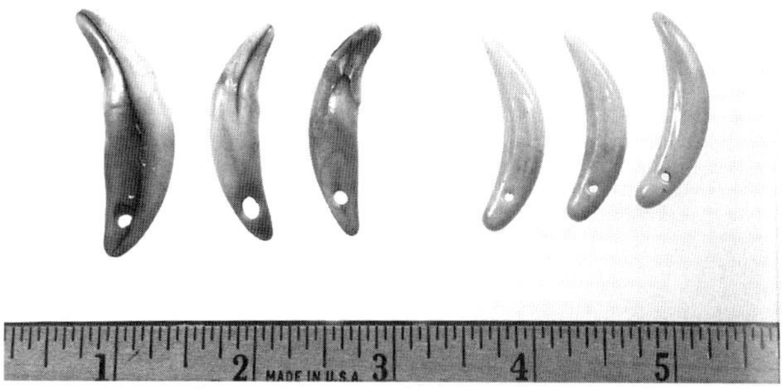

Dog Teeth Money - Left, Genuine Teeth; Right, Porcelain Teeth

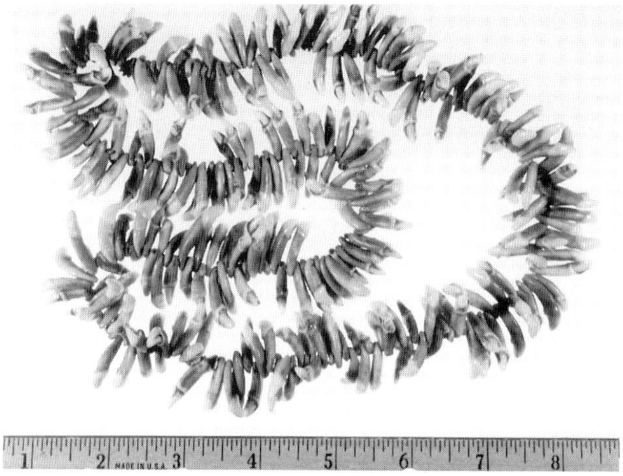

Dog Teeth

Dog Teeth

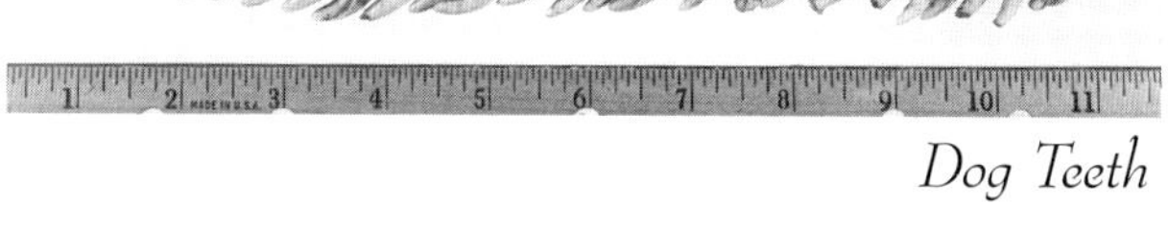

Dog Teeth

instances, dog teeth were valued at a different rate than porcelain teeth.

Sa'a, Solomons

Dog's teeth formed a part of the bride price on Sa'a. Ten monies was the bride price for all. One of the monies would be a unit of 40 dog teeth. Another might be a unit of porpoise teeth. Also included would be seven or eight shell monies. A unit of 40 dog teeth was equal to a unit of 100 porpoise teeth. Dog's teeth were the most valuable teeth. One dog tooth was worth five porpoise teeth at one time. A dog's tooth constituted a *propitiatory* offering when a person had offended or became ill. Two dog teeth were worth one shilling from the 1880s to the 1920s. In the 1890s, traders obtained dog teeth in Sydney, and by the 1900s teeth were coming from London. (See Ivens p.71)

San Cristobal Island

A dog tooth was worth 100 coconuts, 50 porpoise teeth or 10 sticks of tobacco. (See Einzig p. 71) In 1891 one dog tooth was worth one or two porpoise teeth. (Codrington p. 325)

Vitiaz Strait

There were three classes of dog tooth valuables: 1) Woven headbands and belts with rows of dog teeth attached with parallel rows of small cowry shells. 2) V-shaped breastplates of dog teeth with some having 200 to 300 dog's teeth. 3) Woven net bags with several hundred dog teeth on one side. The number of dog teeth determines the value. The age and history also affects the value to some extent. A dog's tooth headband with 40 teeth was at one time worth an average pair of boar's tusks or about $4.50. (See Harding p. 49)

DOGA

Papua New Guinea to 20th century

Necklaces usually consisting of an overlapping string of *sapi sapi* called *wakisowa* attached to a pendant of a circular boar's tusk or imitation boar's tusk were called *doga*. The imitation tusk was made from the *conus, trochus* or *tridacna* shell. The *doga* was also called *dogadoga*. The necklaces circulated counterclockwise like the *mwali*. The boar's tusk pendant pieces are more valuable than the shell pendant pieces. In the old days the *doga* was almost as important as the *mwali*. *Doga* were also highly valued in New Guinea. On Kitava the *doga* could be armshell substitutes, but this was very rarely done. Very few *doga* are left; most were traded out of Kula. Formerly they were important Kula articles, almost as important as the *mwali* and *bagi*, but they are no longer used. They had a value of U.S. $7 but were never sold at that price. See Kula.

DOIT - See Rooster Money

DOLPHIN SHAPE - See Fish Coin

DOLPHIN TEETH - See Porpoise Teeth

DONKEY BEADS - See Beads

DOREI

New Guinea

Coils of red cord made of coconut fiber wound tightly to make a cord was used as money in Dutch New Guinea. The cord looks like a bright shiny string. (See Quiggin p. 134)

DOUBLE SPIRAL

Africa, Zaire

Conjoined spirals of copper wire were a widely traded item. (Per Scott Semans)

DOWEL MONEY

Africa

The rods with a thickened center and ridges at both ends are thought to have been used as bullion or possibly as money in the period 950 AD. to the mid 1500s according to Scott Semans.

DRIED SKIN - See Beaver Skin Money, Raccoon Skin Money

DRUM MONEY

Asmat, Irian Jaya

The drums in this area are normally very tall and decorated over most of the surface of the drum. They were used as wealth.

Papua New Guinea

Drums were used in the Kula. Tami Islands, Arop, and Karkar Islands are the recognized centers of production of superior hardwood hand drums that were traded in the area. When the drums were traded to New Britain, they were worth a dog, and on the New Guinea mainland they were worth a dog's tooth headband.

Garamut drum

Papua New Guinea

These carved slit gongs were considered valuables and were used in trade as money. Only the aristocracy could own these *garamut,* and if a commoner was given one, he must pass it on immediately. (See Lutkehaus p. 131-133) See Kyee-Zee, Moko, Sycee

Doga

Double Spiral

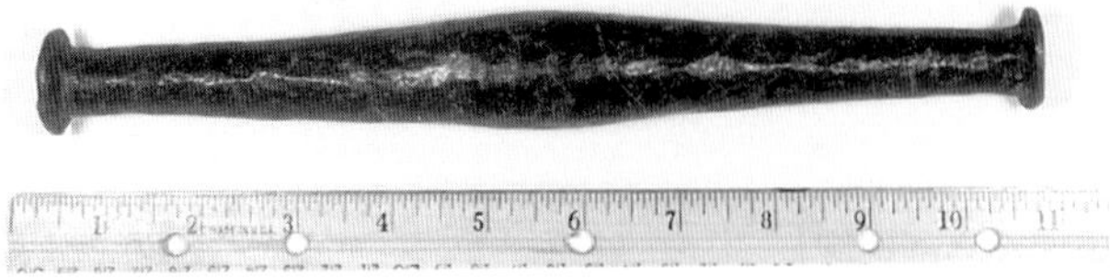

Dowel Money

Drum Money

DUBALIN - See Clam Shell Armbands

DUBIL

Nigeria, Sukur

These iron bars were used as money and were a necessary constituent of bride price in the Madagali area. As early as the 16th century, 13 dubil were the value of a male slave, and 10 were the value of a female slave. They were originally made from native smelted iron. (See Schaedler p. 322)

DUFFLES

Colonial, United States

A coarse trade cloth used in trade with wampum and fur between the Indians and traders. It was probably made in Flanders.

DUGONG TEETH

Solomon Islands

It is believed that these teeth were at one time used as a medium of exchange. The *dugong* is simular to the manatee and is also called a sea cow.

DUPA - See Jembe.

DZI BEADS - See Beads

EAGLE FEATHERS

Pueblo Indians

Article of commerce. (See Einzig)

EAR ORNAMENTS

North Sumatra, Indonesia

Silver and base silver earrings are believed to have been used as a part of bride price.

EARRINGS

Flores, Indonesia

Gold earrings from the Flores Island's Naga culture were used in bride price and given as a sort of advance marriage gift from the family of the groom to the family of the bride. They are called *bela,* and another type is called *wea wunu wona.* (See Rodgers #77 & 85 & 89 & 93)

Flores, Indonesia

Silver earrings from Flores used in marriage gift-giving and as a form of money. Similar pieces were also made in gold. (See Rodgers #98, #156)

Central Sulawesi, Indonesia

The Toradjas use these pieces of jewelry and called these earrings *Tai Gandja.* Most are made of brass, but some are made of silver and gold. They are omega shaped similar to the *Mamuli* from Sumba and the *Laren* earrings from Tanimbar. Most researchers feel the central opening is a stylized representation of the female sex organ. Many *Tai Gandja* are almost completely flat while a few are heavily decorated and three- dimensional. They are used as amulets and also used as a part of dowry payments and fines. They were worn in stretched-out ear lobes and are now worn as pendants around the neck. By 1983 they were not being made anymore. Currently reproductions are being sold in Bali with a small vertical ring at the top to allow the tourists to wear them as pendants. (Information from Bleeg and Rodgers.)

Irian Jaya

Thirteenth century Javanese glass earrings were used as money on Waropen Island off the northwest coast of Irian Jaya. They were called *Dimbo* and were glass rods shaped in a T-shaped cross section, which was then bent into a teardrop shape with the ends just touching. They are clear, green, olive and blue in color. Malay traders brought them to the coast dwellers.

Naga

Rock crystal or glass ear ornament with a hole in the center of the rectangular piece and a slot from the hole to the edge. It was a sign of wealth and possibly was also a form of money. (See Borel p. 152)

Sumatra

Karo Batak women from Sumatra used these heavy silver ornaments. (See Rodgers, Ornament #10, 1986) (Thailand, Hill tribes,P278-279)

Timor, Indonesia

Silver earrings were used in bride price.

EBALE - See Ingonda

EBUNI

Africa

Iron spherical forms were used as money. In Kuba, oral traditions mention the tribute assessment of an iron mining area as having been calculated in standard-sized iron balls. See Kriger, p. 94)

EFUFY - See Ogoja Penny

EGG MONEY - CHICKEN

Guatemala

Maya Indians. Eggs were used as a medium of exchange in small transactions.

Garamut Drum

Dubil

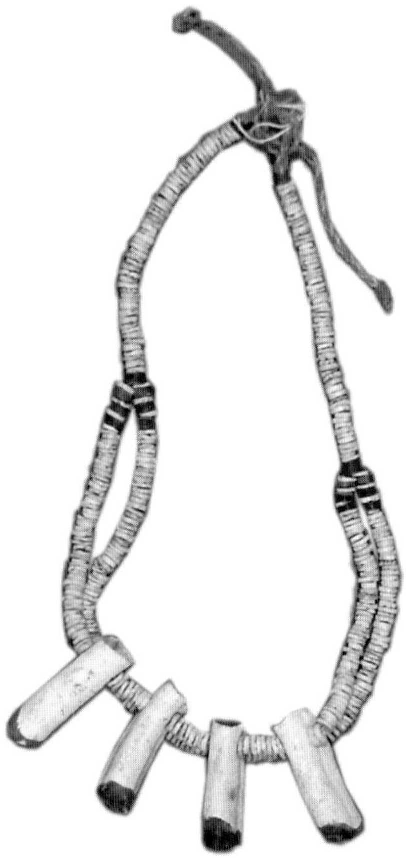

Dugong Teeth - Courtesy of Radford Stearns

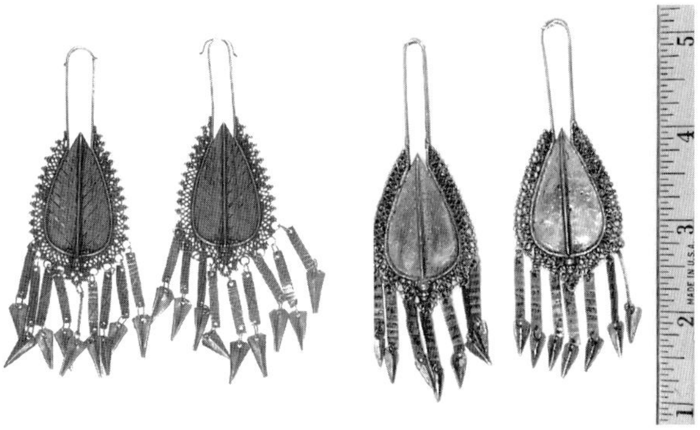
MADE IN U.S.A.

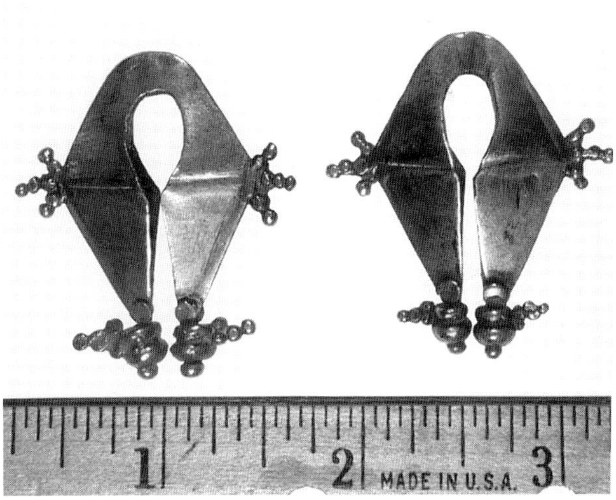
MADE IN U.S.A.

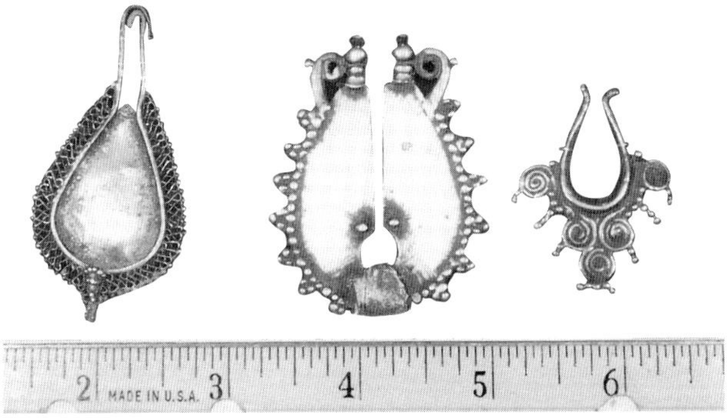
MADE IN U.S.A.

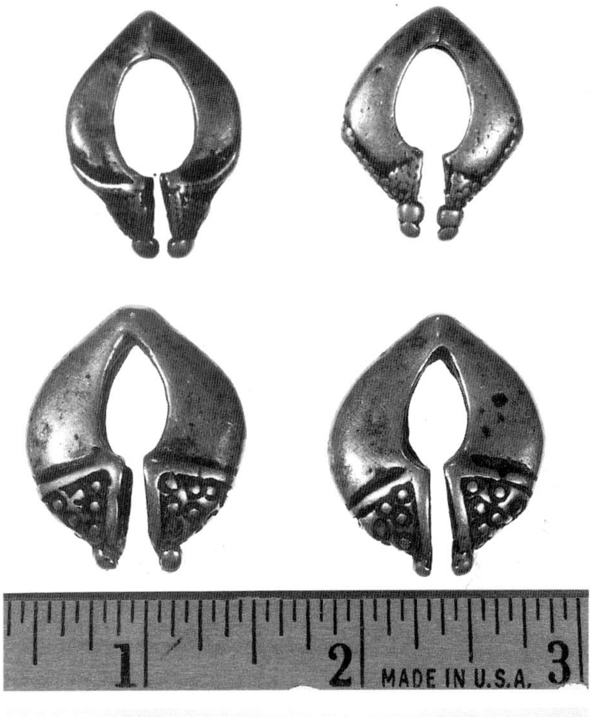
MADE IN U.S.A.

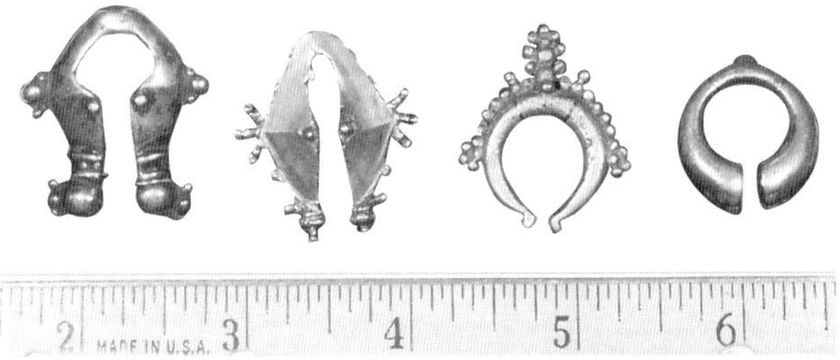
MADE IN U.S.A.

MADE IN U.S.A.

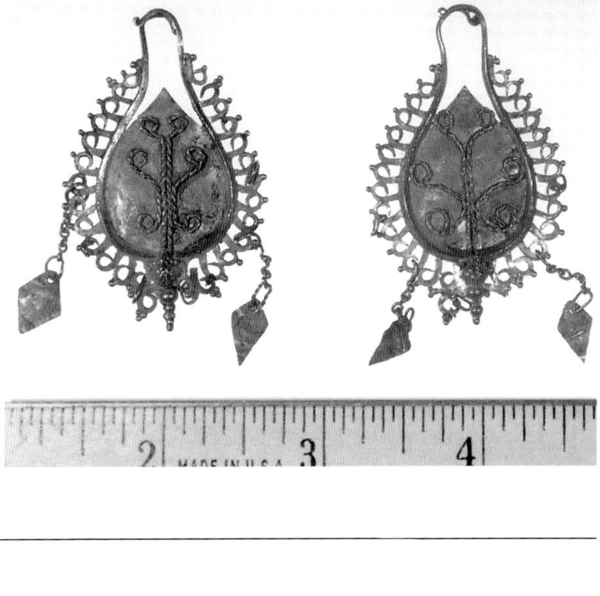

Earrings

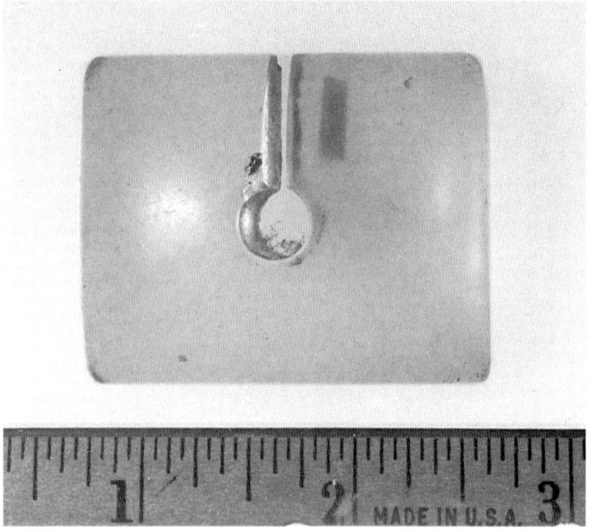

Naga Earrings

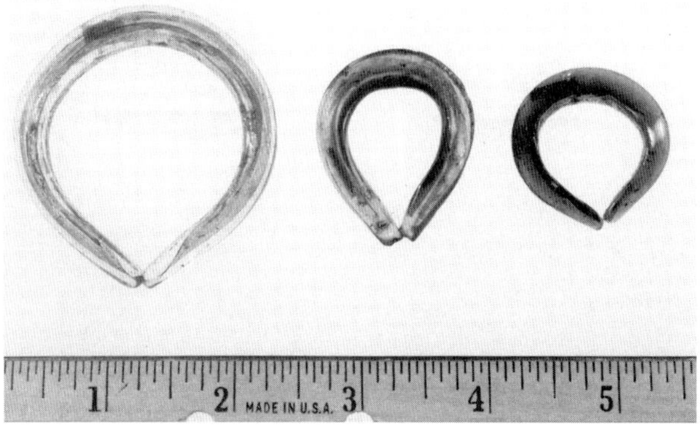

Glass Earrings

Timor Silver Earrings

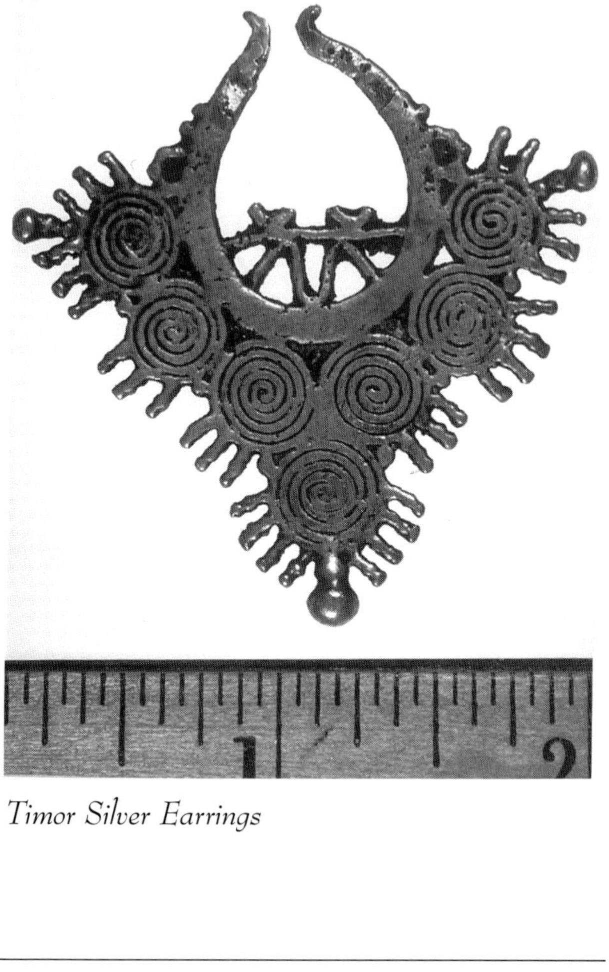

Timor Silver Earrings

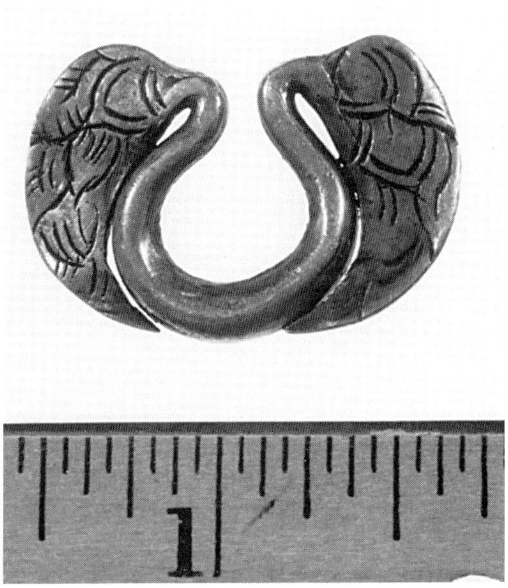

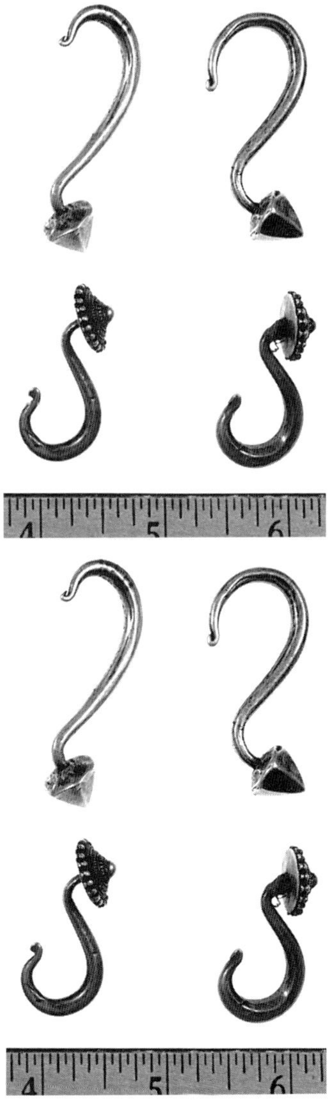

Silver Hill Tribe Earrings

Sumatra Earring

Switzerland

Eggs are said to have circulated in the Alpine villages of Switzerland. See Jevons p. 27.

EKIPA

Kwanyama sub-tribe of the Ovambo of Nambi, Africa

They were worn as ornamentation and status symbols and may have been an item of trade. The pieces were made of elephant ivory, hippo ivory or bone. Most are round or oval with a hole on the under-side and attached to leather thongs. Some had a reddish color from being rubbed with a substance made from the powder of a local wood mixed with aloe juice. Most are more than 100 years old. (See Belding p. 60-61.)

ELEPHANT TAIL HAIR MONEY

Africa, Congo, 19th century

The whole elephant tail as well as individual hairs from the tail were used as money. In the past 600-700 hairs were worth one slave, at one time one tail was worth two-three slaves. Hair was thought to prevent disease. In Durant Lopy's book Kingdom of Congo (1881), he described how natives drive elephants down narrow trails where the elephant would have trouble turning around. Then the natives would creep up behind the elephant, cut off the tail and run before the elephant could turn around. Plastic imitations are numerous. The bracelet is about 3" in diameter.

ELK TEETH MONEY

Idaho, Montana and Wyoming

Shoshoni and Bannock tribes.

The elk teeth were also called *wapiti* (*Cervus Canadensis*). Only the "eye" or canine teeth were used. A prospective husband was expected to own enough elk teeth to decorate his wife's best dress. In 1890 they were valued at $ 0.25 each, and in 1926, 100 teeth were the price of a good horse. Bone imitations were also used. (See Taxay p. 106)

ENSUBA - TRIANGULAR

Bafia tribe, Cameroon, West Africa

This flat, brittle, triangular shaped, rusted iron piece with two small notches near the tip of the two longest sides was used to purchase wives. Very rare. (See Mosher p. 48)

ENSUBA - POTATO MASHER TYPE

Bafia tribe, Cameroon, West Africa

A crude club shaped piece of iron was used as money. Thirty ensuba were worth a wife. They are all very old and rare. 15 pounds weight. (See Sigler p. 16) Currently a new modern form has become available. It is not old or is it very rare.

ERENGE

The most valuable of the three kinds of clamshell rings manufactured in the lagoons of New Georgia. (See Hviding p. 93)

ERMINE

Siberia

The Northern Tungus used ermine skins as money. (See Einzig p. 116)

EVODIA SEED MONEY

Tanes Islands

Small, black, shiny, bead-like seeds were used to trade with the people from the other islands. (See Quiggin p. 164)

EWUL

Papua New Guinea

Another name for kina or gold-lip shells. See kina shells.

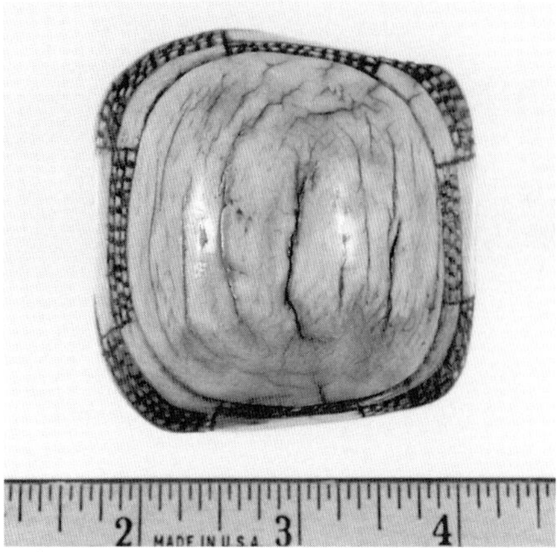

Ekipa

Elephant Tail Hair Money

Elk Teeth Money - Imitation

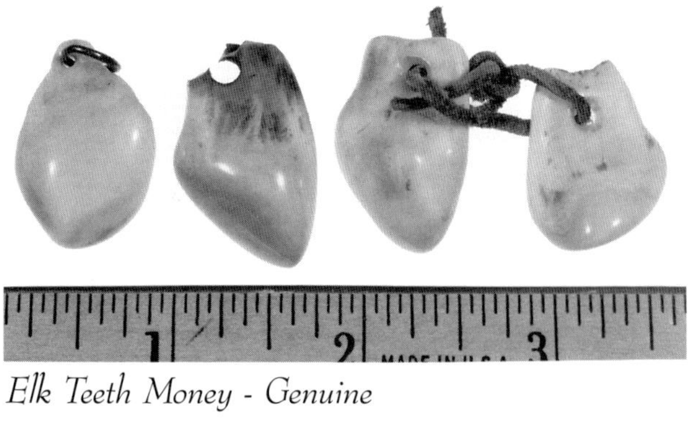

Elk Teeth Money - Genuine

Ensuba - Triangular

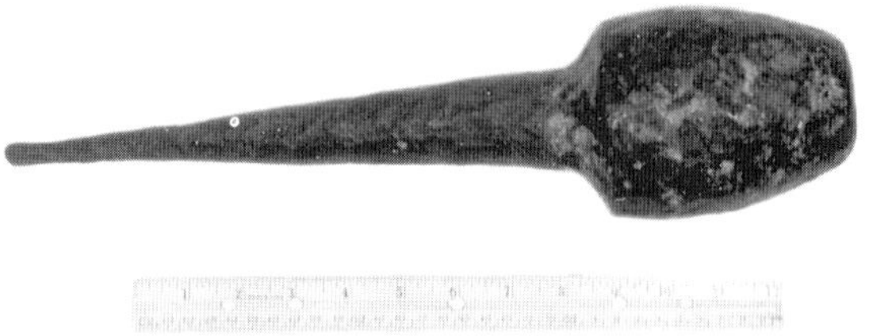

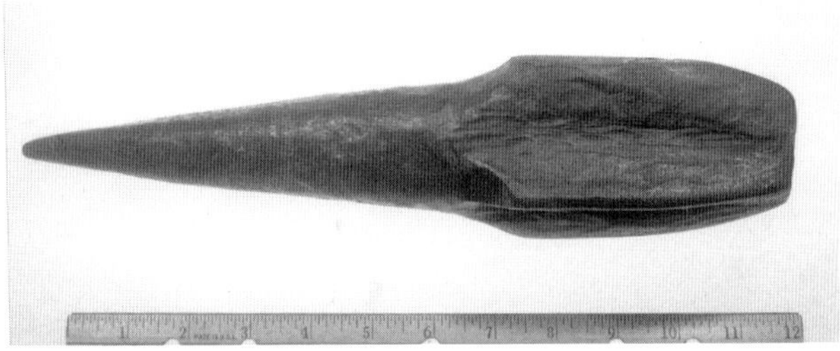

Ensuba - Potato Masher Type

EXCHANGE STONES

Dani tribe, Irian Jaya

Bride price is one of the most important uses for exchange stones. The male stone is narrow and rounded while the female stone is broad and flat. The stones are also called *je* stones. See *je*.

EXECUTION KNIFE

Bangala (Ngala) Tribe, Africa

The execution knife shows some similarities to the throwing knife. It was also known as *ngolo, ngwolo* or *lokula' lombole*. It was a store of wealth but was also used in ordinary trading transactions. It has extensive decoration on the blade. In 1883, a colonial officer at the Equatorville Station identified this knife as a "knife for sacrifice (m'boulou) of Ba-Ngala," and included it in his illustrated description of male slaves being executed at the funerial of a chief, according to Kriger p. 204.

FAE - See Pearl Shell Money

FAI - See Pearl Shell Money

FANG AXES

Fang tribe, Gabon, Africa

Small iron imitation axeheads were tied in bundles of 10, and the bundle was called *Ntet* or *Bikei*. Fang axes could not be used as weapons or tools but were necessary to purchase a wife. They were also used in trade with other tribes in the area for ivory and rubber.

FARAVEL - See Cloth, Mali

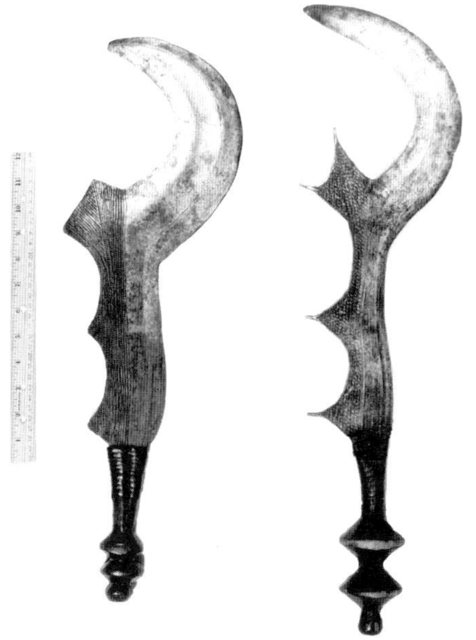

Execution Knife

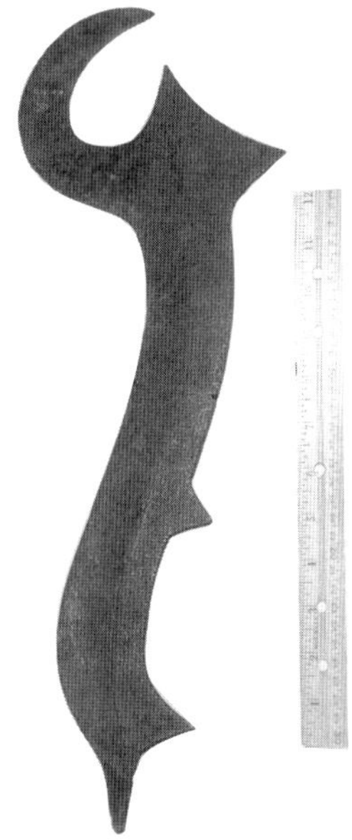

Execution Knife

FE - See Pearl Shell Money, Stone Money - Yap

FEATHER COIL

Santa Cruz, Solomon Islands

The coil was made from the red feathers of the small scarlet honey eater (*Myzomela Cardinalis*). Only the feathers of the breast, head and back of the bird are used. Each coil is two inches wide and about 30 feet long with red feathers on only one side. A considerable part of the 30 feet consists of two bark rings and twine connecting the rings with the feather strip. A coil takes about one year's labor by three specialists to make. The bird snarer catches the birds on a latex covered decoy-baited perch. The platelet maker prepares platelets made of Pacific pigeon feathers (*Broussonetia paoyrifera*), glue and red feather down. The glue is made from the sap of the paper mulberry tree. It takes about 1,500 platelets to make one coil, and one scarlet honey eater produces five platelets. The currency binder assembles the coil from platelets which are secured on two cord foundations with binding. The cords are made of long fibers from the bark of a rain-forest tree (*Gnetum gnemon*). The center of the coil has a scraper with a special platelet with a band of red feathers in the center instead of at the end. At both ends of the feather part of the coil, the cords come together, and a piece of turtle shell is placed on that triangular section. A coil requires a minimum of 300 scarlet honey eater birds. Feather coils (also called *Tau*, *Tirrau*, *Tavau* and *Temotu*) were used in bride price. The bride price always consists of 10 feather coils graduated in value from a new piece or nearly perfect piece (#1) on the bottom to a #10 top piece which is almost completely worn out and therefore worth very little. The pieces increase in value in a geometric progression with the next higher number being worth two of the previous number. For example, it takes 2 #10s to equal a #9 and 2 #9s to equal a #8. Therefore, a #1 is worth 512 #10s. The higher-numbered coils reflect the decrease in value as feathers are lost and the rolls blacken. When the finest feather coil was worth 25 Australian dollars, the #10 was worth one shilling. The coils were also used in trade to buy canoes, pigs, turtles, fish, sago, breadfruit and coconut rope and fiber.

The feathers were traded from the islands of Tikopia, Vanikoro and Utupua. Some of the coils were traded to the Reef Islands. Until prohibited by law in the 1930s, wealthy men or groups of men on Ndendo (Santa Cruz) would pay more than 100 coils to buy concubines from the Reef Islands. This price was more than 10 times the price of a wife. The difference between the two transactions was that all family ties were cut with the concubine, while the bride payment sealed new family relationships. The concubines were treated very well

Fang Axes

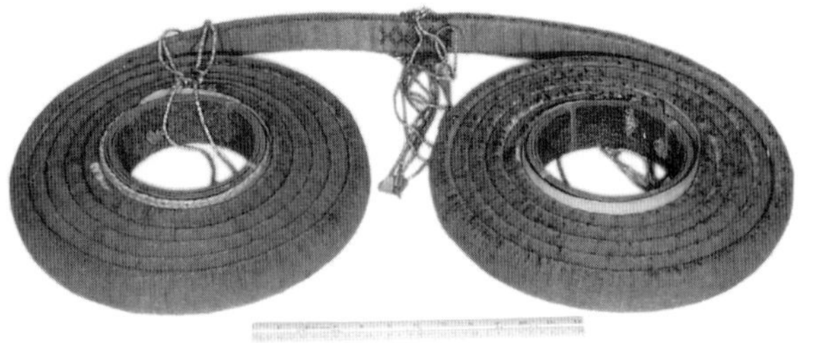

Feather Coil

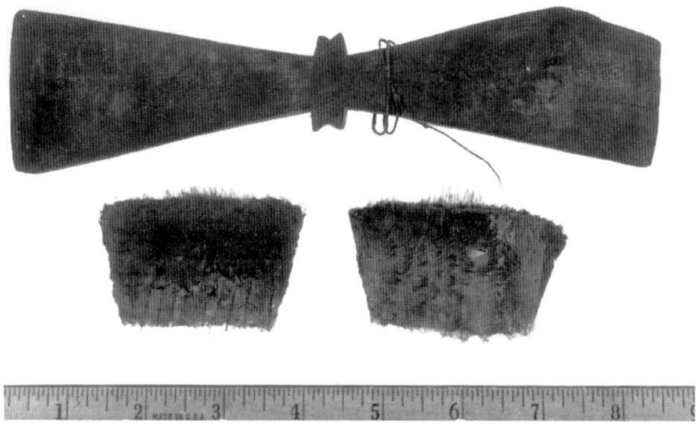

Above: Coil Making Tool; Below: Platelets

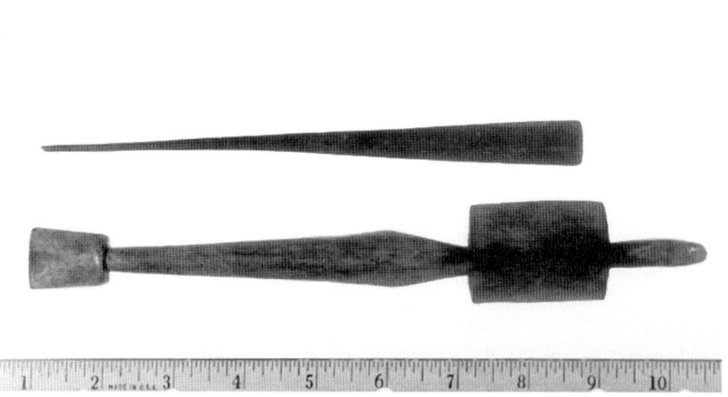

Coil Making Tools

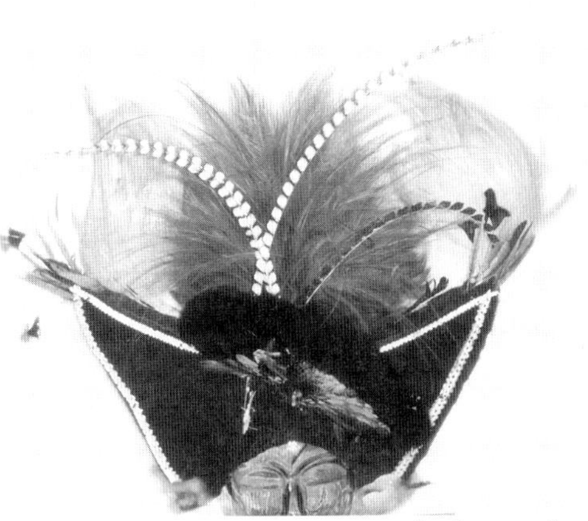

Bird of Paradise Wig

Bird of Paradise Wig

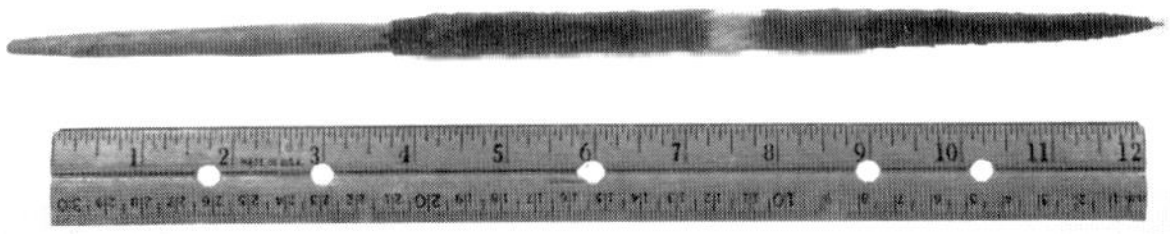

Feather Stick Money

Feather Sticks

and did no work in the house or garden. They were respected by all as extra-special and wore the finest clothing. Sometimes the concubines were hired out to others for a fee. Usually the women later married in the usual way.

In 1962, there were only five men on Santa Cruz who could bind currency. A person may learn this skill only if his father was also a currency binder. The binder needs the inheritance of magic secrets; an unauthorized person making his own currency risks the anger of spirits.

An accessory to the coil is the cross stick called *nomba*. It comes in many shapes, can have three or four arms and may be straight or bowed. The sticks may be plain or carved to show canoes, turtles, sharks or fish. The sticks can be made by anyone. The sticks were not money, but were only to help preserve the coils. (See Scientific American, March 1962)(See Clark, Traditional Money Association Newsletter Vol. 2 Number 1.)

FEATHER MONEY

Timbuktu, Africa

Ostrich feathers were used as money in trade for iron, beads, cotton cloth, tobacco rolls, and clothing. (See Bennett p. 183.)

Nigeria

The feathers of the violet plantaineater (*Musophaga vioacea*) were valued at five feathers for a chicken or a penny at the end of the 1930s. (See Eyo, p.55.)

Papua New Guinea

Feathers of many kinds of birds besides bird of paradise were used as money and for decoration. The following are some of the bird feathers used as money:

Long-tailed Buzzard, Harpy Eagle, Papuan Lory, White Cockatoo, Harpyopsis Eagle, Hornbill, Black Sicklebill, Dwarf Cassowary, Rainbow Lorikeet, Purple-bellied Lory, Black-capped Lory, Fairy Lory, Muschenbroek's Lorikeet, Palm Cockatoo, Pesquette Parrot (*Psittrichus fulgidus*), Red Parrot, Mountain Cassowary, and Brown Sicklebill. The Kundagai use feathers only for decoration and trade. They do not use feathers in ceremonial payments. (Healey p. 71-73) There are many local favorites such as the Vulturine Parrot (*Psittrichas fulgidus*) which are not used by the Maring people but are very popular with the Narak, Kandawo, and other upper-Jimi and Wahgi people. All these groups used the feathers in trade. (See Healey p. 180-181) Bird plumes were the most important trade good over time in terms of the number of transactions. (See Healey p. 256) See Bird of paradise.

Peru, Incas

Feathers of many kinds appear to have been used in trade and probably as money. The feathers were also worn and used as decoration. Macaw feathers along with the feathers of Muscovy ducks, parrots, and paradise tanagers were used to make tunics. (See Bird of Paradise, Eagle Feathers, Ostrich Feathers, Quetzal Feather Money)

FEATHER STICK MONEY

British Solomon Islands

Tiny red feathers from the honey-bird (*Myzomela Cardinalis*) were attached with putty nut to a wood stick. There are various shapes with bands of yellow, white and black feathers. The sticks are worn in the hair over the ear or through the ear lobes. These feathers are the same kind as used in feather coils of Santa Cruz Island. They were money. 13″ length (See Quiggin p. 136)

Santa Maria & Meralava Islands

Dyed red feathers tied to end of stick. The stick was used as money. 5″ length

FEI - See Stone Money - Yap

FELT MONEY

Germany, Inflation period following World War I

Part of the "Notgeld" series of unusual forms of money for the collector, for limited use in various cities. 3″ x 4-3/4″.

FIGURE 8 MONEY

Zaire

The beaten copper figure eight pieces are believed to have been small change in the past. A large number of these has surfaced recently.

FINGERS

Papua, New Guinea, American Indian

In Papua New Guinea the Mariwaka tribe wore finger necklaces made from the smoked fingers of the dead. They were considered a valuable item. Some American Indian tribes used the finger bones in a necklace with a hole drilled through one end of the bone.

FIRAE

Auki Island, Solomon Islands

A *firae* is made up of 10 strings, each one fathom long of special red shell disks which are slightly larger in diameter than normal. It is the highest monetary value and is not very common. The strings are strung similar to the *tafuliaé* and decorated in a similar way. They were worth about 20 pounds. (See shell money, Solomon Islands)

Felt Money

Felt Money

Figure 8 Money

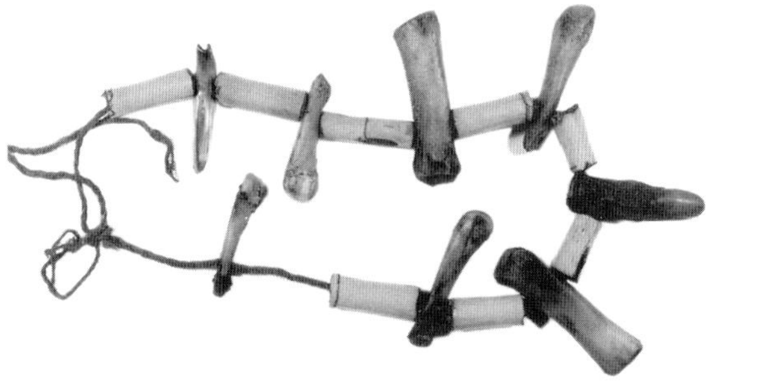

Finger Money - Papau New Guinea

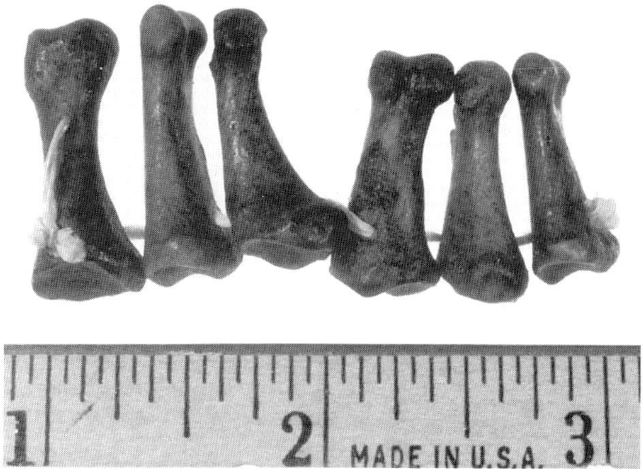

American Indian Finger Bones

Firae

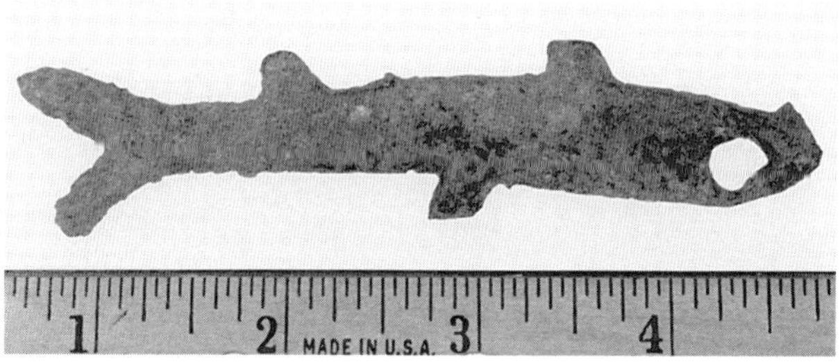

Chinese Fish Coin

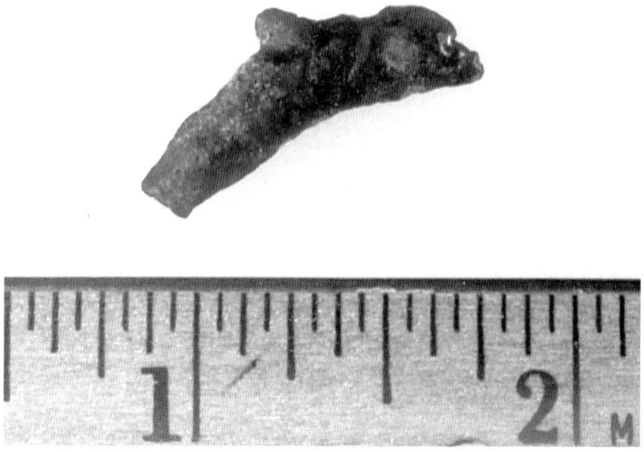

Olbia - Dolphin Shaped Money

FISH

Colonial New Hampshire

Fish was a principal commodity money in this state. (See Taxey p.146)

FISH COIN

China, 1122-255 B.C. Zhou (formerly Chou) Dynasty

Flat copper cast in the shape of a fish with a hole at the eye, probably for suspension as a chime. It may have been used in trade or as bullion. They are found in burials and are in various shapes and sizes. (See Sigler p. 4)

Olbia, as early as 550-525 B.C.

A cast Greek copper token in the shape of a dolphin from about 430 - 410 B.C. They were issued by the Polis (city-state). A few have one of two known inscriptions on them. Possibly used to purchase fish. Large numbers of these pieces have surfaced recently.

FISH HOOK MONEY

Alaska

Eskimos traded furs and goods for metal fish hooks. 1-1/2" to 2-1/2"

Ellice Island

Pearl shell fish-hooks were highly valued on Ellice Island where they were used in presentations to chiefs and dedications to the gods. (See Quiggin p. 142)

Solomon Islands, Guadalcanal

Styles range from a single fish hook to an ornate stylized unusable fish hook. They are in various kinds and sizes and were made from pearl shell in the Marshall and Ellis Islands and in Guadalcanal as late as 1933. These two-piece shell hooks were used as currency. The Torres Straits Islands used turtle-shell fish hooks as a necessary part of bride price. The Solomon Islands have many kinds of fish hooks, and most have names for each type. They are valued items, but their use as money has not been established. (See Larin)

FISH TEETH

Solomon Islands

Fish teeth bound to a cord in short and long strings were used as money. In the early 1900s 4,000 fish teeth along with pigs and shell money, was the price of a white man's head. (See Quiggin p. 128)

Buka, North Solomon Province

Imun, the native money, was made of fish teeth and porpoise teeth bound onto a cord and covered with red ochre. Called *Paiou* (See Quiggin p. 129)

FLINT

Ethiopia

Worked flint used in flintlock guns was used as a medium of exchange. Since the natives had no guns, the flints had no useful purpose other than as a medium of exchange. They are still in use. (See Mosher p. 26)

Colonial America

Flints were used in trade but did not have an established value.

FLOWER MONEY - See Willow Leaf Money

FLYING FOX FUR

New Caledonia and Loyalties

Fur from under the ears of flying foxes was inserted between two strands of fine cord and braided. It was used as money and in necklaces, purses, and a *becket* (spearthrower). *Miu* is the general name of money in New Caledonia. Both black money (*Miu Bwarre*) and white money (*Miu Me*) had tails made of flying fox fur strings. (See Codrington p. 324-325) (See Quiggin p. 168-169) See *Miu*

FLYING FOX JAWS

Bougainville, New Ireland and parts of Papua New Guinea

A string of flying fox jaws was used as money. The jaws are really from small fruit-eating bats. (See Quiggin p. 128)

FLYING FOX TEETH

Papua New Guinea

The flying fox is also known as a fruit-eating bat, or *Pteropus*. The teeth were strung on necklaces and used as money. (See Quiggin p. 111)

New Ireland

The flying fox teeth were bound on a cord called **Agut** or *Angut* and were used as money.

Solomon Islands

This necklace had dog teeth and porpoise teeth pierced and strung together. One necklace with 400 flying fox teeth was called *rokke* and was used as money. A unit of four flying fox teeth was called one *quanamanu*.

FOX FUR

Lithuania, Livonia (Up to 13th century), Swedish Colonies, British Columbia

The fur served as currency in the Swedish colonies along the Baltic. The unit was a bundle of 40 furs called a *Zimmer*.

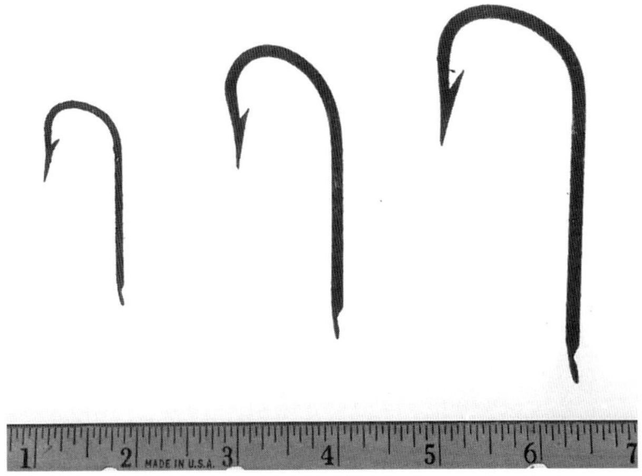

Alaskan Fish Hook Money

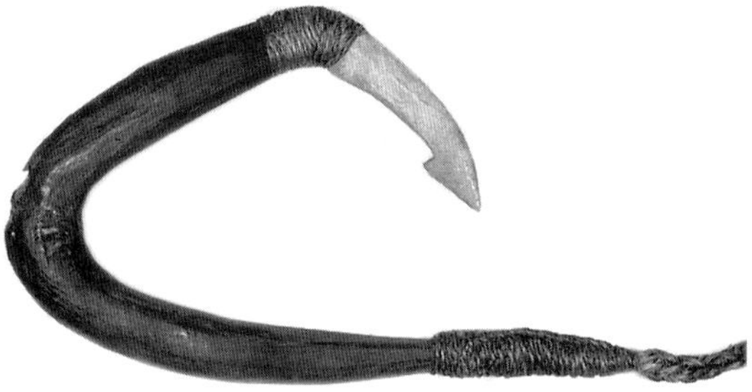

Fish Hook Money

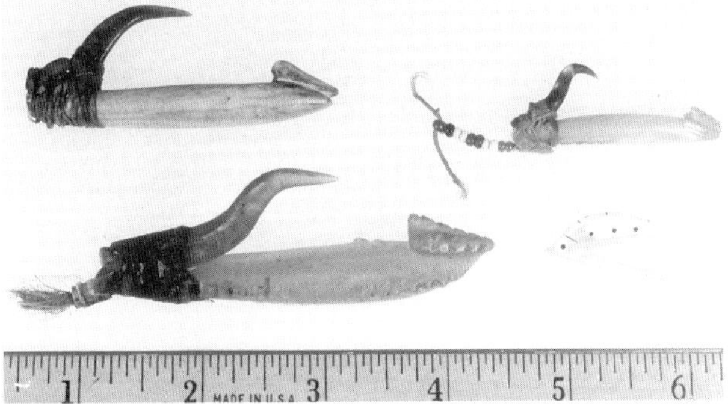

Solomon Islands Fish Hook Money

Marshall Islands Fish Hook Money

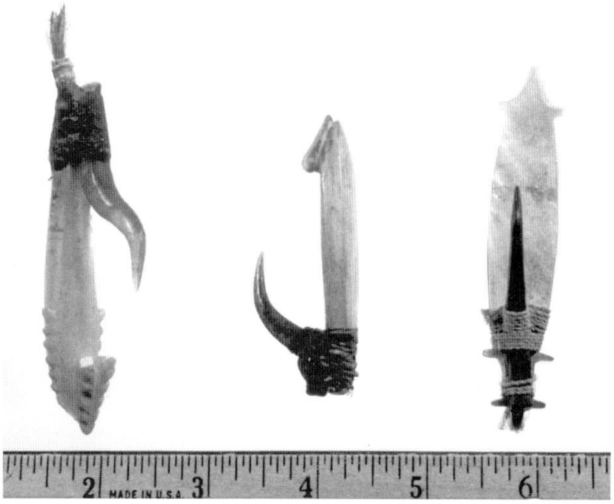

Solomon Islands Fish Hook Money

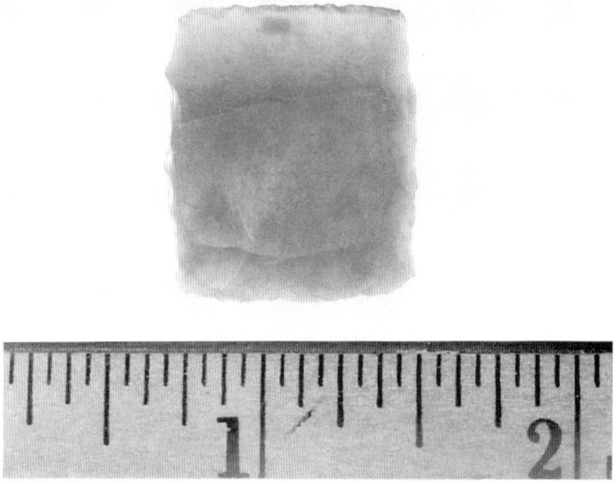

Flint

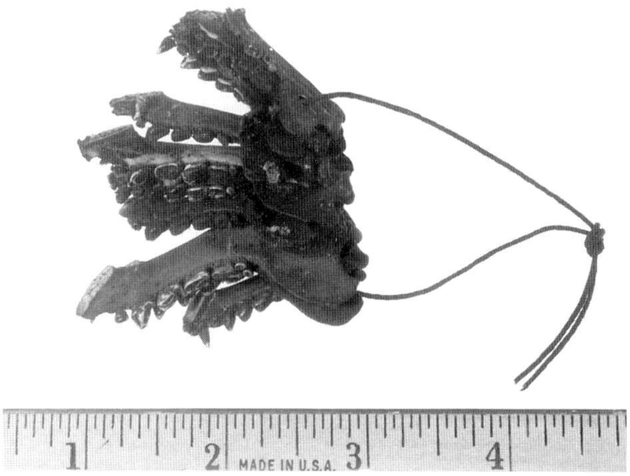

Flying Fox Jaws

The white fox skin was used as money by the Indians of British Columbia. (See Einzig p. 281)

FUNERAL MONEY - See Burial Money

FUR

Many kinds of fur were used throughout history for money. In some cases the entire fur was used while at other times only a part of the skin, such as a head, ears, claws or other part was used. Bearskin, beaver, chamois, fox, martin, moose, raccoon, sable, sea otter, seal, squirrel, walrus and white stag are some of the furs that were used.

FURA

Auki Island, Solomon Islands

Four strings of white shell disks that are each three feet long are tied together. The individual strings are called *galia*, and four of them make the *fura* worth four shillings. They were made and used on Auki Island as bride price. (See shell money, Opitz, Solomon Islands)

FUSIL - See gun money.

GABAELA

Louisiade Archipelago

This turtle-shell ceremonial spatula had incising decoration on it with lime filling the incised area. The *gabaela* was used for display and for trade in the kula. It became a part of a woman's dowry, and its value was enhanced with *spondylus* shells attached in the holes at the edge. (See Wardwell p. 92)

GABAGA - See Cloth, Nigeria

GAJAH - See Gambar

GALIA

Auki Island, Solomon Islands

A single three-foot string of white shell disks valued at one shilling was used in bride price and made on Auki Island. Four *galia* tied together formed a *fura*. (See Bartle p. 382) (See Shell money, Opitz, Solomon Islands)

GAM - See Bailer Shell

GAMBAR

Malaya Peninsula, before the 15th century A.D. to 20th century

There are 10 models of animals, birds and insects and they were possibly used as money and as weights. *Gambar* were used to regulate the ingot currency by giving it a standard form and weight. The animals represented are: crocodile, buaya cock, *ayam*, elephant, *gajah*, tortoise, *kuradura*, mantis and *belalong*. They were made of tin from ore of newly opened mines. Supernatural powers were attached to them. They weighed from 25 grams to 1700 or more grams. The cock style had from one to five rings at the base. The *gambar* crocodile was used as money. (See Singh p. 174 & 179-195) Rare

GANEKHE - See Je stone.

GAU

Yap Island

Strings of reddish shell beads with a few beads having a purplish-grey tinge. The disks of *Spondylus* shell from the Etal Atoll in the Mortlocks, Eauripik Atoll or Udot Island inside Chuuk Lagoon are very crude, and many have a honey comb look to them. The beads are one cm in diameter and three mm thick, and the string is 1 1/2 meters long and is called *"Anagumang."* These are the same beads as the *bungau* of Pelew Island. Many times the necklaces are interspersed with sperm whale teeth. Only the most important Yapese chiefs had custody of *gau*. It was only employed during serious threats of war. They are exclusively possessed by owners of important lands. At the time of the German rule, the necklaces were hidden, probably for fear they would be confiscated by the government as a form of punishment. The writer, Furness, was unable to purchase a string for any price when visiting in the early 1900s. When he was able to purchase an inferior string he was told it was worth the price of a murder. If you offer it to a man and tell him whom you want killed it will be done. In the 1930s the Japanese imported necklaces to Yap. The Chamorro, who settled in Yap, then produced some. Very few necklaces currently exist on the island. Probably fewer than 10 strings are on the island. (See Chappell p. 150.) (See Lou Tsu-k'uang.) (See Berg p.150)

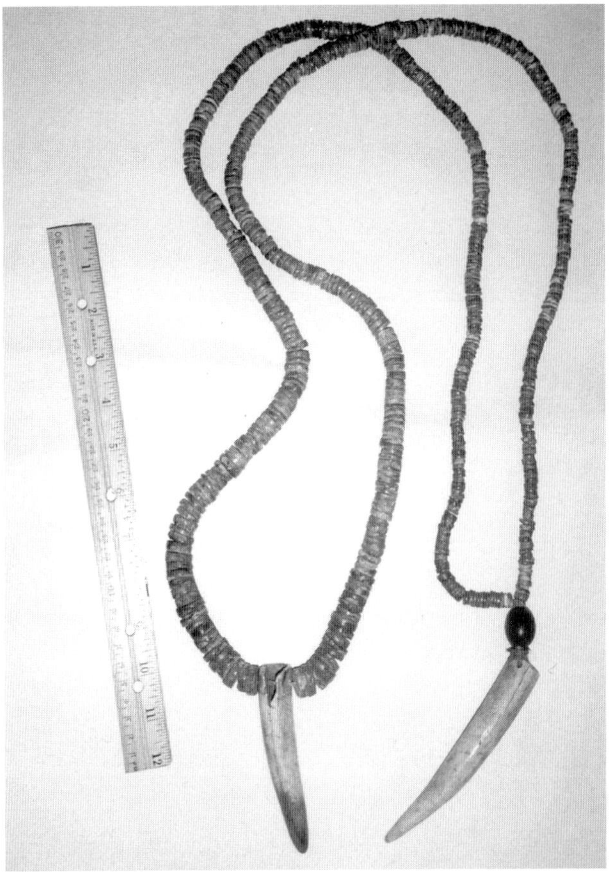

Gau

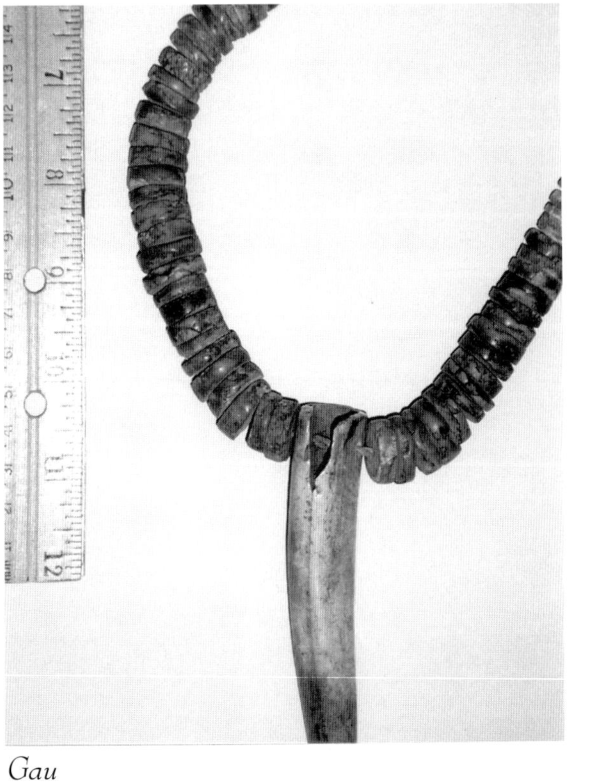

Gau

GEBI - See Halberd-Head Money

GHISI - See Kissi Penny

GHOST-FACE MONEY

China, 770 - 220 B.C.

Also called ant-and-nose money. Twelve inscriptions are recorded with three being collectible. They were issued in the State of Ch'u during the Zhou (formerly Chou) Dynasty. The term applied to imitation cowries made of bronze.

GILE
Sudest Island, Louisiade Archipelago

A vegetable peeler made of a polished and shaped pearl-shell. Considered a ceremonial valuable. Also called ginuba if it is a particularly large and fine one. (See Shack p.93.)

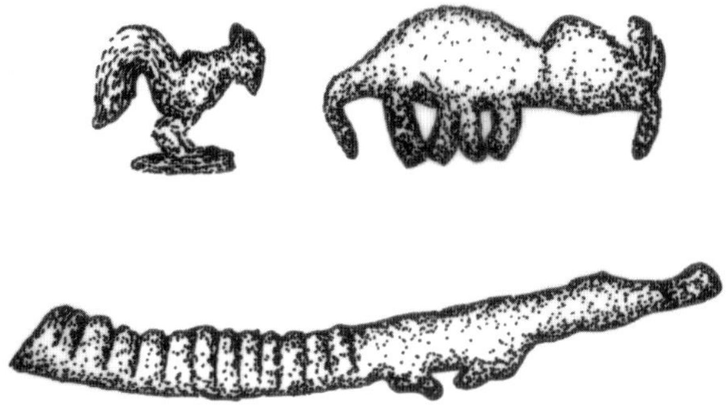

Gambar

Ghost-Head Money

GIN CURRENCY
Nigeria, Until 1914

Gin served as money as well as a store of value. Many chiefs had most of their wealth in gin as late as World War I. Unopened bottles and crates were used as money for many years without being consumed. The value of gin increased as the government increased the duty on the imports. It was used as money even after 1914, when importation was prohibited by the government. It also served as a bride price by the Yorub and Ekoi tribes. A bottle was worth one shilling. In 1905 a crate of 12 bottles was worth 40 copper rods. Farther inland the price went up to 60 rods of copper. As late as 1930, the people of Yenogoa still insisted on their brideprice being settled in gin. (See Johansson p. 47-48)

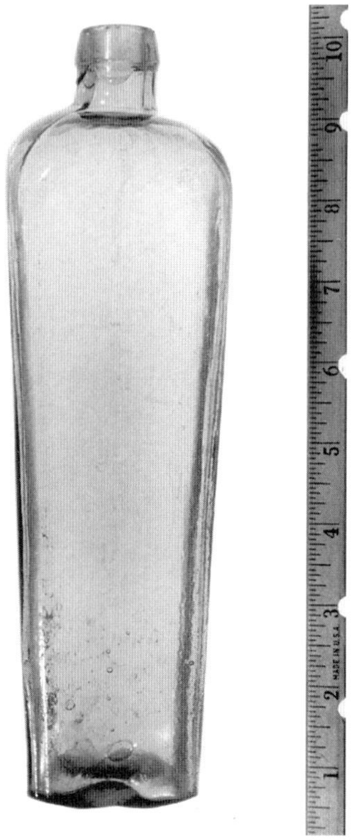

Gin Currency

GINIUBA - See Kula.

GIN KWAN - See Ring Money - Japan

GIQUIPILLI - See Cocoa Bean Money

GIRAFFE'S HAIR AND TAIL MONEY
East Africa

Most tribes used giraffe tails and tail hair bracelets as money. To protect giraffes from being killed, the government outlawed the use of tails as money. However, this did not entirely stop their use. (See Mosher p. 27)

GIRAGIRA
Gela (Florida) Solomon Islands

Four white shell bead strings, each one fathom long, were called a *giragira.* It is one of the many different names for shell groupings used as money from the area. See shell money.

GIRDLE MONEY - See Belt Money

GITZI - See Kissi Penny

GLASS WEIGHTS
Thailand

Green glass and light brown glass disks with inscriptions on them may have been gambling tokens. There are reports that the weights circulated as "palace money."

Egypt and Arabia, 3rd century B.C. to 4th century A.D.

Disk-shaped glass pieces with designs and inscriptions were cast in molds. They exist in various sizes, shapes and colors. Some are considered tokens. Similar pieces are vessel seals.

Germany, 1919-1922 Inflation period following World War I

Part of the "Notgeld" series of unusual forms of money for the collector or for limited use in various cities.

GOAT

Cordoba, Argentina

As early as 1574 goats were decreed to pass as currency. (See Taxay p. 58)

GOBAELA

Kaerihe, Sudest Island, Louisiade Archipelago

Wood or turtle shell wealth presentation scepter sometimes with shell - money disks and fiber attached were lime spatulae. The spatulae were considered as wealth and money in many cases in the kula. See Meyer Fig. 153 and 512.

GOLD DUST MONEY

Africa

Many times gold dust was weighed out instead of being valued by the pinch. It was used for bride price, tributes, fines, and compensation. The Asante of West Africa used gold dust from the 15th to the 20th centuries as money. The men could dig and the women could pan for gold as long as they gave the government 1/3 of what they mined. The weighing of the gold was done with scales, and the goldweights made in the shape of brass figures by the lost wax process were also used as money. Brass geometric weights were also used as weights and money. See weights. (See Quiggin p. 29)

Africa, Ashanti tribe, Baule tribe

In the eighteenth and nineteenth centuries, gold dust and cowries were used as money. (See Guyer p. 99.) In 1889, gold dust was abolished as currency. (See Schaedler p. 166)

Africa, Mande tribe, Akan tribe

It was used as currency in exchange for brass or copper. It was weighed with brass goldweights and scales.

Giraffe's Tail with Hair

Giraffe's Hair Bracelet

Glass Weights

Gong

California, 1849

During the gold rush, gold dust and small gold nuggets were used as money until they could be fabricated into bars or coins. A translucent bird bill was used as a holder for gold dust, closed at the end and used as a form of money. A pinch of gold was worth $.25 (See Taxay p. 106) See Quill Money

GOLD CUBS - See cubs - gold

GOLD LIP SHELL - See Kina Shell

GOLD WEIGHTS - See Weights

GONG

Alor Island

Gongs were used as a part of bride price and dowry payments along with *mokos* and pigs. (See Du Bois p.85)

Borneo

The brass gongs (*tawak*) can still be found in many longhouses. They no longer are used for making music but only as stores of wealth. They had recognized standards of value. Their traditional value was calculated by their relative width, weight, tone, age and pedigree. The gongs with embossed dragon designs are the most valuable. The cheapest ones were used to settle fines and as marriage gifts. The very old ones with beautiful tones were once worth a good male slave. (See Traditional Money Association newsletter, Vol. 12 Number 2, Traditional Money of Borneo, Graeme Krake.)

Laos

The Lamet people in the extreme northwestern area used gongs as money, according to Kemper,s p. 400. See Buffalo Bell,bell, Kyee-Zee

GOOSE QUILLS - See Quill Money

GRAIN CURRENCY

American Colonies, 1690-1709

Massachusetts used wheat, Indian corn, barley, peas, oats, and rye as money in 1690. New Hampshire used peas and Indian corn as money from 1701 to 1709. North Carolina used corn and South Carolina used rice. (See Einzig p. 292-293)

Babylonia

Barley was used as a subsidiary currency to silver.

Quebec, Canada

Wheat, corn and peas were used as money. (See Taxey p.146)

Ceylon, until late 1800s

Grain was used as money and to pay taxes.

Egypt

Grain banks were used as a store of value.

India, until present

Grain banks set up for loans and payments in terms of grain. (See Einzig p. 113-114)

GRATER MONEY - See Gridiron money.

GREEN SNAIL SHELL

Highlands, Papua New Guinea

They were also called atana shell and were traded from the Sepik River area into the highlands. They were used in bride price payment. The green snail shell (*Turbo marmoratus*) was prized by the Tsembaga people of Papua New Guinea. The shell was valued in terms of small gold-lip shells, pigs, cowry shell headbands or feather headdresses. It was also used as money by the Latmul, Aibom and Tchambuli people of the Middle Sepik River region. The shells were collected and exported by Wallis Island people and were attached to the ends of coiled basket work masks. The Kundiawa and Chimbu tribes formerly used the large green snail shell as their main currency. At one time a green snail shell was worth a pig. In 1900 the green snail shell was the most valuable item exceeding even pigs, stone axes, dog teeth and Bird of Paradise feathers. (See Healey p. 134-135) With the coming of the kina shell, the green snail shell was no longer desired and by the middle 1940s was of no importance. (See Spirals From The Sea p.79-80)

GREENSTONE - See Axe Money, Nephrite

GRIDIRON MONEY

China

Native treatises agree that this item has some connection with currency according to Ramsden p. 16. Coole called it "grater money". Many consider this the oldest kind of money in ancient China.

GRIVNA

Russia, 11th to 14th centuries

This silver bar was in the shape of a bag used to transport wheat down the Volga River. It is also called "bag money." There are two different weight standards. The Kievan *grivnas* weighs 160 grams and is a hexagonal ingot of the pre-Mongol period. They were cast in open molds. The second type is the Novgorod *grivnas*. It weighs 200 grams and is shaped like a circular bar. Starting in the second half of the 13th century, the bars were called rouble. Later this name became the main monetary unit of Russia. See *kapa*. (See Schulman p. 11-34)

GRIWNA KUN - See Squirrel Skin

GUADALCANAL SHIELD - See Shield Money - Guadalcanal

GUBKAS - See Cloth money - Africa, Lake Chad area

GUM MONEY

Australia

Natives used triodia gum as a medium of exchange for centuries. Standard units of measure were wrapped in plaited human hair coils. 1-1/2" x 4-1/2" (See Mosher p. 55) (See Schulman p. 23)

GUNS

Canada, 17th and 18th centuries

The Indians of the area traded furs of all kinds to the traders and the Hudson Bay stores for guns and ammunition. In the early period the guns were valued by the length of the gun. They were 3 ft., 3 1/2 ft., 4 ft., and 4 1/2 ft. All the Indians did not adopt the use of guns for several reasons. If the gun failed they had to take it to the trading post to get it fixed. This was normally quite a long distance to travel. The flint lock gun also did not work well in the extreme cold of Interior Western Canada. From a high in 1691, the trading of guns decreased in the 1700s. The stories that the trade gun was of poor quality and light so it could not be easily used in warfare against the settlers were not true. The trade gun was a sound, dependable gun that the Indians used to hunt. The barrel's length was from 30 to 48 inches. All the organized trading companies sold them at a fixed price and not at a price equivalent to a pile of beaver skins the height of the gun. That might have taken place very early on, but it was not the normal way of pricing the guns. The Hudson's Bay Company valued a gun at 20 beaver skins. A pound of powder would cost 10 to 12 guilders. The "London *fusil*" was originally developed for trade in the Northwest Territory. The Hudson's Bay company sold the "Hudson Bay gun," and the Mackinaw Company of Michilimackinac sold the "Mackinaw" gun. Hanson says the trade guns used from 1775 to 1875 can be identified by a few common similarities. The trademark on the side-screw plate is in the form of a sea serpent or dragon. The barrel is part octagon with a smooth bore and is 24 gauge. They are 46 to 64 inches in length and have a small die-stamped sitting fox on the lock, barrel or butt stock. They are also full walnut or maple stocked with a flat brass butt plate. The gun in general was cheap compared with the muskets and rifles of the same time. The trade guns were popular, and by 1630 the Iroquois Indians had traded enough guns from the Dutch to tip the balance of power to their side over the powerful Algonquins. The quality of the trade guns did go down as time went on. They became flimsier and cruder. Hanson says in 1742 the French Trading Company was selling a pound of shot or three flints for one beaver skin. A few trade guns were also brought from Mexico by the Spaniards.

The Hudson's Bay Company continually increased its importance in the fur trade from its start in 1670 to the end of the western Indian trade in the 1870s. Guns always were an important part of its trade. There were many makers of guns and their list would be extensive.

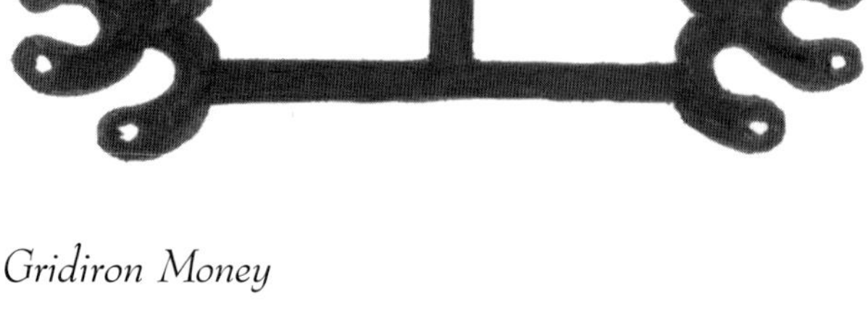

Gridiron Money

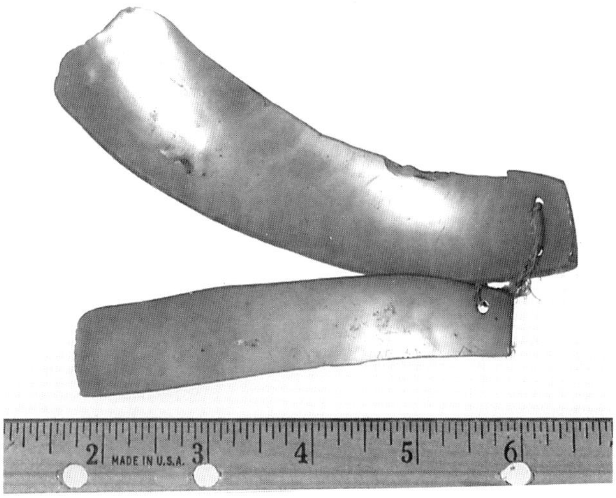

Green Snell Shell

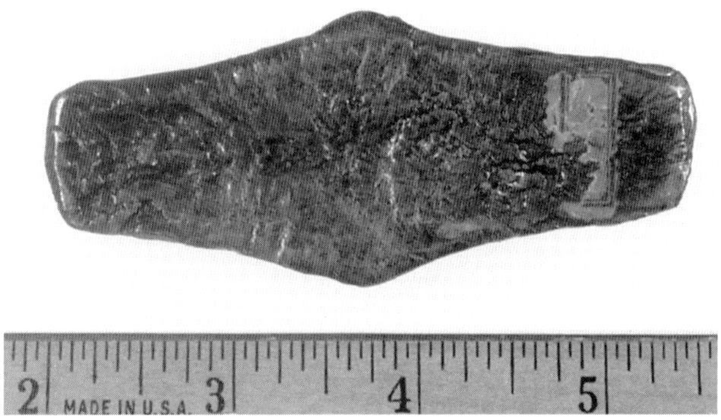

Grivna

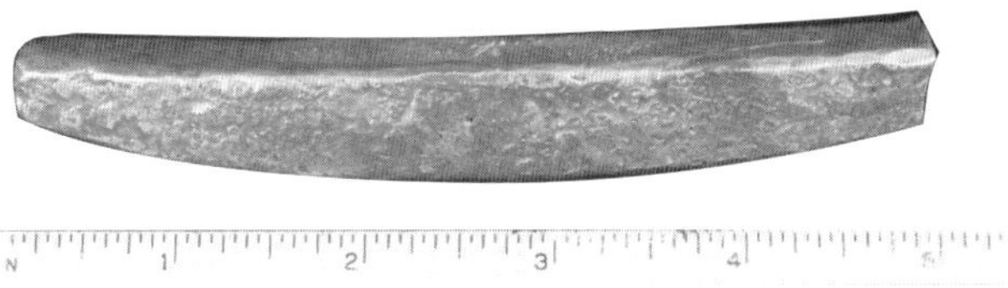

Grivna

Gum Money

Each maker and style had its own special characteristics and marks, but most fit a rather common set of parameters. The cheap trade guns and liquor were used on a large scale to obtain the furs from the Indians. Most of the trade guns have not survived. It was estimated by Hanson that less than one out of one hundred guns survived. There were many suppliers of guns to the Hudson's Bay Company, and most of them had their name stamped on the butt plate. They were originally all flint-locks. After 1830 the guns all had fitted trigger plates engaging a tang screw from above, and the butt plates were attached with screws instead of square nails. After 1821 all Hudson's Bay guns were dated. After 1861 the percussion gun was used. The flint lock did not die as it was still the favorite of many Indians.

In 1808 John Jacob Astor formed the American Fur Company. The company expanded in some measure by absorbing the Northwest Company in 1817. In 1830 the Missouri Fur Company went out of business. In 1827 the Columbia Fur Company was absorbed by the American Fur Company. Finally in 1834, John Jacob Astor sold his company. Other companies such as Pratte Choteau & Company, Hubbel, Hawley & Co., Bent & St. Vrain, Fox Livingston & Co., Harvey, Primeau & Co., Frost, Todd & Co., Clark, Primeau & Co., and Durfee & Peck formed and merged or dissolved. In 1829 the guns would cost the trading company from $4.50 to $5.75 each. Others purchased from 1826 to 1858 cost from $7.50 to $11.50. In the years following 1836, the American Fur Company purchased several hundred guns from British gun makers and, if more guns were required, from American importers of Belgian guns. English guns were the preferred kind. After 1860 the Northwest gun rapidly declined in use. The Hudson's Bay Company used flintlock *fusils* until at least 1876. Hanson states, "Among experienced collectors much can be accomplished in gun identification by simply considering the "general lines" of the piece. The earliest guns have the general lines of the Revolutionary fowling piece-wide but drooping butt stock with slender wrists coupled with extremely thin barrels and forends. This tendency gradually diminished until about 1830. The guns of the 1830-1860 period have noticeably thicker wrists and heaver forends with a more military style to the butt stock. After 1860 the gun as a whole appears quite thick and the butt stock has very little drop. The earliest guns had rather plain details about the tang, lock and side plate. Those of the 1830-1850 period had prominent tear-drops on the top and each side of the wrist. By 1860 this prominent relief carving was still being done around the tang but the finials on each side of the wrist had become short, round, and abrupt." The lock plate of the Northwest Company gun had a sitting fox or fox-like animal facing right on a wreath or chaplet with a circle surrounding the animal and stand. After 1821 the Hudson's Bay guns have the letters EB with a tiny sitting fox facing left with a unlifted tail on top of the letters. This is called the tombstone plaque. Many trade guns were decorated with brass tacks by the Indians. If the stock of the gun broke, it was repaired with rawhide. Many of the guns in existence have cracks repaired with rawhide. Many rifles were given to the Indians by the Indian Bureau for treaty payments or annuities. The East Indian Company trade musket was also used in the Canadian fur trade. The discarded gun barrels were used as tent stakes, pry bars and hide scrapers. The lead balls were melted down and used to inlay catlinite pipes and the handles of tomahawks.

GUN MONEY

Ireland, July, 1689 - October, 1690

James II established mints at Dublin and Limerick and issued token coinage of half crowns, shillings and sixpences. They were struck from base metals (mainly brass) from obsolete cannon and church bells. A second issue was also produced in greatly reduced size. The pieces give the month as well as year they were minted. The gun money was never redeemed in silver as James had promised. Instead, William of Orange, the victor, exchanged the large size half crowns for three quarters of a penny each, the smaller halfcrowns at a halfpenny each, large shillings at a halfpenny each and small shillings and six pence at a farthing each.

Gun Money

GUNPOWDER - West Africa, 19th century.

H CROSS - See Cross "H" Shaped

HABO - See Je stone.

HACIENDA TOKEN - See Leather

HAIR MONEY - See Human Hair Money

HAIRPIN MONEY - See Larin, See Kapkap, New Guinea

HAKATA - See Shell Ring

HAKUNA - See Needle money, Ethiopia.

HALBERD-HEAD MONEY

China

This weapon contains a large quantity of bronze, but its use as money is in question. Some collectors do include it in their collections. (Ramsden p. 22-23)

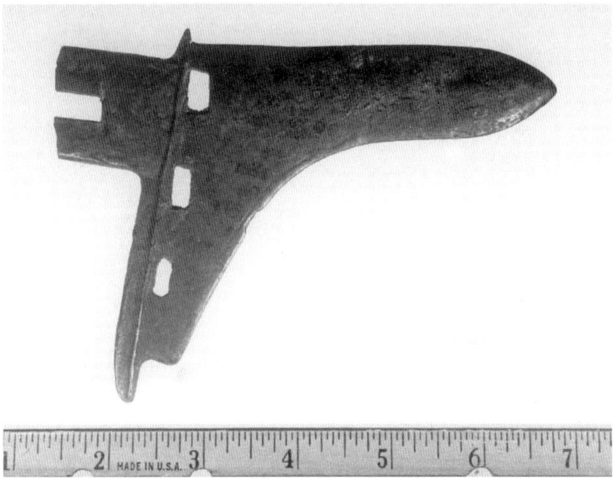

Halbeard Head Money

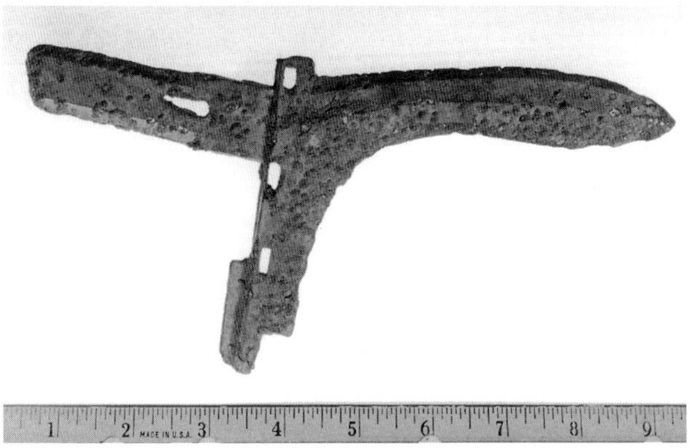

Halbeard Head Money

State of Yue, China

In 1986 a new type of *halberd,* in miniature called "Gebi" meaning "Dagger-Axe Coin", was discovered in the present-day city of Shaoxing, Zhejiang Province, China. The shape is different than the other *halberds.* (See Jen, p.5)

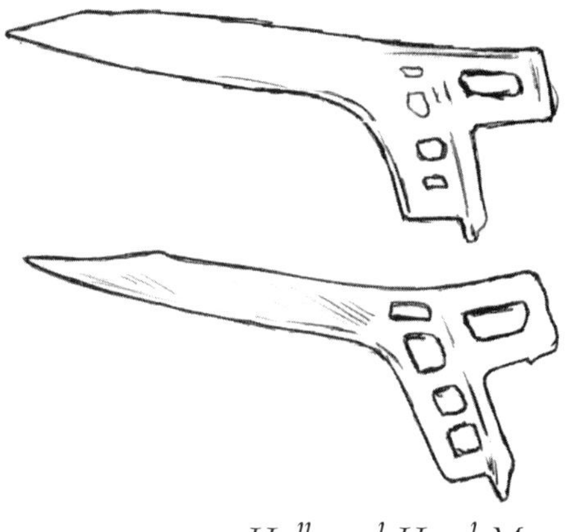

Halbeard-Head Money

HANDA

Africa, Late 1800s

The handa is also called Urua cross, Katanga cross, and St. Andrew's cross. It was the main form of money in the region of Lake Tanganyika. It weighed 2-1/2 to 3 pounds. Many have a raised rib along the center of each arm. In some parts of Africa, copper was preferred to gold. (See Quiggin p. 78) (See Cross, Katanga.)

HANG - See bar money - Annam (Vietnam) - banana bar.

HANSATSU

Japan, 1680-1870

It is also called "bookmark" money from its shape and size. The notes were issued by numerous feudal clans, mostly in pre-Meiji times (both "clan" and "stamped," among many other words, are pronounced "han," but in no way can the characters be confused). It was printed in one or two colors by woodblock on both sides of rough paper. The designs included drums, turtles, rice bowls, and other images. It usually promised to pay a set amount in silver to the bearer. It was based on the MONNE currency system. In it one MOMME was equal to 3.75 grams of silver. The notes were issued by stable local institutions such as clans, merchants, pawnbrokers, temples, money changers and village cooperatives. *Hansatsu* means "clan bills" or "clan notes" because they were issued in the districts, called *han.* After the introduction of a new monetary system in 1870, many *hansatsu* were overprinted with a new denomination based on the new system. The notes are now rare, especially the overprinted notes. About 1,700 different kinds were issued.

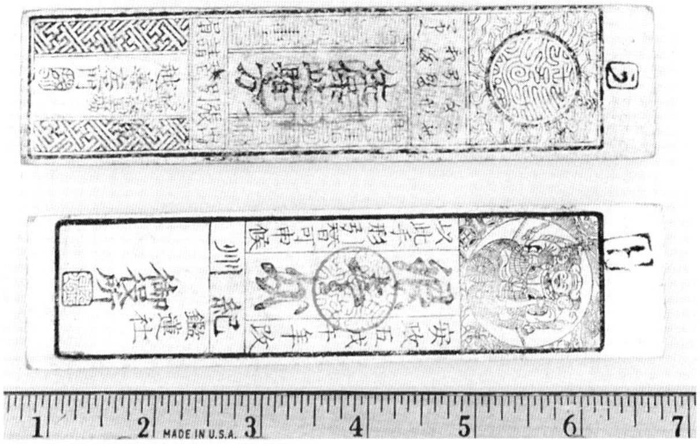

Hansatsu

HASHSHASH

Kordofan and Darfar tribes, Africa, Late 1800s

Iron hoes were used as money. Some are larger and are only a blade with a binding for a wood handle. Those blades are eight inches and a crescent shape. Many varieties. (See Quiggin p. 95) (See Ratzel Vol. 1 p.91)

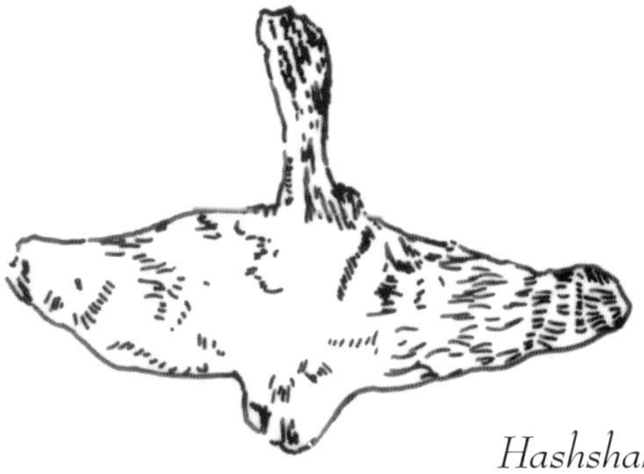

Hashshash

HAT MONEY

Pahang, Malay, until 1893

Tin mixed with lead molded into a hat shape were issued in four sizes 1, 1/2, 1/4, and 1/8 tampang. A hole for stringing is in the outer lip of most hollow hat money.

Hat Money

Solid tin ingots were used first in a truncated pyramid and then in a pyramid shape with a small lip at its base. The smaller hat money shape followed. (See Tin Ingot Money) (See Quiggin p. 253-255)

HATO IME

Clam shell ring with a concave circumference.

HAWKBELL

America

Small bronze hawkbells intended for falconry were traded by explorers, such as Columbus, to the natives. The Narvaez expedition to Florida also used hawkbells. The Europeans used them in most places that they traded with the natives. (See Francis p.29)

HDE - See Kundja

HEAD - See Cowry Shell

HEAD MONEY - See Human Head Money

HEAD TAX TOKEN

New Guinea

From 1921 to 1941 the Australian civilian administration of the Mandated Territory of New Guinea issued head tax tokens. All are made of aluminum and are uniface. There are three types with the first two types having a holed loop at the top. The third type was issued by the *kiaps* (patrol officers) without a hole, but many had holes added by the natives. The basic tax was 10 shillings for all male New Guineans over 12 years of age and fit for work. The tax exempted natives serving under indenture, sick, officials and students at missions or government schools. The money went to the Native Welfare Fund for the maintenance of hospitals, schools, etc. (See Mira p. 307-313)

HEADBAND MONEY

Irian Jaya

Plaited sago fronds with cassowary feathers attached were sometimes worn around the waist as a belt as well as around the head. They were called *momogo* and I believe were a valued item and could possibly have been used in barter. (See Konrad p. 158)

HEAVEN BANK NOTES - See burial money

HELL BANK NOTES - See burial money

Hato Ime

Hawkbell

Head Tax Money

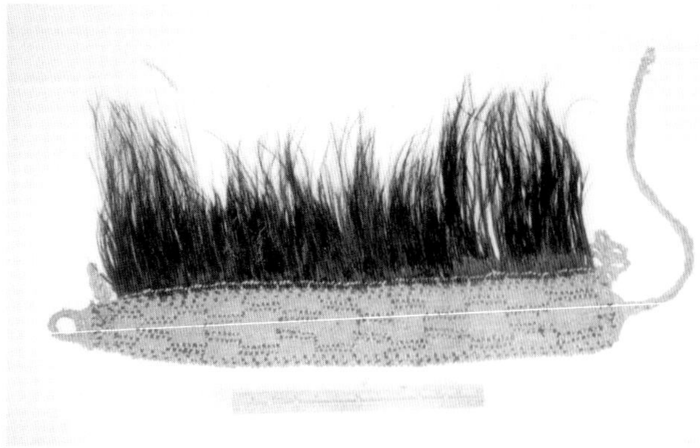

Headband Money

Hinuili

HINUILI

Solomon Islands

A small ring made from *trochus* or *conus* shell was mainly used as a *votive* offering or as part of a charm. (See Miller p. 292)

HIPPOPOTAMUS TOOTH

Africa

The teeth were used in trade for iron, tobacco rolls, cotton cloth and clothing in Timbuktu. (See Bennett p. 183)

Hippopotamus Tooth

HIRI TRADING SYSTEM

Papua New Guinea

An annual overseas trading expedition between the Moto people of the Port Moresby area and along the Papuan coast to the Trobriand Islands. Thousands of pots were transported on large sailing canoes in exchange for sago. The women made the pots, but the men acted as their agents on the *hiri.* In August the canoes were overhauled and caulked and tied together in groups of from four to eight canoes to form a raft to hold the pots in the center. The trips started in September or October. There was much ceremony and ritual in most aspects of the *hiri.* During the trip only certain foods could be eaten, and they must always be cooked. At the end of the voyage the bowls were ritually broken and thrown into the sea. They took pots, stone axes, adzes, shells, shell ornaments and shell necklaces. They returned in November with sago. A large canoe called a *lakatoi* held as much as 34 tons of sago on its return. The hiri did not survive the disruption of World War II.

HO - See DE.

HOBO NICKEL

United States

Buffalo nickels were carved to look like various people in place of the Indian or buffalo. The pieces were carved by hobos to trade for money or a meal. The most famous and one of the best was Bo. They are not considered a part of primitive or traditional money but are included in many collections.

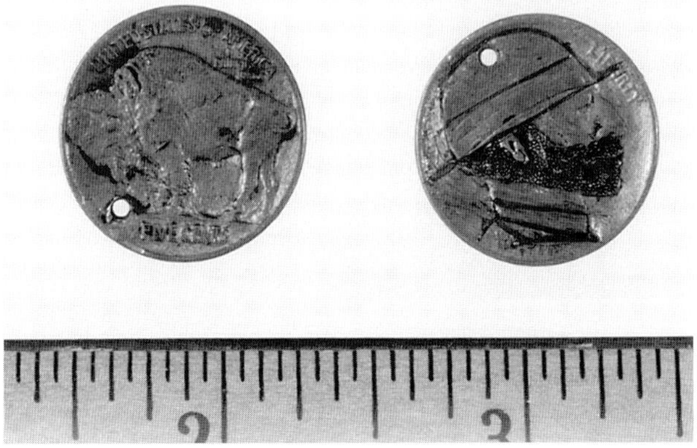

Hobo Nickel

HOE MONEY

See Axe Money, Hashshash, Jembe, Khasu, Sakania, Shoka, Spade Money

"Semifinished hoe blades were commodity currency units that found widespread acceptance in the agriculturally-based economies of the Zaire basin. Nevertheless, some scholars designate hoe currencies as "special use" currencies. But the 19th and early 20th century evidence for west central Africa shows hoe currencies having circulated more generally and widely, along overtly commercial avenues in addition to the ones for bridewealth," according to Kriger, p.99. Hoes were valuable both as iron and as a useful commodity.

Africa, Cameroons, Mambila

Double iron hoe money that is a good example of a non-functional hoe used strictly as money.

East Africa

Hoe money was a local form of iron forgings exchanged for goods by the tribes in the districts where iron was plentiful and worked elsewhere into other implements, weapons and ornaments by the local smiths. (See Quiggin p. 93)

Nigeria

Ten different hoes, each being a very local variety with limited use, were used as money. (See Johansson)

Nigeria

Narrow iron hoes were used as money. Many kinds and shapes of hoes were used in Nigeria.

Africa, Sudan

In the Kordufan, area iron hoes used for weeding which have a socket made of a strip of iron at the end of the blade that could hold a wood handle were used as money. (See Schaedler p.323.)

Uganda

This special "marriage hoe" was too large for practical use and was made solely for payment to the father of the bride. In 1909 this hoe had a value of 10 shillings. It was made of copper.
(See Quiggin p. 98)

HOKATA

A *Tridacna*, *Conus* or *Trochus* shell ring armlet was used as money as well as personal adornment. It was made in eastern and central Marovo. The armlets were often attached to the ridge pole, gable, or edge of the skull hut roofs. They were widely traded and were considered small change and were used to pay for prostitutes. See Poata. (See Waite p. 153) (See Miller p. 292)

HONEY

Yucatan, the time of the conquest.

One of the main export items at the time was honey. It was used along with flint, slaves, cloth and salt in trade. Honey was probably used as a form of money. (See Polanyi p. 133)

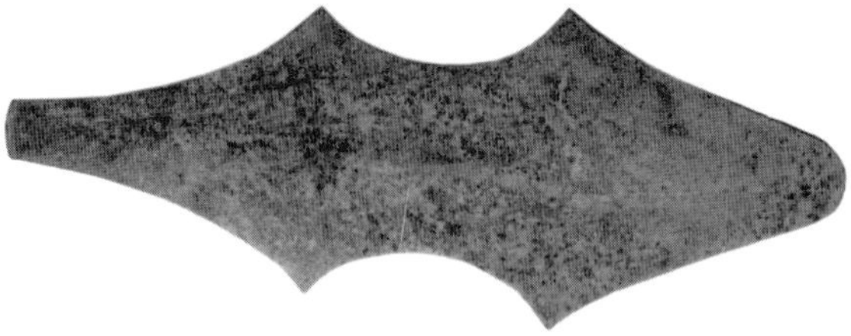

Double Hoe Money

Nigeria Hoe Money

Nigeria Hoe Money

Nigeria Hoe Money

Nigeria Narrow Hoe Money

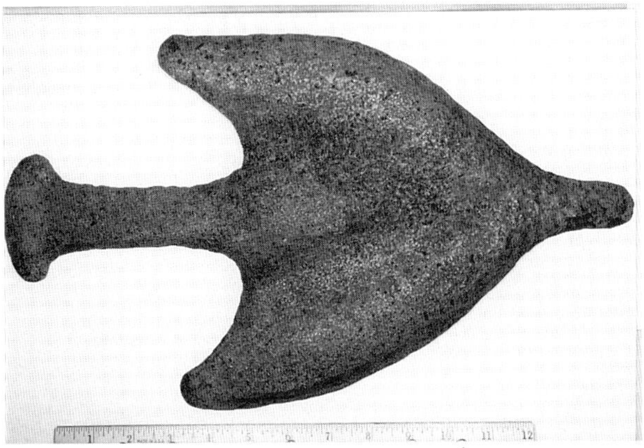

Uganda Hoe Money

Hokata

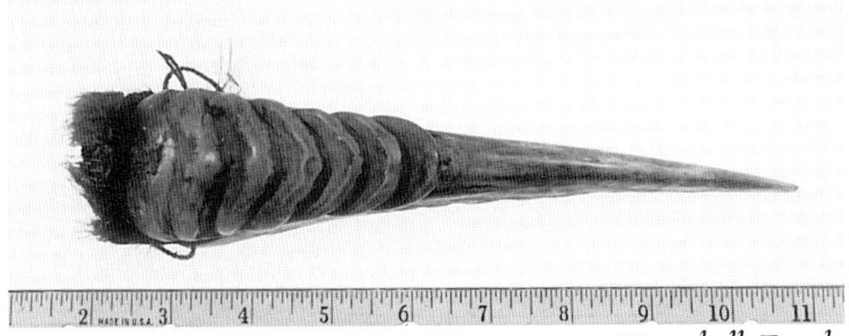

Hornbill Beak

HOOK - See Fish Hook money

HORIM

Irian Jaya

All men but the youngest boys wore an elongated gourd on their penis. It was tied in an erect position by a fine thread of twig fiber secured around their chest. A second thread was looped through a small hole in the rim and down around the scrotum. They are included in money collections, but because of their low value it is doubtful if they were frequently used as money. (See Matthiesen p. 12)

HORNBILL BEAK

Trobriand Islands

HORSE

Africa. 1455

Wolof trading with both the Moors and the Europeans valued the horse as wealth and a limited form of money with 14 or 15 slaves being the value of one horse. (See Bohannan p. 31)

American Plains, 1800's

The local Indians traded horses solely for European goods. The Indians obtained one gun, 100 charges of powder and balls, a knife and other items for one horse. As late as 1854 slave traders made annual trips to Sever Valley paying horses in the value of $100 for boy slaves and $200 in horses for girl slaves. (McNitt p. 18) (See Jablow)

Russia

The Kirghiz used the horse as the main monetary unit until the 20th century, according to Davies p. 42.

HORSESHOES

Cordoba, Argentina

As early as 1574 it was decreed that horseshoes should pass as currency. (See Taxay p. 58)

HUBBELL BEADS - See Beads

HUDSON BAY BEADS - See Beads

HUDSON BAY BLANKET - See Blanket Money - Hudson Bay

HUMAN BONE - See Dagger Money

HUMAN HAIR MONEY

Australia, Taurna Island

Strings of plaited human hair were used as money.

HUMAN HEAD MONEY

Borneo, Papua New Guinea, Philippines

It was an essential item in bride-price. The skull was covered with clay and decorated. Taking a head helped in courtship but it was not an essential qualification for marriage. (See Quiggin p. 263, 266)

Malay Peninsula

Around 1000 A.D. human skulls were used as a special purpose money and as an exchange media. (See Wicks p. 241)

HUMAN TEETH

Congo, Papua New Guinea

Strings of human teeth are one of the oldest forms of currency in the Congo. They were also used in Papua New Guinea until recently.

HUON GULF TRADE NETWORK

The voyages of the Huon Gulf trade network are reciprocal, with natives from one village visiting natives of another village. The north coast villages traded mat and string bags to Labu for baskets, purses and handbags which were traded to Buakap for sago with the southern villages trading food and poor pottery. Tami Islands also traded food and poor wooden bowls to the northern coast villages. Busama gave 150 pounds of taro for one large pot or one small canoe for 24-30 large pots. They would also give 50 pounds of taro for a small pot or one mat. They also paid 10-12 shillings for a Tami Islander bowl. The northern coast villages gave four string bags for a large pot or 10 mats for a basket. Labu gave one basket for two large pots or four purses for a small pot. The pottery villages gave one large pot for 150 pounds of taro or three mats. They gave a small pot for one mat or four purses or 50 pounds of taro. Except in the exchange of bowls, money was rarely used in the trade. The Huon system was not entirely closed. They also traded with other villages in their area. (See Sahlins p.283-284)

HUT TAX TOKEN

Africa

The token was issued to the headman of the village and it was worn by him around his neck. They were made of copper or bronze in several shapes around the beginning of the 20th century.

I'A'AFU

Malaita, Solomon Islands

A *biru* made with 1,000 porpoise teeth. See Porpoise teeth

Human Hair Money

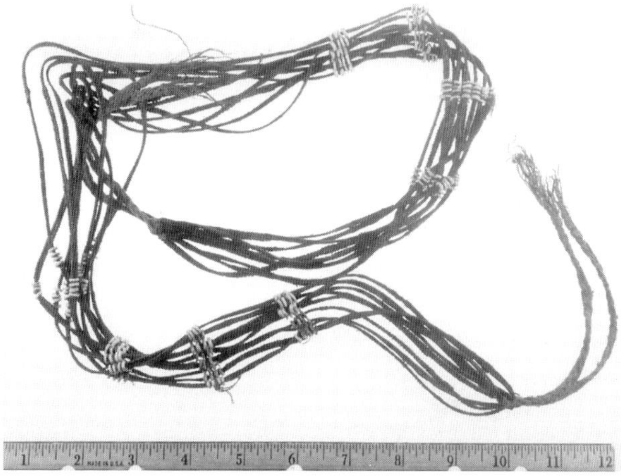

Human Hair Money

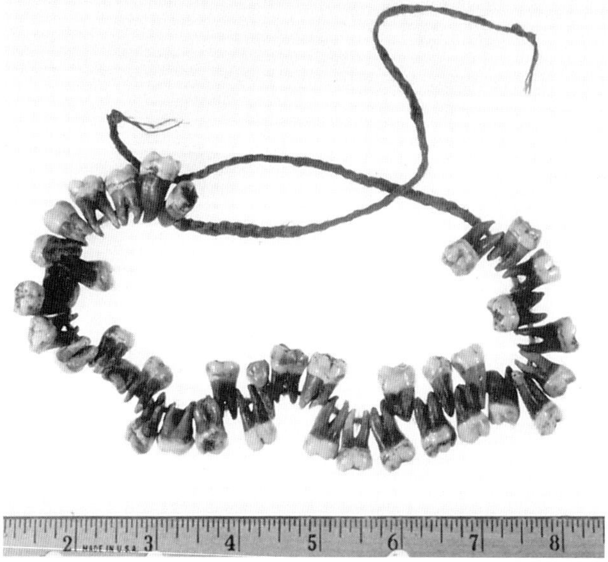

Human Teeth

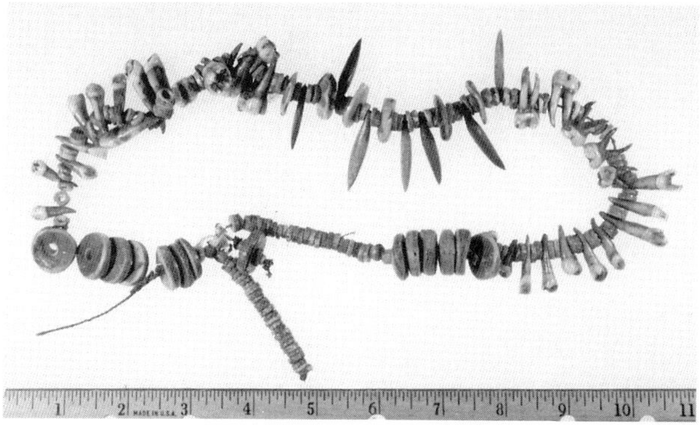

Human Teeth

Hut Tax Tokens

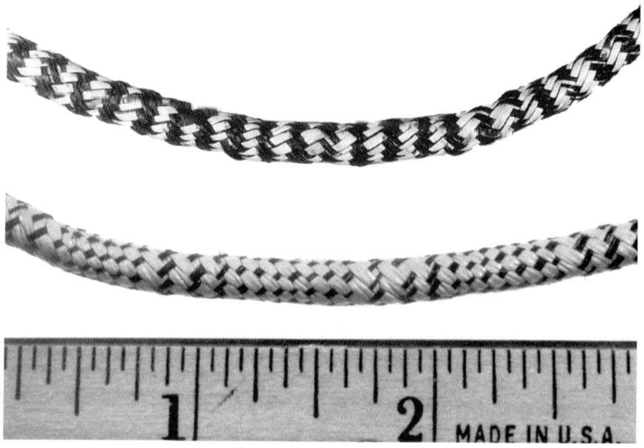

Ihrik

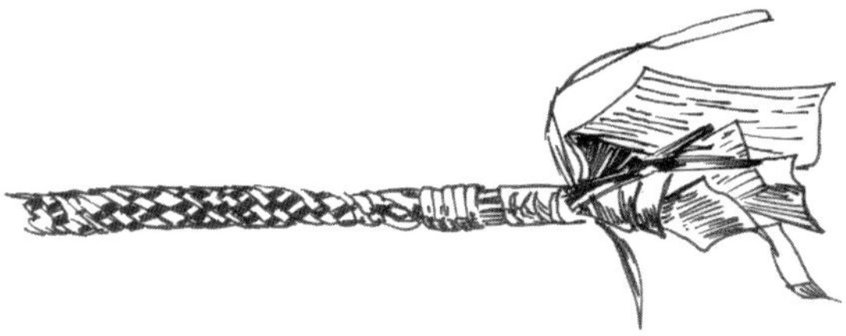

Ihrik

IBAKA

Zaire, Africa

This knife is a personal dagger with a rounded point. At its lower center, near the handle, it has an area of surface patterning in parallel incised lines. The knife was carried by men in a carved wooden sheath under the arm, both sheath and handle often embellished with brass tacks. It was also called *empute.* See Kriger p. 211-212.

IHRIK

Marshall Islands

Plaitwork of black and white palm leaf strips woven over a base of twisted coconut fiber cord were made by the natives. The coils were used as money and also worn as a girdle. The same technique of cylindrical plaitwork in short, stiffer lengths and in gaudier colors is used in the Solomons for ear-sticks. (See Quiggin p. 133)

IKAKALAKA

Zaire, Africa

The knife was made in the late 19th century around Lake Mayi Ndombe and Lake Tumba. The knife was split at the tip into two points and came in two different sizes. The heavier size style was associated with judicial authority and the position of chief. The lighter style was used as a prestige knife by chiefs and other important people. Unlike most knives, this knife was carried by women who were also holders of titles based on their position as the principal wife of a powerful man. (See Kriger p.210-211)

IKAT CLOTH

Indonesia

In Central Sulawesi large pieces of *ikat* cloth were used to pay fines and make peace, but were seldom ever worn as clothing. This kind of cloth has not been made since the 1800s. There are many kinds of *ikat. Ikat* refers to a kind of cloth made by tying and dyeing the warp threads prior to weaving. The design appears fuzzy in a length-wise direction. See cloth money (See Taylor)

IKONGA

Congo

The *ikonga* is a spearhead decorated near the base with simple decoration and worth one fowl. At one time two or three *ikonga* were worth a dog, and five or six were the price of a male slave. (See Quiggin p. 65) Four iron spears were worth one cast copper cross ingot. The iron and copper both weighed about the same. (See Kriger p. 89)

IKUL KNIFE

Kuba Tribe, Africa

Kuba blacksmiths produced these iron knives as prestige items and embellished the blade by heavily blackening the blade surface and then selectively polishing certain areas. The name comes from the Mongo language. The *ikul* was considered an essential aspect of Kuba male identity and status. The lower quality knives have wood handles while the higher quality knives have decorated iron handles. (See Kriger p. 15 & 170.)

IKUMI

Africa

The Wasongola on the Lualaba use strings of snail shells as part of bride price. They are the African snail and are of poor workmanship, only worth about 10 cents per string. The *kiringi* (plural *viringi*) is a bunch of 16 strings worth 16 francs. After 1914, traders paid as much as 25 francs per bunch. (See *Musanga*.) (See Quiggin p. 49.)

IKUL IMBAANG

Kuba kingdom, Africa

The blades were made of iron with copper medallions inset at the center, while in other cases the entire blade was of copper. These knives were probably traded for cloth, carvings and ivory, according to Kriger p.177.

Ikat

Ikonga

Ikul Knife

ikumi

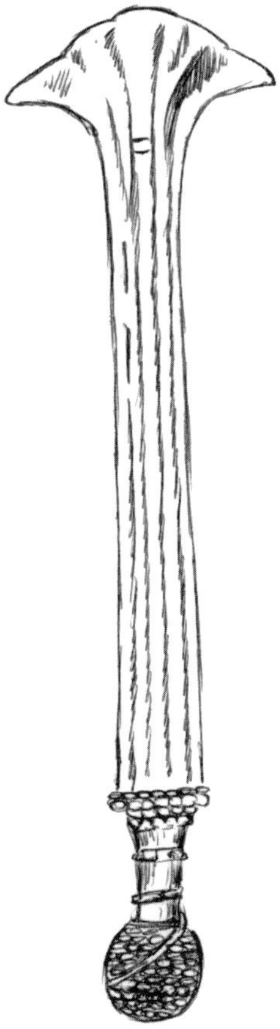

Ingonda

ILOON
Kuba tribe, Africa

The Kuba war sword is a ceremonial or parade sword made with an iron blade and wood handle. They were large enough to have at one time been used as a weapon. The iron *iloon* swords were massive enough to have been used as weapons in the past. (See Kriger p.175-178)

IMPANDE SHELLS
Northern Rhodesia

These shells were used along with cattle, salt, tobacco and beads for marriage payments. Natives, having no concept of the value of silver, gold, and copper, believed white men were digging for *impande* shells. (See Quiggin p. 103)

IMUN
Solomon Islands

Strings of porpoise teeth and bat teeth were used as money. Some strings have 80 to 100 teeth in them. It was the native money of Buka and Northern Bougainville. (See Quiggin p. 126 & 129)

INDIAN CORN - See Grain Currency

INGONDA
Zaire, Africa

This double-edged sword was made of iron and had a splayed, fan like shape at the end of the blade. It was also called *ebale*. Most also had two or more ribs from the handle to the end of the blade. It was a weapon as well as having a number of significant social values. The swords could probably be considered a form of currency because traders also used them, and they had a high trade value. The sword was never used for work and women could never use one, only wealthy Twa men, with permission, could carry one. (See Kriger p. 206-210)

INGOTS - See Mint Bars

INK
China, 1932

it is a compressed-powder bar that must be mixed with water for use.

IRON
Africa

Many shapes, both worked and unworked iron, were used as money in most parts of Africa. Iron was used to purchase slaves, wives, pay taxes, fines and ivory. (See Quiggin p. 101)

IRON BULLET OR BALL - See antimony lump.

IRON DISC CURRENCY

Ashanti, Africa

It is believed that roughly circular iron disks about 2 5/8 to 2 7/8 inches in diameter were at one time used as money at Juaben, the native capital of the district. One source stated that his father handed one to him and stated they were money and valued at 6d. (See Wild.)

IRON STRIP MONEY

Brunei, early part of 19th century

Iron strips one inch wide and 1/4 inch thick circulated as money. One inch square was worth one cent and 100 pieces were worth one dollar. (See Singh p. 568.)

ISAGALIA

Auki Island, Solomon Islands

The *isagalia* is ten *fura,* which is actually 40 *galia.* A *galia* is a single three-foot string of white shell disks. The *isagalia* is made and used on Auki Island as bride price and is worth two pounds. (See Bartle p. 382) (See shell money, Opitz, Solomon Islands)

ITUMA P521

Africa

Wanande tribe. This small spearhead with only one tine was used as money and valued at one fowl or six pence. (See Payne A-33)

IVORY

Africa, until recently

Forms: full tusks, spans (sections), disks and rings. It became the money of the chiefs, as commoners were not allowed to have ivory in their possession without the chief's approval. Its value was due to the knowledge required and difficulty involved in the killing of elephants and the cutting of their tusks. Slaves and ivory were the two most important items wanted by Europeans. A pair of tusks paid for room and board for an entire caravan. The tusk could grow to more than 12 feet in length. Ivory rings were used as money, and some had nail encrustations for decoration. Some had lines cut into the outer surface. Elephant tusks were also used for bride price.

There is much fake ivory on the market. The word ivory has traditionally applied only to the tusks of elephants. Technically it can be applied to any mammalian tooth or tusk of commercial interest that is large enough to be carved or scrimshawed. Some sources of ivory other than elephant teeth are whale teeth (sperm or killer

Ink

Isagalia

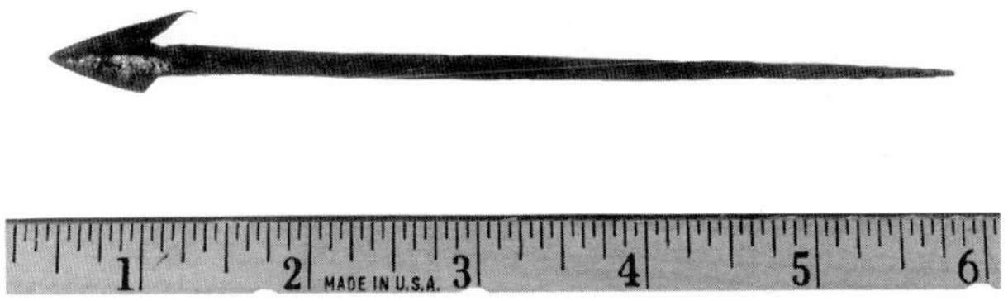

Ituma

whales only), hippopotamus teeth, wart hog tusk, narwhal (upper incisor), and mammoth upper incisors. There does not appear to be any one test to determine what animal the ivory came from or if the ivory is genuine. Some of the substitutes are bone, nut, shell, hornbill ivory, vegetable ivory, ivory dust in styrene resin, and plastics of many kinds.

Bone can many times be detected by observing a series of canals through which fluid flowed. These are the Haversian canals, and they can be seen on a polished bone surface with a 10X hand lens.

Shell is a calcium carbonate. It may present color mottling when viewed through an ultraviolet light.

Most plastics can be detected with a hot pin which in many cases will melt the plastic and not ivory.

Vegetable ivory or ivory nuts are primarily the nuts of the Tagua palm tree. Sulfuric acid applied to the surface will turn the item an irreversible pink after about 12 minutes. You can also see a series of fine, regularly spaced concentric lines similar to those seen in the hippopotamus.

Polished cross-sections of elephant and mammoth ivory display Schreger lines which look like crosshatchings. The outer Schreger pattern should have lines at 90 to 115 degrees.

The walrus tusk has a generally oval shape with concentric rings showing the cementum in the outer ring with a transition ring next to it and a primary dentine in the center.

The sperm whale tooth is conically shaped and will show prominent concentric dentine rings in cross-section.

The narwhal is a rarely seen arctic whale. The male has a single left tusk that is spirally twisted in a counter-clockwise direction. It may be from 6 1/2 feet to 22 feet long. In cross-section the cementum is separated from the dentine by a clearly defined transition ring and has peripheral indentations.

The cross-section of a hippo tooth shows a tightly packed series of fine concentric lines under a 10X hand lens. The orientation of the lines will follow the overall shape of the tooth.

Wart hog ivory tends to have a mottled appearance, and a cross-section will show irregularly spaced concentric lines of varying thickness under a 10X hand lens.

Hornbill ivory is in a very distinct shape and has a bright red peripheral color. (See Espinoza p. 2-26)

Ivory Ring Money

India, Naga

Thick ivory armlets worn above the elbow were highly desired ornaments for men. It is not certain if they ever truly became money.

Indonesia

Ivory tusks were used as money and as important bride price items. Ivory rings were also used in this same manner. Some ivory rings have nail encrustations as decoration. Although ivory in the form of elephant tusks could be obtained from Borneo and Sumatra, they were also brought by ship from India as far back as the days of the Dutch East India Company. (See Rodgers p. 151)

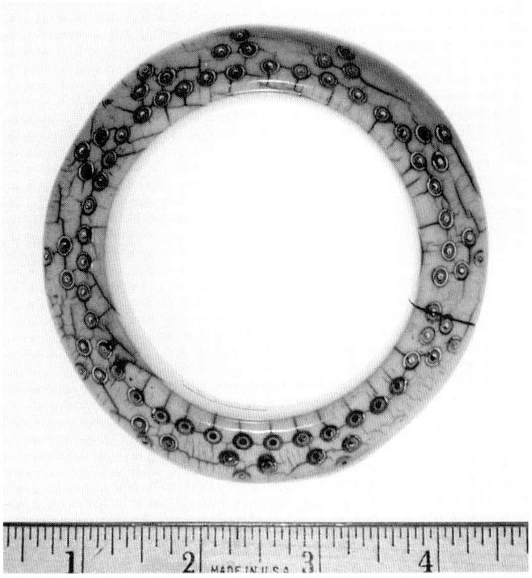

Ivory Ring Money - Indonesia

Keeling Cocos Islands

Ivory or bone (ivorine) tokens were issued by John Sydney Clunies Ross in 1913 and dated the year he became governor, 1910. They were produced in England by a button manufacturer and were used until 1955. While they are not technically primitive money, many collectors include them in their collections. They were made in the following denominations: five (oval), 10 (round), 25 (square), 50 (octagonal) cents, and one (square), two (round), and five (octagonal) rupees. In 1966 the Clunies Ross family released 208 pieces to the collector market, which more than doubled the known pieces in the market. In 1968 newly designed plastic tokens were issued.

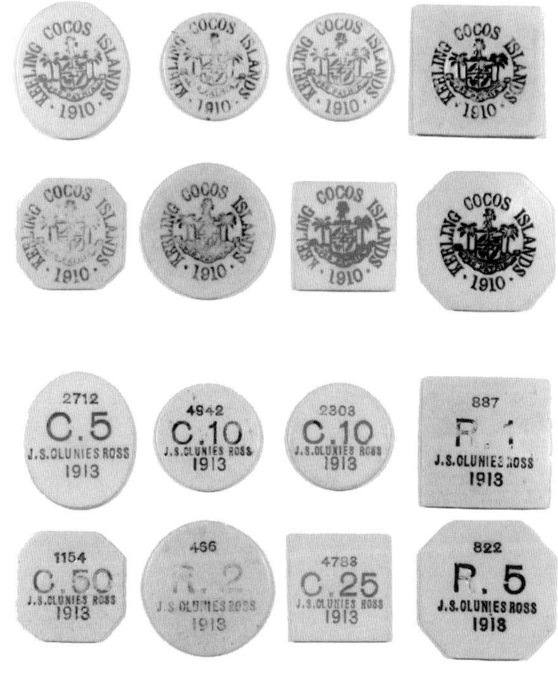

Keeling Cocos Islands Tokens

IYAYAW - See Ogoja Penny

IWENGA - See Kundja

JACKET

Northern Taiwan, Atayal Tribe 1800s

This homespun cloth coat with 2,600 strings of beads was used as money. There are 20 to 25 beads per string and with 2,600 strings of beads, the coat contains more than 50,000 beads. They are polished stone or shell beads. A coat was valued at five cattle and several wives. The beads were sewn onto rectangular pieces of cloth, and the pieces of cloth were sewn together to make jackets and kimonos. (See Dubin p.236-238)

JAD STONE - See Je Stone

JADE MONEY

Jade is a popular name for two mineralogically distinct but similar stones. The more popular nephrite is called the true jade of China and the Orient, and jadeite, which is less popular, was commonly used in Mexico, Burma, and Central America. Jadeite is harder than nephrite. Jadeite varies in color from the rare spinach green of

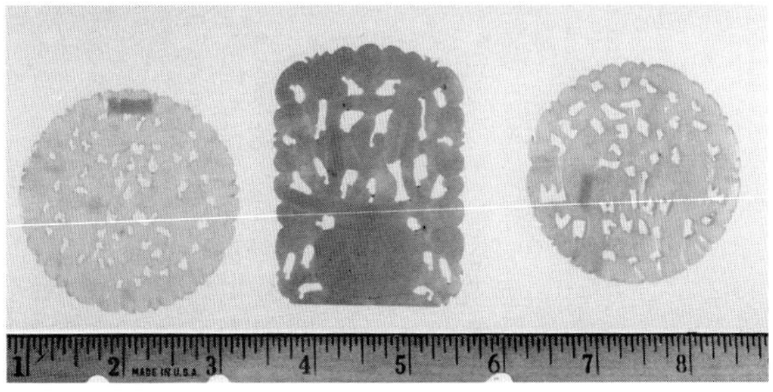

Jade Money

Central America to a grayish green or bluish gray. American jadeite contains diopside, which is not found in the Asian variety, and Asian nephrite contains phosphorous, which is not found in the American variety. Nephrite is most commonly white but comes in a variety of colors with yellow being the rarest (and thus it was reserved for the emperor). Jade showed wealth and also indicated the high social status of its owner. (see Francis)

Mexico

Jade was more valuable than gold in Mexico and was used in the form of beads called *chalchihuitl*. The Indians believed they were a remedy for colic and other intestinal disorders. Francis states that it is believed that the Aztecs valued a single jade bead at 50, 100 or even 200 pounds of gold. Jade was also used to pay tribute to Montezuma in the 1500s and was used as money. (See Taxay p. 38)

Orient, 3rd millennium B.C. to modern times

Jade is found in the form of rings and disks and were symbols of rank or office. It is highly valued. Patterns of coins were made in jade for presentation to the throne. Production of jade pieces as a regular trading medium is still not thoroughly established. One expert states that jade coins were used in the Wang Mang period (7-24 A.D.). Jade rings were used as coins and were strung together in the hundreds during the time of Emperor Wu (265-285 A.D.) In ancient China, jade took the place of valuable money and was occasionally turned into coinage. Jade was used extensively as evidence of indebtedness, certifying that a specific amount was due. This piece could be sold, transferred, or inherited much as a promissory note or bill of exchange, according to Haynes, World Coins. February, 1971, p. 126-127. Many jade pieces have coins in their design. (See Quiggin p. 241-242) (See Haynes p. 124-125).See Nephrite

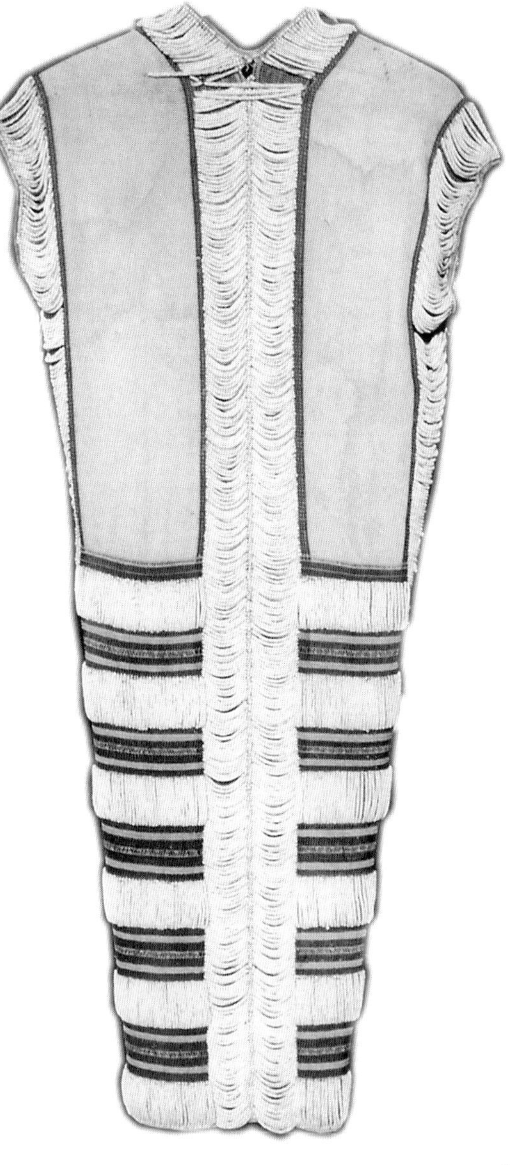

Jacket

JADEITE - See Beads

JAM

Arctic, Siberia, 1930s

It was introduced by Soviet Trading Stations to the natives and was recognized as currency. (See Einzig p. 116)

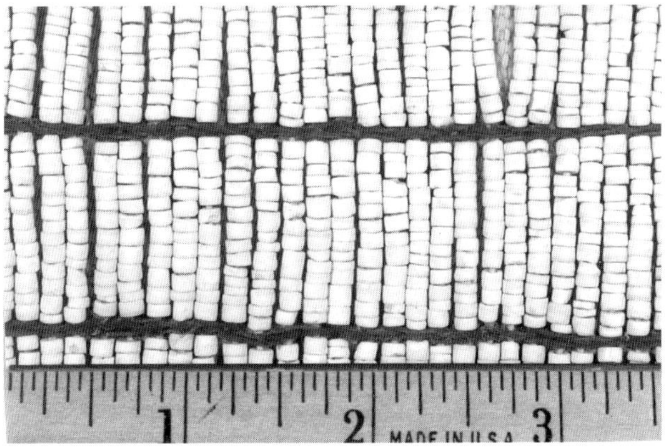

Jacket

JARS

Annam

A large pot was worth seven gray glazed earthenware jars large enough to hold 15 liters. One jar was worth four *muk* and one *muk* was worth 10 mats or hoes, which were used as agricultural implements, according to Ridgeway p. 24. The *Mnong* used tall jars called *yang mei* and small neckless jars called *yang dam tei.* A jar called *rluung* was worth an adult buffalo. Besides being used as money, the jars were also used to prepare and hold rice beer. Some jars are worth as much as a large elephant.

Borneo, until recently

Byaks used jars as a form of money and store of value before 1600. The importation of earthenware and common glazed pottery appears to have ceased about 1600."The old jars just increased in value through the years to the point that at one time $20,000 was offered (and refused) for a particularly renowned jar. Other jars were worth from four to 16 buffaloes. In 1912, the Sea Dayak used jars formerly imported from China and also made by the Chinese in Borneo as money. The most common jar is a plain brown brightly glazed earthware jar about three feet high with a flat bottom and is ornamented with a Chinese dragon molded in relief on the side. Some have scroll designs instead. In 1912 this common jar was worth 200 to 400 dollars. The more valuable jars come in both dark brown and dark green and some have no decoration except for some obscure markings. It is believed that much of their value comes from their age. They were probably imported from China or Siam centuries ago. (See Quiggin p. 260, 264) Rare

JASPER

Benin, West Africa

The King of Benin in the 17th century considered jasper and coral to be the two items of great wealth. The beads were considered a form of money. See Beads, jasper.

JAWS - See Flying Fox Jaws

JAWBONES

Torres Islands

Pig jawbones were used as money.

JE STONES

Irian Jaya, to present

The *je* stones were made of slate and were usually flattened or elongated egg oval shape. They were black, green or dark green in color. The stones were imported from the Jalemo people who live northeast of the Balim Valley. They were sometimes decorated with fur tufts, braided strands of bark fiber, yellow colored braided orchid fiber, red ochre, feathers or cloth around the middle of the stone. There are two kinds. The male is thicker and narrower than the female piece which is

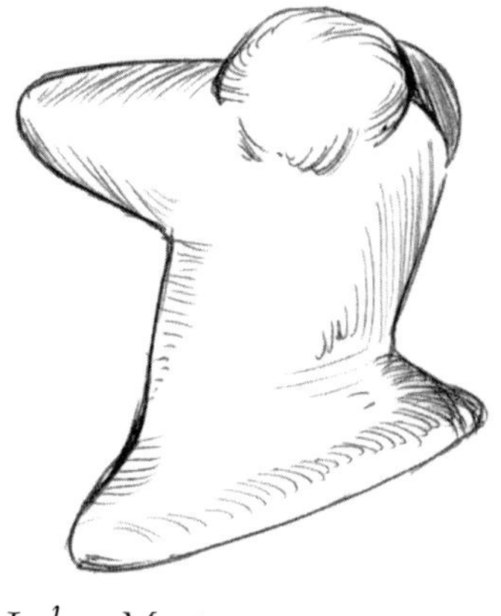

Jade - Mexico

Jade

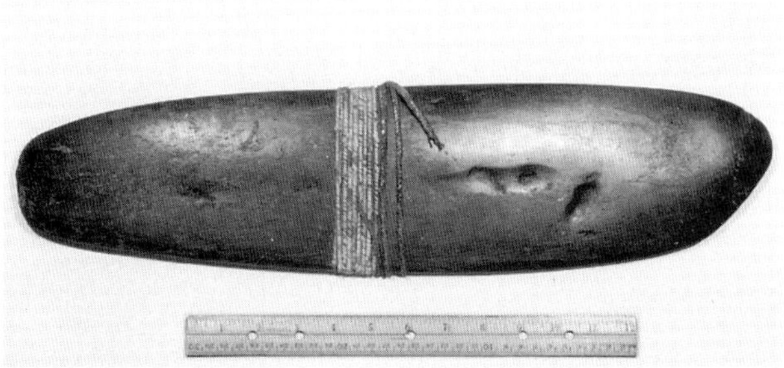

Je Stone

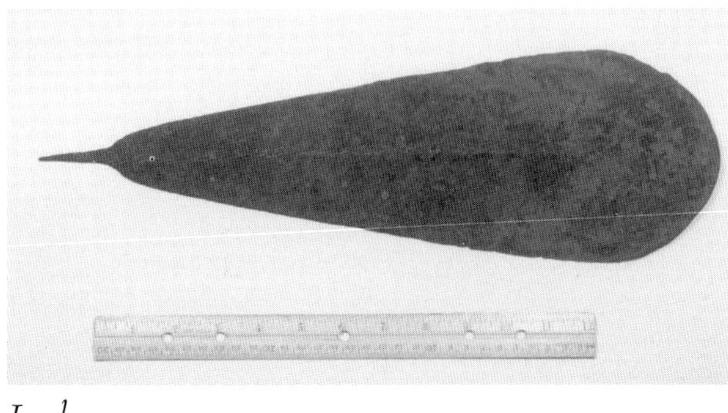

Jembe

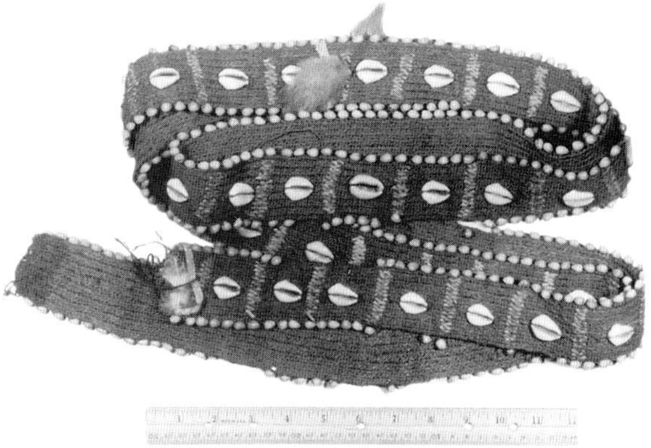

Jetak

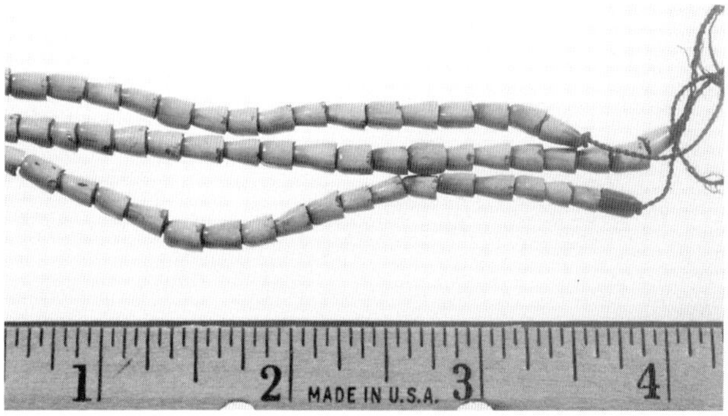

Cut Job's Tears

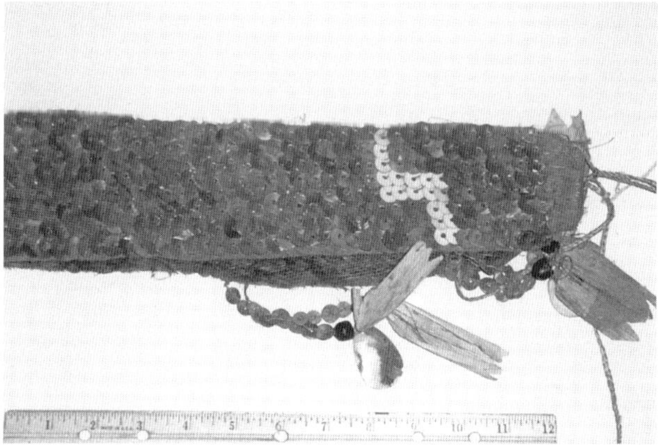

Kaipwesi

wide and thin. They are also called exchange stones or *Yao* stones . The *je* stones were used in ceremonial payments, in funerals and as a currency for important commercial activities as well as bride price. They were used by the Dani tribe who thought the stones had no magic power and regularly passed them from owner to owner calling them exchange stones. The most important ones are the largest and are called *je oak*. The next least important ones are called je *ai*, and the small stones are called *ogosi*. There are at least 14 specific names for the different kinds of *je*. The small pieces were called *holi* and were never over 40 cm. long. The longest *je* were 68 cm. long. (See Heider p. 288-289) The *ganekhe* includes a small flat slate stone called *habo*. They are similar to the *je* stone but are never used in exchange or displayed publicly. They are a powerful sacred stone and they are kept wrapped in a cabinet in the men's house and never seen by women. (See Heider p. 288-289)

JEMBE

Africa, until 1900

Lomami area. Mouloundou. *Jembe* is a form of iron hoe money. In 1894, they were used in payment of a hut tax which was two jembes or three rupees. David Livingstone, the explorer, wrote that "he paid three such iron hoes to have his party of 36 men and several animals ferried across Lake Bemba." Various forms are still being made by the Labwar tribe for trade with neighboring tribes. It was originally a farm implement called *dupa* and was used in bride price. (See Mosher p. 24)

JETAK

Irian Jaya, to present

Long knitted bands with cowry shells sewn in the center of the band at regular intervals along its length are called *jetak*. Job's tears, orchid fiber, feathers and furs are attached to the knitted bands. The cowry shells were called *jetak-egen*. The Dani use several terms to describe the cowry. They do not, however, have a system of classification like some of the other tribes. They call a white cowry *haboke*, an ivory one gut and a discolored one *gusa*. The elongated cowry is *jako*, the broad split cowry is *mogen*, and the small knobby one is *hepugen*. *Jetak* were exchanged at funerals. The *jetak* was also used as a measuring device to determine the price of pigs. (See Heider p. 290-292)

JIBBU

Bubi, Africa

Strings of Achatina shell disks were plaited into broad flat plaits with the ends tied to form circular bands or belts. (See *Bubi* currency.) (See Quiggin p. 49-50)

JOB'S TEAR NECKLACE

Papua New Guinea

This seed necklace was used as money and considered valuable in about 1900. (See Healey p. 134-135) Later it lost its value as money and is only used as decoration at present. Large numbers of strings of Job's tears are presently worn as a sign of mourning.

JOM

Vanuatu

Shell money made on the island of Malo. The shell money was used in necklaces, armbands, and waistbands. The shell money was used to purchase pigs, for bride price, and display status. (Huffman)

KAFA

Solomon Islands

This woven rope was used primarily in fishing, as money, and in bride price on Tikopia. The rope is made from the fibers of coconut husks. The fiber is buried in sand, exposed at low tide and left for three months. The fiber is then made pliable by pounding it with a stick. It is then dried, and the shorter, weaker fibers are removed. The remaining fibers are woven by rolling the fibers across the thigh with the hands to form rope. Three strands of this rope are then plaited together to form a stronger rope. It takes six months to one year to make one unit of rope. There are more than four kinds of *kafa*, each having different values and uses. Four kinds are listed in order of most valuable to least. #1) *Kafa Nopaito* - Used to tie down houses so they do not blow away in storms and for shark fishing; #2) *Kafa Tukukau* - Used for shark fishing and as the main part of bride price; #3) *Kafa Taki* - Used for line for fishing behind a moving canoe; #4) *Kafa Kuani* - Used in fishing with a small net; #5) *Kafa Tauvai* - Used as line in fishing near the reefs. *Kafa* is also used to buy a canoe, pay a man for digging a grave, to complete the adoption of a child, as compensation for an injury or death inflicted on someone, and in custom ceremonies. The unit can vary in length from 200 to 300 fathoms for the smaller ones to 400 to 500 fathoms for the larger ones. (Per communication with Betty, Solomon Islands resident.)

KAIN TIMOR CLOTH

Irian Jaya

This cloth was used as an important item in bride price. It was normally in red, white, and blue and was a traded item rather than a locally made cloth. (See Taylor p. 276)

KAIPWESI

Papua New Guinea, to 20th century

This belt was made of *kaloma* shell disks attached to a broad band of European cloth. Older varieties were made of a woven vine backing instead of cloth. The *kaloma* shell is the shell from which *sapi sapi* were made. It was used as a *pokala* (offering) in the Kula cycle. See Kula.

KALO - See Whale teeth.

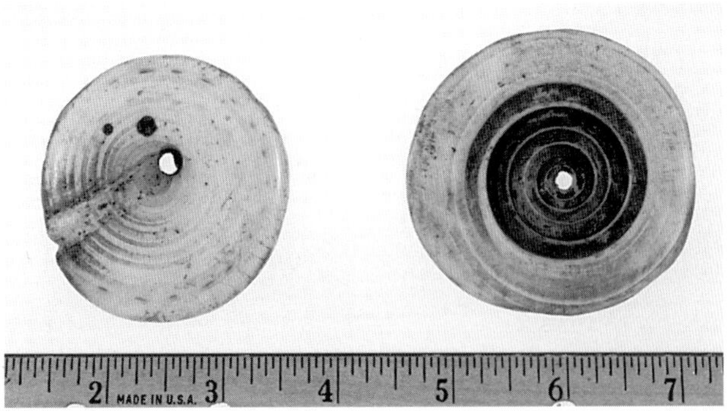

Conus Shell Disks

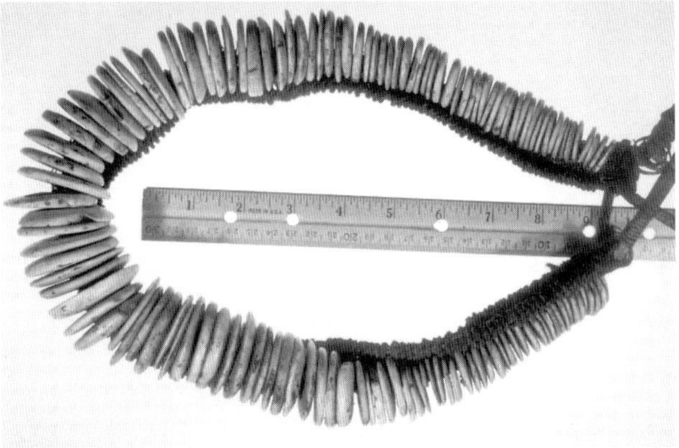

Kandandei Shell Money

Kanotar

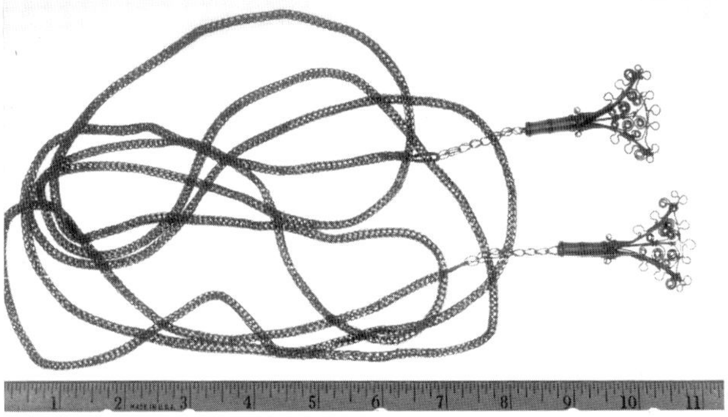

Kanotar

K'a K'im

K'a K'im Marks

KALOMA - See Kula.

KANDANGEI SHELL MONEY

Papua New Guinea, Still Used in 1973

The Village of Kandangei on the Sepik River used this shell belt as money. The shells are 1/2″ to 1 1/2″ in diameter attached end on end to a 3′ woven belt. It was highly valued and used as money. In 1973 when I was in the Village of Kandangei, the natives had these belts and said they were money.

KANOTAR

Sumba, Indonesia

A snake-like metal chain with flared ends and decorations attached to the flared ends. Most are made of tin, but a few are made of gold. They were used in bride price and other transactions.

K'A K'IM

Siam, Early as 13th century

They are also known as *tamlung*, which is also the term for the denominations in which they exist. They were stamped as flat rings, cut at the back and bent into the shape of a women's pelvis. *K'k'im* are counter stamped with the denomination (usually four baht), dynasty mark, and city name. Common cities are Chiang Mai and Chiang Sen, all other cities are rare. Fractional and zinc (lead) pieces are rare. They are the forerunner of packsaddle money. The standard size is 61.2 grams = four baht = one *tamlung*. The zinc - lead pieces are 3 (45.9 gm) or 4 bahts (61.2 gm) and are the earliest pieces. The silver pieces were made from circa 1325 until the demise of the realm in about 1545. They belong to two geographical groups - the northern cities Chiengmai (common), Sak (very rare), and Chiengsen and the southern cities Sawanalok, Lakhon (rare) and Prae (rare)). Other pieces were also issued in Muang Fang (east of Lakhon) and Muang Han (N.E. of Muang Fang). The Chiengmai *Ka'kim* has three stamps on each arm: the stamp at the base gives the denomination of four in a stylized form, the center stamp gives the name of the issuing city, and the upper stamp is an issue mark. Some *Ka'kim* (tamjung) have one or more extra issue marks on the inside face. The fractional *tamlung* were issued in denominations of 1/2 to 1/24 *tamlung* (1/6 *tamlung* weighs 10.2 gm, 1/12 *tamlung* weighs 5.1 gm, and 1/24 *tamlung* weighs 2.6 gm). Some have the name of the issuing city, while many do not have any inscription. (See city marks above.) Counterfeits exist. (See LeMay p.57 and Mitchiner p.330, 347-353)

KAPKAP

Kapkaps were traded from one island to another and used as a form of money in trade. They were used for a variety of occasions and worn by many people from chiefs in some areas to girls at an initiation ceremony in another. In some areas they were worn as breast ornaments, and in other areas they were worn in the hair or on the forehead. The mount is made of any of many different shells. The *tridacna* shell produced the finest pieces, but the *conus, cymbium,* and *Melo diadema* were also used. The openwork piece mounted to the shell base was made from the tortoise-shell in a variety of intricate carved styles. The quality of the carving varied by area.

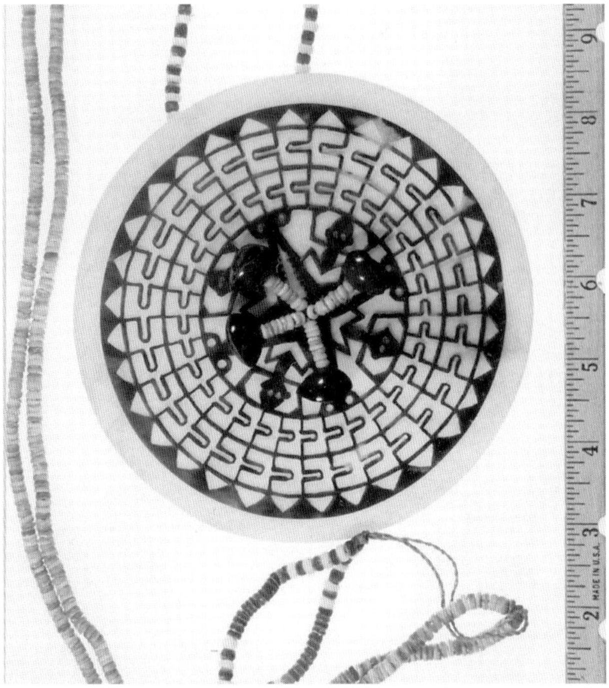

Admiralty Islands

One of two main centers of manufacture. The mount is made from the *tridacna* shell. The *kapkaps* were worn as breast ornaments hung from one or more strings of beads. A poor quality *kapkap* was made from a *conus* shell and used here. All *kapkaps* from this area are not as fine as the kapkaps from New Ireland or the Solomons. The tortoise-shell was also of a coarser carving technique. Many of the bases are much larger than the tortoiseshell carved piece attached. Many of the carved tortoise-shell pieces have little triangles with a center diamond that has edge arcs with teeth facing a smooth center. Much of the tortoise-shell remains in the piece with only small amounts of shell carved out.

Assam

Naga tribesmen made and used the *kapkap* which was worn by headhunting warriors. (See Waite)

Celebes

The *kapkap* used here is similar to the kind used in the Solomons. The *conus* shell base was overlaid with a horn disk that was perforated with openwork designs and attached to warriors' jackets. (See Waite p. 177)

Moluccas

Their *kapkap* is similar to the kind used in the Solomons. The warriors wore round *kapkaps* called *tjidako* on their belts, which were also headhunting symbols. (See Waite p. 177)

New Guinea, Central and Coastal Sepik areas

The *Cymbium* shell was used as the base of the *kapkap* in Papuan Gulf area. The *conus* shell was also used in this area to make a poorer quality *kapkap.* The *Melo diadema* shell was also used in this area. Some of the *kapkaps* have coconut shell carving instead of tortoise-shell.

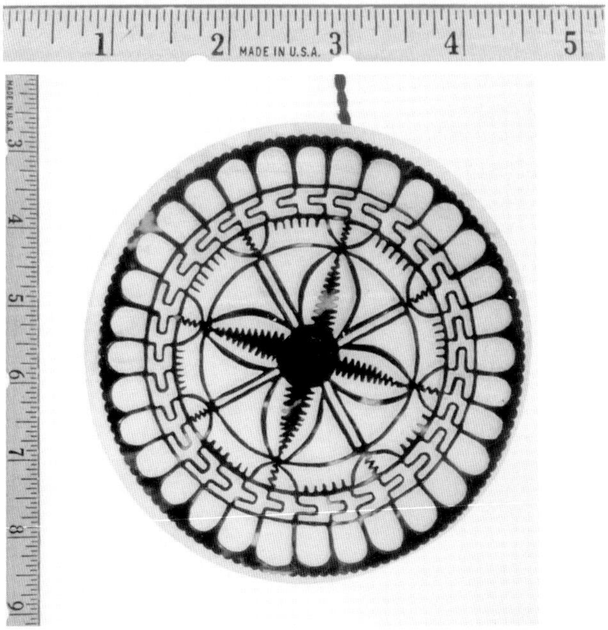

Solomon Island Kapkap

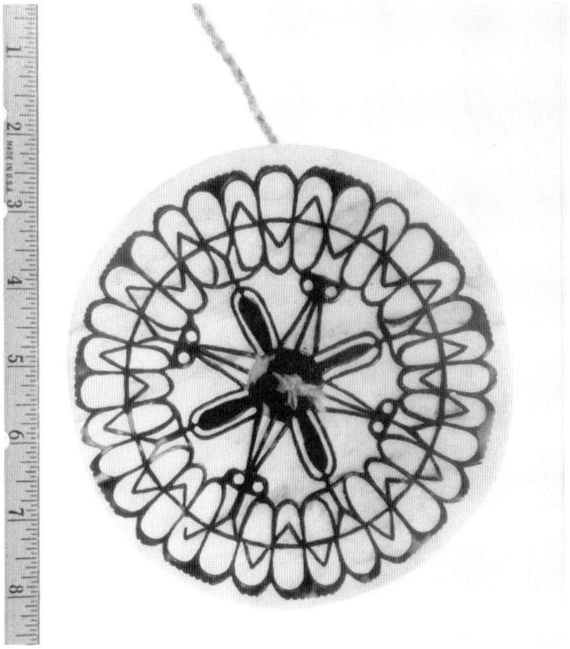

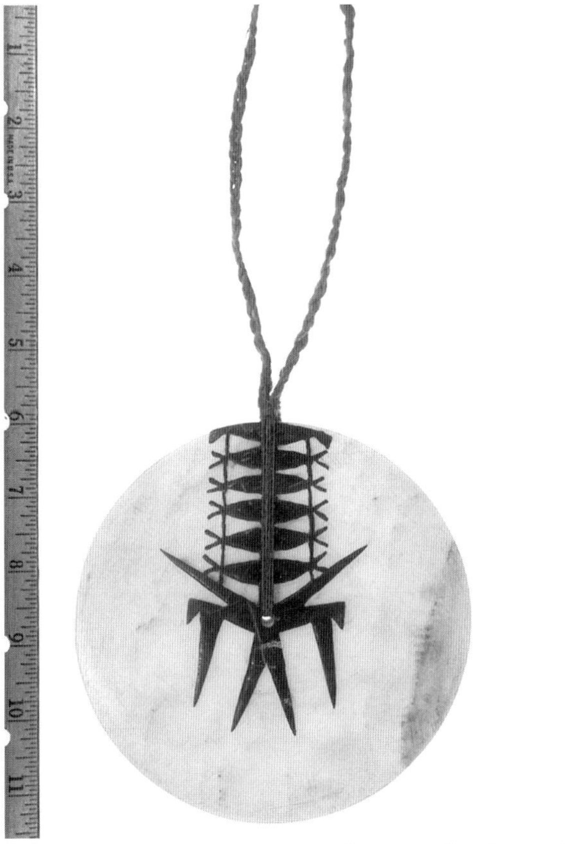

Solomon Island Kapkap

New Ireland

One of the two main centers of manufacture. The most beautiful *kapkaps* come from New Ireland. They were worn as a breast ornament and were hung from a string or strings of beads. The base is normally a finely polished plate of tridacna shell. Generally the tortoise-shell piece on the shell base is normally smaller in proportion than the *kapkaps* from other islands. Most have fine line decoration with most of the tortoise-shell removed and only very fine lines remaining.

Santa Cruz

This is the most easterly island where *kapkaps* occur. The base is polished *tridacna* shell with a tortoise-shell carving mounted on it. The tortoise-shell carving consists almost exclusively of an arrangement of triangles that run in a band from the edge of the shell disk to the center in a broad band. The carving is not circular like most other *kapkaps*. In many cases the heavy piece of twine also runs on top of the tortoise-shell piece from the edge of the base to the center. In some pieces the sticks form symmetric x's or crosshatching with most of the bottom sticks pointing down.

St. Matthias

These *kapkap*-like pieces consist of a thin cut-out piece of tortoise-shell with much open-work and a slit from the edge to the center to allow these pieces to be worn as ear ornaments.

Solomon Islands, Bismark Archipelago

In the Western Solomon Islands the *kapkaps* were worn as head and breast ornaments on ceremonial occasions and formerly in battle. In the Nasioi and Numanumu districts of southern Bougainville, the *kapkaps* were worn as breast ornaments. In northern Bougainville they were worn by young girls in puberty initiation ceremonies. They were made of a disc of turtle-shell cut into an intricate open-work pattern like a filigree design, superimposed on a disc of white tridacna shell. Most of the mounts were smoothly polished thin mounts made of a semi-fossilized variety of tridacna shell. Many of the shells for this base were traded from New Hanover Island and New Ireland. It is said by some they are objects of prestige and wealth and to be used in trade. On the Marovo Lagoon on Rubiana, New Georgia men of high rank bartered for *kapkap* called *Ndala*, their wealth being determined by the number of *ndala* they owned. On the Western Solomons they were called *pirir* and were of two different styles. The first style had fine, regular, web-like designs in the turtle shell filigree design. A bird is also used in the design along with arcs or bands. Double and triple zigzag lines are also used. Symmetry is a very important part of most of these designs. The second style had large and comparatively crude anthropomorphic or star-shaped motifs in the turtle-shell part. They were both made on the island of Nissan and traded from Nissan to Buka and Bougainville. The tridacna shell base originally came from the island of Tanga off the coast of New Ireland and was traded to the island of Nissan where the turtle shell disks were carved. 2" to 5 1/2" diameter.

Torres Straits

Pearl-shell filigree ornaments without the shell backing were used here. (See Haddon Vol. 6 Pl. 24 fig 1-4)

Truk Island

Turtle shell ornament similar to *kapkap* used on this island. (See Damm p. 34-37)

KAPA

Lithuania, Middle Ages

Silver sticks were used as money in the early centuries of the Middle Ages until modern times. They were cast from almost pure silver with the small *kapa* weighing 100 grams and the long *kapa* weighing 200 grams. The Slavs adopted this kind of money in the 12th or 13th century, and the long *kapa* were called *grivna*. The small *kapa* were called rubles. See *grivna*. (See Karys p. 365)

KAPUT

New Ireland

See *mis*.

KARIBUTU - See Kula.

KASUYU - See zappozap.

KATALU'M BUL

Tanga

This necklace consists of an egg cowry with several two-inch or three-inch pieces of red shell disk strings (kemetas) attached to it. Each string has a brown seed case (*kotkot*) attached with dog's teeth inserted in the seed. They are worn at important mortuary feasts. See Kula.

KATANGA CROSS - See Cross - Katanga

KATONGA RING - See Nsambu

KATUDABABILE - See Samakupa

KEELING-COCOS MONEY - See ivory.

KENA - See Bosu

KESA

Choiseul Island in the Solomon Islands

Kesa consists of sets of thin-walled cylinders which were once thought to be made from the fossilized shell of the giant clam *Tridacna*. It is now thought that they are the shell of a sea worm. The natives believe, however, that *kesa* were not made by men. They feel the *kesa* were made by a water god residing in the sea. A set of *kesa* consists of nine cylinders, but the value varies with the size and quality of the pieces. Formerly a set of *kesa* was worth 10 men's *ziku* arm rings. The two classes of *kesa* were the exchange or working class and the large *kesa* or prestige set. The working class *kesa* have five sizes with the smallest size worth three Australian pounds and each larger size worth three pounds more than the next smaller size with the largest size therefore worth 15 pounds. The large or prestige *kesa* varied more in value with its own reputation and the context of its use. Each cylinder was called an eye or *mata*. Three *mata* were bound together in ivory-nut palm leaves and called *salaka*. Three *salaka* were bound with a cord and called one *kesa*. The *kesa* were measured by standing the *mata* on top of each other with an ivory-nut palm midrib between each *mata* to steady it. The smallest *kesa* was about 14 inches, and the largest of the prestige class was six feet. Most *kesa* appear to be very old, and most appear to have been buried at one time.

Managerial wealth consisted of land and *kesa*. *Kesa* was obtained from inheritance from your father or a kinsman with you taking over his position and control over the *kesa* in the descent group. It was also obtained by rearing and selling pigs. Bride price transactions were another a source of *kesa*. Acting as a paid killer or helping in warfare was another way of acquiring *kesa*. *Kesa* was also used to pay fines for many things including stealing property or committing adultery. If the guilty person did not pay the fine he could be killed by the victim. They preferred to settle disputes peacefully if possible. To the Choiseulese, *kesa* was everything; a man who had no *kesa* was a nobody and a weak man. A man's wealth consisted of land and its improvements and *kesa*.

An ordinary girl formerly was worth from three to five *kesa* as bride price. The daughter of a big man was sometimes worth considerably more because of the potential value of the possible relationship with her father. There is bargaining in determining the bride price, with the bride's parents setting the price and the groom's parents offering less. The price goes to her parents and is not divided among her relatives. The bride's parents present baked pig and taro to the groom's parents at a later time after the receipt of the *kesa*. The bride's mother is given one *ziku* (a shell bracelet) or *kesa* to pay for the nourishment of the girl as a baby. In the past *kesa* was highly meaningful, and giving a woman in marriage was one way to get *kesa*. Normally a portion is paid when they agree on the price, and the balance of the *kesa* is paid at the end of a one to four month-probationary period. If they find they are not matched, they separate, and the deposit money is refunded.

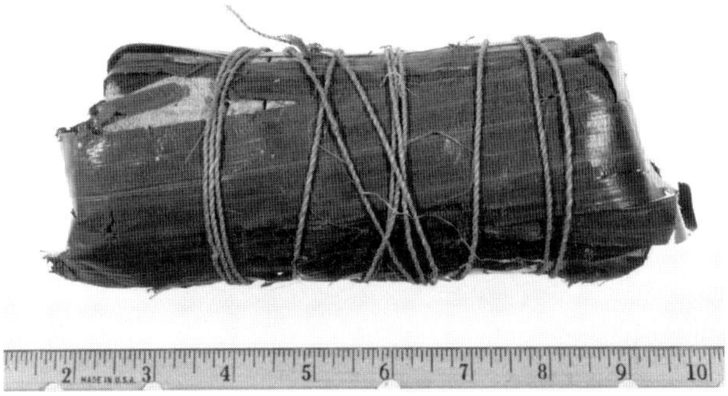

Unit of Three Kesa

The Choiseul Council established that one *kesa* was worth three Australian pounds, and the standard bride price was three *kesa* (nine pounds). The natives who have become Methodists or Seventh Day Adventists are forbidden from paying or receiving bride price. The Catholics are free to pay and receive bride price. The payment of bride price gave the husband exclusive sexual rights over the woman as well as primary claim to the possession of his children by her and rights to her productive labor. She retained her social identity.

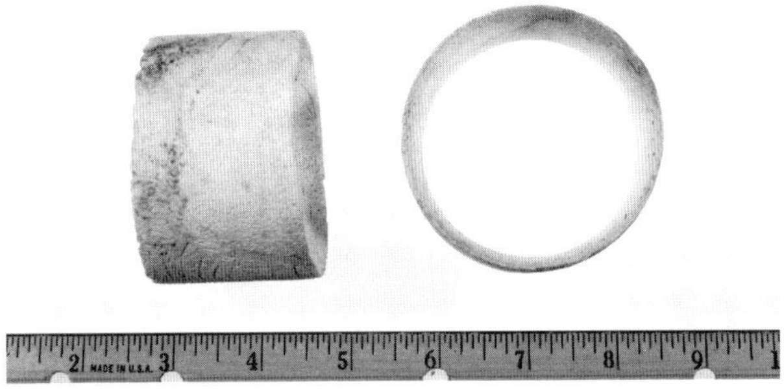

Kesa

Kelo transactions were the most important and prestigious form of giving or receiving *kesa*. *Kelo* was a feast-giving during which *kesa* was exchanged in a competitive manner. If a man built a canoe for another man, he might receive payment at a *kelo*. If a father died before his end of the exchange was completed his son inherited his father's debts. Men tried to come out ahead and therefore profit in all *kesa* exchanges. Just participating in a *kelo* even if you made no profit was better than never participating and being called a "no account man." Past activity as well as *kesa* on hand helped determine a man's prestige. The exact amount of *kesa* held by an individual or a group is kept secret, and the *kesa* is normally stored in several different places so it cannot all be stole at once. The hiding places were normally shown to sons and especially trusted members of the group. It was an honor to be shown the hiding places. Because it was a high value money, it was not used for everyday transactions. Bride price and forming alliances for purposes of vengeance were its main uses. The highest value *kesa* was called *kalusape* and was worth 20 *tuekesa*. The next highest value was called *kalumiinava* and was worth 10 *tuekesa*. The other values are: *kalulomma*, worth five *tuekesa*; *putakavaiti*, worth four *teskesa*; *putapossa* worth three *tuekesa*; and *putakakere*, worth two *tuekesa*. A perfect *kesa* consisted of nine *kesa* that could be in a stack all balanced and level. All must be the same diameter. (See Scheffler)

KETE KOME

Baelelea North Malaita, Solomon Islands

This piece was made of shell rings fashioned from clam shells and was used on Baelelea, North Malaita Island. The strings of shell rings came in pairs and were worn around the leg just below the knee by warriors in pre-battle ceremonial dances. The dances were to gain the

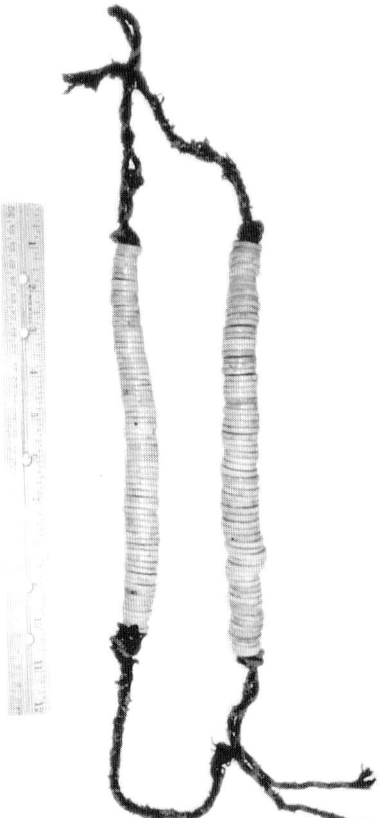

Kete Kome

support of the warrior's ancestors. All pieces were made and used prior to the 1900s. The shell disks are from 5/8″ to 1″ in diameter. (Per. comm. Betty)

KETTLEDRUM - See *Kyee-Zee* and *Moko* and *Sycee* - Kettledrum

KEY MONEY - See Knife money and Lotus root money.

KHASU

Africa

Large hoes were worth four yards of calico or one shilling. (See Quiggin p. 98)

KILINDI - See Ring Money and Kissi penny

KILONDA

Zaire, Africa

Songye or Tetela people. These axes or hatchets, having blades with special designs and inlaid with copper or brass, were used as money. The term kilonda is the generic name for iron. (See Hurst p. 38.)

KIN - See Ring Money

KINA MOKA

Papua New Guinea

It consisted of a thin board, oval in shape, a thin layer of resin, a *kina* shell in the center, and bamboo sticks next to the shell. The resin was covered with red ochre, and a cloth cord was attached. The *kina* shell was used as money by itself. The *kina moka* is used as money and bride price by several tribes in large area of Western Highlands Province and some parts of Enga Province. They were used in the ceremony of Muga (*Moka*) consisting of the laying out of the mounted *kena* (*kina*) in four long rows and the process of presenting the shells. They were only presented in lots of 10, called a *moga*. The record of these transactions was recorded on an *omak*. All items were presented and not lent. It was hoped that the other party would not be able to present an equal or greater value at a future time and thus lose power, with the first presenter gaining the power or influence.

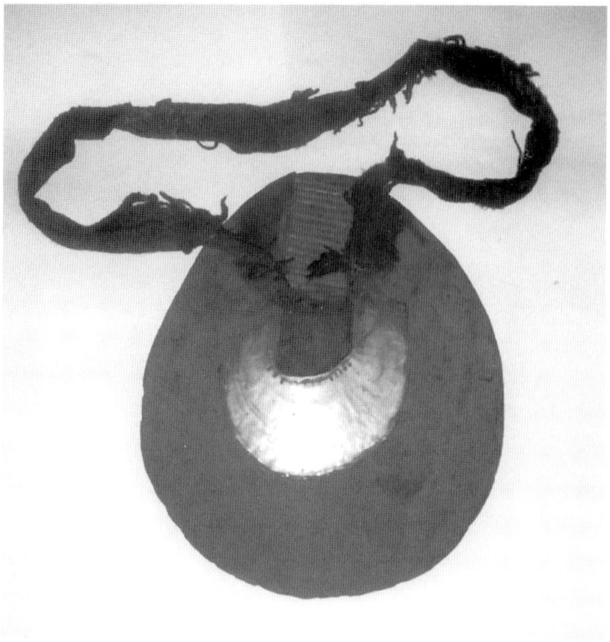

Kina Moka

KINA SHELL MONEY

Papua New Guinea

The gold lip shell (*Pinctada maxima*) is called *kina*. It was used to purchased brides. The shells come in many sizes and widths. They have been in use for only 100 to

Kina Shell

Kina Shell - Front

Kina Shell - Back

200 years. When Europeans first came to the highlands, only the very rich and powerful men had whole shells. *Kina* was the preferred item of trade. The shells came primarily from Manus Island and Thursday Island in the Torres Strait. In the Arawi district the natives would dive for the shells, which were known as *ewul* in 1925. They were rubbed with a stone until perfectly clean, which usually took about two days, and a loop of plaited yellow fiber was attached through small holes drilled at the ends. (See Chinnery p. 23) They were valued by size and the condition of the shell skin. The best are large with ruddy color. They were most prized in the Mt. Hagen area. In the Sepik area, pieces have nassa shell decorations attached at the end holes. Women wear *kina* shells as decoration and as a display of wealth. The Wiru tribe exchanges center around life cycle payments. Pearl shells were also given at ceremonial pig kills. They were considered as male wealth. The red pearl shells were considered very valuable. The shells came into circulation when they were yellow, and they were soon rubbed with red ochre powder. This process was repeated over a period of time, which increased the value of the shell. At one time a *kina* was normally worth a small pig. The *kina* was legal tender into the 1960s at a fixed exchange rate of 12 shillings per pair. The shell was the center piece in the *kina moka*. If a man gave a very valuable red pearl shell to someone, he would receive much prestige. A person can attach a marker to his pearl shell, such as a special knot in the string attached or the bristled end of a pig tail. These pearl shells recorded debts, deaths and exchanges, and the more markers and knots a pearl shell had, the more valuable it was. The bottom edge of the pearl shell crescent is called the *pouwe* and many times was coated with white tree sap which turns black. Red ochre powder called *lokeo* was then rubbed in, and the band turned a dark red. A pattern may be incised into the shell under the top rim. Some pearl shells are given names. *Yobo maiyo* is a very valuable kind of pearl shell. It can be owned only by a group of individuals and not by only one person. It was not used to pay bride price or death payments as other pearl shells were. It was used only to exchange land or for alliances. The pearl shell is smaller than an ordinary pearl shell but is better quality because it is more symmetrical and has a finer and smoother skin. The shell is mounted on a stiff board of bark cloth, and a white sliver of pearl shell is mounted at the bottom. The bark cloth is decorated with Job's tears and painted with various combinations of black, white, yellow and red. A woven vine edge and special leaves are attached where the bark cloth joins the pearl shell at the two sides. In Mount Hagen a good price for a girl was 10 gold lip (*kina*) shells and 10 pigs. A low price was five *kina* shells and five pigs. All her relatives received the bride price,

not only her father. Sometimes a girl would bring 10 pigs and five bailer shells or five pigs and five *kina* shells. The amount would vary by quantity and item. The installment plan was also available where the boy agreed to work for her parents until the amount was paid. The ceremony started with the girl's father killing a pig, smearing the grease on the girl and taking her to the boy's home. The ceremony was solemnized with the feast of the cooked pig. The girl's father gave the boy three or four pigs after he had received the bride price. They were now married. Before 1933, a bride price was normally two or three pieces of gold lip shell (not whole ones), a cowry shell necklace, at least one pig and some bird of paradise feathers. Father Ross stated that in 1935, one ordinary *kina* shell would buy a pig weighing 200 pounds. Within 10 years even a superior *kina* shell would buy only a small pig. The green snail shell would no longer be accepted. The *kina* shell was a common measure of value in trading for other items as well as a medium of exchange. In 1925 a ball of red earth (used for body paint) the size of a coconut was worth one *kina* shell. One *kina* shell (gold-lip shell) was also worth a three-foot string of dog teeth. (See Chinnery p. 24) In 1950 a native returning from indentured labor could buy a large gold lip shell or full size axe at a trade store for a one pound note. The pound notes, as well as coins, were considered as valuables and not considered as a medium of exchange in the 1950s. The *kina* shell, a pig and a bailer shell were roughly equal in value. In 1947 a good price for a girl was 10 *kina* shells and 10 pigs. As late as 1968 *kina* were still used as currency in the Southern Highlands. In the 1930s the value of *kina* shells dropped dramatically due to the large influx of shells from the white prospectors. Initially the natives only knew the finished *kina* shells but later saw the unfinished shells and preferred them to the finished shells. The Enga valued an uncut *kina* shell as worth two cut shells. Ten kina may be in some general way equal to a woman. Formerly three dog-teeth head-bands served the same purpose. It is also called *euk* and can have an "ear" called *kinan*. The shells should pass through a minimum of three new owners before being offered to a previous owner. A recipient has the right to return a shell at any time in the future if he feels the shell is not an acceptable payment. The central highlands used the larger *kina*, while areas such as the Simbu, Kuma, and Melpa used the smaller *kina*. (See Healey p. 193) In the 1960s and 1970s marriage payments were in part large wooden display boards decorated with many *kina* shells and some feathers at the edges of the board. I saw the boards in use in 1973 while on a trip to Papua New Guinea. By 1985 the shells were no longer of value or a form of money.

On Lake Kutubu the shells have a finely woven band for the neck which has been reddened with ochre. The

Kina Shell

Black Edge Pearl Shell

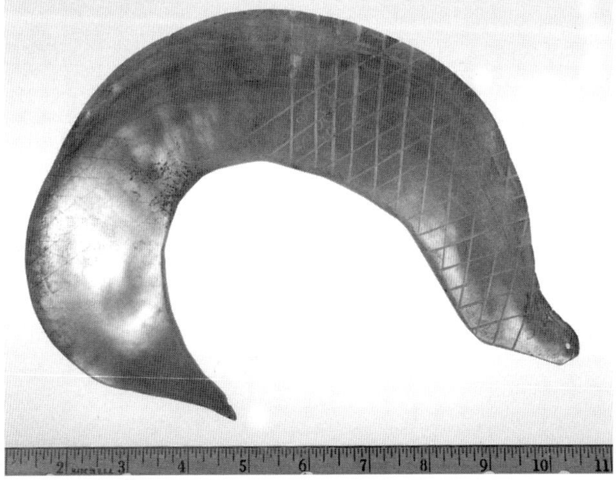

Kina Shell

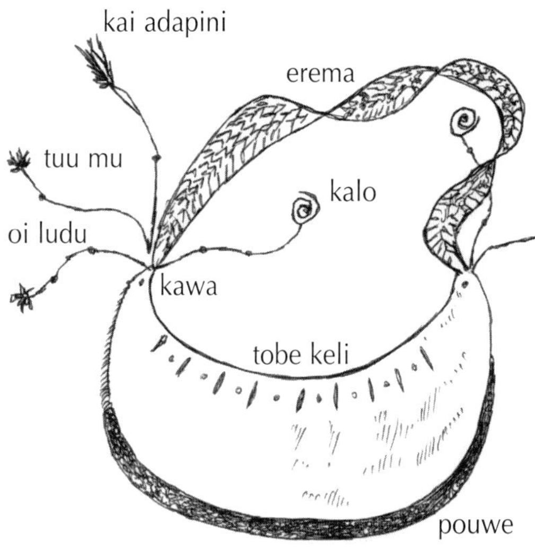

Kina Shell with Names

Kiringi

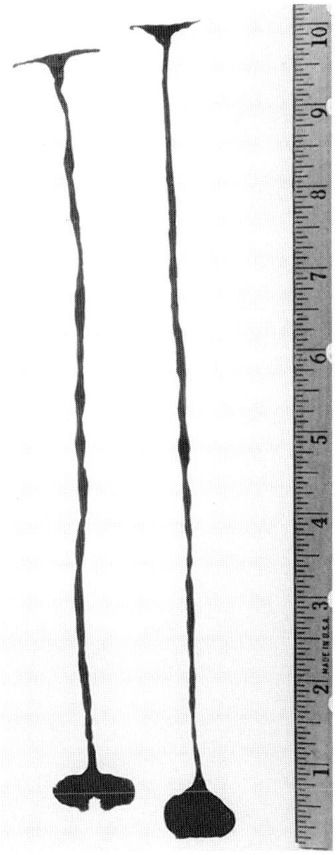

Kissi Penny

shells are normally kept wrapped in voluminous wrappings. Some of the shells are broken and mended, and they still retain some of their value. (See Clark)

The Wola people use *kina* as money, and they distinguish between different kinds of pearl shell. The very fine pearl shells they give names to and do not exchange. Instead, they hide them away. Ordinary shells are regularly exchanged and used as money. The men also repair broken shells using a stick with tree resin on the back of the shell. When the Australians increased the supply of *kina*, the people no longer valued them so highly, and at present they have a low value. (See Sillitoe p.145-147) The *kina* is compared with the human body. The tips of the shell are known as its *kawa*, or legs, and the iridescent surface of *maiyo* with its brilliance enhanced by ochre is called *kepene*, or skin. The back of the shell is called *tepe* and is associated with the stomach area and is also identified with female qualities. The rim, or *pouwe*, is analogous with semen and is associated with the male colors of red and black. It was coated with white tree sap which turned black after setting. Sometimes an incised pattern is made under the tip rim of the crescent. This pattern is said to represent the larval stage of a certain beetle which is yellow at that stage of its life cycle. (See Clark p. 317)

KING MANILLA - See Manilla - King

KIRINGI

Africa

This African snail shell string was from Ponthierville but was used by the Wasongola on the Lualaba. It was a bunch of 16 strings of shells worth 16 francs. Later, when it was found they could not buy ivory without them, the value rose to as high as 25 francs per string. (See Quiggin p. 49.)

KIRKUB

Torres Straits

Nose sticks made of various shells were used in trade. (See Haddon Vol. 4 p. 24)

KISSI PENNY

Sierra Leone, Liberia, and French Guinea

They are also called *Kilindi, gitzi* and *ghisi.* It is a "coin with soul" (if broken a witch doctor must repair and restore the soul). The kissi penny was worth about two cents. It was used by four African tribes: Kissi, Loma, Kpelle and Bande. The iron was smelted by the Mandingoes in the villages of Bakpapa and Nemisola in Guinea. They were first used in 1900, and until the 1920s they were the only money in the area. In 1918, 30 or 40 bundles of 20 pieces each would buy a cow, and

60 or 80 bundles would buy a wife. As late as 1915, 100 or 200 bundles would buy a slave. Two Kissi pennies were worth a yard-long piece of striped country cloth. In 1919 a one franc coin was worth 40 to 50 Kissi pennies. In 1940 Kissi pennies were no longer accepted for the payment of taxes or fines. At present they are not used as money but continue to be used for cult rituals. (1970) Modern pieces exist. (See Quiggin p.92)

KITOMA - See Kula.

KLILT

Pelew Islands

Quiggin (p. 119-120) states that the earliest reference to rings in Micronesia is the picturesque description of the "Order of the Bone" by Captain Wilson of the Antelope, who was one of the first Europeans to make a protracted (though involuntary) landing on the Pelews in 1783. The ring, or *klilt,* was of bone, the atlas vertebrae of the Halicore dugong, but there were rings of stone and shell as well, used as currency. A century later Kubary dispelled much of the picturesque mystery surrounding the *klilt.* The dugong was rare in the Pelews, and a chiefly prerequisite, but the "bone" was not, in his time, the insignia of rank, or even a special mark of honor. It was only a valued ornament which could be worn by anyone who could afford the high price.

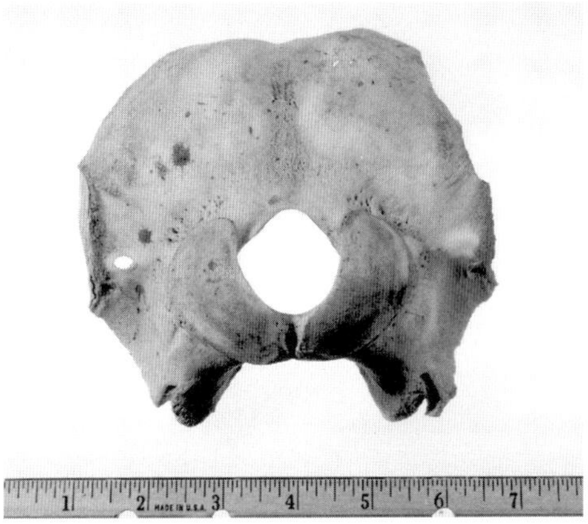

Klilt

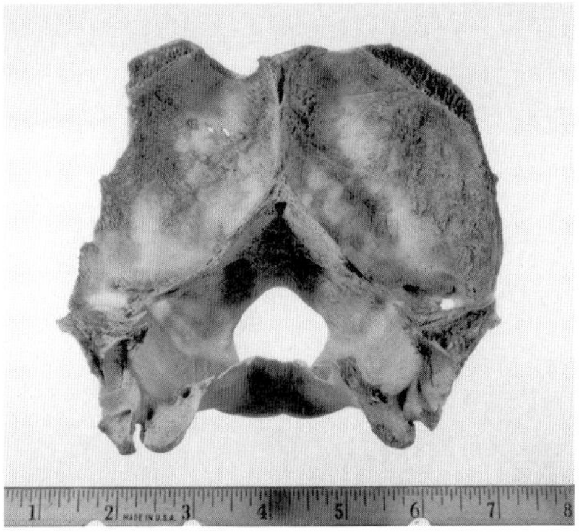

Klilt - Back

KNIFE MONEY

Many of the African knives cannot be defined as either weapon, ornaments, status symbols, or currency with any degree of certainly. Most knives exhibit two or more of these classes. During a period of time many knives would pass from one of these classes to another. In many cases the knives started as weapons and because of their high value or extraordinary workmanship became primarily status symbols or currency. A knife that had a very high value would not be used as a weapon because it could then be damaged or lost and much value would be lost to the owner. Later some of these knives would be made without sharp edges, from soft metal like brass or copper, or of a size or shape that would not allow the knife to be used as a weapon. Most knives seem to have some or most of these properties. Many of these items were used as money before the coming of Europeans to the area. The items were used to buy slaves, get married, become a member of a secret society, or for birth and death ceremonies. Following are a list of some of the knives that have some claim to use as currency or high value status knives. Because opinion plays an important part in defining these knives, experts do not all agree on the uses many of these knives are claimed to have.

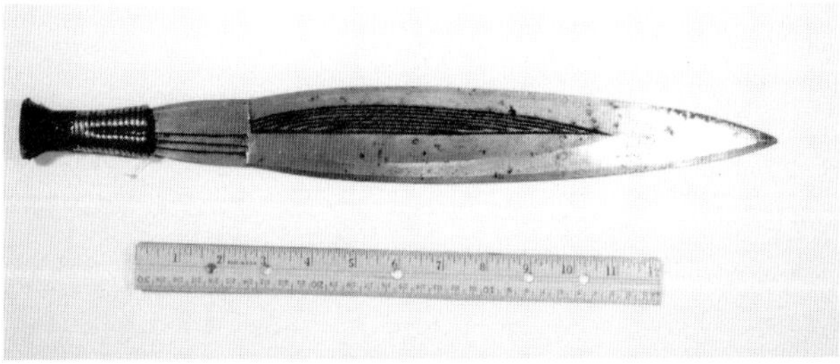

Azande Tribe Knife Money

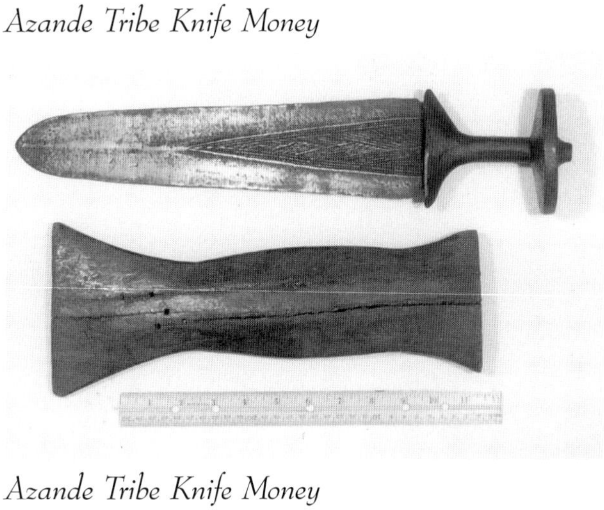

Azande Tribe Knife Money

Azande Tribe Knife Money

Africa, Azande tribe

Used as weapons as well as for bride price. A bridegroom might give 40 blades to the father of the bride. (See Fischer p.55-63)

Africa, Azande tribe

These knives were also known as sabers. There are many different varieties. (See Fischer p. 60-61)

Africa, Bangala

The iron execution knife was highly decorated and used as a store of value and a limited form of money. (See execution knife, Bangala.)

Africa, Banza tribe

These iron throwing knives were probably used as currency. (See Fischer p. 98-99)

Africa, Benge tribe

Known as the Mobenge in the past, this tribe lives in Zaire and produced this forged iron ceremonial saber. The protruding triangular piece was used to tie the saber to the waist. This weapon was probably used as a currency. (See Ballarini p. 80)

Africa, Bwaka tribe

Iron throwing knives like these are believed to have been used as currency. See Fischer p. 91-94

Dahomey (Benin), The Fon, an Ewe tribe

The iron knife has the design of a lion in the outline of part of the blade. The coat of arms was a stylized lion. It was a status weapon because it was only carried on festive occasions and only had a dull blade which precluded its use as a weapon. (See Zirngibl p. 18.)

Africa, Gaboon, Kota/Fang tribe

The bird's head knife is actually an iron throwing knife which served as a form of money. (See Fischer p. 186-189)

Africa, Konda tribe

Collectors now classify all of these knives as currency knives. Because of the branches of knives on the knife the pieces could not have been used as a weapon. (See Zirngibl p. 98-99) (Fischer p. 169-175)

Africa, Konda tribe

The Konda and Mongo use this forged iron knife as currency and in dances. The unusual shapes show that the African producers made the knives to satisfy the needs of the European buyers instead of the native needs. (See Ballarini p. 103)

Africa, Kuba tribe

This knife (*ikula*), meaning knife of peace, replaced the legendary *shongo* throwing knife which was banned by the king. The blades are found in steel, copper, aluminum, bronze, and wood. Many served only an ornamental or monetary function. The handles are particularly well designed and ornamented including the end of the handle. In 1907-1909 the Torday English expedition to the Congo found that this knife would cost 5,000 shells. (See Zirngibl p. 61 and Ballarini p. 91 and Fischer p. 148-159)

Africa, Kundu tribe

The knife was used during ceremonies as a symbol of rank and was probably used as a currency. The forged iron double-edged blade has engraved lines vertically up the center with a flat end and two points to each side. (See Ballarini p. 67)

Africa, Kundu tribe

The Konda and Ngata groups, as well as the Kundu which belong to the larger Mongo group, used this knife in tribal, ceremonies as well as a symbol of rank. It was also probably used as a currency. (See Ballarini p. 68)

Africa, Kusu tribe

The steel pommel knives of the Mbole tribe are similar to this knife. This knife has a smaller iron or copper butt. The impact force was quite large, even though the butt seems small. (See Fischer p. 123)

Africa, Lobala tribe

In the northern part of Zaire this double sided forged iron blade with a wood hilt was a ceremonial knife. It was probably used as a form of currency. There are several styles of this knife. (See Ballarini p.53-54)

Africa, Mangbetu tribe

See Trumbash

Africa, Mbole tribe

The base of this double-sided forged iron blade is a forged iron prism that is very large and heavy. Some experts think the knife was used to kill by dropping it from a tree, and the weight of the iron base would drive the blade deep into the victim. Some feel it was also used as currency, but I have not seen verification of this theory. Earlier it was known as the Stanley-Pool Knife. (See Ballarini p. 70), (See Fischer p. 120-122)

Azande Tribe Knife Money

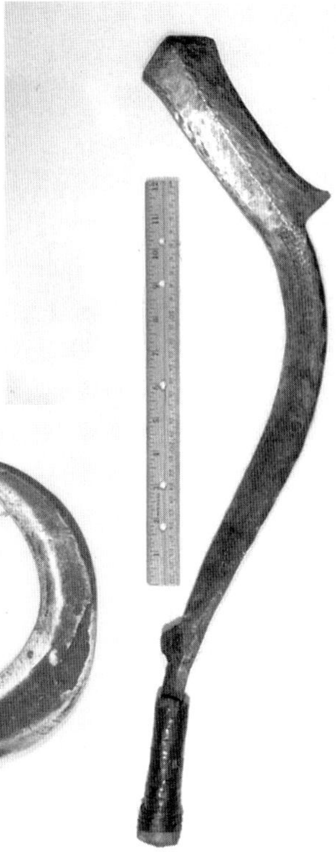

Banza Tribe Throwing Knife

Banza Tribe Throwing Knife

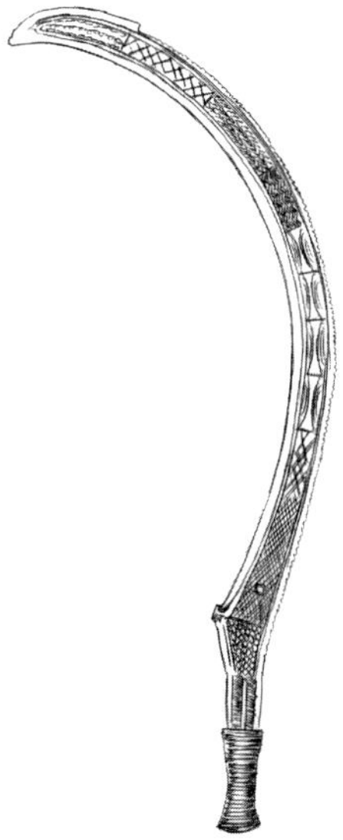

Benge Tribe Knife

Bwaka Tribe Throwing Knife

Bwaka Tribe Throwing Knife

Bwaka Tribe Throwing Knife

Konda Tribe Knife

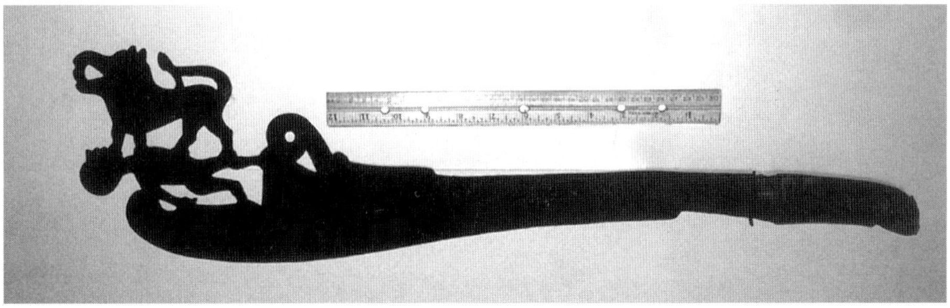

Ewe Tribe Knife

Africa, Mongo tribe

This double-edged forged iron knife was a ceremonial knife and as such probably was used as a currency. (See Zirngibl p. 65)

Africa, Ndjembo tribe

The influence of the Ngala execution knife is seen at the upper part of the knife. There are several varieties of this knife. The chieftain's knife could only be used in a symbolic way. It had no practical use. (See Fischer p. 113-115)

Africa, Ngala tribe

This forged iron knife was used during the ceremonial occasion of an execution of a captured prisoner. One type was also known as a Bangala execution knife. The Ngbaka women wore them in their dances and 20 of them were a wedding dowry price. There are several varieties. See execution knife - Bangala. (See Ballarini p.57-58), (Fischer p. 109-112)

Africa, Ngombe tribe

The double-sided forged iron knife has a large ball covered with animal fur, and it is said to contain magic substances. The scabbard is covered with leather that is sewed on in a particular way. (See Ballarini p. 59-60)

Africa, Poto tribe

Several varieties of the double-edged forged iron blades were used as ceremonial knives. Most have copper or brass winding on the handle. Some have balls covered with fur at the end of the handle. There are many varieties. (See Ballarini p. 61)

Africa, Topoke tribe

This is another example of a double-sided forged iron knife that was used as a ceremonial knife and probably served as currency. (See Ballarini p. 71)

Africa, Yakoma tribe

The knives come in a variety of shapes with both iron, brass and copper winding on the handle. It is believed they were used as currency. (See Fischer p. 78-79)

Africa, Zande tribe

The tribe made many kinds of throwing knives and daggers. An explorer visiting the tribe in 1864 stated that 30 pieces of iron was the bride price, and the iron was also used to buy slaves. See Azande tribe (See Ballarini p. 81-86)

Bird's Head - Kota Tribe

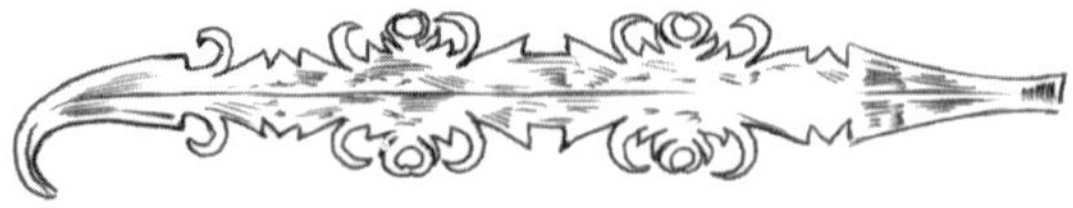

Konda Tribe Knife

Kuba Tribe Knife

Kundu Tribe Knife

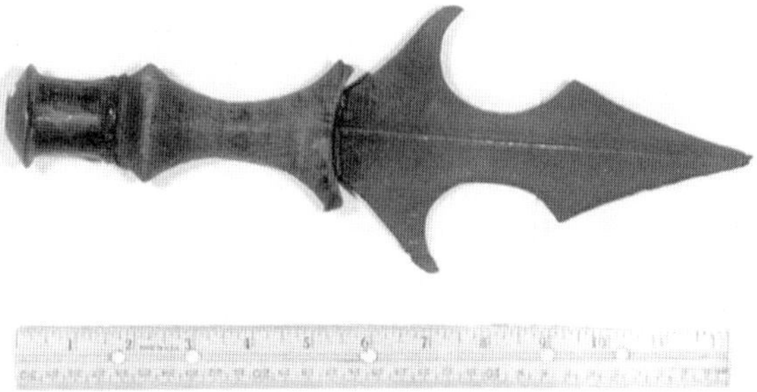

Kusu Tribe Knife

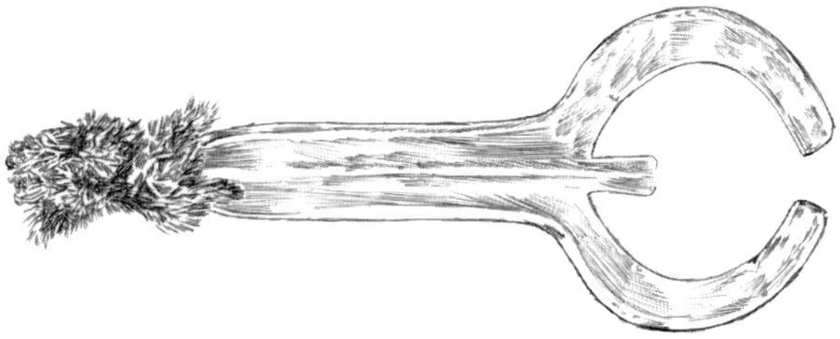

Lobala Tribe Knife

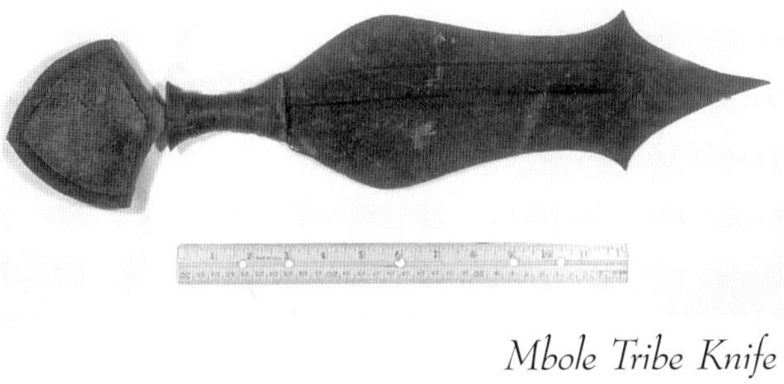

Mbole Tribe Knife

Mongo Tribe Knife

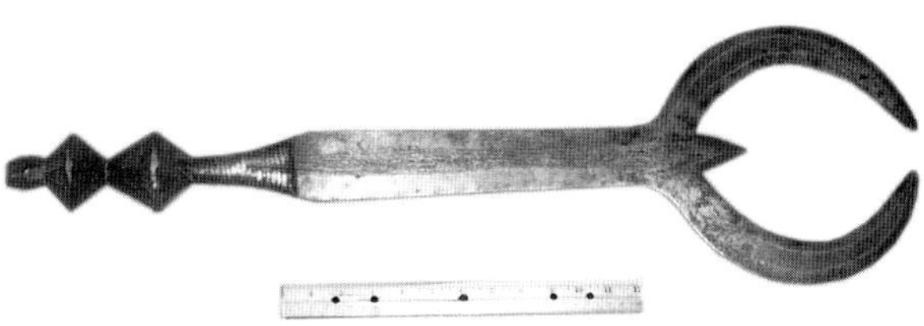

Ndjembo Tribe Knife

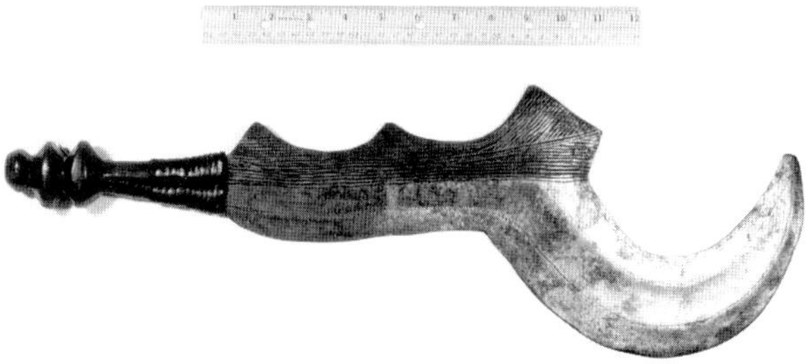

Ngala Tribe - Bangala Execution Knife

Ngombe Tribe Knife

Topoke Tribe Knife

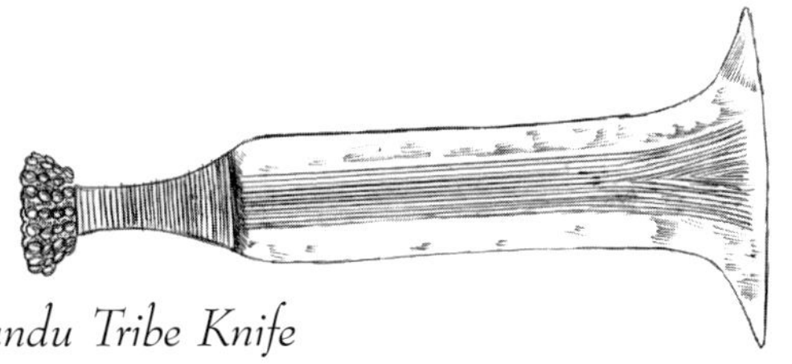

Kundu Tribe Knife

Africa, Zulu tribe

Brass wire bindings cover part or all of the wood handle. This former war hatchet later was used at dance festivals and probably as currency. (See Fischer p. 197-199)

Africa, Zaire

Prestige objects like this knife have been considered as currency by many. This iron knife belonged to chiefs and was used for social control. (See Fischer #197)

Africa, Northern Zaire, Ngbaka people

Travelers coming up the Zaire River exchanged beads, wire and cloth for soft iron blades which were used as currency in eastern Zaire. (See Blackmun p. 40.)

Africa, Zande

Copper blades with copper-wrapped handles made by the Boa (Ababua, Babwa) and the Binja were most likely used as currency knives, according to Zirngibl (p. 80). Most Zande knives including those with iron or steel blades were primarily ornaments or currency.

China, 500 B.C.- 23 A.D.

Small cast bronze inscribed pieces called *dao*, razor, bill-hook, or sword money were used in China. Dao (formerly *tao)* means knife. The knives are considered early barter currency by Ramsden (p.12). There are five main types:

1) *Qi*; large knives of Ch'i principality were first produced about 675-500 B.C. An old legend that may not be true says that Duke Huan of Qi in about 679-675 B.C. issued metal knives as money because his soldiers did not like the use of the current copper ring money. The earliest knives were quite large and well cast of bronze in clay molds. All of these knives have three to six characters on the obverse and one or two characters on the reverse. The common type with nine characters is a fantasy or amulet.

2) Pointed-blade type was introduced around 400-300 B.C. but soon became obsolete. The area of usage expanded during this period to include some of the areas where spade money was formerly used.

3) Straight knives were made in short and long sizes, and all are rare. They were made approximately from 400 B.C. to 250 B.C.

4) Ming knives were made after 400 B.C. They are the last major series and are very common. They have the Chinese character "Ming" on the obverse, with many different reverse inscriptions believed to be accounting terms; some are blank. They have no connection with the Ming Dynasty, which occurred much later. Some

Yakoma Tribe Knife

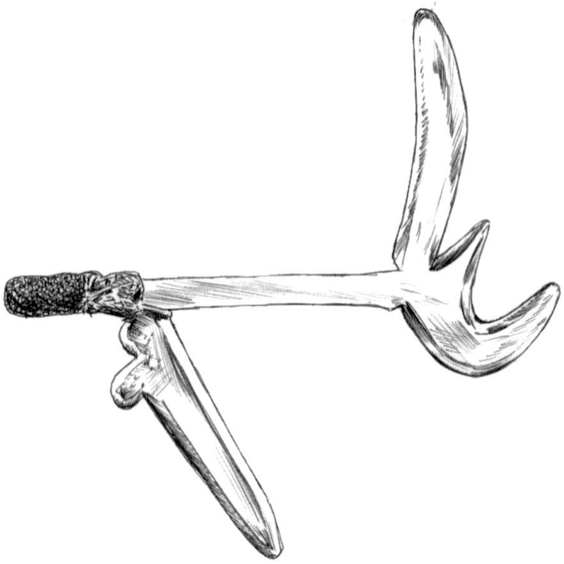

Zande Tribe Throwing Knife

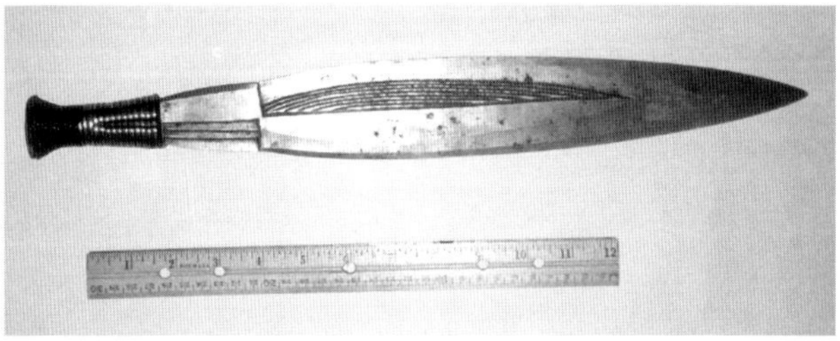

Zande Tribe Knife

Chinese numismatists believe the obverse character is not "Ming" but "Yi" or something else.

5) Key money was made by Wang Mang the Usurper from 7-24 A.D. in two denominations: 500 cash and 5,000 cash. The 5,000 cash key was the only denomination with gold inlaid characters on it. Although round coins had been issued prior to these pieces, Wang Mang admired all classical Chinese items and issued ancient-style spade money followed by this modified style of knife money. In 23 A.D. he was overthrown, and this form of money was terminated.

Congo

Bapoto tribe. Decorated iron knife (some with fur balls). Used as money. 3 1/2" x 24" (See Schulman p.38) (See *Mimboss, Pinga, Trumbash, Woshele*)

United States

Indians used obsidian and jasper in the form of knives both for ceremonial purposes and as money. The large knives, up to 15 inches, were used only for ceremonial purposes, while the pieces about six inches in length were used as money and were worth $2.50 each. (See Hodge p. 102.)

KO - See nko.

KOBAN - See Plate Money

KOFU

Kwaio, Solomon Islands

Shell money consisting of small gray cone shell beads was manufactured on the island. The beads were made by gathering the shells on the beach and making each shell into only one bead. A string of *kofu* would buy enough raw shells to make a string four times as long. It is perceived as "Kwaio money" and anyone can make it. The beads are strung on weak fiber so that short lengths can easily be broken off for small purchases. It is used to purchase everything and is very liquid. There are standard prices in the market for items like betel nut, taro, lime and pigs. It is also used in bride price and most important feasts. (See Akin p. 106-107)

KOKO - See Rice

KOKONON

New Ireland

The shell money is make of disks two to four mm diameter. The shells are dark brown with reddish tints. (See Lewis p. 20-21)

Zulu Tribe Knife

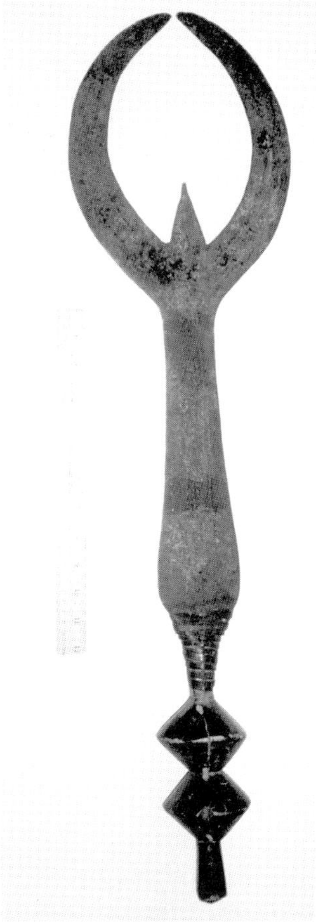

Chief's Prestige Knife

Chi Large Knife

Pointed Knife

KOKONON LULUAI

New Ireland

The beads are white disks with alternate black seeds. Strings of the beads were also attached to a *manun.* A *manum* consists of a pendant of a large reddish black seed, somewhat kidney-shaped, opened at the base to allow for making holes for fastening the attached ornaments. (See Lewis p. 21-22)

KOLA-NUT

Africa

This nut was traded to the Mossi with a unit of 100 kola-nuts being worth 500 to 800 cowries with the going price as high as 4,000 to 5,000 in times of shortage. (See Thurnwald p. 256)

KONGA - See Boloko

KOSO

Bougainville

It was the generic name for the more valuable types of native money such as *mauai* and *kuriri.* All this money was made of *tridacna, spondylus,* or mollusc shell. *Koso* was also the name of a fathom of the largest and least rounded white mollusc disks and had a value of 10 manuai. Also see *mauai.*

KPINGA - See throwing knife

KRIS

Malay

This dagger was made from iron and thought to have many powers and to bring good luck. Many have a squiggled or wavy blade and a handle ornamented with ivory and inlay. Many also have decorated scabbards. The old ones are highly valued. They were a limited form of money and were used in bride price. Beware of modern counterfeits. (See Quiggin p. 257)

KROO - See Palm Oil

KUDATAMA

Japan, 1,500 years ago

Small, cylindrical, crystal, agate or jade beads were used as a limited form of money. (See Quiggin p. 249)

KUE

Australia

The kue is an elaborate ceremonial exchange of gifts between the bridegroom and his relatives on the one hand, and the bride and her relatives on the other. *Kue* is not expected to be made until a few years after

Straight Knife

Ming Knife

Key Knife - 5,000 cash with Gold Inlay

Bapoto Tribe Knife

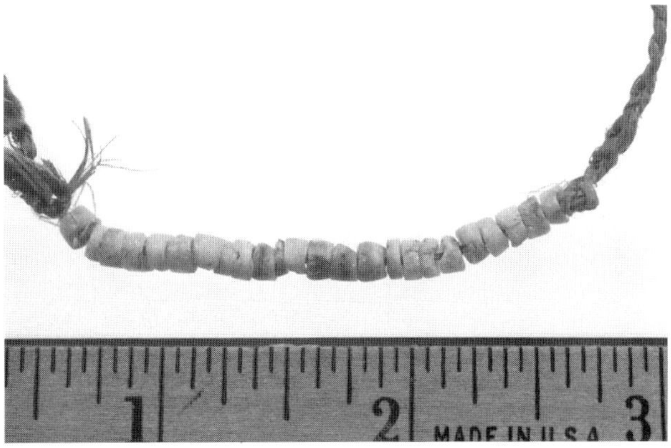

Kofu

Kris - Several Kinds

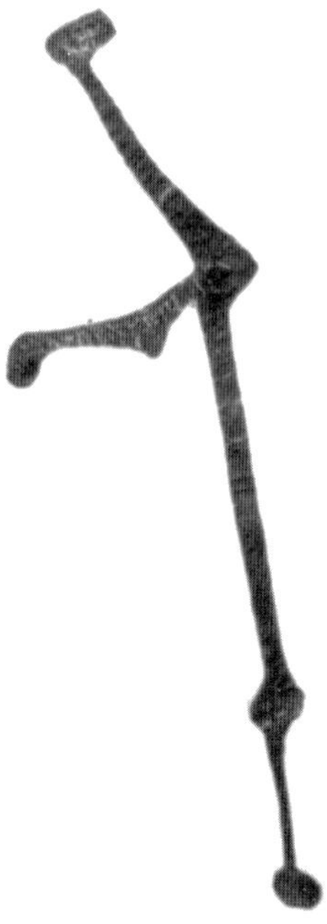

Kul

marriage when a man has several children. (See Stanner p. 458-468)

KUKUMALI - See KULA.

KUL

Africa, Ngama tribe

An iron throwing knife that was unsuitable as a weapon but was used as money. (See Schaedler p. 321)

KULA RING

Description

The Kula is a form of alliance by traditional ceremonial trading and exchange of extensive inter-tribal character, in public, in a closed circuit of islands in the Pacific consisting of the Trobriand Islands and the Massim district of Papua New Guinea. In its simplest form it is a gift exchange of white arm shells (*mwali*) and red shell necklaces (*bagi* or *soulava*). The Kula trade consists of a series of periodic overseas expeditions which link the various island groups. The Kula exchange has always been a gift followed by a counter-gift. It is never barter, and there is no haggling. The ring also functions as a network for trading food and raw materials. The amount of and sophistication of gifts demonstrates the donor's wealth and greatness. It embraces the whole of Trobriand cultural life from birth to death. The trade items take from two to 10 years to make the complete circle. All the main transactions are public and ceremonial and follow definite rules. The Kula items (*vaygu'a*) are never used or considered as a medium of exchange or as a measure of value when in the Kula. They exist only to circulate within the Kula. When the items are owned or removed from the Kula, they can then be considered as money and a store of wealth. No native at Malinowski's time had any idea how the Kula ring worked or what its scope was; they mainly knew their part and not much else about the remainder of the ring. A principle of Kula is that it is a gift repaid after an interval of time with a counter-gift. The equivalent is determined by the giver, and disagreements as to value cannot be enforced nor can any haggling take place; there are customary and usual ways to bid for a particularly valuable piece. Any matching of gifts is in quality and not in quantity. The Kula is a constantly changing system that continues to this day. The Kula has existed for at least 500 years, and the valuables are known to have existed for over 2000 years.

Anthropologist Bronislaw Malinowski spent from 1910 to 1918 in New Guinea and North Melanesia doing research which later resulted in Argonauts of the Western Pacific. This book of more than 500 pages describes the Kula. Even it is not complete or even completely accurate as Jerry and Edmund Leach discussed in their book in 1983, The Kula, New Perspectives on Massim Exchange, which also contains more than 500 pages.

Giving gifts takes place at the home base receiving when abroad. The area is called Melanesia, a vast area northeast of and including Papua New Guinea. The ring is divided into the northern section and the southern section. The northern section covers the Trobriands, the Marshall Bennets, Woodlark Island and Panamonti. The southern section covers the Amphletts, Tubetube and Dobu. The area is 3,300 miles long and 700 miles wide, almost as large as the continental United States. There are about 40 islands in the ring. Leach listed the Kula communities in the 1970s as follows: N. Amphletts on Nabwageta, Gumawana, and Wamea, Basima, Bubibud, Bwaiowa, Bwanabwana on Koyagugau, Tubetube (main center of Southeastern branch), Naluwaluwali, Kwalaiwa, Dobu, Duau, Gawa, Iwa, Kaileuna, on Kaileuna Island, Mnuwata Island, Kuyawa Island, Kilivila on N.E. Kiriwina, Kulatanawa on N.W. Kiriwina, Kummwagea on S.W. Kitava, Kwatoita, Kweawata, Lalela on S.E. Kitava, Nasikwabu, Nayem on Madau and N.W. Woodlark, S.E. Normandy, Okabulula on N. Kitava (every piece of value had to pass through Kitava), Sanaroa, Sinaketa on S.E. Kiriwana,Tewara, Tewatewa, Kitai, and Anagusa, Vakuta, Wamwan on Central Woodlark, Yanaba, Yeguma.

Island Life

The Trobrianders are matrilineal. They trace descent and settle inheritance along the line of the mother instead of the father as we do. The child belongs to the clan and village of its mother. The people are excellent gardeners and because much of the land is very rich, the people grow about twice the amount of food they can eat. In Malinowski's time the food not eaten was allowed to rot. Yams were an important part of their lives, and special yam houses were built to hold the yams until they were eaten or thrown away because they had rotted. Today surplus food is exported to Europe. About half of the natives' working life is spent in the garden. It must be remembered that all of the people in the Kula do not live or act like each other, and there are many different lifestyles and outlooks among the different societies. In many of these islands chastity is not practiced, and the unmarried become initiated into sexual life at a very early age.

Social Aspects of Kula

During the Kula expedition, trade is an important part of the activity. At ceremonies many of the Kula items are worn by someone other than the item's owner. A person in the Kula would have a number of partners that they have for a long time, and sometimes they have them for life. Common people have only a few partners, while important people like chiefs have many partners. Partners are obtained in a defined, regulated way. Partners act as friends and have a number of mutual duties and obligations. They have a special bond. A partner never keeps a valuable for a long time, as it results in a loss of reputation. A Kula community consists of an island or group of islands that go together on big overseas expeditions and act as one body, performing their magic in common and having common leaders. A person can become a Kula partner when he has passed the adolescence. He must have status and rank and know the magic of the Kula. He must also be in possession of a Kula valuable that was gotten in an accepted, traditional manner. A partner does not, however, trade with his Kula partner. Men often try to keep track of valuables they once owned and try to obtain the same item when it comes around again in from two to 10 years. Kula partners normally trade for life. Properly traded Kula valuables follow a specific path known as keda. At death the one who inherits a valuable also inherits the keda, which is really the exchange position the dead person had. When the canoe voyagers arrived at their destination, they gave their partners landing gifts called *pari*. They included small objects such as a comb, lime stick or lime pot. Occasionally a high-value gift was also included, such as a stone blade or good lime spoon. Solicitory gifts were used for this. The solicitory gifts consisted of the *pokala* (offerings) and *kaributu* (solicitory gift). The *pokala* consisted of pigs, taro, yams or fine bananas. The *kaributu* consisted of *beku* (large axe blades), *bosu* (lime spoons made of whale bone), or *kaipwesi* (belt of *kaloma* shell). Another kind of gift is the *korotomna*. It usually was a *bosu*, and if a man received a *samakupa* (coarse shell string) in the West and also received a minor valuable from his other partner in the East, that minor valuable would be given to the Western partner as the *korotomna* of his necklace. These *bosu* were not, strictly speaking, Kula articles, but they were gifts associated with it. When a death occurs in a Kula area, all Kula activity ceases for a minimum of six months. It must be remembered that comparing of gifts as to value must be considered as a flow over a lifetime instead of as a single event. Haggling and bargaining are not used in Kula. There are regulated and customary ways of bidding for a nice item. The etiquette of the transaction is that the gift is given in an off-hand, abrupt, and almost angry manner and it is received in a nonchalant manner almost with disdain. Normally the item is only placed in easy reach of the recipient and an insignificant member of his following would pick it up. It must be remembered that most areas of the Kula and the ceremonies are filled with witchcraft and sorcery. They believe in flying witches who are women with the power to make themselves invisible and fly through the air. Also they believe in jumping stones that live in the water and lie in wait for sailing canoes. The stones run after the canoes and smash them to pieces.

Kula Preparations

Kula expeditions are scheduled and fixed. Preliminary preparations include building canoes, preparation of the outfit and supplying the expedition. The first part of the Kula which consists of building the canoe, is done in two stages. The first stage includes cutting the tree and shaping the various parts, including carving the canoe prow. These activities are done over a period of several months. The second stage is done over a week or two of intense work by the whole community and consists of piecing together of the parts, making the sail, and painting the canoe. On the overseas expedition there must be two ritual halts. The preliminary halt is to perform magic over the canoes while the second is for magic to aid in the wooing of the Kula partner. The opening gift is called *vaga,* and the closing gift is called *yotile.* They are both ceremonial gifts. It must be understood that the entire circuit does not revolve in a regular procession from one district to the next.

Kula Ceremonies

The men of each island make two overseas expeditions annually. One trip is to receive one kind of valuable and the other trip is to receive the other kind of valuable. A great deal of mythology, ritual and magic are associated with the Kula. Expeditions begin with the participants going single file and silent to the beach for departure in the canoes. The men huddle quietly for a period, after which there is noisy excitement for the unfurling of the sail and launching. At the landing at their destination, the men bathe and adorn themselves on the beach and then march single-file to the village. The *vaga* is the opening gift in the exchange. It must be given spontaneously, and there is no duty to give it, nor can there be pressure to give it. The *basi* is an intermediary gift. The *yotile* is the valuable given in return for the valuable previously received, and it is given under pressure. The partners going to the Kula do not take any Kula valuables as they will be receiving *yotile* from the previous visit when their partners came to their island. They will, in addition to *yotile,* also receive *vaga* so there will always be an imbalance. This delay occurs only on overseas trades and not on internal trades. A gift of food called a *pokala* or a minor valuable called a *kaributu* may be given to obtain a *vaga* gift. The *pokala* is later returned, but not necessarily on an equivalent basis. The *kaributu* is normally considered as part of the *yotile. Pari* gifts (landing gifts) made at Dobu are balanced with farewell gifts called *talo'i* made by the Dobuan hosts. The *talo'i* always exceeds the *pari.* There are departing gifts given to the visiting partners. The gifts are mainly tobacco but can also be betel nut, cassowary or cockatoo feathers, piglets, red banana-fiber shirts or canoe-lashing vines. The Kula cycle still continues to this day. It has adapted to modern improvements and has not died out as many had predicted. Every two or three years a big competitive Kula expedition is held, called a *uvalaku.* On this kind of expedition, all the canoes in the district are expected to participate. It occurs when a special event happens such as when one of the head men has an exceptionally fine pig or high-value object. At the end of the expedition all the gifts are compared and counted. That is why it is called a competitive expedition.

Kula Preparations

The two main Kula articles are the *mwali* (arm shells) and the *bagi* or *soulava* (necklaces). The *mwali* were thought of as female and the *bagi* were male. Associated important Kula items are *samakupa, doga, kaloma, beku,* and *bosu.* Long necklaces of red shell called *bagi* move in a clockwise direction from island to island (see map) while shell armrings called *mwali* move in a counterclockwise direction from island to island. Other items are also exchanged, but these two are the most important. The valuables are called *vaygu'a.* Particularly old and valuable pieces each have their own names. In olden days the *doga* (necklace with a boar's tusk or shell pendant) was almost as important as the *mwali,* and traveled in the same direction. Now it is hardly ever used. A possible reason for this is that the *doga* became more valuable on the mainland of New Guinea and most of the *doga* were drained off and out of the Kula ring. The *bosu* is often not actually a Kula item, but it traveled in the same direction as the *mwali* and it also is not now used much in Kula. Leach estimates from Malinowski's data that at his time there were about 3,000 pairs of arm shells and 3,000 necklaces in circulation. Arm shells now trade as single pieces rather than as pairs as they did in Malinowski's time. Also at that time there were sixty canoes for Kula operations. In the 1870s there were about double the number of canoes in Malinowski's time. To be successful in Kula, a person has to understand the ground rules for Kula and the full range of possibilities in the exchange. There are more arm shells than there are necklaces. No one knows why this has happened nor why arm shells have become unpaired since Malinowski's time. In Malinowski's time Kula gifts were ranked as follows:

1): big arm shells and necklaces
2): small arm shells and necklaces

3): whalebone spatula
4): polished axe blades
5): pigs, yams, and bananas.

Shell valuables in general are called *kitomu* and they may be purchased with yams, pigs, or large quantities of betel. All *bagi* and *mwali* are either *kitoma* or *kunedawesi* valuables. They are *kitoma* if the holder of the item is the owner of the item. Then the item can leave the Kula ring and can be sold for money. They are less likely to follow a *keda*. If the item is *kunedawesi* it is a pure Kula valuable and is not actually owned by the holder of the valuable. It cannot leave the ring nor be sold.

Kula items as money

When Kula items like *mwali* and *bagi* are not included in the Kula ring, they are called *kitom*. This means they are owned by a person and can be sold or used as money in trade and for bride price. *Kitom* can also be shells that have not yet entered the ring, or it might be shells on which all reciprocal claims it have been met. At that time it may be outside of Kula and may be used in a mortuary presentation or land presentation. Many fights result from *kitom* because some of the partners may not feel that all obligations are completed, or an old partner may try to reclaim the item, and because the item was sold out of Kula, it is not possible to reclaim it. Malinowski once said that an item once in Kula was always in Kula. This does not hold today. On Kitava, *mwali* and *bagi* are also used in marriage, acquisition of sorcery and Kula magic, and in canoe presentations. Normally the medium or low value shells are used for these purposes, not the famous ones. On Dobu the groom uses the *mwali* and *bagi* as bride price when the groom does not inform his Kula partner that he is getting a wife — if he did he would not get the Kula pieces from his Kula partner because he would know that they would not be returned quickly. On Sudest bride price is called *vazavo* and normally consists of one *bagi* and two large or ten small greenstone axeblades called *tobotobo*. *Bagi*, *tobotobo* and pigs are also used to pay house builders. Most of the items in Kula are considered money at some time.

Trade and other trade items

An important part of the Kula expedition is the trade that occurs on it. Many items were considered valuable and traded. Canoes, clay pots, wooden dishes, ebony lime pots, turtle-shell earrings, special nose sticks, red ochre, tobacco sticks, pumice stone, and obsidian were used in trade. The islands of Tubetube and the Amphletts are short of food; therefore, others trade food to them. The rich Trobriand Islands must import stone to make axes. The axes are polished with special sand from Fergusson Island. They also import pottery from the Amphletts and sago from Dobu. Sinaketa and Vakuta made red shell disks. Kayleula traded betel nut, sago, pottery, and turtle-shell for their produce. Misima built canoes. Sinaketa received arm shell from Luba, Kulumata, and Kiriwina. Boyowa, the Amphletts and Dobu trade necklaces to Sinaketa. The purchase of several acres of good garden land might require 30 *tobotobo*, several *bagi*, ten *daveri*, many baskets of produce, dozens of bundles of sago and other valuables.

Canoes were made on the Islands of Gawa and Panayati. The clay pots were manufactured on the Islands of Tubetube, Amphletts, and Wari. The finer clay pots came from the Amphletts. They were up to a yard in diameter and were extremely thin and yet had good durability. The natives traded them along with turtle shell earrings, special nose sticks, red ochre, pumice stone, and obsidian for wooden dishes, mussel shells, ebony lime pots, folding baskets, and three-tiered baskets. There were also regular trading expeditions between the western villages of the Trobriands to Fergusson Island and Goodenough Island. Sago, betel-nut, pig, cassowary feathers, red parrot feathers, rattan cane belts, plaited fiber belts, obsidian, red ochre, pumice stone, and fine sand for polishing axe blades were traded for arm shells, valuable axe blades, boar's tusks, and imitation tusks, as well as less valuable items like wooden dishes, combs, lime pots, armlets, grass skirts, baskets, mussel shells, ebony, lime spatulas and wayugo creeper. Cash has recently become a part of some of the gifts and trading in some areas. Also, European commodities are now being accepted in some areas. Yams are a major wealth object and are traded for shells to gain entrance in the Kula. Woodlark produced axe blades. Molima produced obsidian from local sites. Misima Island traded pigs, axeblades and wooden bowls. Panaeati manufactured canoes and pottery. In the old days the standard was one *bagi* for each prow of a canoe. Older builders asked two or three. Others now ask five to seven *bagi*. A canoe purchase takes about five years, and they last for seven to 10 years with some lasting as long as 20 years. The Rossel Islanders will give a large pig with tusks for four Brooker Island clay pots. The Sudest currency is called *daveri*, and it is identical to the Rossel Island currency called *ndap*. Sudest Islanders traded *conus* shells, which they found in plenty. In many areas the people import the same kind of item they export. The Woodlark people trade clay pots to the Panaeati people, even though the Panaeati people make and export their own pots. Turtle shell rings are also traded along with red shell disks by some of the people. Items such as mussel shells, knives, combs, lime pots, and plaited fern have dropped out of the Kula with the easy availability of modern substitutes such as steel knives, etc. Pigs are normally traded for two reasons. One reason has to do with what the pig will be used for after it is exchanged. Two frequent uses are cementing outrigger canoe exchanges and assisting in mortuary obligations. The other reason to exchange pigs is to sustain or develop a Kula exchange. The Southern Massim purchased from the Mailu many items including dogs, small pigs, boar's tusks, shell disks, and clay pots. Tobacco sticks were also used in the islands to purchase most items. The village of Kuboma was known for its production of quicklime for betel chewing, and the village of Kudukwaykela produced the burn-in designs on decorated lime pots. The Luya villagers were producers of finely plaited basketwork. The village of Kavaataria produced arm shells. The settlement of Sinketa was the site where some of the main sailing expeditions started. The Molima in the past have suffered droughts so bad that they sold their children (to be eaten) in exchange for vegetables for the islanders to eat.

Modern Kula

Malinowski thought of the Kula as a static system that would stop with the coming of the Europeans. Instead the Kula grew because it actually is a changing system that adjusts and adapts to changes. In the 1880s money began to be a minor item in Kula. It also caused many disputes when valuables were sold to Europeans instead of being passed along on the traditional Kula paths. Problems also developed when natives tried to purchase shells with modern money to gain entrance to Kula. They many times had poor exchanges because it was perceived that their entrance into the system was illegitimate. In the 1960s women were allowed to take part in the Kula on Dobu and Fergusson Islands. In the 1970s boys as young as seven have also taken part in the Kula. The canoe has also given way to modern means of transportation. Now motor boats and even airplanes are used in the Kula. Letters and telegrams now make known the whereabouts and movements of important pieces. With the arrival of Europeans, peace came to the area, and the *bagi* and *mwali* that previously had been used in the wars were now used in the Kula. This allowed more people to own the valuables and therefore participate in the Kula. This increase in pieces took place in the early 1900s. During World War II the Kula was suspended from 1942 to 1945 due to the dangers from the war. During the late 1940s Kula reached a peak because of all the cash earned during the war. In the mid-twentieth century the pottery tradition of Collingwood Bay disappeared. Also, the pearlshell knife or scraper disappeared. The actual Kula valuables also changed. First, glass trade beads replaced the seeds and shell pieces, then plastic beads replaced the glass beads. These changes did not alter the value of the valuables. Now plastic crescents have replaced the shell crescents, and these uses of plastic have reduced the value of the valuables. Now Australian coins, Papua New Guinea coins, rubber and metal disks and other modern items have been added to *bagi.*

Listing of Kula items and terms

Bagi (red shell necklace) also called *soulava;* major Kula valuable traded in clockwise direction from island to island. The terms *soulava* and *bagi* describe different items in different places and at different times. Sometimes it is said that more valuable pieces are called one name or the other. I have used *bagi* as a general term to describe all necklaces of the *bagi* and *soulava* type. The *bagi* consists of four parts: head, abdomen, ear, and tail. The head is always a cowry and the abdomen and ear are the red shell disks and is marked by two white shell disks. The tail is the pearl shell. The best *bagi* have decorations suspended from the tail. The whole decoration is called *dauyoyo,* and the cowry is called *surasura.* The *sapi sapi* shells are attached to a pendant made from the interior of a helmet shell with black banana seeds and beads strung end to end as tassels with *ovula ovuna* shells at the end. The other ends are attached to the edges of the helmet shell. The sapi sapi shells are now made only on Sudest and Rossel Island and some surrounding islands. Some are considered so valuable they are worn only on very festive days and have a name and history of their own. They are used for payments of bride price, canoes, pigs, mortuary commitments, and land access. The shells (*Chama*) are collected in Yela (Rossel Island) and Vanatinai (Sudest Island) and made into disks there. Some informants have stated that in early times *bagi* were from Sinaketa. The men do most of the shell diving, but women are expert *bagi* makers. Each *bagi* has a name, and they are ranked into three classes. The best *bagi* have very thin shell disks and smooth edges from much handling and travel around the Kula ring. The older *bagi* from the time of Malinowski had helmet shells instead of the modern gold-lipped oyster or pearl shell. *Bagi* are ranked from lower to higher as follows: Bagitorobwa, Taituyanabwa, Bagisam, Bagiyeru, Bagidou, and Bagiriku. The criteria are age, history, color, and size of the disks. The best color disks are salmon-red, with brown-red and dark red being lower in value. A high-ranking shell string will look thin as a fine fishing line and feel like oil. Only the women wore the *bagi.*

Kula Items

BANANA SEEDS: used for personal adornment and to decorate Kula necklaces (*Bagi*) and armshell (*Mwali*)

BASI : an intermediary gift given as a token of good faith. This gift must be repaid by a minor gift (*Kudu*).

BEKU: (axe blade) greenstone axe blade used in bride price and for canoe purchase, used by white traders to purchase pearls, for performance of sorcery, payment for gaining allies in war, payment for killing someone, and performance of magic spells. They start out as rough pieces of green-stone which are then polished in the Trobriands and used as stone implements. The biggest of them, which are very thin and well polished all over, are considered a very important valuable in the Kula ring. The blades were also used to form alliances in fights as well as arranging a battleground in another area so your village and gardens would not be damaged. They were quarried on Woodlark Island and polished on Kiriwina. They were used as *kaributu* gifts. In Kiriwina they are male valuables. *Beku* are individually owned and inherited by men. The blades are not being manufactured at present, but they still are being used. A man that had five *beku* was considered wealthy. *Beku* is considered an exchange object only on Kiriwina. In 1970 the blades were small, not used much, and few in number. During exchange, the blades were inserted into wooden handles which were only props. On Sudest Island greenstone axe blades were called tobotobo. Long, thin, dark green axeblades were called Giarova. There are many other names for various axeblades used in the many islands. Each seems to have its own common size, shape, and color, but most seem to have at least some green in them.

BOSU : an associated Kula article (*vaygu'a*). It is a lime spatula made of whale bone and often decorated with sapi sapi shells. They travel in the same direction as the mwali. They are not now encountered much in the Kula.

BUNDLES: Banana leaves were rubbed on a piece of wood that had a design on it, and the design was transferred to the leaves. These leaves were used as an important form of women's wealth on the Trobriand Islands. They were also used in mortuary ceremonies. They are not described in most books on odd and curious money. They are women's money. See Bundles

CANOE: a large sea-going canoe was an important article of exchange. They were made on Gawa and Panayati.

CHAMA SHELL: used in making *bagi*. They were mistakenly identified as *Spondylus* shell by Malinowski.

CONUS SHELLS: used in making the armshells (*mwali*). The Kavataria and Kayleula people had the monopoly over fishing for them.

DAVERI: shell money from Sudest Island that is virtually identical to the Rossel Island shell money called *ndap*.

DOGA: (necklace) boar's tusk pendant or shell ring pendant and *Chama imbricata* (*sapi sapi*) shell disks overlapping on the string called *wakisowa*. The necklaces circulated counterclockwise like the *mwali*. Sometimes an imitation tusk made from a *conus, trochus* or *tridacna* shell was used as the pendant. The boar's tusk pendant pieces are more valuable than the shell pendant pieces. In the old days it was almost as important as *mwali*. *Doga* were also highly valued on New Guinea. On Kitava the *doga* can be arm shell substitutes, but this is very rarely done. Very few of the *doga* are left; most were traded out of Kula.

DURIDURI: (belt) made of fern and orchid fiber.

GIGI'U: (pump drill) used to make shell beads.

GILE: Polished and shaped pearlshell called a vegetable peeler or spoon.

GINIUBA: a large pearl shell knife. It was a Kula valuable that was also used by the Kinaketan people in magic to help them find the *kaloma* shells for use in the manufacture of the *bagi* necklaces. They were also used in internal exchanges by the Kuau and Normandy people and in marriage and mortuary exchanges. They are not used at present.

KAIPWESI: Belt of *kaloma* shell disks attached to a broad band of European cloth. Older pieces were made of a woven vine backing instead of cloth. These shells are the same ones used in *bagi*. The Sudest people used to make these belts, but at present only one belt is on the island.

KALOMA: (shell beads) red shell disks from *Chama Imbricata* used to make *bagi*, belt, bracelets and other valuables. The Sinaketan people used to dive for the shells and along with the Vakutans specialized in the drilling and grinding of the disks. *Kaloma* is not being manufactured at present, but it is still being used. It is also called *kalomwa*.

KARIBUTU: a solicitory gift which can be *beku, kaipwesi*, or *bosu*.

KATUDABILE: (necklace) *Chama Imbricata* shell and bead necklace. It is a Kula valuable.

KAYEKI: pearl shell used in ornament manufacture. Also an important Kula valuable.

KEMA: axe with greenstone blade used in gardening and cutting trees.

KENA: (spatula) wood carved lime spatula

KITOMA: shell valuables which are the property of the holder of the shells. Many times these items leave the ring for intra-district exchanges. They may be purchased for money. The items can then be used as money because they do not have to remain in the Kula.

KUDU: the gift given to complete an exchange.

KUKUMALI: (stone) roughly shaped piece of green

stone. When they were very thin and well polished, they were called *beku*.

KUNEDAWESI: shell valuables that are pure Kula valuables existing solely to be traded within the Kula ring. Unlike *kitoma* shell valuables, they are not actually owned by the holder. Therefore the owner does not have the right to sell the items. These items cannot be considered as money.

KURIA: (clay pot) traded for yams and sago. Manufactured on Tubetube, Wari and Amphletts. Amphletts was the only supplier to the Trobriands, Marshall Bennett Islands, and Woodlark.

KWASI: armlet made of fern and orchid fiber.

LIGOGU: (adze) wood handle with *conus* shell blade

MWALI: (shell armring) major Kula valuable circulated in counterclockwise direction from island to island (see map). They are made by knocking out the circular base along the rim of the *Conus millepunctatus* shell (also called the Leopard Cone shell) with a stone. A groove is made parallel to the knocked-out base with a stone. This creates a cross-section which is then polished on the outside by rubbing it on a flat sandstone. On some rings holes are made in the side of the shell where one rim overlaps the other. Black banana seeds and sapi sapi disks are attached as ornaments. The decoration can also consist of up to six cowry shells depending on its size and a larger number of small cowry shells bound together by trade beads. Also, suspended ornaments of seeds, beads and cowries were added to give the *mwali* a rattling sound when you walked with it. The lip of the shell is called a *kudula*. Depending on the size of the cut shell, a number of egg cowries called *buna kudula* are attached. The size of the cut conus shell determines the number of *buna kudula* that are attached. The circumference of the *mwari* is called the *pwala*, and a number of egg cowries (*Ovula ovum*) called *mwaridoga* are attached to it according to its size. The smaller circumference of the *mwari* is called the *wadola*. Men who are knowledgeable with *mwali* can have a fairly good idea as to the size of the shell by how many *buna kudula* and how many *mwaridoga* are on the shell. Smaller *mwali* are probably made from the *Conus litteratus*. The rope it is suspended by is called *kaipwesi*. Most of the *mwali* were too small to wear and the ones that were large enough to wear would not be worn except once in a decade by a very important person. Originally they were circulated as pairs until 1896 in the North and 1910 in the South. The right-hand one is larger and finer than the left-hand one. The shells come only from Kavataria and Kayleula. *Mwali* were previously made on Woodlark. Valuation criteria are size, circumference, and width as well as age as determined by color. Red striations begin to form on the surface of the shell. The classifications are from lower to higher as follows: *Gibwagibwa, Tomorimwaiya, Mwarigidageda, Mwaributu, Mwarikau.* Most men never touch a *mwarikau* class *mwari*. On the other hand the *gibwagibwa* is the lowest ranking class, and it is considered ugly because it is unpolished, brown and small, and not considered worth cleaning. The arm shells were worn by both the men and women. This is the kind that many times young men use to enter the kula. In 1970 a *mwali* was used to purchase a canoe. The value of a *mwali* is estimated according to the position it is able to occupy on a man's arm. The higher up it will go, the more valuable it is. In 1970 the smallest low-quality shell was worth $10 and the largest and finest about $190.

PARI: a landing gift given by the voyagers upon arriving at their destination, such as lime pot, lime stick or comb.

POKALA: a solicitation of valuables offering such as taro, yams, pigs, or fine bananas.

SAKUSAKU: (canoe finial) wood canoe finial attached to the top of the prowboard.

SAMAKUPA: a bigger, coarser *sapi sapi* shell string made in Sinaketa from *kaloma* beads. The strings never complete the Kula ring and therefore are not truly a Kula article. They were, however, given as a Kula gift. The diving, breaking, and drilling are done by the men, while the polishing is done by the women.

SOULAVA: (red shell necklace) also called *Bagi*. A major Kula valuable used in clockwise direction. See *Bagi*.

SPONDYLUS SHELLS: Malinowski incorrectly reported that these shells were used in *bagi*. Liep reports that the *Chama* shell is actually used. A necklace made of these shells was called *kuwekuwa* in Kiriwina and *samakupa* in Dobu.

SPOON: pearl shell spoon formerly used as ceremonial valuable.

TABUYO: (canoe prow) wood, used to protect the canoe and increase speed.

TALI'I: farewell gifts given by the host when the travelers leave.

TANEPOPO: (baskets) three plaited pandanus leaf baskets used by men of high rank to store personal belongings like lime gourds and spatulas.

TRUMPET: (shell trumpet) made of *Turbo Marmoratus* shell used to announce the arrival of the Kula expedition.

VEGETABLE PEELER: used as ceremonial valuable. Oyster pearl shell. Was used until 1970s in trade between Kiriwina and Kitava. As availability of modern knives increased, the shell knives were no longer needed. They are still used on Sudest as a ceremonial valuable spoon or vegetable peeler, where they are called *Gile*.

WAKALA: minor valuable consisting of a double-rowed *Spondylus* belt of broad disks. They formerly circulated like necklaces in a clockwise direction and dropped out of Kula after World War II. They placed a value of $63 on one in 1970. Another use for them was in mortuary rites.

KUMAL

Ireland, 1st century, A.D.

Slave girls served as a medium of exchange and unit of value. An Irish king had a chess set with each piece worth six *kumals* (slave girls). Later blood money consisted of seven *kumals* of silver. A *kumal* was equal to three cows. The *kumal* was a unit of value.

KUNDJA

Africa, Congo

The iron hoe type item was a unit of value, made by a Bankutu tribe farther inland and bartered for salt. The Nkutshu used them as a standard unit of value. Ten would buy a male goat or one *boloko*. Four to six would buy an indentured servant, and 20 were necessary to enter marriage negotiations. One *oshele* was worth 500 *kundja*. (See Quiggin p. 66-68) (See Kriger p. 109)

Kundja

KUNE TYPES I & 2

Trobriand Islands

Two types of ceremonial trading rings similar to but not overlapping the kula. The islands of Ware and Misima and possible also Sudest are the only islands in the ring. Shell beads are given by the Ware Island natives to the Misima Island natives when they visit Ware Island. The Ware islanders receive 60 heirloom units and a new necklace when they visit Misima. The Misima Islanders receive 60 heirloom units when they visit Ware Island. Canoes are also used in the transactions. (See Belshaw)

KUNEDAWESI - See Kula

KUNGA - See Boloko

KUNTU - See Cloth, Nigeria

KURAKANIKANA

Bougainville

A fathom of very small red disks made on Banoni that have been on Bougainville for a long time. A good span was worth from 100 to 500 *mauai*. Some spans have some white poponi interspersed. *Kurakinikana* is the most valuable shell money in Bougainville. (See *mauai*)

Kuria

Kyee-Zee

KURIA

Trobriand Islands

A clay pot traded for yams and sago and manufactured in Tubetube, Wari and Amphlett Islands. It was also used to a limited extent in the kula. See Kula.

KURIRI

Solomon Islands

Whitish string made of unpolished mussel shell disks. The disks are smaller than the disks used in *mauai*. One fathom of *kuriri* is worth five fathoms of *mauai*. (See Quiggin p. 162)

KWA

Africa

In parts of the upper Zaire river basin Y-shaped iron objects were used as money. There are two different sizes. The smaller one was between six and 10 grams, and the other weighed about 20 grams. Knife blade currencies were valued as a number of *kwa*. (See Kriger p. 109-110)

KWALOI'A

Malaita, Solomon Islands

A ring of porpoise teeth. See Porpoise teeth

KWARI'INARI

Malaita, Solomon Islands

An elaborate ear ornament used as money. See Porpoise teeth

KYEE-ZEE

Burma

Karen Hill Tribe. The gong was made of thick copper with a small open bottom and larger closed top with four frogs on the top edge. They were valued at $25 to $250 depending on the size and sound. There were 10 classes with names known by their sounds which could be heard for several miles. Many drums have three-dimensional frogs on the rim, and the four frogs are equally spaced around the outer top edge of the drum. Some of the drums have a top that comes to an edge at the circumference, while others have a rounded edge that is about three inches or more high. Kempers refers to the drums by type based on an earlier researcher, Heger. Many times there are from two to four frogs sitting on top of one another in gradually decreasing sizes. Inferior *kyee-zee* were not one of the 10 classes, not given names, and had low values. They were and still are used in bride price and are also called rain drums. The Karen used the drums, but they were made by the Shan and Intha of eastern Burma until the beginning of the 20th century. Around 1970 the drums were again made for sale to soldiers, traders, and travelers by people in Laos or northern Thailand. The drums were also made in Burma by persons of the Karen ethnic group. Most drums now seen outside of Asia were from this later production. The makers never used the drums themselves. The original kettledrums are found throughout the area. Twenty-six have been found in Indonesia. The largest known drum is called The Moon of Pejeng and it was found on Bali in the city of Ubud. The descendants of this type are represented by the *mokos* of Alor Island. The Moon of Pejeng is nine feet long and is currently in a temple in Ubud. This large *kyee-zee* is the largest in existence, and it is unique. Prehistoric trading was probably responsible for the scattering of the drums from their original area. They were made with the lost wax method of casting. For a hollow object like a drum, the artist makes a clay sculpture the shape of the object and then covers the mold with a thin layer of wax that is decorated as desired. Then the wax is covered with clay. Molten bronze is then poured in the mold, which replaces the wax. The clay is then removed, leaving the bronze shell which can then have additional decorations added. They are all of one piece and are all metal. The *kyee-zee* had great value among the Karen, and if one was stolen, revenge would be handed down from generation to generation until it was returned. Sometimes the debt was paid by giving a man to replace the drum. The drums were also insurance against crop failure and famine, as they could be sold to purchase food. The Karen recognized drums as tall drums or short drums and as male drums (with frogs) and female drums (no frogs). At one time, one drum was worth eight to 10 oxen. It is said that the price of the drum was determined by the the number of frogs on the drum. A drum with two frogs would cost 20 rupees. Much of the value of the drums is based on the sound of the drum with the best sounding costing 1,000 rupees and the poorest costing 100.

The Lamet people of extreme northwestern Laos also possessed and valued *kyee-zee* drums like the Karen people. They purchase their drums from the Karen for use in bride price. One drum was worth four buffaloes and one buffalo was worth 30 piastres in 1937 according to Kempers (p. 397). A rich man had at least two drums and five or six buffaloes.

The Kammu and the Khmu people also value the *kyee-zee*. They valued the drums according to their size, decoration and material from which they were made. They classified the drums as old, middle, and new style. The old style had the frogs while the middle and new styles had three elephants. There were at least seven different types according to Kempers (p. 399). They valued the oldest type at 200 buffaloes and the newest at two buffaloes. They are also used in dowry but not in bride price. They also used gongs as money.

There are also miniature drums which were used as token drums and were buried with the dead. They are solid and therefore could not produce a sound like the larger hollow drums. Kemper (p. 45) suggests the miniature drums could have been used as money and as imitations of ordinary drums to be included in the grave goods that accompanied the deceased to their final destination. 10" to 27" diameter. Many reproductions. (See Kempers) (See Quiggin p. 208-209)

LALAI

Siassi Islands, Papua New Guinea

Arm shell made from sections of trochus shell and decorated with patterns etched in the surface were traded for food and other items. They are properly called *Mbi*. There are two kinds - men's and women's. Men's are called *Lokoloko;* women's are called *Mbi*. Men's have decoration of shell and beads. 4" diameter

LAND - SNAILS - See Kuriri

LANGTANG - See Cloth money, Nigeria

LA'ONIASI

Malaita Island, Solomon Islands

The East Kwaio people of Malaita Island made this pendant from clam shell. They ground down a piece of shell which was up to one inch thick using a flat stone called a fou'ute until it was a thin disk. The design of a frigate bird was inscribed into the shell with either a

Lalai

La'Oniasi

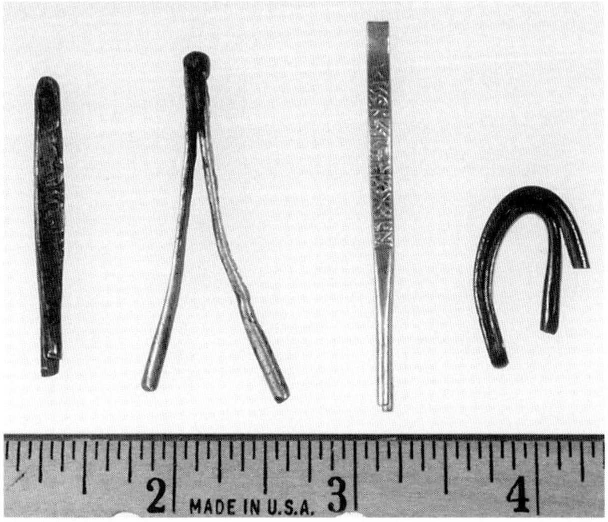

Larin - Note varieties - Center Piece is Gold

Tiger Tounges

Lower Two - Canoe Money *Upper Three - Varities Of Tiger Tongues*

piece of flint or the tooth of a *kivete*, which was a large rat that has now been hunted to extinction in most areas. At present modern European tools are also used. The design is blackened with either muki (putty nut) or a tree berry called *alamakwana*. The excess is rubbed off so only the incised design has the blackened material. The pieces are considered as a valuable by most tribes. They are given away during feasts and as part of compensation payments along with shell money, but shell money is still considered more important. A smaller type of *la'oniasi* is called *madu* and is used or worn like the larger *la'oniasi*. They come primarily in round or oval shapes with a hole for hanging as a pendant. (Per comm. Betty)

LAPLAP

Papua New Guinea

This article of clothing worn by men and women was considered a valuable as well as basic clothing. They were also used in bride price and as decoration. They were valued at six shillings in 1950.

LARIN

Persian Gulf, 965-1067 & 1557-1672

Thin strips of nearly pure silver stamped with inscriptions and bent double were used as money. The name Larin or Lari, said to have been derived from Lar in Persia, where they were first struck, is the general appellation given to these pieces, according to Wood (p. 9). Many gauges of wire were used in making *larins*. I have a *larin* made of low grade gold. In 1785 half-*larins* were struck in the shape of small copper bars rated at 4 3/4 Indian stuivers, according to Codrington (p. 125). Early tweezer types are approximately 2 1/4". Shorter pieces (called *toweelah*) made after 1700 are billon or bronze and shaped like a cotter pin. They are found primarily in the al-Hasa area, generally at Hofuf, and are thought to have originated from one of the Corinthian princes about 920 A.D.

India, Ceylon, 1500-1700

Larin of India are shorter and thicker than Persian types. They are approximately 1 1/4" x 1/4" and are made of good silver, with clear inscriptions. Ceylon pieces are long and thin but bent in the shape of a fish hook.

Maldive Islands

In the Maldive Islands a silver *larin* was worth 12,000 cowries. (See Quiggin p. 194-195, Mitchiner p. 179 & 265, NNM #61)

LAT

Laos, 1353-1889

Found primarily in Thailand, tiger tongues have two or four lines of raised bumps the length of the obverse.

Canoe money has a depression the length of the lat with raised the ends. The stamped bar has a smooth surface with stubbed ends and elephant and other symbols stamped in top surface.

1353-1571 Leech money. Smooth top, no central depression. Raised ends.1 tamlung (72 gm.) elephant is one of several stamps, good silver. Rare.

1353-1571 Leech money. Smooth top, no central depression,. raised ends.1/2 tamlung (36 gm) elephant is one of several stamps, good silver. Rare.

1353-1571 Leech money. Smooth top, no central depression, raised ends. 1/4 tamlung (18 gm.) elephant is one of several stamps, good silver. Rare.

1525-1571 Tiger tongue top. one tamlung (61 gm.) elephant is one of several stamps, good silver

1571-1592 Tiger tongue top. one tamlung (60 gm.) one - three wheel stamps,good silver.

1591-1707 Tiger tongue top. two tamlung (120 gm.) three wheel stamps,good silver.

1591-1707 Tiger tongue top. two tamlung (120 gm.) three snake stamps,good silver.

1591-1707 Tiger tongue top. two tamlung (120 gm.) three symbols, good silver.

1591-1707 Tiger tongue top. 1 1/2 tamlung (90 gm) three symbols, good silver.

1591-1707 Tiger tongue top. one tamlung (60 gm.) no stamps, good silver.

1591-1707 Tiger tongue top. two tamlung (120 gm.) no stamps, good silver.

1707-1828 Tiger tongue top. 90 gm. falling to 60 gm. Billon lat, much debased, no stamps

1707-1828 Tiger tongue top. 90 gm falling to 60 gm. Billon lat, much debased, three snake symbols.

1707-1889 Smooth top. 90 gm. falling to 50 gm. Billon, copper or brass,. no stamps.

19th century. Smooth top. 50 gm. falling to 14 gm. Billion, copper or brass. Broad central depression with raised ends, no stamps. Called canoe or boat money.

Kingdom of Lanchang (Laos) 1353-1571 Smooth top, stubbed ends, elephant stamp. Base silver or silver washed. (See Mitchiner p.355-356, 386-390)

LEACH MONEY

Lanchang, Laos, 15th century

See lats

LEAF MONEY

Siam, Nan Region ,1200 A.D.

The solid, heavy disk has a leaf-rib pattern on the convex

Smooth Top Lat

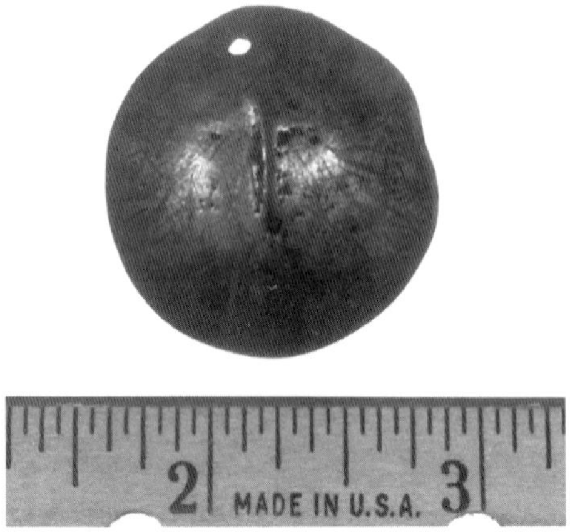

Leaf Money

Leather Money

side and is plain on the concave side. It is similar to the willow leaf (flower) money and tok. It is also called "line money." They are always perforated. Leaf money was made of light colored alloy of base metal often with a silvered surface. (See Quiggin p. 218)

LEATHER MONEY

Europe

Philip of France in 1060-1108 and the Doge Michieli of Venice in 1122 used leather money. It has been said that Edward I of England used stamped leather as money in the late 13th century. Many pieces were issued during this period. (See Del Mar p. 64-65)

King John II of France used small leather coins in 1360 with slim gold threads sewn into the coins or stamped on them. (See Carlton p. 161)

Germany, Austria, 1919-1922 Inflation period following World War I

Part of the "Notgeld" series of unusual forms of money made for collector or for limited use in various cities. Several sizes and shapes. Some are shaped like the heel of a shoe.

Leather Money

Mexico, early 20th century

Hacienda tokens were made of leather as well as many other materials for payments to ranch workers. Rawhide.

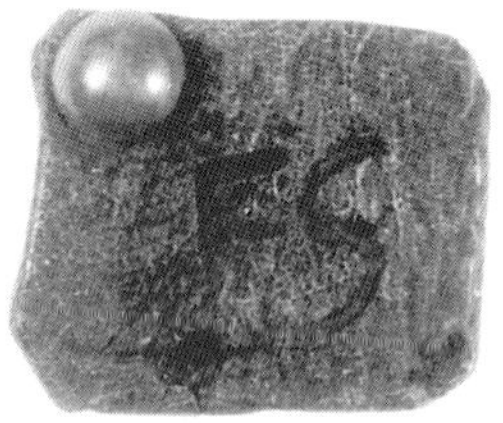

Leather Hacienda Token

Ancient Romans

Stamped leather skins were used as currency.

Russia

In the ninth century and shortly thereafter, one inch square pieces of leather were stamped by the government and used as money. Leather in various forms was used as late as the reign of Peter the Great. (See Del Mar p. 294)

LEECH MONEY - See lat; smooth

LEGBAND

Africa

The Mbole people use these copper legbands in marriage transactions. The five different sizes each had names and different values. They were worth from two to 10 *onglese*. (See Ballarini p. 115)

Legband

Africa , Ekonda tribe, Zaire

Bronze legbands with ribs on the outside were used as a form of money. A wood form was pressed in the earth and hot copper or brass was poured in the mold and while still hot it was wrapped around a log to form a cylinder. It was originally called *konga.* (See Ballarini p. 116) I believe they were called *bakonga,* and in the first half of the 20th century, five to 20 *bakonga* would pay for a wife. Later the price increased from 200 to 300 *bakonga.* One *bakonga* was also worth 10 *engetele* or *bingetele.* (See Ballarini p.116) (See Schaedler p. 322)

LELA - See cannon money, Irian Jaya.

LENDU

Santa Cruz, Solomon Islands

Small pieces of feather coil were called *lendu* and were used as small change. (See Quiggin p. 136)

LEOPARD TEETH

Congo

Strings of leopard teeth were used as money. They are one of the oldest currencies in the Congo. (See Johnston Vol. II p. 792)

LERALE

Transvaal, Africa, 1800s and later

This copper rod with one end like a flattened cone with root-like bars protruding from it that appeared to look like a funnel. It was used as money. They were cast and came from Pallaboroa, Haenertsburg District, Zoutpansberg, Northern Transvaal. One piece was valued at two cows and three goats. At another time one *lirali lerale* and 20 hoes would purchase a bride. The number of cattle it was worth varied from time to time. Some rods have 10 imperfect raised bands near the cone and also an indistinct groove running down the shaft. One informant said that by the middle of the 19th century, one was worth ten cows. This value seems too high. Another person said that 30 *marale* (plural for *lerale*) were worth one ivory tusk, eight to 10 cattle or 55 iron hoes. It is also believed that they were used in bride price payments. Only about 15 pieces are known to exist in collections. (See Herbert p. 194) (See Haddon #65) (See Quiggin p. 107) (See Schaedler p.322)

LIDERAN

New Ireland

This kind of shell money is composed of different kinds of broken flakes which are ground down into circular form to the size of ordinary glass beads. Holes are drilled through the center. The string of beads is measured from the nipple of one breast to the nipple of the other. Seven to eight of them equal one fathom. In New Ireland one fathom of *diwarra* was equal in value to one fathom of *lideran. Lideran,* however, was only of value in New Ireland. Outside of this area it had no value. (See Danks)

Legband

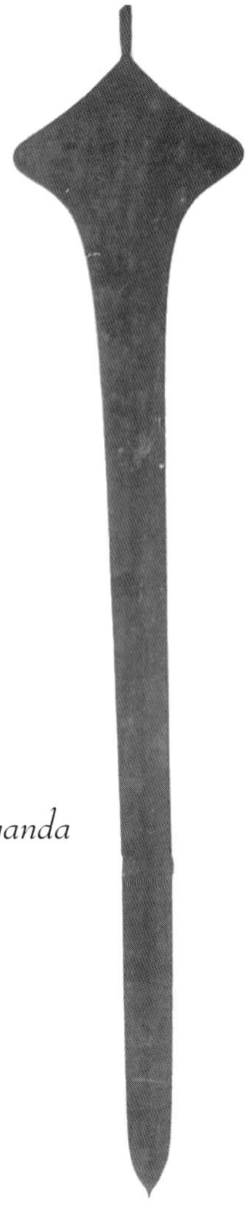

Liganda

Wood Mold for Legband

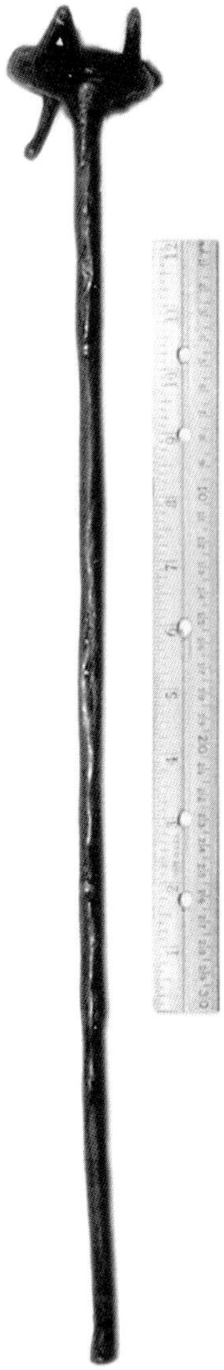

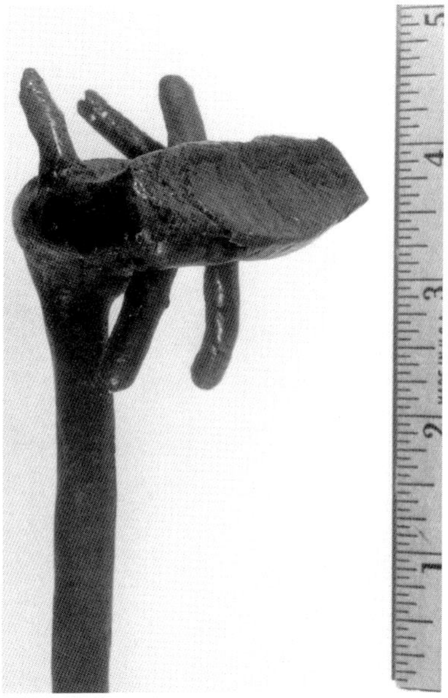

Lerale

LIGANDA

Congo and Lomami

This iron spearhead was made by the Turumba. The large pieces were called *doa* and the small pieces were called *dihunga*. They weigh 4 1/2 pounds. They were worth 10-25 *shoka*, 100 to 250 mitako or up to five shillings. *Liganda* were used as bride price and in the purchase of canoes. The Topoke of the Lomami valued a male slave at 30 *liganda* and a female slave from 40 to 100 in 1907. The *liganda* were made until about 1920 and were then worth about five Belgian francs. They were also called *ngebele* (*ngbele*) in the Stanley Falls area. The Topoke in the Lomami area called them *ndoa*. They are approximately 60″ long. A large hoard was found in 1989. (See Quiggin p. 64)

LIGOMO

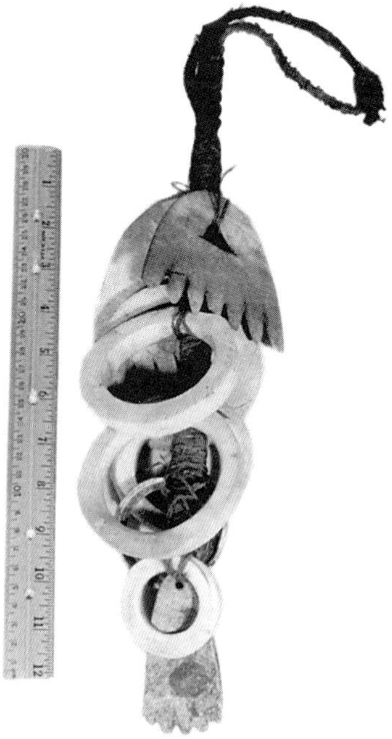

Ligomo

This grave ornament is from Roviana, Western Province, and it consists of a notched black wood stick with a number of shell rings and one to three *barava* attached. The *barava* look like a comb with very short and wide teeth. They are also made of shell and are from 1/4″ to 3/8″ thick. All the shell pieces are very old, but the wood stick and native twine are new. Although the piece is used as a grave marker, the components are all money items, and the piece itself represents great wealth. (Per Betty from the Solomon Islands)

LIKONGA BLADE MONEY

Mobenge and Zande people, Northern Zaire

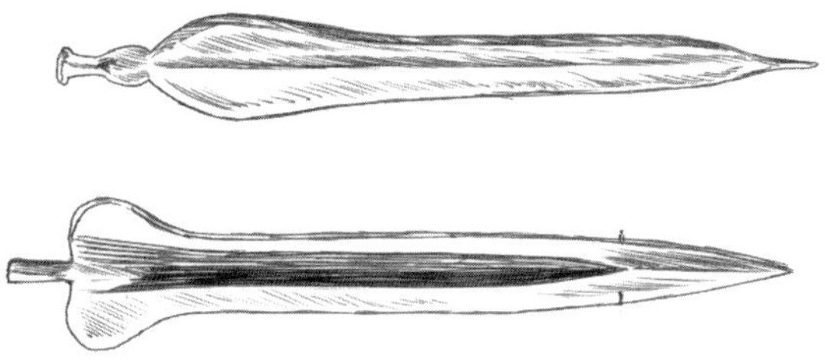

Likonga Blade Money

This hand-forged iron blade was used in trade. They had a definite value and were used in making traditional marriage payments. The currency blades each have a definite value based upon its size and shape. Most are modest in size, while some are over five feet long. (See Blackmun p. 36.) (Quiggin p. 65.)

LIMA ABALA

They are similar to *tafuliae* except they have only five strings. They are used by the Baega tribe from Baelelea in North Malaita, Solomon Islands. They have the same value as the *tafuliae* and are used for the same purposes. (Per Betty from the Solomon Islands)

LIME STICK - See Bosu

LIMESTONE RING MONEY

Palau Islands

The white limestone ring was made with fine workmanship. The ring was worth 10-12 chickens. 7″ diameter (See Quiggin p. 120)

LINDERAN

New Ireland

The shell money is in the form of a girdle with ten to 16 strings. The disks vary from dirty white to a very light red or pink. The pieces looks like a very small *tafuliaé* with very small beads. (See Lewis p. 18)

LINE MONEY - See Leaf Money

LINEN MONEY

Germany, 1919-1922 Inflation period following World War I

Part of the "Notgeld" series of unusual forms of money for collector or for limited use in various cities. Fancy woven or lace borders are in some cases attached to the edges of the linen money.

LINOLEUM MONEY

Germany, 1919-1922. Inflation Period following World War I

Part of the "Notgeld" series of unusual forms of money made for collectors or for limited use in various cities. There are several sizes and shapes.

LILY ROOT MONEY - See lotus root money.

LIPSTICK

French Indochina

A favorite medium of exchange for purchase of almost anything. Lipsticks changed hands many times without being used. (See Einzig p. 313)

LIQUOR

America, 1600-1700

Traders used liquor, rum and whiskey to trade with the Indians. It was used in payment for furs and to pay early railroad workers. (See Mosher p. 41) (See Schnapps)

West Africa, West Indies

Trade gin was used to pay fines and for other transactions. Many bottles were traded unopened for years. See Rum Money

LIRALE - See lerale.

LITLATLA

Portuguese East Africa

Large brass rings weighing more than two pounds were worth a wife in the old days. They were very popular. (See Quiggin p. 104)

LOAF - See Sycee

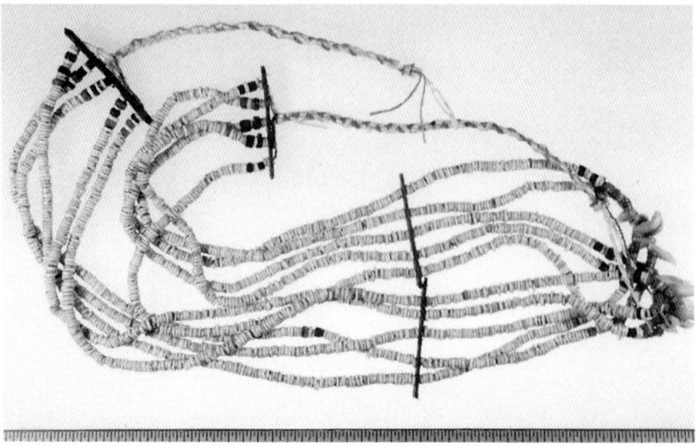

Lima Abala

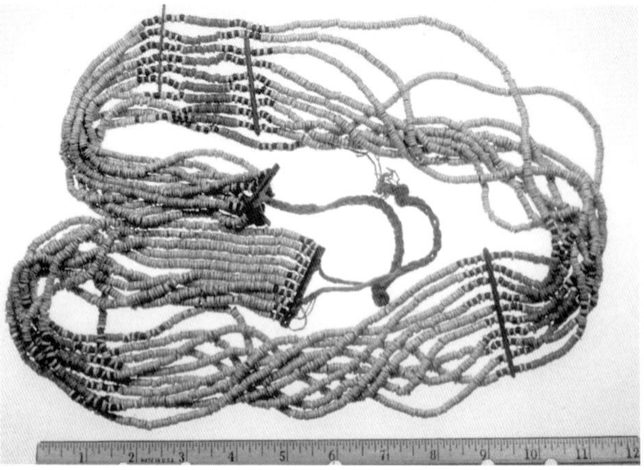

Linderan

Linen Money

Loda

LOBOLO

Portuguese East Africa (Mozambique)

The term was used for bride price. *Lobolo* did not refer to any one kind of money, as many items were used. *Lobolo* included brass rings, oxen, hoes, goats and white beads. It was used in large parts of Africa. (See Quiggin p. 104-105)

Loda

LODA

Sumba Island, Indonesia

The copper wire woven chain with thick woven ends was used as money. It is a hollow rope made with four strands of copper wire and was used in Sumbawa and Sumba islands for marriage gifts or in ratification of a contract, though not in ordinary exchanges. It, along with *mamuli* and horses, was a traditional component of the bride price. The piece exists in copper, white metal, gold-plate, and solid gold. It is similar to the *kanotar*, except the thickness of the wire and the ends of the chain rope are different.

Loggoh Kullet

LOGGOH KULLUT

Africa

Iron circular heart shaped piece was used as money.

LOGWOOD

Honduras

Mahogany logs were one of the main currencies in Honduras. Before 1784, they were used as a medium of exchange as well as a unit of measure. In 1766, the chief town of Honduras actually decreed that all debts would be payable in logwood unless special agreement was made between the parties. After 1784, all debts contracted in logwood were payable at the rate of six pounds per ton for chipped and four pounds per ton for unchipped logwood, with all wood under 15 inches not to be used in settling debts. (See Einzig p. 304) (See Tukula)

LOIN-CLOTH

New Ireland

This piece of clothing worn by men was used as money, particularly in bride price. (See Powdermaker)

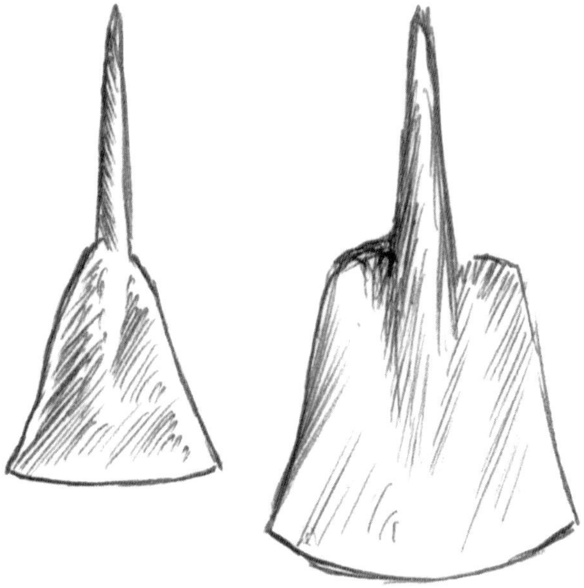

Lokongo

LOKONGO

Zaire basin, Africa

Iron hoe (*lokongo* or *longo*) money was used in the late 19th century. In this area, these two kinds of hoe were used along with the *shoka* as money. (See Kriger p. 102)

LOKULA' LOMBOLE - See throwing knife - Africa, Ubangi, Bubu

LOLOE AMAS - See Loda

LOLOI - See Diwarra

LONGO - See Lokongo

LORAN EARRINGS
Tanimbar, Indonesia

Solid-cast earrings made of gold or silver were used as money. They were also used as a male valuable which was given by the groom's family to the bride's family. They were considered as male money because they were solid and heavy. Similar earrings like the taijana and the mamuli from adjacent areas were considered female money. (See Taylor p.244)

LOSIL - See Sek

LOST WAX - See Animal Money

LOTUS ROOT HEART MONEY
China, before 300 B.C.

The lotus root is also called a corrugated key coin, key coin, and lily root heart money. Many numismatists doubt its use as money. It may have been a barter item. There are many different shapes. It is included in many collections. (See Quiggin p. 234)

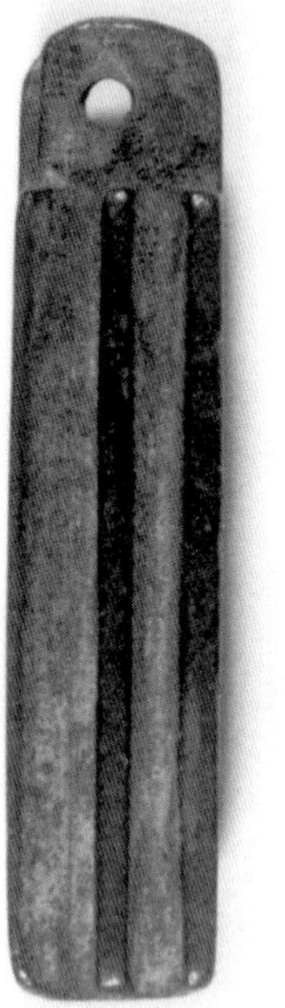

Lotus Root Heart Money

LUKASU
Africa

At least a dozen contiguous language groups share the term *lukasu* to mean hoe. (Kriger p. 101.)

LUMBER
Colonial New Hampshire

Lumber was a principal commodity money in this state. (See Taxey p.146)

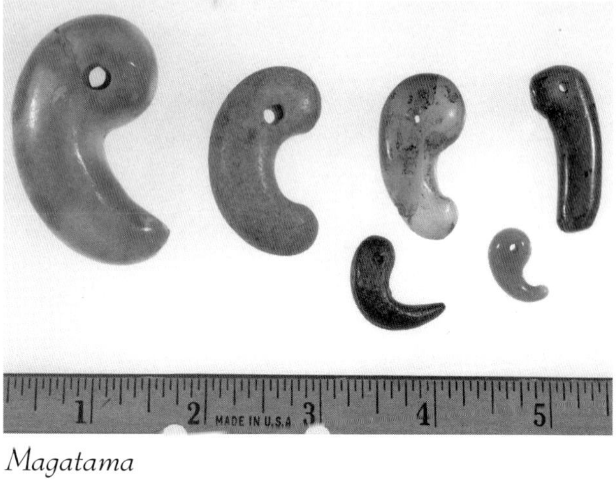

Magatama

MACKINAW BLANKET - See blanket

MADIBA - See Cloth, Raphia, Zaire

MAE EXCHANGE
Western Highlands District, Papua New Guinea

The *mae* exchange takes place between the Mae Enga language-speaking group numbering about 30,000 people. The exchanges as well as the valuables presented are ranked in terms of importance and desirability. The most important items are pigs and cassowaries. They are used in the Te ceremonies for homicide at the clan level. They are also used at the sub-clan level for death and the patrilineage level for marriage and illness. Pearl shell pendants, stone axes,

Mairi

cassowary feather plume headdresses, dogs, pork sides, and cowry shell headbands formed the second level of valuables. They are only used in the sub-clan and patrilineage levels. The third level of valuables is the bailer shell pendants, bilum bags, bird of paradise plumes, hand drums, cowry shell necklets, and bows. There are other levels of valuables and levels of relationships. (See Meggitt) See the Te ceremonies

Tin Plated Mamuli

MAGATAMA
Japan, before 700 B.C.

Gem-stone carving resembling claw of a tiger or some animal was a valuable trade item but probably was not used as currency. It is included in many money collections. (See Munro p.5) (See Quiggin p. 249)

MAGNESITE
North America

Beads made of this material were extremely valuable. See wampum.

MAHEE
East Africa

The iron spearhead was made by the Bongo tribe and used as money. 12″ - 24″ (See Quiggin p. 96)

MAHOGANY - See Logwood

MAI
Torres Straits

Crescent chest ornaments made of pearl-shell were used as decoration and a valuable item. The term *mai* is the same name as the shell itself. (See Haddon Vol. 4 p. 43)

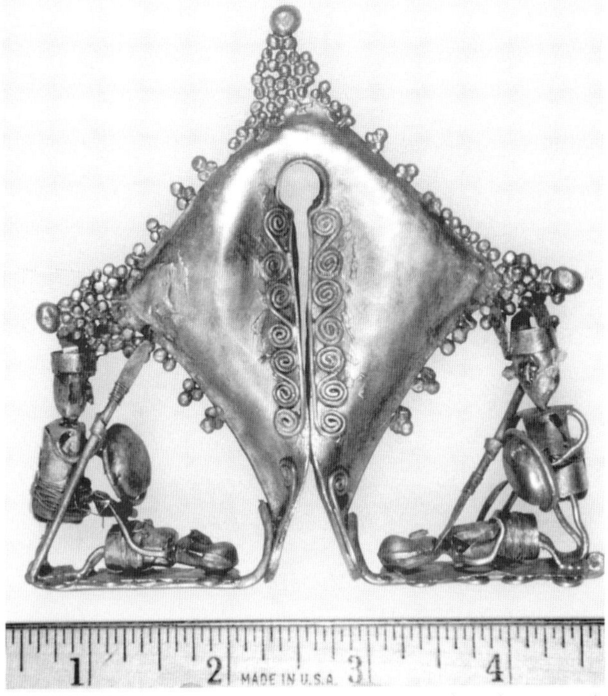

Tin Plated Mamuli

MAIRI
Torres Straits, Papua New Guinea

Crescents made in Port Moresby to accompany arm-rings in the hiri voyages were called *mairi.* They were used in bride-price and exchanges for sago. 4″ x 8″ (See Quiggin p. 179)

MAIZE
Guatemala, late as 1930s

Corn was valued by the gourd, which weighed a pound and was worth one peso. It was traded along with the peso as money, and the corn was readily accepted, as it was part of the daily diet. (See Einzig p. 185)

MALAKI
A complex exchange system from central Africa.

MAMEITAGIN - See Bean Money

MAMULI

Sumba, Indonesia

Omega shaped gold, silver, bronze, or brass earrings are used in bride price. They are crucial bride price goods. Some pieces are made from tin plate. The most valuable *mamuli* are heirlooms and are almost never traded. The active pieces are used in marriages, buying land, peace offerings, and for minor offenses. They say the shape represents the female sexual organs. They are only worn as earrings in a small part of West Sumba by the Lamboya, Anakalang, and Lauli cultures, but in some instances they are worn on a cord or on clothing. On Samba the prospective groom's family presents *mamuli* to the bride's family. Other components of the bride price are water buffalo, dogs, horses, other gold objects, and weapons. The bride's family gives cloth, ivory, pigs, rice, beads, and sometimes gongs. (See Rauus, 1990)

Copper Mamuli

Tin Plated Mamuli

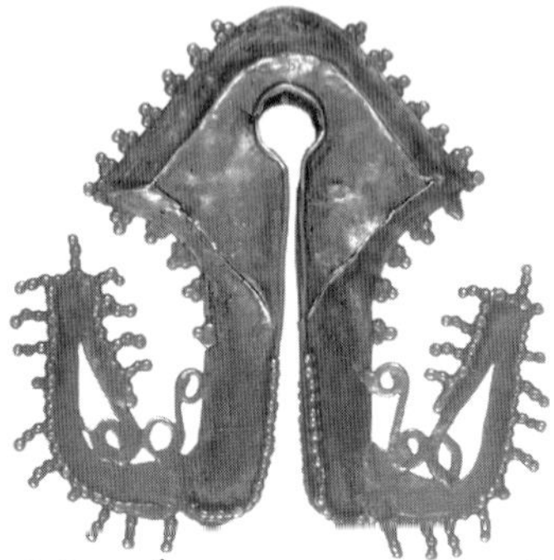

Silver Mamuli

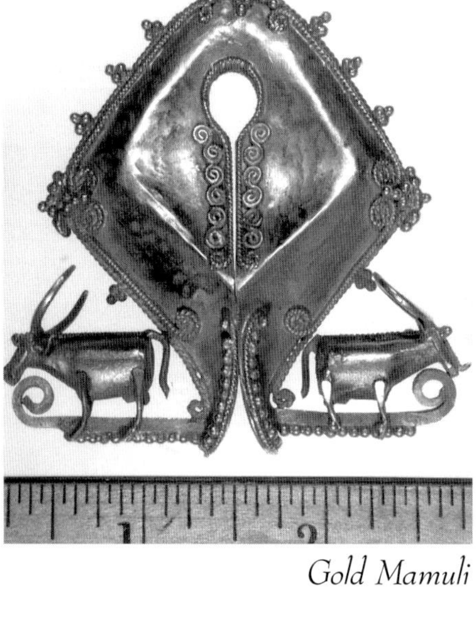

Gold Mamuli

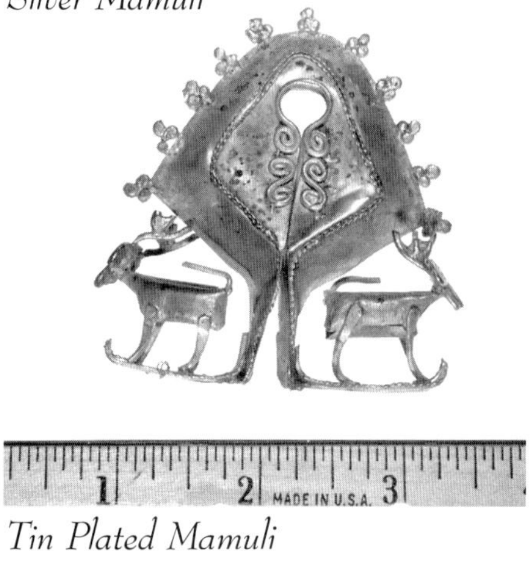

Tin Plated Mamuli

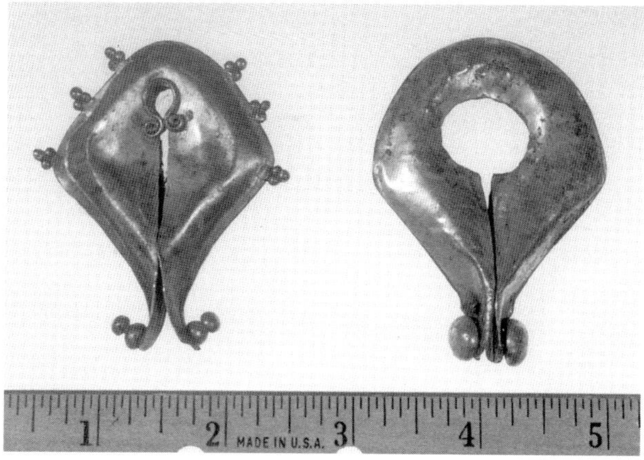

Tin Plated Mamuli

MANDJANG

Africa, Kwele, Gabon, Congo Brazzaville

An anchor shape (*mondjo*) stamped out of a sheet of iron which at one time had a value of 1/4 to 1/2 franc. It was introduced as money by the traders of N'Goko Sangha Company at the beginning of the 20th century for exchange of rubber and ivory. The older pieces are called *zong*. The company called them commodity currencies. They were used until recently, some say, as marriage payments among the Bendjabi and the Nzabi of the Ogooue' Basin. They are also called *Bitchie* by the Djem and *mandjong* by the Bakwele. This piece is very similar to the *zong* but has ears on the ends of the head portion which is also larger. If the ears are not present, the piece cannot be used in bride price. (See Guyer p. 78-93) (Schaedler p 321)

Mandjang

MANGANESE EARTH

Papua New Guinea, New Britain

A loaf of manganese earth 15 inches long and six inches in diameter was worth a 15 to 20-inch string of tali. The manganese earth was used in a paste form to blacken the teeth of young males before they were eligible for marriage. This item was almost as important as salt in intertribal trade. (See Panoff p.13)

MANILLA

West Africa, end of 15th century to 1948

The word "manilla" means bracelet. It is an open bracelet like a horse-shoe with flared end. Manillas were originally made of copper or brass and later a mixture of other metals (copper-lead hardened with arsenic). In 1439 the Portuguese crown ordered manillas from Venice. The earliest manillas were illustrated in Benin panels showing a European holding one. These were early large Portuguese manillas. The later manillas can be classified as follows:

Small manilla - early, probably Birmingham
Small manilla - middle period, probably Birmingham
Small manilla - late period - 1840 - 1900, Birmingham
Small manilla - early, probably French
Small manilla - late period, French popo

Johansson shows many different manillas with native names. It is not a complete list. Until a trader's reference collection from the period is discovered we will probably not have all the types identified correctly. I am showing some probable types from my collection. It is not complete and some could be misidentified.

During the period of their manufacture manillas grew smaller and their metal content from copper, to brass, to highly leaded brass. This shows the gradual lowering in value due to size and cheaper metal usage. In the 1720s, 50 pounds of lead were mixed with a ton of copper. Later

Manilla - Possibly an Old Original

the manillas were 25 to 30 percent lead. Some iron manillas are also known to exist. The first manillas may have been bolts from ships wrecked on the West African coast. Later traders had the pieces manufactured in Birmingham, England, for export to Africa. Irregularities occurred at the mold joints, leaving extra metal called "flash" protruding from the surface. It was very important that this "flash" not be removed because natives would not accept manillas without "flash." A good ringing quality was necessary, and it is believed that the ring could be as good as an assay to determine metal quality. Inferior cast iron pieces were made, some in Birmingham, which were rejected by the natives because of their poor ring. Manillas were the main currency of West Africa and were used for most purchases and bride price. There are a variety of types, and they all fluctuated in value. At many times it was considered a unit of value in which the values of other items was calculated. In 1505, one manilla would purchase a large elephant tusk, and 12 - 15 brass manillas would buy a slave. Later it would take 50 for a slave, which would then purchase 9,000-18,000 reis of gold at Elmina. As more pieces were traded the value fell. Herbert stated that in 1556 the Portuguese paid 40 manillas for an ounce of gold. Later one ounce of gold was worth 20 pounds of copper. In 1750 manillas were imported in strings containing 10 manillas, and four such strings were valued at one iron bar. (See Jones p. 48) In 1911 they stopped being legal tender, and in 1919 foreign traders were prohibited from using manillas in trade with the natives. In 1940 a manilla was worth one calabash of corn.

Portuguese Manillas.

The earliest pieces date to 1439. By the 1470s copper bracelets and legbands were the main currency along the African coast. In the 16th century, manillas were used in the slave trade and made in several European areas. The Mkporo in Nigeria were made in Antwerp, with a few being made in other areas. Originally they were larger, but by 1548 they weighed about 250-280 grams. In the 1400s four manillas would purchase a slave. By 1522 it took 57 manillas. The Portuguese monopoly was broken in 1550. The early manillas were made of copper and brass, while the later ones were all brass. The early manillas were used along the coast from Liberia to Nigeria. At that time, especially in the city of Benin, they were used as money and not for decoration. Their value depreciated as time passed because so many were imported that the market became saturated. Hundreds of thousands were imported each year. The finest manillas were made by Erasmus Schetz of Antwerp until 1547. After that the wealthy Fugger family of Augsburg produced them. By 1550 their monopoly was broken by fierce price competition. The *mkporo*, believed to be the Portuguese manilla, is rare today.

Birmingham Manillas.

The English started trading in Africa in 1550 using many different kinds of manillas to trade for gold, ivory and pepper. By the 1780 the Birmingham manilla became the standard with the *Mkporo* becoming a standard of wealth and burial money, according to Semans. Initially production of manillas was in Bristol by the firm of R. & W. King in the latter part of the 18th century and then in Liverpool. By 1836 Birmingham was producing the manillas for the British for trade in Nigeria. In 1856 the *onoudu* piece was being produced. It was made in several sizes and shapes. Copper, brass and tin manillas were used in Gambia before 1712. Later lead was also used in the copper to reduce the cost. By 1800 the manillas contained 30 percent lead. In Birmingham dozens of varieties of manillas were produced with Johansson showing nine named pieces. Most could be used in only certain markets. In 1902 the import of manillas was prohibited and in 1911 their legal tender was also prohibited. They did, however, continue to circulate as money. In 1948, the government decreed that manillas should be withdrawn from circulation. Their use was prohibited and the possession of more than 200 manillas (for ceremonial purposes) was a punishable offense. A total of 32 1/2 million, manillas weighing 2,460 tons, were withdrawn. When redeemed in 1948, 80 - 480 were equivalent to an English pound depending upon the type.

French Manillas.

This type was called *Popo* and was probably cast in Nantes, France. It is the most common type today because they were used as late as the 1950s in parts of French West Africa and were never withdrawn from circulation or destroyed in quantity. That is probably why they are now the most common type available to the collector. There are four varieties according to Semans. Iron manillas were also used. The French did not become serious traders until after 1550. The manillas were used to purchase palm oil and ivory. When the price of palm oil fell in the late 18th century the import of manillas ceased.

Dutch manillas.

Most of the Dutch trading in manillas started in the 1590s and peaked during the mid 1600s. They traded the manillas from Sierra Leone to Cameroon. The manillas were small (about 43 grams), and it took 120 for a male slave and 100 for a female slave. In 1646 they were said to weigh 151 grams. By 1717 the trade stopped as the natives would not pay the price the Dutch West India Company charged.

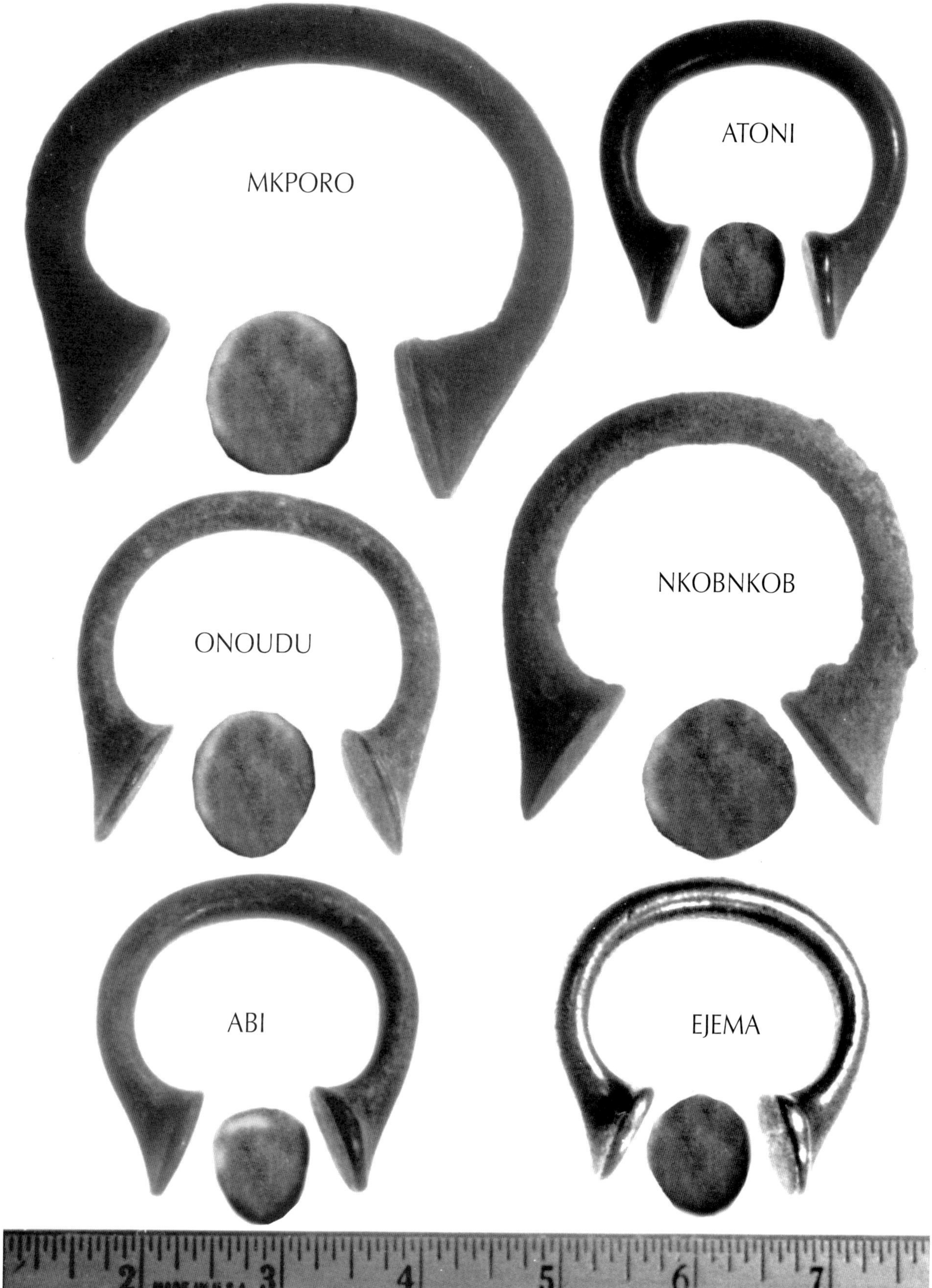
MKPORO
ATONI
ONOUDU
NKOBNKOB
ABI
EJEMA
2
MADE IN U.S.A.
3
4
5
6
7

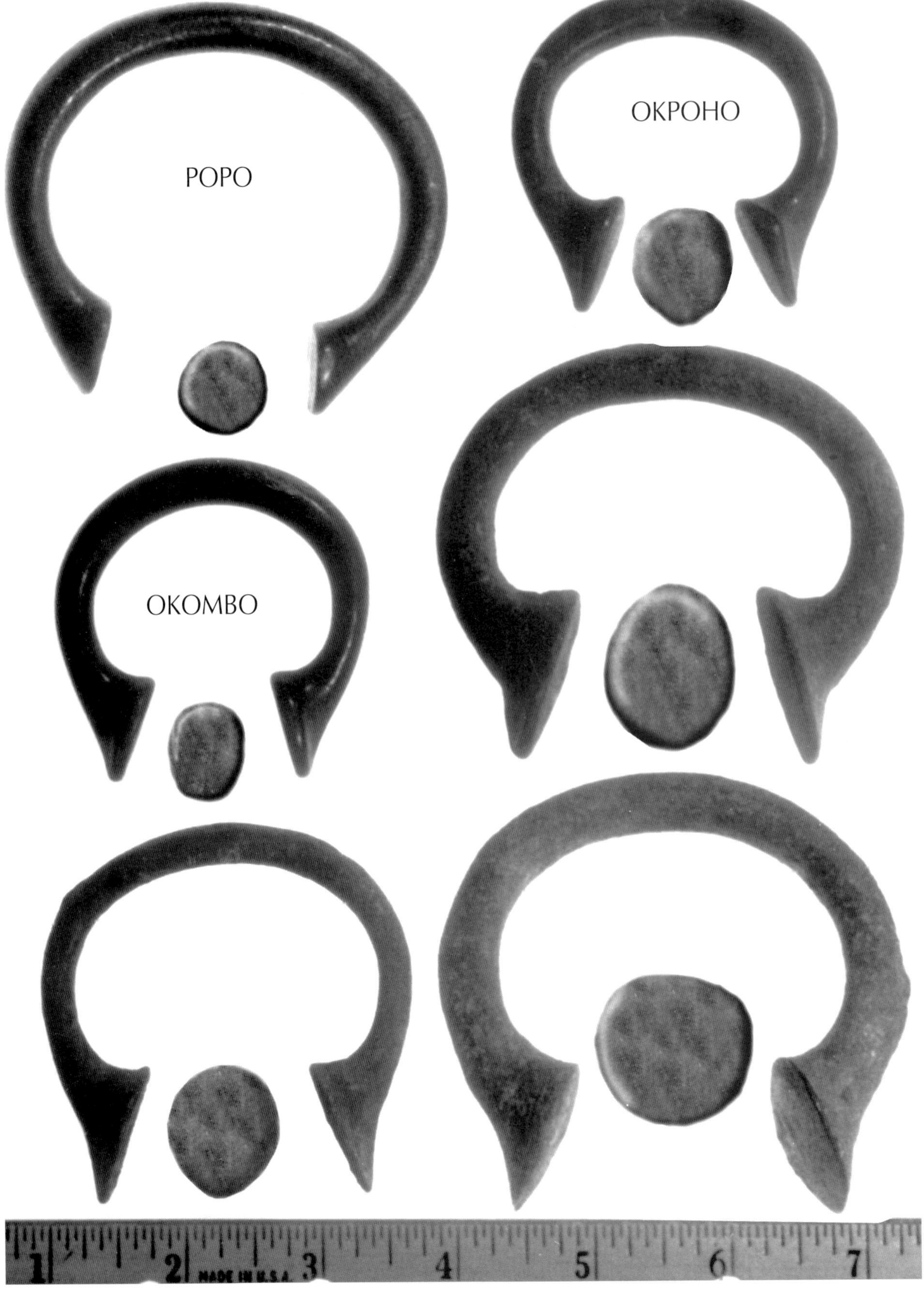
POPO
OKPOHO
OKOMBO
1 2 MADE IN U.S.A. 3 4 5 6 7

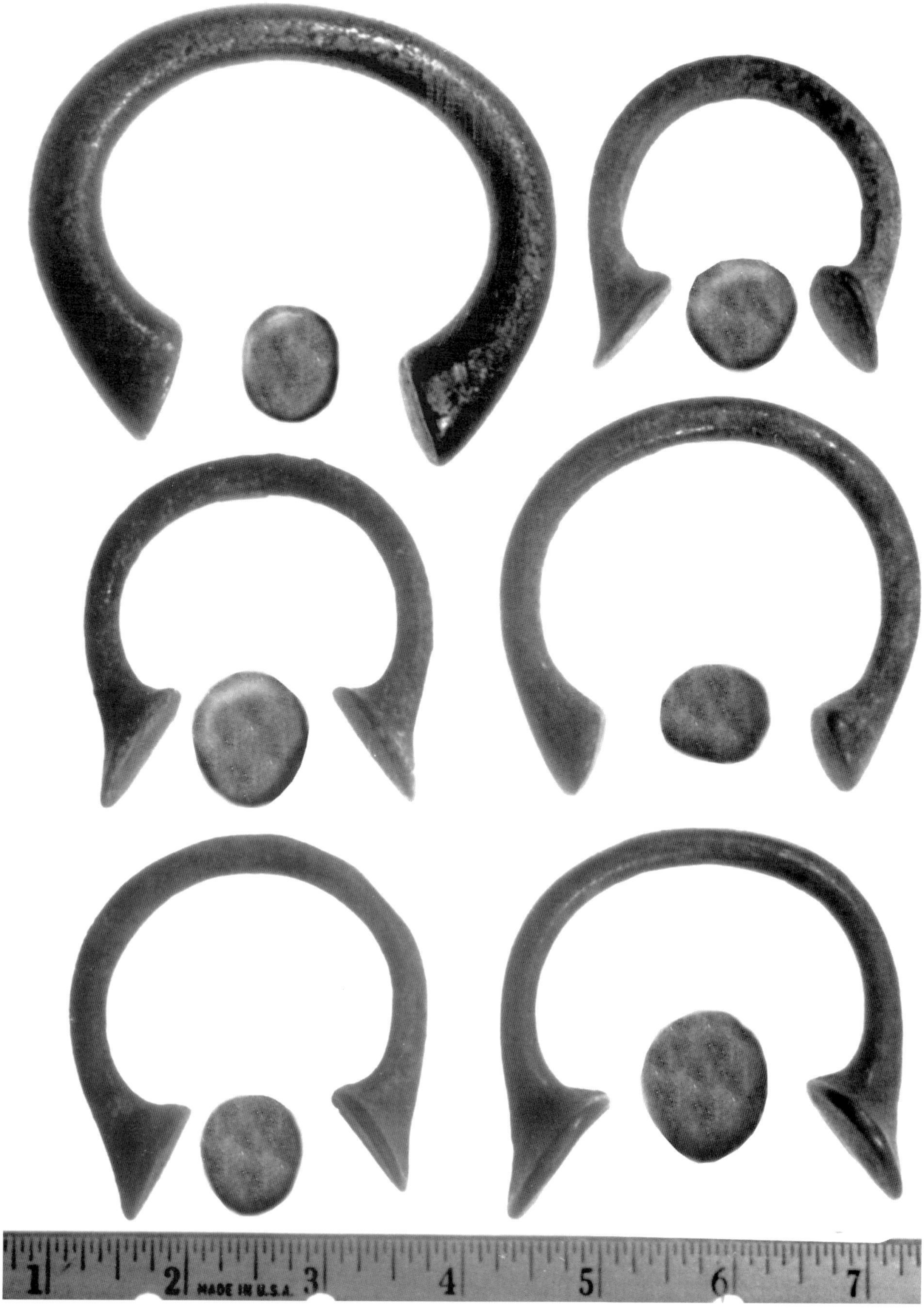

1
2
MADE IN U.S.A.
3
4
5
6
7

MANILLA- KING

Africa

The King manilla was not used in daily trade but was a store of wealth and bride price. One piece was worth 100 manillas. It is difficult to differentiate between King, Queen, and Prince manillas, as these are not native terms and do not have natural fixed physical limits. 10 1/2" (See Johansson p.19-20) (See Akanbiemu) (See Herbert p. 202)

Manilla - Queen

MANILLA - QUEEN

Africa

The Queen manilla was extremely valuable and was used as a store of wealth. It was worth 75 manillas or two slaves (a man and woman). 8" across (See Johansson p. 19-20) (See Akanbiemu) (See Herbert p. 202)

Manilla - Prince

MANILLA - PRINCE

Africa

The Prince manilla is smaller than the King and Queen manilla and also less valuable. It was worth 50 manillas. 6" across (See Quiggin p. 90) (See Akanbiemu)

There are many other types of manillas, including the standing manilla and coiled manilla. The brass spiral coiled manilla, *Nja,* from Ugbbahu in Igboland was usually worn on the leg.

Coil manillas. Thin and heavy-gauge round and twisted copper or brass wire was formed in the shape of a coil or spring. Some have bulbous ends.

Elongated Manillas. Semans calls the King and Queen manillas by this name. He says they were probably introduced by English merchants in the early or mid-19th century. They were royal dowry and were an important part of the dying ceremony for royalty. The King is 10 1/2" across and the Queen is 8" across.

Royal hemp manillas. These twisted manillas came from Opebo, a former kingdom in southeast Nigeria. The piece was very valuable and was used as money until the early 1900s. (See Eyo,p.64-65) (See Johansson p. 11-27) (See Semans info sheets and pamphlets) (See Leonard and Chicago Coin Club)

Twisted Manilla

MANTIS - See Gambar

MANUM

New Ireland

It was a very valuable possession and was called money by Parkinson. It is an elaborately constructed pendant attached to the ends of a string of white shell money with alternate black seeds called *kokonon luluai.* The center of the pendant is a kidney-shaped large reddish black seed with openings in the seed to attach ornaments.

Manilla - King

Coiled Manilla

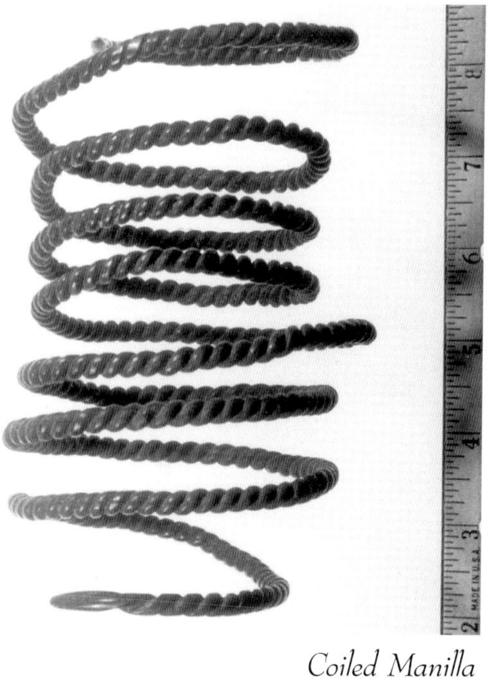

Coiled Manilla

Coix seeds, both whole and cut, were attached to the pendant. Strings of shell money called *kokonon luluai* were attached. Also called *kaput*. See *mis*.

MAPLE SUGAR

Nova Scotia

Maple sugar was used as commodity money. (See Taxey p.146)

MARALI

Transvaal, Africa

The copper ingot rod has protruding parts on its head. It was formerly used as bride price for wives of chiefs and was worth 10 cows, but it later was reduced in value to two cows and three she-goats. (See Quiggin p. 107) (See lerale.)

MARANGGA

Sumba. Indonesia

The *marangga* is a beaten gold piece in the shape of two joined triangles with a beaten loop at the top. It is very similar to the *taka*, but the loop is flat instead of round like a wire. It is considered part of the treasure of the important families. Some large and important pieces are considered holy. (See Rodgers #139 & 140)

MARIA THERESA THALER

1780, Europe, Ethiopia, Africa.

This .833 fine silver coin was originally minted in Austria but later was minted in other countries when the coin became a respected bullion piece. It was used extensively in Ethiopia as money and was also used in some of the silver crosses used in Ethiopia. The thaler originally gained prominence in the Arab world around the Red Sea coast for use in the slave and other trade. The thaler was first minted in 1751, was never legal tender and had no official value. The value of the thalers rose in relation to their distance from the coast, due to transportation costs. The value of the thaler would rise during the dry season because at that time the merchants needed them to purchase goods and do business. Coins that were considered defective in any way lost 10 percent of their value. The coins that had the portrait of the Austrian Emperor instead of Maria Threasa were worth 25 percent less in value. Starting in 1935, Italy struck 20,000,000 thalers over the next four years. They were used for the invasion of Abyssinia. The Ethiopians insisted that from five to eight pearls must show in the Empress' diadem, nine pearls must show on the oval pin on the shoulder and the letters S.F. must appear under the bust. By the mid-1940s, London, Utrecht, Paris and Brussels made their own dies to strike thalers. Later they were also struck in Bombay as well as at other mints. They are still being minted. (See crosses.)

MARTIN SKIN

Canada

A "made beaver" skin was worth two martin skins. The skin was a form of currency. The Hudson's Bay Company and the Northwest Company traded European wool blankets and many other items for animal skins of all kinds with the Indians of Canada. All were valued in terms of a "made beaver" skin, which was the standard of value. (See Taxay p. 96)

China

In the early Mongol period a martin skin was worth 10 squirrel skins, according to (Rockhill p.202.) (Aring p.6.)

Russia, 14 - 16th century

Martin skins were valued at six groschen and they circulated along with silver, according to Einzig p. 305.

MARSUPIAL FUR MONEY

Papua New Guinea, Kundagai tribe

Phalangers or *cuscuses* of the species *Phalanger maculatus* furs were used in trade. (See Healey p. 199-200)

Manum

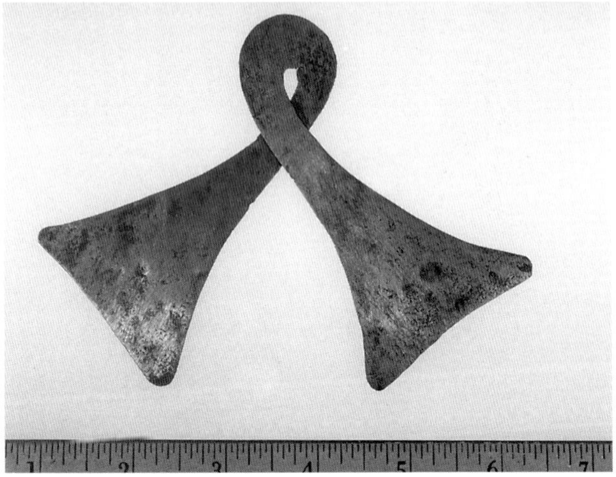

Maramgga

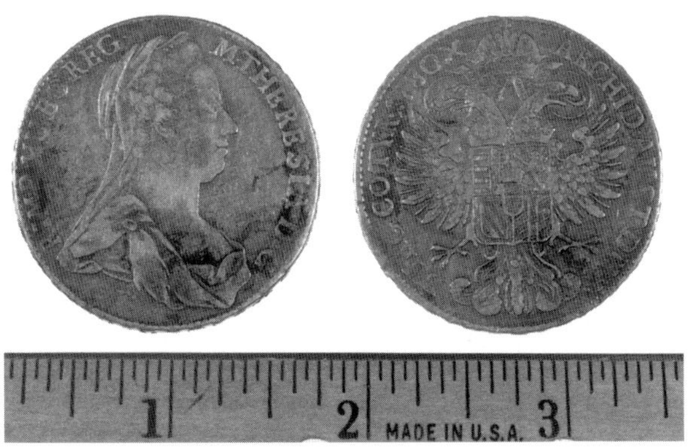

Maria Theresa Thaler

Ethiopean Crosses made from Maria Theresa Thalers

Masks

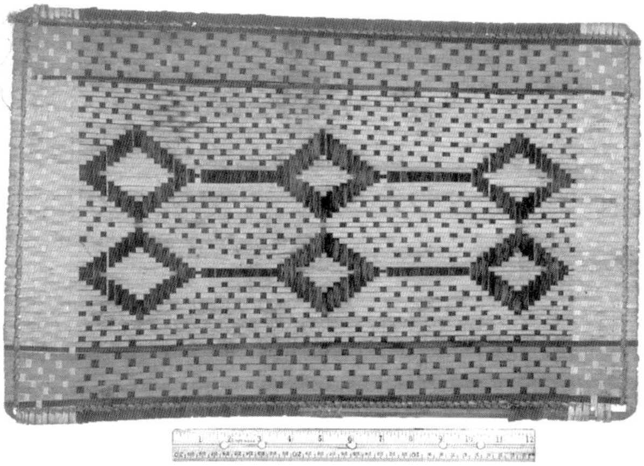

Mat Money

MARSUPIAL TOOTH NECKLACE

Papua New Guinea, Kapauku tribe

The necklace is called *kedege ego dope*. It is a very valuable possession and was used in trade and as money. (See Pospisil)

MASKS

Papua New Guinea

Ceremonial masks, made of carved and painted wood, were family heirlooms. They were used as a part of bride price, a store of wealth, and to gain admittance to secret societies. Many styles, sizes, and shapes are used. (See Moore p. 36) If they were money they were a limited form of money.

MAT MONEY

Africa, Congo, Until 1900

The woven fiber mat was valued at 50 mats for a string of blue beads. Small mats sewed into a unit called the *NTA*, worth one franc, contained three rows of 10 mats sewn together. The mats were used for fines, compensation, bride price, and wrapping the body in a funeral. 100 *NTA* = average bride price. (See Quiggin p. 57-58)

Central Africa

Raffia cloth has been used from the 16th century to the present time as currency. In the Kuba area, square pieces of raffia were used as money. Tribute was also paid in raffia cloth, with one village paying a raffia cloth for each adult man. The Bushoong used it along with many other items in bride price. Today it is used mostly for funerals. Skirts made of raffia are also used as money. (See Cloth - Zaire.) (See Weiner p.128)

Banks Island

Mat money will buy anything but is primarily used to purchase rank in the Suge Club.

Kazakstan

The Kazak people used wool felt mats as money. The felt mats were valued by size, workmanship, availability of material and quality. A small average mat was worth a sheep or goat. Their most prized animal, the camel, was worth a large beautifully embroidered mat. (See Siebert)

New Hebrides, Aurora, Pentecost and Leper's Islands

The mats were long and narrow and were made to be money. The mats were kept in a special house used only to hold the mats. A fire was always burned in the house to blacken the mats and make them more valuable. Their value was determined by the number of folds in the mat. The folds were counted in tens. They were used to buy anything but were mainly used to buy steps in the Suqe Club. The mats were called *maraha* on Penecost and Lepers' Islands, and the red ones were called *bwana*. The red mats are more valuable. Some of the mats can be 600 feet long and two feet wide. The mats could also be lent at interest and used to buy pigs. A medium-size mat would purchase a tusked pig. (See Codrington - 1891)

Nigeria

Round mats and rectangular mats 12 inches by 18 inches were used as money and worth eight shillings, four pence. A small one was only worth 1/2 pence. (See Siebert)

Papua New Guinea

On Umbio Island a fine *Siassi pandanus* mat was worth less than one dollar.

Penecost

The mats are long and narrow, and the older ones are worth more than the newer ones. They are called *maraha*. The red ones are more valuable and are called *bwana*, which means *pandanus*. They serve no purpose other than as money. (Codrington P. 323)

Samoa

Fine mats were made of fiber and were two-three yards square. They were worth \$5 each in the early 20th century. Some old torn ones were worth as much as \$80 - \$100. The price was determined by the fineness of the plait, the size of the mat, and the sentimental value based on that individual mat's history. The mats required many months or years to make. They were used in bride price, fines, blood money, and elections. At one marriage 3,000 fine mats were distributed because the marriage consolidated a tie between traditional political districts that had been separated for a long period of time. The fine old heirloom mats had their own value and could not be considered as money. New mats were sold in the capitol, Apia, with a cost of at least \$150 each. The value of a fine old mat can never be replaced with a new mat. A woman's mats are used to support her husband and her brother when they need wealth. (See Einzig p. 41-43)

Santa Cruz

Mats were narrow variegated strips like book-markers. 1″ x 8″

San Matthias

Finely woven with fine *Pandanus* fibers and dyed red and orange. 2″ x 46″

Sam Mathias Mat Money

Vanuatu Mat Money

Maulavata

Mauwai

Sumba, Indonesia

A marriage payment includes a basic price of at least 10 horses and buffaloes. It is reciprocated by an equivalent payment in cloth and pigs. Cloth is considered female goods, along with pigs.

Tikopia

The islanders used three basic kinds of mats in this area. They are: *pandanus* mat, the blanket of bark-cloth and the long strip of bark-cloth used as a man's waist-cloth. Mats made of *pandanus* were used in bride price as well as for ceremonial gifts. The mat must be unused and newly made. It is eight feet long by four feet wide and composed of quarter-inch strips of *pandanus*. It takes about three months of part-time work by a woman to make one mat. When bark-cloth is presented in ceremonial form it is known as *maro*. It only takes three days to make and they are used extensively for gifts. The barkcloth is not as valuable as the *pandanus* mat. (See Firth p.250)

Vanuatu

Mats are plain and narrow (6-8 inches wide) with fringes two-three feet long. The mats were used as money and in bride price. On Ambae, a new mat was valued more highly than an old mat. An old mat can be considered new if it has been redyed recently. In the past, men made trading expeditions to other districts to trade mats. There are many styles of mats, and they have individual names. The mats were only made by women, never by men. (See Bonnemaison)

Yap Island

Special mats called *mbul* or *ambul* have been described as currency but were seldom bartered. They were made of the extremely fine soft threads of banana fiber. The mats were kept rolled and out of sight. Large rolls were worth seven to 10 pounds. (See Quiggin p. 147)

Vitiaz Strait

A basket or leaf packet of taro was worth a *pandanus* mat.

MATTY ISLAND BELT MONEY - See Belt Money - Matty Island

MAUAI

Bougainville

Mauai consists of one fathom of bits of unpolished mussel shell disks. In Bougainville there are many kinds of shell money other than *mauai*. Some of them are *kurakanikana, sansai, mimis, kurireu, tomo, poponi, sariai, karoni, runnaku and momoru*. All are valued in terms of *mauai*. The most valuable is *kurakanikana*. It is worth 100 to 500 *mauai*. One fathom of *mauai* is worth any of the following: a medium pot, a *bilum* bag, two decorated arm bands, a hunting spear, a bow, two opossums, a plot's yield of taro, 20 coconuts, or 10 arrows. Ten fathoms of *mauai* also buy a suckling pig, and 50 fathoms will buy a large sow. Six fathoms of *mauai* will purchase the average acre of land, although most land is purchased in conjunction with *nori*, which is a kind of inheritance and mortuary feast transaction. In 1955 Oliver recorded 78,000 units of *mauai* among the Siuai of Bougainville. He also found 41,000 units of high value shell money. (See Oliver p. 339-348)

MAULAVATA

Choiseul Island

Shell rings made by Pongo, a foreigner who settled on Nuatabu Island, an island near Choiseul Island, are called *maulavata*. The natives feel that Pongo was the man who made all the shell money on Choiseul Island. (Per. Comm. Betty)

MAUWAI

North Solomons Province, Papua New Guinea

A string of speckled tops of *conus* shells broken into square bits, holed and strung is called *mauwai*. It is also called *abuta* or *aputa*. Better *mauwai* are used to purchase pigs. A fathom of *mauwai* is worth one shilling, a good arm-ring, a large pot, a large basket of taro, a large bailer shell, a club or a spear; 10-12 fathoms of *mauwai* are paid for a large pig or a murder. (See Quiggin p. 161-162)

MBADI

Africa, Zaire

Bundles of raphia fibers were a unit of value and were used as money. See Quiggin p. 56

MBARI - Also called mbadi. See mbadi

MBAKIHA

It is called *erenge* in Marovo has a yellow to red streak along one side where the ring often dips in and has a lustrous polish. It is also called *tarkola*. (See Waite 1983 p. 32) When it was worn as a necklace it was bound with turtle shell and fringed with opossum or flying fox teeth and modern glass seed beads. The yellow stain comes from using the hinge portion of the clamshell. Only a single ring of this kind could be made per valve. The *mbakiha* was a major symbol of the bigmen. It was used to hire an assassin or to make peace. It is the most valuable clamshell ring manufactured in the lagoons of New Georgia. It was probably manufactured by slaves who were captured on raids, bought or adopted. Some traders had manufactured porcelain copies of the shell ring complete with yellow streak hoping to trade for turtle-shell. The copies were accepted by the natives and were given a fixed money equivalent. (See Poata.) (See Miller p. 288)

Mbakiha

MBARAKE

It is called *tinete* in Marovo and is a ring where the natural clamshell contours often markedly distort the shape. The surface tends to be rougher in texture, and they are normally the larger of the kinds of *poata*. All are plain with no embellishments or decoration. The hole was made by either breaking and chipping the clamshell into a rough circle or by pecking and drilling with a bow drill. The ring was then ground on a black stone called *patu hokaram*. Slaves who were captured during raids, bought or adopted were probably used to make the rings. They were used as money with relatively fixed values, in marriage payments and for land purchases. Many people consider it the area's oldest form of money. While most people considered it the poorest form of shell ring, a few thought that because of its use, it could be considered one of the most valuable. It was used as a presentation to a conqueror as a last resort. (See Miller p. 289)

Mbakiha

The Roviana shell rings were traded for *kesa* and slaves from Choiseul Island; girls, megapode eggs and necklaces from Simbo; slaves, dyed barkcloth and turtles from Isabel; shields, baskets and barkcloth from Kolombangara; ndala and girls from Ranongga; blackstone from Rendova; and greenstone from Ghizo. As missions became well established, the use of shell rings for money diminished. (See Poata)

MBOKOMO

Solomon Islands

A *tridacna gigas* clam shell plaque carving was used as chief's money and in some cases as ornaments for small mortuary huts built to hold the skulls of chiefs and other important people. All plaques have rings or circles in some part of them and resemble the shell money rings *bakhia* or *hokata*. The Central Bank money exhibit in Honiara, Solomon Islands, describes these items as

Mbarake

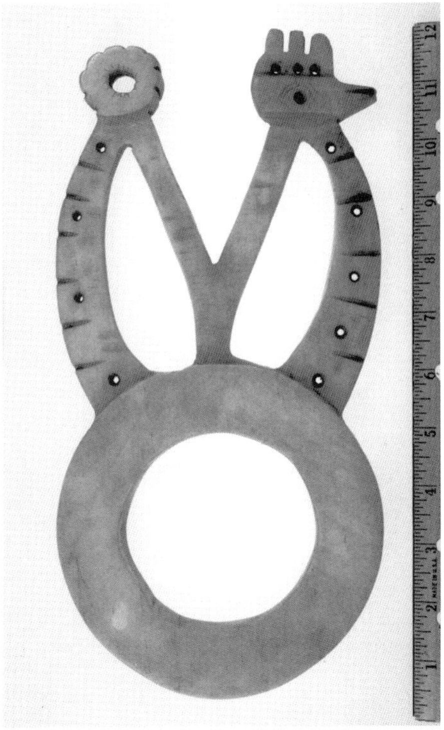

Mbokomo

Mbole

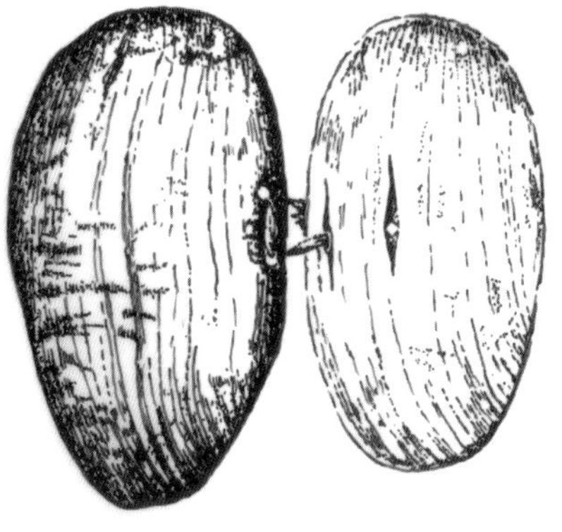

Melo Shell

chief's money and very valuable. There are two general types of plaques, with the first type having horizontal rows of small motifs like stylized identical humans. The second type has one or more anthropomorphic figures, like roosters, above a ring with a series of small holes along the sides of the figure or figures. All the plaques appear to be very old and have an overwhelming preoccupation with head hunting and the dead. According to a note on a broken plaque in the Solomon Islands Museum, most of the plaques were deliberately broken on the graves of the deceased chiefs. (See Waite p. 152 and 1983 p. 124)

MBOLE

Africa, Zaire

A bronze ingot in a U shape with five ridges on the outside. The pieces were used as money. (See Ballarini p. 117)

MBOSSO

Cameroon

Iron currency blade used as money. (Per. comm. Kurt Koschatzky)

MEJIT - See beads, jade

MELEGRINA - See Kina Shell Money

MELO SHELL

Papua New Guinea

Melo shells were rare and hard to obtain. They were worn as breast ornaments and formerly were used in bride price. (See Healey p.134-135). They were also called bailer shells because they were used to bail out canoes in the Fly River area. (See Quiggin p. 175)

Papua New Guinea, Kapauku tribe

The large *woti* shell (*Volutidae, Melo hunteri Perry*) (bailer shell) was a trade object, that was cut into sections, ground and polished to make wotiimo necklaces. Their value fluctuated considerably. (See Pospisil p. 312) (See Bailer Shell)

MELOTE

Central Africa

This spade was made by the Bongo tribe and used along with the Loggoh-Kullutty and Mahee for trade. It was used as an implement and also as money. (See Quiggin p. 96-97)

MERBOK

Australia

This is a complex system of delayed economic exchanges between individuals in the same tribe and different tribes. The tribes participating are the Mulluk Mulluk and the Madgella tribe of the Daly River, North Australia. A large variety of articles of intrinsic utilitarian basis are used. *Merbok* partners trade with each other. They are friends and partners. Some of the items traded are spears, hair belts, beeswax, stone axes, knives, and red and yellow ochre. A gift of *merbok* has always been an affirmation of friendship and attachment. There are many rules in its use. (See Elkin p. 156-164)

Melote

MEZONG - See Zong

MIDJOKO
Africa

A spiral copper bracelet worth two francs was used as money. (See Guyer p.80)

MIKAK
Irian Jaya

The huge baler shell was spoon-shaped and eight or more inches long and was worn with the white concave surface outward just under the chin. A single *mikak* would purchase a large pig. (See Matthiessen p. 12.)

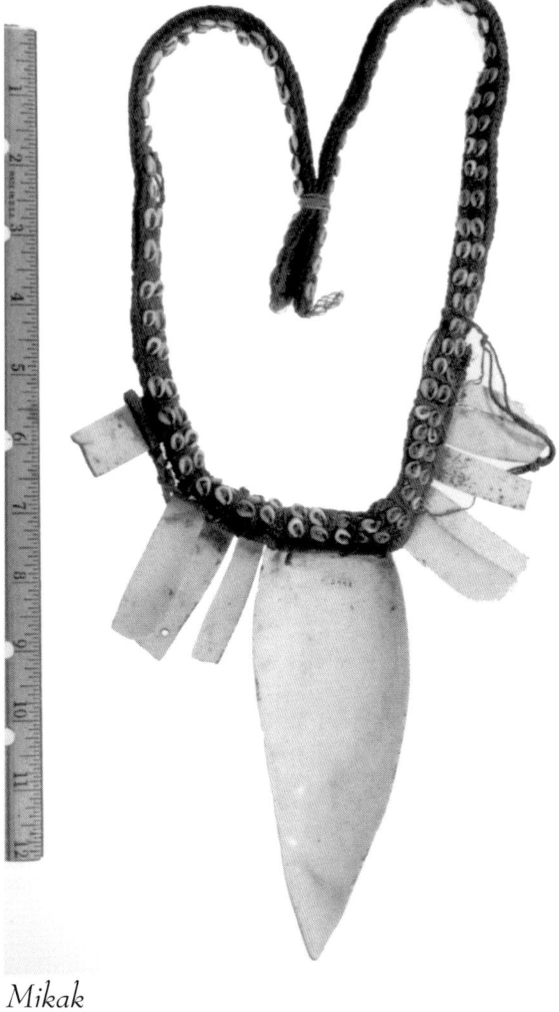
Mikak

MIMBOSS
French West Africa

Gabon tribe. Small iron rods that appear to be degenerated arrow points were used only as money. They were kept in bundles of up to 75 pieces. They were also called *bikie*. See *Bikie*. (See Mosher p. 27)

MING BANK NOTE
China, 1368-1399 A.D.

Paper money was made from the bark of the mulberry tree and stamped in a printing press. The note was printed on a coarse dark gray paper with uneven edges. It nominally had a value of 1,000 cash. The note was issued by the Chinese Imperial Government's Board of Revenue during the period of Hong Wu. By 1448 the notes had a real market value of only three cash, and after that they were not mentioned as a circulating money. Marco Polo reported the use of paper money in China while visiting there in the 13th century. It is estimated that only about 100 pieces are known today. They were all found under a Buddha figure in a Chinese temple by European soldiers looting the temple in Peking after the Boxer Rebellion in 1898. The notes were valued at 10 strings of cash pictured on the notes, but all known notes are only specimen notes never having been issued for circulation. Despite being paper money, Ming Bank Notes are often included in collections of odd and curious money because of their age and size. (8 3/4" x 12 1/4"). Deceptive replicas have

Minkata

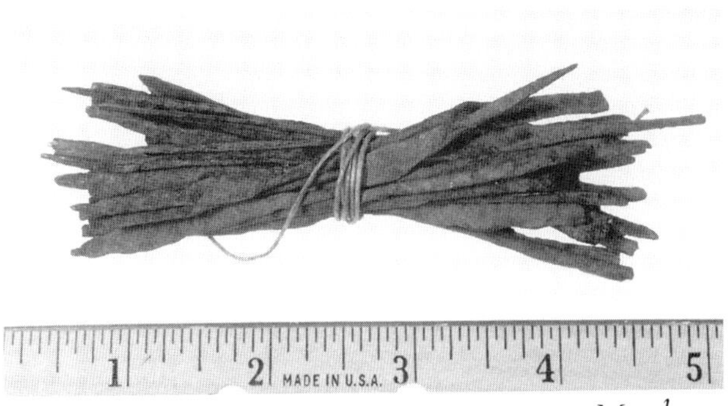

Mimboss

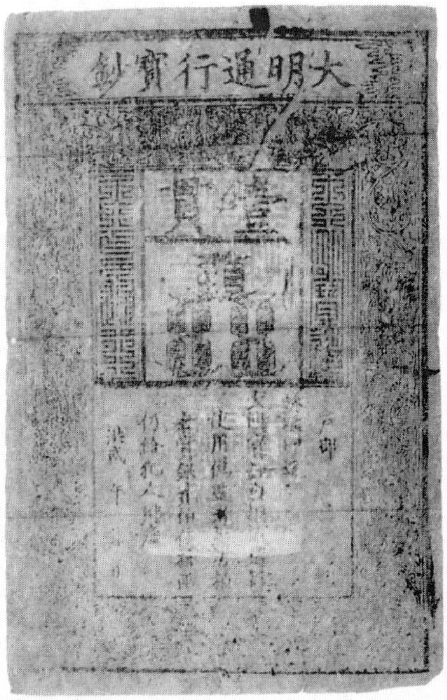

Ming Bank Note

Mint Bars

been sold as originals. The earliest paper money was made by Mangu, the grandson of the great Mongolian Ghengis Khan in 1254. None of these notes are known to exist, but some of the copper printing plates still exist. Ming notes in smaller denominations were recently discovered in China. (See Mosher p. 21)

MING TAO - See Knife Money

MINKATA

Wangata tribe, Congo

Coiled iron or brass arm or leg rings made in various sizes and weights were made by the Wangata tribe. The pieces were worn and also served as money. "When Chief M'kuba was asked if such a weight on his leg did not make it awkward for walking, he replied that it suited the dignity of a chief to have a slower and heavier walk than that of ordinary mortals." (See Quiggin p. 80)

MINT BARS

Southwestern America, 19th - 20th century

San Francisco mint silver bars. Traders exchanged silver bars with the Indians for jewelry, turquoise, etc. The Indians melted the bars for use in making jewelry and other ornaments. Many of the bars are small bars of about five oz. in weight. Many fakes are known.

MIS

New Ireland

This shell money is also called *manum, mangin* or *kaput.* It was originally made on the offshore islands of Tabar; but later made on the Lihir Islands which are now the main source of the new *mis.* It is believed to be made from the *Chrysostoma paradoxum* of the family Trochidae found on Dyaul (Djaul) Island off the west coast of northern New Ireland. There are two kinds of *mis* (*mangin*): heirloom *mangin* and circulating *mangin.* The heirloom *mangin* is no longer made or used and is often pure white or brilliant, translucent salmon in color. The circulating *mangin* have several grades. The color is most important, with the size of the disk second in importance. The most valuable ranking to the less valuable are : 1.) *pabang*: red-orange, large disks, 2.) *kuwas*: red-orange, smaller disks, 3.) *emeras*: red-brown, 4.) *sili-uro*: alternating bands of gray and pink-white, large disks, 5.) *lolot*: alternating bands of gray and pink-white, smaller disks. A large home- grown pig was worth $288, which was also equal to 50 *kina* and five strands of *mis.* After 1975 the government encouraged the people to again take up the craft of making shell money. *Mis* sold for $43.20 in 1979. The Lihir strands are slightly shorter than the Mandak, so the Mandak restring the strands to the preferred length. A decorative piece is called *urakembaum*. The piece is said to speak out during public exchanges and attract shell money. This pendant consists of a large kidney-shaped reddish-black seed with two rows of black seeds strung around the circumference of the large seed and the small black seeds radiating out. On the outer circumference of these two rows of black seeds is a row of white shell disks followed by two more rows of black seeds all radiating from the large center seed. Some pendants are simpler with varying numbers of rows of seeds and shell disks. At the two ends of the rows of shells and seeds are attached bead strings with either seeds or pigs' incisors attached. The red *mis* is called e*warendinpuruk* and is the highest value *mis*. Now red *mis* is the only kind made and used. The white variety was made taboo shortly after World War II.

Mint Bar

MITAKO

Africa

Short lengths (about six inches) of copper wire (*ngiele*) in the form of rings were called *mitako*. Imported brass (*mitako*) also were used later as well. They are also called *teke*. Every area had its own standards, which also changed as time passed because people cut off small pieces for extra profit. In 1890, the Bangala standard *mitako* was 20″ long and worth 15 centimes. The Lower Congo *mitako* was 27″ in 1884, 10″ in 1894, and 4-1/2″ in 1909. At one time a male slave was worth 600 *mitako*; a female slave, 200; a fowl, 10; and an egg, one *mitako*. Ten *Nzimbu* (cowries) were worth one *mitako*. In 1905 the Bahuana values were 10 olive shells, (*nzimbu*) worth one *mitako*, and 20 *mitako*, worth one fowl. One hundred *mitako* were worth two or three pounds of salt. Twenty salts (worth 2,000 *mitako*) were worth a male slave. (See Quiggin p. 47 & 76-77) (See Payne A-25) (See Ballarini p. 119)

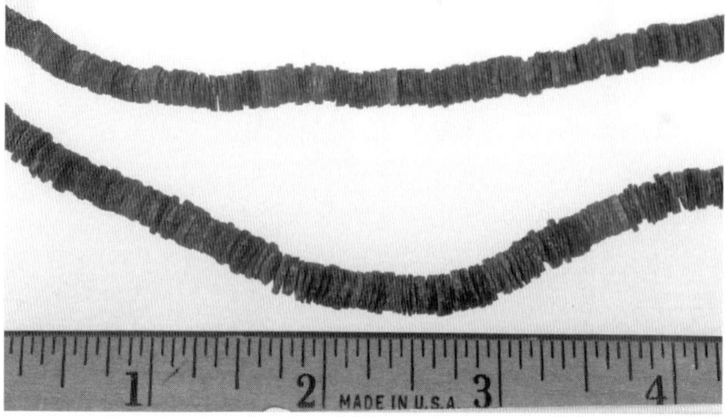

Mis

MIU

New Caledonia

The general name for money in New Caledonia is *miu*. Originally bits of tarsal bones of lizards were used to produce it. It was also imitated with conus shell tips, less than one millimeter. This was attached to a tail of plaited flying fox fur. *Miu bwarre* (black money) is the most valued. The darker the color, the higher the value. *Miu* was used by great chiefs for fines and trading. Many natives never even saw a string because it was so rare. White money, called *miu me*, is lighter in color but not white. A 6″ piece is worth one pound. *Go miu* (head of money) is most valued. It is a piece of bark cloth or wood with flying fox fur string. An opening in center exposes a face in the wood core. Shell money dangles below. (See Quiggin p. 170)

Mitako

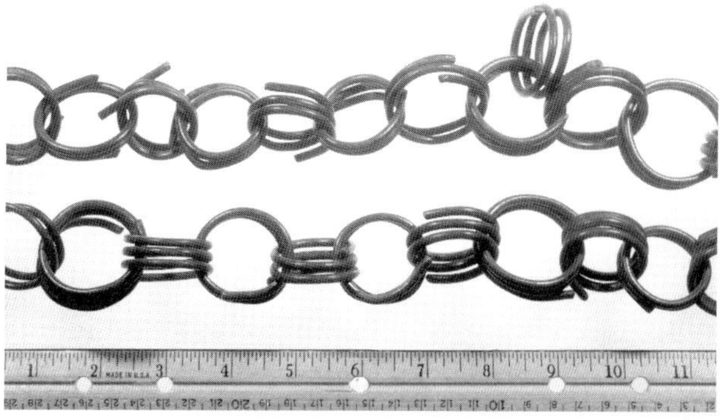

Mitako

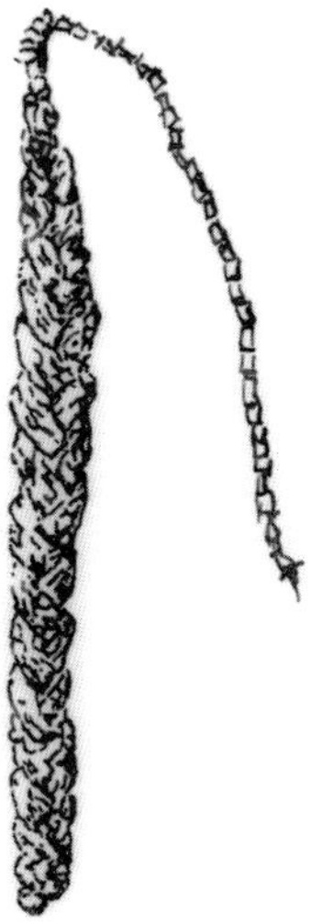

Miu

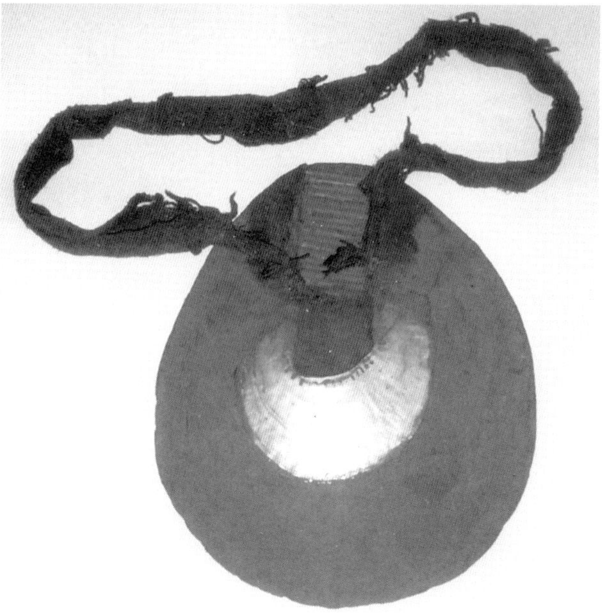

Kina Moka

MLE - See Cloth Money - Papua New Guinea

MMBUL

Yap Island

Money about two feet in diameter used on Yap Island. (See Ashby p. 46.)

MOKA

Highlands, Papua New Guinea

Moka is the pidgin English term for the ceremonial exchange festivals of the Enga, Gawil and Metlpa people. A moral obligation based on relationship by blood or marriage underlies a *Moka* partnership. A *Moka* relationship always involves three parties, never two. The Central Enga call their exchange festival the *Te*. Individuals and groups try to outdo each other returning more gifts than they received in the previous exchange. Kina *moka* and pigs are the most used gifts. At one time one pig and two kina shells was worth four *kina* shells. Later one pig and two *kina* shells was worth eight *kina* shells. The value of the *kina* shells had fallen due to an abundance of shells. The *kina* shells were obtained from Manus Island and Thursday Island in the Torres Strait. Later cowry shells, *nassa* and green snail shells were all eliminated in use as money due to their low value because of the increase of the shells in the area. The shells continued to be used in decoration, not as money. Other gifts may be salt, shells (up to 1960), cash, cassowaries and oil. In *moka* exchanges, at each stage more is given than was received the last time. (The *moka* part is the more part, and the rest is just repaying debts.) Over-giving is a means of humiliating a recipient, and under-giving is a means of sabotaging his plans. Without giving more, a man cannot achieve status as a big man. Every cycle of the *Enga Moka* has three main phases of activity. The first phase of solicitory gifts consists of live pigs, pearl shells, axes or legs of pork. They are passed from partner to partner in the same direction as the main items made in the previous cycle.These solicitory gifts are given both publicly and privately over a period of from several months to over a year. During this time, preparations are also made for the second phase which is the main presentations or true *Moka*. Dance grounds and special houses are prepared for this true *Moka*. During the true *Moka* the gifts are passed in the opposite direction as during the solicitory gifts. Gifts to important men can be as much as eight to 10 pigs or other valuables like cassowaries or shells. The pigs are then killed and eaten. The whole process will take place again in three or four years. The *Moka* partnerships outside the clan are between brothers-in-law or father-in-law and son-in-law. The *Moka* is actually a chain of exchange partnerships. A man who gives or receives a

Moka can wear another omak-stick. (See Omak.) During a pig *Moka*, a man must give at least eight live animals for it to be considered a true *Moka*. A shell *Moka* has no less than eight pearl shells given for it to be called a true shell *Moka*. The pearl shells have a ring of resin coated with red ochre because the red is considered an excellent bearer of power. The *werma* carrying strap and bark bag are also rubbed with red ochre. The great *Moka* can have several hundred pigs and in recent times can have thousands of gold lip pearl shells. The great *Moka* lasts for eight days. (See Kina Moka) (See Safer and Gill p. 64-66)

MOKO

Island of Alor and surrounding islands,

As late as 1914. This bronze drum was the main currency on Alor Island and is still used today in the remote areas in the purchase of brides. It is involved in a complicated financial system administered by men who then leave all the gardening and other work to the women. *Mokos* were used as part of bride price as well as in other exchanges. The earliest drums were called *Dongson* and probably were produced during the Bronze Age. Later *mokos* are called "additional" *mokos* by Kemper (p. 365) to avoid calling them "fakes." The old *mokos* are made of bronze while the later, modern ones are made of brass. While *kyee-zee* were made in one piece, *mokos* were made in two or more pieces. The pieces were fitted together to appear to be one piece, the handles were soldered on and the horizontal parts were occasionally riveted on. Du Bois gives the following names and values in the 1920s for the various *mokos*:

Mokos	*Rupiahs*	Dollars
Lasingtafa	1	.50
Salaka	2	1.00
Fatafa	2.5	1.25
Kabali	3	1.50
Piki	5	2.50
Tawantama	5	2.50
Hiekbui	6	3.00
Tamamia	8	4.00
Maningmauk	10	5.00
Kolmale	13	6.50
Hawataka	15	7.50
Yekasing	25	12.50
Fehawa	30	15.00
Aimala	65	32.50
Afuipe	70	35.00
Makassar	130 and up	
Djawa	500 and up	
Itkira	1000 and up	

A pig was worth a *Piki moko*, which is five *rupiahs* ($2.50), Du Bois states. *Mokos* were imported from Java by Makassarese traders. The importation was stopped

Moko

Dongson

Old Bronze Moko

Moon Over Pejeng Moko

before the turn of the 20th century. This caused the value to rise due to a shortage. Some *mokos* were worth as much as 50 pigs. By 1900, new copies of the old drums were made in Java, and they were traded as money for agricultural produce. The large increase in drums created disarray in the monetary system. The natives valued the older drums at much higher values than the modern Java pieces. The possession of an old valuable drum was sometimes a joint ownership of an entire family. The *mokos* were mostly kept in the loft of the house. In about 1905 there were about 20,000 *mokos* on Alor Island. Consequently in 1914, the Dutch Colonial Government banned the import of *mokos* from East Java. Hoping to encourage the use of modern money, they banned the use of *mokos* for money except to pay taxes and then scrapped the 1,660 mokos received in payment of taxes. They still allowed the *mokos* to be used in bride price, however. *Mokos*, along with pigs and gongs, were the most highly prized money on the island. They were worth one to 3,000 rupiahs each. An inventory taken in 1916 showed there were still 2,164 *mokos* remaining. It can be assumed that many mokos were in hiding and not counted. The ornamentation on the newer drums was more floral and Chinese or Indian-influenced than found on the earlier Dongson drums. The old residents of Alor said they could distinguish genuine old *mokos* from imitations by passing their hands over the drum's surface and then smelling their palms, according to Kempers (p. 382). *Mokos*, pigs and gongs were used in bride price and in dowry, which is separate from bride price. The engagement gift starts the procedure, and it consists of a *moko* worth from $1.50 to $2.50. This is given to the bride's father, and a shawl is given to her mother. The bride price is usually about $60.50 in *mokos*, which is three times as much as the dowry, which is $20.10. If the marriage does not take place after the payment of the first and largest *moko*, the groom can ask for its return. Wealthy brides' families require the groom to pay much more than families that are not as rich. The most valuable *mokos* were never used in bride price, however, because no girl was worth that much. There are other gifts and requirements the groom also must participate in, such as the giving of at least four piglets as well as food gifts such as corn and rice. Some kinds of *mokos* were used only in commerce, while other kinds were used in bride price as well as in commerce. There are many sizes of *mokos*. The largest of all is the Moon of Pejeng (dia. 63″ length 120″) of which only one exists. It is located in a temple on the island of Bali. Next there is the large *Manuaba* (dia. 39″ length 42″) and the medium size *Manuaba* (dia. 20″). Next there are the old mokos made of bronze (dia. 25″ length 24″), followed by the brass *mokos* which we commonly see (dia. 14″ length 24″ with some being even smaller). Most have four handles which are on the upper part of the mantle and equally spaced around the circumference. The miniature *mokos* are dia. 1 1/4" length 2", and only a small number have handles. (See Kempers) (See Einzig p. 95-97)

MOMOGO - See headband

MONDJO - See Mandjong

MONDONO

Papua New Guinea, Gende

This whitish powder is used as a tonic dietary supplement for pigs to make them grow fat. The powder comes from an opening in the ground caused by a nocturnal earth tremor common in this area. It is traded by the Gende for salt, dog and possum teeth, small axe blades, and pigs. See Hughes p. 112-113.

MONEY COWRY - See Cowry Shell

MONEY SWORD

China, until recently, if not still being made.

The sword was made of cash pieces attached to a bamboo or iron frame with string. Also they are called *quian* meaning cash or money sword. The sword was used as a gift to the bride from her family to bring her health, wealth, happiness, and many children. Then it was hung at the entrance of the wedding carriage and later in their home or business. Others say it was used as a pension for wounded or retiring soldiers. It was thought to bring good luck, but the swords are essentially amulets to ward off evil spirit, and to protect a couple, a house, or a child as the case may be. They were never used as money in the sword form, so they were not a trading medium or unit of measure. Some say they were hung above the bed of a sick person. They were thought to banish the spirits that caused the illness. The earliest known pieces are from the 1890s; some have Northern Song Dynasty coins from a thousand years ago. They were considered a store of value. They are included in many money collectors.

MONEY TREE

China, Japan, before 1850

Cash coins were cast in molds with the coins on a "tree" so that many coins could be made in one mold. Pieces were then broken off and finished prior to circulation. Few original trees remain. Souvenir and novelty trees with false coins were made for decoration and as charms but not intended for circulation. Beware of fakes. (See Payne A-19)

Dongson

Money Sword

Novelty Money Tree

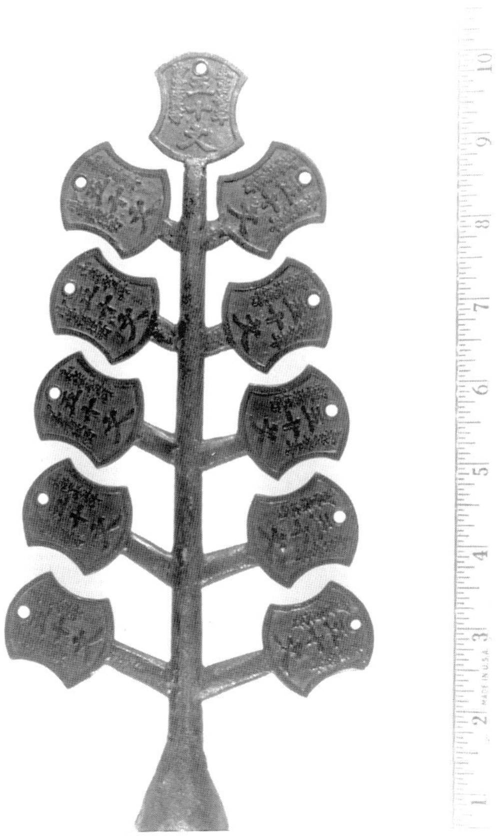

Money Tree - China

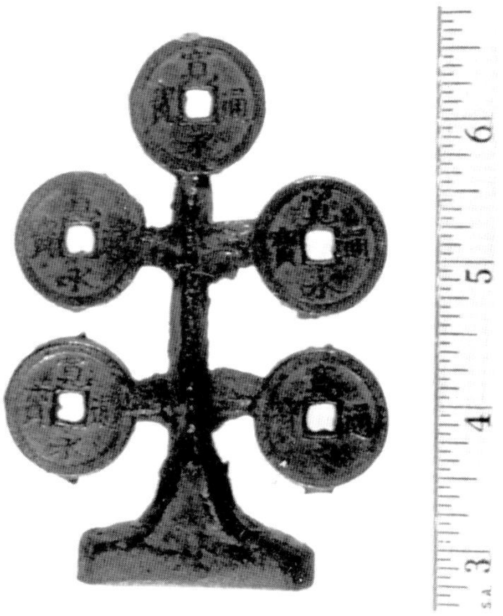

Money Tree - Japan

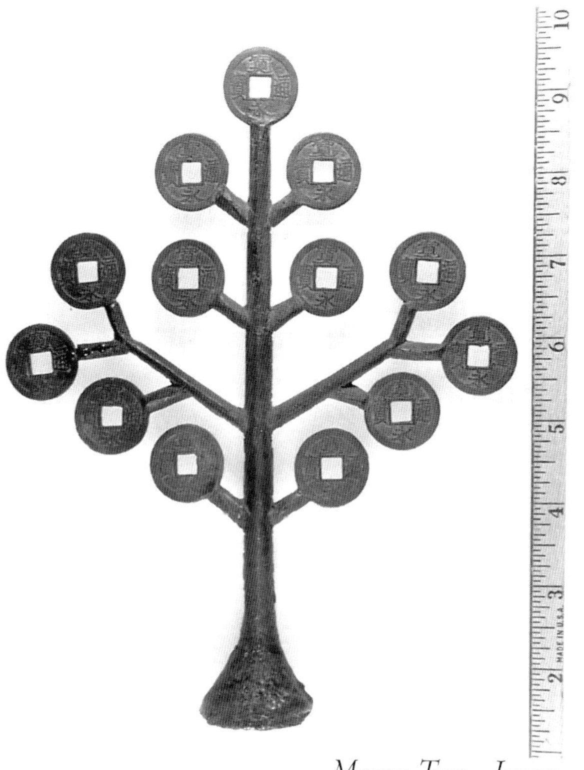

Money Tree - Japan

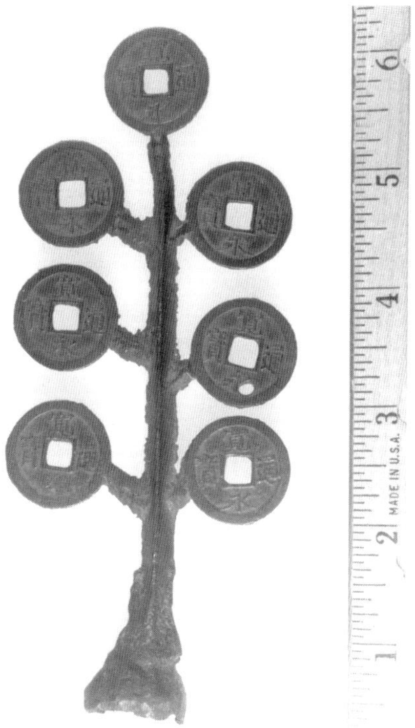

Money Tree - China

Malaysia, 1883 - 1919
Money trees made of tin, 13 to 17 coins. They are called a *pitis* tree. All very rare. (See Mitchiner p.409)

Morocco
1790 - 1873
Bronze. Three rows of four Falu coins each. Some partial and entire trees exist.

MOON MONEY - See Tingle Dangle Money

Money Tree - Morocco

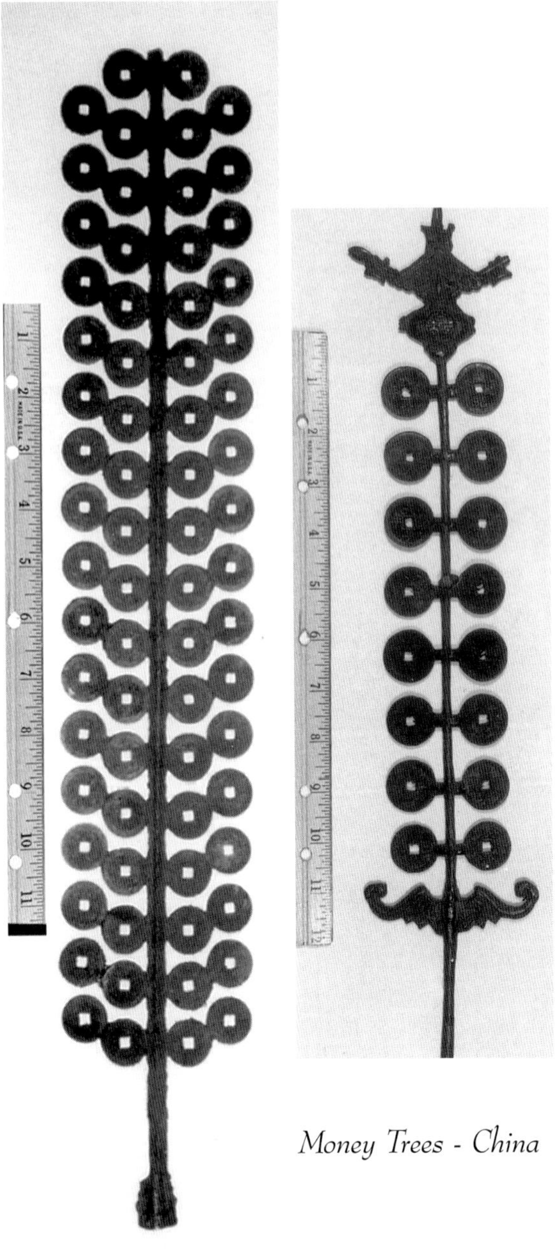

Money Trees - China

Money Tree - Malaysia

Mortor and Pestle

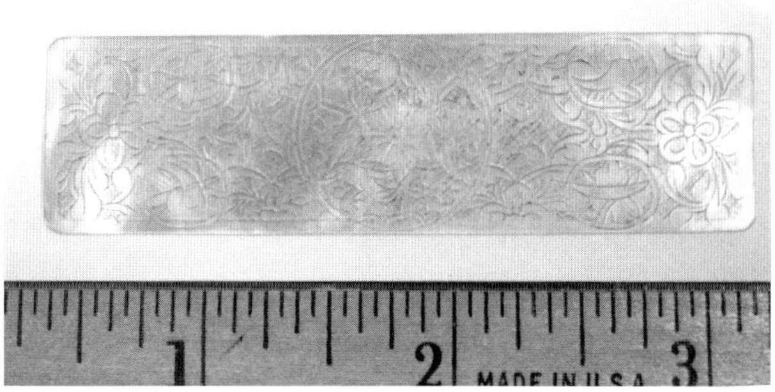

Mother-of-Pearl Gambling Token

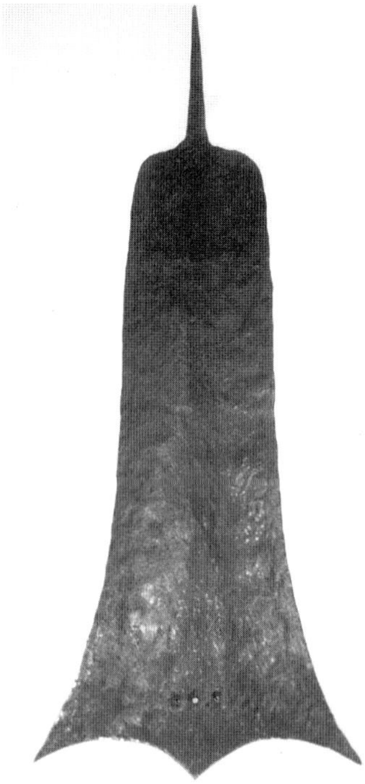

Munesia

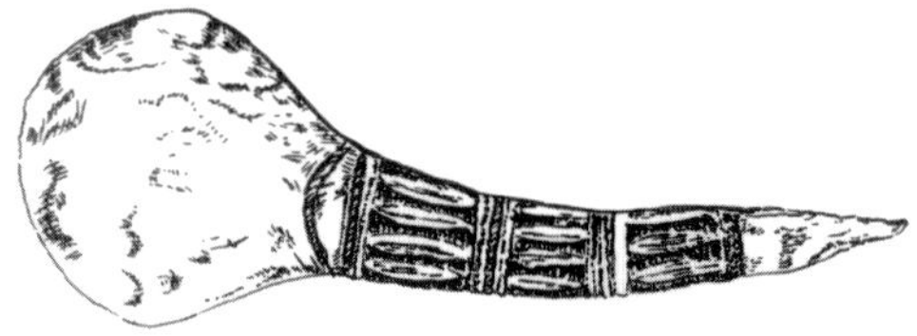

Munshi Axehead

MOOSE SKIN

Quebec, 1674

Moose skins were made legal tender at one time. (See Taxay p. 145) (See Quiggin p. 308)

MORTAR AND PESTLE

Yap Island

Large mortars made of soft wood and pestles (called *ma*) from *tridacna* shell and firmly bound were recognized as wealth, though not as a circulating medium. Mortars are 1′ high and wide; pestles are 1′ - 2′ long and very heavy. They have a high value, and have some symbolic meaning. (See Quiggin p. 147) Very Rare

MOTHER OF PEARL - See Abalone Shell

MOTHER-OF-PEARL GAMBLING TOKEN

It was believed that these tokens were from Siam, but they were actually made in China for use in America and Europe as gambling chips as early as the 1700s and were never used in Siam. Hand engraved round, oval, rectangular, and fish-shaped. 2 1/2″

MUNSEIA

Zaire

Munseia is part of a four iron blade monetary system. The first has a value of 1/2 and is called *nkwa* (pl. *lokwa*). The next has a value of one and is called *bokona* (pl. *makona*). The next has a value of two and is called *lingeme* (pl. *mangeme*), and the last has a value of four and is called *munseia* (pl. *minseia*). The *bokona* is the most common blade. The pieces were used until 1940. One *bokona* had a value of five Belgium francs. A bundle of 10 *bokona* was a common unit. The blades were also collectively called *mpata mine*. (Per. comm, Kurt Koschatzky)

MUNSHI AXEHEAD

Northern Nigeria

The Munshi tribe used this axehead as currency. 12″ (See Quiggin p. 89)

MUSCAVADO - See Sugar

MUSKET BALL

Massachusetts, 1635

Musket balls of a full bore were made legal tender. They had a value of one farthing but were not legal tender in quantities of more than 48 at one time. (See Einzig p. 291-292)

MUKUBA WA MATWI
Katanga, Africa

Also called the copper bar with ears and was in the form of the capital "I". Produced by the Sanga. They range up to four feet long. A bar three feet long was the price of a female slave in the 1800s.

Mukuba Wa Matwi

Mukuba Wa Matwi

MUSANGA
Africa

This string of snail-shells was used as money by the Batetela of the Upper Lomami.They were made from the African snail and served no other purpose than as money. The string was originally worth one franc. It was worth as high as 25 francs when traders found they couldn't purchase ivory with money alone unless supplemented with some of these shell strings. A string measured from the big toe to the heel and was worth a *doti*, which was one yard of indigo-blue cloth. Ten yards of indigo-blue cloth were worth any other piece of cloth. They were also called *ikumi* and *viringi*. (See Quiggin p. 48-49) See Snailshell

Musnaga

MUSINA - Plural for lerale. (See lerale.)

MUSKET
Fiji, 1800s

One musket would purchase 12 to 20 pigs. One to five muskets would purchase a young girl from 15 to 20 years old. One musket would also purchase 12 160-gallon casks of *beche-de-mer*, a Chinese aphrodisiac. Muskets would also purchase labor to work for the planters. Also see guns (Clunie, p.81-82)

MUSUKU
Transvaal, Africa

This ancient copper ingot looks like a top hat with finger-like protrusions coming from the top. It was used as money. Each stud in the top represented 1/4 pound of copper in the ingot. An ingot with four studs was valued at one cow, or 20 bracelets or 10 anklets. By the 1930s they were considered sacred. (See Herbert p. 192)

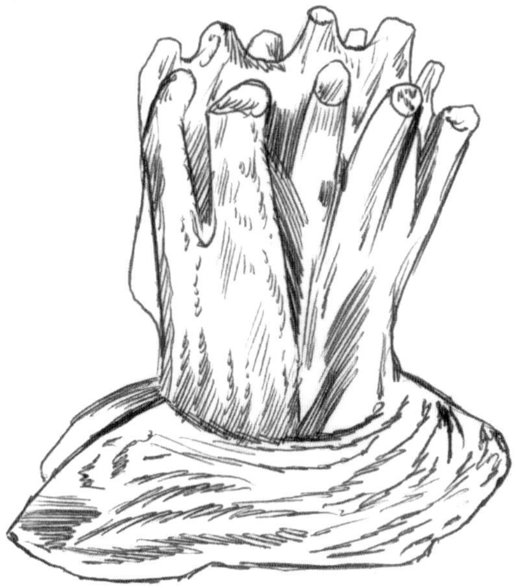

Musuku

MUTAGA
Yeke Tribe, Africa

Their most common currency was thin copper wire wound around a vegetable fiber mixed with goat and animal hair. It was the form of a bracelet. (See Herbert p. 191)

Mwali

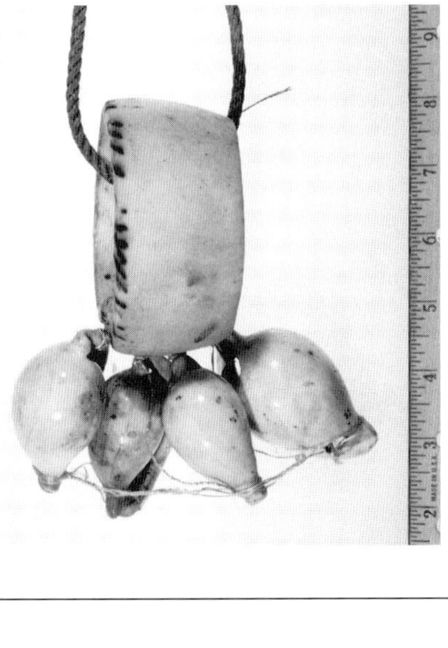

MWALI

Trobriand Islands, to the present

It was called *Toea* in the Motu language. This major Kula valuable circulated in counterclockwise direction from island to island. This arm shell ring was made by knocking out the circular base along the rim of the shell with a stone. A groove was made parallel to the knocked-out base with a stone. This created a cross-section which was then polished on the outside by rubbing on a flat sandstone and the interior polished with a long cylindrical piece of stone. The larger rings were made of *Conus Leopardus* (*Conus Millepunctatus*). Smaller rings probably were made with *Conus Litteratus*. On some rings, holes were made in the side of the shell where one rim overlaps the other. Black banana seeds and *sapi sapi* disks were attached as ornaments. The decoration could also consist of up to six cowry shells, depending on its size, and a larger number of small cowry shells bound together by trade beads. Also, suspended ornaments of seeds, beads and cowries were added to give the *mwali* a rattling sound when you walked with it. The lip of the shell was called a *kudula*. Depending on the size of the cut shell, a number of egg cowries called buna *kudula* were attached. The size of the cut conus shell determined the number of *buna kudula* that were attached. The circumference of the *mwari* is called the *pwala* and a number of egg cowries (*Ovula ovum*) called *mwaridoga* were attached to it according to its size. The smaller circumference of the *mwari* was called the *wadola*. Men who were knowledgeable with *mwali* could have a fairly good idea as to the size of the shell by how many *buna kudula* and how many *mwaridoga* were on the shell. Smaller *mwali* were probably made from the Conus litteratus. The rope it was suspended by was called *kaipwesi*. Most of the *mwali* were too small to wear, and the ones that were large enough to wear would not be worn except once in a decade by a very important person. Originally they were circulated as pairs until 1896 in the North and 1910 in the South. The right-hand one was larger and finer than the left hand one. The shells came only from Kavataria and Kayleula. *Mwali* were previously made on Woodlark. The rings were made in three stages.The rough ring was called *makavayna* and was made in the vicinity of Kayleula. It was then given as a *kula* gift in the Amphletts where it was polished and given as a *kula* gift in Dobu. The holes were made in the side of the shell where one rim overlapped the other, and black banana seeds and *sapi sapi* disks were attached as ornaments.This did not affect the value. Originally they were circulated as pairs, but this seems to have stopped about 1896 in the northern area and about 1910 in the southern area. In 1904 it was reported that a bride price consisted of 43 arm shells, three pigs and 100 dog teeth.

In 1975 it was reported that a bride price consisted of 836 arm shells, 67 bags of rice, 14 hands of bananas, 31 bags of sugar and 3,245 *kina* in money. In 1957 one *toea* was worth one pound. Valuation criteria were size, circumference, and width as well as age as determined by color. Red striations began to form on the surface of the shell. The classifications were from lower to higher as follows: *Gibwagibwa, Tomorimwaiya, Mwarigidageda, Mwaributu, Mwarikau.* Most men never touched a *mwarikau*-class *mwari.* On the other hand, the *gibwagibwa* was the lowest-ranking class and it was considered ugly because it was unpolished, brown and small, and not considered worth cleaning. The arm shells were worn by both the men and women. This was the kind that many times young men used to enter the *kula.* In 1970 a *mwali* was used to purchase a canoe. The value of a *mwali* is estimated according to the position it was able to occupy on a man's arm. The higher up it will go, the more valuable it was. In 1970 the smallest low-quality shell was worth $10 and the largest and finest about $190. (See Kula.)

Mwali

NADJATA - See Trombash

NAGA

Assam

The *naga* is a spearhead that was used in bride price, fines, and compensation for adultery. It is related to the *dao* and *chadili* from the same area. 19" (See Quiggin p. 205-206)

Naga

NAGATA - See Trombash

NAILS

Greece

In ancient times, nails or iron spits were used as money, according to Davies (p. 45.)

North America, Colonial Period

Hand-wrought iron nails were scarce and expensive until a nail-cutting and heading machine was invented in the late 1700s. Nails may have served as a barter item or in trade but not as true money of fixed value. Their cost was stated in pence according to size, the same as it is today. A tenpenny nail is approximately 3". Old pieces are square with a "butterfly" head. (See Sigler p. 35-36)

Colonial Period Nails

South Seas Islands

In 1643, nails were traded for fish hooks in the Friendly Islands. In 1778, Captain Cook traded a sixpenny nail for several small pigs. In 1791, nails were used to obtain coconuts, fish, and bread-fruit in the Marquesas Islands. There are many other instances of nails being used as money or in trade in the early days. (See Rickard)

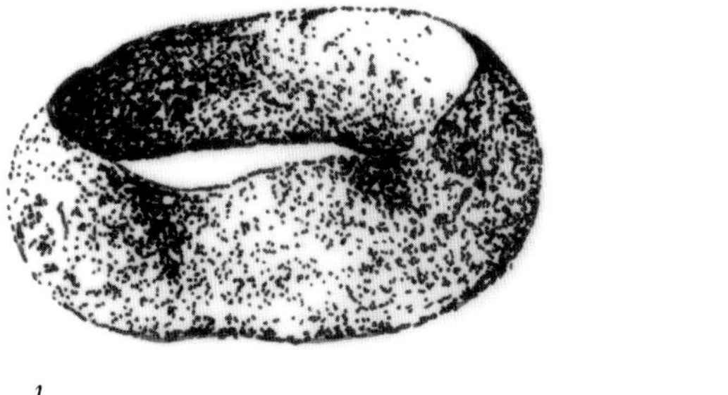

Navela

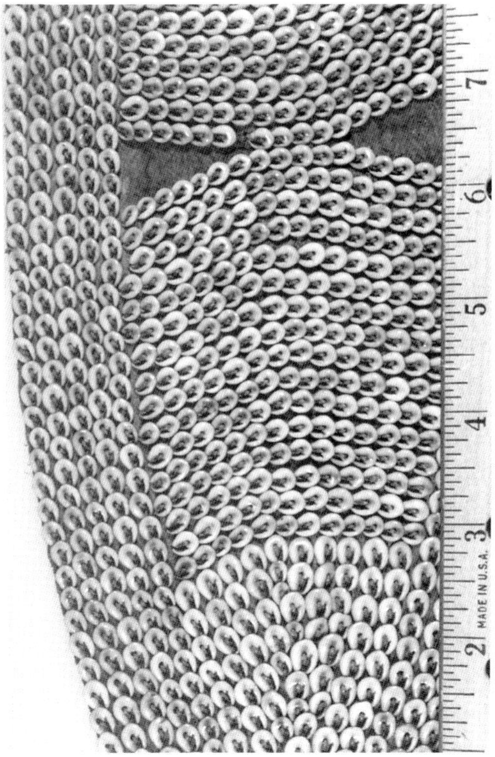

NAMATAWUK

Siassi Islands, Papua New Guinea

Small brown shell disks were used to buy food, dogs, pigs, and in bride price. 1/10 " diameter.

NASSA SHELL MONEY

Papua New Guinea

Backs of *nassa callospira* shells (dog-whelk) were broken and threaded on a cord. The cords were used for money. The overlapping design is found in the Lower Ramu area of Madang Province and in East Sepik Province. *Nassa* shell money was used for bride price. The Min people used them as a store of wealth before modern money was available. The shells were also counterfeited unsuccessfully when the German administration was in control as well as in the late 1930s. In Pidgin it is called *tambu.* Some shells are sewed on barkcloth and arranged in designs. The headbands of *nassa* shell (dogwhelk) shells were formerly used in bride price. By the 1960s the *nassa* shells were no longer used as money. (See Healey p. 134-135) If the shells are fixed onto a stiff cane, the cane is called *diwarra.*

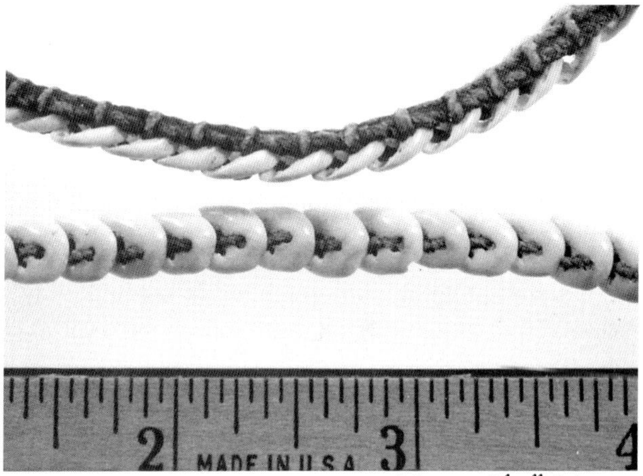

Nassa Shell Money

Papua New Guinea, Kapauku Tribe

Necklace, called *dedege* was made of the small white cowry-like shell (*Nassariidae, Nassarius*). A necklace that consists of two strings which pass through the two perforations in each shell is called *dedege woja.* It is the length of a man's arm and is worth 30 glass beads. Pospisil describes them as being used in bride price. The longer necklaces, he says are six feet long and worth 90 glass beads. In 1955 necklaces consisting of many kinds of glass beads were also considered as money. (Pospisil p. 304) The Europeans introduced a cylindrical or spherical light blue glass bead called *dau,* which was money, and 30 of them were worth one *dege bomoje* cowry. See *Diwarra.* (See Quiggin p. 173-174) See *Tau Tau*

NAVELA

Vanuatu

The *navela* is a stone ring, up to 5 feet in circumference, weighting 40-50 pounds. A man could crawl through the piece. It is also called *navela ornavilah.* Each piece had its own name and history and was believed not to have been made by human hands. Chiefs presented *navela* at feasts, thereby necessitating another exchange at a return feast. It was used in bride price. (See Quiggin p. 167-168)

Navoi

NAVOI

New Britain

Tortoise-shell armbands were used as currency and bride price. Patterns were scratched on the surface and filled with lime. (See Quiggin p. 155)

NDALA

A forehead ornament of turtle-shell fretwork over a clamshell base. It was worn as a major symbol of the bigman.

NDAP

Rossel Island

One of two major forms of money. See *nko*. *Ndap* are triangular or oval-shaped pieces of spondylus shell with hole in corner and polished, round edges. The colors vary from white over yellow and orange to red. There are 22 different kinds or grades. Certain of these are further subdivided into two or three classes. About 40 different distinctions of value exist. The pieces are identified by number. The higher numbers are more valuable. On all numbers above seven no new pieces have been added to the number in existence. All the existing pieces were obtained in the far distant past. All pieces of numbers 13 to 22 are known to all the natives who have above-average knowledge in financial affairs. All the pieces in classes 15 to 22 have an individual name in addition to their class name. There are a total of only 81 total pieces in classes 15 to 22. They exist as follows: #22 - 7, #21 - 10, #20 - 10, #19 - 10, #18 - 20, #17 - 7, #16 - 7, #15 - 10. There are more #4 than there are #1-3, yet the #4 is more valuable. The unit is 10 disks. High valued pieces are treated with religious reverence and do not circulate freely like the lower values. It is one of the most complicated monetary systems in the world. The values cannot be exchanged for other values. Pieces are borrowed and interest paid or discounted. If a piece is borrowed, interest is calculated and paid by repaying a higher number piece. For numbers above 17, the interest is paid with lower numbers, and only the same number piece as was borrowed is repaid. If the loan period is for several years, the interest will be paid several times during that period. Security, in the form of a ceremonial stone axe, is given for the time the *ndap* is borrowed. At present there is very little use for values above number 18. Presently number 18 is used in payment for wives. A number 20 was used as compensation for ritual murder. The numbers over 18 are kept enclosed and are not to see the light of day. *Ndap* money is known as man's money, while *nko* is known as women's money. Most values have a limited purpose. If a man buys a pig for a feast, it is ceremonially divided into 10 portions, and each portion is paid for with a different item of currency. The better parts of the pig are paid for with the higher value *ndap*. Today all of the low ranking *ndap* have a cash equivalent, but not the higher values. It has been called a prestige money and is not directly comparable to our Western monetary systems.

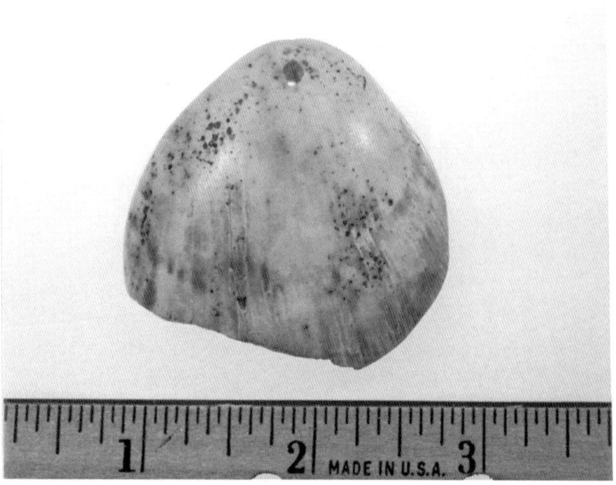

Ndap

Another expert, John Liep, feels that Armstrong didn't interpret the basic forms of exchange correctly. Armstrong based his model on the principle of interest. Liep feels the socio-political control in Yela formerly was connected to the control over trade relations to Sudest. The rigid system of exchange in Yela was dominated by the minority of men who possessed the scarce high-rank *ndap*. It seems probable that their position was based on the control over the import of foreign goods and valuables from Sudest. A complex exchange economy had evolved in Yela. Various valuables were used for bride price, houses, canoes, pigs, crops, mortuary presentations, and homicide payments associated with cannibalism. The big men took the high-ranking *ndap* out of circulation. The high-ranking *ndap* were still required for bride price and other high payment events. The high-ranking *ndap* was still transferred, but only for one night. It was then returned to the original owner and other items substituted. A pig was the payment for the transfer. This system allows the big men to control the wealth. In everyday life, food is passed by the means of kinship reciprocity without the use of money. Liep estimates in the early 1970s there were 15,000 to 20,000 *ndap* in Yela. The highest ranking are individually named and are considered as ancient. Lower ranking *ndap* were still circulating freely. Some were still being produced. Liep feels *ndap* were not a media in the commodity exchange of a developed market. The *ndap* up to the *chaamo* were worth 14 cents in 1973. The value of the higher pieces was exceedingly vague.

The list of the names of *ndap* starting with the most valuable are:
kuchem - out of circulation

Neck Ring Money

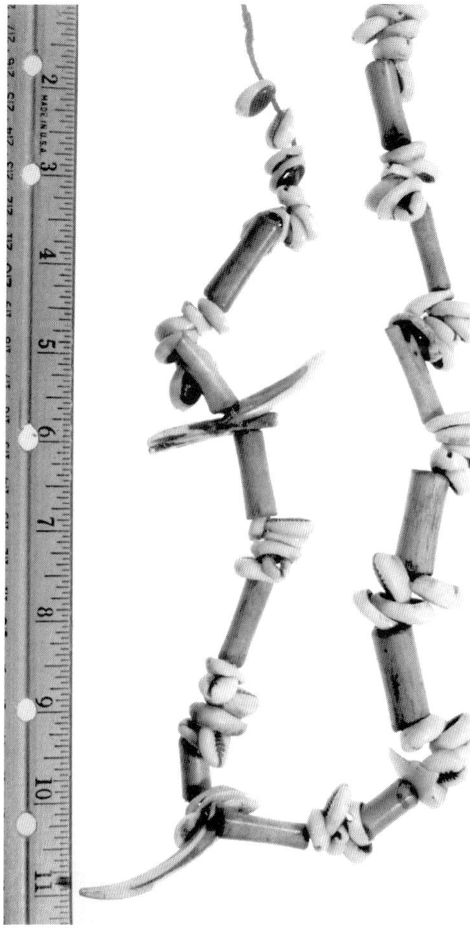

Dani Neckalnce with Bamboo and Cowry Shells

poochem - out of circulation
nggemita - out of circulation
techem - out of circulation
chaamandu - out of circulation - nominally involved in payments
nggomindo - out of circulation - nominally involved in payments
tpimbaa - out of circulation - nominally involved in payments
kweronundo - out of circulation - nominally involved in payments
tangwolundo - out of circulation - nominally involved in payments
tcputundbo
yeranggewindo
chaamo
tepute
wope
kpoya
kpomondap
kechem
ghaamo
mdbono
(See Armstrong) (See Einzig p. 73-75) (See Liep) (See Piddington p.276-277) See *Pko, Pwomondap*

NDOA - See Liganda

NDOVU

Guadalcanal

This is a unit of money used to pay fines and bride price on Guadalcanal. A *ndovu* consists of 40 strings of shell disks, 40 dog's teeth and 100 porpoise teeth. In 1964 the natives could purchase a fathom length of shell disks for 70 cents or five shillings. The bride price could consist of more than 100 shell strings as well as hundreds of porpoise teeth and dog teeth. More than 25 people could contribute to this bride price. The bride price was split into two portions, with one portion going to her mother's relatives and the other to her father's relatives. (See Hogbin p.21-48)

NECK RING MONEY

Africa, Congo

Copper and brass neck rings weighing as much as 28 pounds each were worn by women and used in bride price. In a raid on an enemy village the victors simply cut off the heads of the women to take the neck rings back to their village. A husband can remove the neck ring from his wife by having his wife lie on the ground and attaching vines to the ring and to stakes in the ground about ten yards apart. The vines are then turned, forcing apart the ring. 7-1/2" diameter.

Africa, Nigeria
This neck ring was used by the Yoruba tribe. See Schaedler p. 241.

Irian Jaya P1194
The Dani highly prize this necklace which is made of small pieces of bamboo alternating with cowry shells. (See Borel p. 210)

NEEDLE MONEY

Ethiopia
Iron needle money called *hakuna* was used as money. A cow was worth 5,000 needles in the 14th century. (See Gill, p.10)

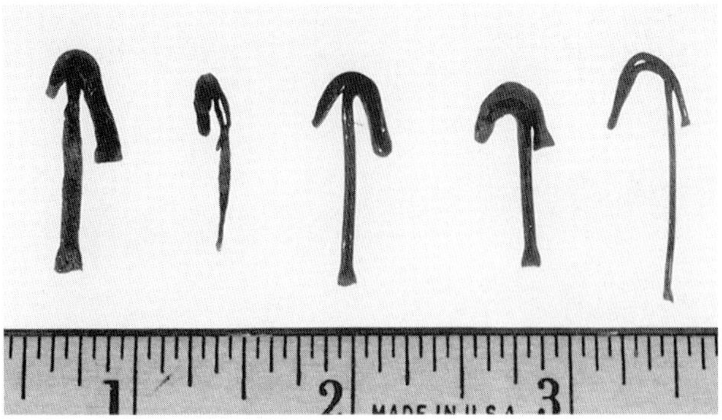

Needle Money

Eastern & Southern Nigeria
Small iron arrow or needle shaped pieces also called *anyun, aiyu, ozala, umumu* or *aiyu* and are valued at three shillings per pound. The exchange value was roughly 45 to the penny or twice as much as cowries. They were at one time used to buy slaves, but it took hundreds of thousands to purchase just one slave. (See Quiggin p. 88-89) They were used in sacrificing and juju, although formerly they were used as money. Johansson says there are at least five main types, but it is hard to find two alike. (See Johansson p. 42)

NELO

Nendo Island, Solomon Islands
A nose pendant made of turtle-shell or occasionally clamshell worn when performing a dance also called *nelo.* They are treated as family heirlooms and occasionally traded.

Nelo

NENENENE - See Porpoise teeth

NEPHRITE

New Zealand
The Maori tribe used nephrite weapons and ornaments as money. They are true jade. A nephrite club called a mere was a well used form of money and store of wealth. It was thought to contain *mana,* a kind of psychic force or magical essence. Force gave the owner special powers. Nephrite was also made into adzes, *tiki,* and other items. Some people feel that greenstone (nephrite) was the money of the Maori. While it was not true money, it comes as close to money as the Maori have. It was not a medium of exchange, nor did it have a fixed value. (See Quiggin p. 13)

Nephrite

NEPTUNES - See Basins.

"All the News That's Fit to Print."

The New York Times.

CITY EDITION

ITALIANS DRIVE GERMANS FROM SARDINIA; ALLIES AGAIN WIDEN SALERNO BEACHHEAD; RUSSIANS CAPTURE 1,200 TOWNS IN SWEEP

MIGHTIEST FLEET IN HISTORY CREATED IN NAVY EXPANSION

DRIVE ON SMOLENSK

ITALY DRIVE GAINS

NEW GAINS RECORDED IN THE ITALIAN CAMPAIGN

ISLAND JOINS ALLIES

SWARMS OF PLANES STRIKE AT EUROPE

U. S. Forces Raid Gilberts, Hit 2 Central Pacific Bases

BIG GERMAN DRIVE ON IN YUGOSLAVIA

War News Summarized

Churchill Arrives Safely in London; Faces Debates on Italy and Labor

Newspaper

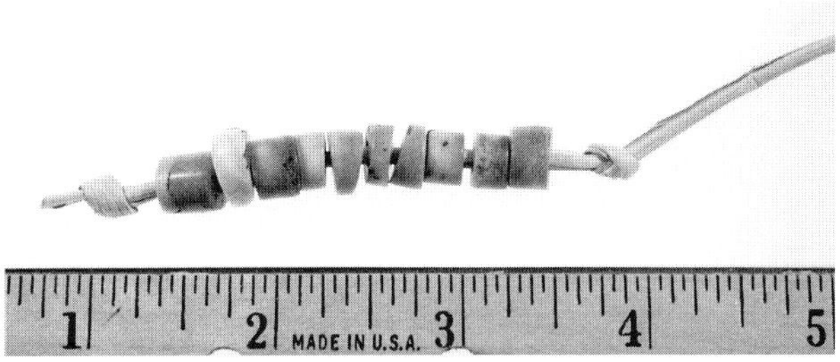

Nko

Nose Ornament - Papau New Guinea

NEWSPAPER

Papua New Guinea, Mount Hagen

During World War II the natives were introduced to cigarettes and liked them. After the war the natives had no access to modern cigarettes when their services were no longer needed in the war effort and therefore went back to their local tobacco, but they needed paper to wrap it in to form a cigarette. Father Ross's mission station in the Mount Hagen area had a large supply of newspapers left by American servicemen after they left the area. The mission's stock of trade items like *tambu* shells, salt, and cowry shells was depleted at about the same time. Father Ross then traded his newspapers for food and labor. A quarter sheet of The New York Times was worth five pounds of sweet potatoes, eight ears of corn, a large bundle of firewood, a small bunch of bananas or two six-foot lengths of sugar cane. A half sheet was worth a large bundle of bananas or one half day's labor working on the mission's lawns. (See Gitlow p. 80-81) Newspapers were later used in death payments as well as betrothal payments. (See Du Toit p. 175-177)

NET BAG - See Bilum

NGALA

Africa, Zaire

This iron ceremonial execution knife was used to execute captured escaped slaves. Twenty knives were the cost of a wife. (See Ballarini p. 57) See execution knife- Bangala.

NGBAKA

Africa, Zaire

This iron throwing knife was used as money and also in bride price. The handle is bound with copper bands, fiber, or animal hide. (See Ballarini p. 73)

NGBELE - See Liganda.

NGEBELE - See liganda.

NGERN RING - See Bar Money

NGIELE - See Mitako

NGINDZA - See throwing knife - Africa, Ubangi, Bubu

NGKE - See bell money.

NGOLO - See Execution Knife - -Bangala

NGON HOI - See Tok, Willow Leaf Money

NGWOLO - See throwing knife - Africa, Ubangi, Bubu

NICKELS - See Wooden Nickels

NJA - See Manilla - coiled

NKO

Rossel Island

One of two kinds of money on Rossel Island. It was made from the giant clam, and there are 16 different values, all of which circulate freely, unlike *Ndap*. They are regarded as women's money. (See *ndap*) (See Einzig p. 73-75)

An expert, John Liep, calls it *ko* and sets a unit as a set of 10 disks of shell on a string of dried banana-leaf. The higher the rank, the wider the disk. The diameter runs from 12 mm to 40 mm for the highest ranking. The rules of exchange are similar to those of *ndap*. Sometimes a number of *nko* are strung together to form a long rope. The higher-ranking *nko* circulate, but there are many limitations on their exchange. (See Liep)

NNABUO

Ashanti tribe, Africa

The earliest medium of exchange among the Ashanti were iron rods called *nnabuo*. They ceased to be used as money by the 18th century. (See Guyer p. 98.)

NOSE ORNAMENT MONEY

Asmat, Irian Jaya

Many styles of carved pig, human or cassowary bone nose pieces were used in trade and were worn through the septum of the nose. The Asmat also used a shell nose ornament made from the cymbium shell. See bipane and *otsj*.

Papua New Guinea and Solomon Islands

Seashell or tortoise shell were worn through the septum of the nose. There were many different designs and cutouts on the surface of the nose ornament. "At Wagawag (New Guinea) the blood-price for a man killed in a brawl was quoted as a pair of really good shell armrings, one shell nose-stick and one Samakupa necklace of Sapi-Sapi" according to Quiggin p. 174.

Philippines

These pieces were made in both bronze and gold.

Solomon Islands

Nose sticks were made from tortoise-shell and seashell See *usu usu*.

Nose Ornaments - Phillapines: Left, Bronze; Right, Gold

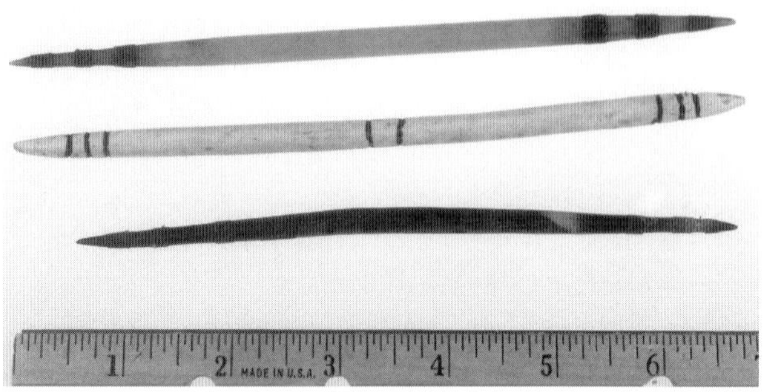

Nose Ornaments - Solomon Islands

Nose Ornaments - Dugong Bone

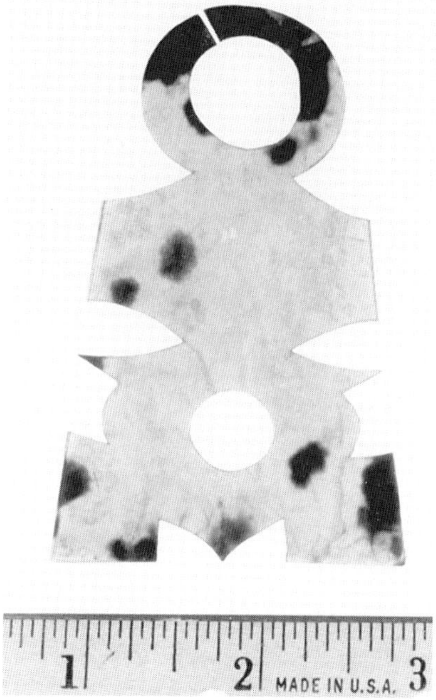

Nose Ornament - Tortoise Shell

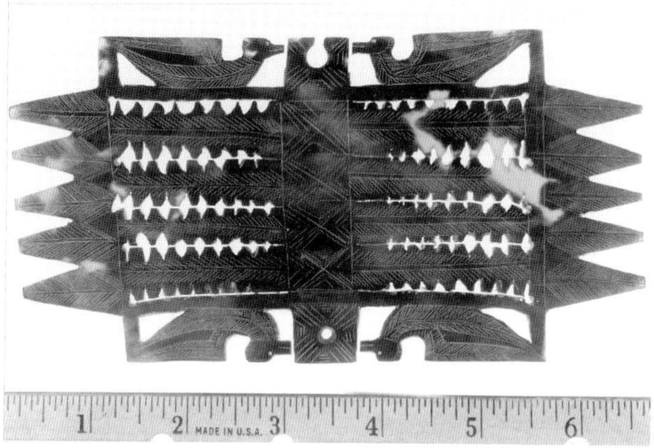

Nose Ornament - Paraparanaiga

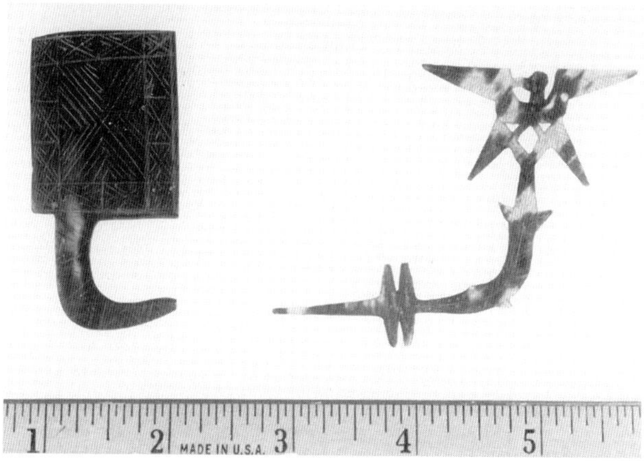

Nose Ornament - Left, Taumono; Right, Maurakoura

Solomon Islands

This *dugong* (manatee) bone nose ornament was used as money . The small teeth are flying fox teeth.

Solomon Islands

A tortoise shell nose ornament (*asana maka lua*) whose custom name was *Keasanga* was worn by both men and women for different ceremonies and celebrations. Only the high-born men wore these pieces. Special value was attached to the light yellow or amber color of the shell which occurred with limited exposure of the turtle to sun light. They were considered a valued item.

These Santa Ana Island nose ornaments were made from tortoise shell and had incised decorations over the entire piece. Some of the different kinds known are: *Paraparanaiga, Taumono* (left) and *Maurakoura* (right).

Torres Straits

Nose sticks called *kirkup* were traded with New Guinea.

NOTGELD -

Notgeld is emergency money issued in primarily German-speaking countries. After World War I an estimated 175,000 different issues were made by German private issuers alone. Most pieces are low-priced and found in excellent condition. They are not primitive money but are collected by many collectors. (See Aluminum Foil Money, Leather Money, Linen Money, Linoleum Money, Porcelain Money, Silk Money)

NOVEAPU

Solomon Islands

Another name for feather money sticks. See feather sticks.

NSAMBU

It is also known as a Katanga ring and was worn on the ankles as rings, coiled wire or bangles. 3″ diameter, 3″ height (See Quiggin p. 79)

NTA - See Mat Money, Africa, Congo

NTCHANG

Cameroon

It consists of a brass, copper or iron wire 1/4″ diameter rolled into a spiral with four or five twists about 3″ in diameter. In 1899 one *ntchang* was worth five bags of salt or 20 large beads. (See Schaedler p. 324)

NTET - See Fang Axe

NTUM IRON MONEY

South Cameroon

Thin iron rod was wrapped with strips of rattan. It is a pure form of money. (See Schaedler p. 322)

NUTMEG-GRATER MONEY

China

It is doubtful if this item was ever used as money in China. Some do feel that if it was used, it was used in the time of barter (Ramsden p. 18.) It is believed the item was in fact used as a grater.

NUTS - See Almonds, Areca Nuts

NZIMBU SHELLS

Africa

The name covers any shells used as currency, not only olive shells. One hundred *nzimbus* would buy a fowl. A male slave was worth 10,000 *nzimbu*. See Quiggin p. 47

NZUNDU

Congo, Africa

A bride price was six *nzundu*, which were metal anvils. (See Guyer p. 114.)

O SHELL PENDANT

Torres Straits

Triangular pieces from the outer whorl of the large cone shell, *wauri* (*Conus litteratus var. millepunctatus*) were worn as a pendant by brides. No unmarried girl could wear them. They formed a part of the bride's decoration. The number and variety depended on the wealth of her parents. (See Haddon Vol. 4 p.47-48)

OATS - See Grain Currency

OBAN - See Plate Money

OBSIDIAN

Northwestern California, Europe

Since ancient times, hand-formed blades of natural obsidian were used by natives. A barter item in ancient times, it was also used in trade by North American Indian tribes. It was valued by color (black or red), length and finish. Medium-sized black blades passed at $1 an inch, while the ratio lessened below the length of 6″ or 8″ and increased sharply above that of about 15″. A 20-inch blade was worth about $50, and blades that reach 30 to 33 inches did not have a value placed on them. Red blades were rarer than black and were worth at least 1 1/2 times as much. Strings of small blades were also used as money. White flint blades called *ne-gam* were also used as money and were more valuable than the other color blades. (See Taxay p.80)

O Shell Pendant

O Shell Pendants

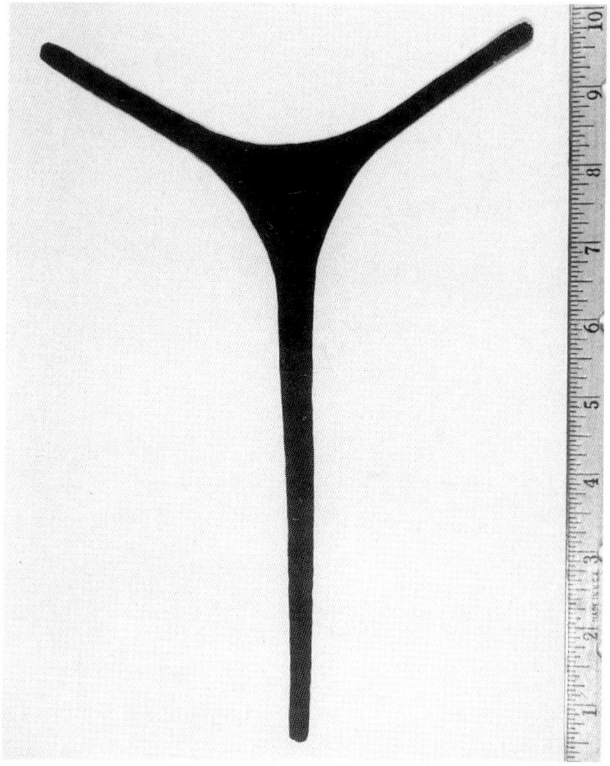

Ogoja Penny

Ogoja Penny

D'Entrecasteaux group

Obsidian was used as an item of trade and was valued at one plaited fiber belt. (See Malinowski p. 245)

Papua New Guinea

In Maenge country the people of Mukulu village made expeditions once a year to the north coast to trade obsidian from the Nakanai of the Ulamona area, who received it from the Talasea. A block of obsidian eight to 10 inches square was traded for a roll of tobacco leaves three feet long and 12 inches in diameter. The blocks were then split into flakes and traded to other villages to carve. Slivers of obsidian were used for tattooing and bleeding themselves.

The Siassi and then the Tami traders brought obsidian from the Willaumez Peninsula in New Britain to the Huon Gulf. A cubical piece the size of a coconut was worth a single pot in northeastern New Britain but was worth a dozen or more pots at Sio.

OCHRE

Australia

The principal trade routes in South Australia seem to have been focused around the red ochre deposits at Parachilina Gorge in the Flinders Range according to (Elkin p. 427). Ochre could be considered as a medium of exchange, depending on your definition of money.

Arizona, New Ireland, Africa, Europe

Red clay containing iron was used for face paint and money. In Papua New Guinea the value is for the work done to make the ochre by wrapping the clay in wild asparagus leaves and baking it on a wooden trestle over a fire. The clay material can be obtained by anyone in the area of the deposits. By the 1960s the trade stores brought commercial paints to the natives, and the traditional pigments were abandoned. (See Quiggin p. 199)

Papua New Guinea

On Umbio Island a hard-packed ball about three inches in diameter was worth one clay pot or a basket of betel nut. A large lump of 50 to 60 pounds was worth a pig or a dog.

Papua New Guinea, Chimbu area

Red ochre was prepared by Chimbu men of the Gena Nogar tribe in the north-central part of the Wahgi region. It was called *gawagamba* and was traded throughout central Chimbu. (See Hughes p. 108-109).

Blue ochre, called *gamba kum*, was made and used like red ochre.

Vanuatu

Ochre for paint was widely traded. Much of it originated in Santo and Malakula and was traded with Ambae, Ambrym and Epi. (Rodman p. 178)

OGOJA PENNY

Africa

Y shaped piece of iron. Worth from one penny to less than a 1/2 penny. The sizes varied by tribe. The Akuju tribe called them *Iyawa*; the Nkun tribe called them *Efufy*; and the Munshi tribe called a similar Y-shaped piece *Yakaro*. They were also used in Nigeria and Zaire. The native names were also *iyayaw* or *akaju*. (See Johansson p. 36 & Quiggin p. 87)

OIL - See Palm Oil

OKPOHO OKUK

Nigeria

Brass rods bent in a U shape were used as money. These bars were used as early as 1698 and as late as 1907. At one time 38 bars would buy a male slave, and a female was slightly less. In 1856 a bar was worth one shilling in Old Calabar. (Eyo p.67)

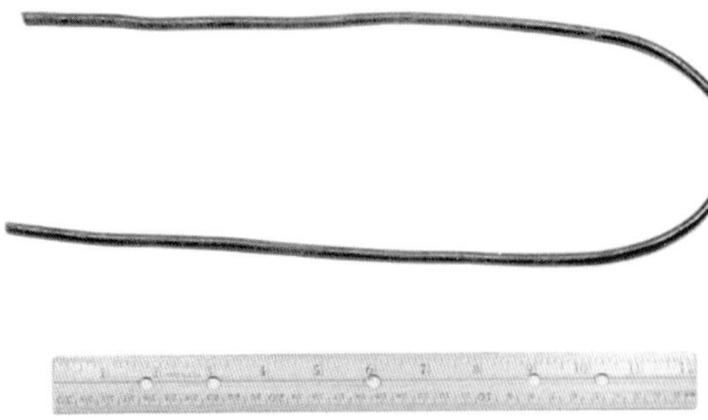

Okpoho Okuk

OLIVE OIL

Ionian Islands and Aegean Islands, 1944-1945

Values were fixed daily in this standard, and all things were valued in terms of olive oil. Prices varied with the fluctuation in the price of olive oil. The sovereign replaced oil in 1945. (See Einzig p. 310)

Olive Shell - From Burial

OLIVE SHELLS

Africa and North America

The shells are also known as *Oliva Nana* or *Olivella* shells. The olive shells were extremely popular in trading, second only to the cowry shell. In Brazil they were used along with cowries in the slave markets. They were traded as individual shells, in strings strung end to end, and also by breaking the shells, holing the pieces and then stringing them. The Indians used the shells in all three manners in their trading. Beads were made from the wall of the shell, and the bead retains the slight curvature of the shell. Large quantities of these beads have been found, indicating that they were very popular with the Indians. They were also called *simbos, simbu, nzimbu mbudi,* or *jimbu* shells in southwest Africa. This shell was used until the 16th century in the Kongo kingdom as money. They were also used in Bantu. One hundred olive shells (*nzimbu*) would buy a fowl, while a male slave was worth 10,000 shells, and a female slave was worth 10,000 to 30,000 shells. (See Quiggin p. 47)

Olive Shells

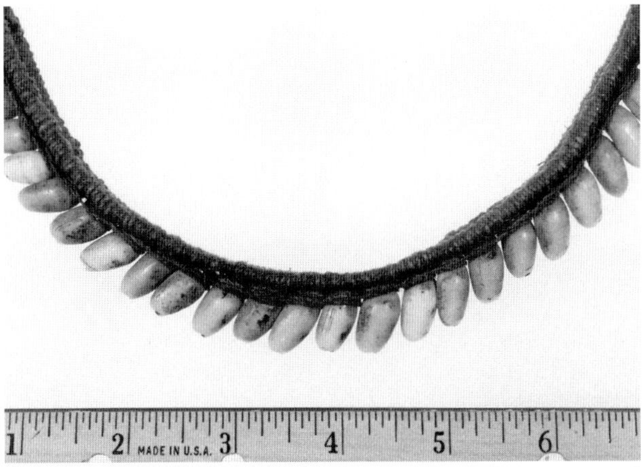

Olive Shells Bound In A Cord

Torres Straits

Strings of olive shells (called *waraz* or *uradzi*) had a high value, with a good necklace worth a canoe in 1912. Two or three ordinary strings would also equal one canoe. (See Haddon Vol. 4 p.42)

OMAK

Papua New Guinea

A series of bamboo sticks about four inches long attached parallel to each other and suspended by a cord from around the neck was called *omak* or *omaak*. Each bamboo stick represents an amount of wealth in pigs, shell, axes, etc., presented with the expectation that they would be repaid in a future ceremony. It was not a loan, as it was hoped that the other party would not be able to equal the presentation in value and thus lose power, with the first party gaining more power or influence. This ceremony is a "*moga*." The presenter wore the bamboo stick around his neck and it was a matter of great prestige and indicated a "big man." The transactions recorded occurred at the ceremony of Muga (*Moka*) in the Mt. Hagen area of the Highlands. The piece was not money itself but merely showed the giving away of wealth. Gitlow states that the bamboo slats represent the number of *moga* ceremonies in which he participated as one of the two principals. Both participants may add a bamboo slat to their *omak*. Each slat represents that at least 10 *kina* shells has passed through his hands. (See Gitlow p. 83-85)

Oamk

ONGANDA

Africa

A bronze rhomboid bar in a U-shape was used as money, and its value was based on a decimal system of values based on weight. In 1950 this piece was worth 10 Belgian francs. One *onganda* was worth between two and 10 *onglese*, depending on its size. (See Ballarini p. 114)

Onganda

OPIUM WEIGHTS - See Weights

OPOSSUM TEETH - See Cuscus Teeth

ORCHID BARK

Papua New Guinea

Strings of orchid bark were used as decorations, necklaces and barter. The strings are yellow and usually are multiple stranded.

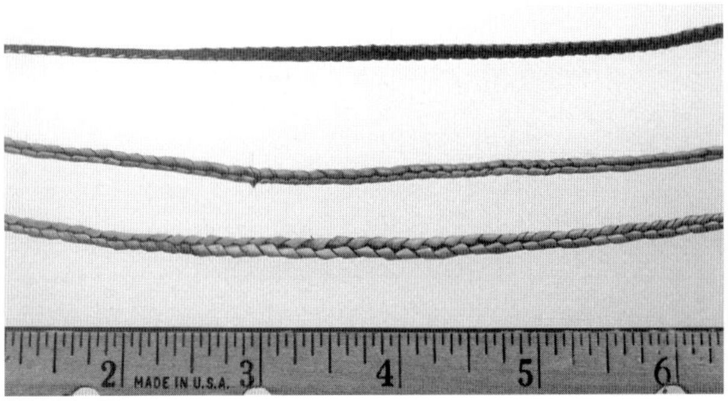

Orchid Bark

O-RINKA - See rhinoceros horn

OSHELE - See Woshele.

OSTRICH EGG SHELL BEADS

Africa

The disks were used among the Ovambo, Herero, Nama, and Bergdama tribes. The disks, fashioned from the egg shell, were pierced and strung. They are also called "bushmen's beads" and were used as ornaments and as a medium of exchange. (See Beads - ostrich egg shell).

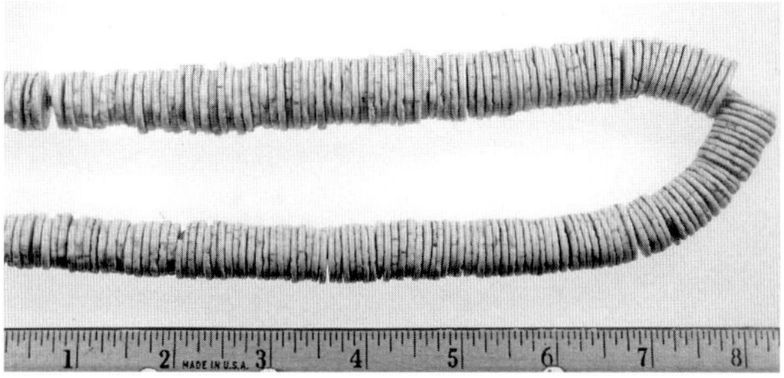

Ostrich Egg Shell Beads

OSTRICH FEATHERS

South Africa

Nama tribe. Medium of exchange. (See Einzig p. 169)

OTSJ

Asmat, Irian Jaya

The nose pieces were made of pig, human or cassowary bone. There are seven different varieties. The bones were worn through the septum. (See Konrad p. 147)

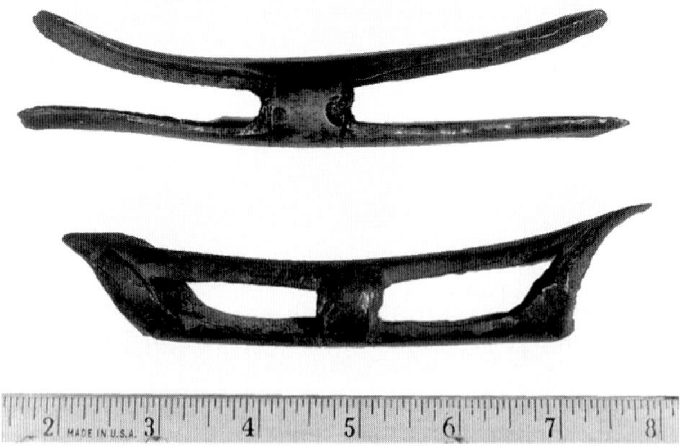

Otsj - Nose Ornament

OTTER - See Sea Otter

OXEN

Ancient times

In the Homeric poems oxen are distinctly and repeatedly mentioned as the commodity in terms of which those to be worth nine oxen, and compared with those of Glaucos, worth one hundred. (See Jevons p. 21)

PAAZONG - See Mandjong

PACK SADDLE SYCEE MONEY

China 1875 - 1933

These *sycee* were issued by many banking houses in China. Virtually all the pack saddle sycee of this type were made in Yunnan Province. Most have a weight of five taels fine silver (175 - 195 grams). The stamp of the banking house was stamped three times on the hump. The inscription of the Government Assay Official was stamped twice on the hump of some pieces issued in the 1920s and have the inscription "Fine silver, (money)-exchange house manufactured in the era of the People's State," instead of the standard Banking House inscription. From 1912-1925, packsaddles were minted which cited that they were manufactured in the era of the Republic. There are hundreds of varieties known. (See Mitchiner p. 520-528& LeMay p. 9-11)

Pack Saddle Sycee Money

PADRE BEADS - See Beads

PAGE

New Britain

Massive *tridacna* shell rings were used in bride price and on ceremonial occasions. They originally came from

New Ireland. One page was worth 20 to 40 coconuts. (See Panoff p.8)

PALAY - See Rice

PALM OIL

Nigeria

Palm oil was the principal standard of value. The kroo was the unit of value, and it varied from village to village. In 1830, the kroo was worth 12 gallons of palm oil in Calabar. This equaled eight to 12 copper bars. In 1886, a case of gin was worth 27.9 gallons of palm oil. (See Johansson p. 48) (Guyer p. 17)

PANDANUS MAT - See mat

PANTS - See Pu Money

PAWN - See Turquoise

PEAS

Quebec, Massachusetts, 1690

Peas were used as currency in 1690. (See Taxay p. 145-146)

PEARL BUTTON MONEY - See Buttons

PEARL SHELL MONEY

Caroline Islands

They were called *Fae*, *Fai* or *Fe*. This spade-shaped shell was pierced at the end and hung by a thick cord. Larger pieces had a higher value. The piece pictured has a native woven handle. Imitations were made of aragonite (like the Yap stone money). It was also used to make fish-hook money. 5-1/2" x 9" (See Quiggin p. 141-142)

New Guinea & Solomons Islands - See kina shell

PEACE PIPE

Northern Canada, America, North Manitoba

Indians used peace pipes as gifts with ceremonial significance and as a trade item. The most valued pipes were made of catlinite (pipestone) or steatite (soapstone). (See Quiggin p. 317)

PEARL

United States

American Indians used natural fresh-water pearls as a trade item. The Maidu carried on a trade with the Wintun in which they received pearls and shells that were considered as money. (See Thurnwald p. 252) See Beads - fresh-water pearls.

Peace Pipe

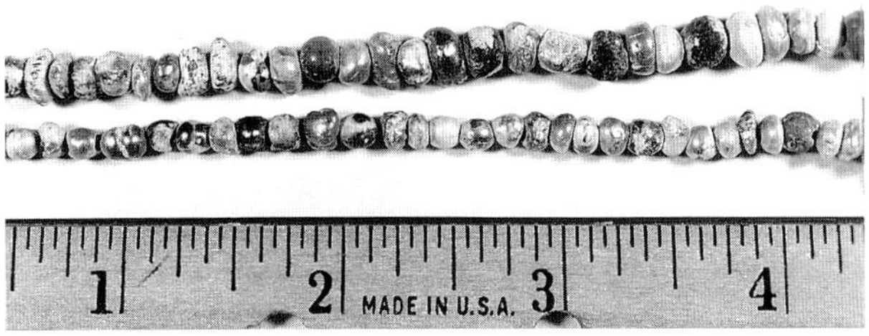

Pearls

Pearl Shell

PEARL SHELL

New Britain

Gold lip shells in the shape of pendants with nassa shells and other decorations attached were highly valued for ornaments in many places and also served as money. See Kina. (See Lewis p.11 Plate 4)

PELE STRINGS

Duke of York Islands

Many different kinds of shells were used to make *pele*. Orange-red (highly prized), white, light purplish-gray, or dark brown (most common) were some of the valued colors. The shells are rough, thin, or smooth. The strings were made in Mioko in Duke of York Islands. *Pele* strings were used as money in the trade for *diwarra*. *Diwarra* was the real money on Duke of York Islands. The government (German) prohibited the use of *pele* in 1902. It was also used on the southern part of New Ireland. *Pele* was the money of the Tolai people on New Britain who made the *diwarra* to trade for the *pele*. It was made from the walls of the very common pearl shells. Eleven types of *pele* were used. The strings varied in length from less than six inches to almost 10 inches. The strings were then bundled into groups of from four to ten strings. *Pele* strings were measured from one nipple to another nipple, with four or five lengths of *pele* being enough to purchase from Nakanai the shells that will make two to three fathoms of *tambu*. The most important variety, called *pirr*, is made from the top of the shells *Cypraea annulus L.* and *C. moneta L.* Another type, mbiu, is made from *Modiola plumescens*, and mui is made from the thick walls of *Strombus luhuanus L.* and *C. moneta*. *Munbun* is made from *Chrysostoma paradoxum* Born. A pig was worth from 12,500 to 25,000 disks. (See Quiggin p. 156) (See Lewis)(See TMA April, 1986)

PENDANTS

Mauritania.

Silver pieces like these were considered valuables and served as a limited form of money.

PEPPER MONEY

Baltic Sea Coast, 15th Century

Pepper was used for currency and tax payments at a fixed rate. (See Einzig p. 281)

Italy, 1378

A loan was issued to be paid in pepper or gold. Pepper was a standard of value.

Sumatra, 17th Century

People of Jambi priced items in gold but paid in pepper. Two taels of gold were worth 100 piculs of pepper. (See Einzig p. 100)

PESTLE - See Mortar and Pestle

PIG MONEY

Alor Island

The most important currencies on Alor were *mokos*, with pigs being second in importance. A pig was worth a *piki moko*, according to Du Bois.

Bougainville

Pigs were valued by their girth. Their average value was 50 to 100 spans of shell money. A pig with a 30-inch girth was worth 10 spans of mauai shell money. Native bred pigs were worth less than European-bred pigs of the same girth, and native pigs normally were also smaller than European pigs.

Buin, Papua New Guinea

Pigs were used as money and bride price. They were worth from 10 to 100 fathoms of shell money called abuta. They were always valued in units of ten, never odd units like 15 or 45. Pigs were also used in magic. (See Thurnwald)

Fiji, 1820s

Twelve to 20 pigs would purchase one common musket.

Irian Jaya, Dani Tribe

Pig feasts were held periodically, and at these feasts debts were paid off in pigs as well as with cowry shell bands and *bilum* bags. (See Heider p. 132)

New Hebrides (now Vanuatu) until World War II

In some areas the pigs were valued solely as animals, while in other areas they were valued solely for their tusks. They served as a standard of value and as a means of deferred payments. Interest was the growth the tusks would have grown if the pig would had been kept. They were used for bride price, blood money, ransom, fines for infringing taboos, admission into men's clubs and secret societies. The value of the pig was based on the curvature of its tusk more than its size. The bride price was two pigs. Pigs were graded, and the bride price required one of each of two grades. The pigs were given up to 11 different names, depending on the size, curvature, and projection from the month of the tusks. The value of each increase in grade of pig increased by five pigs. The difference in value between the lowest grade and highest grade was 55 pigs.

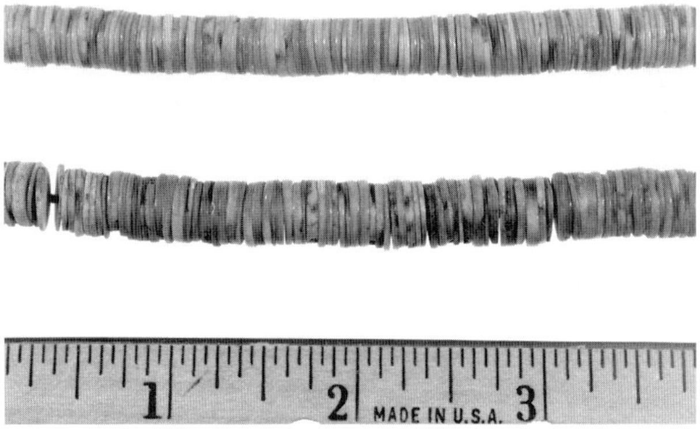

Pele Strings

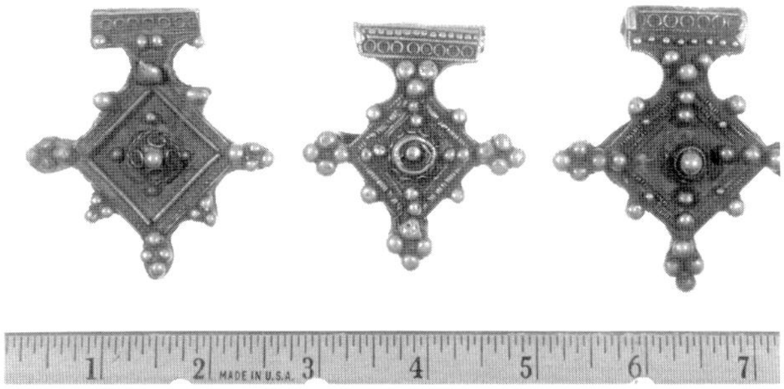

Pendants

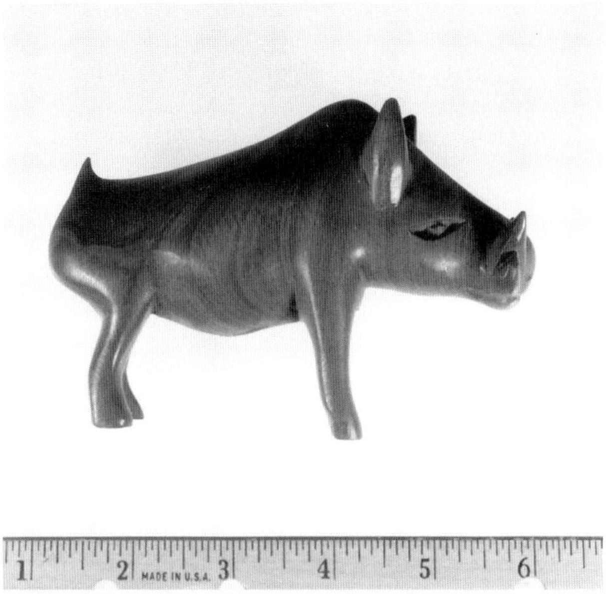

Pig Made of Wood

Papua New Guinea

Live pigs are a unit of value, store of value, and a trading medium. They form an important part of bride price as well as the main food at most important feasts called pig killings. They were eaten in a Roman style orgy. Pigs were also used in compensation for deaths. In a sense, the bodies of pigs and people were interchangeable, as they represented a negotiated value between the two. The value of the pigs varied by area. The Melpa of Mount Hagen and the Kakoli of Kaugel Valley valued pearl shells greater than pigs, while the Laiapu Enga to the east of Wabag valued them equally, and the Mae Enga to the west valued pigs greater than pearl shell. The pig was a major item in bride price in the Mount Hagen area. A good bride price would be ten pigs and ten *kina* shells. The pigs were a major wealth item and means of payment for doctors, priests, and workers. The small pigs were treated like human babies. Pigs were killed for many events such as: at big singsings; marriage feasts; building a new house;, when someone dies; naming a baby; payment for rape; theft or wrongs; giving thanks for a good harvest; and before a big hunt. They were also an important part of the kula trade cycle. A full-circle tusk formed in seven years. The entire pig was valued by the size of the tusks. Example of value: 1/4 circle tusk - four pounds, 1/2 circle tusk - six pounds, 3/4 circle tusk - 10-15 pounds, full circle tusk - 30 pounds and 1 1/2 circle tusk - 50-60 pounds. The interest on tusks was greater than normal interest: 100 percent per year in primitive communities due to this growth of the tusks. The pig was worth about one kina shell or one bailer shell. (See Einzig p.48) (See Boar Tusks)

Papua New Guinea
Huli tribe

The bride price depended on the status of the woman by the Huli tribe. A spinster was valued at 15 items. Most of the items were pigs. A man of high status would voluntarily pay more than a person of low status. In one area the average bride price was 21 or 22 pigs.

Papua New Guinea
Mae tribe

During the period prior to heavy European influence (pre 1940) an average of 9.5 pigs, one half pearl shell, 2.4 axes, and 4.8 other things like money, steel spades, steel knives, or shell decorations would be the bride price. Between 1940 and 1950 the average was seven pigs, .9 pearl shells, 2.3 axes, and 7.1 other things. Between 1950 and 1970 the average bride price consisted of 7.9 pigs, 1.8 pearl shells, 4.1 axes, and 11.2 other things. (See Meggitt p.121)

Papua New Guinea. Garia tribe

In 1949 a pig was worth $5 Australian, while in 1970 a pig was worth $40. They were used in bride price. The initial negotiations and first installment consisted of a pig, taro, clay pots, cooked food, wood plates, bowls, and, after the 1930s, money. Later installments would total about 10 pigs. The main use of pigs was in pig exchanges. They took place from late May to late August. The exchanges were complex due to rules about what pigs a person may eat. A person may not eat any pigs they have raised themselves. It would be considered cannibalism. You were considered the father or mother of the pigs you raised. In their way of thinking, wealth was traded for wealth on the basis of equivalence. Pigs were also used to buy the rights to a particular dance. In 1950 the price was four or five pigs along with $10 cash, 20 clay pots, wood plates, taro, tobacco, and other items. (See Lawrence)

Papua New Guinea

This pig made of wood was said to be valued the same as a real pig. It represented wealth, but is questionable if it was used as money. Schulman said it was. (See Schulman p.63)

Papua New Guinea

Shell beads strung end to end are called pig money. See Birok.

Siassi Islands

Off the coast of Papua New Guinea, the natives of the Siassi Islands traded with the other islands in the area. For example, one pig would be traded for five to 10 packages of sago on Umboi, which would be traded for 50 to 100 pots on Sio-Gitua, which in turn would be traded for five to 10 pigs on New Britain. Other items were also traded with the resulting profit in comparable proportion. They also used the curved pig's tusks in bride price. (See Sahlins p. 283-284)

Vitiaz Strait

Pigs were the supreme object of wealth. They were exchanged for dogs, canoes, wood bowls, pots, and now cash. A one year old pig was worth five pounds, a two-year-old pig was worth 10 pounds, and a three-year-old pig was worth 15 pounds. Boars with curved tusks were worth more.

Solomon Islands

A live pig was worth 30 to 50 fathoms of shell disk money. Pigs were valued in terms of their girth. They were worth from 10 *mauai* to 100 *mauai*. When European breeds were introduced, they were worth more than native pig breeds because they were larger, and the natives found the European breeds of better quality. The tusks of pigs were worn by warriors and elders during ceremonies or during courtship. They were worn through the nose, through the base of the ear, and integrated as part of an elaborate chest hanging. In 1847 a 100-pound pig was worth five pounds of tobacco. In the 1850s one pig was worth 20 steel fish-hooks, five strings of red corals, five strings of green and red glass beads, or five packets of needles, according to Bennett (p. 42.)

Pig Mouth Money

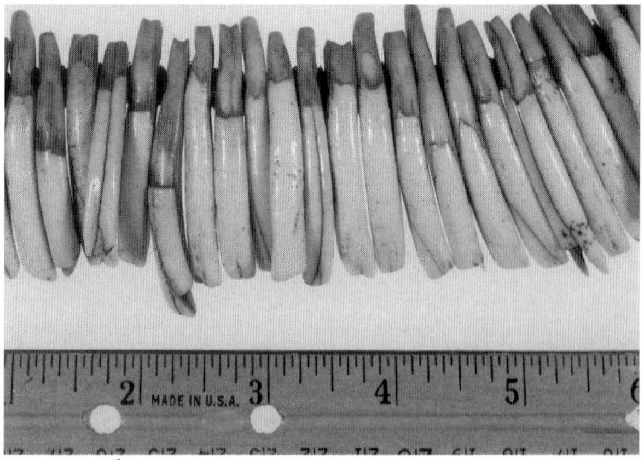

Pig Teeth

PIG MOUTH MONEY

North of Siam, 1615-1871

This disk of cast silver with an arcuate opening below, a hollow interior and a very high domed top was used in the area from Chiang Mai in the east to the Shan states in the west. It was used as money and in bride price. Approximately 2″ diameter (See Mitchiner p. 360 & LeMay p. 123) See Tok

PIG TEETH

Africa, Congo

Wild pigs' teeth were one of the oldest currencies in Africa. (See Einzig p. 163)

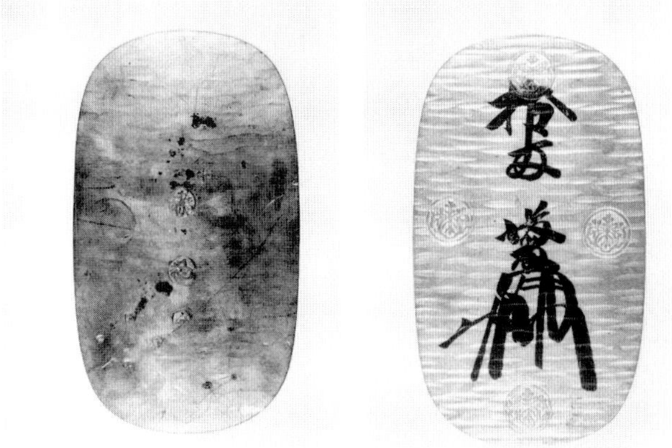

Plate Money Oban, Copy - Courtesy of Ken Bressett

Plate Money - Silver Piece

1726 10 Kopek Original Plate Money, Russia - Courtesy of Charles Stearns

Papua New Guinea

Pig teeth were used in a necklace and were a very limited form of money. Necklaces were also used as decoration. The pigs' teeth formerly were worth a carved bowl but are not used as money presently. These teeth are not to be confused with boar's tusks, which are much larger and longer. 2-1/4″

PIG TUSK - See boar tusks

PINGA - See pingha.

PINGHA

Azande tribe, Africa

The throwing knife was used by the Zande people where the unmarried men served as royal bodyguards and court attendants. The blade was iron, and the handle was covered with hide. In 1887 a trader told of his difficulty in buying grain because the traders would take nothing but throwing knives in trade. He needed two knives per day to live. The knives are now carried as emblems of authority and used as currency blades with a generally recognized value. See Throwing Knives (See Quiggin p. 68)

PINYON PINE NUTS

Washo, Northern Paiute, and Great Basin Shoshone tribes in the State of Nevada made pinyon nuts, also known as pine-nuts, into beads and classed them as trade items. They were also found in late prehistoric sites.

PLATE MONEY

Japan, 1600-1867

Large flat oval plates (3 3/4″ x 6″) of gold, called *oban,* were made from 1600-1837. Most of these have hand-punched stamps and characters written in India ink. There were several sizes and weights. Smaller pieces (1 1/2″ x 3″) made from 1819-1867, called *koban,* have only punch marks. Similar gold and silver pieces are provincial coins made before 1867 in various denominations and sizes. (See Krause)

Oban are all very rare. While they are not primitive money, they are included in some collections.

Russia. 1725-1727

Russia produced large quantities of copper at its mines at Ekaterinburg. The plates were to use some of the large amounts of copper Russia produced. Peter I passed the law authorizing plate money on February 4, 1726. Some plates were dated 1725. By January 1727, the whole experiment was called off. The experiment lasted only one and a half years. One reason was that the Russians encountered many technical difficulties in making the plates, even with the help of Swedish technicians. The plates were intended to circulate along with copper coins of the same value but with lower intrinsic values. The five kopek (20 grams) coin had only one-fourth as much copper as the five kopek plate money (80 grams). The plates were minted at Ekaterinburg and were intended to circulate mainly in the local area. The plates produced in 1725 were the grivna (10 kopeks), 1/4 rouble (25 kopeks), and one rouble. In 1726 1/2 rouble (50 kopeks), five kopeks, and one kopek pieces were also produced. The one rouble plate was to be the same size as the two daler Swedish plate money. In 1726 the minting was ordered to be halted, but a few pieces dated 1727 were produced. All plates that could be found were withdrawn and destroyed. All pieces are very rare. Many forgeries exist.

SWEDISH PLATE MONEY

Sweden, 1644-1776

The plate money was also called *kopperplatmynt* after the very large copper mine Stora Kopparerget at Falun. The four stamps in corners have a crowned monogram of the ruler and the date. The corner stamps generally give the name of the Sovereign in Latin either completely, partly abbreviated with a monogram, or only with the initial letter followed by R. S. (Rex Sveciae - King of Sweden) and the date. The fifth stamp in the center gives the denomination. The 10 daler denomination, the largest produced, was minted in Avesta. It weighed 48 pounds and was only minted in 1644 and 1645 and thus is very rare. It was 12 inches by 27 1/2 inches. In 1644, 26,539 plates of the 10 daler denomination were struck. In 1645, 235 plates were made. Only seven from 1644 and one from 1645 survive to the present. In 1649 the eight, four, two, and one daler denominations were minted. In 1674 the three and five daler pieces were minted, with the 1/2 daler piece being minted in 1681. In 1666, the Stora Kopparberg Company (the oldest company in existence) was granted permission to strike plate money. Only the copper plate money was made because Sweden had no silver, but it did have large copper mines. In the 17th century the Falu Mine produced about two-thirds of the copper used in Europe. At that time money had to contain the value in metal, and these pieces contained their value in copper. Unusual denominations of three and five were daler made in 1674 (both are exceedingly rare). In 1718 an extra counter stamp was added to the older 1/2, one, and two daler plates to revalue them to 3/4, 1 1/2, and three dalers respectively. This was due to a large increase in the price of copper. To distinguish the plates owned privately from the plates owned by the State, the privately owned plates had an extra stamp of the Lion of Gota on a shield and dated were 1718. At that time all unstamped plates could not be exported. Only 25 percent of the plates owned by the public in 1718 were counter-stamped. A total of 48 million plates were issued.

Over 18,000 plates are known to exist today excluding the "Nicobar" sea salvage pieces. In 1987, 3,000 pieces with varying degrees of sea damage were recovered from the "Nicobar," a cargo ship that sank in 1782. Denominations recovered are 1/2, one, two, and four daler. Plate money was never popular, but the plates were considered a commodity, and owners could profit when the price of copper rose. A government statement made in 1672 said the plates should be regarded as a commodity. From 1714 -1716 plates were also made of cannon metal (bronze) obtained from rejected pieces of artillery and were worth only 2/3 as much as copper.
The cannon metal plates only have a Royal crown except for 1718-1719 with a triangular center-stamp and the date in the corner stamp. The center stamp always gives the denomination, date and symbol for the mint or place of origin of the copper. There are several exceptions to the above stamp rules. Tingstrom gives the mint marks by date.

The last regular date was 1759, with one known from 1760 and one each of the 1/2 daler and four daler from 1768. (See Tingstrom, Plate Money)
LIST OF DATES AND TYPES KNOWN:

1/2 Daler
Karl XI, (Charles) copper, Mint: Avesta
Corner stamps: Crowned C R S, date
Center Stamp: 1/2 daler, SolffMyt, three stars
1681,1682,1683,1685, 1686, 1687,1689, 1690, 1691

Karl XII, copper, Mint: Avesta
Corner stamps: Crowned C R S, date
Center Stamp: 1/2 daler,SolffMyt, crossed arrows
Copper from Stora Kopparberg & Ljusnarsberg
1710, 1711, 1712, 1713, 1714, 1715

Karl XII, copper, Mint: Avesta
Corner Stamps: Crowned C R S, date
Center Stamp: 1/2 daler, Star, SolffMyt, crossed arrows
Copper from Garpenberg
1710, 1711, 1713, 1714

Karl XII, copper, Mint: Avesta
Corner Stamps: Crowned doubled C superimposed on date
Center Stamp: Diamond reeded outline around 1/2 daler S.M
1715, 1716, 1717

Swedish Plate Money - 4 Daler

Swedish Plate Money - 2 Daler

Swedish Plate Money - 1 Daler

Karl XII, copper, Mint: Avesta
  Corner Stamps: three crowns above date
  Center Stamp: Triangular reeded outline, 1/2 D S in corners with lion in shield in center
1718

Ulrika Elonora, copper, Mint: Avesta
  Corner Stamps: three crowns in circle above date
  Center Stamp: Triangular reeded outline, 1/2 D S in corners with lion in shield in center
  1719

Ulirika Eleonora, copper, Mint: Avesta
  Corner Stamps: Crown over V with double E monogram over V, date split by double E
  Center Stamp: 1/2 daler, Slif:Mynt, crossed arrows
  1719, 1720

Fredrik I (Frederick I), copper, Mint: Avesta
  Corner Stamps: Crowned FRS, date
  Center Stamp: 1/2 daler, Slif:Mynt, crossed arrows
  1720, 1721, 1722, 1723, 1724, 1725, 1726, 1727, 1728, 1729, 1730, 1731, 1732, 1733, 1734, 1735, 1736, 1737, 1738, 1739, 1740, 1741, 1742, 1743, 1744, 1745, 1746, 1747, 1748, 1749, 1750

Fredrik I , copper, Mint: Ljusnedal
  Corner Stamps: Crowned FRS, date
  Center Stamp: 1/2 daler, crowned L
  1746, 1748

Fredrik I , copper, Mint: Husa
  Corner Stamps: Crowned FRS, date
  Center Stamp: 1/2 daler, crowned G
  1748

Adolphus Fredrik (Adolphus Frederick), copper, Mint: Avesta
  Corner Stamps: Crowned AFRS, date
  Center Stamp: 1/2 daler, Slif:Mynt, crossed arrows
  1751, 1752, 1753, 1754, 1755, 1756, 1757, 1758, 1759, 1768

Adolphus Fredrik, copper, Mint: Ljusnedal
  Corner Stamps: Crowned AFRS, date
  Center Stamp: 1/2 daler, Slif:Mynt, monogram L
  1753

Adolphus Fredrik, copper, Mint: Semian
  Corner Stamps: Crowned AFRS, date
  Center Stamp: 1/2 daler, Slif:Mynt, crowned G
  Copper from Gustavsberg Mine
  1752

Adolphus Fredrik, copper, Mint: Semian
  Corner Stamps: Crowned AFRS, date
  Center Stamp: 1/2 daler, Slif:Mynt, crowned G
  Copper from Carisberg Mine
  1752

3/4 daler
Countermarked 1/2 daler in 1718
Additional stamp: 3/4 daler SM, 1718, in circle
Orig. date: 1689
Copper from Stora Kopparberg & Ljusnarsberg, Orig. date: 1710, 1711 (Unique), 1712
Copper from Garpenberg Mine, 1710, 1714 (Unique)

1 daler
Queen Christina, copper, Mint Avesta
Corner Stamps: crown over date, legend around crown & date
Center Stamp: one daler, Solff:Mint, M.K.
1649, 1650, 1652, 1653, 1654

Carl Gustaf, copper, Mint: Avesta
Corner Stamps: crown over date, legend around crown & date
Center Stamp: one daler, Solff:Mint, M.K.
1655, 1656, 1657, 1658, 1659, 1660

Carl XI, copper, Mint: Avesta
Corner Stamps: crown over date, legend around crown & date
Center Stamp: one daler, Solff:Mint, M.K.
1660, 1661, 1662, 1663, 1664, 1667, 1668, 1669, 1672, 1673, 1674, 1675, 1676, 1677, 1678, 1679, 1680, 1681, 1682, 1683, 1684, 1685, 1686, 1687, 1688, 1689, 1690, 1691,

Carl XI, copper, Mint: Avesta
Corner Stamps: crown over date, legend around crown & date
Center Stamp: one daler, Solff:Mint, M.K.
Copper from Garpenberg
1674

Carl XI, copper, Mint: Kengls
Corner Stamps: crown over date, legend around crown & date
Center Stamp: one daler, Solff:Mint, AIR monogram
1675

Charles XII, copper, Mint: Kengis
Corner Stamps: crown above date, legend around date & crown
Center Stamp: one daler, Solff:Myt, AIR
1702

Charles XII, copper, Mint: Avesta
Corner Stamps: crown above date, legend around date & crown
Center Stamp: one daler, Solff:Myt, crossed arrows
1710, 1711, 1712, 1713, 1714, 1715

Charles XII, copper, Mint: Avesta
Corner Stamps: crown above date, legend around date & crown
Center Stamp: one daler, Solff:Myt, large star
1710

Charles XII, copper, Mint: Avesta
Corner Stamps: crown above date, legend around date & crown
Center Stamp: one daler, Solff:Myt, crowned B between roses
1711

Charles XII, copper, Mint: Avesta
Corner Stamps: crowned mirror C, XII monogram, date
Center Stamp: one daler S.M. in diamond reeded outline
1715, 1716, 1717

Charles XII, copper, Mint: Avesta
Corner Stamps: three crowns, date
Center Stamp: one daler D S in triangular reeded outline
1718

Charles XII, cannon metal, Mint: Stockholm
Corner Stamps: crown in circle reeded outline
Center Stamp: two daler, Interwoven 3 crowns, date
1715

Ulrika Eleonora, cannon metal, Mint: Avesta
Corner Stamps: three crowns, date
Center Stamp: 1 D S in the corners of a reeded outline triangle with a shield in the center
1719

Ulrika Eleonora, cannon metal, Mint: Avesta
Corner Stamps: three crowns, date in circle
Center Stamp: one daler, Sllf:Mynt, crossed arrows
1719, 1729

Fredrik I (Fredrick I), cannon metal, Mint: Avesta
Corner Stamps: Crowned FRS, date
Center Stamp: one daler, Sllf:Mynt, crossed arrows
1720, 1721, 1722, 1723, 1724, 1725, 1726, 1727, 1728, 1729, 1730, 1731, 1732, 1733, 1734, 1735, 1736, 1737, 1738, 1739, 1740, 1741, 1742, 1743, 1744, 1745, 1746, 1747, 1748, 1749, 1750

Fredrik I (Fredrick I), cannon metal, Mint: Ljusnedal
Corner Stamps: Crowned FRS, date
Center Stamp: one daler, Sllf:Mynt, monogrammed L
1746, 1749

Fredrik I (Fredrick I), cannon metal, Mint: Husa
Corner Stamps: Crowned FRS, date
Center Stamp: one daler, Sllf:Mynt, crowned G
1748

Swedish Plate Money - 1/2 Daler

Adolphus Frederick, cannon metal, Mint: Avesta
Corner Stamps: Crowned AFRS, date
Center Stamp: one daler, Sllf:Mynt, crossed arrows
1751, 1752, 1753, 1754, 1755, 1756, 1757, 1758, 1759, 1768

Adolphus Frederick, cannon metal, Mint: Ljusnedal
Corner Stamps: Crowned AFRS, date
Center Stamp: one daler, Sllf:Mynt, mirror L monogram
1753

Adolphus Frederick, cannon metal, Mint: Semian
Corner Stamps: Crowned AFRS, date
Center Stamp: one daler, Sllf:Mynt, crowned G
Copper from Gustavsberg Mine
1752

Adolphus Frederick, cannon metal, Mint: Semian
Corner Stamps: Crowned AFRS, date
Center Stamp: one daler, Sllf:Mynt, crowned C
Copper from Gustavsberg Mine
1752

Adolphus Frederick, cannon metal, Mint: Semian
Corner Stamps: Crowned AFRS, date
Center Stamp: one daler, Sllf:Mynt, crowned C
Copper from Carlisberg Mine
1752

1 1/2 daler
Countermarked one daler in 1718
Additional stamp: 1 1/2 daler SM, 1718, in circle
Charles XII, copper, Mint: Avesta
Corner Stamps: crown above date, legend around date & crown
Center Stamp: one daler, Solff:Myt, crowned B between roses
Orig. dates: 1710, 1711, 1712, 1713, 1717

2 daler
Queen Christina, copper, Mint: Avesta
Corner Stamps: Crown, date
Center Stamp: two daler, Soliff:Mynt, M. K.
1649, 1651, 1652, 1653, 1654

Karl X Gustaf, copper, Mint: Avesta
Corner Stamps: Crown, date, legend around crown & date
Center Stamp: two daler, Solff:Mnt
1658, 1659

Karl XI, copper, Mint: Avesta
Corner Stamps: Crown, date, legend around crown & date
Center Stamp: two daler, Solff:Mnt, shield or rose between stars or lilies or three stars
1660, 1662, 1663, 1664, 1667, 1669, 1672, 1673, 1674, 1675, 1676, 1677, 1678, 1679, 1680, 1681, 1682, 1683, 1684, 1685, 1686, 1689, 1690, 1691

Karl XI, copper, Mint: Avesta
Corner Stamps: Crown, date, legend around crown & date
Center Stamp: two daler, Solff:Mnt, star between lilies
Copper from Garpenberg Mine
1673, 1674

Karl XI, copper, Mint: Kenglis
Corner Stamps: Crown, date, legend around crown & date
Center Stamp: two daler, Solff:Mnt, monogram AIR
Copper from Garpenberg Mine
1693

Karl XI, copper, Mint: Kenglis
Corner Stamps: Crown, date, legend around crown & date
Center Stamp: two daler, Solff:Mnt, monogram AIR
Copper from Garpenberg Mine
1700

Karl XI, copper, Mint: Avesta
Corner Stamps: Crown, date, legend around crown & date
Center Stamp: two daler, Solff:Mnt, three stars
Copper from Garpenberg Mine
1702

Karl XI, copper, Mint: Avesta
Corner Stamps: Crown, date, legend around crown & date
Center Stamp: two daler, Solff:Mnt, crossed arrows
Copper from Stora Kopparberg Mine and Ljusnarsberg Mine
1710, 1711, 1712, 1713, 1714, 1715

Karl XI, copper, Mint: Avesta
Corner Stamps: Crown, date, legend around crown & date
Center Stamp: two daler, Solff:Mnt, crowned E between roses
Copper from Basinge Mine
1711, 1712, 1713

Karl XI, copper, Mint: Avesta
Corner Stamps: Crown, date, legend around crown & date
Center Stamp: two daler, Solff:Mnt, large star
Copper from Garpenberg Mine
1710, 1711, 1712, 1713, 1714

Karl XI, copper, Mint: Avesta
Corner Stamps: Crowned mirrored C monogram, date
Center Stamp: two daler S.M. in diamond shaped reeded edge outline
Copper from Garpenberg Mine
1716, 1717

Karl XI, copper, Mint: Avesta
Corner Stamps: three crowns, date
Center Stamp: 2 D S in corners of triangle with reeded outline and shield in the center
Copper from Garpenberg Mine
1718

Karl XI, cannon metal, Mint: Stockholm
Corner Stamps: crown, date
Center Stamp: 2 D S M, three crowns, date
1714, 1715, 1716

Ulrilka Eleonora, copper, Mint: Avesta
Corner Stamps: 3 crowns, date
Center Stamp: 2 D S in corners of triangle with reeded outline and shield in center
1719

Ulrilka Eleonora, copper, Mint: Avesta
Corner Stamps: Crowned V, double E monogram, date
Center Stamp: two daler Silf:mint, crossed arrows
1719, 1720

Fredrik I, copper, Mint: Avesta
Corner Stamps: Crowned FRS, date
Center Stamp: two daler, Silf:mint, crossed arrows
1720, 1721, 1722, 1723, 1724, 1725, 1726, 1727, 1728, 1729, 1730, 1731, 1732, 1733, 1734, 1735, 1736, 1737, 1738, 1739, 1740, 1741, 1742, 1743, 1744, 1745, 1746, 1747, 1748, 1749, 1750

Fredrik I, copper, Mint: Ljusnedal
Corner Stamps: Crowned FRS, date
Center Stamp: two daler, Silf:mint, two L monogram
1746

Fredrik I, copper, Mint: Ljusnedal
Corner Stamps: Crowned AFRS monogram, date
Center Stamp: two daler, Silf:mint, two L monogram
1751, 1752, 1753, 1754, 1755, 1756, 1757, 1758, 1759, 1760

3 daler
Countermarked three daler in 1718
Additional stamp: 3 daler SM on two daler, 1718, in circle
Karl XI, copper, Mint: Avesta
Corner Stamps: Crown, date, legend around crown & date
Center Stamp: two daler, Solff:Mnt, crossed arrows
Copper from Stora Kopparberg Mine and Ljusnarsberg Mine
Orig dates: 1710, 1711, 1712, 1713, 1714, 1715

4 Daler
Christina, copper, Mint: Avesta
Corner Stamps: crown, date with legend around
Center Stamp: four daler, Solff:Mnt, MK
1649, 1652, 1653

Karl Gustaf, copper, Mint: Avesta
Corner Stamps: crown, date with legend around
Center Stamp: four daler, Solff:Mnt, M K
1656, 1657, 1658

Karl XI, copper, Mint: Avesta
Corner Stamps: crown, date with legend around
Center Stamp: four daler, Solff:Mnt, M K
1663

Charles XII, copper, Mint: Avesta
Corner Stamps: crowned mirrored C XII, date
Center Stamp: four daler S M in diamond shaped reeded outline
1716, 1717

Charles XII, copper, Mint: Avesta
Corner Stamps: three crowns, date
Center Stamp: 4 D S in corners of triangle with shield in center
1718

Ulrika Eleonora, copper, Mint: Avesta
Corner Stamps: three crowns, date
Center Stamp: 4 D S in corners of triangle with shield in center
1719

Ulrika Eleonora, copper, Mint: Avesta
Corner Stamps: crowned V over double E monogram, date
Center Stamp: four daler, Silf:Mynt, crossed arrows
1719, 1720

Fredrik I, copper, Mint: Avesta
Corner Stamps: crowned FRS, date
Center Stamp: four daler, Silf:Mynt, crossed arrows
1720, 1721, 1722, 1723, 1724, 1725, 1726, 1727, 1728, 1729, 1730, 1731, 1732, 1733, 1734, 1735, 1736, 1737, 1738, 1739, 1740, 1741, 1742, 1743, 1744, 1745, 1746

Fredrik I, copper, Mint: Avesta
Corner Stamps: crowned AFRS monogram, date
Center Stamp: split four in four daler, Silf:mynt, crossed arrows
1753, 1754

Fredrik I, copper, Mint: Avesta
Corner Stamps: crowned AFRS monogram, date
Center Stamp: solid four in four daler, Silf:mynt, crossed arrows
1753, 1754, 1755, 1756, 1757, 1758, 1759, 1768 (Unique)

5 daler
Karl XI, copper, Mint: Avesta
Corner Stamps: crown, date with legend around crown & date
Center Stamp: five daler, Solff:Myt, three stars
1674

8 daler
Christina, copper, Mint: Avesta
Corner Stamps: crown, date with legend around date & crown
Center Stamp: eight daler, Solff:Mnt, M K
1652, 1653

Karl X Gustaf, copper, Mint: Avesta
Corner Stamps: crown, date with legend around date & crown
Center Stamp: eight daler, Solff:Mnt, shield between roses
1656, 1657, 1658, 1659

Karl XI Gustaf, copper, Mint: Avesta
Corner Stamps: crown, date with legend around date & crown
Center Stamp: eight daler, Solff:Mnt, roses
1660, 1661, 1662, 1663

Karl XI Gustaf, copper, Mint: Avesta
Corner Stamps: crown, date with legend around date & crown
Center Stamp: eight daler, Solff:Mnt, 3 stars
1681, 1682

10 daler
Christina, copper, Mint: Avesta
Corner Stamps: crown, date with legend around date & crown
Center Stamp: 10 daler, Solff:Mnt, shield
1644, 1645

MINT	PERIOD	MINT-MARK
Avesta	1644-1645	
	1649-1657	
	1658-1664	
	1667-1669	
	1672-1673	
	1673-1674	
	1674-1691	
	1710-1715	
	1702 and 1712	
	1711-1713	
Bäsinge	1710-1714	
	1715-1717	
	1718-1719	
	1719-1768	
Huså	1748	
Kengis	1675-1689 and 1693	
	1700-1701	
Ljusnedal	1746, 1748 and 1753	
Semlan	1752	
	1752	
Stockholm	1714-1716	

PLAYING CARD MONEY

Austria, 1920

The City of Steyregg issued money on the backs of playing cards in denominations of 10, 20, 30, 40, 50, 80, and 90 heller. Only four designs were used on the reverses: a castle, a church, a village and a factory.

Canada, Nova Scotia, French Louisiana, 1685 - 1763

Prior to 1685 the French government advanced funds six months in advance to meet government and military expenses in Canada. For some reason the practice was changed in 1685, and no funds were received until September 1685, instead of in January, 1685. First the Intendants used their own private funds, but by April the money ran out. In June 1685, the King's Intendant (De Meulles) started to issue money on playing cards because there was no other suitable paper. The cards had the denomination on them as well as the signature of the Intendant, De Meulles, and his own seal with his own wax and the signature of the clerk of the treasury (according to McLachlan). Later issues were also signed by the governor. When the ship arrived in September with the money, all the playing card money was redeemed. It is not known for certain, but it is believed the Intendant was forced to issue more money again in 1686 as well as in 1690 and every year thereafter to 1719. Each year all the cards were redeemed. By 1706, the French financial difficulties did not allow all the cards to be redeemed. In 1709 there were cards from 1703, 1705, 1707, and 1708 still unpaid. After 1708 the cards were paid in French paper money, which the public had already discounted. In 1702 there were only 120,000 livres in card money, but by 1714, because of the lack of French funds, there were more than 2,000,000 livres in cards. A complete set of the 1714 issue consisting of four, six, 12, 20, 40, 50, 100 livres, as well as 10, 15 and 20 sols, has been preserved in the archives of the Department of Marine in Paris, according to McLachlan. This increase in card money with no means of conversion to silver or gold caused inflation to increase prices by fourfold between 1709 and 1712. The playing card money did not, however, depreciate as fast as the French money. The playing card money was finally all redeemed at one-half the face value and burned by 1720. After that time the card money was declared worthless. So complete was the redemption that none of the cards remained, and the country had no currency. In 1728 the merchants in Canada petitioned the colonial authorities to again issue playing card money to increase the supply of money in Canada. In 1729 the King of France issued a royal ordinance to reestablish playing card money. They were written on the plain back of white cardboard. The King authorized

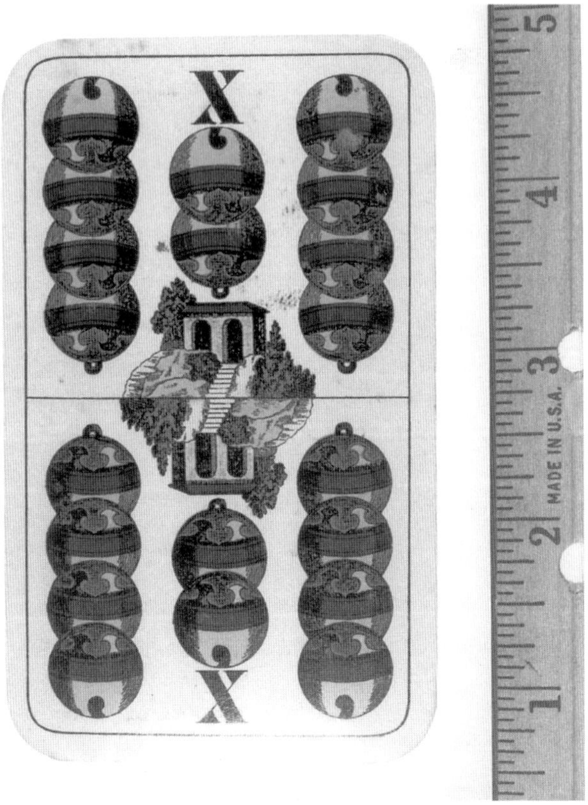

Playing Card Money - Austria

Playing Card Money - Canada

Playing Card Money - Austria

Playing Card Money - France

Playing Card Money - France

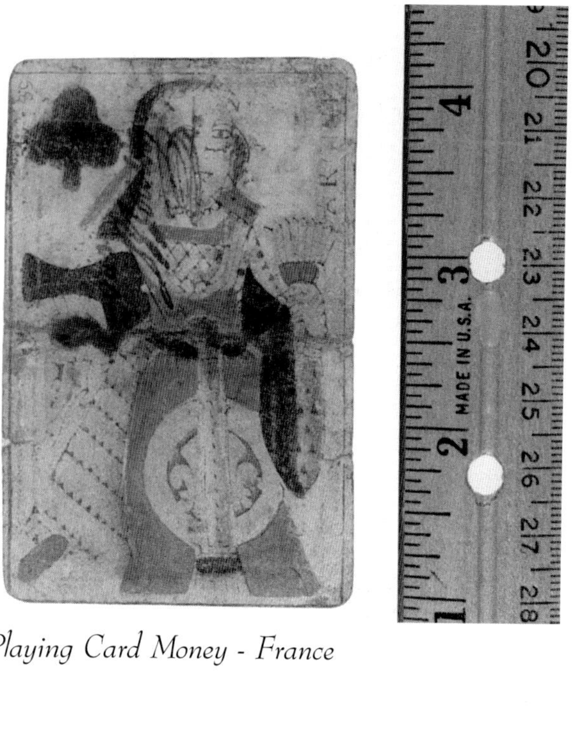

Playing Card Money - France

an issue of 400,000 livres of card money. Thousands of notes were issued but few survived as most notes were redeemed and burned. The denominations of the cards were seven sols six deniers, 15 and 30 sols, and three, six, 12, and 24 livres. There were 22 issues of card money with the later cards being on plain white cards instead of playing cards. During the period of peace until 1744, the card money was used and considered as excellent credit and was as good as gold or silver. At this time, 250,000 livres of bills of exchange could be drawn, but 400,000 were actually issued. When the Intendant questioned this practice, he was told this is the same practice the banks have been doing for centuries. In 1741 there were 600,000 livres of card money issued but only 200,000 in circulation. The remainder was being hoarded. In 1742 the total issue was 720,000 livres, and in 1749 it was raised to 1,000,000 livres. The amount of "orders" or "army-made" money constantly increased so that by 1747 there were 55,000 livres of cards and 2,669,000 livres of "orders." From 1755 on, the issues of paper money "orders" and bills of exchange on France increased due to the war between England and France. After peace was declared in 1763, the cards were redeemed at one quarter of their face value in coins. British subjects holding card money were paid in full.

In summary, playing card money circulated in Canada in 1685 and 1686. From 1690 to 1720, blank card money circulated from 1730 to 1763, a total of 65 years. During that period, no less than 22 issues, valued at many millions of dollars were issued. Examples of cards issued under the ordinances of 1729 (issued in 1729 and 1730), 1733 (issued in 1733, 1735, 1738, and 1739), 1742 (issued in 1742 and 1747), and 1749 (issued in 1749, 1752, and 1757) are known to exist, according to McLachlan. They are of seven, 15, and 30 sols and three, six, 12, and 24 livres. The record of playing card money was very good, as it broke down only twice during that period, and both times were during periods of warfare. Because there were stiff penalties for not turning in old cards when a new issue came out, there is not a single specimen of any of the first eight issues known to exist. Each card gave its value and was signed and sealed in wax by the Intendant and countersigned by the Clerk of the Treasury. Later issues also had the governor's signature. Playing card money was also used in the war between France and England. France decided to use the playing card money instead of sending coins to Canada to prevent losing money if the English won. McLachlan believed that the card money was used in most of the western posts controlled by the French at Detroit, Fort Duquesne, and possibly at St. Louis and Louisiana. By 1763 the intendant had issued more than 80,000,000 livres of playing card money worth $14,000,000. Major Sheldon Carroll stated in 1967 that

Playing Card Money - Germany

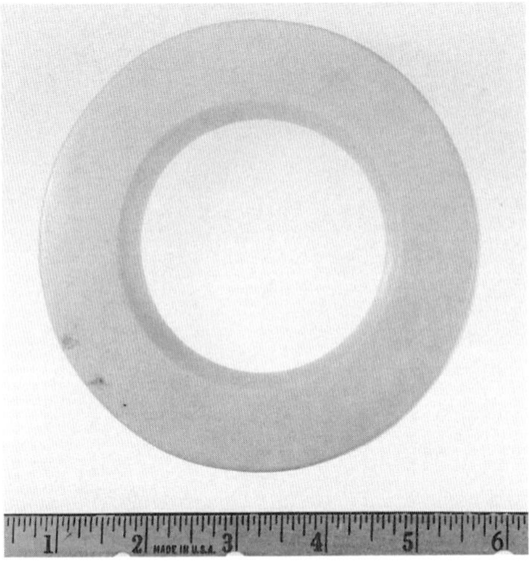

Poata

Andana

there were only 50 genuine specimens of card money in existence. (See Neufeld, p.9-p.23)(See McLachlan)
Very rare

France, 1791 - 1792

Called *Billets de Confiance*, they were issued by a body called Societe Patriotique which later changed its name to Caisse Patriotique, also known as Association Patriotique. They were issued in denominations of three, five, six, 10, 12, 15, 20, 30 sols and three livres. The printed notes were hand-numbered and hand-signed, and often a counter-signature appeared on the front of the card as a ratification.

Germany, 1922

Gustav Habeck issued money on backs of colored packs of playing cards and always divided the backs into 4 parts. There are four denominations: five, 10, 25, and 50 pfennigs.

Surinam, 1761- 1828

They were issued by the Governor during shortages of small coins. The denomination was recognizable by the size of the government seal embossed on the card. They had a hand-written serial number and signature.

POATA

This shell ring was made from the giant clam, *Tridacna gigas. Poata* is the generic term for most types of Solomon Islands shell rings. There are three types of poata.

1. *Mbakiha* - It has a yellow to red streak and has highly lustrous polish. When it was worn as a necklace it was bound and fringed with opossum or flying fox teeth.

2. *Poata* - A plain white ring well polished. It is a plain white shell ring less well-polished than the mbakiha with a rectangular cross-section and no yellow to red streak along one side often where the ring dips down.

3. *Mbarake* - The natural contour of the shell distorts the shape of the ring. It is the oldest form of ring and is rough. It generally is larger than the other rings.

An extension to a fourth level to this class would be the *hokata*. It is an associated form. It is a smooth thin ring. It was often called "small change." Large numbers were given to prostitutes who were brought to the manufacturing centers by their owners.

Other rings are as follows:

Umbu - A *poata* of large dimension.

Andana - A *poata* which is notched, but not enough to be a mbarake.

Hinuili - A small ring from a *trochus* or *conus* shell.

Hokata

Mbakina

Mbarake

Pangusia, Mbarava, Porobatuna - Three further forms of clamshell object sometimes based on the ring form, but often carved with a high degree of elaboration.

Poata was used as money in payment to have a man killed, to repay a blood debt, to purchase alliances of nearby villages, to buy canoes and slaves, and to intercede with the ancestors so that they would bring success in future ventures. A good quality ring was worth a life. The older and more valuable *poata* were worth a head, a very good pig, or a middling youth, according to Quiggin (p. 123). The rings were worn only by chiefs. Some rings have a native fiber wrapped around 1/3 of the ring and fiber to form a necklace from the ends of the wrapping. Many items in the general area were traded for clam shell rings. The ring was then worn as a necklace. One ring was worth 500 - 1000 pounds of sago. The rings were traded for many items, depending on the island. In Choiseul Island it was *kesa* and slaves; in Isabel it was slaves, turtle and dyed barkcloth; in Simbo it was girls, necklaces, and megapode eggs; in Kusaghe it was shields; in Ghizo it was greenstone; and in most of these islands canoes, armbands, and nali nuts were also traded. After the missions were established and warfare and head-hunting were eradicated, the use of these shell rings stopped. Roviana and Marovo seem to have been the main manufacturing centers for these rings. Originally the fiber from a bush creeper was used to cut the ring, but later metal wire was used, which greatly reduced the time necessary to make a ring. (See Miller p. 289-295) (See Quiggin p. 122-123)

Umbu

POLAR BEAR TEETH - See Bear Teeth

POLYCHROME BEADS - See Beads

PONY BEADS - See Beads

PORCELAIN COINS

Japan, 1945

Clay and feldspar were used to make porcelain coins called toka. The one sen piece was chocolate or red. The five and 10 sen were dark reddish brown. They were never issued for circulation. They were only made during the waning months of World War II due to a shortage of all metals. They are not odd & curious money, but are included in many collections. All white pieces are patterns.

Siam Porcelain Tokens

Siam Porcelain Token - Fakes

Germany, after World War 1, 1920-1924.

Germany issued hundreds of porcelain pieces in varied sizes, thicknesses, colors, and denominations. Most were made at the Meissen porcelain plant. The crossed sword design is the trademark of the Meissen plant.

Siam Porcelain Token - Fakes

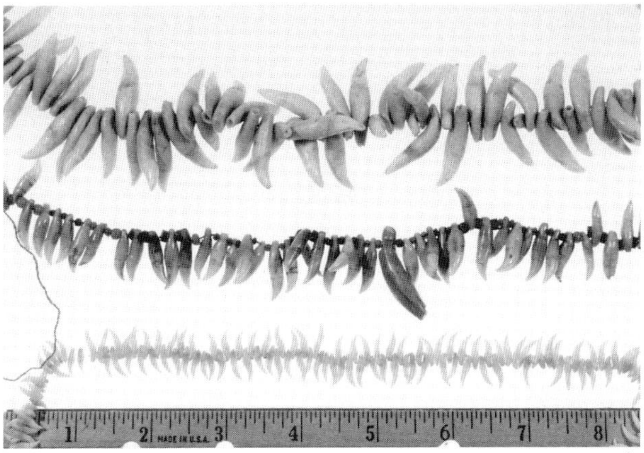

Porpoise Teeth

Porpoise Teeth

Some pieces have gold edges and gold or painted designs on them. The Hohr Central Pottery Works near Coblenz also made some pieces. Most of them are rough with large, thick devices and many have a shiny glazed finish. Saxony coins of 1920 and 1921 are the most familiar to collectors. (See Sigler p. 26) They are not odd & curious money, but are included in many collections.

Siam (Thailand) 1760 - 1875

Most Siam pieces are white porcelain. There are many shapes, including circular, star, flower, pillow, fan, kite, bird, peach, squid, scroll, diamond, oval, gourd, fish, butterfly, leaf, rectangle, five-sided, six-sided, seven-sided, eight-pointed star, and scalloped. The designs on the tokens include plants as well as tigers, cats, horses, bats, fish, rabbits, frogs, crabs, lizards, shrimp, butterflies, deer, spiders, dragons, elephants, monkeys, chickens, peacocks, birds, and many zodiacal animals. Humans including Queen Victoria, Buddha, a Thai queen, and King Chulalongkorn are also pictured on the tokens. They were made in China for use by the Chinese in private gambling houses in Sia, but were also used in the surrounding area as small change. The gambling houses were "tax farms" where every one year, or some say every three years, the government accepted bids for the right to operate the gambling monopoly for the next period. There were between 500 and 1,000 different firms, called *hongs*, that issued tokens. In many cases the *hongs* would issue new counters and give holders of the obsolete counters only 48 hours to exchange the old ones for new ones. A special clay token, made in the 1760s, is believed to be the first token made. In 1875 the government prohibited the circulation of the tokens to facilitate the circulation of the government's new flat metallic coinage. (See Smith p. 61) In 1907 the government prohibited gambling everywhere except Bangkok, and in 1917 it was prohibited there also. To reduce counterfeiting, issues were recalled frequently, and new pieces were issued to replace them. More than 10,000 different varieties are known. They were issued in denominations of from one Att to one Salung. The inscriptions were usually in blue or black, while the red inscriptions are uncommon, and most green are rare. It is believed that between 2,000 and 6,000 pieces of each design were minted. The tokens are also known in ivory, gold, silver, and sealing wax. Other series are in brass-bronze, iron, lead, stoneware, and glass. The mother of pearl tokens are not from Siam, as is commonly believed, but are from China for use as gambling chips in America and Europe from as far back as the 1700s. There are many modern fakes. Many of the modern fakes have no glazing on the back of the token. Instead there is incising in various patterns. Some also have dabs of blue on the front under the glazing, but the blue does not

Porpoise Teeth

follow the outline of the figure like the original tokens do. These tokens are found in Thailand where they are sold to tourists because the original tokens were taken to the United States many years ago. Original tokens have recently been sent from the United States to Thailand, where they are worth more than in the United States. (See Ramsden) (See Mitchiner p.379-382) See Dog Teeth Money - porcelain

PORCUPINE QUILLS

Sioux Indians

The quills were used in barter from tribe to tribe. They were a popular exchange item and used to decorate belts, clothing, etc. (See Quiggin p. 310)

PORPOISE TEETH

Kwaio of East Central Malaita, Solomon Islands

Porpoise teeth are used throughout the Solomons and are used in bride price as well as in payments to burial parties at mortuary feasts. There are four types of porpoise teeth in Kwaio. They are *lobo, unaburu, nenenene,* and *rii*. The lobo teeth are the rarest. In the Lau Lagoon area to the north of Malaita. great porpoise drives were held to obtain the teeth. The teeth were also exchanged for shell money. The teeth were used in ear ornaments. The Ba'o was made by cutting a thin piece of turtle-shell into a ring with a wide base in which designs were cut and holes were drilled from which to hang the teeth. The *kwari 'inari* was a more elaborate ear ornament made by inlaying the shell of *nari* (canarium almond nut) with designs of mother of pearl. About 100-250 porpoise teeth were hung from short strings of white shell beads. One nut shell was attached on the outer side of the ear, and another nut shell was attached on the inner side of the ear. A small stick was inserted through the ear and the two shell nuts to hold them to the ear lobe. Nose pins consisted of *rii* or *nenenene* porpoise teeth inserted in the nose with the tip of the tooth pointing out. Six *nenenene* stuck in the nose in a line are called *baru'ilaa.* A ring of porpoise teeth is called *'waloi'a.* It is used to decorate bows, plaited combs, war clubs, and for protection against sorcery. The *biru* neck bands and head bands were made by weaving from 200 to 1,000 *unaburu t*eeth into a strip of *tatai* vine. These were used both as a body ornament and as a type of money. A biru with 1,000 teeth is called *to'onilobo* or *i'a'afu.* One porpoise tooth would purchase one bundle, cut rolled, and tied. (See Bundles) Ten teeth would also hire a big overseas canoe. On Sa'a, Solomons, a unit of 200 porpoise teeth was one of 10 monies used for bride price. Another unit was 40 dog teeth. Seven or eight shell monies also was part of the price.

In 1933, 50 porpoise teeth were worth five shillings. The teeth were also used as bride price, for ceremonial payments and in the purchase of pigs. The groom's mother produces one fathom of shell money and combines it with 1,000 porpoise teeth and some bark cloth as a present for the bride's mother. This bundle is called a "bundle of cloth" according to Ivens - 1930. The bride price for a widow was one shell money and 100 porpoise teeth. The bride price was two or three shell monies and 200 or 300 porpoise teeth in 1930. The teeth usually come from Mwanasike. At one time 100 porpoise teeth consisted of a unit. Each porpoise has

Copper Potlatch Shield - Pieces

about 150 teeth. There are three different sizes of teeth used as currency. The small size is called *raa*, the medium size is called *una bubu*, and the large size is called *robo*. The small size is used for body ornamentation. The medium size is used for bride price and as part of blood money. The large size is used to hire canoes, to pay wages, and all other purchases. In the past the porpoise came from the North Mala area. In the 1930s the teeth were imported from some of the Micronesian Islands. In 1968, porpoise teeth were worth one Australian shilling each. A *quanaiga* was a unit of four porpoise teeth. When visiting the Solomon Islands in 1995 I saw porpoise teeth used in bride price. On that visit our taxi driver explained that bride price was still used to purchase wives. He further explained that the purchase of the wife was to validate the marriage. We purchase a marriage license to get married they pay bride price. They do not have a marriage license to make the union official. With the bride price the two families are united through the marriage. In this case the bride price is not an economic purchase of the wife like in some other societies. It only validates the marriage. (See Ivens - 1930) (See Akin, Traditional Money Association Newsletter. Vol 2 Number 1.

Malaita, Solomon Islands

The teeth are worth one shilling each and 50 teeth for $6 Australian. The bride price was negotiated in porpoise teeth and shell money.

Guadalcanal

Porpoise teeth and dog teeth plus 40 strings of *ndovu* shell money was the fine for seducing a single girl. Her bride price was also reduced.

POSTAGE STAMP MONEY - See Stamp Money

POTATO MASHER - See Ensuba

POTLATCH SHIELD - See Shield Money

POTLATCH

The potlatch was a fundamentally hostile gift-giving ceremony of the Canadian Northwest Indians. Its primary purpose was the repeated and public reaffirmation and validation of both the horizontal lineage system and the vertical hierarchy of rank. Potlatches were occasions for passing on inheritance and ceremonial wealth to oncoming generations. It was economic to the extent that it transferred material goods, and the recipient was obligated to return the gift at some future date. Most kinds of potlatches, items used, and item values varied by tribe and period of time.

The potlatch existed in the context of a large surplus economy. The surplus food supply was transformed into potlatch goods, and reserves of food were expended in potlatching, marriage gifts, and other ceremonies. The potlatch ceremony consisted of three main parts: (1) the feast, (2) the dances, songs, and theatricals, and (3) the presentation of the ceremonial gifts. The preparations for a potlatch could take many years. They had to compose songs, teach them to the singers, rehearse dances, commission carvings, plan speeches, and obtain the gifts to be given away at the ceremony. A person's rank determined the order of everything from the distribution of the gifts to the seating of the guests. When the position of chief is passed to a successor, the potlatch serves to validate the successor as the legitimate heir. The lineage chief, therefore, invited other lineage chiefs with their linear relatives to a feast which lasted several days and where the guests were assigned seats strictly in accordance with their social positions. A potlatch has been described as a congregation of people, ceremoniously and often individually invited to witness a demonstration of family proration. Normally the entire kin or local group acts as host to the visitors.

A father or matrilineal uncle would hold potlatches at regular intervals during a childhood to confirm the legitimacy of the child's future rank. The naming of a child, the acquisition of a traditional family name, a girl's first menses, marriage, the redemption of the bridal payment, and the completion of house building were all points in a life when a potlatch would be held by some of the tribes. Also, death with the raising of a memorial pole and the assumption by a relative of the name and position of the deceased was a time for a potlatch. Sometimes potlatches were given just because the local clan felt rich enough to do so. All people other than slaves could participate. Women and children freely participated. By strict custom the potlatch lasted four days. The first day was for speech-making by both sides, feasting and dancing. The feast started with large bowls of water being passed around for the people to wash their hands. Then dried salmon was served, with the highest-ranking visitor receiving the first dish. Then various kinds of seaweed were served, followed by boiled clams, sea urchins, mussels, salmonberry stalks, and berries. The whole meal took three to five hours. The food was always cooked, never raw. The second day was used for the visitors to perform dances for the hosts. The third day was for theatricals and contests, such as eating. The main contest was fish-oil eating. The fourth day was for making presentations of goods. At this time the coppers, slaves, blankets, and money were given.

Some tribes had potlatches at more frequent intervals than other tribes. The Kwakiiutl and the Bella Colla held frequent potlatches. Native tradition says that the Quinault held their first potlatch around 1800. The Haida had five principal forms of potlatch: house-building, totem pole, funeral, vengeance, and face-saving. The house-building was the most important type. The totem pole potlatch was used to raise a totem pole and tattoo the children. The amount of property given away depended on the type of potlatch. For example, the totem potlatch requires only one half as much property as the house-building potlatch. The vengeance potlatch was given by a high-ranking person who had been insulted or whose honor had been injured. The injured party then destroyed property such as killing a slave or cutting up a copper. The party causing the injury then must destroy the same amount of property. If he did, the matter was settled. The Haida had two main types of potlatches: the house-building potlatch and the funeral potlatch. The Nootka had their potlatches mainly to honor children and individuals. The Tsimshian had potlatches to honor one's father's lineage.

At a time before access to European goods, one recorded potlatch distributed 50 seals, 10 sea otter blankets, 25 martin blankets, 20 black bear blankets, and some slaves. At another later potlatch a chief gave away 100 muskets, 400 yards of cloth, 20 casks of powder, 100 looking glasses, and many other items. Much of the goods given at a potlatch were valued as wealth rather than for their usefulness. Blankets came into popularity as potlatch goods when the sea otter and bearskin robes formerly used were traded to ships. In 1895, silver bracelets, brass bracelets, calico, kettles, abalone shells, and wash basins were given away. The interest rates on potlatch loans could vary. For under six months it normally ran 20 percent. For six months it was 40 percent. The normal rate for one year was 100 percent, but could go as high as 233 percent for a borrower with poor credit. The majority of the goods distributed were treasure items for the most part and were mainly used to confer prestige rather than for consumption. Even the practical items were given in quantities out of proportion to their practical use. Some anthropologists feel that the loan and its high interest was not a part of the actual potlatch but was preliminary to it to accumulate the amounts necessary for the actual potlatch. The goal was to publicly dispose of wealth and not to merely acquire and accumulate items. Men, women and children could freely participate in the potlatch. Only slaves were excluded. The giving of a potlatch was merely to establish position; it did not validate position. Position could only be validated by other members of society. It depended on the good-will the claimant was able to establish among other members of society. The Kwakiiutl potlatch was based on credit. There never were enough potlatch items in the Kwakiiutl tribe area to cover all the transactions in the potlatch.

Coppers played a prominent part in the potlatches of the Southern Kwakiiutl, while the Lekwiltok Kwakiiutl primarily used canoes and only later changed to coppers. A major potlatch was one involving guests from another tribe as well as the home tribe. A minor potlatch was one involving only guests from the local tribe. A major potlatch called the *Khatashi* (to raise the dead) was only given by very wealthy chiefs, and one has not been given since 1828. When invitations were given they did not specify the persons, but it was understood that the invitation included wives and children. A potlatch canceled old debts and created new credits. Only the potlatches given by one's parents determined one's position; a potlatch given by you would only affect the status of your children. One writer has said the potlatch is an example of conspicuous consumption.

Some of the tribes that participated in the potlatch were: Kwakiiutl, Niska, Haida, Tlingit, Bella Coola, Salish, Chinook, Tsimshian, Stikine, Tongass, Nuuchahnulthaht, Quinault, and Upper Skagit.

Potlatch Articles

Coppers, blankets, canoes, slaves, and abalone shell ornaments were the most important articles in the potlatch. The Tlingit also used moose and caribou hide shirts, trousers and moccasins. Modern potlatches use money and other items as discussed later.

Changes in Potlatch

The Kwakiiutl had their first contact with Europeans in 1792. A change came to the potlatch when the flow of European goods increased, and the goods did not go primarily to the established chiefs and other heads. Then a social upheaval occurred when small-pox and measles reduced the Indian population in some villages to as little as 10 percent of the original population. Because there was a lack of appropriate heirs, conflicts arose over the assumption of hereditary rights. The newly wealthy men then tried to show their new found wealth, and the traditional way of doing this was with the potlatch. At this time the competition started to take the form of destroying property such as slaves, coppers, canoes, and blankets. This was a so-called rivalry potlatch. Prior to 1849, potlatches were not the big ceremony they were later. The Canadian government used the rivalry potlatch as a reason to outlaw all potlatches. The great wealth from the fur trade made possible larger and more frequent potlatches. Until 1849 the Kwakiiutl used native blankets, but these were replaced by the Hudson's Bay Company's woolen ones. Now, Pendleton Company woolens are used. Once a trading post came to an area, the frequency and size of the potlatch increased.

After whiskey was introduced to the Indians, some potlatches often deteriorated into drunken orgies with the whole affair ending in a fight.

One chief thought he was insulted by another tribe. Rather than raid the other village and have trouble with the Canadian government, he told his tribe to have a potlatch with the other tribe and destroy them with property. They killed a large number of sea otters and at the potlatch slashed the skins and threw the pelts overboard. When the other side did the same and ran out of hides before the first chief did, the first chief avenged the insult.

Most potlatches were planned for and preparations started many years before the actual potlatch was held. One chief started to prepare for the announcement of his daughter's puberty, and therefore her readiness for marriage, shortly after her birth.

Among the Kwakiiutl the rank of "eagle," which was a position belonging to some head chiefs, was also allowed for some whose wealth and liberality gave them a status that was inappropriate with their heredity.

At later potlatches, blankets and cloth were torn instead of killing slaves. Also, slaves were freed from their slavery in some instances. This was really the destruction of wealth, as the slaves were considered wealth. By making them free, the slave owner lost wealth that was not in turn given to another potlatch recipient. To acquire the goods needed for the potlatch, many women turned to prostitution to earn enough money for a large potlatch. In 1906 a number of girls were sold for $300 to $1,200 each. In some cases they were used as prostitutes. The Indians stated that the potlatch was a "method that we have of showing our good-will toward one another, and we believe that it is our just right as much as it is the right of our white brethren to make presents to each other." The Kwakiiutl thought of the potlatch as a way to fight with property instead of weapons. Potlatches were a planned campaign against the enemy. The Kwakiiutl were encouraged by the cheap goods from the traders. The Indians' own people could not produce the quantity of goods the later potlatches required.

The size of the potlatch increased over the years from 1849 to 1936. Prior to 1849 the largest potlatch was valued at 320 blankets. By 1890 that number was 18,000 blankets, and in 1936 the number was 33,000 blankets. It is true, however, that the early potlatches were valued in mountain goat hair blankets, while later ones were valued in modern woolen blankets. Trade took the form of exchanging food for wealth, such as slaves, canoes, and blankets, which were then given away at the potlatch for prestige.

Canadian Government Laws

In 1885 the Canadian government outlawed the potlatch because it felt the ruinous gift-giving ceremony was destroying too many of the goods that the Indians needed to prosper. It was also said that at some ceremonies of initiation, "dog-eating" rites and the taking of bites from arms and chests of witnesses and a corpse was done. There is no conclusive evidence of the flesh actually being ingested, however. The conflict of the natives and the Canadian government was a clash of values. The natives considered their potlatch a time-honored and beneficial institution that did no harm. The banning of the potlatch tore away most of the traditional social fabric of the Northwest Coast Indians. The government had difficulty enforcing the potlatch laws and as early as 1886 there were complaints about lack of enforcement. Many tribes decided to continue the potlatch even if it was against the law. The 1895 amendment instructed the agents to use "great circumspection, exhausting every means of bringing the Indians to abandon the custom, through moral session, before instituting prosecution."

The Indians did not stop the potlatch with the passing of the Canadian law. The potlatches were primarily done in secret, and in the early 1920s the potlatches were greatly reduced and to a large extent faded away.

In 1951 the Canadian government changed the law to again allow potlatches. They did that simply by omitting the Potlatch Law from new legislation. Since that time, potlatches have grown larger and more elaborate as the years go by.

One of the Largest Potlatches

In 1922 at Village Island, Emma Cranmer held a "repurchase" followed by a distribution by Dan Cranmer of the goods received from his wife and her family as well as some of his own items. He first repaid earlier loans with a copper changing hands several times. He then paid out 24 canoes, three pool tables, four gas boats, dresses, shawls, bracelets, sweaters, shirts, blankets, gas lights, violins, guitars, basins, glasses, washtubs, teapots, boxes, 300 oak trunks, sewing machines, gramophones, bedsteads, bureaus, and between 400 and 1,000 sacks of flour. The government arrested the Indians and threatened to put them in jail. Some did go to jail. As a result the Indians once more signed an agreement not to hold any more potlatches. They also reluctantly agreed to finally turn in their coppers and dancing gear. The material turned in consisted of over 450 items, including 20 coppers, along with masks and hamatsa whistles. This was the last large potlatch that the government was aware of.

Modern Potlatches

Since 1951, potlatches now use store-bought blankets from Hudson's Bay Company or Pendleton Company. They also use bedding, china, glassware, T-shirts, flour, silk scarves, brass bracelets, kettles, sewing machines, dishes, pails, zinc wash boilers, shotgun shells, coins, fish knives and some native art. The modern potlatch is again an important part of the Indians' lives. It appears that, except for substituting modern goods, no great changes have occurred between modern potlatches and the old ones. In 1950 in the Alert Bay area, a potlatch occurred in which $15,000 changed hands. In 1933, it was stated that a 33,000-blanket potlatch took place.

Bride Price

Among the Kwakiiutl, marriage must be considered a purchase. However, the object bought was not only the woman but also the right of membership in her clan for future children of the couple. The bride groom's family paid from $500 to $1,000 to the bride's family, mostly in blankets. Repayment by the bride's family was required. The Tlingit did not return gifts as the other tribes did. Part of the payment was made at the time of the marriage and the remainder later. When the bride price was repaid, the marriage was ended. Often after the completing of the marriage, the girl was married to another man, and the bride price was again paid and repaid. This increased the prestige of the family. Some girls 13 years old and younger were reported to be sold without their consent. Some marriages were sham marriages and were done only for the exchanging of privileges. An individual was worth the amount of the bride gift of his mother.

Abalone Shell

Earrings and nose rings of abalone shell were used as important potlatch gifts.

Blankets

Chilkat blankets were of highest value in the potlatch. They had a crest of the owner on them. The blankets were produced by the Tlingit tribe and were the most original ceremonial robe. They were made of the wool of the mountain goat. The weaving of this type of blanket was originated by the Tsimshian and taken to the Tlingit. The men provided the mountain goat wool as well as the cedar bark, frame, and painted pattern board. The women did the weaving. Three goat skins were used to make one blanket. Cedar bark was gathered in long strips in the spring-time of the year. Only the inner bark was used. It was first dried, and when actually used to make the blanket, it was boiled in water for up to two days to remove the sap. Then it was washed and left soaking in the water until it was pliable. Then it was shredded to separate the fibers which were made into a continuous strand and covered with loose wool. It was again twisted so that the cedar bark core was covered in a layer of wool. The various parts of the wool were dyed different colors by the use of natural dyes. The black dye came from a long process of heating the bark in various combinations of old strong urine and copper. The yellow dye came from tree moss. Greenish-blue and yellow green were obtained from a complicated process using urine, copper, and tree moss. By the late 19th century, commercial dyes from trade stores were used instead of the natural dyes. When the blanket was woven, the design was taken exactly as it appeared on a painted pattern board. The color scheme on all the blankets was the same even though the pattern changed. The field was a natural white of the goat, and the figure was outlined in black bands with the parts filled in with yellow and blue. An experienced weaver could produce a blanket in five or six months. The blankets were used in ceremonies and dances, and the wealthy used them as ceremonial robes. They were given to the most honored guests at a potlatch, and in some cases they were cut into two or three strips and given away. These strips were especially valuable as they could later be combined and made into dance aprons or caps or leggings. The strips were always divided evenly at a potlatch, while the whole blankets were given to the recipients as the host designated. Some blankets had strips of fur such as mink or otter attached to the upper border. Some older blankets were rectangular and did not have the cedar bark mixed with the wool. Some authorities think the classic Chilkat robe was a 19th century development from 18th century blankets. A Chilkat blanket was worth two black fox furs. Four blankets would also purchase a slave.

Woolen blankets were used by the Indians as a store of wealth and also as a unit of value and form of money after the Indians came in contact with Europeans. One report in 1859 announced the conversion from furs to blankets. Some tribes like the Kwakiiutl may have made the conversion even earlier. Cheap white wool blankets were used among the Kwakiiutl as money and valued at 50 cents each. A double blanket was worth three single ones. Taxay writes that between 1849 and 1850, Hudson's Bay Company purchased 200 square miles of land for 950 blankets. Two blankets would purchase a gun, and 12 blankets would purchase a sea-otter skin. The Hudson's Bay trade blanket at one time was priced at 50 cents for a single blanket and $1.50 for a double blanket. In 1888 a new blanket had a price of $2.50 for a double but was worth only $1.50 in trade. Therefore, no new blankets were entering the trade because of this difference in value. Money gradually took the place of the blanket. Blankets were used extensively in the potlatch. Some were covered with large pearl buttons. In the modern potlatch, Pendleton Company blankets are used. The blankets used for potlatching were never used for economic purposes or to keep warm. In 1859 a bear or land otter fur was worth one blanket. A beaver fur was worth two blankets. Lynx and fox furs were three blankets each, and a mink was 30 blankets.

Canoes

Large and small canoes were often used in trade and in potlatches. A large canoe was worth $150 or 10 to 15 slaves. For some tribes the canoe was the second most important potlatch gift.

Shield Money

Northwest Coast Indians, particularly the Kwakiiutl and Haida tribes, used the copper shield, also called *tinneh*, *tinnah* or "Chief's coppers." They were a form of wealth equivalent to high-denomination paper money. They were more the property of the family than that of an individual. Shields were the supremely valuable item used in the potlatch, where they were given to a rival tribe with the understanding that at some later date the value of the shield would be returned with 100 percent or more interest. Failure to accept the shield was an admission of being poor, as it showed the entire rival tribe did not have sufficient wealth to return the value of the shield and 100 percent interest at a later date. If a shield was broken into sections, a prescribed sequence was followed. The upper right corner was always broken first, then the lower corner diagonally opposite from it, then the upper left corner and finally the lower right corner. The T-shaped center which was left was worth two-thirds of the total value. The design on the copper usually represented the crest animal of the owner. Other shields did not have any design on them. The shields were made of pure copper. Many were painted or engraved with symbolic or totemic devices. Black lead was painted on the front side of the whole shield, and often a design was incised by scraping away the black lead to show the design. Some said that the Indians covered the copper with spruce gum and heated it, leaving a black enamel. Coppers were used as late as the 1930s. They were first outlawed in 1898. The value of a copper depended entirely on the amount of property that was paid for it and then given away in a potlatch. Some coppers were valued as high as 7,500 blankets, worth $3,750, and weighed 90 pounds. One copper was valued at $20,000. In 1866 one sold for 15 slaves and 200 blankets. Another copper was worth 10 slaves. In 1936 one copper sold for 25,000 blankets and another sold for 33,000 blankets. The copper was also used in the dowry of an Indian bride to give to the groom's family. The bride's family would also "buy back" the bride with a copper and other wealth items. It was also a store of wealth. Small coppers three or four inches long were used by the Kwakiiutl tribe for decoration on ceremonial costumes and ornaments. Larger ones five to seven inches long were worn on a headdress of fur. A copper shield increased in value every time it was given away, but if it were spent it was discounted by fifty percent in value. Shields were normally valued in blankets. The shields were valued at very high values, but the amount could vary considerably. One copper went for 14,500 blankets. A wealthy chief might own as many as 24 to 36 shields at one time. The only time the value of a copper decreased was when the copper was totally destroyed. Then it had no value. This was a surpassing feat that the rival could only match by destroying a copper of equal or greater value. If he couldn't, he was beaten and disgraced. They were considered property above all else. Shields made by Europeans were discounted by 95 percent or more over the value of shields made by the Indians out of native copper. The ring of the shield when struck was different. The native copper originally used in a shield to a large extent came from the Copper River valley and the White River valley. It was exchanged for cedar bark baskets, oil, iron, fish, and shell ornaments. It was said that the many coppers were made from native copper, but in all the museums there is currently not one example of a copper shield made from native copper. There are reported to be 135 coppers in museums at present. One expert has said that it appears that no present coppers seem to have been made before commercial copper was available to be used. See Shield money

Slaves

Many tribes of the Canadian Northwest had slaves as property before the Europeans came to the area. The slaves had neither rank nor rights and received no legacy. Most were taken as booty in raids or were the descendants of such slaves. A high-ranking person captured as a slave could be ransomed for a high price.

Kirk states, "There are accounts of 140 feet of strung dentalium shells, 10 sea otter skins, or 100 or more wool blankets being exchanged for a healthy slave." One chief stated that in his grandfather's time, a slave was usually purchased for 600 to 700 blankets and that previously canoes, house planks and various other goods were used. Kirk also states, "Slaves could be used or given away, discarded or destroyed just like any other property; most were treated fairly well, and their lot was not sharply different from that of low-ranking commoners." There was a close relationship between predatory warfare for the acquisition of slaves and the maintenance or enhancement of high social status. Much of the warfare among the Indians was for the main purpose of obtaining slaves for trade or to potlatch. In a potlatch the Tongass gave 20 slaves to the Stikine. One report states that slaves formed the principal article of trade on the whole coast and constituted the greater part of their riches. Wars were waged more to profit from the sale of slaves than to avenge aggressions. The Tsimshian and Haida tribes bartered for slaves with the Kwakiiutl, who got their slaves by raiding the villages of Puget Sound and from the mouth of the Fraser River. Slaves also served as trade goods between the various Tlingit villages. They were a medium of exchange. The Tlingit purchased most of their slaves from the Haida. Others were taken in warfare. In some cases they also enslaved other Tlingit. The slaves were children and women of other Tlingit tribes with whom they had been at war. The children of slaves were also slaves. The hardest thing about slavery was that slaves were the absolute property of the owner, and therefore the owner was able to kill the slave at a potlatch. Many times when a slave owner died, his slaves were killed so they could attend to him in the spirit world. Slaves were valued at different amounts by different tribes at different times. A man was valued at 20 pounds of copper or six prime sea otter pelts. A woman was valued at 10 pounds of copper or five normal sea otter pelts. In another area a man was worth one Chilkat blanket, 30 fox skins, 10 moose skins or two martin skin blankets. In 1860 a man was worth $200 or 40 blankets. Twenty slaves would pay for a medium copper. A large copper was worth 40 slaves. In the 1880s a slave was worth 30 to as much as 60 blankets, and most chiefs owned 50 to 100 slaves. In the 1840s it was estimated that one third of the Indians in one area were slaves. Slaves to be used in a potlatch were always purchased just before the ceremony and were not the slaves kept in the houses for labor. According to Mitchell, a single slave had the following values among the various tribes:

Tribe	Value
Stikine	18-20 skins
Tsimshian	15 elk skins
Haida	150-200 blankets
Bella Coola	10-20 blankets
Kwakiiutl	100 blankets
Quinault	80 blankets
Chinook	20-100 blankets

There are many instances of trading slaves for furs by many of the tribes. Some of the tribes- the Bella Coola, for instance- varied the value of a slave based on the general supply, age, sex, ability, and industriousness. Slaves were some of the highest-valued items the Indians possessed.

POTS

Amphlett Islands

Women manufacture cooking pots which measure as large as three to four feet in diameter. They are generally acknowledged to be the best in the area. The Amphletts occasionally trade pottery to Goodenough Island in the west for pigs. The majority of pots of non-European origin in many of the Trobriand Islands come from the Amphlett Islands.

Bougainville

Surplus pots were produced to exchange for shell money, pigs, and taro. They were also used to give a renowned spring feast. All valuables, such as pots, were called *manunu.*

Kiriwina Island, Trobriand Islands

Clay pots, along with stone axe blades, are the major source of wealth for internal exchanges.
(See Inalienable Possessions P.139)

New Britain

A dog or a pig were each worth 10 pots in the old days. More recently, only two pots would purchase a piglet. Over the years the prices and values have changed substantially. A boar's tusk pendant was worth three or more bowls. While some of the pots were actually used for cooking, most of the pots were wealth objects and used in trading. Ten pots were worth a block of obsidian. The items went in a series of trades from island to island, and the trading profit made was substantial.

Papua New Guinea

Pots come in a variety of sizes and shapes. Cooking and storage pots were made for trade. All of the different villages and areas make different styles and types of pottery with different quality and durability because of techniques and varying clay deposits. Many villages specialize in pottery. Pots were traded for lower-ranked *mwali* and *bagi,* food items. The pots were considered a trade good. They were also given in bride price payments and figure strongly in many rituals and

Amphlett Island Pot

Pot - Papau New Guinea

customs. The raw clay itself is now traded or sold in many areas. In the past, pots were the stock-in-trade of fleets of *lakatoi*. The Siassi people obtained pots from the Sio people which they traded to the West New Britain coast, where they were used for bride price, and in return they obtained pigs. They considered pigs to be the most valuable item. Of lesser importance were wooden bowls and dogs. Pots were considered wealth objects and played an important part in bride price transactions. Ten Sio pots were worth one dog, one pig or one boar's tusk. A Sio pot was also worth two to four coconuts. These values varied from area to area. Pottery was used in the **hiri**, kula and the complex system of the Vitiaz Straits as a form of money in trade. In the *hiri*, thousands of pots were transported on large sailing canoes in exchange for sago. The coastal dwellers traded pottery, fish, shells, and shell jewelry for betel nut, bird feathers, taro, yams, dogs, and dog teeth to the mountain dwellers. The strongest and best pottery came from the Amphlett Islands. Tubetube Island was the dominant pot-producing island in the kula ring. In 1935, Wari pottery was traded to the mainland and also Tubetube, Wagawaga, Suau, Samarai, and Normanby. Rawa pots were traded to the Benabena people and then across the Ramu River into the Eastern Highlands. The Benabena people gave dogs, dog's teeth, small pigs, bows, arrows, bilum bags, salt, stone axes, and lime for the pottery. Madang pots were traded into Goroka and Chimbu on a small scale. The Wanitzir and Biampitzir people supply pots to the Tangu people in trade for bilum bags, tobacco, betel nut, pandanus, and sago. The Tangu people then trade the pots to many others, some from as far away as Manam Island. The Jitibu people traded pots from many villages, including Nodabu. They gave a canoe for 20 pots, a large bundle of bark for five to 10 pots, and a large fish for four pots. The Kwoma people trade their pots for mussel shells to the Mayo villagers. The villages of Koiwat and Kamanggaui produce cooking pots and sago storage vessels for trade to northern villages for dogs, tobacco, and tubers. Aibom pottery has always been a valuable item of trade. They trade it along the Sepik River, and, with the help of middlemen, they obtain sago. Formerly, Yaul pots were traded to villages on the Keram in exchange for bows, arrows, bilum bags, and dogs. Pottery is made in the villages of Terebu, Samap, and Kapak 1 & 2, traded to the Wewak area for wooden plates or cash sale, and exchanged with the Murik Lakes people for pearl shells, fish, and baskets. A small pot was worth 50 pounds of taro. A medium size pot was 100 pounds, and a large pot was 150 pounds of taro. A large pot was worth four *bilum* bags or three mats. A canoe was worth 24 to 30 pots.

Panaeati Islands

Their pottery was traded in the kula for betel nut, food, and sago prior to the larger transactions of kula. Panaeati was known as the source of pots.

Vitiaz Strait

Large canoes were used to carry 200 to 300 clay pots or two tons of taro. The communities of Siboma, Lababia, Laukanu, and Buso on the south coast of Huon Gulf as well as Sio, Nambariwa, Gitua, and Sialum on the north coast of Huon Peninsula and also Bilibili and Jabob in Astrolabe Bay supply the people of the Vitiaz Strait. The pots were treated as bride price payments on Umboi Island and in western New Britain.

Wooden bowls were also manufactured in the Tami Islands and traded to eastern Vitiaz Strait. The bowls were made of hardwood and expertly carved with excellent designs. Large Tami Islands bowls were worth 5 to 10 pounds. The Tami style bowl has come to be known as the Siassi bowl because they now supply many of that style bowl. Four pots and eight coconuts were worth two *bilums* of taro and three packets of tobacco. One pot was also worth one packet of tobacco or two to four coconuts and a small pot was worth three to six shillings.

Tubetube Island

A pot was worth six yams, a bunch of bananas or a bunch of areca nuts.

Wanigela area

These people made pots for trade with the inland people for reptile skins, tapa cloth, and feathers. They also traded with the people along Collingwood Bay for shells, canoes, and obsidian. (See Tuckson) (See Rogers p.88, Newton p. 14, Cranstone p. 23)

POTUMA - See Bosu

POUND BEADS - See Beads

PRAKAB

Siam, About 1744

Baked clay coins were used in place of cowries during a shortage of the shells. (See Gear p.30)

PRAYER BOOK MONEY

Netherlands, May - October 1574

For a five month period, two provinces of the Netherlands, Holland and Zeeland, were under siege. When metal became scarce, five Stiver and 20 Stiver coins were made out of pages of Church books glued together or the covers of religious books. Disks were cut out and stamped with dies from coins. If the piece is split you can see the wording from the pages of the book. The coins are also known in silver. (See Sigler p. 24)

PRINCE MANILLA - See Manilla - Prince

PU MONEY (now BU)

China, 350 B.C - 23 A.D.

Cast bronze pieces, also called shirt, pants, spade, or cloth money. Pu now means "cloth" or "silk." Many

Wang Mang Reform Bu Money (Courtesy Shanghai Museum)

Prayer Book Money

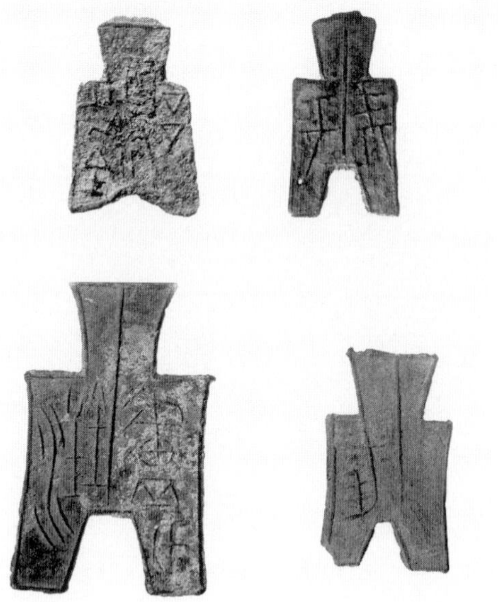

Han State By Money (Courtesy Shanghai Museum)

Chu State By Money (Courtesy Shanghai Museum)

have rounded or angular shoulders, feet or heads. Various inscriptions. Imitations were made by Emperor Wang Mang in 9-23 A.D. See Spade Money

PUMTEK - See Beads, Burma

PURR-PURR
Nigeria, as Late as 1939

They were used in the area around Gwosa. They were considered a currency bar and valued at 3d. In the last few years a hoard has come on the market. (See Johansson p. 41)

PWOMONDAP
Rossel Island

This item is a piece of *spondylus* shell, triangular in shape with rounded edges and a hole in the corner. Two hundred of this value *Ndap* exist on the island. It is the most common value of *Ndap*. (See Quiggin p. 184)

QUARTZ BALLS
Gold Coast

The balls are from the Stone Age, and it is believed they were used as currency. 2" - 2-1/2" diameter (See Quiggin p. 60)

QUARTZ DISK
Ghana, Togo and Sierra Leone, as early as 1600 A.D.

Accans, Baoula, and Ashanti tribes used these donut shaped quartz disks as money. They have a high value and are thought to have medicinal healing powers. The natives believed the disks had fallen from heaven to bring good luck. 2" diameter. Also called Togo Stone.

QUACHTLI
Mexico

A large cotton mantle that would purchase a canoe. Thirty were the cost of an ordinary slave. (See Taxay p. 29)

QUEEN MANILLA - See Manilla - Queen

QUETZAL FEATHER MONEY
Mexico, Guatemala

Among the Aztecs, the quetzal feather was the most valuable trade article. Green feathers from the tail of the Quetzal bird (*Trogon Resplendens*) were used. The feathers were very rare. Mayans also used these plumes as money. "The only legal way to capture a bird was to stun it with a clay pellet shot from a blow gun. It was a capital offense to kill the bird" said Taxay, p. 30

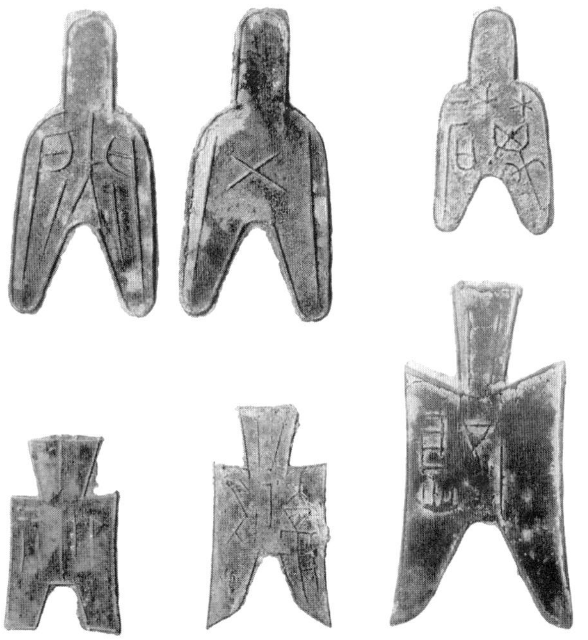

Zhao State Bu Money (Courtesy Shanghai Museum)

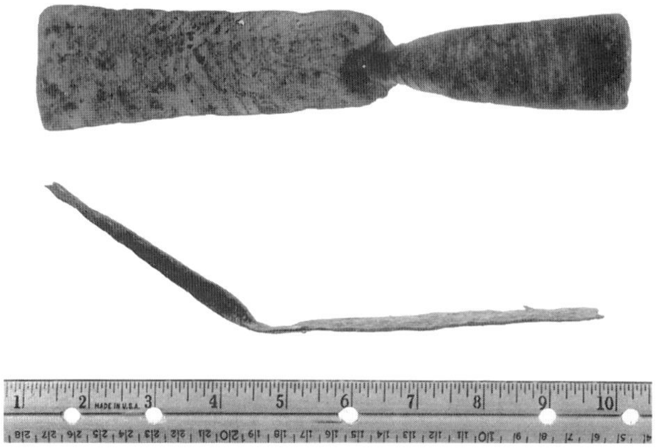

Purr Purr

Pwomondap

QUILL MONEY

Mexico

Goose and other quills filled with gold were a circulating medium of exchange. (See Gibbs p. 34) See Gold Dust Money

QUIRANDA - See Bubi currency.

RACCOON SKIN MONEY

Tennessee and surrounding area, 18th &19th century

During pioneer days the raccoon skin was a unit of value, store of wealth, and medium of exchange. In 1789 in the State of Franklin, which is now known as Tennessee, The General Assembly set the salary of the Clerk of the House of Commons at 200 raccoon skins per annum. (See Dillingham)

RAFFIA CLOTH - See Cloth - Zaire

RAI - See Stone Money - Yap

RAIN DRUM - See Kyee Zee

RAPHIA CLOTH - See Cloth - Zaire

RAT MONEY

Easter Island

Edible rats were a delicacy and were eaten raw. They were a favorite medium of barter and exchange. (See Einzig p. 45)

RAWHIDE TOKEN

See Leather

RAY - *Yap Island*

Monet that is 12 feet high and 12 feet wide. (See Ashby p. 46.)

RAZOR - See Knife Money

REINDEER

Siberia

The entire economy is based on the reindeer. The reindeer was a store of value, and each reindeer was worth five rubles. They were used in bride price and for payment of taxes. (See Einzig p. 116)

RHINOCEROS HORN

Africa

Some Africans thought that water drunk from rhinoceros horn cups would not kill you even if the water contained poison. Powdered rhinoceros horn was thought to cure disease and was used for medicinal purposes. The horn was a valuable item and was used in barter. The o-rinka is a stick with a knob at one end, all in one piece, carved from a rhinoceros horn and used by the Maasai. The o-rinka is very rare and could be owned only by the most outstanding leaders. There are many imitations. The rhinoceros is an endangered species. (See Turle)

China, 180 B.C.

Rhinoceros horns were used to pay tribute to the emperor. They are also a valuable item even to the present time, as the horn is still used in many Chinese medicines. Recently, steps have been taken to remove it from most medicines in China because the rhinoceros is an endangered animal. (See Wicks p. 28.)

RICE

Burma, 1797

Useless, broken rice was used as money (See Temple p.111) Unhusked rice, called paddy, was commonly used as a measure of value and a medium of exchange in 1000 A.D. (See Wicks p. 154)

Cambodia

The size of the transaction determined which medium of exchange was acceptable. For small transactions cereals in the form of rice were frequently used. (See Wicks p.206)

Japan, 16th century - World War II

Rice was the principal means of payment in many areas. In towns metallic money replaced rice by the 18th century but not in the villages. As early as the 17th century, the national wealth of Japan was calculated at 28,000,000 koku of rice. A koku of rice was equal to 5.12 bushels. Until prohibited in 1760 because of abuses, notes were issued by the landowners with rice as the unit of account. These notes were to represent rice held by the landowners. (See Einzig p. 313-315)

Java

In early Java rice probably served as a medium of exchange and in a very limited sense as a measure of value. (See Wicks p. 308)

Naga

Rice was used as money and wealth as well as in bride price. (See Quiggin p. 203)

Philippines, Early as 1775

Unthreshed rice, called palay, was used to pay taxes and was the principal currency. Igorot and Tinguian used palay in fixed denominations from one to 1000 handfuls.

Quartz Disk

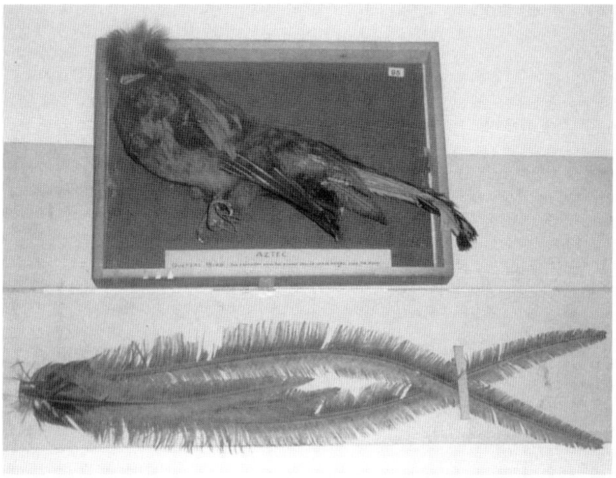

Quetzal Bird

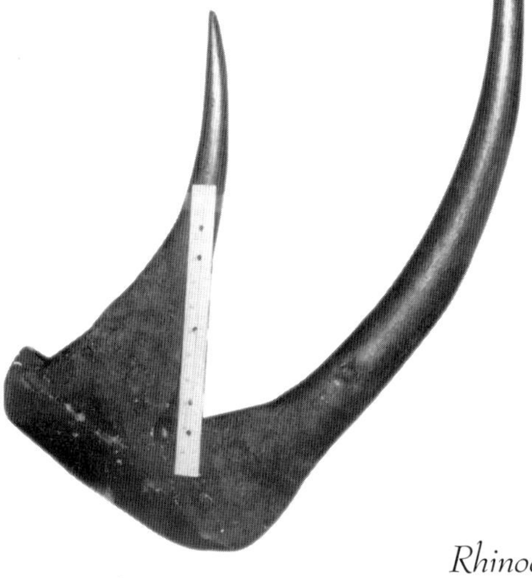

Rhinoceros Horn

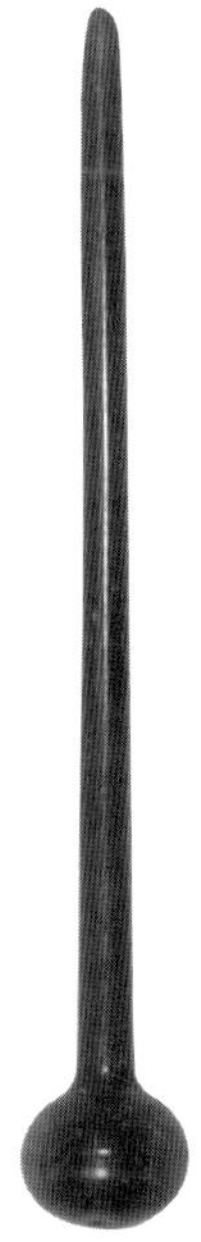

Rhinoceros Club (O-Rinka)

Cleaned rice was measured in units of one coconut shellful. Rice was used as a standard of value. In 1919 a bundle of rice was worth from 2 1/2 cents in one area to five cents in another. (See Einzig p. 93-95, Barton p. 428-429)

United States, South Carolina, 1719

The Assembly of South Carolina made rice receivable for taxes. Rice orders were issued to public creditors, and rice was receivable for all purposes. (See Angell p. 97).

RII - See Porpoise teeth

RING MONEY - See Mutaga

Africa

Various sizes and shapes of metal rings were used for decoration and as money by many tribes. The Arab traveler Al Bakri noted that rings of copper functioned as currency at Silla in Takrur in 1068 A.D., according to Herbert p. 113. The H-shaped copper ingots were believed to have been mined as early as 9th-12th century A.D. in the Katanga area. It is believed that heavy bracelets and beads first appeared in about the 8th century. From early on the bracelets served as a medium of exchange and also as an ornament. In the West we differentiate between money and ornament. Many areas of the world do not. In Takkeda, Herbert (p.195), says thick copper rings were used to buy slaves, wheat, ghee, and millet, while thin copper rings were used to buy meat and firewood. In most cases the bracelets were not worn and were 2" - 4 1/2" in diameter. There were two principal methods of manufacturing rings or bracelets. They were: (1) drawing wire to form bracelets and (2) casting. The Dan tribe and their neighbors used the lost wax technique to cast heavy bronze anklets, which became part of the woman's dowry. The Ibo tribe women also used anklets. The copper trade with Africa was large, and during the 1700s 16,000 tons of brass and copper were traded to Africa by the English alone. In 1698, a male slave was worth 38 copper bars, and a female slave was worth 36 or 37 copper bars. One iron bar was at that time worth four copper bars. Copper rings were also used during this time, but they were worth so little that one iron bar was worth 40 copper rings. (See Jones p. 44) Manillas were also a form of copper ring.

Africa

Rings of brass covered with decoration and twisted with overlapping ends were used as money. Many parts of Africa used them.

Africa
Iron rings with sharp points were used as weapons. It is also believed they were used as money.

Africa, Ashanti
The bell brass bracelet was probably made in Europe. Some bell bracelets were used in other areas of Africa. (See Semans p. 7-8)

Africa, Baoule
The anklet was traditionally part of the woman's dowry. It was made by the lost wax method and was hollow.

Africa, Benin
Large bicone shaped bronze bracelets were used as a form of money. (See Semans p. 5)

Africa, Benin
The twisted plain cast brass manilla has a mock twist at the top. (See Semans p. 6)

Africa, Berber tribe
Completely decorated hollow silver bracelets and rings were made and used by the Berber people in dowry and as a form of money.

Africa, Congo
Conus shell disk cut from the thicker end of the shell served as money.

Africa, Congo, Welle Tribe
Iron rings with two large or three small hollow enlargements were possibly used as money. (See Semans p. 12)

Africa, Congo
Rough cast brass semi-circle crescents were used as money. They had no other use than as money.

Africa, Ethiopia
Ornate silver wedding rings were worn on a cotton cord around the neck. The rings were never worn on the finger as we do; the hole was too small for any finger. It was considered a valuable, and some say it was used as money.

Africa, Ethiopia, beginning of 20th century
Gold rings were used in the Walaga and Beni Sshagul areas and southwest area of Ethiopia. The gold rings were worth from one dollar to 32 dollars each. No gold was mined in Ethiopia, so all of the gold came from

Brass Ring Money

Iron Ring Money

Ashanti Bell Bracelet

Baoule Anklet

Benin Bicone Bracelet

Twisted Brass Manilla Ring

Berber Silver Bracelet

trading with other areas. The rings were finger-ring size. (See Gill, p.12) (See Quiggin p. 94)

Africa, Hausa

Fancy white brass small bracelets with complex cast designs were used to purchase brides and cattle. The Fulani women wore them. (See Semans p. 9)

Africa, Marka of Dafing

The ornamental double bracelet is a broad, fancy brass with interior and exterior lengthwise grooves and raised cuffs. (See Semans p. 7)

Africa, Mbede tribe, Congo Brazzaville and Gabon

This bronze or copper anklet was used by the Mbede / Kota people and was used as an important currency and during marriage transactions. They were cast in flat earth molds and bent to form an anklet. They have three to six ribs. (See Borel p. 73) (See Schaedler p. 290-291)

Africa, Mbole tribe (Jonga, Nkutshu, Mongo)

Large copper spherical-shaped split rings were used as money and in matrimonial transactions by the Jonga. They were worn by both the men and women of the Mbole tribe. They vary from 18 to 35 cm in diameter. Their names were based on their size: *Diako,* (small) valued at two *onglese; Ambi,* (medium) valued at three *onglese; Ehuke,* (large) valued at four to eight *onglese; Hatakataka,* (very large) valued at nine *onglese;* and *Batataka,* (gigantic) valued at 10 *onglese.* (See Schaeder p. 292), (Ballarini p. 115)

Africa, Mongo tribe

Copper and zinc were poured in a horizontal press molded in the earth from a wood mold. While the ingot was still hot, it was wrapped a round a log to form a ring. The Mongo and Konda rich women wore these legbands, and using large rolls of vegetable fiber to protect their legs and help support the weight over a larger area of the leg. (See Ballarini P. 116). (See Schaedler p. 293.)

Africa, Namibia

Tiny silver twisted rings were used as bride money in the early 1900s. The wire was thinly drawn and twisted into a double strand and joined to form a ring. (See Crawford p. 478)

Africa, Nigeria, Bidda tribe

The wide crescent with flared ends was a well-cast, fancy, manilla-like brass bracelet was used as currency. (See Semans p. 6)

Africa, Nigeria

In the early 1600s, 120 brass rings would purchase a slave. 3″ diameter. (See Johansson p.45)

Africa, Nigeria

The bracelet was designed to imitate a stack of wire bracelets. It was used by the Hausa who used rod currencies. (See Semans p. 5)

Africa, Nigeria, Igbo

Decorated copper anklets were used as money. (See Eyo p.66)

Africa, Nigeria, Yoruba tribe

The entire outer surface of this copper or brass bracelet was covered with etched and punched designs. The broad-faced, squared body has curled-back ends. It was used as money. (See Semans p. 7)

Africa, Nigeria, Nupe type

Spatulate-ends with heavy yellow brass ring. (See Semans p. 8)

Africa, Pahouin

Decorated brass rings were used as a medium of exchange. (See Farr p. 46)

Africa , Rashaida

Ornate silver rings were used in bride price and as jewelry. This wide ring is given to the bride by the groom.

Africa, Senufo tribe

The boat anklet has pointed ends and was used as a form of money. (See Semans p. 6)

Africa, Senufo tribe

This rounded boat anklet was used as a form of money. (See Semans p. 6)

Africa, Yoruba tribe

This bronze ring was used as a part of dowry. (See Schaedler p. 241)

Africa, Zaire

This chief's neck ring was made of bronze. The number of notches denotes the number of villages under his jurisdiction and therefore his prestige. There is some doubt about the use of this item as currency. (See Quiggin p. 76)

Conus Shell Disk

Congo, Welle Tribe

Congo Ridged Crescent

Ethipia Wedding Ring

Namibia Silver Ring

Mbede Tribe Ribbed Angled Anklet

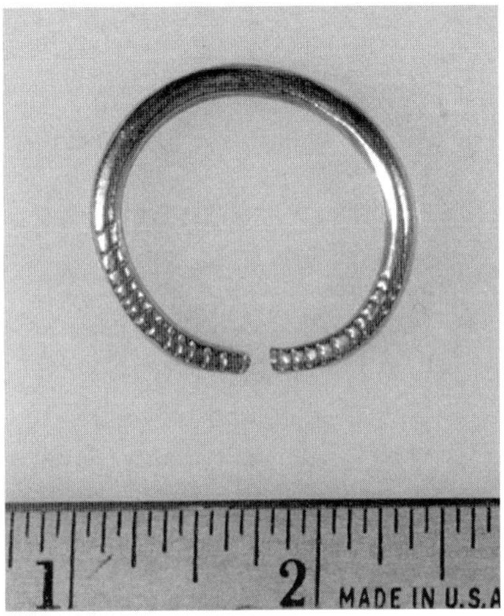

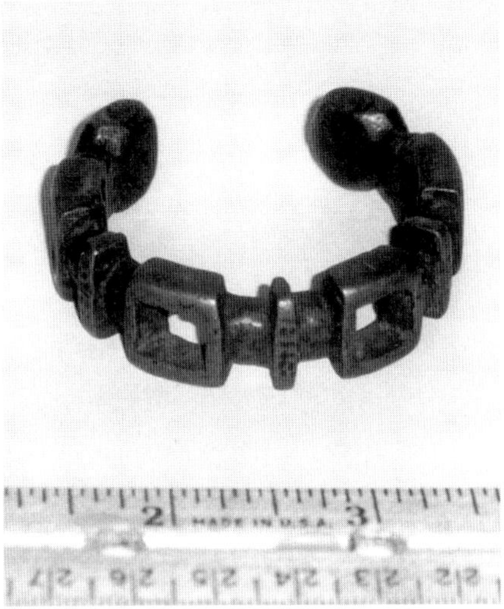

Gold Ring - Abyssinia

Hausa Fancy Bracelet

Ornamental Double Bracelet

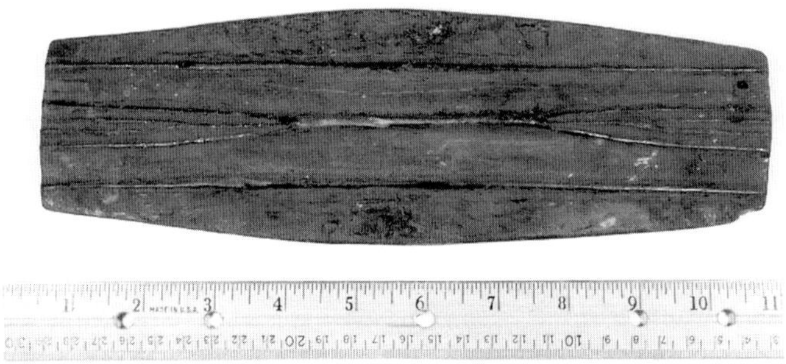

Mold for Mongo Ring

Congo, Welle Tribe

Africa, Zaire
Inter linked clusters of small red-copper rings were used as money in Zaire. Both hammered and drawn-wire rings were used.

Africa, Zaire
Bullion bronze fancy bracelets with many different designs were used as money.

Armenia, 800 B.C. and earlier
Smooth-surfaced, coarsely hammered rings are thought to have served as money. The bronze rings were considered a store of wealth. (See Saryan)

Burma, 750 - 1253 A.D.
Kingdom of Nanchao. Crescent-shaped silver rings were used as money until Kubla Khan conquered Nanchao in 1253. The flat bracelet had two cuts on the upper surface and five symbolic stamps. 2 inch diameter. (See Mitchiner p.329)

Indonesia, Sumba Island
Bronze and cast-iron rings were worn by women of high rank. Even to this day they are sometimes worn during wedding processions. Some of the designs are almost identical to Dongson bronze ware. I found bronze rings in several villages on Sumba in 1996.

Irian Jaya, Sentani Tribe
Transparent glass rings of Javanese origin that are more than 1,500 years old were used in bride price. They have also become traditional valuables for the people of the Vanimo region, who continue to obtain them from Jayapura. In 1980 a glass bracelet was worth 400 - 700 kina. Similar rings were made before 1656 at Biak. Dutch traders had green glass bracelets made in the Netherlands in the 18th century. They are highly valued and have been copied from shortly after they were first introduced to present times. The glass is transparent green. The modern rings are of light green glass with flat sides and rounded apex. (See Traditional Money Association Newsletter Vol. 10 Number 1, April, 1989)

Ireland, ancient times, Celtic, Anglo-Irish, 1st Millennium B.C.
Gold and bronze rings were used for bride-price. Wealthy ladies used them to reward poets, musicians, and story-tellers. The bronze Celtic ring circulated as a form of token currency.

Japan, 2500 years ago
Copper rings were covered with silver or gold. The silver rings are called *Gin*, and the gold rings are called *Kin*.

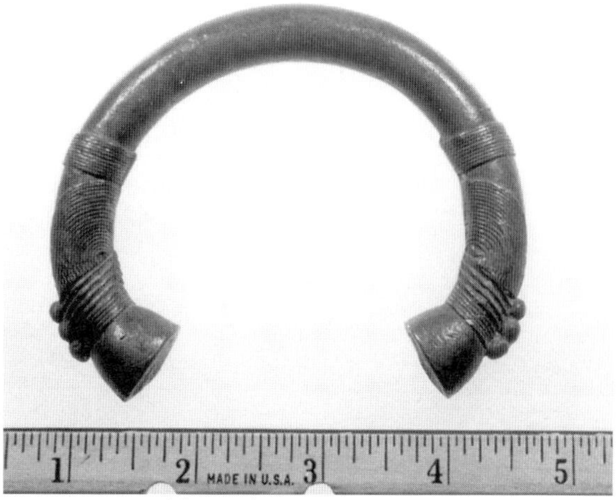

Nigeria, Bidda Tribe

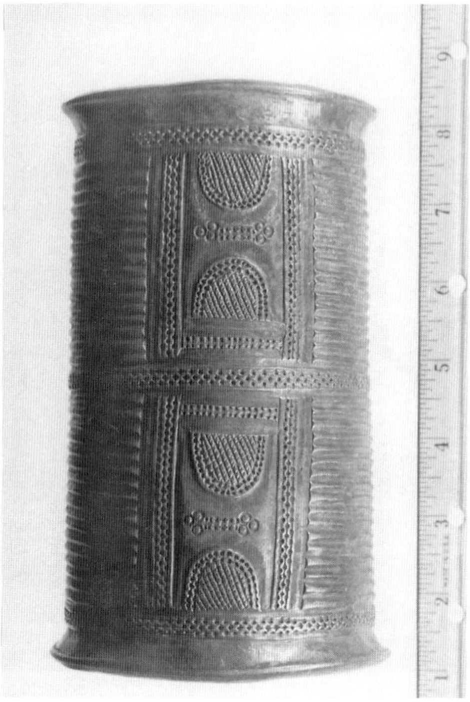
Nigeria, Igbo Tribe

Nigeria, Nupe Type

Rashaida Silver Ring

Senufo Boat Bracelet

Senufo Rounded Boat Bracelet

Nigeria, Bidda Tribe

Nigeria, Bidda Tribe

Nigeria, Bidda Tribe

Malay 1511 - 1556

Silver open bracelets in a quadrilateral cross-section with a cut at the apex were used as money. The sides of the bracelet have a formalized number "4," two issue marks, and the Sultan's formula on them. The piece became obsolete in 1556 when the Burmese occupied Chiengmai. (See Mitchiner p. 398).

Sumba Island Bronze Ring

Melanesia

Clam shell ring. See *Amfat*

Philippines

Igorot tribe, As early as 500 B.C. probably 200 AD - 600 AD

Hammered interrupted gold rings of various sizes dating from before the arrival of the Spaniards served as barter items. They were used for payment of the bride's dowry. (See Alexander, The Philippines A Multi-cultured Numismatic Mosaic)

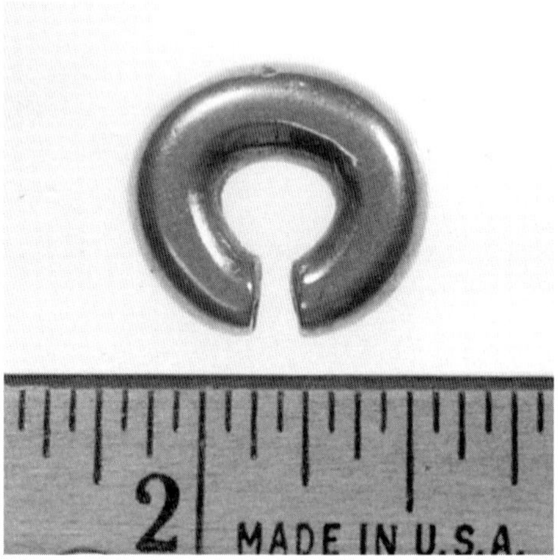

Ireland Gold Ring

Thailand

Rounded bracelet

Lahu, Akha & Lisu hill tribes

Silver tapered or flattened ends with a thick body with fancy designs along the entire length of the bracelet. The decoration includes double beaded ridges, pinches and smooth ring areas. (See Semans p. 5)

Faceted bracelet

Lahu, Akha & Lisu hill tribes

Six facets with slightly tapering ends. Most are plain and small. (See Semans p. 5)

Squared bracelet

Lahu, Akha and Lisu hill tribes

Most are plain with squared body with even ends and chased design. (See Semans p. 5)

Japan Gold Rings

Squared/flared bracelet

Hmong & Mien hill tribes

Squared sides with flared, flat ends. (See Semans p. 5)

Pointed end bracelet

Lawa hill tribe

The six -facet body with enlarged pointed ends has chased designs on more than half of the bracelet. (See Semans p. 5)

Hollow bracelet

Lahu & Akha hill tribes

Silver sheet was formed into a bracelet with all areas

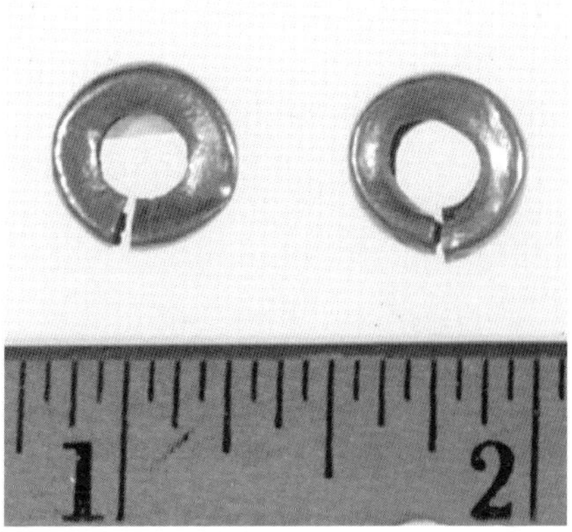

Gold Rings - Philippines

Rounded Bracelet

Faceted Bracelet

Twisted Wire Bracelet

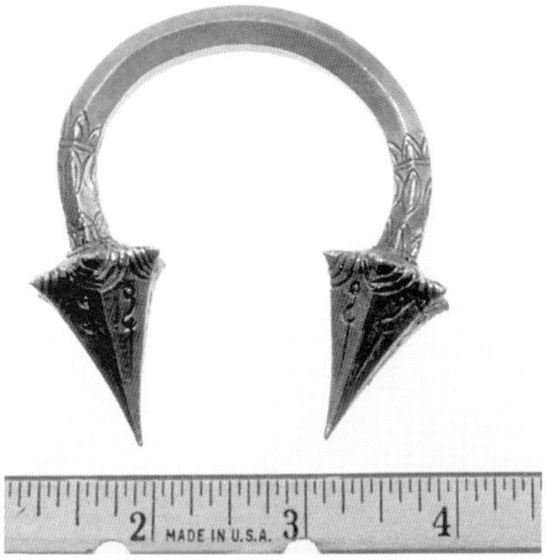

Pointed Ends Bracelet

Hollow Bracelet

Squared/Flared Bracelet

Twisted Wire Bracelet

Twisted Bracelet

Clasped Ends Bracelet

Flat Spiral Bracelet

covered with silver. It was made by the Chinese or Shan and was most likely a later type. Many have decoration on the surface. Some have knob ends and ridges. (See Semans p. 5)

Twisted wire bracelet
Akha hill tribe
Coils of tightly twisted silver wire was coiled around an imaginary bracelet to form a flexible body tapering to solid ends. They were made in Yunnan. (See Semans p. 5)

Twisted bracelet
Lawa hill tribe
Tightly twisted silver wire was formed into an overlapping ring and had smooth flat squared ends. (See Semans p. 5)

Clasped ends bracelet
Lawa hill tribe
Rounded or faceted silver bracelets have coiled or crossed silver wire wound around the tapered silver bracelet ends. (See Semans p. 5)

Flat spiral bracelet
Lawa hill tribe
Flattened silver wire was made into 3 to 4 coils with some having chased designs. (See Semans p. 5)

Solid neck ring
Hmong (Meo), Mien (Yao) & Lahu hill tribes
Plain solid silver torque with flattened back-turned ends. Some ends have a chased design on them. (See Semans p. 5)

Multi-tiered neck ring
Hmong (Yeo) & Mien hill tribes
Five attached solid silver neck rings in increasing size held together at the ends. Some have etched designs on the neck rings. It is a very impressive piece. (See Semans p. 5)

Hammered neck ring
Hmong (Meo), Mien (Yao) & Lahu hill tribes
A solid neck ring faceted by hammer blows. Similar to the solid neck ring. (See Semans p. 5)

Hmong and Mien bracelet
Round silver wire with bulb ends and minor decoration near the ends were used as money. (See Lewis 41.)

Hmong and Mien bracelet
Twisted round silver wire with smooth ends in the form of a bracelet were used as money. See Lewis p. 41.

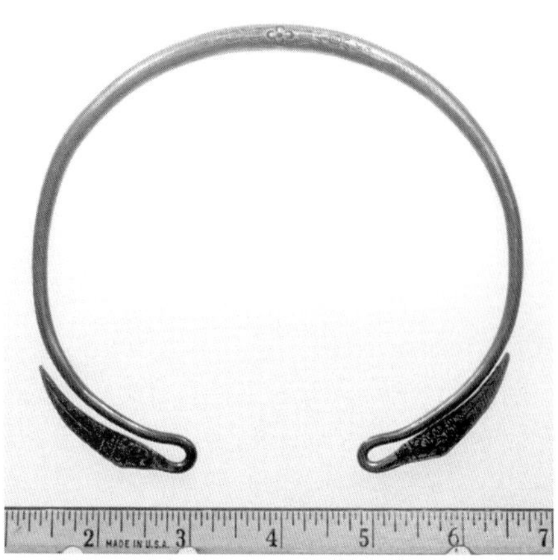
Solid Neck Ring

Multi-Tiered Neck Ring

Hammered Neck Ring

Twisted Ring

Solid Ring

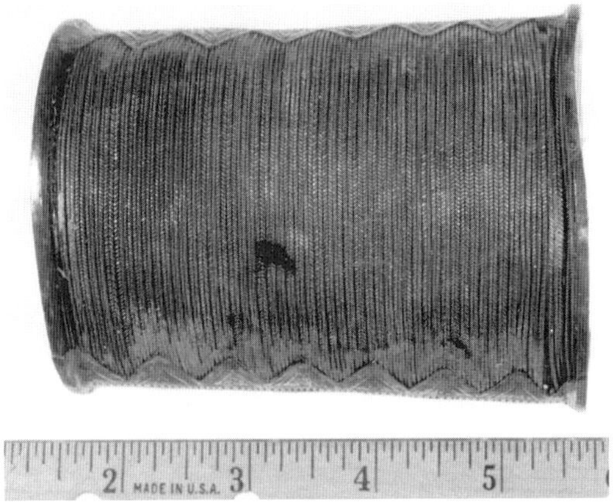

Shan Bracelet

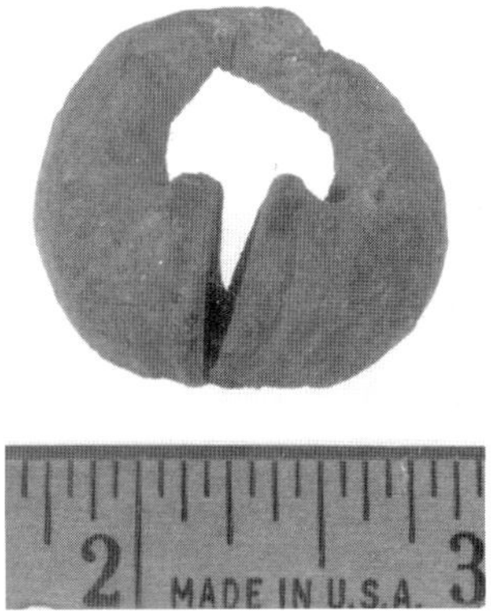

Mon Coinage - Lead

Twisted Neck Ring

Hollow Neck Ring

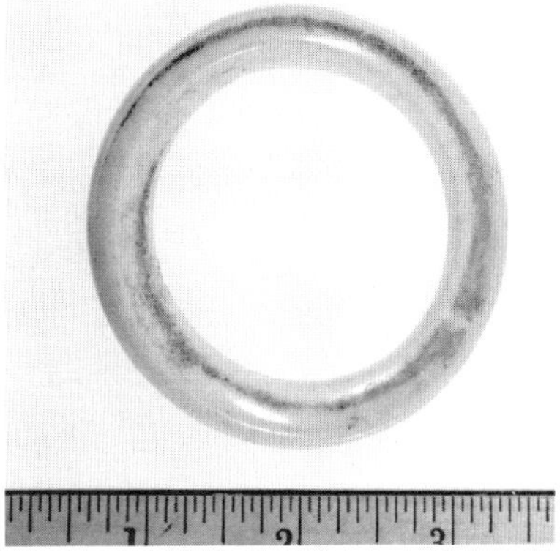

Glass Ring - Papau New Guinea

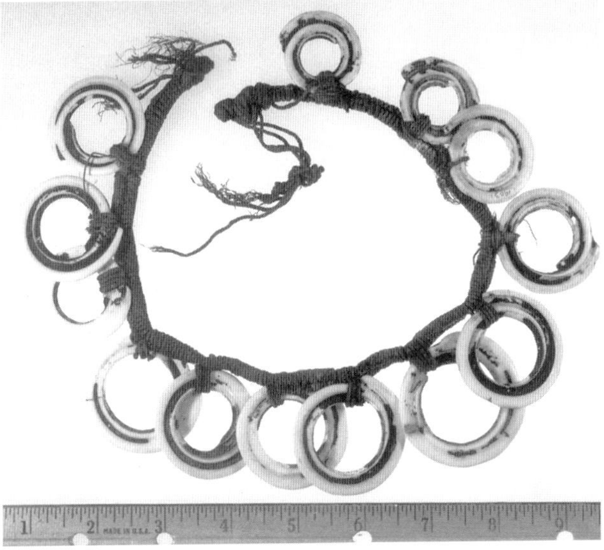

Conus Shell Rings - Papau New Guinea

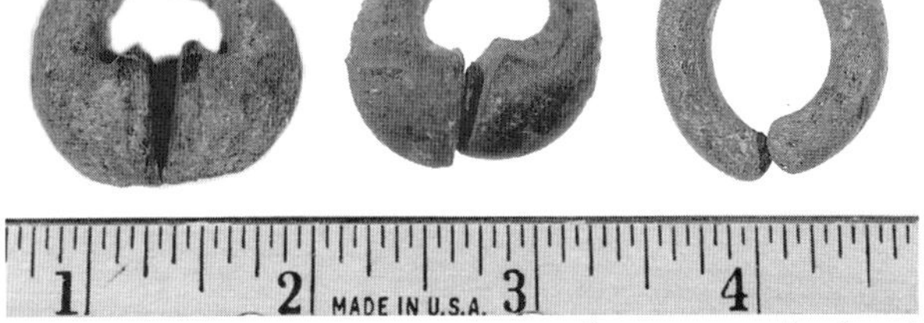

Lead Rings - Thailand

Twisted neck ring

Hmong (Meo) hill tribe

A solid neck ring that has been twisted most of its entire length. Some have decorated chased grooves. (See Semans p. 5)

Hollow neck ring

Hmong (Meo) & Mien hill tribes

It looks much like the solid neck ring although most are thicker in the diameter of the silver. (See Semans p. 5)

Shan bracelet with wire embellishment

The bracelets have a smooth flat interior with simulated wire on the top and decoration on the sides. See Lewis p. 40

Thailand, The Kingdom of Dvaravati: circa 550 - 1050 A.D.

Mon coinage was made from lead. It is a roughly shaped tapered broken ring, some with rough dumbbell expansions of the open ends. It was used as money. (See Mitchiner p. 665)

Papua New Guinea, Abelam Tribe

Mussel rings made from the Tridacna Gigas were called *Yua*. There are two basic types: the smooth ring without projections from the outer edge, and a ring with projections from the outer edge, part of the projection being smooth and part granular. The smaller rings were used as money while the large rings with a pedigree were not because they could only be inherited within the family. Several factors determined the value of the ring besides its size, age, texture, whiteness, and regularity of shape. Warped rings that were not ground smooth were especially valuable, while the translucent ring without flaws in the shell was even more valuable. The Arapesh manufactured the rings and used them as money to purchase pigs from the Abelam. A pig was worth six rings. The rings were used in bride price, adultery, at the birth of of a child and at a death. Rings that were smaller than four cm were not money and were only worn as jewelry.

Papua New Guinea

Conus shell rings were used in necklaces and served as decoration as well as a form of money by many tribes throughout Papua New Guinea.

Papua New Guinea

Tribes on the Sepik River used glass rings in trade and as money. The rings were made of white glass, and many were in imitation of shell rings. (See Meyer Fig. 15.)

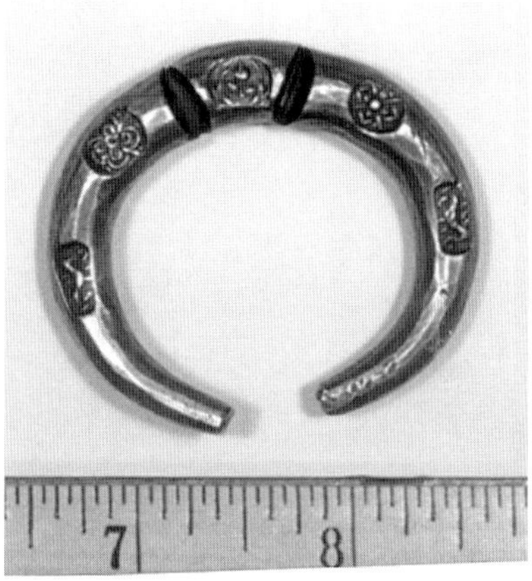

Kingdom of Nanchao - Silver Bracelet

Silver Bracelet - Timor

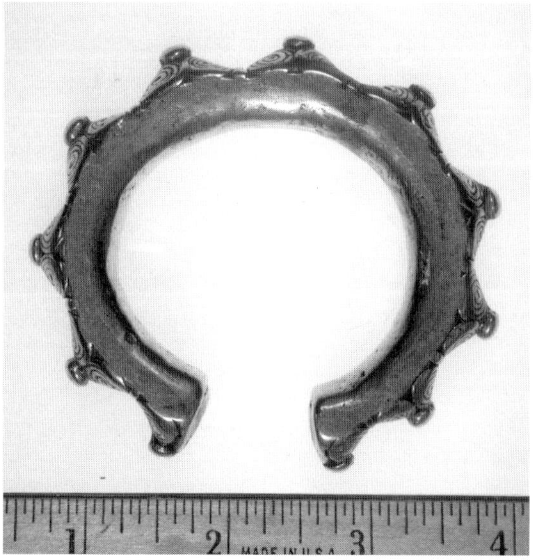

Silver Bracelet - Timor

Silver Bracelet - Timor

Syria, 3500-3000 B.C.

Shell rings were made from a cone-shaped shell during the time of the Sumerian settlements of Kish, Larsa and Ur. It is not known with certainty that the rings were actually used as a medium of exchange.

Thailand, Kingdom of Lavapura, circa 1050-1350

Various shapes of lead rings with a cut through the ring were called dumbbell rings. (Mitchiner #2610-11). Another style was called a serrated broken ring. (Mitchiner #2609). There were several similar rings, including a thin plain ring.

Kingdom of Lannathai, 1300 - 1350 (see Burma)

A flat silver bracelet with two deep cuts and three pairs of stamps on the upper surface was valued at one tamlung.

Shell Ring - Trobriand Islands

Timor

Silver bracelets were used as money and in bride price.

Trobriand Islands

Thin shell rings were used as money on many of the Trobriand Islands. Some of the rings had black cut lines on the outer edge. The rings are still being made and are now used for decoration.

Burma - Silver Bracelet

Yunnan, Burma, Thailand trade route, 1364-1555

This silver bracelet with a single cut and three pairs of stamps was worth one tamlung. (61.2 grams) Mitchiner p. 340.

Zhenlifu Kingdom, ca. 1200

This small non-Thai kingdom on the Gulf of Thailand used lead rings as money. (See Semans p. 2).

See Legband, Limestone Ring, Litlatla, Manilla, Mbakiha, Mbarake, Minkata, Mitako, Navela, Neck Ring Money, Nsambu, Poata, Shell Money, Tridacna Arm Ring, Unus

Zhenlifu Kingdom Lead Bracelet

ROANOKE

Virginia, Colonial times

A cheap kind of wampum made from oyster shells. (See wampum)

ROD MONEY

Africa, Calabar

In the 1660s copper rods were used as currency. The rods weighed 1 1/4 pounds and were red and smooth.

Fourteen or 15 would buy a slave. Local smiths would beat them to form long thin wire, which was then braided with two other pieces and made into bracelets and necklaces which served as money.

Africa, Calabar

Nineteenth century

Imported rods were split into a number of wires about 18 to 24 inches long and bent like a hairpin. These pieces were money and were called "black copper." (See Herbert p.197)

Africa, Congo

Among the Mboshi in 1885 two brass rods would buy a sleeping mat, a chicken or a bunch of bananas. (See Harms p. 60)

Africa, Frafra

A brass rod was worth from eight pence to one shilling, depending on the area. In one area, two would buy a sheep.

Africa, Tiv tribe, Nigeria

Brass rods were used as money and as a unit of account by the Tiv. Five brass rods were worth a bull. The rods were also used to purchase a wife. The rods were imported from Europe and were 1/4 inch in diameter and about three feet long. By 1910 the Europeans replaced the rods with pounds and shillings because they knew the rods were currency. Because they felt they could not control the rods but wanted to control the currency, they eliminated the rods. (See Hammond p. 138-141)

Africa, Upper Congo, latter part of 19th century

The length of the rods got shorter through time. In 1890 the rod was 15 inches long, but by 1905 it was only 11 inches long. One egg was worth a rod, while a female slave was worth 2,500 brass rods. Two yards of cloth were worth 20 rods, and a male slave would have cost 600 rods at one time. The brass got its value originally because it could be melted down to make the brass arm rings, leg rings, and necklaces they valued. (See Havemeyer p.61) See Lerale, Mitako, Ngiele

Africa, Central Zaire Basin

In 1885 a 30-kilogram elephant tusk was worth 350 brass rods. At that same time, a glass bottle was worth 10 brass rods, a small mirror was worth three brass rods, and 10 cowry shells were worth one brass rod. The brass rod traded in different lengths at different places. At times the lengths were up to one-third less. In 1888 the chiefs of all the component villages of Bolobo held a meeting and set the price for an upriver slave at 1,000 brass rods and 500 for a down-river slave. (See Harms p. 86-87)

RONGEI NA GAUNI

Papua New Guinea

A string of 30 dog teeth in a necklace was called *rongei na gauni* and was used as money. It was also used as bride price. (See Quiggin p. 127)

ROOSTER MONEY.

Malay Peninsula, Kedah, during reign of Sultan Muhammad Jiwa Abidin Muazzam Shah (1710-1773)

A tin rooster perched on a number of rings was money. The fighting cock was worth five cents of the Spanish dollar. Each ring attached to the rooster was worth one cent. They circulated as late as the 1850s. There were one to six rings on each piece. (See Singh p. 329 - 333).

ROTL

Bornu, Nigeria

In pre-colonial times it was a unit of measure worth one pound of copper. Later the value of the *rotl* fluctuated from 45-100 *rotls* to a dollar. A large shirt was worth 50 to 60 *rotls*. The values fluctuated from as low as 45 to as high as 100 *rotls*. The *rotl* consisted of a string of 32 interwoven cowries. (See Quiggin p. 33) (See Johansson Fig 8)

RUBBER

Amazon River

A ball of rubber was a medium of exchange and was used for tithes and fines. (See Quiggin p. 314)

RUG MONEY

Kazakstan

Kazak nomads made wool felt mats from goat and sheep hair. Some had silver and gold threads and were well made with intricate designs. They were used as a medium of exchange and store of wealth. A large embroidered mat was worth one camel. (old oriental rug) (See Siebert)

RUM MONEY

Australia, early period of British colonization

Rum was a universal medium of exchange. (See Einzig p. 298)

RUSSIAN TRADE BEADS - See Beads

RYE - See Grain Currency

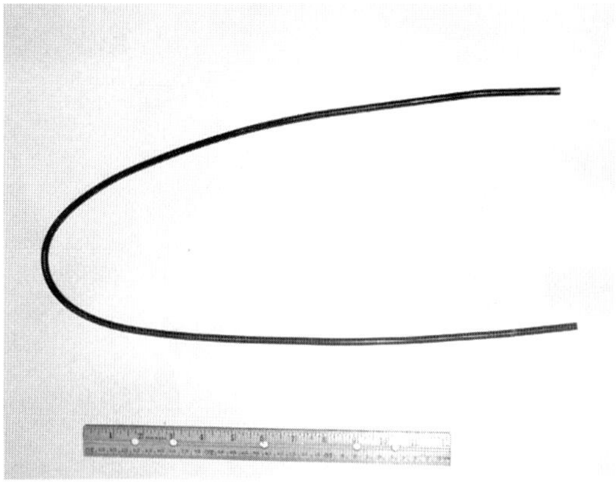

Rod Money

SABAGORAR

Torris Strait, Papua New Guinea

Turtle-shell ornaments shaped to resemble a canoe shield were used in bride price and as a form of money. (See Meyer Fig. 513)

SABER MONEY - See knife money

SABLE

Poland, 1471

A Polish king imposed a tribute in fur and required the "plaintiff in courts of justice to deposit with the judge three sable or martin skins," which were returned if the action were won. (See Einzig p. 281)

Rooster Money

SADDLE SYCEE MONEY - See Pack Saddle Money

SAK - See Sek

SAKANIA

Lake Chad area, Africa

This hoe was currency. 5" across (See Quiggin p. 95)

SAMAKUPA - See Kula.

SALT MONEY

Salt has been used in many parts of world for money. Roman soldiers were paid "salt money" in addition to their regular pay when sent to foreign provinces. In Latin, salt is called salarium. By the third century, "salary" was used to mean "payment of money at specific intervals." In the 13th century Marco Polo, observed the importance of salt in Asia. Salt cakes were officially stamped with the head of the Great Khan and then used as currency. In Papua New Guinea, sodium salts as well as potassium salts were used as money. The potassium salts were from plant material. Sometimes plant material was soaked in salt water and then burned to retrieve the sodium and potassium salts.

Africa, Lomami tribe

Two or three pots of salt were worth a good slave. Salt was an important factor in the slave trade in much of Africa. (See Quiggin p. 54)

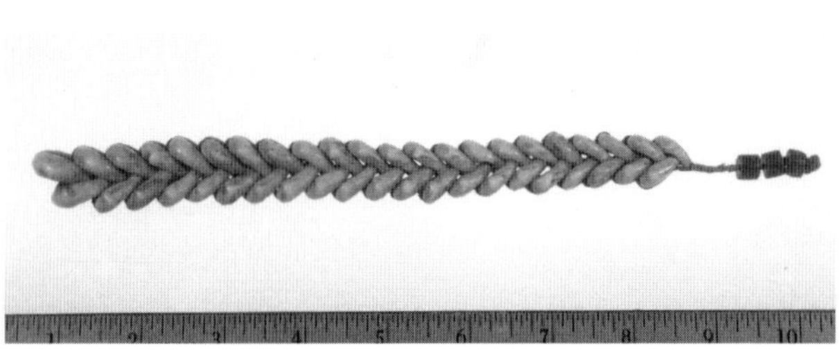

Rotl

Africa, Abyssinia, Ethiopia, 525 A.D. to 1940s

Long rectangular bars of salt were called *amole.* The name was derived from the name of the Amole tribe in the Danakil territory where the salt was quarried. The salt comes from Lake Karum, which is 400 feet below sea level and contains salt to a depth of more than three miles. The salt was cut into slabs and then finished into rectangular bricks with reed or thin wooden strips at the edges to reduce breakage. The slabs are cut into a brick called a *ganfur,* which is eight inches wide, 10 inches long and about two inches in thickness. The *ganfur* are then processed into *amole* in one of the salt markets at Makalle or Aguela. The *amole* is 1/4 the breath of the *ganfur* and the same length and thickness. In other parts of Ethiopia, smaller bricks called *bage* are also used as money. The bricks are eight to 10 inches long and about two inches in thickness. The entire journey from Makalle to Arho takes about four days with stops at Dessa, Berahle, Saba River and finally Arho, according to Giday. The salt caravan consisted of 4,000 to 6,000 pack animals. A camel carried 18 to 24 *ganfur,* a mule carried 16 to 20 *ganfur,* and a donkey carried 9 to 12 *ganfur.* The annual mining season lasts from September to May. The *amole* varied in value depending on the distance from the lake because portering costs and taxes were added to its value. Broken pieces were not considered as money. They were only valued as salt. Beginning in the 19th century the Maria Theresa thaler was also used as money in Ethiopia, and the natives producing the salt bars were paid one thaler for each 300 bars produced. In the 1840s a Maria Theresa thaler was worth from 10 to 12 salt bars in Enarea and from 100 to 110 salt bars in Atsbi, the difference being due to the distance from the mines. In 1869, Munzinger, a Swiss merchant, calculated that the salt trade was about 30 million *amoles* per year. In the early 20th century a mule load of *amoles* was worth $14 and included at least $11 in tax and transportation. During this same period the value of *amoles* continued to fall. In Illubabor, Wallega, Kaffa and Mecha, the salt bar was called *bage,* and it was about one third the size of the *amole* and worth only one twelfth of a dollar. An *amole* was also worth 30 beads. The bars had four different values equivalent to 1 1/2, 1, 1/2, and 1/4 dollars. The salt is still mined and used as in olden days. (See Gill, p.5) (See Giday) (Quiggin p. 55)

Africa, Angola

Salt was used as money during the 1600s in Angola. (See Quiggin p. 54)

Africa, Babunda tribe.

Salt was wrapped in banana leaves and used as money to pay for a murder or preparations for war. (See Quiggin p. 53-54)

Africa, Bambala tribe

The Bambala dealt in livestock, which was exchanged for rubber, which was exchanged to the Europeans for salt, which was subsequently traded for slaves, which were then traded for *djimbu* (shells), which were used as money.

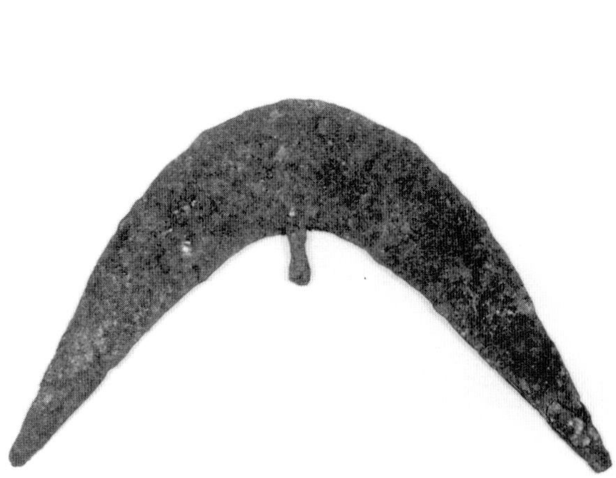

Sakania

Salt Money

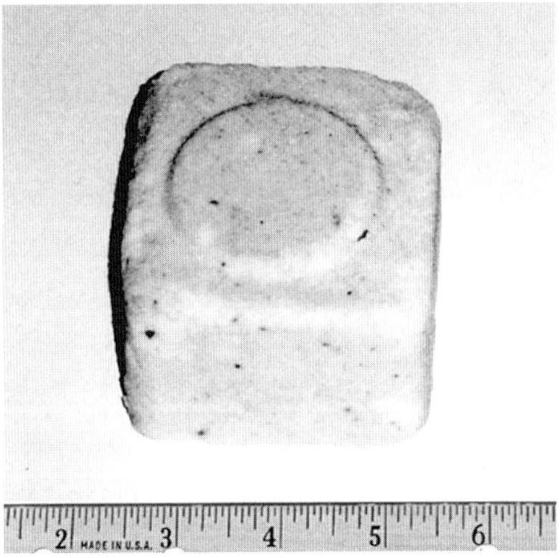

Salt Money

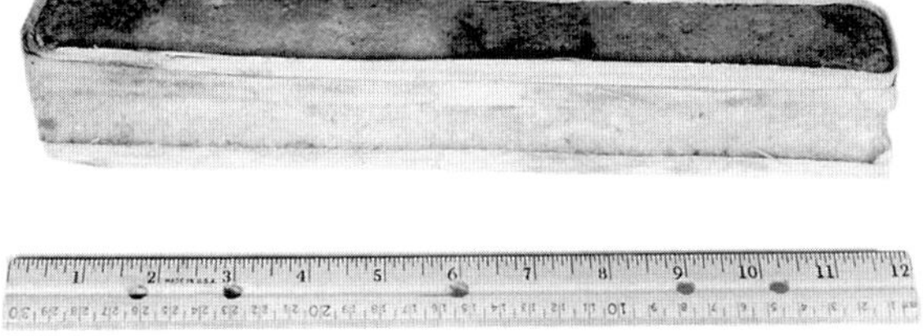

Abyssinia Salt Bar

Katanaga Salt Bar

Nigeria Salt Bar

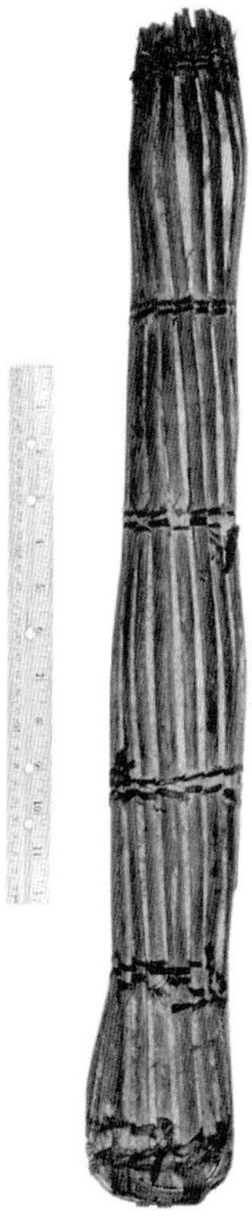

Sierra Leone Salt Basket

Africa, Benin

The natives liked the local salt better than European salt. It was obtained by burning the young branches of the salt bush which grows near salt water. Some salt is also made by evaporating seawater in large brass pans called *neptunes*. (See Roth p. 142)

Africa, Cameroons

Cakes of salt were used as currency and in bride price. 5″ diameter, 9″ height. (See Quiggin p. 84)

Africa, Congo

A salt bar called a dibanda weighing 6 1/2 pounds was used as money. (See Herskovits 214)

Africa, Ethiopia

The salt was dug out of mountains and traded in sizes from five pounds to about 80 pounds. A piece weighing 20 pounds was worth one shilling sterling. (See Quiggin p. 55)

Africa, Gambia River area

In 1620 a poor grade of salt was collected near the mouth of the river and traded into the interior for slaves. (See Bohannan p. 32)

Africa, Katanga, Congo

A 6 1/2 pound bar of salt, called a *dibanda*, was the standard unit of measure. It would purchase an axe, string of beads, hoe, or a calabash of palm oil. Salt bars were also used to purchase slaves and guns. (See Herskovits p.214)

Africa, Mali

In 1455 salt from Taghaza, in the Sahara, was carried to Mali, where it was broken into smaller pieces and carried by porters to the Niger and then to the Sudanic markets, where it was was exchanged for gold.

Africa, Nigeria

Salt was boiled in earthenware pots until hard, and the earthen pots were then broken away. The salt was used to purchase slaves. Ten to 20 bags of salt were worth one slave.

Africa, Nigeria

Cones of different sizes were molded from salt produced from brine and used in exchange transactions and bride price. (See Guyer p. 136-137) (See Quiggin p. 54)

Africa, Sahara, 6th century A.D. to present

Salt was traded to the Sudan in the Middle Ages for its weight in gold. The salt was mined in bars of 140 pounds each. At Taoudeni the bars were 65 pounds each. (See Briggs p. 30)

Africa, Sierra Leone

Cylindrical split bamboo baskets filled with salt were used as money. Ten baskets of salt purchased a wife. 3″ diameter, 25″ length

Africa, Sudan

Slaves were purchased with salt. In peacetime a slave was worth his weight in salt. In wartime a slave was worth less due to the availability of prisoners of war.

China

Salt was used in the ninth century by the Khmers to purchase horses and weapons. During Marco Polo's time, salt cakes weighing about a half-pound, flat on one side and mounded on the other, were traded for gold. Some had a seal of the issuing authority on them. (See Wicks p. 52 & 307)

Irian Jaya, Dani tribe

A salt block was covered in rattan and pandanus leaves and was worth seven pigs. The Dani use the Iluekaima brine pool which is an hour's walk from their territory. They soak banana tree strips in salt brine, let the strips dry in the sun for a few days and then burn the strips to ash. The ashes are then mixed with a little water and made into cakes which are wrapped in banana bark and left to harden. (Heider p. 46) The Fore tribe also produce trade salt by burning indigenous tall grass (*Coix gigantea*) after it has been soaked in salt brine. Sometimes other plants such as staghorns, creepers, ferns, herbs, or barks are used if they want to change the taste. After the introduction of Western commercial salt in the 1950s, the native salt was reduced in importance, and by 1959 it was eliminated.

Mexico, Maya

Salt was an important ingredient in Mayan trade and was produced in limited areas largely on the northern and western coasts of the Yucatan Peninsula. (See Hedges P.500)

New Britain

The bush people made loaves of salt each one worth a piglet or at times an adult pig. (See Panoff p.9)

Papua New Guinea, Enga tribe

Salt was made by burning salt-impregnated wood. The wood was soaked in the salt water pools for two-four months and then dried and burned. A thin package, 1″x15″x18″, covered with banana leaves and thin cane net, weighing about five pounds. It was called *eip* by the Melpa. It was worth one pig, one pearl shell or one good stone axe. Now trade salt has replaced the traditionally made salt, but some Enga still make it and sell it in the Mt. Hagen market for about 10 cents per teaspoon.

Papua New Guinea, Etoro tribe

In pre-contact times the Etoro exported mature pigs for a fist-sized bundle of salt from the Huli, who obtained it from the Ipili, according to Kelly (p. 111).

Papua New Guinea, Lake Kutubu

Packages of a squashed spherical shape neatly bound with strips of pandanus leaf weighing about five pounds were used as money. They were obtained from Augu or the Wage for cowry shells. The salt is gray and powdery.

Papua New Guinea, Baruya, part of Kukukuku people.

The Baruya people numbered about 1,500 and were the last area of the Eastern Highlands of New Guinea to be brought under control by the Australian administration in 1960. The salt was produced from ashes of coix grass. The grass was cut every year during the dry period and left to dry for a week or two. It was then put on a pile of special wood and burned for one or two days. The ashes were left there under a thatched roof for several months. They then built a filter of small gourds with a special plant at the bottom to catch the impurities. Pure water was then passed through the ashes in the gourds and into bamboo tubes. A specialist who was the master of the salt magic would heat the salt water in a special oven made of fireproof flat stones cemented together. There were 15 molds made of waterproof banana leaves in the oven. The salt solution was poured into the molds when the oven had reached the correct temperature. The oven was kept at the same temperature for five days and nights. This was the necessary time to evaporate the water to crystallize the salt. During that time he stirred the surface of the solution to prevent the formation of a film and he took out any impurities. The bars were 60 to 72 cm long and 10 to 13 cm wide. The bars had their edges scraped until they were perfectly shaped and then they were wrapped in dry banana leaves and long strips of wet bark that was carefully sewn together and allowed to harden. The 15 bars weighed a total of 25 to 30 kilograms. Out of a batch of 15 there were three

Dani Tribe Salt Block - End Piece

Samakupa Shell Money

groups of bars according to size. Each had its own name and value. There were four or five small bars, four or five medium bars and six large bars. The 15 bars took a total of 21 days to produce or an average of 1 1/2 days per bar. The bars were used for trade and for ceremonies. A stone adze was worth one to two large salt bars, a pig's tooth necklace was worth 1/2 large salt bar and a bow, and 20 to 30 barbed arrows was worth 1/2 large salt bar. A male pig was worth two to three large bars, a female pig was worth four to six large bars, a male dog was worth one medium bar, and a female dog was worth one large and one medium bar. The salt specialist was given two large bars for producing the batch. The Baruya did not have good stone to produce axes, so they traded salt to obtain the stones to make axes and clubs. A salt bar was worth a round pierced stone for a stone club. The Wantekia people gave five large capes and five bark loin cloths for one salt bar, which is equal to seven *capes*. A *cape* took 3/4 of a day to make. (See Godelier)

Papua New Guinea, Wahgi Valley, to the mid-1960's.

Grasses were soaked in a salt water spring and then were dried and burned. Water was passed through the ashes and evaporated. Tablets were packaged in special wicker containers which were then called *murukakali*. The containers were sometimes decorated with a variety of fibers and weaving patterns which would indicate it was classed as a valuable. They weighed about 4 1/2 pounds. One man working full time could produce 25 cakes of salt per year. In the 1940s the salt tablets were traded over a large area and a tablet was worth a pig or a bird-of-paradise plume. In the mid-1960s a man paid bride wealth of one pig and one cake of salt. By the time it reached the upper Chimbu Valley, the salt was in a small piece of bamboo or gourd and was still worth a pig. The middle Wahgi people traded it for stone axes, pigs, or pearl shell. Used in bride price. (See Barron p. 12)

Papua New Guinea, Yandapu tribe

The package was called *tili*, weighed about five pounds, it was wrapped in banana leaves which were enclosed in an open net of thin cane with part of the cane forming a carrying handle. The package was worth a pig, a good stone axe or pearl shell and is now worth $10.

South America, late as 1949

Many parts of South America, Ecuador, and Andes used salt as money in the past. (See Taxay p. 58)

Tibet, 14th century

Marco Polo described the use of salt as money. It was traded for gold. (See Wicks p. 53)

United States, Ononodaga Indians, 1788

The Ononodaga Indians ceded most of their land for a peck of salt apiece, some yards of calico and an annuity of $4 each.

SAMAKUPA SHELL MONEY

Papua New Guinea

At Wagawage the blood price for a man killed in a brawl was quoted as a pair of really good shell arm-rings, one shell nose-stud and one *samakupa* necklace of *Sapi-Sapi.* It was an associated Kula article. It was called *kuwekuwa* in Kiriwina and was also called *katudababile.* (See Quiggin p. 174)

Sapi-Sapi

SALT WATER SOAP CAKES - See Soap Cakes

SANDALWOOD

Hawaii, 19th century

This hard, sweet-smelling heart wood was used as currency in transactions with traders. The unit of account was the picul, and traders purchased it for trade. It was burned as incense and used in making cabinets. (See Einzig p. 45-46)

SANTA CRUZ FEATHER COIL - See Feather Coil - Santa Cruz

Sauad

SAPI-SAPI

Papua New Guinea

Red shell disks from red spondylus shells were used for ornaments and in making the bagi (*soulava*). Strings of *sapi-sapi* were used as money with a string worth five to 10 dollars. *Sapi-sapi* shells were bought for one pound sterling for 100 shells in 1933 on Rossel Island where the shells were gotten from the sea and made into shell beads for *bagi.* These *bagi* (*soulava*) were then traded to Sudest Island and used in the Kula Ring. As late as 1940 there were still 20 men working on making *bagi* on Rossel Island. A string of *sapi-sapi* was called *wakisowa,* and a belt was called *kaipwesi.* The shells are the same shells used in the *samakupa.* (See Lewis p. 11) See *Bagi* Shell Money, *Samakupa* Shell Money

SAUAD

Torres Straits

Artificially deformed boar's tusks were worn with two pigs' tails as an ornament and at the conclusion of initiation ceremonies by important men. They were highly valued objects. Most were imported from New Guinea. I believe they were from the kula. Imitation pieces were made from the giant clam (*Tridacna*). (See Haddon Vol. 4 p/50-51)

Scarab

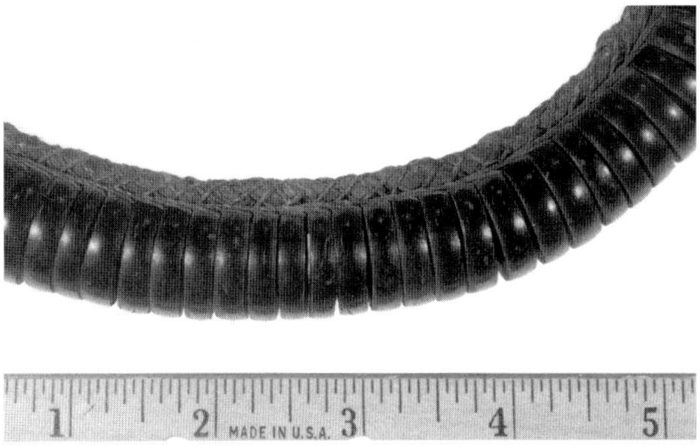

Sek

SAVI
Auki Island, Solomon Islands

A single string, six feet long, of off-white shell disks was made from Kae shell. The strings are made on Auki Island for sale to the natives on Guadalcanal and worth about one pound each. See shell money. (Opitz, Solomon Islands)

SCARAB
Egypt, 1400-900 B.C.

Personal seals in the shape of a beetle were made of faience (glazed and fired clay) or carved bone, crystal, stone, or semi-precious gems. It is highly unlikely that these were ever used as money, but are included in many odd & curious money collections.

Sen Bars

SCHNAPPS
Nigeria

Bottles of schnapps were used extensively as a trade currency until the 1930s. They were also used as a part of bride price. (See Guyer p. 149)

SEA OTTER
Alaska, Tlingit tribe, 1830

The otter skin was used for currency. A sea otter pelt was worth a set number of chisels or sheets of copper. At one time six small copper pots were worth 30 sea otter pelts. Later, caribou skin was substituted for the otter. (See Taxay p. 92)

SEAL SKIN NOTE - See Walrus Skin Money

SEALING WAX - See Wax

SEDABALA
Trobriand Islands

A headband (usually the prerogative of rank) is no longer worn and has become extremely rare.

SEEDS - See Abrus precatorius, Banana Seeds, Evodia Seed Money, Tamarind Seeds

Shark Vertebrae

SEK
Central Caroline Islands, Yap Islands

Black coconut disks, which provide the black in the black and white Tekaroro strings, are used as a currency of their own. They are called *Sek* or *Sak* and were made from a special coconut called *Losil*. *Sek* was traded to Yap Island and took part in the inter-insular trade with the Pelews. 1/4″ diameter. (See Quiggin p. 140)

SEN BAR MONEY
Siam, 1556-1595

The typical C'ieng Sen inscriptions on these base silver cast bars are attributed to Lannathai 1545-56 by Mitchiner (p. 354). They were issued during the Burmese occupation period and all bear the name of Chiang Sen city. The denominations are: four Baht (one tamlung) 61.2 gm, three Baht (3/4 tamlung) 45.9 gm, two Baht (1/2 tamlung) 30.6 gm, one Baht (1/4 tamlung) 15.3 gm, and 1/2 Baht (1/8 tamlung) 7.7 gm. (See Mitchiner p.354) Some experts, according to Semans, might have introduced them to compete with the finer silver C'ieng, and the pieces are not actually indigenous Thai currency.

SHAN SYCEE - See Sycee - Burma

SHARK VERTEBRAE
Melanesia, Polynesia

Shark vertebrae were used as money. (See Mosher p. 55)

SHEEP
Russia

The Kirghiz used sheep as a subsidiary currency, along with horses, well into the 1900s according to Davies (p. 42).

SHEEP SKIN TOKENS
Cocos Keeling Islands, 1887 - 1888

George Sydney Cluinies Ross issued tokens made of sheep skin in the following denominations: 1/4, 1/2, one, two, three, and five Rupees. (See Singh p. 330)

SHELL RINGS

There are three different kinds of shell rings: erenge, poata, tinete. They were used as money, had relatively fixed values and are used in marriage payments and land purchase. The shells were made from *Conus, Trochus*, or Tridacna in eastern and central Marovo, Solomon Islands. (See Hviding p. 93) See Poata

Abelam, Papua New Guinea

The mussel rings were made from the *tridacna gigas* shell. The rings have a high value and are large, ground, flat rings. The rings are very large, ground flat rings known as *Yua* and are made of tridacna gigas. There are two basic types: the smooth ring without projections from the outer edge, and the ring with an outer edge projection. The large rings with a pedigree of previous owners back to the spirits who made the ring cannot be used as money and can only be inherited within the family. The other rings, not having a pedigree, were used as money. Rings having a greater inner diameter have a higher value because of the greater labor used to make them. Translucent rings without flaws in the shell have a high value. Warped rings that are not ground smooth have a high value also. All rings over 4 cm in diameter are used as money, smaller ones are only jewelry. The largest are 25 cm. in diameter. The ring is made by drilling a flat dish-like piece of a *tridacna* mussel with a bamboo pole with splintered bamboo at one end. This is turned while on the shell disk with sand and water until a hole is ground through. The Arapesh use the rings to buy pigs from the Abelam, and the Abelam measure their wealth in rings and use them for bride price. The price of a wife varied from one to six rings. For killing a man the price was 20 rings, less for a woman or a child. Some of the names of kinds of rings are: *pal yua*, magna yua, *mbia yua*, and *mbandi yua*. (See Rabus)

Mailu Island, Papua New Guinea

The Mailu people purchase shell arm rings made by the Southern Massim and regrind and repolish them for trade. Only one arm ring can be made from one shell so that there may be a complete circle inside formed by the joining of the spiral to the side near the base. When the ring is smooth, three small holes are drilled near the end of the remaining portion of the lip. The decorations, which are black wild banana seeds and thin, small discs of shell lip, are attached to these holes. Red glass beads are also used. (See Saville p. 153)

Motu tribe

The bride price is 10 white shell arm rings, two shell necklaces, a pig, and an axe.

Walis and Tarawai tribes

They made the rings from *Tridacna* shells and used a solid piece of bamboo to drill the hole. The rings were used as money and also in bride price along with pigs.

Sepik River, Papua New Guinea

On the Sepik River in the village of Melawei, shell rings were used as personal ornaments and as money. They were too small to wear on the wrist, so they were worn on necklaces by the women. 3″ diameter. See Ring money

SHELL MONEY
Africa

Conus disks or whorls were used as currency in East Africa, now called Malawi and Zimbabwe. They were destroyed by the British in the late 1800s and Czech porcelain copies were made in 1892 to replace the *conus* whorls. The first porcelain copies had serial

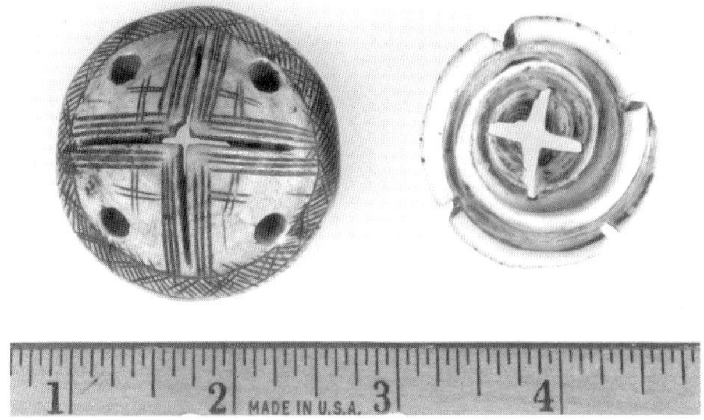

Conus Disks

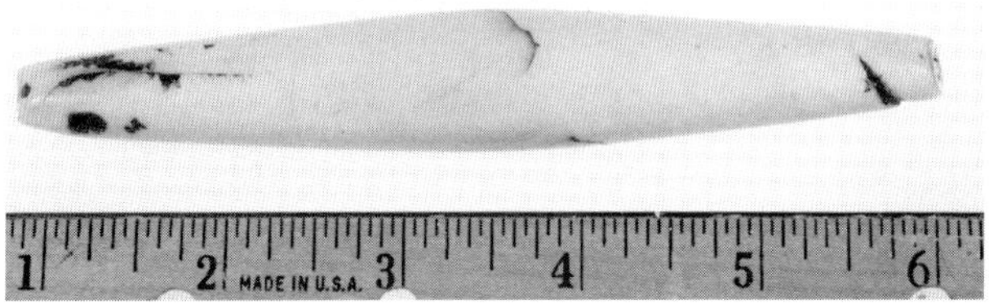

Naga Chank Shell Bead

Breaking Shells Into Shell Disks

Polishing And Smoothing Disk Edges

numbers. Other copies were made in wood, metal, ivory, glass, and plastic. (See Liu p. 29)

Naga

Chank shell beads were made from segments of chank shell, which is *Turbinella*. They were decorated with small indentations in the shell and carnelian beads. (See Liu p. 76)

New Caledonia

There are at least three kinds of shell money on this island. The most valuable is made from the smallest shell disks. It is called *ter mawon* and was used only by the chiefs as money. The second type is called *weni*, and it has shell disks that are two mm in diameter, which is about twice the diameter of *ter mawon*. The disks are a light gray in color. The third type was used by the traders in dealing with the natives and was worth about six cents per foot in 1911. These disks varied from 1 1/2 mm to 3 mm in diameter. (See Lewis p.33-34)

Papua New Guinea

Only seven types of shells were commonly used as money in Papua New Guinea: 1) Large pearl oyster shell (*Pinctada maxima*) which had nine different names. 2) Large volutes (baler shell)(*Melo aethiopicus L.*), which had eight different names. 3) Giant green turban shell (commercial green snail) (*Turbo marmoratus L.*). 4) Dog whelks (*Nassa sp.*). 5) Money cowry (*Cypraea moneta L.*) and ring cowry (*C. annulus*). 6) Leopard cone (*Conus leopardus Rod.*) 7) Large white egg cowry (*Ovula ovum L.*). The olive shell (*Oliva sp.*) and tiger cowry (*Cypraea tigris L.*) were also used to some extent.

Buin, Bougainville, Papua New Guinea

The shell money is called *abuta*. It is used to purchase pigs, with a pig worth 10 to 100 fathoms of *abuta*. They always valued the pig in units of 10 fathoms of shell money. They were never valued at 15 or 25 fathoms, for example. A fathom of *abuta* was worth one shilling. The woman's money called *bum* or *tombu* is worth twice as much as *abuta*. One fathom of red onu was worth 20 fathoms of *abuta*. One fathom of white *onu* was worth 10 fathoms of *abuta*. *Abuta* is arranged in a bundle 10 fathoms long arranged in six strings with one quarter of a string overhanging with an inland snail shell at the end. *Abuta* was also kept in net bags containing 100 fathoms. (See Thurnwald)

Rossel Island

See *ndap* and *nko*

Solomon Islands

Shell money was traded from Malaita to the islands of Guadalcanal, Santa Isabel, Nggela (Florida), Makira (San Cristobal), Russel, Choiseul, Shortland Islands, New Ireland, West New Britain, and Bougainville. Bougainville, in particular, did considerable trade with Malaita. The three production centers were 1) Hounihu, on the southwest coast of San Cristobal, 2) Marau Sound, toward the southern end of Guadalcanal, 3) the artificial islands off the southwest coast of Malaita. The island of Malaita and the surrounding area today produce most of the shell money in the area. This area includes Langa Langa Lagoon and Laulasi Island which is an artificial island in the lagoon. The three kinds of shells used are: a white mollusk called *Kakadu*, a black mussel called *Kurila*, and a red lipped *spondylus* called *Romu*. The red is the most valuable, probably due to the difficult collection process of this shell. The Langa Langa men make all three kinds of shell money called *bata*. The small shell disks are red and white with black vegetable seeds interspersed. The shells to make the disks are obtained by the men diving for the shells in the Langa Langa Lagoon, or, for the highly valued red *romu* shells, arrangements must be made to either buy baskets of the shells from other areas or mount a diving expedition to Lau Lagoon in northeastern Malaita or to Florida Island, Gizo, or Choiseul Island in the Western Solomons and dive for the shells after paying the local people to allow them to dive in their area. The shells are obtained from distant reefs, where they are sold for as much as four shells for 10 cents or $25 for a basket of about 100 shells. Sometimes canoes can be rented for $8 per day. The red shells called *Romu* are about two inches in diameter and are found at a depth of 60 feet. The *Kakadu* shells are found at any depth on the reef. The black *Kurila* shells are about one foot in diameter and are found in shallow water. The black shell money is not used on Bougainville. The black shells can be turned to red if they are briefly heated on a stone. The diving is done by the men, and much religion is a part of the diving operation. Pigs are sacrificed, and the spirits are consulted before any diving starts. Shell beads are made in great quantity as money. Shells are hammered into small pieces and perforated with a twist drill and strings of shells are rubbed on stones to smooth the edges. The shell money is used for bride price, to compensate for injuries, as part payment for carvings, the teaching of magic, buried with the dead, or worn at feasts. Disks are made into strings, belts, necklaces or arm bands. The making of the shell money is normally done by the girls and women. They first break the shells into small circular pieces about twice the size of the finished piece with a black stone hammer called a *falbura*. Now solid metal cylinders are used to make the

Drilling Holes Into Shell Disks

Woman Making Shell Rings

Woman Polishing A Shell Ring On A Stone

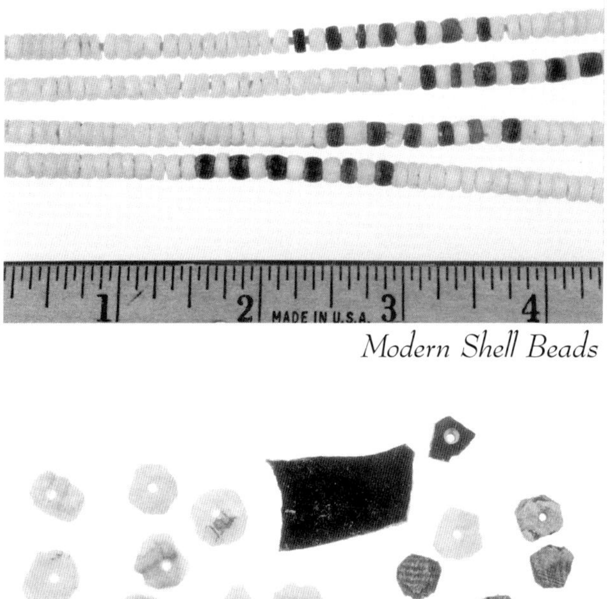

Modern Shell Beads

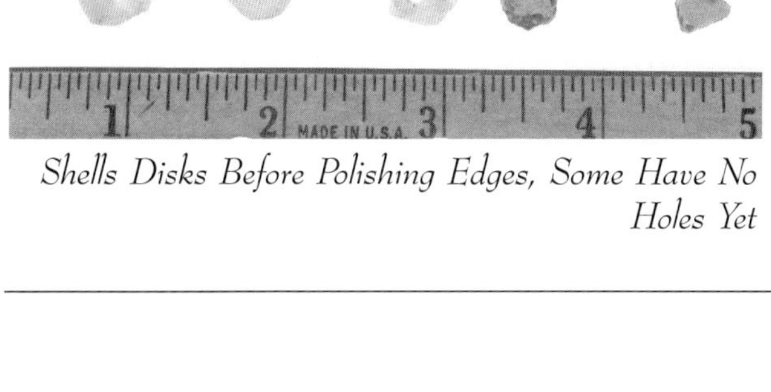

Shells Disks Before Polishing Edges, Some Have No Holes Yet

process faster. The *Romu* shell is then heated by placing the shell on very hot stones which turn the normally pink shells deeper red in color. The circular shells are then placed on a piece of wood called *ma-ai* which has about 50 shallow circular depressions and which is used to flatten the shell disks and make them smooth. The flat rectangular grinding stone used is called *fou-sava*. They then shape them and drill the holes with a pump drill called *futa*. This drill had a flint or chalcedony tip, but now modern drills with steel drills are used. After both sides of the shell are rubbed, the shell is the proper thickness. Then a hole is drilled in the center, and they are strung. They are on a strong bush fiber called *lili* in lengths of four to five feet. They are smoothed by the men with the use of sand and water on a flat board with a grooved stone until they are the correct size and have the proper smoothness.

The smoothing was formerly done by rubbing them with a grooved stone called a *faoliara* using sand and water. Now Chinese grinding blocks are used. Some of the smoothing of the shell edges is also done now in Honiara. At present, Malaita puts so much of its time into producing shell money that it no longer does deep-sea fishing and does little gardening.

The shell disks are made into strings, belts, *tafuliae*, necklaces, or arm bands. Some of the names of different groupings are *Talina*, *Talina Bariono*, and *Tafuliae* (see *tafuliae*). On Sa'a and Ulawa red shell beads are made called *Romo*. The full unit of measure for the beads is a fathom. The most valuable shell money was called *kali awala*, and it consisted of 10 strings of shells each a fathom long. The natives of Buka, New Ireland, New Britain, and Nissan islands regularly traded shell money with each other. Malaita traded shell money to the islands of Guadalcanal, Russell Islands, Choiseul, Santa Isabel, Ngela (Florida), and San Cristobal. In the 1890s shell money was traded from Malaita to New Guinea, where it was used to purchase gold dust. The value of the shell money increased from one shilling per fathom on Malaita to 25 shillings in New Guinea. A particularly well-made span of *spondylus* was worth 50 to 100 times as much of the cruder *mauai*. Later, the government prohibited the use of shell money in trade with Europeans because of trouble with the valuation. The government then forbade the use of shell money in all business transactions.

The shell strings were used in purchasing canoes, buying pigs, compensation for injuries, part payment for carvings, teaching magic, purchasing food, as blood money, in bride price, and obtaining advancement in various social societies. Currently the shell strings are used mainly in bride price. At present, Malaita produces most of its shell money for trade to Bougainville.

Currently there is a $2 duty per string of shell money between Papua New Guinea and the Solomon Islands. In 1964 and 1965, shell money was valued at $10 to $12 per string. The price was then raised to $30 to $35 per string, and they were able to sell it for that amount. Some strings went for a maximum price of $40 per string. At that time the government on Siwai tried unsuccessfully to lower the price of shell money and tried to have the maximum price be $16. In 1975 the Malaita Council did state that they felt there should be a fixed price for red shell money (*L-safi*) of $25 and white shell money (*L-galia*) and black shell money (*dafi*) of $20. In Malaita *L-tafuliae* is used because a *tafuliae* is usually included in bride price. The natives use cash in daily life but continue to save in shell money. Shell money is now restricted to the significant exchanges that maintain social systems and not to run the wheels of business. Bougainvilleans purchase about 3,000 strings of shell money per year. This is more than three-quarters of the total production; two-thirds of that goes to Siwai, and the remainder goes to Nagovisi. Traders take the shell money from Malaita to Bougainville, making the trip for less than $200 and selling at least 100 strings in about one week for about $9,000 with a profit of $2,000 for the trip. In the 1960s shell money production went down, but by the 1980s the production reached its highest level ever. This has changed the family roles with the women now making shell money instead of working in the gardens. The men now increasingly work in the gardens. In 1967 one *tafuli'ae* valued at $10 could be produced by one woman working full time for one month. At present, with the modern methods of making the shell money, a good household can produce four or five strings per month. Each is now valued at $130 US.

Langa Langa shell money was valued at $1 for one fathom of large smooth red shells called a *Galia Bata* and $.50 for one fathom of large un-smoothed white shells called a *Galia*. A *Safi* was one fathom of small smooth red shells valued at $2. A *Isae Bata* was four strings each one fathom long of smooth white shells with black shells in the middle string, and was worth $4. The white shell money was called *forososo* and, in the Gela language, *turumbuto*. The red shell money was also strung in a length of two fathoms called *vinda*. Two strings joined at each end and tied in the center are called *kongana*. Three strings are called *sautolu*, four strings are *matambala*, five strings are *rapakava*, and six strings are *talina*. An *isa* is 10 strings of red shell money. An *isa* is also worth a *talina*, 100 porpoise teeth (*randi*), and four *turumbuto*. The *tafuli'ae* consisted of 10 strings of one fathom each consisting primarily of red shells but interspersed with white and black shells. One *tafuli'ae* was worth 2,000 taro or one pig. The shell money was also used in bride price with the Kwara'ae establishing

Old Belt Made of Shell Disks

Old Armband Made of Shell Disks

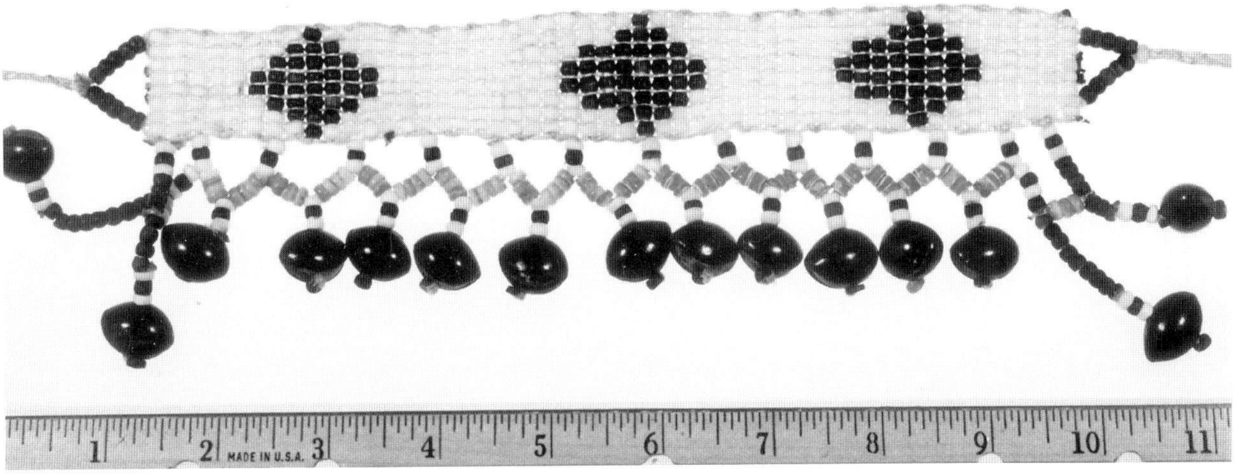

Modern Shell Beads

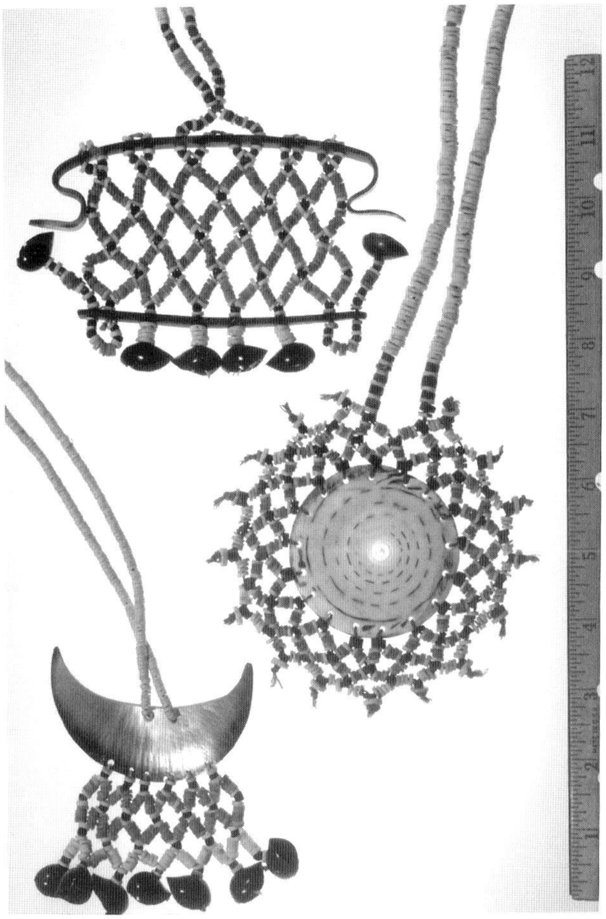

Malaita Island Shell Necklaces

the price at five *tafuli'ae* and the Langa Langa at 30 *Isae Bata*.

On Malaita the shell money is known as *Rongo*. The white shell money is called *Rongo pura,* and the red shell money is called *Rongo sisi*. There is also a kind of shell money which is pinkish-white and the beads are much smaller. It is called mamalakwai and it is made only on Kwa, which is between Onepusu and Bina.

Eastern Solomon Islands shell money belts were made from shell disks traditionally made in the coastal villages of Langa Langa, Auki and Alite in the Langa Langa Lagoon on the south coast of Malaita. The belt consisted of four sections of eight black and white shell disks strung on coconut fiber and interspersed with three shorter bands of predominately orange disks with each section separated by a thin strip of turtle shell or wood, according to Waite. Some belts contain from seven to 10 strings.

On Auki Island, only a single three-foot length of rough white shell disks called a galia is used in bride price. One string was worth one shilling, and four strings tied together were called a fura. When 10 *fura* were tied together they were called a *Isagalia,* which had a value of two pounds. The highest value of all is the *firae* which consists of 10 strings of special red shell disks that are of a larger diameter than normal. This item is quite rare. Each of the individual strings is an individual monetary unit by itself and was worth two pounds, with the *firae* worth 20 pounds. On Guadalcanal a unit called a galiabata which is valued at five shillings is used and consists of a single string of white shell disks, about six feet long that has only been roughly chipped, drilled and unpolished. A batauliuli is a money unit that consists of four *galiabata* tied together and worth about one pound.

Another unit of money used mainly on Guadalcanal is the *savi*, which is a single string of slightly off-white shell disks made from the Kae shell, six feet in length and worth one pound. All these items were made on Auki Island.

Shell disk arm bands, called *abagwaro*, were made in the Malaita area from red, white and black shell disks. They are examples of the finest shell workmanship with the beads being small and uniform and set in intricate designs with the beads at 45-degree angles. This pattern was also used for bracelets, anklets, belts, and necklaces, according to Dubin p. 240. (See Bartle p. 379) (See Davidson, Traditional Money Association Newsletter Vol 1 Number 1.) (See Cranstone p. 38) (See Lewis) (See Connell) (See Waite)

Siwai, Bougainville

There are two major types of shell money in this area. The first major type is *S-pesi*. The most common variety is *mauai*, which is a coarse, unpolished cone shell from Shortland island of Alu. The second variety is *kuriri*, which is more fine broken cone shells. The second major type is *S-koso*. It mainly comes from Malaita, where it is more finely ground, polished shell. There are nine varieties of this type. One variety is the *tomo*, which includes five strips of red shell beads. It can also have alternating white beads or be all red beads. The *mauai* variety was used for general commercial transactions. The more highly valued kinds were used for bride price. During World War II when the war came to the Bougainville area, the people moved to the north and the low valued *mauai* was destroyed, abandoned or hidden. After the war it was not revived as money, and the higher-valued varieties replaced it as money. Australian money was used instead of *mauai*. At present, shell money is used primarily in transactions of social importance but not as true money. Shell money is used to purchase wives, pigs, land, court fines and as compensation for the services of sorcerers and curers.

Solomon Islands

The Solomons had another kind of money that consisted of a polished clamshell incised with a design and the incised area filled with a black substance. Many of the pieces come from Malaita, Ulawa and Arosi further south. The incised figures were mostly birds, fish, and sea-ghosts. They were also important in Bougainville and Buka. (See Reichard p.111)

Tanga

Grooved shell rings called *am fat* are the major shell wealth on the island. They were made by roughly trimming the valve of a large clam (Tridacna gigas) into

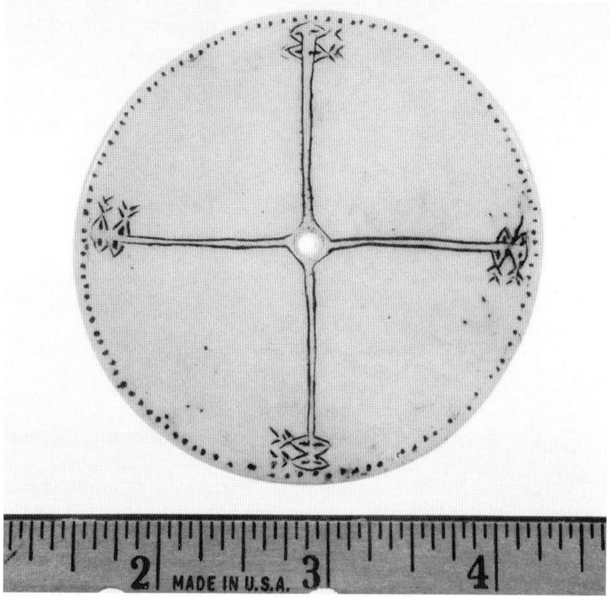

Incised Clamshell Disk

Incised Clamshell Disk

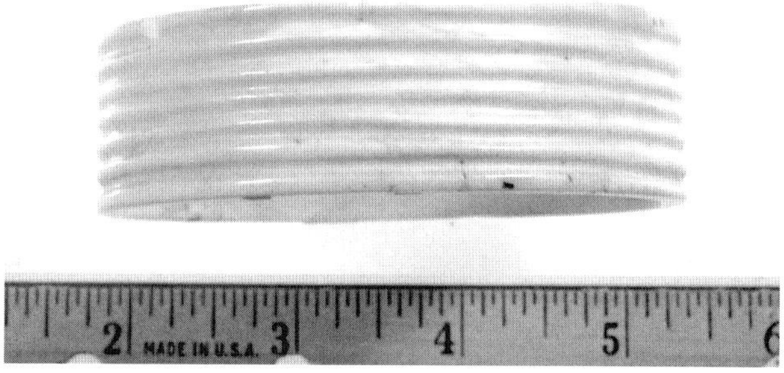

Tanga Grooved Rings

a discoid shape with the aid of water-washed basalt. Then the surfaces were flattened by rubbing the clam on a flat volcanic rock. Then it was finished by making it in a perfect circular shape and smoothing all the edges. Next, the center was created by making a hole in the center and rubbing with progressively larger rods as the diameter of the hole increased. The last step was to make the grooves around the outer edge with a sharp stone knife. A person who wanted an am fat, which required about six months to make, would supply food daily to the maker during its manufacture and upon completion give him a large pig at a feast. There are two basic types of *am fat.* The first type consists of tubes of varying length with thin incised bands around the outside of the ring. Long tubes with up to 25 bands are called *puk sil,* and shorter tubes are called an *malmal.* The second type is called *tintol.* They are single grooved disks and are used in marriage and mortuary exchanges. The larger rings called *tintil dok* are more rare than the medium-sized tintol. The rings without damage like chips or cracks are most valued. The largest rings, called *warantang,* never circulate and are kept as heirlooms. *Am fat* are preferred to other kinds of money because they can be kept for long periods instead of being used up like cash or eaten like pigs.

Tanga Grooved Rings

Tanga Grooved Rings

See the following: Beads, Dentalium, Impande Shells, *Giragira, Hokata, Jom,* Kandangei Shell Money, *Kofu, Kuriri,* Leaf money, *Mauwai, Mbakiha, Mbarake, Mis, Navoi, Ndap, Nko, Nzimbu* shells, Olive Shells, Ostrich Egg Shell Money, *Pele, Poata, Pwomonodap,* Ring Money, *Samakupa* Shell Money, *Sapi-Sapi,* Snail Shell, *Som, Spondylus* Shells, *Tafuliae, Talina', Talina Bariono, Tapsoka, Tekaroro, Tetiti* Shell Belt, *To-Uba, Tridacina* Shell Money, *Ulawa,* Wampum, *Wauri*

SHELL MONEY

Thailand

The piece is solid silver shaped like a shell without a hole a the top. In many ways it is similar to the leaf money. Very rare.

Siam Silver Shell Money

SHIELD MONEY

Aboriginal Australia

Wooden shields were manufactured at Roxburgh and along the Upper Georgina for trade and barter. It is doubtful that they were true money.

Africa

Many kinds of shields made of many different materials in many styles were used in trade by the natives. They also were used for defense.

Canada

Since the abolition of slavery in the 19th and 20th centuries coppers, copper plates and copper shield articles were the most valuable possessions of the upper classes of five ethnic groups of Northwest coast Indians. They are called *tinnahs* or *taus*. They were used in the potlatch where shields were given to a rival tribe with the understanding that at some later date the value of the shield would be returned with 100% interest. Failure to accept the shield was an admission of being poor, as it showed that the entire rival tribe did not have sufficient wealth to return the value of the shield and 100% interest at a later date. They were made with imported copper sheet metal and many times decorated through engraving or painting with stylized faces by the Indians. A copper's value was that of the property distributed at the potlatch in which it had last changed hands, and it could be bought only at double that amount, a fact that so inflated the cost of the coppers that by the 1920s they could not be used. An even more costly gesture than breaking a copper was to destroy it in a fire or throw it into the sea. When the copper was broken, the "t" element was valued at 2/3 of the whole copper. If a shield was broken into sections a prescribed sequence was followed. The upper right corner was always broken first, then the lower corner diagonally opposite from it, then the upper left corner and finally the lower right corner.

African Shield

Shields came in three sizes, with the smallest called a "baby copper." It reached from the fingertips to the wrist. The second size reached from the fingertips to the inside bend of the elbow or the armpit. The largest reached from the fingertips of the outstretched arm to the averted chin and was worth eight or 10 slaves, according to Laguna p. 353. A fourth size exists which is for ornamental shields that are two to three inches long. They were worn as personal adornment on clothing or as earrings by rich people and were not used in the potlatch. (Jopling p. 7)

Copper Shield

The differences between the shields of the Tlingit, Tsimshian and Haida and between those of the Kwakiuti and Bella Colla are hard to discern. The differences between northern and southern shields are more visible. The Kwakiutl and Bella Colla shields are decorated with crude designs of animal or human-like figures. The Haida shields have the centers bulging from the borders, and the majority have decorations of the eagle, bear, raven or killer whale. The Tsimshian shields had representations of the wolf, bear, eagle or killer whale. The majority of the Kwakiutl shields are made of multiple pieces of thin sheets of copper riveted together, although some are made of a single sheet of copper. (Jopling p. 7-10) Some tribes incised the metal, while

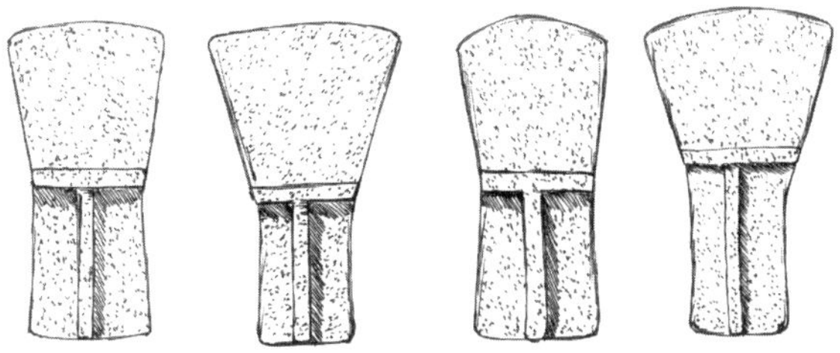

Southern Copper Shield Types

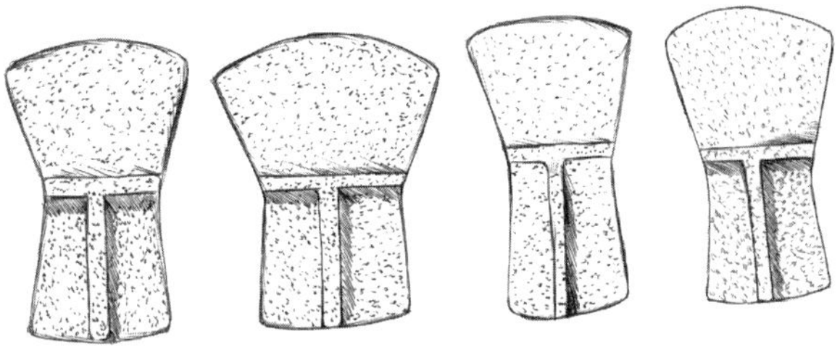

Northern Copper Shield Types

Guadalcanal Shield 1880s

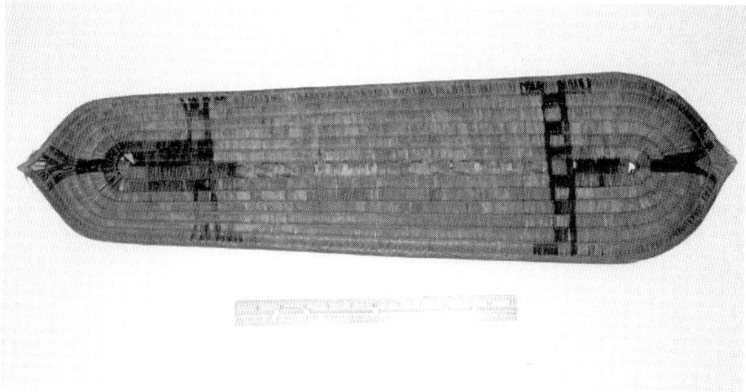

Guadalcanal Shield 1910-1920

others favored a very thick coating of paint and pitch into which they scraped through to the metal to form the design. Some shields had no decoration made in the black coating. Most shields in existence are different from all others, as styles, methods and materials varied. (Jopling p. 10) Only the Haida, Tlingit, Tsimshian, Bella Colla and Kwakiutl used shields. Copper shields were also used as "blood money" after a killing to prevent further killing and loss of property. They also seem to have been substituted as a guarantee or a bond of peace between Tlingit and Tsimshian groups when the human hostages, who had fulfilled this objective, returned home. (See Jopling p. 37) Coppers also served as replacements for slaves in the Kwakiutl hamatsa ceremony. (See Jopling p. 38) Almost all observers noted the existence of "spurious" coppers that were exchanged and used. In 1788, 10 otter skins were worth one six-inch square of copper. In a short time one otter skin would be valued at one large copper sheet. This trade copper became an item of exchange. (See Jopling p. 56) (See Quiggin p. 300-302) (See Potlatch)

Guadalcanal, Santa Isabel Island, New Georgia Islands, and Nggela (formerly Florida Island) The two general shapes of shield are the elliptical shape and the rectangular shape. The long elliptically-shaped shields, called *tako*-were made of woven wicker and rattan, and some were covered with clay and inlaid with nautilus shell decoration. The wicker shields were produced on Guadalcanal and on Ysabel (Santa Isabel), but the inlaid shields were only produced on Isabel and not after 1860. To make them, the wicker shields were covered with a black resinous substance with small square pieces of mother-of-pearl inlaid in intricate linear patterns. Only about 20 inlaid shields are known to exist in the world today and only five shell inlaid bark shields. On Ysabel the natives also made curved rectangular inlaid shields from thin wood or bark. The plaitwork shield was used as money and in barter. It was worth a wife or from one to 30 pounds. Waite said the shield pictured with almost parallel vertical sides was collected between 1850 and 1880 and was made with Lawyer cane for the coiling and *Lygodium* fern (*asa*) for the horizontal wrapping. She also said it was worth one *bakhea*. (7" x 25 1/2" and larger) Modern wicker shields with a point in the center of both the upper and lower rounded ends were made until as late as 1980. These shields are numerous and valued in the lower price range. The shield pictured was made about 1910. (See Quiggin p. 133) (See Waite)

Irian Jaya

Michael Rockefeller felt that wooden shields could occasionally be trade pieces. It is not known to what extent they were used and if they actually served as a limited form of money.

Papua New Guinea

Wood shields made from the trunk of a tree, carved in relief and decorated with paint were used as a form of wealth and limited form of money.

SHIRT - See Pu Money

SHOKA

Africa, Northern Zaire, Mangbetu people

Ten to 25 *shoka* were worth one *liganda*. European-made (Birmingham, England) *shoka* were originally welcome, but later were rejected when it was discovered the commercial sheet iron used was impure compared with the native made blade. The name *shoka* means axe or hoe in Swahili. In the Stanley Falls district, the blacksmiths used *shokas* as the raw material to make axes, knives, spears and arrowheads. Three bundles of plantain were worth one *shoka*. (See Kriger p. 100-101) (See Quiggin p. 64) (See Blackmun p. 44)

Asmat Shield

SHONGO - See Woshele

SIAM (BRASS OR COPPER) GAMBLING TOKENS

Siam, (Ayuthia)

These copper pieces were struck before the Burmese occupation (1350 A.D. - 1564 A.D.). The early pieces are solid, while later pieces are cut out sections so both sides having the same design. Some thought these pieces were used along with the porcelain tokens in the Chinese gambling houses during the late 18th and 19th centuries, but most now feel these pieces became obsolete in the 16th century. (See Mitchiner p. 344-345)

SIAM (LEAD) GAMBLING TOKENS

Siam,

Lead floral pattern tokens are thought to be gambling chips or counters. Most are reproductions.

SIAM (PORCELAIN) GAMBLING TOKENS

See Porcelain coins

SIEGE MONEY

Mostly Europe, 1574 to after 1800

During the 16th and 17th centuries the low countries (region bordering the North Sea and now part of

Asmat Shield or Sago Plate

Papau New Guinea Shield

Shoka

Siam Brass or Copper Gambling Tokens

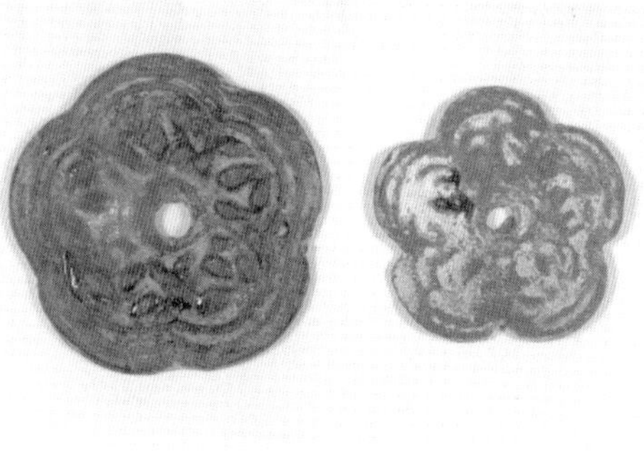

Siam Lead Gambling Tokens

Belgium, Luxembourg and Netherlands) were in a struggle for independence from Spain. The siege pieces were issued by authorities in more than 30 towns and cities surrounded by hostile forces. They were usually made of silver but also were made of paper and other materials. In 1574 in Leyden, prayer book pages were stamped with dies and were used as money. (See Prayer Book Money). From 1702-1713 in Landau, silver plate was used.

SILW'AE

Auki Islands, Solomon Islands

The piece is identical to the tafuliae except there are only nine strings of shells instead of ten. It was worth four pounds and was never actually made on Auki Island. (See Bartle p. 382)

SILK MONEY

China, 24 - 402 A.D.

Raw silk and rolls of woven silk were used as money in ancient China and were reintroduced as money in 24 A.D. and 402 A.D. due to prevalent counterfeiting of metallic currency. It was a medium of exchange between the Chinese and neighboring Mongol tribes to the West. It was one of the few currencies in Marco Polo's time. As late as the 13th century the Chinese Imperial Treasury received silk for taxes and tribute. Up to 1260 A.D, silk was used as a reserve for many issues of paper money. (See Quiggin p. 221) (See Wicks p. 47)

Germany, 1919 - 1922 inflation period following World War I

Part of the Notgeld series of unusual forms of money for collectors or for limited use in various cities. Many silk pieces have fancy woven or lace borders.

SILVER

Mesopotamia

Pieces of silver were weighed in terms of shekels (one shekel equaled one-third of an ounce) which was the standard measure. The pieces of silver were used as a form of money. A slave, for example, was worth from 10 to 20 shekels of barley. (See Pringle p. 60) Pringle also states that in the city of Eshnunna around 2000 B.C., a man who slapped another had to pay 10 shekels. Pringle says that in Mesopotamia, silver in the form of rings or coils, was called *har* and was used by the rich as a form of money. The average and poor person used copper, tin, lead and barley as money, as silver was too valuable.

SILVER BAR - See Mint Bars

SIMBOS OR SIMBU SHELLS - See Olive Shells

SINNET

Solomon Islands

Rolls were used on Santa Cruz Island and made by diagonally winding 3 ply plaited coconut fiber into a solid block, 7″ square and 4″ thick. (See Quiggin p. 134) A roll was 30 to 120 feet long and was only made by men. It was made in their leisure time and took five to six weeks. The rolls were used for ceremonial exchange with the more valuable, heavier sinnet used for shark fishing. Old sinnet as well as new sinnet could be used in exchange. (See Quiggin p. 134) (See Firth p. 252)

Tikopia, Solomon Islands

A coil of sinnet cord is 10 to 20 fathoms long, and a man takes at least five to six weeks working part time to make one coil. They are used for ceremonial exchange. (See Firth p. 252)

SIRIPIYA

Bena-Bena Tribe, Eastern Highlands, Papua New Guinea

The fiber ornament was held in the teeth as a battle ornament by Big Men, was also worn in marriage transactions and served as a bride price item. (See Meyer Fig. 344.)

SITIM

Nigeria

Among the Efiks of old Calabar, copper wire was used as money (See Akanbiemu p.25)

SKIN - See Martin Skin Money, Moose Skin, Raccoon Skin Money, Sable Skin, Sea Otter, Squirrel Skin, Walrus Skin Money

SKIRTS

Trobriand Islands

Women's skirts are objects of wealth. They are made from banana leaves that are cut into long narrow fringe-like fibers and dried. They are then colored with dyes purchased from the trade stores. Traditionally the dyes were made from special roots. The completed leaves are then threaded through three thick fiber cords to make the waistband. Women of rank have tiny white cowry shells woven into the band. The skirts are more valuable than bundles and can be reused. The young girls wear the short red miniskirts, and the older women wear the longer skirts. They were also called *takulakola.* (See Weiner.)

Siege Money

Silk Notgeld

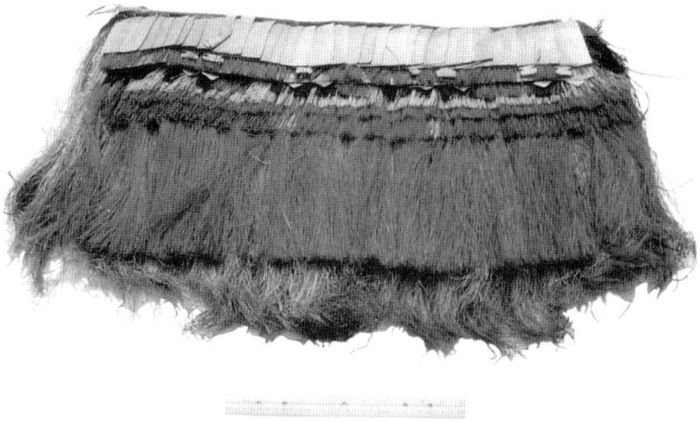

Skirt

SLAVES

Most parts of the world at some time in history had slaves. In a number of cases these slaves were considered as a unit of value. In virtually all cases they were considered a store of wealth.

Africa

Most areas of Africa had slaves for their own use and also sold slaves to other areas such as the United States and Europe. In the Congo area a slave was worth 100 iron bells at one time. It took two or three slaves to equal one elephant tail in the Congo. Among the Bambala a slave was worth 10,000 *Nzimbu* shells. In Ethiopia, eight to 12 iron bars was the price of a slave. The Slave Coast of Africa contained the majority of slaves, which later were sold in the United States. In 1699, a slave was worth two manillas. The areas of Ashanti, Kenya, Uganda and Rhodesia also used slaves as a unit of wealth and store of wealth. As late as 1905 a male slave was worth 10 he-goats. The Tuareg included a slave girl as a part of the bride price. The Bantu people paid the price of two male and two female slaves when a free man married a free woman. No other trade items could be substituted. Among the Kpelle a slave was worth one head of cattle. A male slave was worth 300 packets of salt while a female slave was worth 350 packets of salt. A male slave was also worth 100 iron rods and a female slave was worth 120 rods. The Ila speaking people carried on a brisk trade in slaves with a boy worth five or six hoes and a girl worth 10 to 12 hoes. During the first half of the 17th century in West Africa, a male slave was worth 23 rods weighing one pound each. A female slave was worth only 18 rods. The price was 10 baskets of salt or five bunches of glass beads. The Arabs formerly traded 10 to 15 slaves for one Berber horse. In some places the slave was an abstract, standardized slave unit, not an actual person. It has been argued that only rarely were slaves actually exchanged in transactions. In 1882 a slave was worth less than a donkey, a cow or a sack of salt. In 1888 in Bolobo, an upriver slave sold for 1,000 brass rods while a down river slave sold for only 500 brass rods. (See Quiggin p. 47, 63, 75, 80, 89) (See Havemeyer p.64) (See Herbert p, 139) (See Harms p. 86-87)

Africa, Benin

Slaves were exchanged for European goods by the king and the rich. The price of a Sobo slave was a span cut off the large end of a large tusk of an elephant. (See Roth p. 141)

America, Northwest Coast

Human beings were bought and sold on the North Pacific Coast of North America during the late 18th and first half of the 19th century, according to Donald p. 123. Many tribes of the Canadian Northwest had slaves as property prior to the coming of Europeans to the area. Most of the slaves were seized by force, usually during intergroup fighting. A few were obtained as part of marriage presentations and during potlatch. (Donald p. 136) The slaves had neither rank nor rights and received no legacy. Most were taken as booty in raids or were the descendants of such slaves. A high-ranking person captured as a slave could be ransomed for a high price. Kirk states, "There are accounts of 140 feet of strung dentalium shells, 10 sea otter skins or 100 or more wool blankets being exchanged for a healthy slave." One chief stated that at his grandfather's time a slave was usually purchased for 600 to 700 blankets and that previously canoes, house planks and various other goods were used. Kirk also states, "Slaves could be used or given away, discarded or destroyed just like any other property; most were treated fairly well, and their lot was not sharply different from that of low-ranking commoners." (Donald p. 153) There was a close relationship between predatory warfare for the acquisition of slaves and the maintenance or enhancement of high social status. Much of the warfare among the Indians was for the main purpose of obtaining slaves for trade or to potlatch. In a potlatch the Tongass gave 20 slaves to the Stikine. One report states that slaves formed the principal article of trade on the whole coast and constituted the greater part of their riches. Wars were waged more to profit from the sale of slaves than to avenge aggressions. The Tsimshian and Haida tribes bartered for slaves with the Kwakiiutl who got their slaves by raiding the villages of Puget Sound and from the mouth of the Fraser River. Slaves also served as trade goods between the various Tlingit villages. They were a medium of exchange. The Tlingit purchased most of their slaves from the Haida. Others were taken in warfare. In some cases they also enslaved other Tlingit. The slaves were children and women of other Tlingit tribes with whom they had been at war. The children of slaves were also slaves. Among the Tlingit Indians a slave was valued at from 12 to 20 deerskins. The Clayoquot and Makah also used slaves. During military expeditions and raids, slaves would be taken. Enslavement brought disgrace to the victim and the entire family, so the family would try to purchase the slave's freedom. Slaves were primarily a source of prestige. They would be displayed as a part of the owner's wealth. A chief would sometimes set a slave free or sacrifice a slave to show his disregard for wealth. They also functioned as laborers and trade goods. The economic gain from the labor was in most cases not much more than the cost of keeping them, as in most cases they were women and children. (See Gerber p. 92) Except among the Bella Colla, only chiefs could own slaves until about 1920, after which anyone could own slaves. The slaves participated in the life of the household, performing the drudgery, helping in the acquisition of food and fighting in wars, according to Jopling p. 14. One of the first requirements for a Tlingit potlatch was to capture slaves. The worse thing about slavery was that the slaves were the absolute property of the owner and, therefore, the owner was able to kill the slave at a potlatch. Many times when a slave owner died his slaves were killed so they could attend to him in the spirit world. Slaves were valued at different amounts by different tribes at different times. A man slave was valued at 20 pounds of copper or six prime sea otter pelts. A woman slave was valued at 10 pounds of copper or five normal sea otter pelts. In another area a man was worth one Chilkat blanket, 30 fox skins, 10 moose skins or two martin skin blankets. In 1828 a Chinook purchased a slave for a gun, a blanket and two yards of copper wire according to Donald p. 140. Copper shields were at times valued in slaves. A copper was worth from one to 40 slaves. Canoes and shell money were also used to purchase slaves. Before 1850, 10 to 20 blankets would purchase a slave, while after 1850 more than 30 blankets were needed according to Donald p. 144. At other times and from various tribes a slave was worth 25 beavers or eight beavers, and 15 elk skins. In 1860 a man was worth $200 or 40 blankets. Twenty slaves would pay for a medium copper. A large copper was worth 40 slaves. In the 1880s a slave was worth 30 to as much as 60 blankets, and most chiefs owned 50 to 100 slaves. In the 1840s it was estimated that one third of the Indians in one area were slaves. Slaves to be used in a potlatch were always purchased just before the ceremony and were not the slaves kept in the houses for labor. According to Mitchell a single slave had the following values among the various tribes:

Tribe	**Value**
Stikine	18-20 skins
Tsimshian	15 elk skins
Haida	150-200 blankets
Bella Coola	10-20 blankets
Kwakiiutl	100 blankets
Quinault	80 blankets
Chinook	20-100 blankets

There are many instances of trading slaves for furs by many of the tribes. Some of the tribes, the Bella Coola for instance, varied the value of a slave based on the general supply, age, sex, ability, and industriousness. Slaves were some of the highest valued items the Indians possessed. See Potlatch.

Borneo

A male slave was worth a "Gong *gilan*," which was valued at $150. (See Quiggin p. 260)

Cambodia

Slaves as well as cattle, rice, cereals, gold and silver were used as money. (See Quiggin p. 214)

Europe

In Ancient Europe a slave was worth three cows. (See Quiggin p. 286)

Greece, Homeric

A slave was a large monetary unit worth a number of buffalo.

Mexico

The slave "constituted the wealth of the owner and provided a standard of value." (See Quiggin p. 311)

Papua New Guinea

The slave was the standard of value in western parts of Papua New Guinea.

Northern Siam

Bahnars of Annam valued the male slave as worth five to seven buffaloes. It was the highest monetary unit. (See Quiggin p. 212)

United States

In the southern states before the Civil War, and in the northern states as late as the early 1800s, the slave was a store of wealth but never a unit of value or form of money. Indians in northern California had shell money worth one or two slaves. Slaves and coppers were standards of value in the Northwest. (See Quiggin p. 292, 294) See Kumal

Wales

The slave woman was in the course of time a mere unit of account. Originally the slave was the highest barter unit and equal in value to the Roman libra or pound. A slave was also worth three cows or three ounces of silver. (See Ridgeway p. 33)

SNAIL SHELLS - See Musanga, Ikumi, Kiringi.

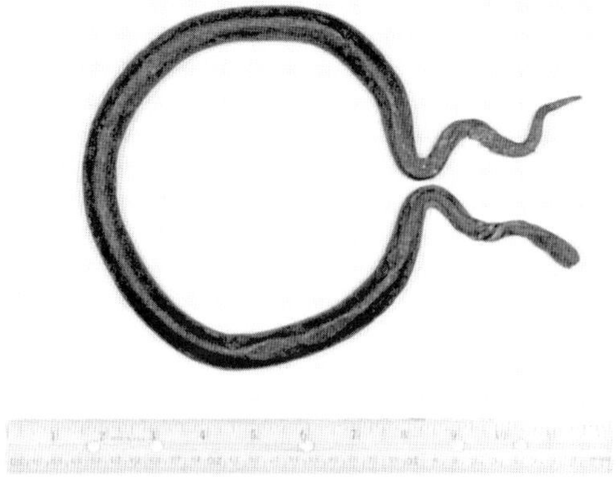

Snake Money

SNAKE MONEY

Africa

Old iron open ended rings were used as money.

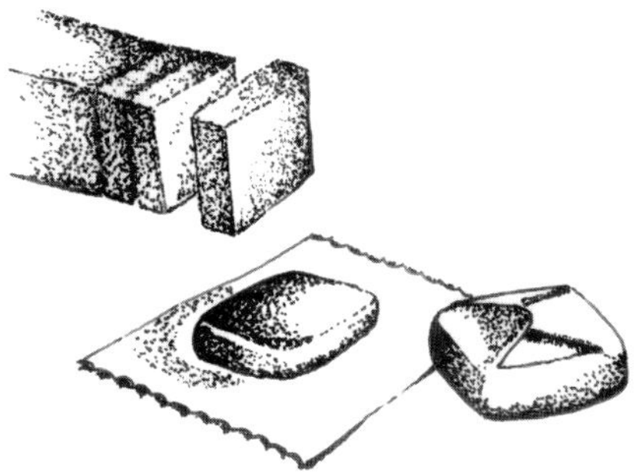

Soap Money

SOAP MONEY

Asiatic Areas

Seamen traded soap cakes with area people for services. The cake was worth five cents. The cake of soap was covered in talcum powder and wrapped in tissue paper. (See Reed p. 56)

China, before World War II

Small inscribed cakes were used in Shanghai for emergency money. (See Schulman and Gibbs, p. 35)

Mexico, 1840s

Cakes were stamped with the name of the town and the person authorized to issue it. Soap was money only in the town and only as long as the stamp was visible. Worth 1-1/2 cents. Legal tender. (See Einzig p. 184)

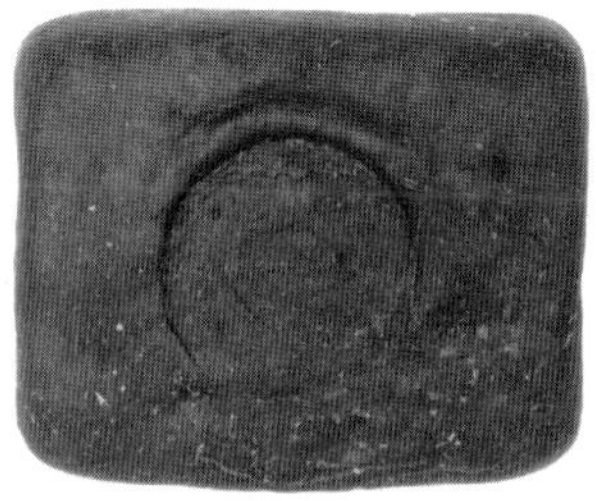

Soap Cake - Mexico

SOLEVU

A formalized exchange between clans in the Fiji Islands was called *soleyu.* Goods were ceremonially presented to the chief of the receiving clan, and a reciprocal gift was expected.

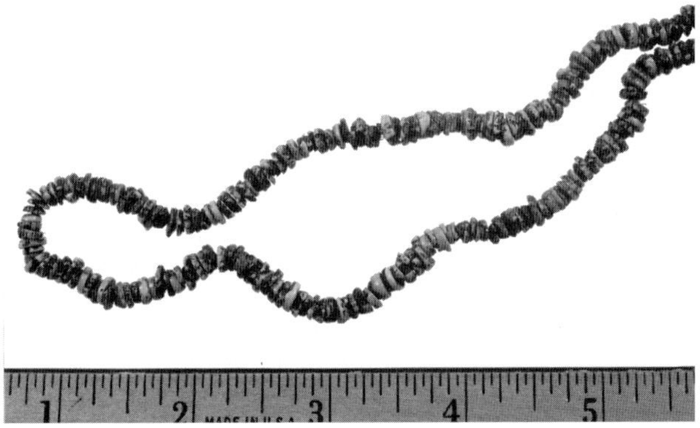

Som

SOM

Banks Islands and Reef Island

There are two kinds of *som.* One kind is rare and consists of finely ground thin discs and the other is a much coarser shell disk which is in general use. *Som* shells (*Conus ceylanensis Hwass*) are gathered by the men and taken to the small coral islet of Rowa. There the women break the shells with a piece of giant clam shell called *chele.* The pieces are then washed and dried in the sun and chipped with a sharp piece of shell until only the tip is left. The pointed surface is put on the end of a stick and rubbed on a stone with water and volcanic sand. This forms a hole without drilling. They are then strung on a fiber of hibiscus called *gaviv.* It is essential for important payments. A string four feet long called *chiregi* would buy 10 yams, which is enough for family of four for week. It was not used as an ornament, only as money.

A woman working from sun-up to sundown could make a string a fathom long. New *som* was worth twice as much as old *som*. A unit of measure ,called a tal ,was two fathoms of *som*. Another shorter measure from the elbow to the tips of the fingers was called *letnovivhe*. The *tarak*, a length of *som* from the waist to the ends of the fingers. *Som* is used to purchase steps in the *Suqe Club*. *Som* is arranged and counted in coils. (See Quiggin p. 165) (See Rivers p. 166 - 170)

SOSOROFA
Trobriand Islands

Conus tips with holes in the center and strung alternately with banana seeds were called *sosorofa*. They are very old and not at present being used as money. In the past they were used in Bauwane village for bride price with three or four needed to purchase a wife. Most of the village is now Christian, and they do not use bride price. They called it custom money. Very few are in existence. In 1995 there were only three strings left on the island.

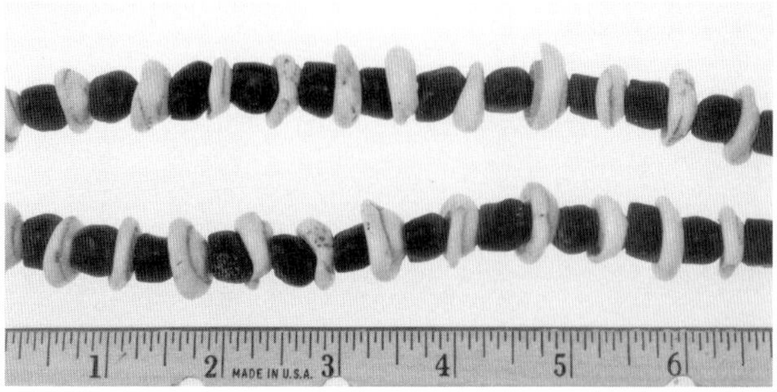

Sosorofa

SOULAVA - See Bagi, Kula.

SPADE MONEY
China, 600-250 B.C.

Hollow-handle spade money was made to imitate old trade items and was introduced about 400 B.C. It was cast in bronze of standard weight and had a hole piercing both sides of the half through which a nail or other pin could pass to hold a wood handle in place. One side also has three vertical lines.There are several types of hollow-handle spade money as shown. Inscriptions denote the district where it was made. Old flat spades with rounded ends were also made until about 350 B.C., and late-style small flat spades were made from 350-250 B.C. The pieces are also known as Pu or Bu (now) money. (See Pu Money) See Melote, Tula

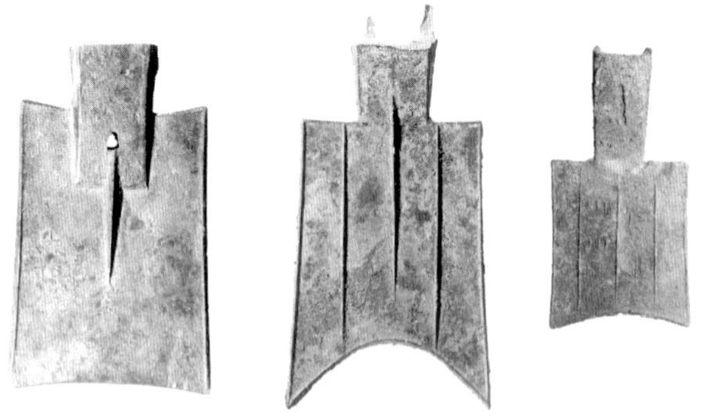

Spade Money - Zhou Imperial Spade Money (Courtesy Shanghai Müseum)

Spade Money - Jin State Spade Money

SPEAR MONEY
Africa, Kenya, Loikop of Samburu District

There are more than 11 different styles of spears used according to the owner's status and age. Most spears had a blade made of iron on one end with a wood center section and a tapered iron rod on the other end. The size and shape of the blade and length of the wood center section varied. New weapons are valued at one, two, or three goats. In 1983 one US dollar was worth Ksh 14, and spears were worth 100, 150, 200, or 250 Ksh. They served as a limited medium of exchange. See Larik

Africa, Nigeria

There are several varieties of this brass ceremonial staff that were used as currency. (See Schaedler p. 254)

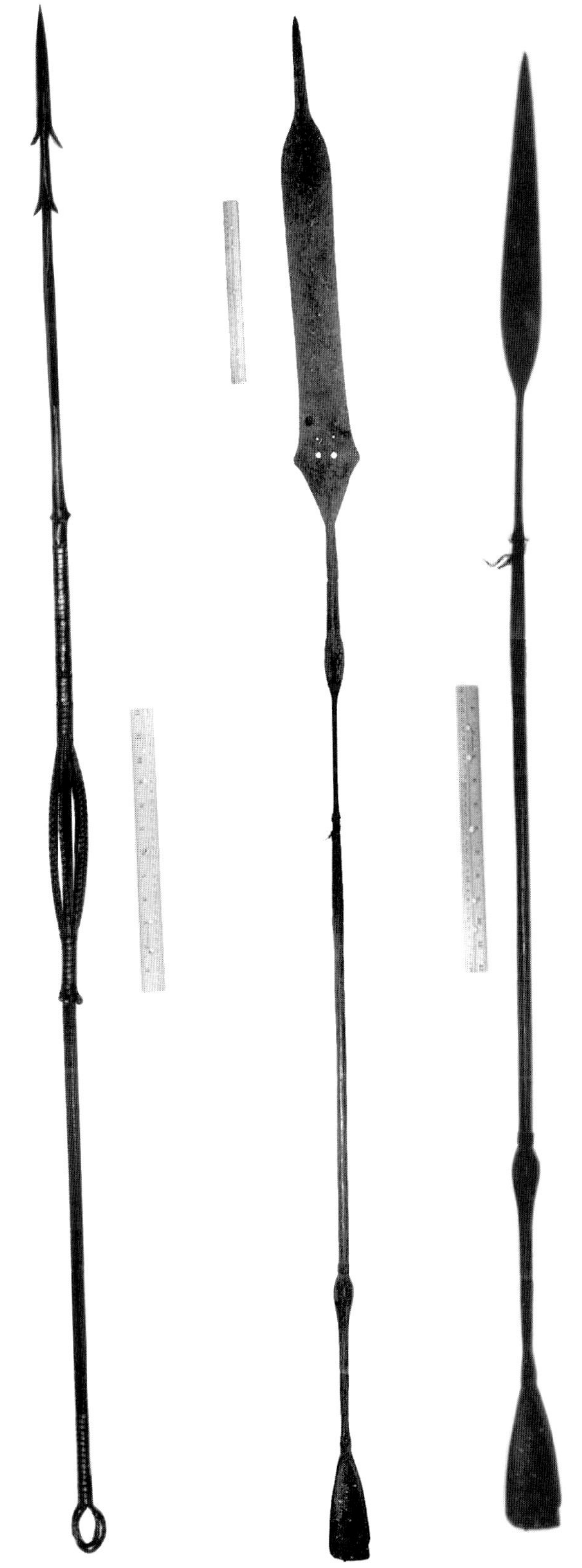

Spear Money - Nigeria

Nkutschu Tribe Lance

Ngombe Tribe Lance

Africa, Zaire

The Nkutshu use this lance in war in tribal dances and as money. The shaft is the most valuable part of the lance and is made of wood bound with woven brass and copper threads and covered with brass in the center section. There is an iron bell at the end and iron blade at the other. (See Ballarini p. 104)

Africa, Zaire

The Ngombe people use this iron blade lance with a wood shaft to pay dowry to the wife's family. (See Ballarini p. 104)

Africa, Zande tribe

Spears were used in marriage payment. Money has now been substituted for the spears in marriage payments, but the money is called spears. (See Reining p. 41)

New Britain

Spears decorated with *nassa* shells were the most important wealth item used by the Lakalai. Pearl shells and disk-shaped shell beads called *bubu* were their minor forms of money. (See Chowning p. 298)

Nigeria, Nsubi and Edo tribes

Large brass spears were used as money. Notice the unusual widening of the shaft near the center of the spear. 63 1/2" (See Schulman item 345)

Papua New Guinea

Bundles of spears made of all wood or bamboo without feathers attached. They were used along with shell armlets and boar's tusks as compensation for serious offenses such as murder or rape. They were also used in bride price. In 1964, one spear was valued at one small pig or six chickens. (See Rogers p. 98)(See TMA Nov, 1987)

SPEARHEAD MONEY

Bangala,Bwaka, Zaire, as late as turn of 19th century

This heavy iron piece with blunt edges had no practical use and was only used as money. Its indigenous name, *mbili ngbaka*, means money of Ngbaka. The current name for the tribes are Ngbaka / Lobele, from Zaire. (See Ballarini p. 120-121) (See Schaedler p. 321)

Africa, Mbole tribe

The rhomboid shape of the head is attached to a rectangular iron bar with two iron spirals attached to the side of the shaft. The large size and delicate design did not allow the spear to be used as a weapon. It was a very valuable currency and was used in bride price. The spear was driven into the ground in front of the bride's home when the bride price was paid. As late as 1975 the spears were still being made in the village. (See Ballarini p. 104-105) See Ikonga, Liganda, Mahee, Naga

SPEARS - See Mimboss

SPEAR THROWER

Caledonia

This interesting item was made by entwining the hair of a fruit-eating bat into a string. The resulting string was woven into a cord. The becket was used as money as well as a spear thrower. (See *Becket*) (See Quiggin p. 169)

SPERM WHALE - See Whale Tooth

SPICES

Orient to Europe

Spices were use to preserve food and mask bad tastes. They were a store of wealth.

SPIKE - DUTSI

Africa, Nigeria

The Dutsi spike was made of iron was iron currency in the Dutsi district in Kaduna State. It is shown in Eyo p.50. A large hoard has come on the market in the last few years.

SPIRAL CURRENCY

Africa, Ngelima tribe

There are several varieties of this copper snake-like coil. It was used in Equatorial Zaire as money. (See Ballarini p. 118.) See mitako

SPONDYLUS SHELLS

Trobriand Islands

The spondylus shell disks were strung on strings and used in ceremonial exchanges, bride-price, purchase of yams, pearl, and part of the kula trade. They were a store of value but not a unit of exchange. (See Einzig p. 80) See Pwomondap

SQUIRREL SKIN

Russia, 1400s

A unit of measure, *Grivna Kun*, was worth a number of squirrel skins. Irregular pieces were impressed with a government stamp and were valued at and convertible into a whole squirrel skin. Tolls, customs, and church donations were paid with squirrel skins. (See Einzig p. 279)

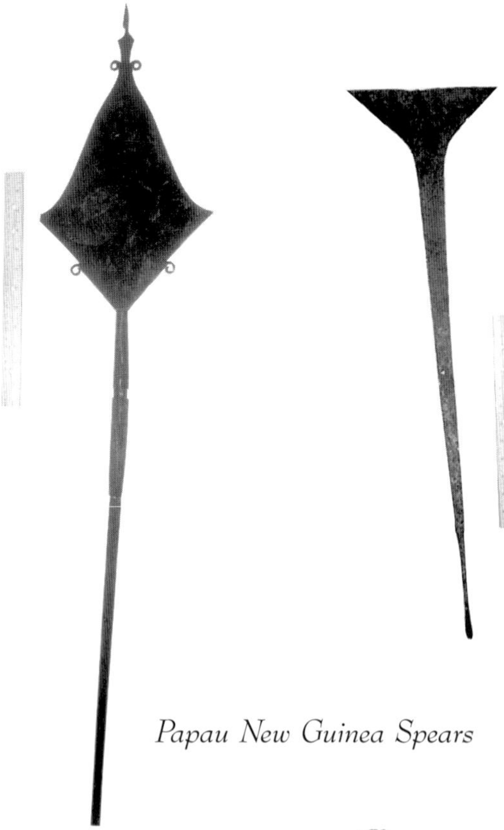

Papau New Guinea Spears

Spear Thrower

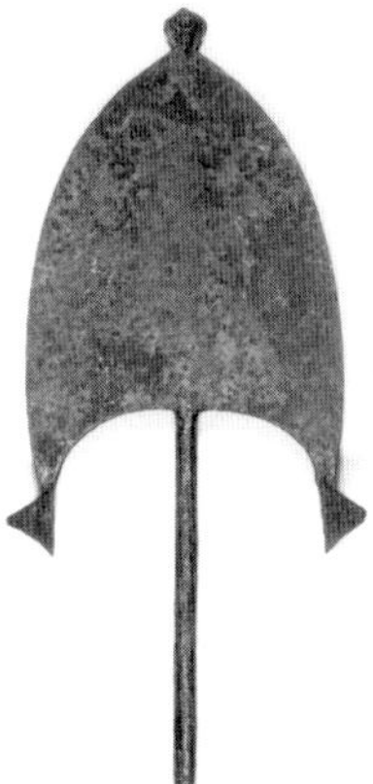

Bangala Spearhead

Papua New Guinea Spear or Arrow Money

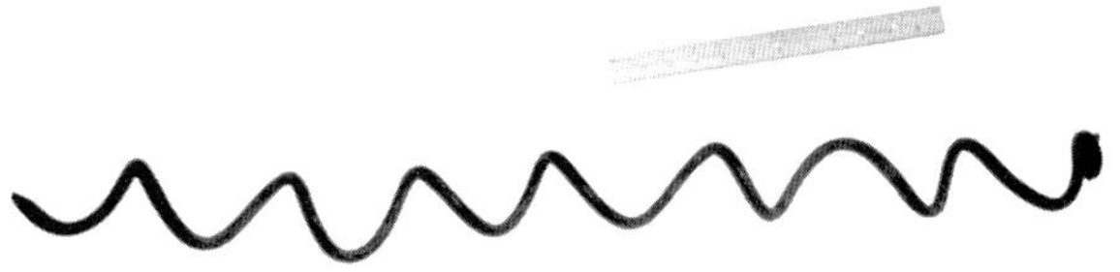

Spiral Currency

Spondylus Shell

Stamp Money

Stamp Money Russia

STAMP MONEY

Stamps and encased stamps were used as money in many countries for temporary use in lieu of small-denomination coins. Many countries have issued postage currency consisting of a postage stamp encased on a round or oblong container sealed with a clear face such as plastic, mica or cellophane. Many have advertisements printed or stamped on the back of the container. Countries who have issued them are Austria, Denmark, Italy, Germany, the United States, Luxembourg, New Caledonia, and Spain. Another kind of stamp money consisted of an actual postage stamp with a notation or imprint on the reverse indicating its use as money. Many times the stamp was on a thick paper or thin cardboard. This variety was issued by Austria, Ceylon, Germany, Madagascar, New Caledonia, Russia, Serbia, and Turkey. Another variety was a piece of printed paper with a stamp or stamps attached. Countries that issued these were Austria, Belgium, Ceylon, Czechoslovakia, Denmark, France, French Colonies (Madagascar, Tangier, Spanish Sahara, Morocco, Guinee), Germany, Italy, Japan, New Caledonia, Norway, Portugal, Russia, Serbia, Spain, Turkey, and Uruguay. Other countries also issued the above stamps.

Russia 1915-1917

Postage stamp images were placed on perforated cardboard. The backs stated their use was on a par with silver subsidiary coins. They were issued in one, two, three, 10, 15 and 20 kopek denominations. The stamp designs belong to the Romanoff issue, and each bears the portrait of a Russian sovereign. One kopek - Peter I. Two kopeks - Alexander II. Three kopeks - Alexander III. Ten kopeks - Nicholas II. Fifteen kopeks - Nicholas I. Twenty kopeks - Alexander I. The backs of the one, two, and three kopek had printed on the them in Russian "Can Be Circulated on Equal Footing with a Copper Coin," and the backs of the 10, 15, and 20 kopek pieces had printed on them in Russian "Can Be Circulated on Equal Footing with a Silver Coin." Pieces were also issued for Ukraine.

Spain

1936-1939

During the Spanish Civil War stamps were affixed to small round pieces of cardboard to circulate as money. One side has the arms of Spain in brick red. It is not known which denomination stamps were used. The practice was also followed in the colonies of Morocco, Spanish Sahara, and Tangier.

Germany & Austria

Stamps were put in cheap transparent holders to circulate as money.

United States. 1861-1865

Stamps were placed in round brass holder with mica on the front. Advertising was sold on the back. They were invented by J. Gault. They were used as a substitute for coins when the coins were hoarded during the Civil War.

Stamps were also used individually and also placed in paper envelopes with advertising on the envelopes. Many varieties exist.

STICKS - See Tally Sticks

STOCKFISH

Iceland

Dried cod was used as money sometime between 1413 A.D. and 1426 A.D. and had set values, according to Wicks p. 12. Stockfish served as a measure of value or a unit of account. A pair of leather shoes was worth four stockfish, and three tons of wheat was worth 120 stockfish. (See Wicks p. 12)

STONE AXE - See Axe Money

YAP STONE MONEY

The stone money of Yap Island is one of the most interesting and unusual kinds of money in the world. The islands were discovered by the Portuguese explorer Diego Da Rocha in 1526. At one time the islands to the east were part of an empire controlled by Yap. The people of those islands brought tribute to Yap's chiefs and in return the Yapese watched over the people of those islands and protected them. The Yapese had black magic and used it to terrorize the other islands with threats of storms. In 1869 the Germans set up a trading post. In 1885 the Spanish occupied Colonia, the principal city, which they sold back to the Germans in 1899. The Japanese occupied Yap from 1914 to the end of World War II. In 1947 the United Nations set up a trust territory which included Yap and was administered by the United States. The district administrator was an American citizen. In 1990 Yap became a part of the Federated States of Micronesia.

Origin of Stone Money

The stones were called *"fe," "fei"* or *"rai"*. They are now called *"rai"*. At one time the Yapese in the southern parts called it *"fei,"* and the northern areas called it *"rai."* The Germans called it *"fa."* It is not known when they did come into existence, but they were known to be in existence more than 200 years ago. "In the early 1800s, Otto von Kotzebue, sailing for the czar of Russia, stopped in the Carolines." In one of his journals of the trip, a reference is made to the stone disks: "Eap (Yap) produces whet-stones, which the low easterly islands

Stamp Money - Russia

Stamp Money - Spain

Encased Stamp Money

Encased Stamp Money

Opitz Specimen, The Piece Described In The Letter. Diameter 23 Inches, Weight 60 Pounds.

obtain from thence. They are a kinder gift of nature than the silver, Cantova, on the testimony of the native, Cayal, ascribes to this island. Kadu has explained to us this tradition. A white stone is found in the mountains of Eap, to which the chiefs have exclusive right; their seats of honor are made of it. One block forms the seat, and the other the back. Kadu has seen this stone; it is neither silver nor metal. A yellow stone the same honor in Pelli (the Palau islands)."

How much earlier the stones were made and used is not known, but they do not appear to have been used to any large extent too much earlier than the 1800s, as other explorers of the time did not even mention the stone money in their writings despite the fact that they made extensive notes about the island and its people. Small stone beads might have been used earlier, but I do not consider them the kind of stone money we are discussing. This conclusion is merely the author's opinion.

Location of Lap Island

Yap is about 450 miles southwest of Guam. It is also 4,400 miles southwest of Hawaii. The state of Yap is comprised of four large adjoining islands and 15 outer islands. The large islands are Yap, Maap, Tomil and Rumung. Except for Rumung, the other three large islands are connected by bridges. Rumung must be reached by boat and is not open to tourists at this time. The principal island is Yap, and on it is located the district center of Colonia.

Opitz Specimens - Left, Diameter 11 Inches, 5 Pounds; Center Piece Diameter 5 Inches; Right Two Specimens - Modern Pieces

The Palau Islands (Republic of Belau)

Now known as the Republic of Belau, it consists of 343 islands. Babeldaop is the second largest island in Micronesia (Guam is larger). It has two elevated limestone islands and a large freshwater lake. Only nine islands are inhabited now. Many of the stones came from Koror on one of the limestone islands of Babeldaop.

Government

Since 1979 the states of Yap, Chuuk (formerly Truk until renamed in 1990), Pohnpei (formerly Ponape until renamed in 1984) and Kosrae have been part of the Federated States of Micronesia. Formerly they were part of the U.S.-administered Trust Territory of the Pacific Islands set up by the UN. In 1990 the UN Trusteeship Council ratified the termination of the trusteeship which the UN had set up in 1947. The capital is Kolonia on the island of Pohnpei. Most of its revenue is U.S. government grants. This is 70% of the gross national product. On Yap there is an elected governor and lieutenant governor. If the governor is from Yap Proper, then the lieutenant governor must be from the outer islands, or vice versa. There are two councils of chiefs: the Council of Tamol from the outer islands and the Council of Pilung from Yap Proper. The councils have veto power over any legislation affecting traditional customs.

In the past a rigid nine-level caste system governed Yap. The highest caste people lived in the strongest and most powerful villages. People took their surnames from their land parcels rather than from their parents. Land was sacred.

Life on Yap Island

The state has a population of approximately 12,000 as of 1988. One third live in the outer islands with the remainder on Yap Proper. 95% are Catholic. The population had dropped from 10,000 in 1869 to a low of 2,500 in 1945. Foreign diseases caused much of this decline. The Yapese use separate cooking vessels and separate dishes for four groups of the family. The four groups are: old males, young males, old females, and young females. Yap has one of the most complex economic systems in the Western Pacific Ocean. Yap society had patrilineal lineages, and everybody was a member of matrilineal, named, exogamous clan. There were also elaborate caste and class systems. There were nine classes, with the last four classes not owning any land. Each household in a village was ranked, as well as each person in that household. Every bit of land and also the fishing areas inside the reef were owned by someone. Men of higher rank had to pay more for everything than men of lower rank. Many times a man of an upper class wore a long wooden comb in his hair. Only upper-class men could wear the comb. At one time the lower castes and tribute payers could not own stone money that was more than four spans in size. The bachelor's houses were called *failu* and *pabai*. They were used for discussing the affairs of the people. They also were a place the tabooed fishermen could stay during their time of rest between fishing trips. The fish were paid for with yar. Stone money was also sometimes used. In the men's houses were also kept *mispils*. They were the mistresses of the men of the men's house. The men supplied the *mispil's* needs such as food and betel nuts. The *mispils* were not required to work in the fields as the wives were. The natives did not bargain, and prices were not set as we are accustomed to. Things were given, and then it was expected that at a later time they would be returned.

Production of Stone Money

A type of calcite, called aragonite, is the material that all Yap stones were made of. Yap Island does not have any stone native to the island. Aragonite has the hardness of marble, 3.75, and a specific gravity of 2.9. A kind of brittle shale is the closest thing to stone on the island. Aragonite to make the stone money came from Babeldaop Island in the Pelew group of islands. A few stones were also made on the island of Guam. The natives thought the stones were of divine origin. Prior to the traders a chief would give permission to some youths to go to Palau to manufacture and bring back stone money. The chief received all the large stones and two-fifths of the smaller stones. The remainder were exchanged for baskets of taro. Hundreds of stones were brought back on each trip, but they were all less than four feet in diameter. The Yapese were required to perform many of the menial duties on Palau in return for permission to use the quarries. They built roads, gathered firewood, carried water, and acted as soothsayers and doctors. The Yapese would also give antique glass beads to the Palauan chiefs for permission to quarry the stone. These beads were then used as money on Palau and are called *udoud*. The aragonite that was streaked with a brownish chocolate color, as well as aragonite with a milky white color with small crystals, were both preferred to any other. The stone decreases in thickness from the center to the outer edge. There were several ways used to make the hole. The hole in a few stones was made with a shell adze called *gi* and was drilled with a reef-stone used as a fire-drill. Many of the stones had the hole made with the *gi* used to drill the hole from both sides. Some stones fashioned with iron implements had a small hole large enough to put a chain through it. Some of the older pieces had names. The names came from various sources. They

Opitz Specimen, Formerly Gill And Mitchell, Weight 78 Pounds, Diameter 21-3/4 Inches

Opitz Specimen, Pre O'Keefe, Diameter 15-1/2 Inches, Weight 35 Pounds

might come from the canoe used to haul the stone to Yap, the name of the chief who gave permission to sail to Palau, the maker of the stone if he died during the venture, or some other famous person. The older stones were rough, irregular, thick and porous, while the O'Keefe stones were smooth and most had a stepped appearance with two distinct planes. The last pieces were produced as late as 1931.

The German Captain Tetens sailed in western Micronesia from 1862 to 1868. He was the first to convey the stones from Palau to Yap along with 10 cutters. He only made a limited number of pieces and therefore the monetary system remained intact. In 1871, David Dean O'Keefe, an enterprising Irish-American sea captain from Savannah, Ga., was shipwrecked on the island. He was called His Majesty O'Keefe by the natives because of the fame and fortune he obtained during the 30 years he was on Yap. He traded safe travel to the Palau Islands to quarry the stone to make the stone money and in return received copra, the dried meat of the coconut, and trepang, a giant sea slug. Both items were plentiful on Yap and were highly prized in China. He also brought iron for tools to shape the stones and dynamite to break the stones loose. O'Keefe died in 1901 at sea during a tropical storm. LeHunte stated, "Almost the whole trade of Yap and Pelew is in the hands of O'Keefe. He also has a monopoly, for a nominal rental, of the produce of St. David's Island (claimed by the Dutch Governor) [Mapia Island, Indonesia] from which he exports about 220 tons of copra per annum. There being no local labor at that place, the inhabitants having been almost killed off by the natives of Ternate and New Guinea. O'Keefe employs in making copra there, natives of Yap and also of Sansoral or Pulo Anna. The arrangements between the Yap natives and O'Keefe is that he conveys the money cutters to Pelew and with their cargoes back to Yap in consideration for which he obtains a proportionate number of laborers to go to St. David's for the term of six months. Both the chiefs and the common people we examined expressed themselves perfectly happy with this arrangement, which had been faithfully carried out by both sides for a considerable time and is likely to continue as long as O'Keefe's interest in St. David's and this demand for Pelew stone money in Yap exists." O'Keefe did not buy or sell the stones but merely held them until he received the copra for his services of transportation.

Uses of Stone Money

The small stones of one or two feet in diameter were not displayed because they did not think they had any reason to be proud of those stones. The larger stones were displayed and in many cases were displayed outside the bachelor's house to show the wealth of the village. The stones had no practical non-monetary use other than as ornamentation. The stones were also used for political payments. A large stone could be used to buy support of a neutral tribe during a war. Many of the older pieces were given names. Sometimes the names were of important people. The German government set fines in stone money. The stone money was purely an internal money and was never used to trade with other islands. The biggest kind of celebration on Yap was the *mitmit*. It was a time of considerable social contact during which a coconut wine called *tuba* was drunk. The intention of the *mitmit* was to give back to the people the stone money (from the women's side) and shell money that were given to them by the recipients' previous *mitmit*. The tradition was that all gifts demanded repayment. Two pieces of stone money were paid to the chief of the village where a girl who was to serve in the men's house was called a *mispil*. This was in no way considered disgraceful and abduction was pre-arranged. The ransom of the corpse of a fallen warrior required the presentation of stone money.

Size of Stone Money

Pieces range in size from two or three inches in diameter to about 12 feet in diameter. Only after traders such as O'Keefe came along would stones of four feet or more in diameter be produced. The Yapese brought pieces back no larger than four feet in diameter, while O'Keefe could bring pieces no larger than six feet in diameter. The larger pieces were brought back by a large German trading ship. The Yapese measured the stones in terms of spans, which were the width of the outstretched fingers. The smallest unit was determined by the width of the finger. The largest unit was the fathom, which was the length of the outstretched arms.

Rarity of Stone Money

The Japanese, who controlled Yap after World War I, did a survey in 1929 and found 13,281 pieces on Yap. Many stones were destroyed and used as anchors, roads etc., during World War II. It is thought that only one half of the 13,281 survived to the present time. The old, traditionally made pieces were called *Fe'Ni Ngochol*. They all have rough surfaces. At the time of O'Keefe the old pieces were worth about as much as the O'Keefe pieces. Within 20 years, however, the natives realized they were rarer than the O'Keefe pieces and were more highly valued, and then hoarded them. These are the pieces the Japanese destroyed most during World War II. The O'Keefe pieces and those from the German steamship Germania were known as *Fe'Ni Dumow*. They all have smooth surfaces. By the 1920s they were of little value and were the circulating stone money on the island.

Value of Stone Money

The value of the stones depends as much on factors such as shape, quality, thickness, hardness, and pedigree as on size. Most foreigners, however, used size to determine value. The value has fluctuated greatly, with the stones first being of low value, then higher value and later low value again. In the early times the writer Kubary stated the stone money had a very low purchasing value considering its size and weight. Furness stated a three span stone of good whiteness and shape would purchase 50 baskets (18 inches by 10 inches) of food, a pig weighing 80 to 100 pounds, or 1,000 coconuts. It is strange that during the 1880's when Captain O'Keefe was transporting large numbers of the stones to Yap, the value of the stones actually increased in value. Normally when a supply increases, the value decreases. That would indicate that during this time the demand for the stones increased dramatically. It seems that in modern times the scarcity of the pre-O'Keefe pieces and the abundance of the O'Keefe pieces has been recognized with the large value placed on the old pieces and the relatively low value placed on the O'Keefe pieces. Kubary stated in 1889 that a three-hand-span stone was worth a pig. He also said that a six-foot stone was worth a common big canoe or a Palau necklace. Price said a one-foot diameter piece from Guam would cost $75 U.S. in the 1940s. Value was also determined by the standing of the men involved in the transaction. Old men and women would receive more for a stone than a person of higher standing. The stones have continued to be used as money and in trade into the present time. In the United States in 1952, the late Gordon Gill tried for some time to purchase a piece of stone money. Many of the important collectors of the day had none for sale and only knew of a few in the United States. He ultimately purchased a stone from Ralph A. Mitchell for $200. It was 21-3/4" in diameter, 4-3/4" thick and weighed 78 pounds. It does not have the ridge but is smooth with an irregular size and almost all white in color. That piece is currently in my collection. In the early 1960s the Yapese valued the stones at $25 per foot while in 1966, when I purchased his piece, they valued the stones at $30 per foot.

Export of Stone Money

Since 1965, it has been against the law to export stone money from Yap without the permission of the paramount chief and the state governor. In 1965, I purchased a 23-inch piece of stone money weighing 66 pounds (see photos). The stone had a cost of $30 per foot plus freight and crating. They also said that my piece being sent to the United States and a piece being sent to the First National Bank of Sweden were probably the last two pieces allowed out of Yap.

Other Forms of Yap Money

Yar is a large polished mother-of-pearl shell with a handle made of woven coconut fiber. They were used to purchase land, for the losers of a war to pay to the winners, and in bride price. *Yar* was also used in funeral ceremonies and to pay the village prostitutes. Four to six shells bound on a second cord is a unit called *Boyha a yar*. A presentation string could have as many as 500 shells on it.

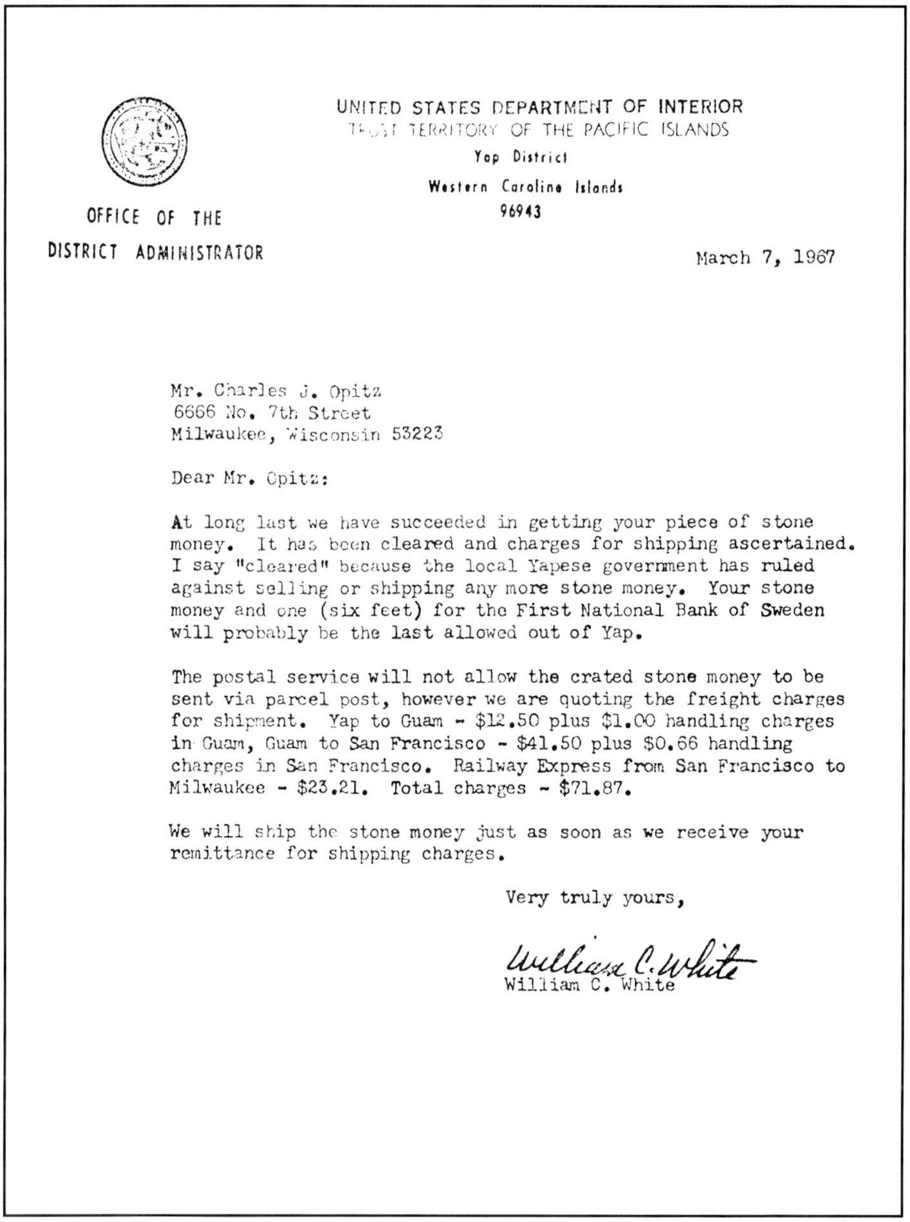

UNITED STATES DEPARTMENT OF INTERIOR
TRUST TERRITORY OF THE PACIFIC ISLANDS
Yap District
Western Caroline Islands
96943

OFFICE OF THE
DISTRICT ADMINISTRATOR

March 7, 1967

Mr. Charles J. Opitz
6666 No. 7th Street
Milwaukee, Wisconsin 53223

Dear Mr. Opitz:

At long last we have succeeded in getting your piece of stone money. It has been cleared and charges for shipping ascertained. I say "cleared" because the local Yapese government has ruled against selling or shipping any more stone money. Your stone money and one (six feet) for the First National Bank of Sweden will probably be the last allowed out of Yap.

The postal service will not allow the crated stone money to be sent via parcel post, however we are quoting the freight charges for shipment. Yap to Guam - $12.50 plus $1.00 handling charges in Guam, Guam to San Francisco - $41.50 plus $0.66 handling charges in San Francisco. Railway Express from San Francisco to Milwaukee - $23.21. Total charges - $71.87.

We will ship the stone money just as soon as we receive your remittance for shipping charges.

Very truly yours,

William C. White
William C. White

Gau is a string of discs made from the shell *Chama Pacica*. The necklaces were loaned out with interest. They were heirlooms and were very old. They were passed down from the father's side. The price of a murder was an inferior string of *gau*.

Reng is the dye stuff and perfume made from the roots of *Curcuma*, which was found on Yap. On the nearby island of Truk it was also used, and there it was called *taik*.

Tobacco was used for goods sold to traders.

Mats were a form of money used in many parts of the Pacific. On Yap Island they were called *mmbul* and were used in funeral ceremonies. They were coarse, shaggy, and white and were made from the beaten bark of the lemon hibiscus tree. It is not known when or where they were made, but it is doubtful they were ever made on Yap. They were kept rolled up and enclosed in matting. Their value was determined by their diameter. They were valued highly, like the stone money.

Huge mortars and pestles were used as money. The mortars were made of soft wood, and the pestles were made from *Tridacna* shell. They were wealth but not considered as money by some.

Baskets of taro were used as a unit of account.

Coconuts and copra were used as payment when dealing with traders.

Stone Money Outside of Yap Island

The Stone Money of Yap, A Numismatic Survey, by Cora Lee Gilliland lists 149 stones outside of Yap in about 1975. Numerous pieces, particularly in the United States, were not included. Her excellent book gives much information on the subject of Yap stone money and is the most comprehensive on the subject.

The largest stone money to leave the island is the Grover Criswell specimen (included in the survey). It is 7-1/2 ft. and weighs 6,000 pounds. Mr. Criswell told me he purchased it from A. Roboman, a chief on the island, in 1960 for a number of farm animals which he had to purchase. He leased the stone money to Ripley's "Believe It or Not" Museum in St. Augustine, Fla. from 1964-1974. It was also displayed at the ANA Convention in Miami, Fla. In 1974 the Bank of Canada National Numismatic Collection purchased it from Mr. Criswell for $11,000. It now is on display in Ottawa, Canada.

STONES

Amazon, 1618 - 19th century

Green serpentine stones in the shape of an animal's head or cylinder shape with an animal or fish design incised are said to be the currency of Matinino tribe, but existence of such a tribe is questioned. (See Taxay p. 51-52)

STONE RING - See Navela

STRAW TIN

Nigeria

The alluvial casseterite from which tin was extracted was dug out of old river beds. The tin was then cast in the form of thin wires by making a hole in the clay with a dry grass stalk. The grass was removed, and the tin was poured into the hole left by the grass stalk. When it was set, the clay was broken open. This form of pure tin was used as currency with the traders. (Johansson p. 57)

STRING MONEY

China

During the late Shang and early Chou dynasties bronze pieces were believed to have been used as money. It was excavated from a tomb in Liaoning Province. Also called "chiuan" money.

SUGAR

Barbados, 1640

Sugar was the principal medium of exchange and unit of account. The legal ratio of *Muscavado* (brown sugar) to the pound sterling was 10 shillings per 100 pounds of sugar. In 1667, this was raised to 16 shillings per 100 pounds. In 1645, swearing was punishable by a fine of four pounds (master or free man) or two pounds (servant). An "able preaching Minister" was obtained for 14,000 pounds of sugar a year. (See Quiggin p. 319)

Brazil, 1712

Sugar was declared as currency in Brazil and to pay salaries of troops. (See Taxay p. 58)

SWEDISH PLATE MONEY - See Plate Money

SWORD - See Knife Money, Money Sword

SWORD GUARD

Japan

Sword guards were not believed to have been used as money, but some collectors include them in their collections.

SYCEE

China

Before 1000 A.D., silver was used as a store of wealth, and later it became a form of bullion. Prior to 1889 only cash coins were issued by the government. For large transactions, private firms produced silver ingots called sycee. Cribb said that in 119 B.C., the Han emperor Wudi experimented with a silver ingot. During the Tang

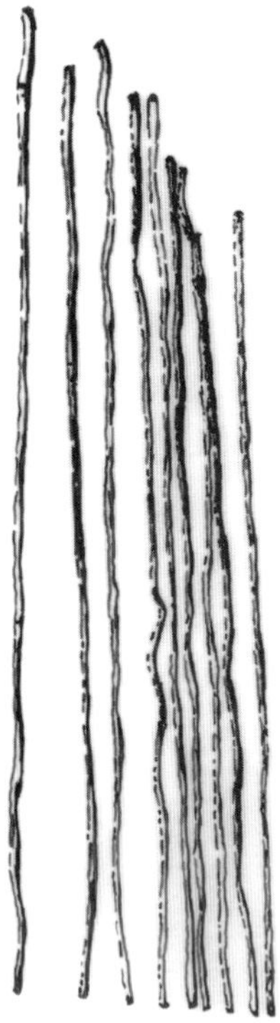

Straw Tin

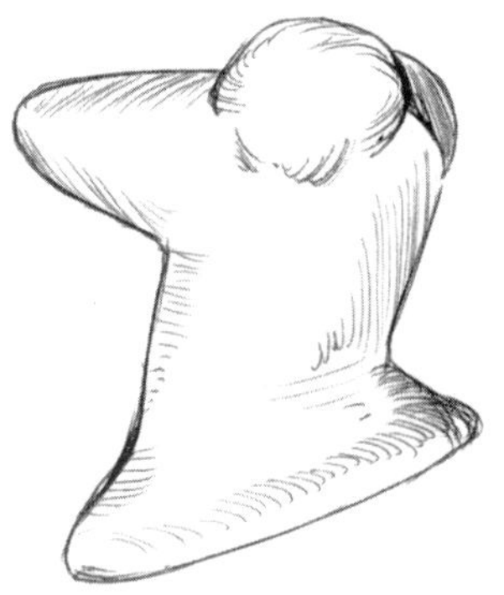

Amazon Stone

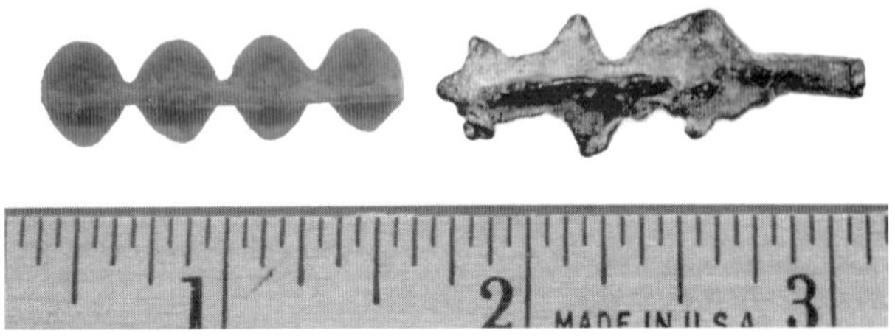

String Money

Sword Guard

50 Tael Sycee - Yuanbao - Dabao - Bank Ingot

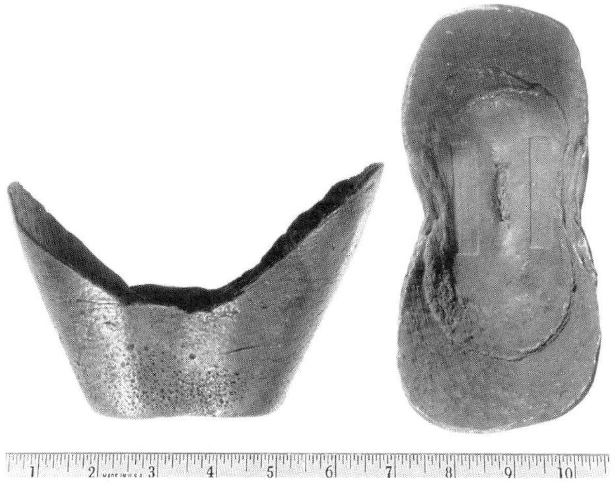

50 Tael Sycee - Yuanbao - Dabao

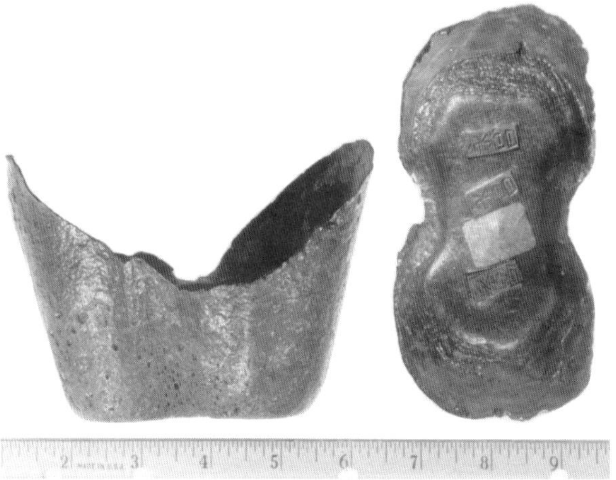

50 Tael Sycee - Yuanbao - Dabao

Dynasty period (A.D. 618-907), silver ingots began to play a significant part in China. By the Mongol period (1280-1368), sycee dominated the trade currency. The majority of pieces now found are from 1820-1925. This increase in the use of silver ingots during this period is due to a sales tax imposed on the people that was payable entirely in silver. Also during this period, other taxes were demanded in silver. These ingots were made by the local banks instead of by the government. They were the most important method of payment for large transactions. During this period the place of manufacture and function were shown by the ingot's shape, size, and detail. Most of the ingots are from 98.5% to 99.5% pure silver. The large, 50-ounce sycee were kept in a box containing 60 ingots, which took two coolies to carry. Sycee were banned in 1933. They were also called "shoe" money and "boat" money. Sycee were cast in iron molds and stamped with inscriptions while still soft. This caused the edges to be higher than the centers. The large sycee did not circulate but rather were used in large transactions and for storing wealth. Most common weights were one, five,10, and 50 taels. Other weights were 1/10, 1/5, 1/4, 1/3, 1/2, 2/3, 72/100, 3/4, two, three, four, six, seven, eight, and 100 taels. The most common shape was boat; other shapes were kettle drum, loaf (rectangular), double-headed axe (oldest type), square, flat, and some fancy shapes. In theory the fineness of silver was .916 2/3. In practice it was .980. Every degree above .935 is marked as a premium on the sycee and charged for. Some sycee have fine ripples on the top surface which were caused by slight movement of the mold just prior to the hardening of the silver. The ripples occur most frequently on high purity silver and some feel the ripples indicate fine silver. The porous bottoms of some sycee probably were caused by the flash boiling of water in the mold that was used for cooling the mold. Some of the holes could also be bubbles due to the release of gases dissolved in the metal. Most kettle-drum sycee were produced in the southwestern Yunnan province and weighed 10 taels. Some were five taels. Rectangular sycee were produced in Southern China (Yunnan Province) in the 19th century. Cribb stated that the sycee have some or, in a few cases, all of the following information:

1) maker's name
2) place of manufacture
3) date of manufacture
4) function
5) name of ingot
6) weight standard
7) weight
8) fineness
9) assay mark
10) good luck motto.

Many ingots have only the first three, some have none.

1) The name was normally the silversmith who cast the ingot or the name of the bank which was responsible for its manufacture.
2) The place sometimes inscribed is the county, district, prefecture or province.
3) The date inscribed is normally only the year or period and not the complete date.
4) Some ingots name the use for which the ingot was cast, such as land tax, salt tax, sales tax, or customs duty.
5) The name of the kind of ingot is sometimes inscribed.
6) The weight standard is seldom stated.
7) The weight is also seldom recorded on the ingot.
8) The fineness also was seldom recorded on the ingot.
9) The assay marks were normally added after the manufacture.
10) Many small ingots have a single character that means good luck. These were presentation types for birthdays and similar happy occasions.

There are 11 main categories of ingots:

1) *yuanbao* - ingot with raised ends, but also the generic term for sycee. There are three types:

dabao - big ingot, weight about 50 ounces; They were used in large scale bank & government transactions

zhongbao - 10 ounce ingots, produced only in north China

xiaobao - small ingots weighting five ounces or less

2) *yaoding* - waisted ingot.

3) *caoding* - oval trough ingot. There are two types:

Sichuan Province weighing five or 10 ounces and having rounded bases, Shaanxi Province weighing four ounces and having flat bases).

4) *yuanding* - hemispherical ingots. There are four types:

1) rimmed edge with a nipple in the center weighing five ounces,

2) rimmed edge flat in the center weighing 10 ounces,

3) rimless with a nipple in the center weighing five ounces,

4) rimless flat in the center weighing five ounces)

5) *xiaoke* - very small ingot There are three types:

Henan Province xiaoke, weighs less than three ounces with four or more side indentations;

Yunnan Province weighing three ounces or less; and oval-shaped and cast in round-bases molds,

Beijing, Hebei Province ingot weighs less than three ounces, either oval or rectangular, made in flat-based molds.

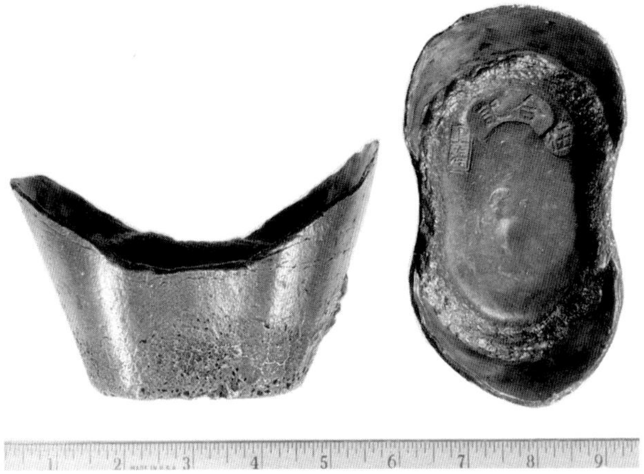

50 Tael Sycee - Yuanbao - Dabao

50 Tael Sycee - Yuanbao - Dabao

11 Tael Sycee - Yuanbao - Zhongbao

50 Tael Sycee - Yuanbao - Dabao

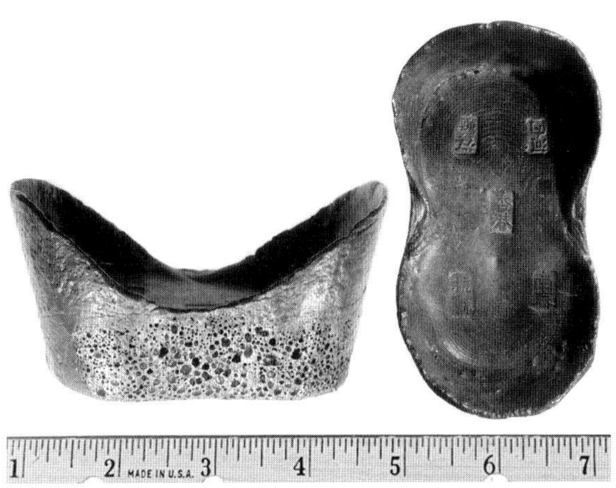

14 Tael Sycee - Yuanbao - Zhongbao

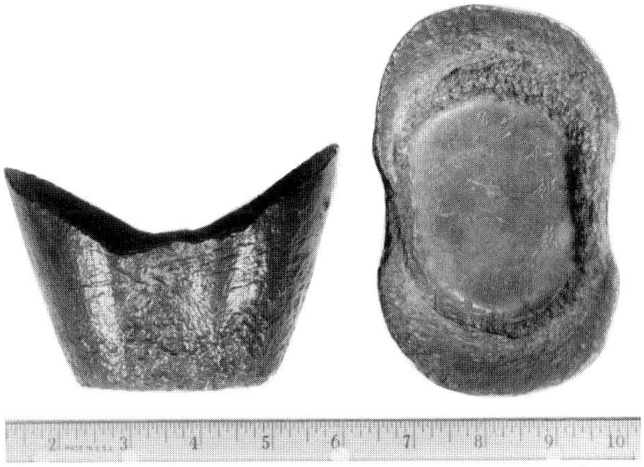

50 Tael Sycee - Yuanbao - Dabao - Local Tax Ingot

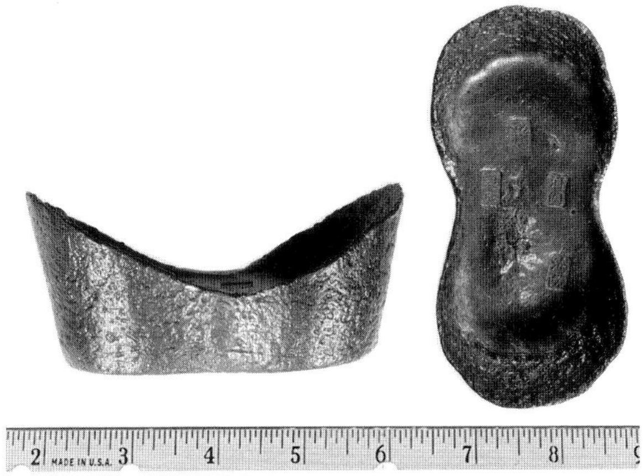

18 Tael Sycee - Yuanbao - Zhongbao

50 Tael Sycee - Yuanbao - Dabao

18 Tael Sycee - Yuanbao - Zhongbao

6) *fangding* - square ingot. There are two types:

fangcao - cast in a deep curved-based mold with indented sides and weighs 10 ounces,

fangbian - cast in flat-based mold and weighs 10 ounces or less with most weighing five ounces)

7) *yuanbing* - round cake-shaped ingot. There are two types:

single-sided

double-sided

8) *yuansi* - fine silk ingot. (All are of various shapes and have concentric ripple marks.)

9) *suiyin* - broken silver. Cut-up silver dollars and cut-up ingots were also used as money in the 18th & 19th centuries.

10) *yintiao* - silver bar. A Shanghai bank manufactured two kinds, and the Shanghai Mint (which was not established until the 1920s-1930s) manufactured one; all three are flat-based rectangular ingots. Their use is unknown.

11) gift ingot. Small ingots made in various shapes, do not appear to have served as money although most weigh about one ounce.

Most of the above information is from *Cribb's, A Catalog Of Sycee In The British Museum.*

In Yunnan Province the rectangular sycee evolved into the "packsaddle" or saddle sycee. The packsaddle (saddle) weighed five taels.

See bar money and pack saddle money. (See Krause & Mishler, and Mitchiner p 519-523)

10 Tael Sycee - Yuanbao - Zhongbao

9 Tael Sycee - Yuanbao - Zhongbao

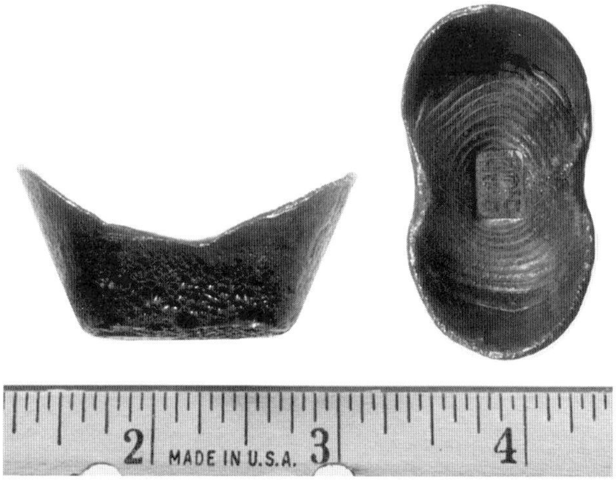

1 Tael Sycee - Yuanbao - Xiaobao

Burmese Sycee

19th century

Miniature version of the kettle-drum type of sycee called Shan, chocolate drop or snail sycee and are oval in shape. They were probably manufactured in the Bhamo region of the Sino-Burmese trade route. They have unusually fine concentric rings on the top surface. They are attributed to the Shan border states of Burma. Some have irregular small raised rims. A few have inscriptions on the top. Silver. 30 - 35 grams.

Kettledrum Sycee. 1874-1911

These 10-tael pieces are rounded hemispheres, usually with a raised rim and a raised nipple in the center. They were primarily used to pay taxes in Sichuan Province and are often found in Thailand. There are two repeated single columns of characters on the flat top. 300 - 400 gm.

1 Tael Sycee - Yuanbao - Xiaobao

Yaoding - Waisted Ingot

Yunnan Province Three-Stamp Remittance Ingot

Caoding - Sichuan Province Certified Ingot

Yunnan Province Single-Stamp Ingot - Fangbianding

Caoding - Sichuan Province Certified Ingot

Caoding - Sichuan Province Certified Ingot

Jiangsu Province Hump Ingot - Xiaoke

Caoding - Sichuan Province Certified Ingot

Yunnan Province Three-Stamp Ingot - Fangbianding

Yuansi - Fine Silk Oval Ingot

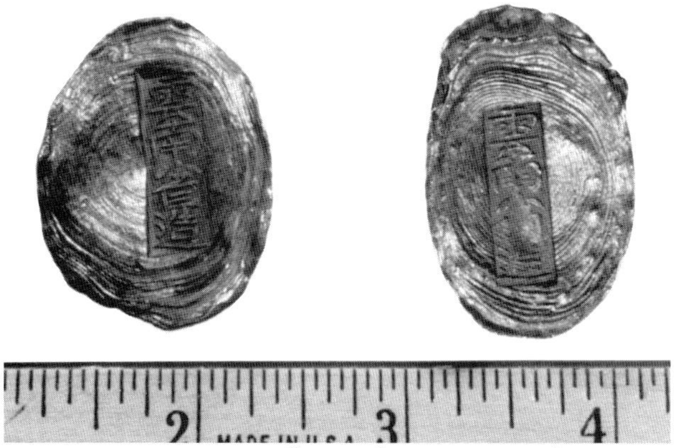

Yuansi - Fine Silk Oval Ingot - Single Stamp

Yintiao - Shanghai City Central Bank Bar

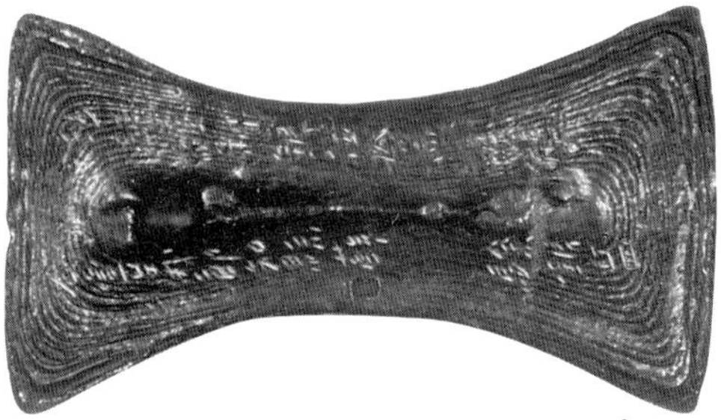

Song Or Yuan Dynasty 50 Tael Sycee

Yunnan Province Two-Stamp Ingot - Fangbianding

Yunnan Province Single-Stamp Ingot - Fangbianding

This Silver Sycee Was Casted In Capital-Lin An Fu Of Southern Song

TABU - Also called tambu - see tambu.

T SHAPED AXE - See Axe Money

TAFULIAE'

Malaita, Solomon Islands

There are at least five different kinds of tafuliae' with the number of strings, length and colors of shells varying by kind. The red-lipped *Spondylus*, white mollusk, and the black mussel are the three kinds of shells used to make the disks. The natives in 1964 could purchase these shell disks for 70 cents (five shillings) for a fathom length. The strings are each about eight, 10, or 12 feet long. The number of shell strings in a tafuliae' varied in some areas. Ten strings of red, black and white shell disks connected with spacer bars of wood or turtle-shell were the most common. Different areas also placed a different value on the various color disks. Most areas considered the red disks (*Romu*) to be the most valuable. Orange (*Faraga*) is next valuable with brown (*Kee*) and black (*Kakadu*) following. The smaller disks are also more valuable than the larger ones because the disks would also be thinner and therefore had more disks per inch. Formerly, a woman working full time could produce one *tafuliae'* in about one month. Modern technology has reduced this time to one half of what it was. Women could be hired for about $1 per day to work producing shell money. The making of shell money is normally done by the girls and women. They first break the shells into small circular pieces, about twice the size of the finished piece, with a black stone hammer called a *falbura*. Now solid metal cylinders are used to make the process faster. The *Romu* shell is at this time heated by placing the shell on very hot stones which turn the normally pink shells deeper red in color. The circular shells are then placed on a piece of wood called *ma-ai*, which has about 50 shallow circular depressions and is used to flatten the shell disks and make them smooth. The flat rectangular grinding stone used is called fou-*sava*. They then shape them and then drill the holes with a pump drill called *futa*. This drill had a flint or chalcedony tip, but now modern drills made of steel are used. You can tell if the hole is drilled with the old or new method by examining the hole to see if the walls of the hole are parallel and smooth. If they are the hole was made with a steel drill and is modern. If the hole tapers and is not even, it was made with a bow drill. After both sides of the shell are rubbed, the shell is the proper thickness. Then a hole is drilled in the center, and they are strung. The disks are strung on a strong bush fiber called *lili* in lengths of four to five feet and smoothed by the men with sand and water on a flat board with a grooved stone until they are the correct size and have the proper smoothness. The smoothing was formerly

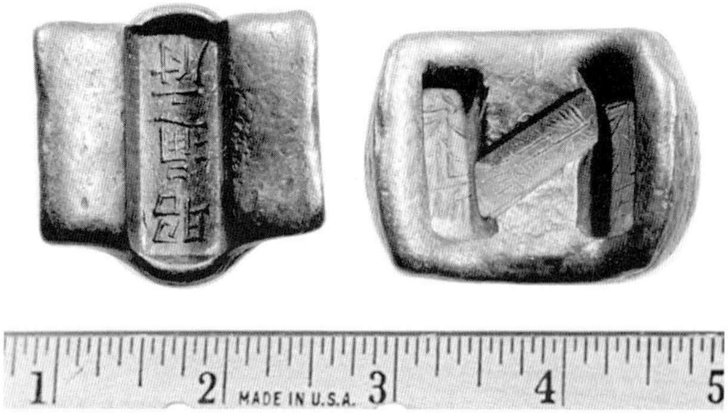

Yunnan Province Sycee

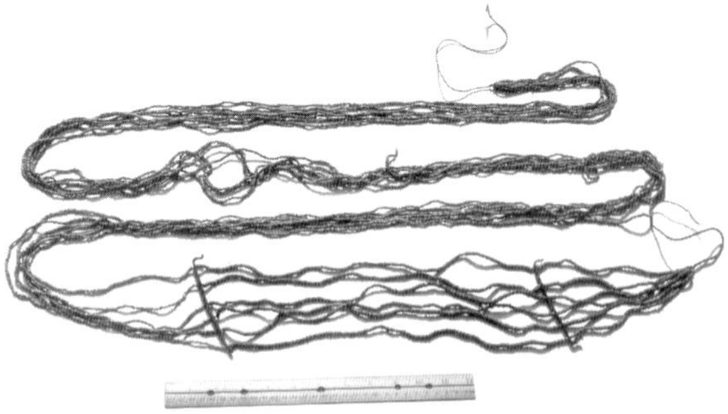

Tafuliae' - Made with stone tipped bow drill. Older and finer - notice the different style.

Tafuliae' made and collected in 1995 on Auki, Malaita Island

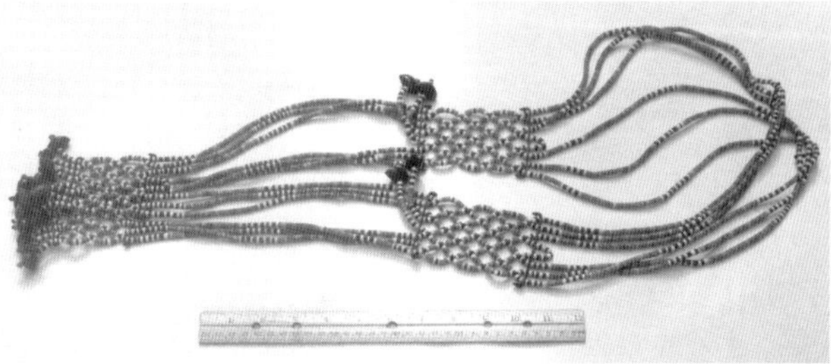

Tafuliae' made and collected in 1995 on Auki, Malaita Island

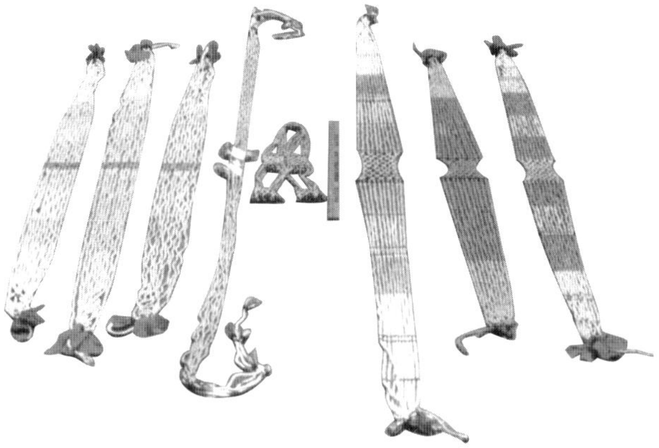

Tafuliae' showing the length and variety - Notice the yard stick in the center to show length.

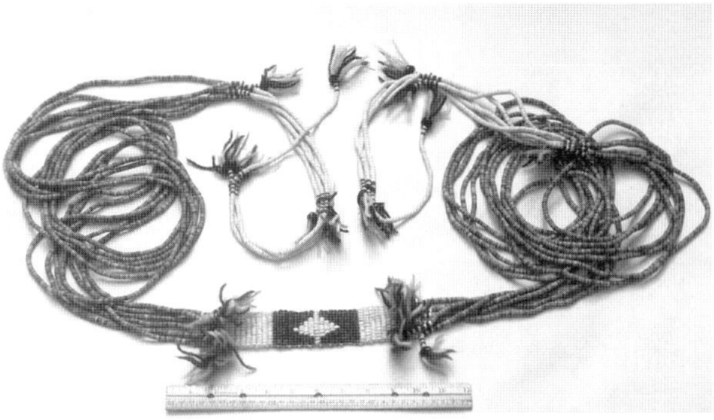

Tafuliae' made and collected in 1995 on Auki, Malaita Island. This variety was used only on Malaita.

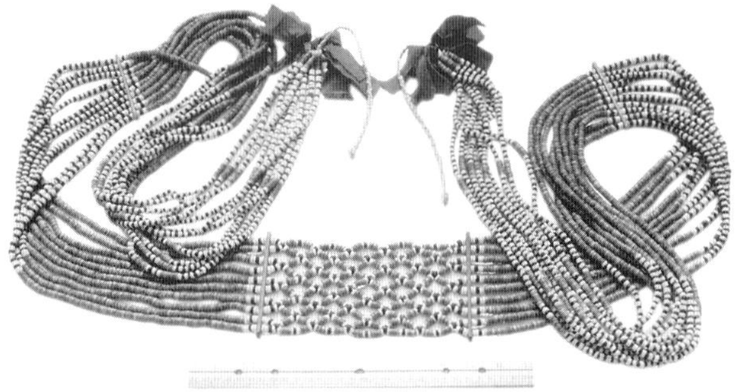

Tafuliae' made and collected in 1995 on Auki, Malaita Island. Note the weaving of strings in the center called Furai. The red cloth at the ends indicates the pieces could be used to prevent bloodshed.

done by rubbing them with a grooved stone called a *faoliara,* using sand and water. Now Chinese grinding blocks are used. Some of the smoothing of the shell edges is also done now in Honiara. The shell beads are then strung onto fiber strings with two or more wood or turtle-shell spacers used to hold the strings of shell beads so they do not bunch up. In the center of the most valuable types of tafuliae' there is a weaving of the strings, and it is called *Furai.* Old tafuliae' is not worth as much as new tafuliae'. It takes an old tafuliae' and cash to obtain one new tafuliae'. The old tafuliae' is then reground for use in the Bougainville market. In 1967 they were worth $10 Australian but it would vary. In the 1980s they had increased to $100 and up to $120. Each is now valued at $130 U.S. At one time a tafuliae' was worth one pig. At another time it took two tafuliae' to purchase one large pig. Both *tafuliae'* and *bani'au* are known as red money. In the 1950s a senior man received 38 contributions to his own marriage including 13 large red money, 23 smaller shell money units and two pigs, according to Burt. Formerly bride price varied from two to up to 100 tafuliae,' but in recent years the price is declining, with five to 10 tafuliae' being an average bride price. Tafuliae' were also used as the compensation payment for many transgressions, such as cutting a banana, ivory-nut or coconut tree; burning a house; trespassing on private land or house; slandering a woman; swearing at a pig; stepping over a woman's feet; and desecration of a burial ground. By the 1980s Burt points out that he had made 70 contributions toward the marriages of others. Bride price and feasting have declined in recent years. If a person feels he has been wronged, he will demand shell money or other goods as payment. Burt tells of a man who was killed in a brawl in 1990 in a suburb of Honiara, and compensation of 57 red money and $2,000 was negotiated as compensation for the death. If it had not been paid, there probably would have been another killing in retaliation. Shell money still serves this function. Tafuliae' are still sold in the general stores in Auki, Malaita Island. I personally purchased them there in 1995. Some were obtained directly from Laulasi Island, which is in the Langa Langa Lagoon off the coast of Malaita. It is an artificial island made in the 1600s. It has no soil for growing crops and most of the income earned by the natives comes from making shell money. They take the shell money to many of the other areas in the Solomons as well as Bougainville, which is in Papua New Guinea. At present most denominations of churches have limited the bride price to five tafuliae' (red money), and this has kept the network of exchanges without causing economic hardship on the young men. A few religions have banned bride price completely. They do not understand that bride price gives honor and legitimacy to a marriage.

Different areas use different kinds, but most all are made by the natives of Langa Langa lagoon on the western coast of the island of Malaita. At present many of the natives still use shell money to purchase brides, even as they use modern money in everyday business. Tradition still demands the use of shell money on many occasions. At present one tafuliae' of 10 strings 10 feet long would be worth one-three-year old pig. While in Honiara in 1995, my taxi driver told me he personally had used shell money to purchase his wife, and just two years ago his son had also used shell money to purchase his wife. One woman told us that just the previous day, there had been a wedding with much shell money, and because it was her niece who had gotten married, she received a porpoise tooth necklace as her compensation by the groom's family. (See Shell Money) (See Burt)

TAI GANDJA - See Earrings, Central Sulawesi, Indonesia

TAIL - See Elephant Tail Money, Giraffe Tail Hair Money, Zebra Hair Money

TAILPUN - See Turbo Shell

TAIJANA

Sulawesi, Indonesia

Ornaments made from gold or silver were used as bride price. Many of them represented the female sexual organs and were used as earrings. They are similar to the bela earrings of central Flores and loran earrings of the Moluccas.

TAJERE

Nigeria

Iron currency rods from the Fulani were made in many different shapes and styles. (See Eyo p.52) They were called *losol* by the Eastern Fulani and *tajere* by the Western Fulani. In 1934 they were worth a penny or less. They were used as currency and ultimately used for making hoes and other implements. (See Quinnin p. 87)

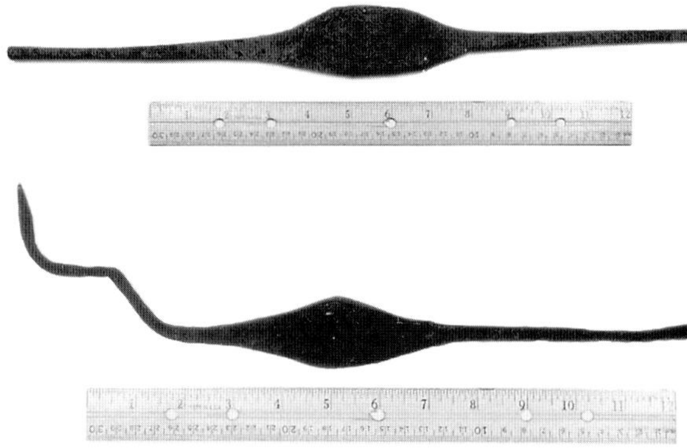

Tajere

TAKA

Flores, Indonesia

Low-carat gold, gilded silver, or silver pendants in this double-axhead shape were worn by men and women around the neck or on headbands. They were also used in bride price. Some have decorations on them. They are similar to the *marangga* chest ornaments except the loop at the joining of the two axehead shapes is not flattened like the *marangga*. (See Rodgers #104 & 105)

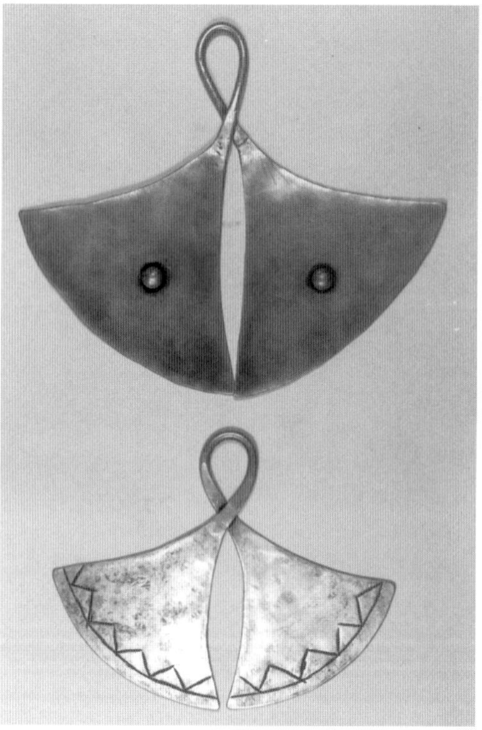

Taka - Silver

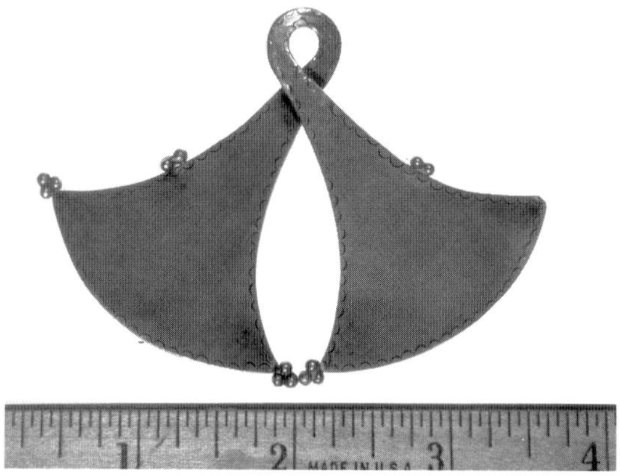

Taka - Low-Carat Gold

TAKULAKOLA - Decorated banana-leaf skirt. See Skirt

Taka - Flattened Loop

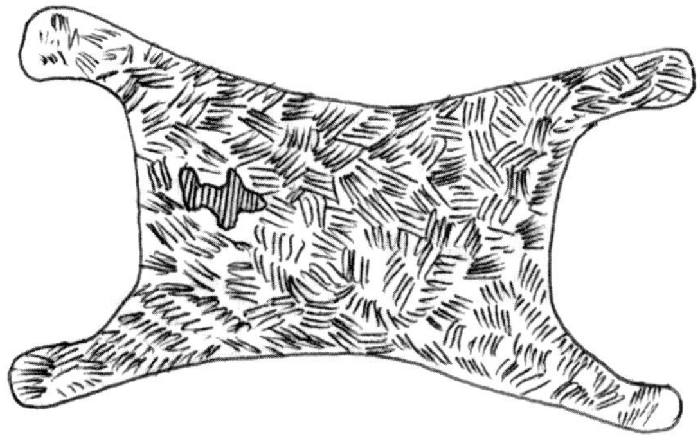

Talent

Tally Sticks

TALARI - See Maria Theresa dollar.

TALENT

England, Iron age

Copper currency bar in the shape of a flat copper plate resembling an ox hide. Weighs 11 ozs.

TALI

New Britain

A string of shell money almost identical to the *pele* of the Duke of York islands. It originated in New Ireland and Duke of York islands and was exchanged for nassa shells in the Nakanai area. The nassa shells were used to make *tambu.* (See Panoff p.7)

TALIBUM - See Green Snail Shell

TALINA

Gela (Florida) Solomon Islands

The *talina* consisted of 12 fathoms each of six red strings of shell disks. It was used like the *Talina Bariono.* See Talina Bariono

TALINA BARIONO

Gela (Florida) Solomon Islands

The *talina bariono* consisted of six fathoms each of six red strings of shell disks. The shells were located in the Gela Island area, but the Malaita people did the diving for the shells. The strings were always hard to obtain. Men would use them as blood money. The owner of the shell strings would say who he wanted killed and someone would kill that person for the shell money. Other ceremonial occasions also required the use of these shell strings. (See Davidson, "Traditional Money Association Newsletter," Vol. 1 Number 1.)

TALLY STICKS

China

Bronze sticks are believed to have been used in trade.

China

Bone or ivory sticks were valued at 50 cash each. Many of the sticks were only game pieces.

China

Lacquered bamboo tallies were carved and inked, or inscriptions were burned onto them. The tallies were issued in the 1890s and later by small banks or merchant associations that apparently were not accorded the privilege of issuing conventional banknotes. There are more than 75 different pieces. The left piece is from 1895 and is 200 cash, the middle is from 1928 and 200 cash, the right piece is from 1929 and is 1,000 cash. They are all from the Guang Shan (Kuang Shan) Bank of Suzhou, Jiangsu Province. (Information from Jim Anderson, Long Beach, CA.)

England, c. 1350 - 1850

Exchequer tally sticks were a medieval method of receipt. When money was paid into the Exchequer, a hazel stick was prepared on which notches were cut to indicate the sum as paid; other details were written on two sides of the stick, which was then split lengthwise through the notches. The pieces were retained in the Exchequer, and the second halves, or foils, were given to the person paying in the money. They could then circulate, claims being evidenced by the coincidence of the two halves. They were used by the Bank of England. The amount of money determined the amount of wood removed to represent the sum. A 1,000 pound amount was a straight indented notch the width of a man's hand (four inches), while 20 pounds was a V-shaped notch, according to Davies (p. 148). A debt owed to the king shown physically by the tally stick held by the Exchequer could be used by the king to pay someone else by transferring the tally stick to this third person. The stick could also be used to pay one's taxes, Davies states (p. 150). In 1830, William IV had the old tallies destroyed to make room in the Parliament buildings. (See Angell p. 87)

Europe, 1100 A.D.

A wand was split down the middle, and when a purchase was made, the two pieces were put together and notched with the customer and merchant each keeping a piece. When the customer had made purchases equaling one denar, the lowest-denomination coin, the customer would pay the merchant, and the customer would receive both pieces and promptly destroy the sticks. The wands were called *kerbholz*.

TAIK

Caroline Islands

Yellow or brown powder made from the root of curcuma was thought to possess protective and healing qualities. It was used to paint the body and was also a unit of account and circulated in cake form. (See Einzig p. 57)

TAMARIND SEEDS

Ceylon, Middle Ages

Used as money.

TAMBU

New Britain

Tiny *nassa* shells (*Nassa Camelus*), also known as dog-whelk, were strung on rattan. Shells must not touch each

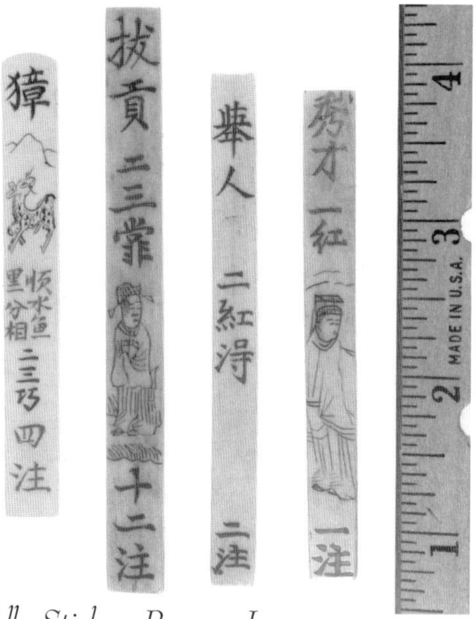

Tally Sticks - Bone or Ivory

Tally Sticks - Bamboo

English Tally Stick

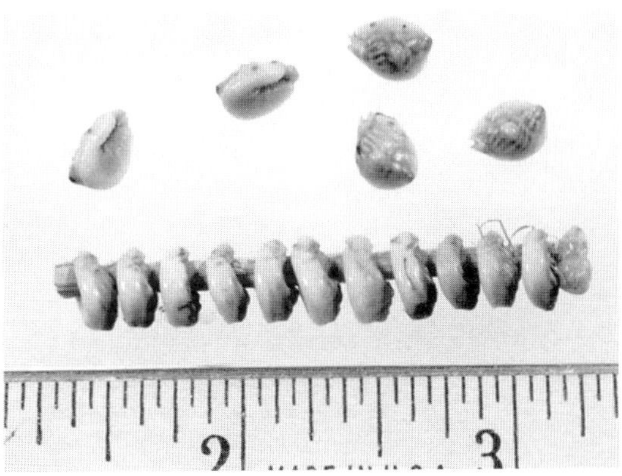

Tambu

other. The pieces of rattan are about two feet, six inches long and are spliced together to a length of 60 feet as the shells are strung on the rattan. The length of rattan is scraped or pared down to the required size, and then the shells are strung on the rattan. The *nassa* shells were collected along Blanche Bay and the north coast shores or traded from the west coast of the Gazelle Peninsula or the north coast of West New Britain and then traded to the Tolai living on the north coast of the Gazelle, according to Neumann. Before the shells can be strung on the rattan, a hole is punched through the backs of the shells. In the 1890s Europeans who wanted to obtain copra or coconuts from the Tolai had to purchase *tambu* from the Nakanai to trade as the Tolai would only accept *tambu*. A fathom of *tambu* was worth 120 coconuts. *Tambu* is still used by the Tolai people as money along with Australian currency. Two hundred yards are currently worth one large canoe. In 1878, 20 to 50 yards were worth one large canoe. In the 1890s it was the only medium of exchange among the Tolai. Today in some transactions among the Tolai, some goods and services can only be purchased with *tambu*. *Tambu* can be gotten by selling garden produce or performing tasks that are paid in *tambu*, according to Neumann. Fines and compensation for the mediators are still paid in *tambu*. Since the 1880s inflation in the value of *tambu* has been 200 to 300 percent. Parkinson stated that in 1887, the bride price was 50 to 100 fathoms of *tambu*, and food and other items were less than one half the price now charged. Now bride price is 100 fathoms of *tambu*. The groom's family pays the *tambu* to the bride's family. The actual amount and customs in the ceremony varies by area. At present time, the bride price that a groom who is not from the Tolai pays is considerably more, as much as 3,000 kina, for a Tolai bride. There is also more *tambu* now than at any time in the past. Large amounts of *tambu* were made after World War II with the war damages payments. In the 1960s there was another large increase in the supply of *tambu*. Neumann notes that during German times a fathom of *tambu* equaled two marks, and in 1960 it equaled 10 shillings. When rolled into a coil, it sometimes contains a mile of tambu which cannot be used for everyday purchases. Most rolls contain from 60 fathoms to 400 or 500 fathoms. It is displayed at all festivals but carved up only at his funeral or at a ceremony he sponsors. Once the coil is carved up at one of these ceremonies, it is no longer thought of as ceremonial money, but only as trading money. At the funeral the *tambu* is given to all the people who attend the ceremony. The people then use the *tambu* they received to buy items they need. The children may use their distribution of *tambu* to purchase candy immediately. An average of 100 fathoms of *tambu* might be distributed at an average funeral ceremony. It is used by the Tolai on the Gazelle Peninsula of New Britain. The shells come from about 200 miles away. *Tambu* is used in bride price and compensation payments like mortuary payments and to pay for goods and services. It also purchases food and other items. In 1987, a fathom of *tambu* was worth two *kina*. At present, natives who have earned modern money working for foreigners buy themselves into Tolai life by converting some of their money to *tambu* so they can participate and be recognized by Tolai society. At present, when a person builds a new trade store or house or buys a new lawn mower, he or she invites neighbors to see it. They will bring *tambu* as a gift. It can be from one to as much as 10 fathoms of *tambu*. In total it could amount to 200 fathoms of *tambu*. The organizer then presents the guests with food. The organizer can also hold a *vuvuai* and give the guests items like axes, loincloths and spades. This would result in the organizer receiving *tambu* at a later time. Recently women have increased their ownership of *tambu*. In the 1960s modern money was used along with *tambu*. In the late 1800s a large salmon was worth 1/2 fathom of *tambu*, a pig from seven to 10 fathoms, a large canoe from 20 to 50 fathoms, a tomahawk from three to four fathoms, and a large fishing net from 40 to 50 fathoms of *tambu*. On the Duke of York Island, natives lend their *tambu* for an interest of 10 per cent. They do not really think of it as interest, but merely an expression of thanks for the favor. *Tambu* is also used to pay for damages inflicted during a war. If a life is taken, payment of 15 to 50 fathoms must be paid. Even wounds must be paid for. If the person later dies, and it is determined that the wound had anything to do with his death, the whole life must be paid for at that time, even if it is many years after the wound was inflicted. *Tambu* was divided into several standard unit lengths.The pindik (15-20 cm.), the peapar (1 m.), the pokono (one fathom), the rip or skein (20 m.), and the lolo, gogo or coil (100 to 1,000 fathoms). The skeins and coils are used only for ceremonial purposes, while the other units are used in everyday purchases. It was believed that when a coil was made, magic was put into the coil, and it would be dangerous to break up a coil before your death. On New Ireland, *tambu* is called *diwarra.* (see Neumann)

Papua New Guinea, Mount Hagen

A string of *tambu* shells about seven inches long is a basic unit of value and traded as such. They are frequently worn as necklaces and bracelets. (See Gitlow p.77-78)

Vitiaz Strait

There are five types of shell valuables: 1) headbands called *matin,* 2) belts called *bukawa,* which consist of rows of nassa shell and dog teeth; 3) a rectangular piece of coconut bast or new burlap about eight inches by 10 inches, covered with rows of nassa shells; sometimes there is an open area covered with blue, yellow or green paint; larger ones are made of two pieces sewn together and called *kinsa;* they have tie strings and are worn suspended from the waist in front, on the buttocks, under either arm or on the forehead; 4) string or span of *tambu* shell used formerly as an important article of exchange; at present the strings are not important as a trade item; and 5) wicker armlets covered with nassa shells. (See Harding p. 52)

TAMBUA - See Whale Tooth

TAMLUNG - See K'a k'im

TAMPANG

Malay

Sugar-loaf shaped tin ingots were called *tampang.* The tampang shape was the oldest with the pyramid or "pagoda" shape coming later. All these ingots were money and were the staple metal product of the peninsula. (See Quiggin p. 253)

TAN - See Feather Coil - Santa Cruz

TAPA CLOTH

Fiji, Oro Province, Samoa, Tikopia, Banyoro Tribe in Africa

Tapa cloth was made from pounded mulberry bark printed with geometric designs drawn with vegetable dyes. Strips of the inner bark of the mulberry tree where pieced together with the natural glue of the inner bark and from a plant. The resulting material is beaten by the women in many different manners. The cloth is then dried and dyed and decorated in brown, yellow, and red. The cloth has been made for thousands of years. It represented wealth and is used in present-giving and bride price and as a symbol of chiefs. Bark cloth was a unit of exchange and used in exchange on several islands, including Samoa. Fiji exchanged its bark cloth to Tonga natives for canoes. On Fiji the value of the cloth increased if it had the purple stamp from the chief on it. Tonga also traded some of its bark cloth to Fiji for the purchase of wood. A small piece was worth one to two shillings, and a large piece was worth $5. In Samoa it is described as paper money. Cloth was worn or piled in the owner's hut. On Tikopia, exchange was done by quantity and not by quality. On Hawaii and the Wallis Islands, bark cloth was mainly used in gift exchange and not as a true form of money. The Marquesas Islands used it as money but only for tattooing the first-born son. The Tahitians used it as a unit of exchange and store of wealth. Their unit was a *ruru vehe,* which was a bundle 12 feet wide and 540 feet long, folded longitudinally, rolled up and wrapped in a piece of matting. The wealth of a chief was measured in the number of bales he had. On Tikopia, tapa is made in strips and squares. It takes about 10 days to make it, and it is used for clothing and in sacred ritual. There are different kinds for the different uses. It is used as money to pay for the services of experts and for such things as cutting trees for a canoe. (See Quiggin p. 111) (See Firth p.252-378)

TAPSOKA

New Hanover, New Ireland, New Britain

Strings of shells (*Chama Pacifica Imbricata*) are the most valuable kind of money in New Ireland. Boys dive for the shells which are broken up and ground down by the women into small thin disks. The men perforate the disks with stone points or nails. The disks are baked on stones to improve the color. Five strings of the best kind were the average price of a woman, and six to seven were worth a pig. That means a pig would be worth 5,000 to 6,500 disks. The strings consisted of alternating stretches of white and red shell disks. They were made on several small islands off the coast of New Hanover. *Tapsoka* was

Tapa Cloth

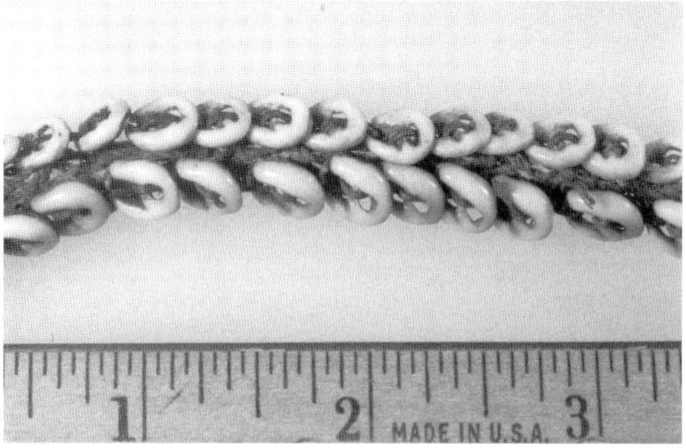

Tautau

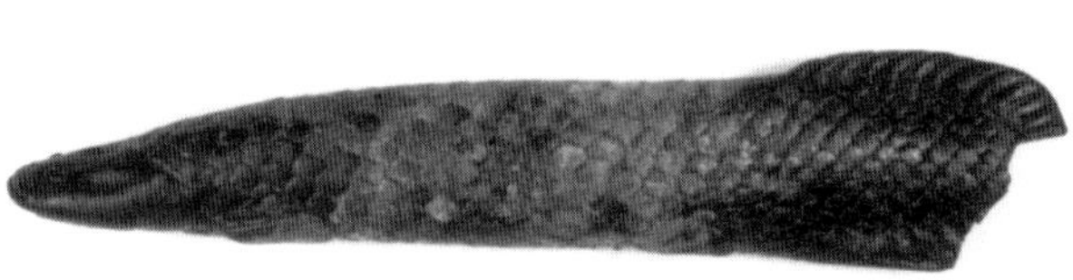

Tea Money - Animals

also called *lolat* and *telenai*. Typical *tapsoka* contains alternate areas of red and white shells also have considerable areas of brown. The brown disks are not as valuable as the red disks. (See Quiggin p. 157) (See Lewis)

TARKOLA

New Georgia

Breast ornament made from shell ring with turtle shell back and porpoise teeth decoration were used as money by the chiefs. It is also called *mbakiha*. See Mbakiha (See Waite 1983 p. 32)

TARNEIH - See Tin ring money

TAU - See Feather Coil

TAUS - See Shield, Canada

TAUTAU

Papua New Guinea

Tautau is the method of attaching Nassa shells to a rope. It makes the nassa shells lie flat and slightly overlap. The method is also used for attaching cowry shells. (See Quiggin p. 115)

TAVAU - See Feather Coil - Santa Cruz

TEA MONEY

Brazilian Guarana

A bitter tea is made from the guarana plant cultivated near Manuas . It is ground up and mixed with coloring and formed into animals, beads, fish, reptiles and other shapes. Figures are made by the local townspeople for the Indians nearby. (See Schulman May 6, 1974, catalog)

China, Mongolia, Tibet, Burma, and parts of Russia, 19th century to recently

The tea is formed into bricks weighing 2 1/2 to 5 pounds. Various grades and sizes are known. Value depends upon quantity available, distance from the market and the quality of the tea. Bricks are made by drying the tea in the sun, beating it with sticks on hot plates to break up the tea, and sifting and steaming over boiling water, then pressing it into molds. A little soot was added to the poorer-quality tea to give it a richer color. About 1850 the Russians began buying tea at Hankou, the great commercial center of the interior of China. In 1861 the Russians opened their first factory to make brick tea in Hankou. They pressed the tea like the Chinese did in a huge lever press, which was similar to a wine press. In 1878 the hydraulic press came into use. Initially odd lots of tea dust were used, but later better-quality tea was used, and the value of the tea brick increased to equal the uncompressed tea. From 1891 to 1901, the Russians developed the brick tea manufacturing in Jiujiang. In the 1870s the Russians produced the tea bricks in Fuzhou. At about that same time, three British firms also started to make tea bricks in Foochow. In 1879, the output in this city was 13,700,000 pounds of tea. In 1891 the Russians moved the manufacturing to Kiukiang. In 1918, the Russians stopped buying tea, and many of the firms stopped production. Some of the better known firms were: A. Goobkin; A. Kooznetzoff & Co.; V. Vyssotzky & Co.; Tea Trading Co.; K. & S. Popoff Bros.; Vogan & Co.; D. J. Nakvasin & Co.; Molchanoff, Pechatnoff & Co., Ltd.; and S. W. Litvinoff & Co., Ltd. Several of these firms had modern factories for the manufacture of brick and tablet teas. The Chinese tea firm of Shin Shang Company owned a factory which made brick tea for Mongolia and Siberia. The French, Germans, Americans, and Chinese also had companies in Hankow to buy or broker tea. In Mongolia 12 to 15 bricks of tea bought a sheep. Some bricks were painted on the design side. In Tibet, wages were paid to laborers and servants in bricks of tea. 20 bricks were worth a horse; 120 to 150 were worth a camel. The bricks of good quality tea weighed 2 1/2 pounds and sold for 10 annas at Tachienlu, one rupee at Batang, and two or more at Lhassa. The poor-quality tea was called wood tea, and that brick weighed five pounds and was worth 12 annas six pies at Tachienlu or one rupee at Batang. The brick tea used in Russia is very high quality, while the brick tea in Tibet is very poor quality. In South China, some tea bricks were made with the leaves, leaf buds and stems all mixed with aromatic herbs, blood and/or yak dung and placed in molds. About the turn of the 20th century, five different grades of bricks were recognized in China, Mongolia, and Tibet. The top-quality brick contained only fermented tea leaves with a nice dark brown color. The lowest grade contained mostly prunings, wood chips, twigs and soot for color. Communist China started making tea bricks after 1949, which are currently available. They have a gateway with a star and trees on either side and 14 Chinese characters below. The top row in larger characters reads Zhongguo Chaye Gongsi (Chung-kuo Ch'a-yeh Kung-szu), meaning "China National Tea Corporation," the Chinese Communist state-owned tea monopoly. The lower row of smaller characters reads "Zhaoliqiao Zhuancha Chang Zhizao (Chao-li-ch'iao Chuan-ch'a Ch'ang Chih-tsao)", meaning "Made by the Zhaoliqiao Brick Tea Factory." Zhaoliqiao is a town in the extreme southeastern Hubei Province on the border with Hunan Province. The design has five five-pointed stars across the top. The first three characters on the right are the name of the town where the brick was made. Several names appear; only Zhaoliqiao (Chao-li-ch'iao) is now used on the currently made bricks, the

Tea Money - China/Sinkiang

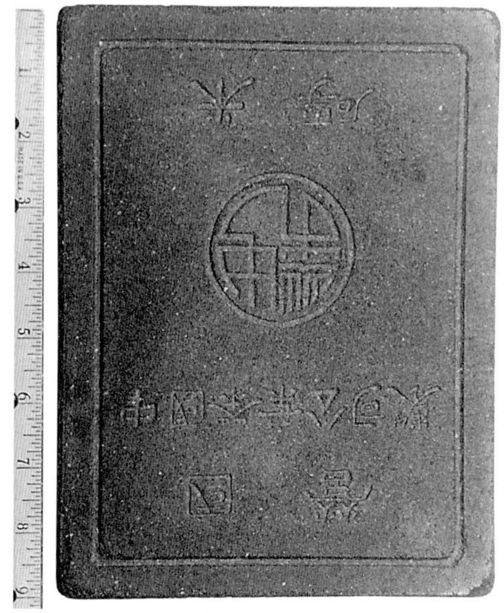

Tea Money - China

Tea Money - China

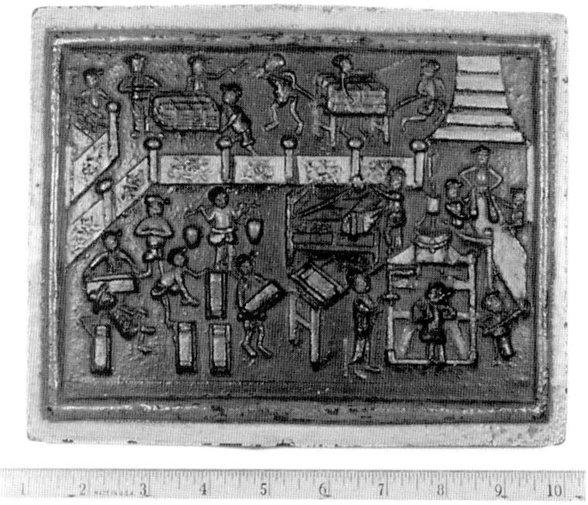

Tea Money - Mongolia - Painted

Tibet Tea Money

Tea Money

Chinese Tea Money - Modern

Tea Money

manufacturing of which has been moved from the Southern Hubei Province town to Shanghai, but the name has been retained. Older bricks with the identical design except for the factory name Yangloudong (Yang-lou-tung), have the back divided into 16 sections. Just prior to Red China invading Tibet, China bought up all of the brick tea available on the market to disrupt Tibet's monetary exchange with foreign trade. (See Dodson p. 53) (See Mitchiner p. 535)

Tea Money

TEE - CEREMONY

Enga tribe, Papua New Guinea

The *tee* ceremony is an exchange system similar to the *moka*. It starts with a solitary gift which has to be returned with pigs; the whole system builds from there. It is also called *te*. It is held in the Eastern parts of the Highlands, while the *moka* exchange is held in the Western Highlands. The *te* is a major ceremonial exchange of the Enga people. It is the only occasion when outstanding debts of all types can be repaid. The backbone is formed by chains of partners called *tee akali*. Some chains are very long, while others are shorter. The kina shell is a very important part of the *tee*, and it is mounted on a plaque of hardened resin and rubbed with red ochre. A cord is hung from the top of the plaque. The whole unit is called a *kina moka*. In recent times the plaque is made from plywood or a hardened form of cardboard. Other kina shells are fastened with woven fiber or bamboo and worn as necklaces. The basic structure of *saandi pingi* is always the same. Pigs from individuals' houses move up the *tee* line step by step between pairs of partners until they are withdrawn. Men solicit *saandi* to take brides and make other obligatory payments. There are many rules for payments and what they mean. The *tee* cycle consists of a four-year cycle of three phases: the first, during which initiatory gifts progress in a given direction; the second, during which the main gifts travel in the opposite direction; and the third, during which return gifts come back in the original direction. The initiatory gifts are many things, including small pigs, pork, packages of salt, well-made stone axes, shells, gold lip shell (kina), bailer pendants, plumes of cassowary and bird of paradise feathers, as well as cowry headbands, necklaces and, more recently, steel axes. Occasionally, tree-climbing kangaroos are also used. When the first group feels they have given enough, they call in their credits. A ceremony is then held in which about half the pigs they are holding are killed, cooked and distributed to their pig creditors. One "side" of pork is payment for one pig. At these ceremonies, 2,000 to 3,000 people can attend, and from 100 to 500 pigs will be disbursed. All pigs given in the *tee* are not killed; only about half are needed to satisfy all claims. Pigs are the focus of the

Tea Money - Mongolia

Tea Money

Tea Money - Mongolia

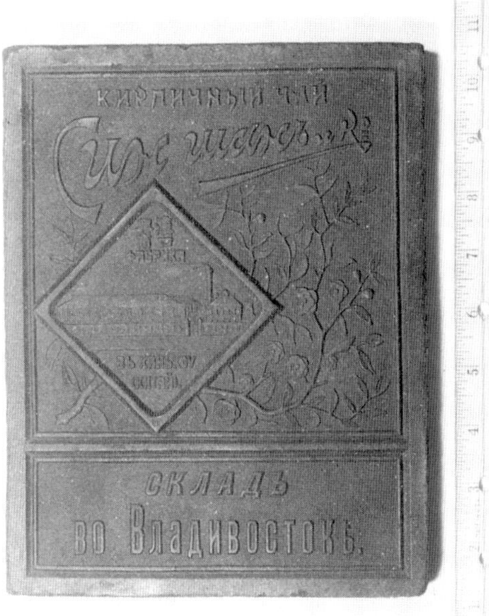

Tea Money

Russian Tea Money

Tea Money

Tea Money - China/Sinkiang

Tea Money

Tea Money

entire *tee* system. Pearl shells, a small number of cassowaries, and other valuables are also disbursed. The Tombema *tee* valuables are pigs, cassowaries, mother-of-pearl shell, bailer shell, *nassa* shell, cowry necklace, *conus* shell, green snail shell, tree oil, stone axes, cassowary feather headdresses, bird of paradise feathers, black palm, tree fruit, modern spinning yarn, ash salt, steel axes, spades and shovels. People try to participate in as many *tee* transactions as possible so that through time their credits will exceed their debts. Many people are not directly in the *te* ceremony, but participate through group payments of bride price and compensation for homicide or death. At the start of the process when the men believe they have enough gifts to pay their debts, they signal the next in line until the signal reaches the end of the network. Then each clan in succession stages an elaborate ceremony to distribute the pigs to the visiting creditors. The receiving clan adds these pigs to the ones they already have and sets aside about 1/8 of their pigs for breeding and use. The remainder are then given at their distribution and this continues until all the clans in the network have had their distribution. Sometimes cassowaries and pearl shells are also given. It takes six to nine months to complete this phase of the *te*. All these items are considered money.

For the Laiapu, the exchange of shells forms the backbone of the *tee*, while the Mae see the shells as an extra gift placed on top of the pigs by Big Men. The actual transactions are made by agents who have built a good reputation or have maintained the good reputation their fathers had built. The ceremony primarily has social and political implications but also provides a means of circulating valuables over the area. *Tee* roads can only be created by women because where the women go in marriage is where the pigs will later go in the *tee*. The women provide the ultimate sanctions of *tee* partnerships.

The ceremony begins at 10 a.m. and might last until 5 p.m. First the pigs are presented, the donor calls out the name of the recipient, and the recipient takes away the pig. Then the cassowaries are handed over. Usually, because of their high value, only about six birds are handed over. Then come the ceremonial stone axes, kina shells and money. The kina shells are also distributed as *kina moka* (see *kina moka*).The money is in the form of bank notes attached to a pole about 20 feet long. Many times K100 in bank notes will be attached to the pole. Recent ceremonies have been lavish, with more than $80,000 in pigs alone being distributed in one ceremony in 1978. The period leading up to and including the ceremony could last for several months, during which the participants do very little if any work.

Russian Tea Money

Tea Money

The greenstone axe similar to the Mount Hagen axe was used in the ceremony. Cowry shell necklaces valued at one pig and normally about 24 inches long were also used. A *nassa* shell forehead band, called *angala lenge* by the Enga, was also used. It was valued at one cassowary and was covered with *nassa* shells in overlap fashion with a thin strip in the center of the band not having any shells on it. A small piece of opossum skin is also attached. A long nassa shell necklace, worn only by the women, was valued at one smaller pig. It was about 10 feet long and was made up of a single row of nassa shells strung overlap fashion to a narrow strip of plaited native twine.

When an old man dies or becomes senile, his son inherits his father's network in the *tee*. Success in the *te* requires the work of women. A man cannot go very far without the labor of wives. Women cannot by themselves participate in the *tee* ceremony. During *tee* festivals, leaders in the clan compete to see who can give out the most pigs. All transactions are carried out individually, but the total amount of wealth given out by a clan enhances the clan's prestige. The whole ceremony and cycle is extremely complex. (See Davidson, Traditional Money Association Newsletter Vol. 1 Number 2.)

Tekaroro

Teke Necklace

Tema

TEETH - See the following: Bat Teeth, Boar Teeth, Cuscus Teeth, Dog Teeth, Dugong Teeth, Elephant Teeth, Elk Teeth, Fish Teeth, Flying Fox Teeth, Hippo Teeth, Human Teeth, Leopard Teeth, Opossum Teeth, Porpoise Teeth, Sperm Whale Teeth, Walrus Teeth, WhaleTeeth

TEKARORO

Gilbert Islands

Alternating white and black disks strung on fiber were used as money. White disks (conus shells) and black disks (coconut shell) form the money. 1/8" - 3/4" diameter. (See Quiggin p. 140)

TEKE NECKLACE

Congo, Africa

Chief's collar of brass decorated on one flat side of the ring. There is a cut with a small space to put on and take off the ring. It is highly incised with varied complex motifs and has alternating rectangular tabs on the outer edge of the ring. It is more a sign of wealth than a circulating medium of exchange and was worn by chiefs. (picture of piece on a chief, Zirngibl p. 97)

TEKE - See mitako

TEMA

Santa Cruz Island, Solomon Islands

Tridacna clam shell breast plates with a turtle-shell decoration in a stick form symmetrically arranged extending from the center of the circular shell disk to the top edge were used as money. (See Waite 1983 p. 96)

TEMO

Africa, Angola

The most common hoe in this area was oval and angled rather than flat across. (See Kriger p. 103.)

TEMOTU - See Feather Coil - Santa Cruz

TETITI SHELL BELT

Torres Island

Snail shells bound on cane were used as money. (See Quiggin p. 164)

THIMBLES

North America

Indians used thimbles as dangles on their clothes. They were popular trading items but not a unit of measure or large store of value. The French thimbles were made of silver, gilded copper, brass, and gold. Many had a hole in them through which a thread was placed with a piece of wampum attached at the end. This formed a tinkler which represented the thunder being who could chase evil spirits away. (See Quiggin p. 299, Hamilton p. 128)

THROWING KNIFE

African metal currencies in general fall into three groups. The first includes items where the distinction between their utilitarian use and money use is minor. Many of these items, such as spears, axeheads, anklets, hoe blades, daggers, and bangles, can function as money as well still having their practical use. These items are hardest to determine if they are money. The second group of items sometimes retain their original shape, but the material will change. Copper or brass might replace iron in the blade. Ivory or iron might replace the wood handle. Others in this group change their shape by having finals of various shapes added so the item cannot, for practical purposes, function in a practical manner. The blade might be made too thin to be useful, or the edge might be dulled. The third group is shaped in such a form as to have lost all form of practically for use in a utilitarian manner. These items have a standardized weight and size so they will have the same value but will serve strictly as money. The lines between these three groups are fuzzy, and experts will not always agree on which group a particular item falls.

The knives were made in many shapes and styles. They were all from the north central area of Africa that includes Cameroon, Equatorial Guinea, Central African Republic, Cabinda, Sao Tome, Uganda, Gabon, Republic of Congo, and parts of Zaire, Rwanda, Sudan, Chad, Niger, Nigeria, and Tanzania. They were considered a store of value, a standard of value, a token of wealth, a treasured heirloom, and were used in bride price. Spring (p. 77 - 78) suggests that most throwing knives (*kpinga*) were never actually thrown, even though they are in a shape to be thrown. Before the widespread introduction of imported scrap metal in the 20th century, metal was an extremely valuable commodity in Africa. Many throwing knives were elaborately decorated to the point that they could no longer be used as weapons. There were two different types of throwing knives. The equestrian peoples of the Sahel, the grasslands which separate the deserts from the sub-Saharan forests, used a throwing knife with a very long handle. The short handle knives were used primarily by the forest dwelling peoples of the Zaire River basin. There are a number of exceptions to this general rule. There are five basic shapes of throwing-blades, and they are in the shape of the letters F (found in the north), Z (found in the eastern central region), Y (found in the southwestern central

Tema

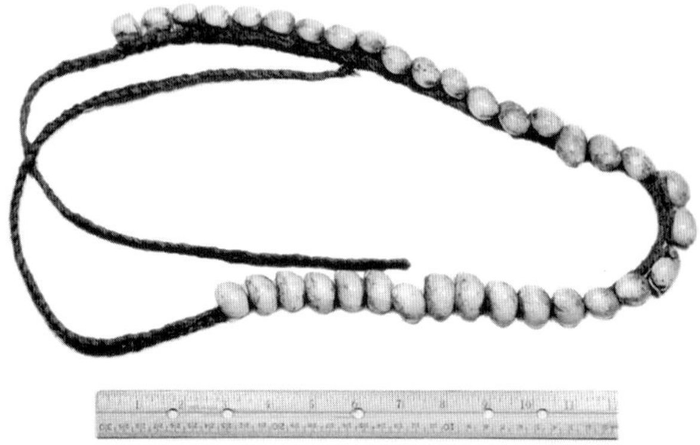

Tetiti Shell Belt

Thimble

A 

B 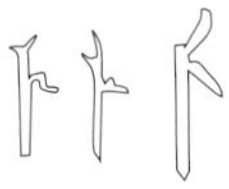

C 

D 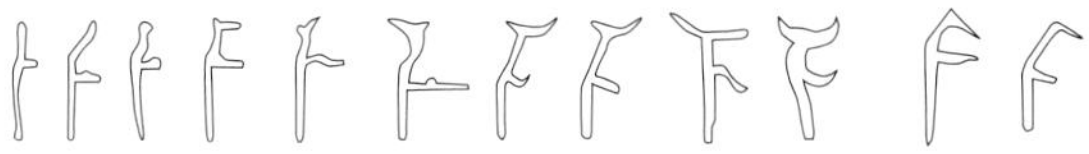

E 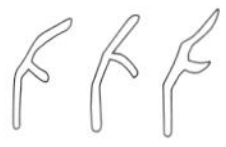

F 

G 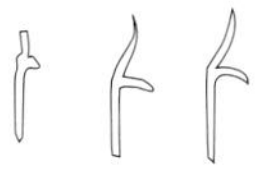

H 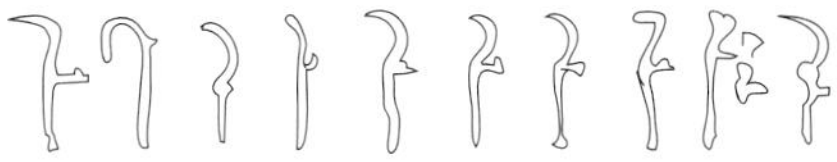

I 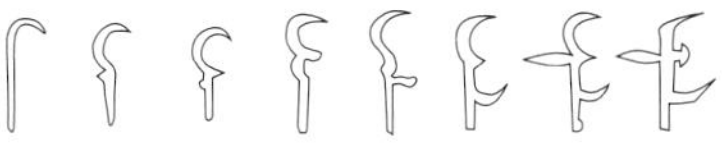

J 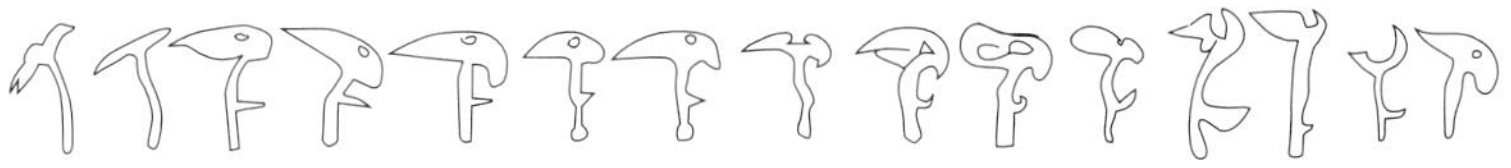

K 

L 

M 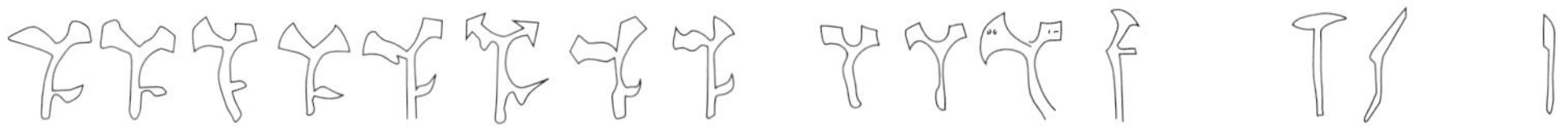

N 

O 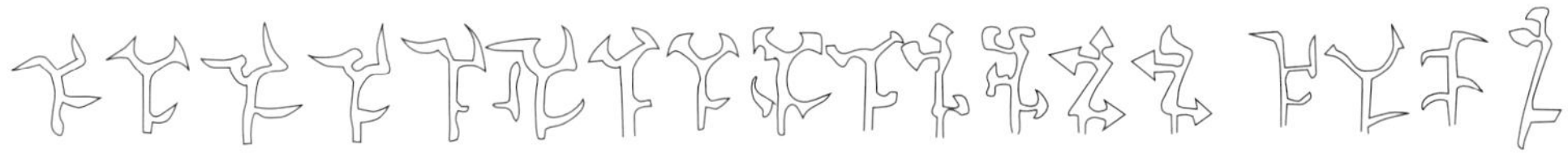

P 

Q 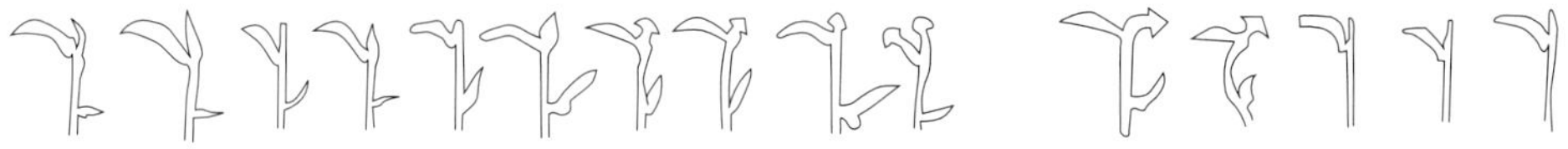

R 

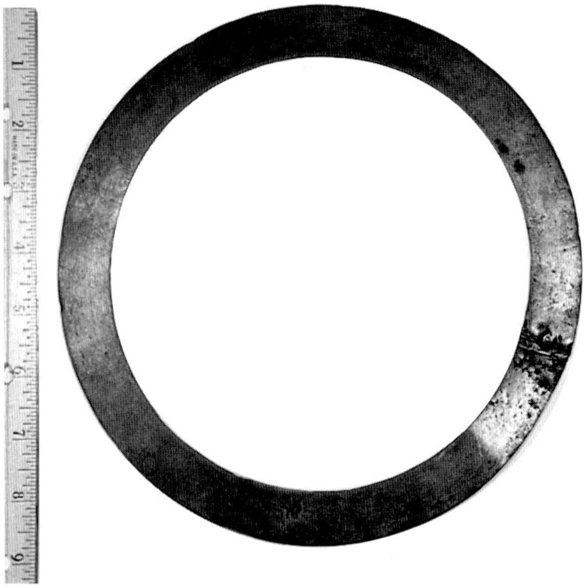

Round Iron Throwing Knife

Azande Throwing Knife

Throwing Knife

Azande Throwing Knife

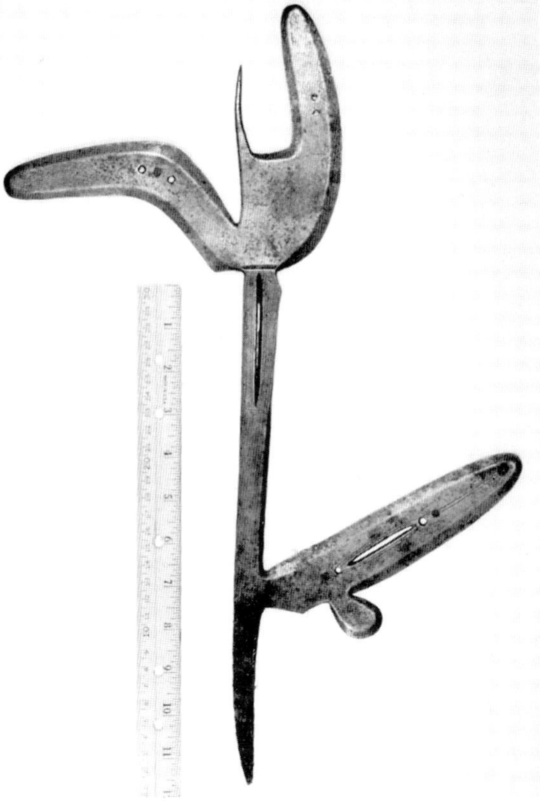

Azande Throwing Knife

Bangi Throwing Knife

Throwing Knife - Bwaka

Throwing Knife - Bwaka

region), E (found in the central region), and I (found in the southwest), as defined by Felix (p. 15). The big F blades are found in open country, while the smaller winged types are found in wooded country. Felix feels these forms have been in use for centuries. Many of the throwing knives were owned by the chief, considered part of the treasury and were articles of ritual and social importance as well as signs of wealth. Most were traded and commonly used as currency for barter, for settlement of debts, or as wedding payments, according to Felix (p. 38). He said that "some very elaborate examples have handles made of wood or ivory and were used exclusively as currency or for show. " He felt this way because it is thought that with these handles the blades could not be thrown and therefore could only be used as money. Felix and Westerdijk describe in their books 14 stylistic provinces and show maps that cover those areas. Throwing knives were known by different names in different areas. The Zande called them *gangoo;* the Bongo called them *mokoongo*; the Kreich called them *pere*; the Zande also called the best throwing knives *kpinga* or *kipinga*; the Banda called them onto; the Ngbaka-Mabo called them *ndo*; the Ngbaka called them *za*; the Gbaya also called them *kpinga*; the Nzabi called the bird beak-shaped pieces *onzil*; the Mitsogho called them *ebasa*; and the Kuba called them *shongo*. The Nzakara and Ngbandi peoples from the fringes of the Zande empire used copper tribute blades. (See Spring p. 46) Generally the best throwing knives were made with native smelted iron, while the poorer knives were made from the dull scrap metal which cannot be burnished the same way. (See Spring p. 74) It took two to four throwing knives to buy a goat, six to eight to buy a slave and up to 30 for bride price. Hurst states (p.12 Ngola) that throwing knives were exchanged as currency, given as rewards for fealty in combat, preserved as heirlooms, and placed on graves of the specially revered.

Ernest Thomas gives a very good chart of types of throwing knives. The following throwing knives are only a representative group of some of the many varities. See Ballarini, Felix, Fischer, Spring, Thomas, and Westerdijk.

Africa, Azande tribe

Their throwing knives were feared by their enemies. The knives were too valuable to throw and were only used to threaten the enemy. (See Fischer p. 56-59)

Africa, Bangi

This is a different kind of throwing knife with a wood handle. (See Fischer p. 100)

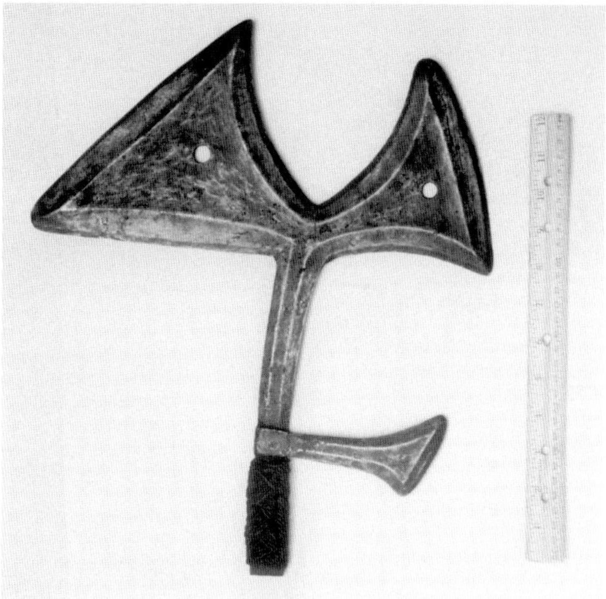

Throwing Knife - Bwaka

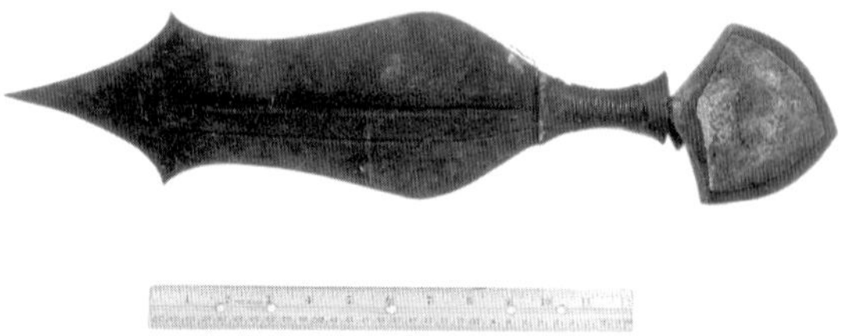

Stanley-Pool Knife

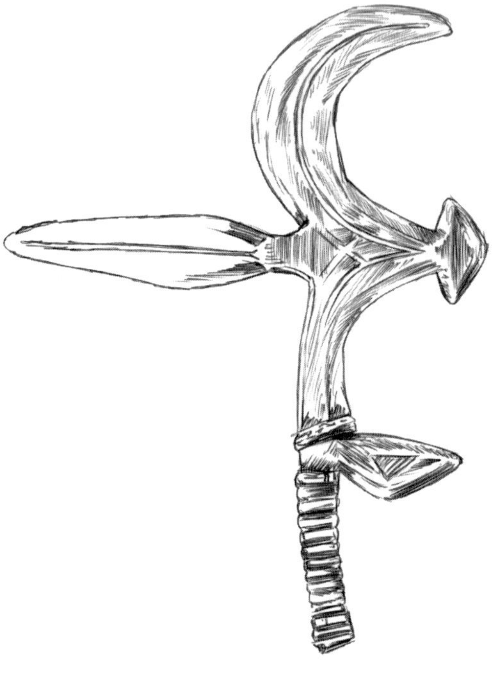

Throwing Knife - Ngbaka Tribe

Throwing Knife - Chad

Matakam Throwing Knife

Bird's Head Knife

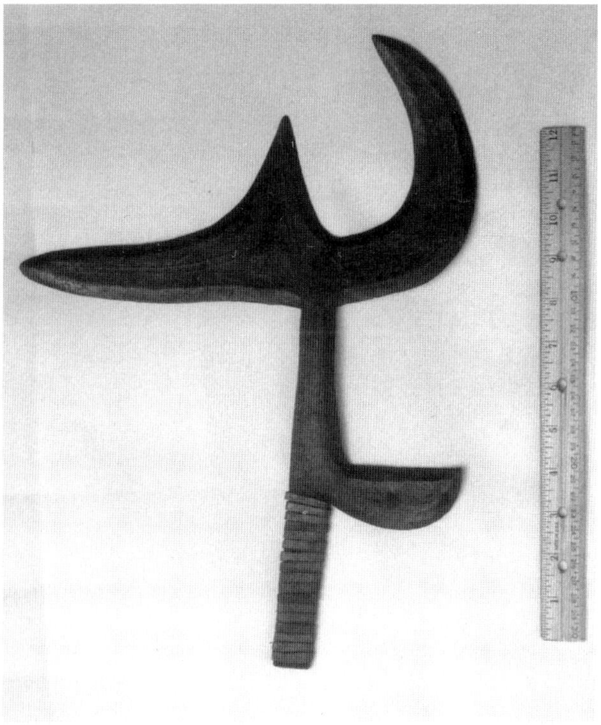

Throwing Knife - Ngombe

Throwing Knife - Sabre Sharp

Africa, Bwaka

The forged iron blade comes in several slightly different shapes. These throwing knives were also used as money. (See Fischer p. 91.)

Africa, Chad

The Potokwo tribe of eastern Lake Chad used this throwing knife. (See Fischer p. 27.)

Africa, Congo

Some Stanley-Pool knives were fitted with heavy steel butts and used as currency. The Mbole may have used them prior to their arrival in the Stanly-Pool area. See knife money - Mbole tribe

Africa, Congo

The various forms of throwing knives were "sabre" shaped and made of iron. (See Fischer p. 60-61.)

Africa, Gabon

The Fang used throwing knives as money and for bride price. A large throwing knife was worth 100 small throwing knives. The bird's head knife was also a throwing knife. (See Fischer p. 185-189)

Africa, Matakam tribe

This iron throwing knife is still used today as an ornament. (See Fischer p. 30)

Africa, Ngbaka tribe

This type of throwing knife was also used and made by neighboring groups like the Togbo, Banja and Ngbandi tribes. The knives were used in bride price and also as money in commercial transactions. This tribe used many other shapes of throwing knives. (See Ballarini p. 73)

Africa, Ngombe

The forged iron blade is engraved on the face and was originally called *ngwolo*. (See Ballarini p. 76-77.)

Africa, Ubangi, Central African Republic, Bubu, Banda Gbugbu, Mbugbu and Nzakkara tribe

The blades are made of very thin metal and are called *ngindza* or *guindza gbo*, which means money. They had no practical value except as money. Some have handles, and others probably never had handles. (See Quiggin p. 69-70) See Knife Money, Trumbash, Woshele

Africa, Zaire, Azande-Vongara

Kpinga is the name of this style of throwing knife. It was made of iron with a fiber handle. Like the other throwing knives, it also was used as money.

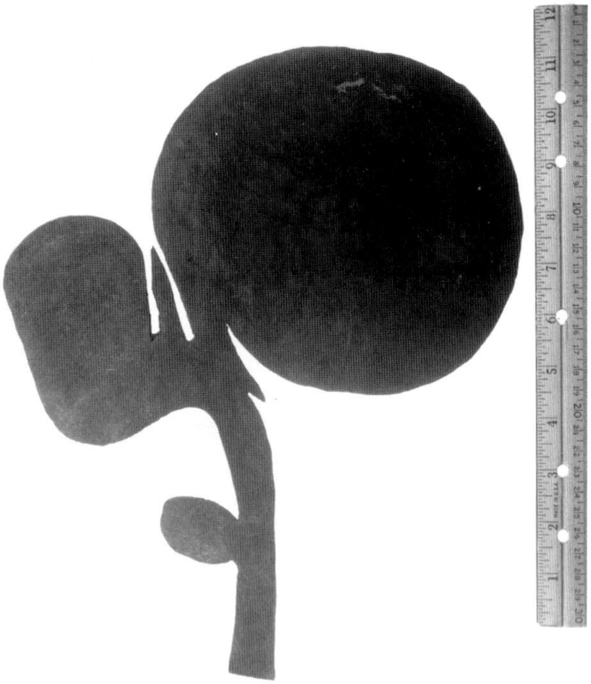

Bubu Throwing Knife

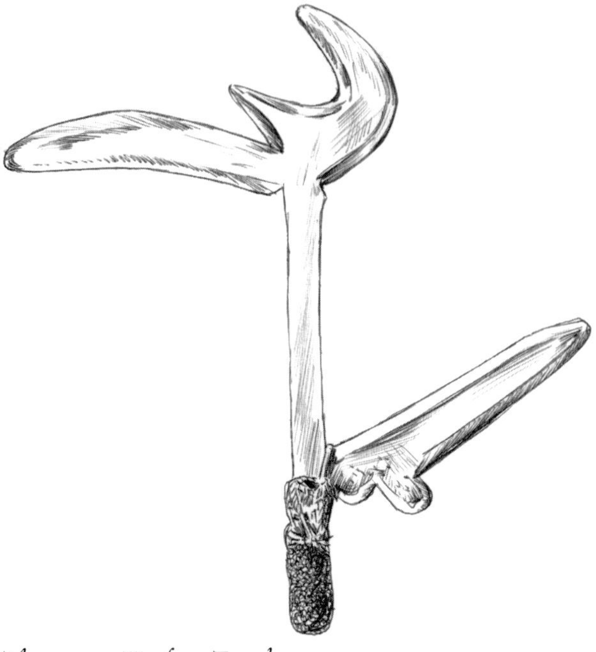

Throwing Knife - Zande

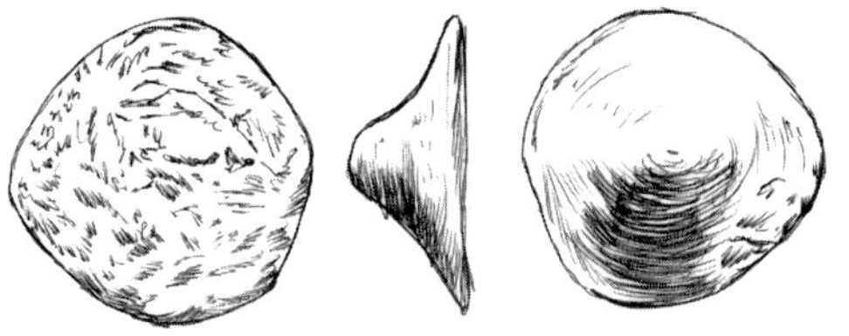

Tin Ingot Money

Pyramid Tin Ingot

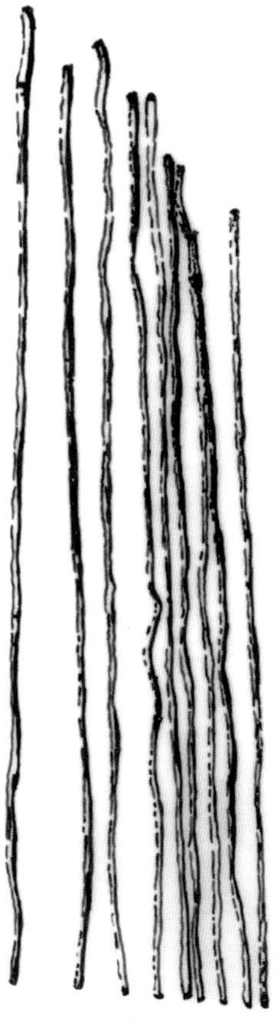

Tin Straw Money

Africa, Zande

The forged iron throwing knife has designs engraved on the face and was originally called *pinga*. (See Ballarini p. 83-84.) See ngbaka, pingha

TIGER TONGUE - See Lat

TIN ANIMAL MONEY - See Gambar

TIN MONEY

Navajo tribe, United States

Slip or tin money was the first money used by the trading posts in the Navajo area. (See Blue p. 11.)

TIN INGOT MONEY

Malaya, 13th - 19th centuries

During the 13th century, dome-shaped tin ingots probably started to be used as a medium of exchange. The ingots continued to be used after the flat coinage was introduced by the Malacca Sultanate (1403 - 1510). The tin was mined in Malaya. Conical ingots and shaped *gambars* were also used as currencies. (See Mitchiner p. 397 - 398)

Malacca, 16th century - 19th century

The tin ingot currency issued by Perak and Selangor come in six main types: 1) irregular mound-shaped ingots; 2) conical or cylindrical ingot;. 3) mountain-shaped fairly symmetric ingots - Chandi; 4) sugar-loaf-shaped solid ingot; 5) pyramid or pagoda ingot-Bidor, has ornamental designs on top of ingot with no or only a small bottom lip, many different designs and styles; 6) pyramid or pagoda, solid *Tampang* with a wide bottom lip. All are rare. See animal currency. (See Singh p. 173-174 & 179-189)

TIN RING MONEY

Africa

In El Fasher in Darfur tin rings, called *tarneih*, were the only currency in that area. (See Quiggin p. 94)

TIN STRAW MONEY

Nigeria

In the tin-producing area of Jos Plateau, casting was done by making a hole in the clay with a grass stalk. Molten tin was then poured into the hole after removing the grass stalk. The tin straws were used as money. See straw tin money.

TINETE

Solomon Islands

The least valuable kind of three different clam shell rings used as money and manufactured in the lagoons of New Georgia is called *tinete*. (See Hviding p. 93)

TINTOL - See shell money - Tanga

TIN FOIL MONEY - See Aluminum Foil Money

TIN HAT MONEY - See Hat Money

Malaya, 13th-19th centuries

Ingots of tin that look like flower money with a raised center were used as a medium of exchange in such tin mining kingdoms as Pahang. They were predecessors of tin hat money. They also developed into gambar, which are tin ingots shaped like canoes, frogs, crocodiles, and other animal shapes. (See Mitchiner p. 397-398.)

TINGLE DANGLE MONEY

China, c.700 B.C.

Bronze Qing (Ch'ing) or bridge money was cast as a flat, curved, bronze item, probably a miniature token representative of the larger musical instruments still used in certain parts of China, according to Ramsden (p. 30). There is no proof that they were used as money, but it is possible they served in trade or barter because of their high value. They are often decorated and usually holed at top for suspension. There are at least five different shapes, including one with dragon heads at the ends. (See Ramsden p. 29-32) Many odd & curious money collections contain these pieces.

Tingle Dangle Money

TINNAH - See Shield

TOBACCO

Tobacco in the leaf or stick form has served as money in many parts of the world from early times to the present. From its establishment in 1818 until the mid 1960s, the Maclin-Zimmer-McGill Tobacco Co. in Virginia was making Lord Beacoinsfield Native Twist Tobacco, which was used as money in parts of the Pacific.

Admiralty Islands

Tobacco sticks became a subsidiary currency upon contact with whites. They were not used in the official exchanges between bride and groom. (See Einzig p. 79)

Angola, 1850 - 1880

Coiled tobacco, about eight feet long, wrapped with fiber, and coiled and fastened together with pegs was used as money. Very rare.

Africa, Hottentots

The sticks were used in trade for oxen. The animal was valued at the number of sticks it takes to reach from the horns to the end of his tail. (See Einzig p. 170)

America, Colonial days

In 1619 tobacco became the legal tender in Virginia. A few years later farmers were buying mail order brides for 120 pounds of tobacco. Tobacco was valued at three shillings for a pound of the best grade and 18 pence a pound for lower-grade tobacco. By 1645 that same pound of the best tobacco was worth only 1 1/2 pence due to over-production. Tobacco warehouses were set up to receive and issue receipts for tobacco, which then circulated as money. These receipts were used as money until the late 1700s. Trading with the Indians was also done with tobacco until the Hudson Bay blanket established itself as the main standard of value. One "made beaver", which was the standard of value with the Indians, and was worth three quarters of a pound of tobacco. In 1785 tobacco was revived as barter for a short time due to the shortage of coins.
(See Einzig p. 290, 308)

Australia

Wild tobacco was chewed as a narcotic and was an important trade article. (See Quiggin p. 108) Some of the Aboriginals of Australia used tobacco as a medium of

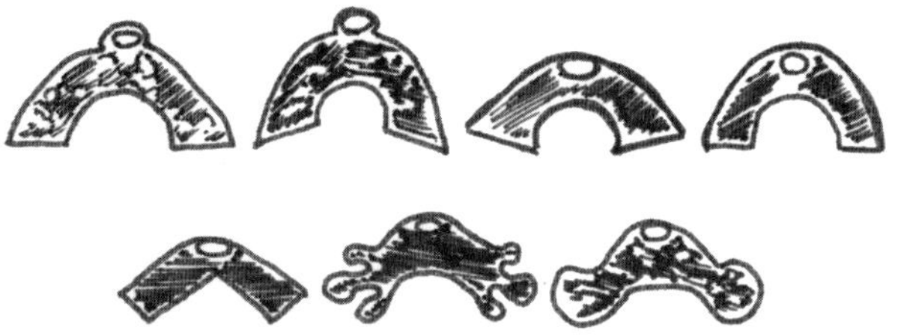

Tingle Dangle Money

Tobacco

Colonial Tobacco Twist

Coiled Tobacco

exchange when it was introduced by the Europeans. (See Elkin p. 421)

Bermuda, Until 1684

It was the main currency in Bermuda. (See Taxay p. 59-61)

Borneo, Kalabit tribe

Two plaited sticks of tobacco, measuring from the first finger round the elbow and back, were worth a large salt cake. (See Quiggin p. 259)

Bougainville

Natives were paid stick tobacco to work on the plantations.

Duke of York Island

Tobacco sticks were used as money along with diwarra. Originally a stick of tobacco was worth one fathom of *diwarra*. Later the value changed so that two sticks of tobacco bought the same one fathom of *diwarra*.
(See George Brown p.296-297)

Irian Jaya

One or two lempeng was a day's pay for paddling a canoe or cutting wood in the forest, according to Michael Rockefeller (p. 11). Alempeng was a flat slab of pressed tobacco leaves about 3″ by 10″ mixed with spices. He said it served as money.

Manus Province, Papua New Guinea

Sticks of tobacco were used in presentations at an engagement with the groom's family giving four or five pounds of stick tobacco to the bride's family. This took place in 1979. There are 30 sticks of tobacco to the pound, and each pound was worth about K2. This transaction was only a small part of a much larger formal exchange that took place for one of many events. Some of the events for which exchanges were held included bride price, weddings, funerals, men's house-raising and others. (See Carrier p.207)

New Hebrides

The sticks served as a universal currency in the import trade with Europeans. One stick was worth three pence. (See Einzig p. 62)

Papua New Guinea

Braided tobacco sticks were the preferred method of small payments. In 1950 a stick of tobacco was worth 4d. (See Einzig p. 91)

Ponape

In the 1830s and 1840s, tobacco sticks would purchase anything on the island. A few sticks of tobacco would supply a ship's mess with vegetables and fruit for several days. A hundred yams, breadfruit, or coconuts cost 10 units of tobacco, according to Hezel (p. 126).

Solomon Islands

Braided tobacco sticks were valued at 3 sticks per shilling. (See Einzig p. 71) In the 1880s, 10 coconuts cost one stick of tobacco. By 1886 one stick of tobacco went for eight coconuts, according to See Bennett (p. 53).

Trobriand Islands

A wooden lime spatula was worth three to four sticks of tobacco, a large pot was worth eight sticks, a basket was worth two sticks, and spoon shells were worth one stick each. (See Einzig p. 82)

Irian Jaya

In 1961, Nelson Rockefeller put up 250 sticks of tobacco for the return of his son, Michael, after he disappeared. Experts recommended this quantity and form of money to generate the greatest interest among the natives to search for Michael Rockefeller.

TOEA

Shell arm rings See Mwali

TOGO STONE - See Quartz disk.

TOK

1615- 1770, Thailand and Burma

The *tok* is domed on one side. This side is said by mythology to be stained with egg yolk and chicken blood. It appears the enamel encrustation is actually caused by impurities in the metal rather than the egg and blood. Two *toks* would buy a wife, and two more would divorce her.There are three types of *toks*:

1) Chiengmai (Chiang Mai) *toks* 1615-1768. Five denominations: one Tamlung, 63-77 grams silver; 1/2 Tamlung, 29-37 grams; 1/4 Tamlung, 15-20 grams; and 1/8 Tamlung six-nine grams. On one tamlung pieces, the dome is often broken and appears hollowed out. It was used in the Chiang Mai area. It was demonetized in 1871. See pig's mouth money.

2) *Tok* of Nan, 1615-1768. One Tamlung, only 62 grams base, from Nan region to the east of Chiang Mai. Similar to the "Chiengmai" *toks* but solid with no break in the dome. Some have characters on them. Also see leaf money and line money.

Chiang Mai Tok

Tok of Nan

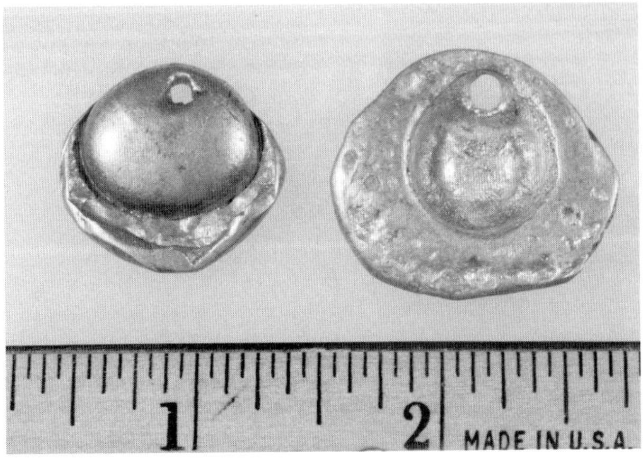

Shan Tok

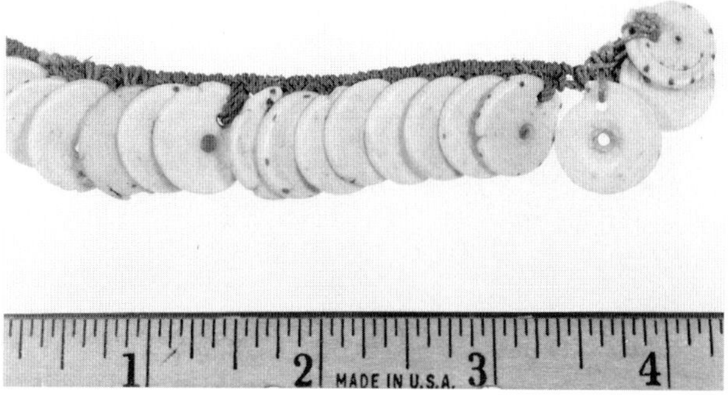

To-Uba

Trade Silver Brooch

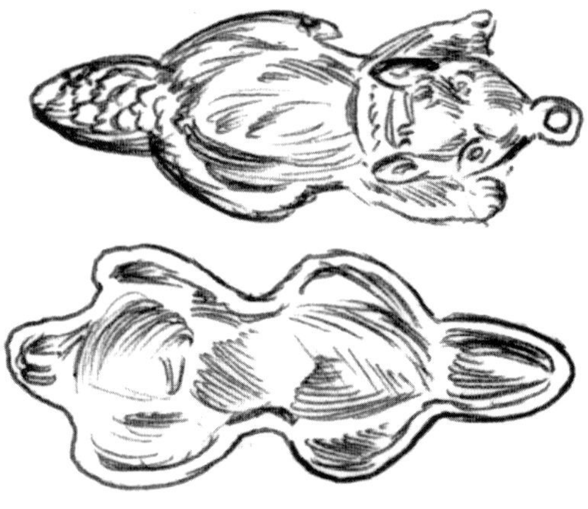

Trade Silver Beaver

3) Shan *Tok*, 1650-1770, 2 - 1/2 - 7 grams. Thin silver shell enveloping a hollow cavity with an opening at the base. Looks like a small shell.

TOKEN - See Head tax token, Hut tax token, Leather, Mother- of-Pearl

TOLUK
Palau Islands

A small plate made from turtle-shell used by the women as money. See Turtle shell.

TO'ONILOBO
Malaita, Solomon Islands

A *biru* made with 1,000 porpoise teeth. See Porpoise teeth

TORTOISE - See Crocodile Money, Gambar, Nose Ornament Money, Turtle Shell

TORTOISE SHELL MONEY
China

The ancients used tortoise shell as currency. The Book of Rites says, "The feudal lords all consider tortoise shells as treasure." It also says that when the Chen Dynasty annexed all the feudal kingdoms about 300 B.C., the use of tortoise shells as currency was prohibited. (See Vissering p. 6)

TORTOISE SHELL ARMBANDS - See Navoi

TOUAU - Another name for a feather coil. See Feather Coil

TO-UBA
Gilbert Islands, 1700's

Disks cut from conus shell (*Conus Eburneus*) and perforated are attached to a cord so the pieces are close enough to overlap. They are said by traders to have been used as money in the 1700s, but later were used as ornaments. They are similar to the *dibidibi*. 1/2" - 1" diameter. (See Quiggin p. 140)

TOWEELAH - See Larin

TRADING AXE - See Axe Money

TRADE BEADS - See Beads

TRADE GUN - See gun money

TRADE SILVER

North American Indians

During the trade period of 1620 to 1820, forms of silver were made based on the Indian's pre-contact religious beliefs. They felt that silver was a gift from the underworld. They believed silver ornaments constituted a power that reflected or blocked evil spirits and radiated good powers of the sun and moon in the Upper World. Silver ornaments served to block the course of evil forces from entering the body at all the entry points. Ornaments of sheet silver were made specifically for use in the fur trade by silversmiths in the United States, Canada, and England. Silver ornaments were used in eastern Canada prior to 1500 but became commonplace in the 1750s when trade silver became cheap. Most were used between 1760 and 1820. Pendants, crosses, effigies, brooches, ear ornaments, gorgets, finger rings, armbands, wristbands, and other forms were made and used during this period. Beaver effigy pendants were also used. Some are solid-cast and others are hollow. They also come in bronze or brass as well as silver. If a beaver effigy was worn, the Indian felt that good beaver hunting could be expected. Many of the items also have identifying marks that show who made the piece. The average Native American wore much more silver than the average white person at that time. The simple, circular, silver brooch embodied many powers and represented nature's many cycles. The simplified brooch was manufactured in both Europe and North America and became a standard trade commodity. Between 1803 and 1811, 31,400 brooches were handled at the Fort Wayne, Indiana, trading post alone. In 1808, 40 silver brooches were worth one dollar. In 1775, silver brooches were used in trade between Indians for deeds, tobacco, and wampum. By 1828, silver brooches up to six inches in diameter, some with cutouts, were common. They were called ear wheels. Silver ear ornaments were also used in trade and as a medium of exchange. When the ring was wide with cutouts, it was called a pierced brooch. They were from one to nine inches in diameter. Ear bobs, nose bobs, wrist bands, finer rings, and ear twists were also used. Small crosses of many designs were as popular as nose bobs. Arm bands of silver, both incised and plain, were also traded but not to the extent that brooches were. The bands were from three to four inches wide. The arm-bands could be shortened to form hair plates.

Shell was a pre-contact term for ornaments made from naturally polished conch shell. Silver moons are concave and three to four inches in diameter with two holes far apart. Later they were called gorgets instead of moons, but this is a misnomer. In 1762, one silver moon was worth nine pounds of skins, and an incised moon

Tridacna Carvings

Tridacna Carvings

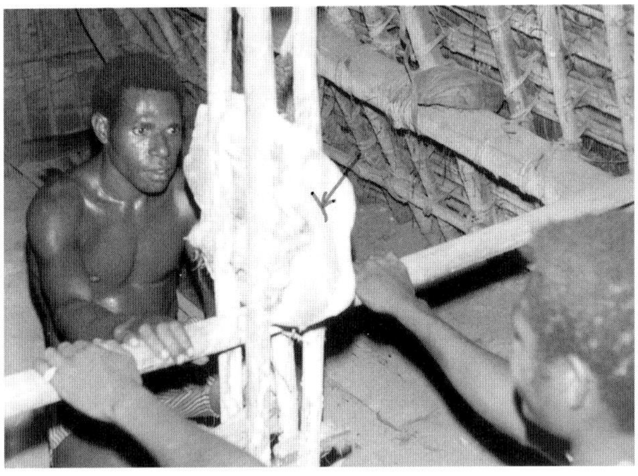

Native Making A Shell Ring

Native Polishing A Shell Ring

Tridacna Ring

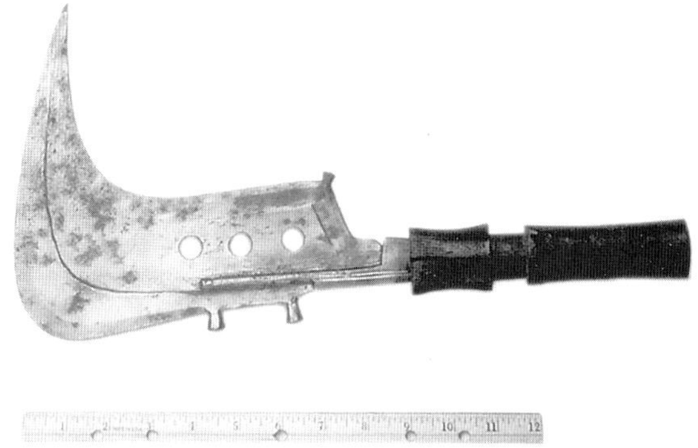

Trombash

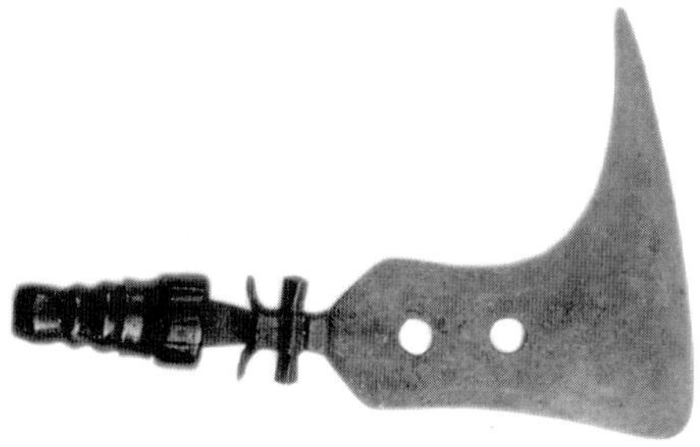

Trombash

was worth 12 pounds of skins. The half moon, or gorget, was used as early as 1580. In 1764 one silver gorget was worth two beavers. Hair pipes of both silver and copper were used by the Indians. They were hollow tubes about the size of a finger, open at both ends, and sealed by being turned back and crimped. (See Karklins p.228, Hamilton p.44-135) (See thimbles and bells)

TREE - See Money Tree

TRIDACNA CARVINGS

Solomon Islands

Natives carved thick slabs of tridacna shell into plaques that formerly served as doors or gable ornaments, according to Waite (Solomon Islands Sculpture p. 151). They have two-dimensional open-work designs. Some of the figures are humans in a hocker position, and the rings are similar to the currency rings like the highly prized *bakhia* and *hokata*. Some believe that these plaques were used as money or wealth.

TRIDACNA RING

Papua New Guinea, Nissan, Tanga, New Georgia, Trobriands, Solomon Islands

The ring was made from the clam shell (*Tridacna Gigas*). The ring was made by cutting and grinding a disk from the giant clam shell. A small hole was pecked or drilled through the disk. The core of the disk was sawed out using a length of rattan which was sawed back and forth with sand and water. It was worth 500 - 1000 pounds of sago. (See Quiggin p. 122-123)

TRIODIA GUM - See Gum Money

TROMBASH

Africa, Sudan and Upper Nile

In the past it was wrongly thought to be a throwing knife. The Mangbetu tribe used the knife (also *trombasc, nadjata, nagata* or *trumbash*) both as a symbol of rank as well as money. The Bushongo tribe, which means "people of the throwing knife," later decided to use the *trombash* only as currency. Only royalty could use the knives made of copper or brass. Iron and ivory handles were reserved for only the most important members of the group. There are two types — one with a large wood cylinder at the end of the handle, and the other with no cylinder at the end. There are many varieties of both of these types. It is believed that the number of holes in the blade could denote the number of wives the owner of the knife had. (See Quiggin p. 68) (See Ballarini p. 87-89) (See Fischer p. 64-73 (See Payne A-4)

TSERA

New Ireland

The unit consists of an arm's length of tiny flat shell discs. There are two kinds. The white *tsera* is called *muning* and one arm length was worth 2 1/2 shillings in 1933. The second kind is red *tsera*, called *bial*, and one arm length was worth five shillings in 1933. A combination of the white and red is called *atok*. An arm's length was also worth five shillings in 1933. Sometimes dog's teeth and an ornament called *urakembaum*, which is a small round fiber object with a mussel shell as an eye, are attached to the *tsera*, as it is supposed to attract more *tsera* to it. *Tsera* is the unit of value that many other items are valued in. A large *kapkap* (breast ornament consisting of a shell with a turtle shell incised overlay) was worth two *tsera*. Large male pigs were worth between two and four *tsera*. A canoe was worth four to six *tsera*. There is never any bargaining, and to gain prestige a person would sell an item for less or buy an item for more than it was normally worth. Payments for all objects are always made in public. No items are sold for a profit. They must always be sold for cost. Sales of items are a continuation of other sales and purchases, and many of the transactions are reciprocal with other relatives and items. Profit comes only through the rendering of services or magic. The price for black magic or war magic was 10 *tsera*. Rain magic was two to four *tsera*, and taro magic was one *tsera*. They were always very careful to not allow anyone to hear the spell so the knowledge would not become widespread and the value of the magic would not decrease. Magic to a new-born infant to make it strong would cost two to three *tsera*. Bride price consists of 12 tsera, tobacco, and seven or eight loin-cloths. (See Powdwemaker p. 146)

TUGUDU CLOTH - See Cloth, Africa, Tiv tribe

TUKULA

Congo

Old redwood trees (*Baphia, Nitida* or Camwood) were ground into powder, mixed with water and formed into cakes. The cakes were stamped with a pattern. The cakes became black and shiny with age and use. They were used as money. The value came from the redwood powder, which was mixed with oil, smeared on the body, used to stiffen the coiffure, dye cloth, and color woodwork and pots. The red camwood powder, called *ngola* by the Bobangi, was used throughout the central basin of Zaire. It was mainly made in spare time and was traded over long distances because the trees did not grow in the savanna area. The main source was the Ubangi, where it was sold in small slabs or in balls. In the Lake Mai-Ndombe region it was made in conic

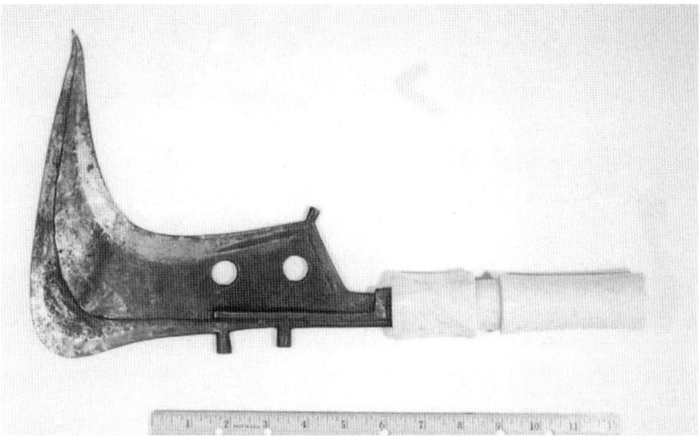

Trombash

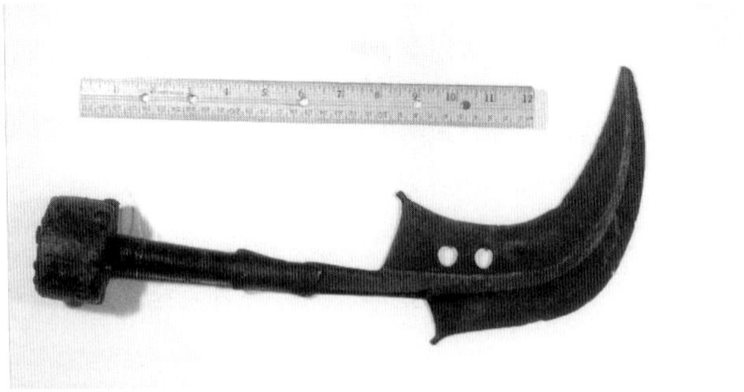

Trombash

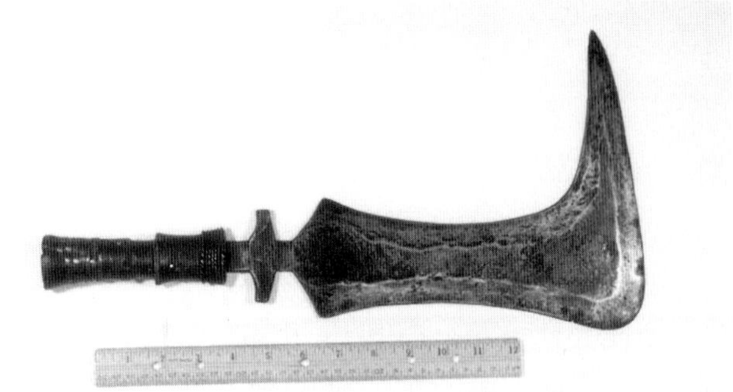

Trombash

Tukula

packages. It was made by one of several methods. The most common was to rub two blocks of camwood against each other with sand and water between them. The Ubangi cut the block into fine shavings and then used a millstone to turn it into powder. There are also several variations of these methods. Most *tukula* have been broken. (See Quiggin p. 80) (See Harms p. 60-63)

Tukula

Tukula

TULA

Africa

The iron spade money was used in trade. (See Quiggin p. 97 fig.33.)

Tula

TURBAN SNAIL - See Snail Shell

TURBO SHELL

Papua New Guinea, Chambri tribe and Tsembaga tribe

Cut green turban snail shells (*Turbo marmoratus*) were used as money and in bride price. Each had its own value based on markings, size, shape, color, luster, and ornamentation. They are also called *talipun*. The Yangoru people believe in two kinds of *talipun*, one male (*hombulyi*) and one female (*horie*). The *talipun* is pictured on the five kina note. (See Safer & Gill p. 63)

Papua New Guinea

The whole turbo shell (*Turbo marmoratus*) was painted with ochre and, with a cassowary feather ornament attached, was used to purchase a wife. See Shell Money, Snail Shell

Turbo Shell

TURKEDI - See Cloth, Mali

TURMERIC POWDER

Micronesia, Truk Island, 19th century

It was the closest thing to a standard medium of exchange on Truk. Two sticks of turmeric were worth one *ceejityr* (*woven lavalava*). (See Quiggin p. 137)

Samoa

Native cloth was exchanged for turmeric from village to village. (See George Brown p. 305)

TURQUOISE

United States, Hopi and Zuni Indians

An Indian pawns his turquoise jewelry to obtain money to grow wool and other crops. When the crops are sold, the man reclaims his pawned jewelry and invests the balance in additional turquoise jewelry. The necklaces are a store of value and could be used as currency. This piece is called concha. (See Erikson p. 111)

TURTLE SHELL MONEY

Africa

Bushmen of the Kalahari District use tortoise shell as money. (See Mosher p. 40)

China, 14th - 2nd century B.C.

Tortoise shell was considered a money of high value and was used along with cowries. After 221 B.C., the use of tortoise shell as money was forbidden except for a four-year period from 10 A.D. to 13 A.D. (See Quiggin p. 224) (See Einzig p. 253-254)

Ontong Java

Nose pendants of turtle shell, called *asanga,* were worn through a hole in the side of the nose and used as money.

Palau Islands

The women made small plates or dishes from turtle shell and used them as money called *toluk.* Most are oblong, about 3/4 inch high, and their diameter varies on the short side from three to six inches and on the long side from 4 1/2 to nine inches. They have a broad lip on the longer ends and a smaller lip on the shorter sides. The older pieces are more valuable, have been polished with sandstone and grit and have a translucent look. The dishes are called women's money and are not considered as valuable as men's money. The dishes were no longer made even in the 1940s and all trading was done with the old dishes still in existence. They are gradually being replaced with foreign goods. The oldest woman among a group of clan sisters holds all the toluks belonging to all of them. At present the dishes are being made by some natives. (See Barnett p.55-56)

Pacific Islands

Most of the Pacific islands valued turtleshell and used it as money in some form. Small disks of turtle shell, called *alas,* were money as well as arm rings, spoons, small trays and saucers. They were also used in bride price. (See Quiggin p. 144)

Papua New Guinea - See Navoi

Solomon Islands

In the 1840s traders would trade turtle shell for iron of all kinds. In New Georgia, the natives only wanted tomahawks for their turtle shell. In 1835, turtle shell was selling for the high price of $14 per pound in North America. (See Roth p. 296) Nose pieces and armbands as trade items and store of wealth. (See Quiggin p. 164)

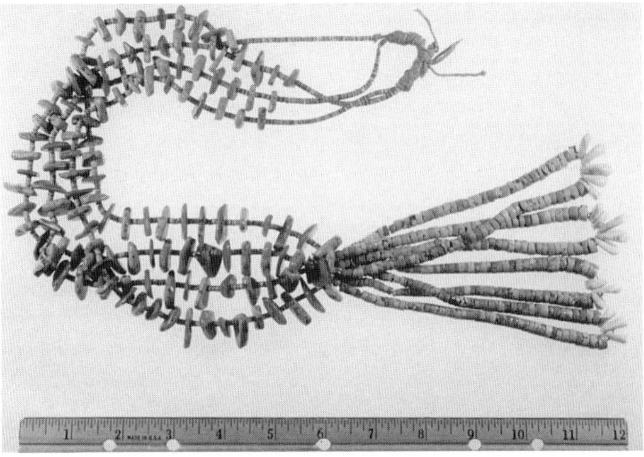

Turquoise

Palau Turtle Shell Disk

Turtle Shell Rings

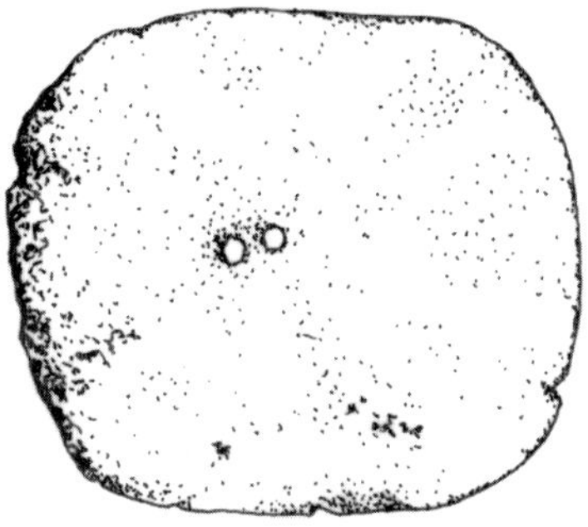

Tyere

Vitiaz Strait

Kombe-manufacture turtle-shell disks for export to the mainland. Necklaces of the disks were used in bride price, and a necklace was worth a small pig. Turtle shell bracelets were worn on the upper arm and were two to eight inches wide. The plates from two sides of the shells of two large turtles are softened in boiling water, cut into wide strips and molded into the bracelets. The outer surface is then incised with geometric designs. (See Harding p. 53)

TUSK - See Dentalium Shell Money, Ivory, Walrus Tusk Money

TUSKER - See Pig Money

TYERE

Nigeria, Birom tribe

Thirty iron disks called *tyere* were worth a wife.

Umbu

UDOUD - See Beads

ULAWA SHELL MONEY

Solomons

This is the finest red shell disk money in the Solomons. There are as many as 50 disks per inch. The ends of the string are whitish gray shell beads called *ngisi*. (See Ivens p.48)

ULOS CLOTH

Sumatra, Indonesia

The cloth is made of cotton formerly grown locally and dyed with natural plant dyes. It is woven with a technique called warp *ikat* where the warp threads are tied and dyed before weaving. It is traditionally made on a back loom with circular continuous warps. *Ikat* is distinguished by a fussy lengthwise design. There are more than 50 kinds of *ulos*. The wife's family traditionally give *ulos*, which are in most instances a kind of cloth but can also be plots of land. The cloth is also used in other trade as well.

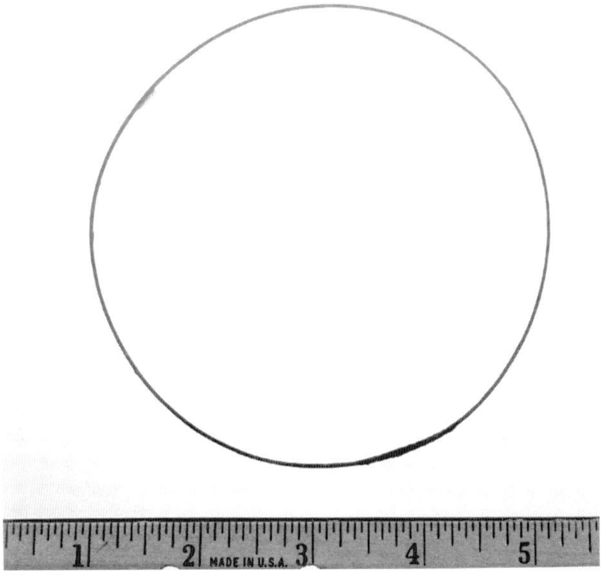

Unus

UMBU

Solomon Islands

A kind of *poata* shell ring which had a particularly large dimension. See *Poata*. (See Miller p. 292)

UMUMU

Nigeria

Y-shaped iron pieces about one inch long were used as money. They were produced by Awaka/Lejja blacksmiths in northern Igboland. See Needle money. (See Guyer p. 137.)

UNABURU - See Porpoise teeth

UNUS

Borneo

Unus are rings of very finely plaited palm fibers. Each was worth 1/5 cent. They were used by the Dyak and worn in large numbers on their legs below the knee and arms below the elbow. Three hundred rings could be worn on one leg. 5″ diameter. (See Quiggin p. 258)

URAKEMBAUM

An ornament attached to a *tsera*. It is not money, but it is an important part of the *tsera*, as it was believed to attract more *tsera*. It is a small round fiber object with a mussel shell as an eye. (See tsera) (See Powdermaker p. 200)

Urakembaum

USU USU

Shell sticks with pointed ends passing through the septum of the nose were also money. Designs and cutouts on the surface of the piece may be rings near the points or more complex decoration.

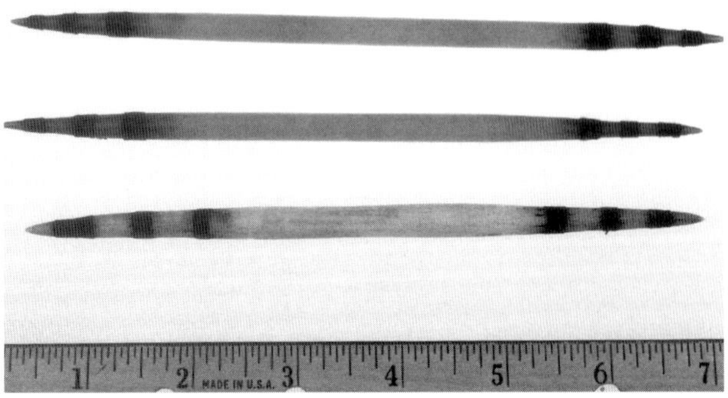

Usu Usu

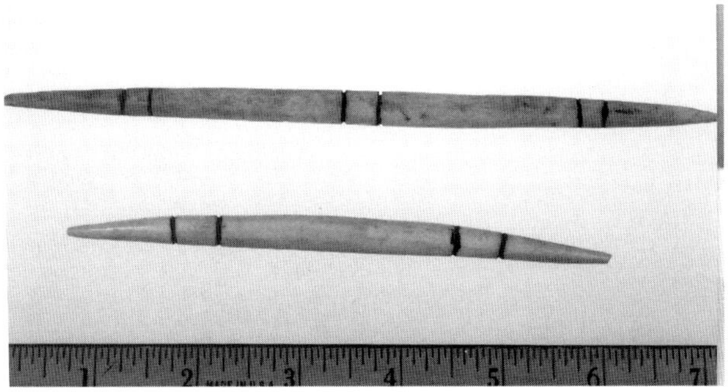

Usu Usu

UTUTE

Tridacna clam-shell circular disks decorated with etched decoration were worn by the men of Malaita, Ulawa, and Maramasike. Most have a cross of some kind and other decoration as well. It is possible they were a valued item or possibly even money. This piece is of pre-European manufacture.

URUA CROSS - See Handa

VAYGUA

Trobriand Islands

Objects or tokens of wealth that consist of classes of highly valued items like big ceremonial axe blades, necklaces of red shell disks, and arm shells of conus millepunctatus shell. See bagi.

VEGETABLE PEELER - See Kula.

VERTEBRAE - See Shark Vertebrae

VULA

New Britain

Shell disk bead money of the Kaliai people of northwest New Britain. It comes in two denominations black *vula* (*vula asona*) and gold *vula* (*vula misi*). It has been used from old times to the present. Lewis states that New Ireland and the small islands off its coast were originally the chief centers for the production of the shell money. The black *vula* comes from a bivalve shell found on the

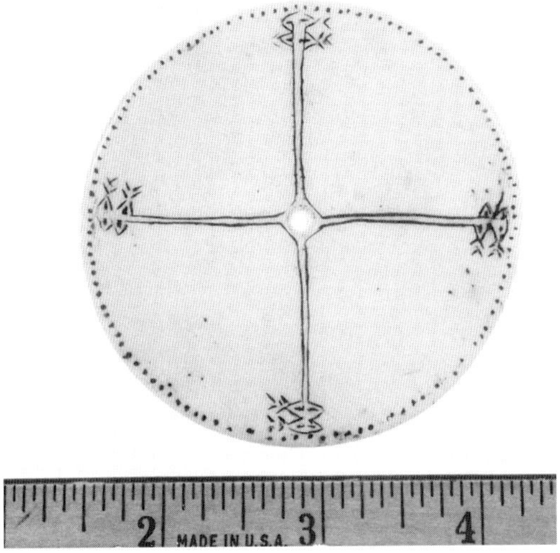

Utute

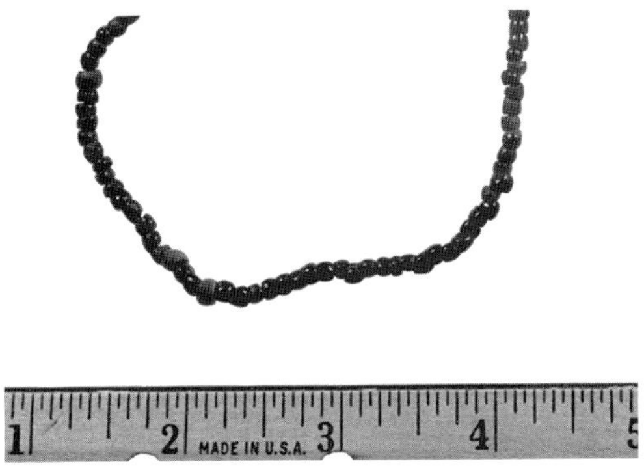

Vula

Walrus Skin Money

island. A bead is 1/8 to 3/16 inch in diameter and 1/64 inch thick. It is strung on pandanus fiber in lengths of about six feet long, and this is called a *pram*. The gold *vula* is usually white or pink in color and is worth five times as much as the black *vula*.The white shells used for making *vula* came from The Duke of York Island and were traded by the Tolai to the region of Open Bay, where they were then traded to the Nakanai, who traded them farther to the west. These beads are slightly smaller than the black *vula*. Shell money is used to purchase masks and for assistance in building men's houses. *Vula* is used in bride wealth presentations as well as at mortuary ceremonies and the initiation of children. It is used along with Australian money in bride price. Some *vula* must always be included because Australian money by itself is not acceptable. It is said that wealth moves in one direction and prestige moves in the other direction. A *pram* of black *vula* was worth one Australian dollar, while a pram of gold *vula* was worth five Australian dollars. The items do not equate as one dollar to five dollars, as both kinds of *vula* are required in bride price. Other items were valued in black *vula* as follows: a 40 foot canoe was 20 *pram*, a pig was five to 10 *pram*, a mask was five *pram*, a spear was 1/2 *pram*, and a Siassi wooden pot was one to five *pram*. The value of *vula* has decreased due to the use of steel tools, which make production much faster and easier. The current value is about one half of its former value. That has also made more people produce it. Fifty years ago bride price was five *pram* plus three or four pots and spears, while now it is about 100 *pram* of black *vula*. *Vula* is used to obtain turtle shell arm rings, Siassi bowls, Sio pots, sago, and tobacco. Among the Sio a string of *vula* is worth a small pig. The Sio use modern money as a wealth item instead of as a medium of exchange. The *vula* is the medium of exchange. In 1970 a pram *vula* (six feet) was worth $1 Australian. A mase *vula* (15 inches) was worth $.20 Australian. A Siassi wood bowl was worth one to five pram of black *vula*, depending on the size of the bowl. A Sio pot was worth about the same amount. A mask was worth five *pram* of black *vula*, and a large 40-foot canoe was worth 20 pram. Pigs went for five to ten *pram* each, and a mask was worth five *pram*. (See Counts)

At present *vula* is made by the Kove people for their use. In the past, the Kove state they did not manufacture the disks but traded them from the east. The Tolai people obtained the shell disks from the Duke of York Islands, especially Mioko, where they were manufactured and called *pele*. It is believed that *vula* and *pele*, as well as *bubu*, are the same shell bead. There are several kinds of *vula*: *vula misi* (gold *tambu*) is light colored, usually white or pink, and *vula kasoka* (black *tambu*) is low-valued and dark-colored. There are many minor varieties, and it is believed that not all kinds came from the same areas. (See Chowning) 3/8″ dia.

WADMAL

Iceland

In ancient times cloth, spun from the fleece of sheep was called *wadmal* and was money. (See Quiggin p. 284)

WAKALA - See Kula.

WALRUS SKIN MONEY

Russia, 1816-1852

Parchment notes were first made in 1826, and the paper notes were issued in 1816 and 1822. They were made for the private Russian American Company, which was chartered in 1799 by the Russian government as a joint-stock company with the power of a trading monopoly like East India Companies and the Hudson's Bay Company. The firm's income was from hunting fur-bearing animals and seals for export of the fur. In 1797 the Commercial American Company was formed by a Russian named Mylnikoff in Irkutsk, Siberia. In 1798, it combined with another company to form the Russian-American Company. In 1816 the company printed 12,000 rubles of walrus skin money printed. A second printing took place in 1822 and another printing in 1826. Zander states that during this period and up to 1860, the amount of notes in circulation varied from a low of 12,000 rubles to a high of 80,000 rubles. When a new series came out, the old notes were called in. Zander says notes were issued in 1816, 1822, 1826, 1834 and 1852, and correspondence also shows notes in 1842, 1845, and 1858. Because the company did not provide the number of notes needed, the Governor produced local currency from time to time. The notes were issued in seven denominations, which were 10, 25 and 50 kopeck notes and one, five, 10, and 25 ruble notes. The serial numbers are all hand-written on the notes. On the face of the notes it states in Russian "Note in America" along with the denomination. The reverse of the notes has the double-headed eagle around which in Russian it states, "Under the High Patronage of His Imperial Majesty." There were five to possibly eight issues with a total value of from 280,000 to 3,109,000 rubles, according to Zander. The notes are known in mustard, blue, green, brown, red, and tan. Later notes are black printing on light color parchment. All the notes were redeemed for Russian credit notes. All notes are rare. Most notes have holes and clips as follows: 10 kopeck notes have a hole in each upper corner; the 25 kopeck notes have all four corners clipped; and the 50 kopeck notes have the two upper corners clipped. There are also some oval shaped notes. There are only about 100 to 120 notes in existence, and about one half are in private collections. Uhl believed the notes were made from waterproof bags made of walrus skin used to ship

Walrus Tusk Money

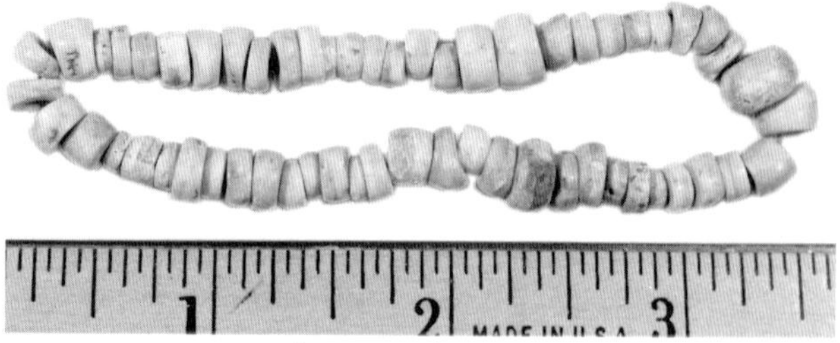

Wampum - Temple Mounds

Wampum - Shell Beads

Wampum - Square Cut Olive Shell Beads

Wampum - Pomo Indian Shell Beads

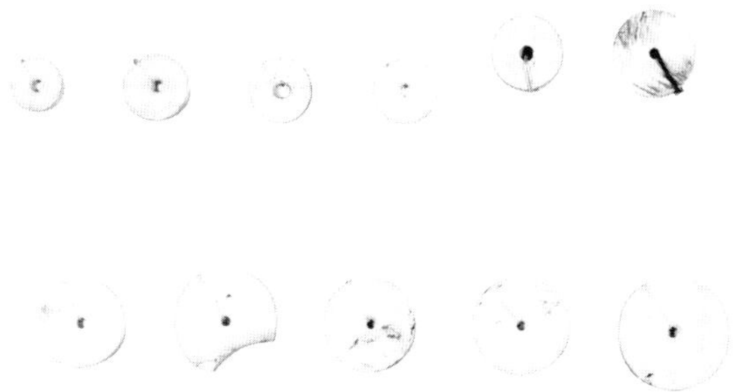
Wampum - Pomo Indian Shell Beads

Magnesite Beads - left, Heated Natural Bead; right, Natural Magnesite Bead

Wampum - Ohio Mounds

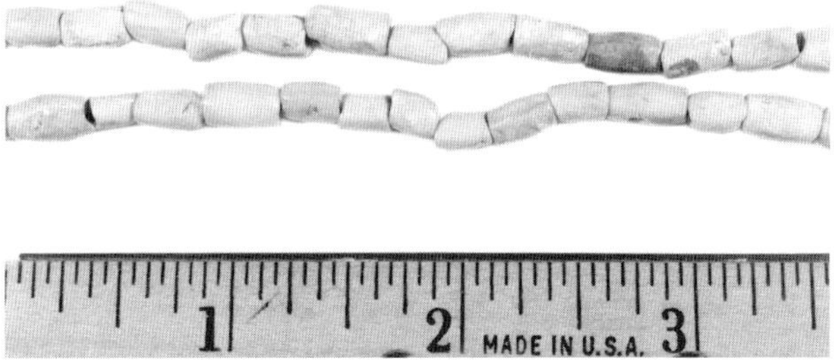

Wampum - Temple Mounds

otter skins to China. The Chinese then used them to ship tea and spices to Russia. In Russia they were cut and stamped with values and devices of the RAC. Anders Bergland, Tuukka Talvio, and Randolph Zander published an article in 1987 stating they felt that the notes were made of paper, cardboard, and parchment or walrus hide. (See Zander) They were erroneously referred to as "seal skin money" in several past articles. Only three of the 1816 issue are known, one each of 25 and 50 kopecks and one ruble. The Company phased out its activities in 1867-68 after the sale of Alaska to the United States, and it redeemed the outstanding notes. Very rare

WALRUS TUSK MONEY

Alaska

Indians used whole tusks and pieces of tusks as money. Hudson's Bay Company accepted walrus tusks in all of its stores as money. (See Payne A-11)

WAMPUM

New England, until late 19th century

The Merriam Webster Collegiate Dictionary defines wampum as "beads of polished shells strung in strands, belts, or sashes and used by North American Indians as money, ceremonial pledges, and ornaments. Money." The word "wampom" is an Iroquois word meaning mussel. It is shortened from *wampumpeak* which is Algonkian for white shell beads. It is also called *peage, peake* or *peg,* which are abbreviations. The Dutch used the term *Sewan, Sewant* or *Zee* wand. Wampum was the English term for the Algonkian "*wampumpeak.*" The French called it "*porcelain.*" True wampum refers only to a particular type shell-bead of unique importance to the Iroquois Indians, and it is called belt wampum or "true wampum." (Ceci p.63)

Indian Use Prior to European Contact

Taxey feels that wampum was used as money in pre-contact times, mostly for small transactions, but in most cases barter was used instead. He feels this is true because of the tight supply of wampum, and it was therefore saved for such transactions where the debt could not otherwise be settled, such as in the payment of blood money.

Prior to Europeans coming to North America, the Indians, in some cases, made their wampum from small pieces of wood which they stained white or black. The Iroquois claimed to have invented wampum. One story states that Hiawatha, the founder of the Iroquois League, first made and used wampum. This cannot be verified. Another story says that porcupine quills were used. Since the Iroquois Indians did not have access to the shells used in wampum, it seems unlikely that they actually invented it but instead got it from the wampum makers of Long Island. (Fenton p. 440)

Orchard feels that the Indians did have cylindrical beads in the pre-contact period, while other experts do not agree. Only a few beads were made from mussel shells because the Indians lacked proper tools. To substantiate this feeling, it is known that few shell beads are found in prehistoric Onondaga Indian village sites. After the coming of the whites, it is felt that the Indians, as well as the Dutch and English, made wampum. Beauchamp feels that owing to the large number of beads required and the regularity of their size, it is doubtful whether wampum belts were used as necessary or ordinary parts of Indian councils before the coming of the whites.

When a bargain was made, a string of wampum was given by the buyer to the seller as an evidence of good faith, not as a part of the price. "The Iroquois tribe had a custom that all important statements should be accompanied by a gift, the gift indicating that the statement is a serious one and is a true one. In time wampum came to be regarded as the most appropriate and customary gift. It also served as a letter of introduction and a certificate of authority. This custom started as late as within the last 450 years." (Tooker p. 422)

Trade existed prior to the coming of the Europeans and was described as early as 1606. (Salwen p. 166) Wampum caused some confusion with the colonists because when they first noticed wampum, they regarded it as pieces of natural pearls. Prior to the coming of the European trader, the Indians used wampum as a source of prestige and as a badge of authorization or identification as well as a mechanism for recording and binding treaties in the form of belts. Only when the white traders came did the wampum become a media of exchange.

What is Roanoke?

Roanoke is a cheap kind of wampum made from oyster shells from an area south of the Delaware Bay and used in Virginia by the neighboring Indians.These shell beads were worth less than one fourth as much as wampum. Their disks were not as finished as wampum, but were used in the same manner. The edges of *roanoke* are rough, while the edges of wampum are very smooth. *Roanoke* was also more wheel-shaped than cylinder-shaped like wampum and shorter in length than the diameter of the bead. (Swanton p.482-485)

Was it Money?

"Wampum was a repository of value among the Indians before white contact, but its use as money is probably the result of the diffusion of the Western European idea of money as part of the acculturation process between Indians and whites. Later, through the influence of the monetary customs of the English in Virginia, wampum began being used in money transactions between Western Europeans and Indians." (Slotkin p. 223 & 226) There is not much evidence that wampum was used as money by the Indians prior to the arrival of the colonists. Wampum was actually "white man's money," more so than the popular notion that it was "Indian money."

Use By Indians

The great attraction of wampum was its value to the Iroquois Indians of New York. They were one of the most powerful native tribes in North America. Therefore, the beads had value in all of the surrounding area. They used wampum in nearly every stage of their life and public action. They did not then use it as money as we use the term but as a kind of seal to mark agreements and milestones in life. Wampum was used in adoption rites, invitations of importance, condolences for the dead, to seal contracts, to pay tribute, and to purchase land. They also used wampum to announce the death of a sachem, to hire other tribes to fight, to make war and peace, to pay tribute, to pay indemnities for casualties, to record speeches made at ceremonial occasions, as bridewealth, to save a captive from death by torture, to make belts by Indian converts as gifts to the Church, ransom captives held by the Indians, to establish boundaries between enemy tribes, as gifts between friends, to adorn prisoners about to be tortured to death, as a fee to have an enemy murdered, as a sign of status and wealth, and in a marriage proposal. Wampum was also given to atone for a murder and could prevent retaliation. The Iroquois Indians used wampum extensively for many of the normal activities, such as obtaining permission to speak at council meetings. In condolences when a chief or sachem died, all activities in that nation were suspended until the condolence had been completed. A runner bearing special wampum carried it to each of the other nations. In the case of a principal chief, three strings of purple wampum united at one end were used. The death of a war chief was announced with one string joined at the ends to form a circle with a small stick with a number of notches on it indicating how many days remained until the condolence ceremony. The Iroquois valued a human life at ten strings of wampum a cubit in length. The wampum was thought of as an act of atonement rather than as compensation. The Iroquois later valued a life at six strings of white wampum, and the strings were sent by the killer to the relatives of the deceased. If that was not done, the murdered person's family could kill the man or a member of his family. If a man killed a woman,

Wampum - Olive Shell Backs

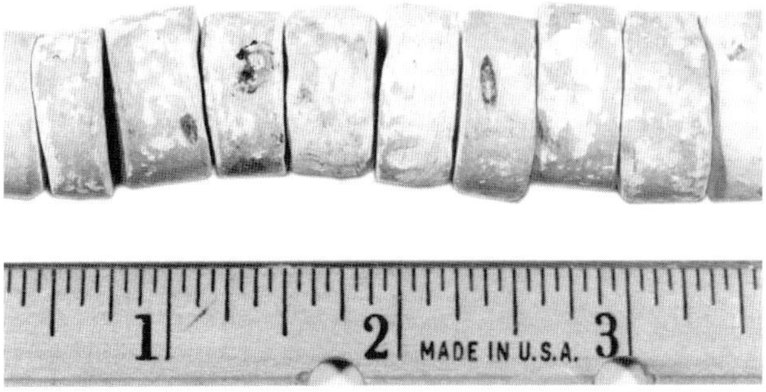

Wampum - Large Shell Beads

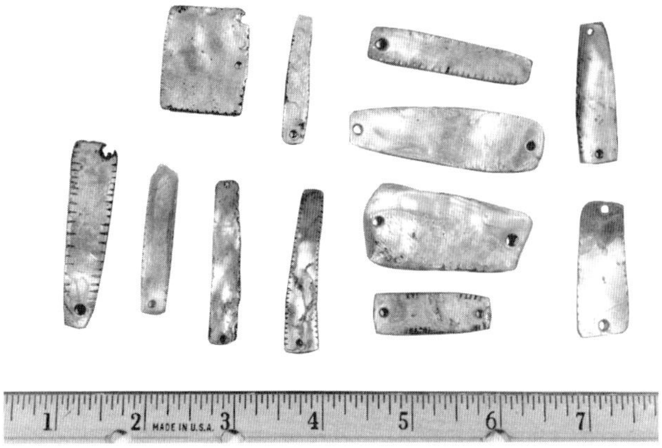

Maidu Shell Beads

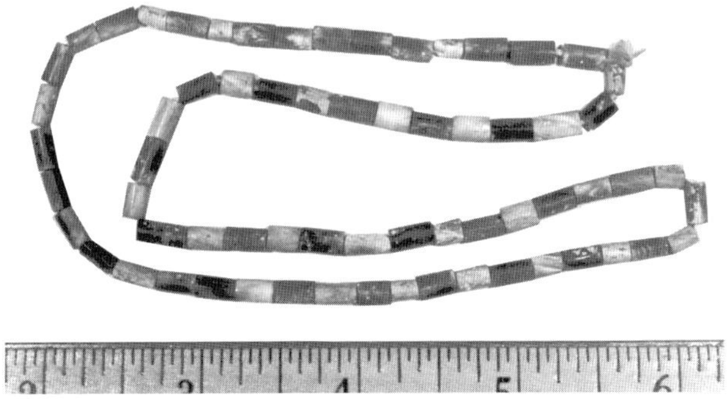

Wampum - White & Purple

he could give 20 strings of wampum for the life of the woman and 10 strings of wampum for his life because if he didn't, his life would have also been taken. The Huron tribe valued a man at 30 presents, with each present being 700 wampum beads. A woman's life was worth 40 presents. Wampum was also used in ransom. If a chief or sachem was captured and condemned to die, a certain amount of wampum would ransom him. Wampum was also used in tribute. After 1637, the Long Island Indians made the wampum and were required to pay large sums of it annually to both the Narragansetts and the aggressive Pequots, as late as 1756, and they traded the wampum for furs. The English also required the Long Island Indians and others to pay annual tribute to the English for protection. A girdle was one yard long and 14 pieces wide. It had squares of black and white over most of the length. The girdles have been identified as made by the Iroquois Indians, and they were all very valuable.

The names "Wapanoos," "Pequats," and "Sequins" were used to describe wampum and were also some of the important suppliers of the wampum. The Pequots also acquired wampum from other tribes that they had conquered or subjugated. The Narragansetts as well as the Pequots used the wampum to obtain furs and European goods.

In 1628 wampum was used in bride price, enabling men to buy three or four wives. In that same year, the first Anglo-Indian war, the Pequot War, was fought over control of the wampum trade. The Pequots were the most powerful Indian competitor for wampum. To try to settle the war, the Pequots sent 70 beaver and otter skins and 400 fathoms of wampum to New England authorities to restore friendship. The fighting continued, and eventually the English demanded 6,000 fathoms of wampum to pay for damages. This demand was worth 3,000 English pounds. The military campaigns continued until the Pequots were destroyed and dispersed. The English then controlled the wampum as well as the other wampum-producing Indian tribes formerly controlled by the Pequots. After the Indians saw what the English did to the most powerful tribe, the Pequots, they were not going to fight the English. In 1645 the Narragansett Indians had to pay the Connecticut colonists 2,000 fathoms of wampum because of the expenses they caused by persisting in fighting the Mohegans. All this resulted in lower values for wampum and therefore furs. This also led the way for wampum to be used as money in the colonies at lower prices than when the Pequots were competing with the English. The Indians were also charged a tribute of one fathom of white wampum for every Pequot man and 1/2 fathom for every Pequot youth. Fines were also charged to the Indians of 560 fathoms for the murder of an Englishman, as well as fines for other damages. Total fines were in excess of 17,000 fathoms worth 9,500 pounds English. The English demanded and received from the Indians much wampum as tribute and in fines for offenses and damages. These annual payments of tribute continued until 1651 when the English told the Indians that they needed to pay for another 10 years, but children born after this time would not be subject to assessments. In 1656, Farmington Indians were forced to pay 80 fathoms of wampum annually for seven years for murdering a white man. Fines and assessments for damages, such as an Indian burning English property, continued as late as 1657. In 1639 the Dutch also started to charge the Indians in the form of wampum and corn. By 1643 this had gotten out of hand, and the Indians attacked the settlers and forced the governor to pay the Indians wampum to try to establish peace. The killing continued on both sides for many years.

Wampum was also used for sending messages. The runner orally delivered the specifics, but he would use a belt or string of wampum to recite the message, which validated his message. Small strings of wampum were used as decorations and in barter or trade. Imitation beads were made in Europe from porcelain and sent to America to be used as wampum. The colonists used the imitations, but the Indians refused to accept them. Indians made wampum in their primitive way as late as 1700. Wampum was also at times buried with the dead. As wampum became rare, this practice was stopped.

Use By Colonists

The first European to encounter wampum was Cartier in Montreal in 1497. (Francis p.22) A man named Johnson is credited with calling attention to the value of wampum in a letter to Clinton, the Governor of New York. The governor wrote to the directors and stated that wampum was the mother of the beaver trade, and without it they could not obtain beavers from the Indians. Smith (who quoted Williams, p. 144) stated that the fur trade existed with the coastal tribes buying furs from the interior tribes for wampum prior to the whites coming to America. Some traded a heavy, coarse trade cloth called "duffles" to obtain wampum, which was then traded to obtain beavers. The English traders were late to recognize the importance of wampum in the beaver skin trade. Furs were important in the history of the North American colonies, and the easiest way to obtain them was by trading with the Indians. In the early 1600s the colonists purchased much land from the Indians. In 1622 the Dutch trader, J. Elekes, held the chief of the Sequin tribe hostage and demanded 140 fathoms of wampum, which they called *Zeewan*, or they would decapitate the chief. Wampum eventually became a universal currency, exchangeable for merchandise, labor, and for taxes.

The Indians measured the beads according to a span which extended from the end of the little finger to the elbow joint. Because this measurement varied according to the size of the Indian, the colonial authorities fixed the value by the number of beads instead of the length. The colonists demanded wampum as compensation for damage, for pillaging property, raiding settlements, and killing settlers. In 1625, the English traders used Indian corn, which the Plymouth farmers raised, to exchange for beaver skins at the rate of one bushel of corn for one pound of beaver skins. A single beaver skin weighed about 1.7 pounds. Ten bushels of corn were worth six fathoms of wampum. A fathom of wampum consisted of about 360 beads. A fathom of wampum also required from eight to fourteen mature shells to make. It also took from seven and a half to 10 days of labor to make the beads after the shells were collected. The Dutch monopolized the trade in wampum when they recognized its importance. Records show that most of the land both the Dutch and English purchased from the Indians was purchased more for the production of wampum rather than to farm or settle colonists. In 1628 the Dutch sold some wampum to the English. By 1636 both the English and the Dutch were using wampum to trade for furs to send to Europe. Because furs could always be obtained for wampum, it became the most important currency for all of the colonists, even those who had no interest in the fur trade. "In 1640 one tract of land that was one day's walk across was purchased for eight fathoms of wampum, six coats, 10 hatchets, 10 hoes, 10 knives, 10 scissors, 10 jews harps, 10 fathoms of tobacco, three kettles, six hands and 10 looking-glasses." (De Forest p. 177) Many other parcels were purchased for approximately those same items, including wampum. The production of wampum and trade for furs with the Indians were the most important concerns of the Europeans in the area. Much of the land was purchased with the drills used to make the wampum beads. The deed included clauses excluding the right to trade wampum. By 1648 the English passed rules that regulated the quality and stringing of wampum. In 1648, four beads were valued at one penny in Connecticut. All the colonies used wampum at one time. Because the colonies were restricted by England from coining their own money to a large extent, and because few coins and other money came from Europe, there was little money to carry on commerce in the colonies. The legislatures of many of the colonies then established wampum as money within the colony and established a set value on the wampum. Beaver skins were valued in wampum using the guilder denomination.

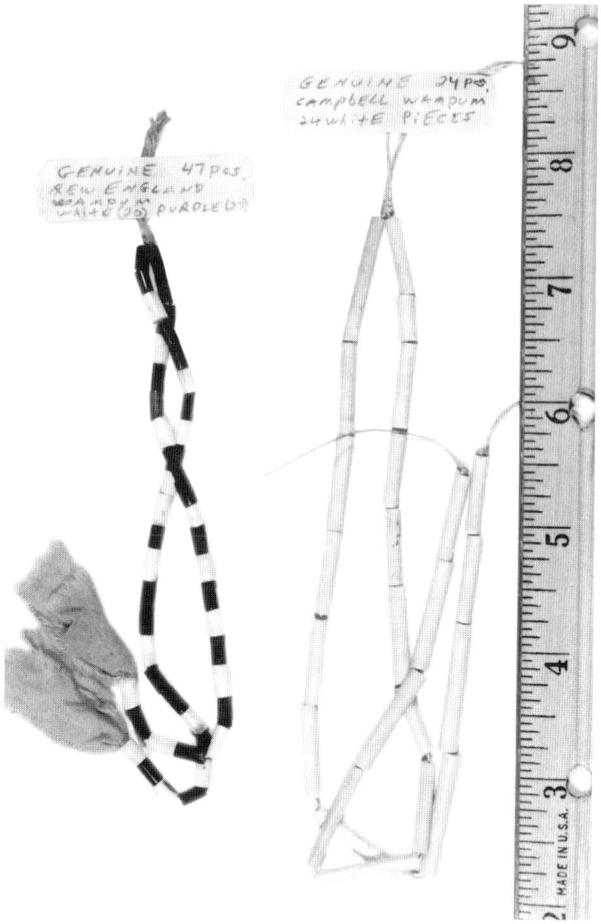

Wampum - Genuine & Campbell

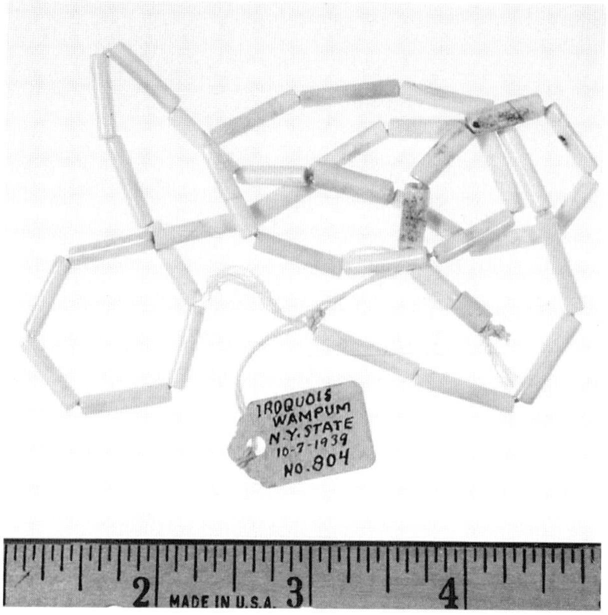

Wampum - Iroquois Indian

However, by 1648 wampum started to gradually lose status due to counterfeiting and the 1652 issuance of the silver pine tree shilling in Massachusetts. In 1650, bad wampum was devalued to one-half the value of good wampum. Control of wampum and the Indian lands was an important factor in the English overthrowing the Dutch. In 1650, much of the wampum in circulation was only half-finished, and some was made of stone, bone, glass, and even wood according to Francis. In 1658 the value of a beaver skin rose to 16 guilders. Later the beaver skins rose even more in value. Wampum changed in value between 1628 and 1673 from a low of three white beads for a penny to a high of 12 white beads for a penny. A big problem was the large number of bad or imperfect beads in circulation. In 1661, legal tender status was revoked by Massachusetts and the other colonies. As late as 1683, the salary of a schoolmaster was paid in wampum. As late as the 19th century a string of white Campbell wampum was valued at a bit, or 12-1/2 cents, and still circulated widely. (Taxey p.135-136) Wampum was used for ornamentation into the early part of the 20th century, long after most economic and ceremonial uses had disappeared. The rough, unpolished beads were traded, while the good, polished beads, called "Manhattan wampum," were exported or saved.

How It Was Made

Cylindrical beads from the quahog clam shell (*Venus mercenaria*) were used to make the black wampum. and the columella of univalves, periwinkles and conchs, like *Buccinum undatum*, were used to make the white wampum. It was produced by the Indians of Long Island, coastal Connecticut, and Rhode Island, including the Pequots, Narragansetts, and Shinnecock. The shells were not found in quantity north of Cape Cod, so the shells were traded to the northern areas.

The tools used for making Dutch wampum consisted of a double-bladed adze with a short handle, a hickory stick about 14 inches long with a notch in the center (which allowed the shell to be placed in the notch and held in place by pulling on the two ends), a drill made from a saw file, a bow drill to revolve the drill, a wire to hold the rough ground beads, and a grind stone to smooth and polish the edges. The hickory stick was only a cleft stick, but it formed a clamp or vise to hold the shell. Hickory was used because it has "give" and will spring back to its original shape. The drill was sharpened to a point, heated to red-hot and put into tallow to give it the required hardness or temper. The Indians originally drilled the shells with a stone or reed drill. Later iron drills were used. The east end of Long Island was the original location of wampum trade. The Iroquois said that peach pits were broken and boiled in water, and the liquid made the shell soft to drill.

Purchase of Manhattan

The question of whether Manhattan Island was purchased for $24 worth of beads or wampum can best be answered by the fact that there is no documentation that beads or wampum purchased the island. We do know that the purchase price was 60 Dutch guilders, as dollars were not used at that time. What is known is that the island was purchased in 1626 for a variety of trade goods. Which trade goods were used are not documented, but beads were a popular trade good, so part of the purchase price could have been beads. Some of the other trade goods that could have been used were axes, knives, rolls of cloth, pots, and coats. It is also clear that the natives misrepresented themselves as the owners of the entire island, which in fact they did not own. Francis states that in 1626, Minuit bought Staten Island from the Indians and gave them wampum, probably to seal the agreement. The English have said that the items paid were more to promote good relations than to actually pay for the land because the Indians did not actually own the land they sold.

Use of Belts

Some authorities have said that Hiawatha was the inventor of the wampum belt. This information is contained in Iroquois legend, but many of the legends have not proven to be true. Even though the Indians believe some known belts were prior to 1600, no beads of the type found in the belts have been found in any sites in upstate New York pre-dating 1600. (Fenton p. 449) There do not seem to be any wampum belts which appear to have been made before the European period in America. In 1624, Governor Burnett presented a belt to the Five Nations. As early as 1641, the Mohawks presented belts to the French. One belt given in the mid 1700s consisted of 30 rows of wampum and was five feet long. In 1701, the Onondagas announced the death of an old chief and the appointment of his successor by giving a bunch of wampum to each nation. To some councils they were taken almost by the bushel, more than 100 being used sometimes, but nearly all these were taken apart afterwards or made to do duty on some other occasion. It is to be remembered that very few belts were preserved. (Beauchamp p. 11) Hundreds of wampum belts of varying size, design, and color were exchanged to attest to political agreements. Most wampum belts were later broken up to form new belts, or the supply of wampum would not have been sufficient to make all the belts needed. That is one reason few really old belts survive. The widest known belt was 50 rows wide and measured 31-1/2 by 14-1/2 inches. The Washington Covenant Belt was given to the Iroquois either at a conference or at a treaty in 1775 or 1789 and is 6 feet 3-1/2 inches long by 5-1/4 inches wide with 10,000 beads and is the longest Iroquois belt extant in the U.S. It testifies to friendship between the 13 colonies and the Six Nations. Belts were made from wampum and varied in length, width and the kind and style of beads used. Many of the belts were seven rows wide. War belts were made of dark beads with a series of white tomahawks, and the peace belts were in white beads with a pipe in dark beads, according to Speck. Message belts were sometimes sent to the white colonists by the Indians. One of the most important belts known is the Penn Wampum Belt. It was supposed to record a treaty made by William Penn and the Delaware Indians in 1682, but it appears that the belt was actually made at a later date by the Iroquois Indians. It is said that Washington persuaded the Indians of western Pennsylvania to break the alliances they had made with the French and to return all the wampum belts they had received from the French to record the treaty. The Grand River Territory of the Iroquois Confederacy was established in the late 18th century and it became the repository for the wampum records of the Confederacy. It held three kinds of wampum records: the Confederacy constitutional records, the treaty records with the British Crown and other Indian nations, and the ceremonial wampum. There were a total of 20 belts located there in the 1870s. The belts were later stolen and sold to various museums. During the 1980s, many were returned to the Confederacy Chiefs at the Grand River.

Where it Was Used

Wampum was eventually used as money throughout the continental United States. Shell beads and actual whole shells were traded in ancient times, as shown by the ancient shells found great distances from their source. They had been traded to that area by tribes along the way. The majority of wampum was used, made, and traded in the New England area by the Dutch and English. The French also used wampum in trading with the Indians over a larger area. As early as 1715, New England wampum was used as money in Wisconsin. In 1804 Lewis and Clark used wampum with the Sioux and the Aricaras in the Dakotas. In 1819 the Osages knew about wampum. Wampum was also used in Arizona, California, the Carolinas, Florida, Georgia, New Mexico, Ohio, Oklahoma, and Tennessee. The Indians used six fathoms of wampum on the Colombia River to purchase a canoe. The Cherokee used it for money. The mound-builders and other tribes of the Mississippi area, including the Lenape Nation, used flat disk beads of

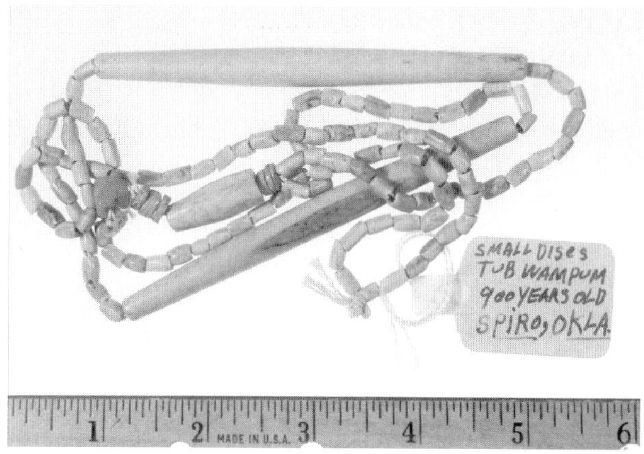

Wampum

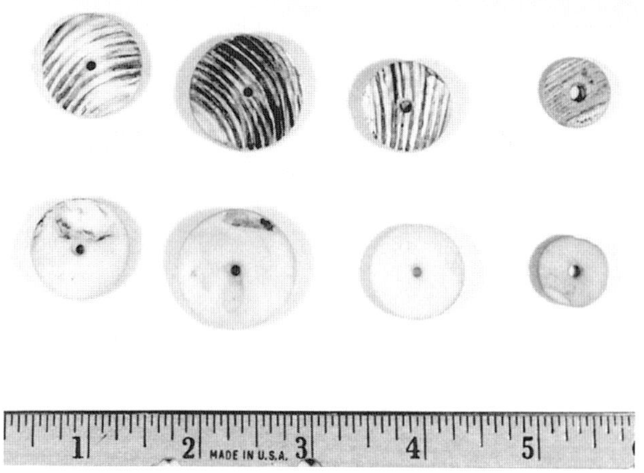

Wampum - Pomo Indians

shell as treasured possessions and for decoration on the dress and in the hair of the women. They were also made into belts to exchange at ceremonial or tribal conferences.

Arizona

The Pima Indians would only use clam shell disks as money. The Navahos used olivella shells as money. In the later 1800s a small string of olivella shells was worth a good horse.

Carolinas

The Indians of Carolina and Virginia used two different kinds of shell money called *peak* (wampum) and *ronoak* (*roanoke*). *Roanoke* was worth only 1/4 as much as wampum.

California

Discoidal shell beads ranging from 1/8 inch to 1-1/2 inches in diameter were made and used by the California tribes as a medium of exchange and have been called wampum. As early as 1792, Jose Longinos Martinez observed shell beads being used by the Chumash Indians in lower California. They were made from a small sea snail called *caracolito.* It is believed they were made on the Santa Barbara Channel. Eight strings of the shell beads, each one a yard long, were worth one silver dollar.

In central California the Pomo Indians used shell beads as money. The beads generally are about 1/2 inch in diameter. A bead two inches in diameter was valued at one dollar, a bead the size of a quarter was valued at 25 cents, and most 1/2 inch beads were valued at only four cents each. It appears that their value was based on the size of the denomination of the coin of that corresponding size. At one time the half-inch beads were only worth 160 to the dollar. The values did not remain constant. The Pomo Indians also produced and used clam shell cylinder beads which were made from the thick heel of the shell. They obtained them from Bodega Bay (Sonoma County) in Coast Miwok territory from the shell called *Saxidomus nuttallii*, or *aratus*, or *gracilis*. Every man manufactured the beads for himself. In former times the Indians traded for the shells, as it was too dangerous to go to the shell's source. The northernmost Pomo got their shells from the Athabascan coast near Shelter Cove. The Pomo supplied the disks for the northern half. They were broken, and the rough outer surface of the shell was rubbed off down to the white inner layer. The shells were then ground approximately round on a sandstone, bored, strung, and then finished by being ground on a fine- grain sandstone. Enough water was always used to keep the beads and the stone well dampened. In ancient times the drill was a piece of chert stone. When whites came, the small three-cornered steel file replaced the chert drill for drilling the holes in wampum. The value of wampum was based on the diameter, thickness, and the degree of polish on the beads. The older valuation was 400 beads for $2.50, or about $1 per yard. The value varied by time and location. It took about 800 regular beads to equal one magnesite bead which was the Pomo's high value currency. These magnesite beads, called *po*, *pol*, or *fol*, were made by baking raw nodules of magnesite in a fire and then shaping and drilling the piece to form a bead. The magnesite, which was dull grayish-white, turned beautiful shades of orange which polished up well. Magnesite beads were also used by the Yuki, Wintun, Kuhlanapo, Habenapo, Miwok, and Maidu.

The Yuki Indians used clam shell disk beads as money, which they obtained from the Pomo Indians. They also used dentalia as well. The Yokuts used shell disks of the wampum type for money, and they called them *keha*.

The Yokuts valued a string from the middle finger to the elbow at 25 cents. Clam-shell disks were a staple currency in central and southern California and were known as *hawock* or *hawok*. A particular necklace of these shells was 10 yards long with 1,160 beads and was worth $225. Some disks were two inches in diameter and 1/2 inch thick and were worth $1 each. (See Taxey p.68) The Chumash furnished the bulk of the supply of clam-shell disks used as money in the southern half of California.

Other tribes that also used the clam-shell disks as money include the Migueleno, Salinans, Gabrielino, and Luiseno. The value among these tribes varied considerably with a yard of the beads worth from 12-1/2 cents to $25. The disks also varied within the same tribe with different values at different times.

The Maidu used shell disk beads as money, and they counted them instead of measuring them by the length of the string. The Miwok Indians valued the shell beads at $5 per yard of beads. They also valued shell beads believed to be olivella shell at $1 per yard.

Oblong strips of abalone shell with a hole in one or both ends of the strip were worn as pendants or hung end to end to form a kind of necklace. They were a currency of the Miwok Indians of California. The Maidu Indians also used these pieces as money. A piece one inch to two inches by 1/2 inch wide was valued at one dollar and other sizes were valued proportionately. A string consists of 10 pieces making a string worth about $10. Only pieces that were polished to a beautiful iridescence were highly valued and used as money.

Oklahoma

The Temple Mounds yielded more than 5,000,000 shell beads in the 1930s. It is widely believed that the Indians used them as a form of money or for trade.

What Was Its Value?

In 1626, a fathom of wampum was purchased for five guilders and would buy 2-1/2 beaver pelts, while in 1641 six fathoms of wampum would buy only one beaver pelt. In 1662, 16 to 18 fathoms of wampum were needed to purchase one beaver pelt. (Ceci p. 101) Two hundred pieces of duffles (cloth) could be traded for 10,000 beaver skins. In the eight-year period from 1624 to 1632, 97,000 beaver skins and 8,500 otter skins were sent to Holland alone. Other goods like hatchets and linens were also used. In Massachusetts, the official exchange rate in 1637 was two white or one black bead per farthing, or six to eight beads for a penny for any sum under a shilling. In 1637, Connecticut received wampum for taxes at the rate of four beads to a penny. Later the rate was raised to six to the penny and then reduced again to the original four to a penny. In 1641 the legal tender of wampum was increased from one shilling to 10 pounds.

Purple beads were valued at twice that of white beads. At one time, three purple and six white beads were worth an English penny. In the mid 1600s the value of wampum fell by 50 percent, but by 1673 there was a severe shortage in wampum due to the sudden and general movement of the Indians toward the West and the placing of large amounts of wampum in Indian graves. In 1648, one beaver skin was worth two fathoms of white and one fathom of black wampum. In 1657, a beaver skin was worth two strings of wampum. In 1658 the old township of Bergen was purchased for 80 fathoms of wampum and other items. In 1660 the Mohawks wanted 30 handfuls of black wampum for one beaver skin. There were single strings that were valued at five shillings for a fathom, with the purple going for 10 shillings per fathom. A wampum belt five inches wide was valued at 10 pounds. In New Jersey, one fathom of wampum was valued at five Dutch guilders. In Virginia, a yard of purple wampum was valued at five Dutch guilders, and white beads were worth nine pence. In 1667 the town of Newark was purchased from the Hackensack Indians for 850 fathoms of wampum.

Campbell Wampum Factory

All persons were free to make wampum. Wampum was made in Bergen County, New Jersey, by the Campbell family starting about 1735. William Campbell started making wampum, and his son John set up a wampum factory in Park Ridge, New Jersey. His business was continued by his sons Abraham and William until 1899. There were five generations in total. Their beads are 1/2 inch to 7/8 inch long and a diameter of 3/16 of an inch. No bead of this size (small) appeared before the Campbells started making wampum. This small "belt wampum" does not appear until about 1650, which indicates the Indians did not make or use it before the coming of the European settlers. Some of the Campbell wampum was used to establish the John Jacob Astor fur business, and some of the wampum also was used as far west as Oregon. During the best wampum producing years between 1835 and 1866, one million dark beads were produced.

The Campbells got some of their shells from sailing ships from the West Indies, that used them as ballast as well as purchasing all the clam shells from the Fulton Fish Market in New York. They also had free clam- opening feasts when they imported the shells from Rockaway (N.Y.) Beach. The people in the area could have all the clams they wanted as long as they left the shells and did not break them.

They made the wampum by using a hammer to split off the thin part of the shell. It was then clamped in a hickory stick with a slit in it which held the shell secure. It was then ground smooth on a grindstone until it was made into an eight-sided piece about one inch long and 1/2 inch in diameter. A drill made from an untempered handsaw was tempered in the flame of a candle. A bow drill was then used to bore the hole. About every other sweep of the bow, the drill was withdrawn, cleaned and cooled by dripping water on it. They had to watch that excess heat did not break the shell and also had to remove the shell pieces that were drilled out. The hole was drilled halfway from each direction. A wire was then threaded through the unfinished beads, which were then ground on a grooved grindstone until smooth. The Campbells later discovered that buttermilk could be used to soften and bleach the shells, allowing them to make the beads faster and better. Many women worked in their homes for the Campbells. A woman could make five to 10 strings per day, and each string sold for 12-1/2 cents. The company sold black wampum for $5 per thousand. A string 12 inches long was counted as 50 beads. In 1869 James Campbell devised a machine that would drill six beads at one time. The Campbells made only two of these wampum-making machines. At one time they were said to have refused $10,000 for one machine. The length of the Campbell wampum is probably its most distinguishing characteristic as it is about three times as long as the Indian-made wampum. Westervelt states that the Campbells sold their wampum to John Jacob Astor, P. Cheauteau & Co. New York, Secter, Price & Co. Philadelphia, Robert Campbell, Chicago, and a firm in Texas. Astor is said to have opened the way for the Campbells to sell their items to the Indians in the plains and far West. Wampum started to decline around 1830, but moons and pipes continued until about 1899 (Westervelt p. 23-24). Wampum moons were made by the Campbells from conch shells brought from West Indian ports as ballast. Five to ten thousand shells were received at a time. The concave disks for the moons were made from the centers of pink shells and ranged in size from 1-1/2 inches to five inches in diameter. They were a natural, highly glazed pink and white with the side tied with a bright red worsted tassel through two holes in each center. Moons were very popular and were worn mostly as breastpins. A full set of moons consisted of three to five different size pieces. They were valued at $3 for a five-piece set, $2 for a three-piece set and $1.50 each. (Westervelt p. 16-19) Westervelt also states that wampum pipes were made by the Campbells from the large ridges or ribs on the lips of the conch shell. The large five-pound shells worked best because they yielded the largest pipes and moons. The pipes were from 1-1/2 inches to six inches long and larger than a lead pencil tapering from the center to each end. They were bleached with buttermilk and polished with sand and water. They were also called hair pipes and were used in breast plates in rows of from one to four rows wide, worn mainly by the Plains Indians. Sometimes hair was run through them and tied with brightly colored strings for ornament. Each pipe, up to 4-1/2 inches long, was worth six cents per inch, and larger pipes up to six inches long were worth eight cents per inch. Later the pipes were made from cow bones by white manufacturers. In the 1800s the use of cow bones greatly increased the supply of pipes, and large breast plates were possible and also were cheaper.

A farmer by the name of Johannes Stoltz had a large wampum-making business in the hamlet of Goffle, New Jersey, from 1700 to 1770. This factory started operation prior to the Campbell factory, and it is believed that it did not have power equipment like the Campbell factory. These beads were slightly larger than the native pieces and made use of purple pieces with traces of white. Other wampum factories were reported in Philadelphia, Staten Island, Babylon and Oyster Bay on Long Island, Keyport, Egg Harbor, Cape May, Absecon and Hakensak, New Jersey. (Francis p.26)

Abalone (Haliotis) Shell

The mother-of-pearl-looking shell was a barter item that was used on the West Coast and New Mexico. It was shaped into pendants, beads, and oblong pieces. At the turn of the 19th century, the Indians valued the shell at $6, which was equal to the value of a horse. Some consider the abalone only as a favorite barter item instead of as money. I feel that it was a form of money at times and only a form of barter at other times. (See Taxey p.73-74) Haliotis (abalone) was also used for ornamention by the Yurok but not as money.

Dentalium Shell Money -Indian Money But Not Wampum

Dentalium shells were called *allicotsik*, which means "Indian money" in the Yurok language. In northern California the species *D. indianorum* and in the south the species *D. hexagonum* was used as money. Both shells live in the sand in comparatively deep waters. Most of the shells came to the Yuroks from the Indians of Vancouver Island. The shells were valued more highly in the south than in the north. Larger shells were considered more valuable. Prices varied from $.25 to $5. Value was determined by how many shells it took to make a string of standard length (27-1/2"). Yurok Indians valued a house at three 12-shell strings, a bride from a wealthy family at 10 strings of various sizes, and a fine for adultery at five strings. A small boat was worth a 13-

shell string, and obsidian blades were worth two to 10 strings. A slave was worth one or two strings, while a headband called *sraisplegok* made from 50 woodpecker scalps was worth 10 strings of probably small shells. (Kroeber p. 27) They tried to have all of the shells on a string be the same size. The *Kergerpitl* shell was 2-1/2 inches long, and it took only 11 shells to make a string worth $50. The *Tsepupitl* shell was 1-1/2 inches, and it took 15 shells to make a string worth $2.50. Twelve-shell strings were worth $20, 13-shell strings were worth $10, and 14-shell strings were worth $5. Shells shorter than 1-1/8 inches long were not used as money. By 1920 the value of these strings was cut in half. A longer string was more valuable.

The Nootka of Vancouver Island, the Nuu-chah-nulth and also probably the Makah were the tribes who collected the shells. They devised complicated dredges to collect the dentalia from depths of 20 to 30 feet. They ate the meat and traded the shells to their southern neighbors. The Indians used a strip of wood with bone or wood teeth on it. They attached it to a pole, carefully probed the sand at the bottom of the water a number of times and then raised the strip to see if any shells were brought up. The farther from the source, the more valuable the shells were. The marriage price for a woman among the Shasta Indians in California was 15 or 20 large dentalium shells, 10 to 15 strings of disk-shaped beads, and 20 or 30 woodpecker scalps. Each shell was approximately 2" long. The shells were some of the wealth items used to proclaim rank and uphold prestige. The Shasta Indians engraved their dentalia with fine lines and angles and wrapped some of their shells with narrow strips of snake or fish skin diagonally along the shell. These decorations did not increase the value of the shells but were mainly decoration. Dentalium shells were used to pay for blood payment, murder, religious trespass, adultery, or the most heinous crime, which was to utter the name of another person's deceased relative. The Chinook Indians to the north also used dentalium shells as money and called them *hiaqua*. (To be considered as *hiaqua* there could be no more than 25 shells to the fathom. Forty shells to the fathom was considered a fixed standard.) Fifty shells to the fathom was worth only half as much as a 40 shell fathom. A fathom of 40 was formerly equivalent to a slave. Strings of smaller shells were called kop kop and were worth only one fortieth as much as a string of 25 shells to the fathom (hiaqua). Very long shells were worth more than one dollar in Washington. The longest shells known were about 2-1/2 inches long. (Hodge p. 447)

OLIVELLA SHELLS

Olivella or olive shells which have been ground down at the top to permit stringing were used as money. The

Olivella Shells

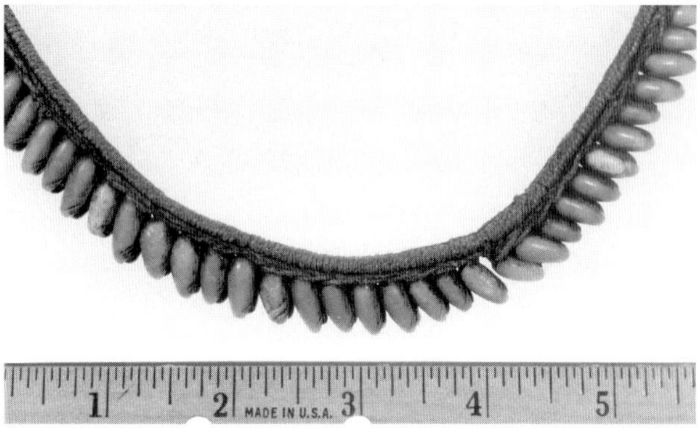

Waraz

Maidu used them as money and called them *kolkol*. They were valued at one dollar per yard in 1875. *Halitis* shell were called *ulo* and were strung in a double row in lengths as long as 15 feet. The shells were valued at one-fifth the value of the regular 1/2 inch shell disks. The Yurok Indians used *olivella* shells for ornamentation but not for money. In general the *olivella* shell beads were not considered as valuable as the clam shell beads or in some cases not even as money by some tribes. The beads were used in some areas as trade goods and in other areas as money. The Chumash used *olivella* shell beads as one of their less- valuable money beads. (King p. 61)

WAPITI - See Elk Teeth Money

WARAZ

Torres Straits

Another name for the string of olive shells used as money in a necklace is waraz. See olive shells. (See Haddon Vol. 6 p. 24)

WAURI

Torres Straits

The *wauri* is the first step toward actual money. This Conus shell has a token value and parts were used to

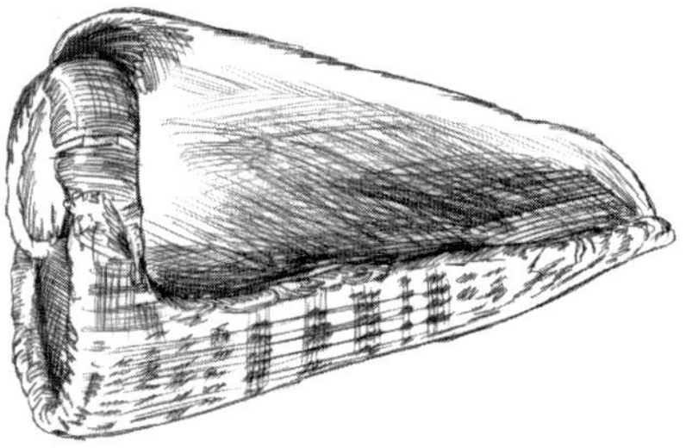

Wauri

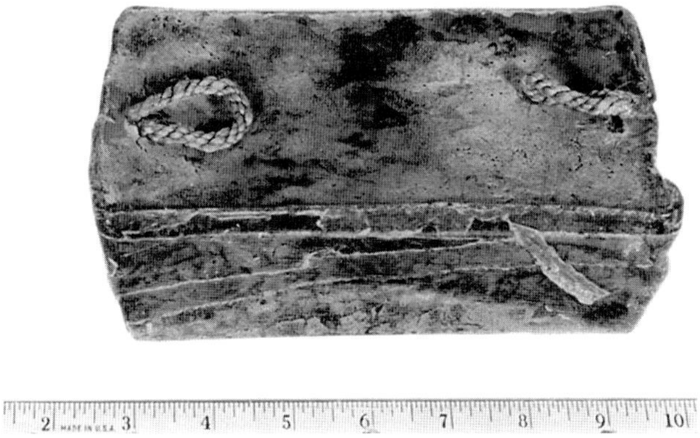

Wax

Ashanti Geometric Weights

Ashanti Weight Figures

make *wauri* o, shell ring and *Dibidibi*. A *wauri* was worth 10 to 12 large *dibidibi* or a wife. It was also an upper armband. (Quiggin p.17) (See Quiggin p. 181-182)

Cone shell arm ring used as money on both Torres Straits and parts of New Guinea. They were also part of the kula. A ring large enough to go on the arm was the highest unit of exchange in Torres Straits. It was worth a canoe. (See Haddon Vol. 4 p.56)

Triangular white shell pendant hung on the bride's chest. They were called o, *wauri* o, and o *kaukau*. Some had incised decoration on them. (See Haddon Vol. 6 p. 114)

WAX

Borneo

Blocks of beeswax weighing eight to 34 pounds were valued at 40 shillings.

Brazil

Round white cakes weighed one pound and were worth $1. (See Taxay p. 57)

Sweden

Tokens of sealing wax mounted on bases of iron, wood, or ivory were used as money. (See Schulman p. 35)

WEIGHTS - GOLD

Ashanti, Ghana, Togo, and Ivory Coast

The Akan occupied the area of Ghana and the Ivory Coast. They developed a weighing system based on the Islamic, Portuguese, and English systems and introduced weights around 1400, which spread rapidly in use until the 1750s. The Asante were the last of the Akan people to use the weights, starting after 1700. The Akan ceased using the weights about 1900. The weights are called Asante or Baule gold weights. Brass, copper, or bronze was used to make the weights by the lost wax method. A wax model was made and covered with clay and baked to melt the wax. Molten brass was then poured into the mold and allowed to harden, and the clay was then broken away, leaving an exact copy of the wax figure.The ornamental and geometric weights are considered to be the oldest. They were used to weigh gold as well as for trading purposes. The oldest Akan gold weights, among Islamic weights, are plain in the form of a truncated double cone, four-sided pyramid weights, weights with indented edges, polygonal weights (usually five or nine sides), or square or rectangular weights decorated with one, two, three, or four simple parallel bars. Many of the geometric weights show that they once had a lead filling which has since been removed. The Akan had weights in Islamic, Portuguese, troy, and mitkal weight standards. Almost all weights

now found are modern. They are cast into small animals, squares, rectangles, triangles, beetles, and people. The weights are still being made at the present time. Each weight had a name, and the Asante had 54 names describing weights from .02 to 352 grams. It is believed that the geometric weights were made and used earlier than the figure weights. The designs on the weights had no relation to the size or value of the weight. Metal boxes were used to hold gold dust and were also used as weights. There were also shovels or scoops used for lifting the gold dust and putting it on the scales. Items pictured were purchased in Africa in 1974. (See Nitecki)
Akan gold weights - (following from Garrard p. 275-299)
Early geometric weights

Cone forms - circular pellets, plugs, truncated cones, etc., circa 1400-1700.

Simple engraved forms - square, rectangular, circular with some engraved lines and dots, circa 1400-1700.

Polyhedron forms - eight sided cube from 1400-1700

Cogwheels - circular, rectangular, square all with cut cog teeth, circa 1400-1700

Notched forms - notches stamped in flat side at edge, square, rectangular, or circular, circa 1400-1700

Carved polygons - thick polygon base with carved designs on top. Made by lost wax method, circa 1500-1720.

Carved rectangles - similar to carved polygons but more common.

Variant carved rectangles - similar to carved rectangles, circa 1500-1720.

Pyramid forms - truncated pyramid and triangular pyramid, circa 1500-1720.

Late period geometric weights - square, rectangles, triangles, circles all in high relief, circa 1700-1900.

Early period figurative -shapes of animals & implements, circa 1600-1720.

Direct castings - seeds, insects, nuts, fruits, etc.

Late period figurative - more ornate and well made, circa 1700-1900.
Human figures - both early & late periods. Some are still being made for tourists.

Burma, Siam, Laos region, 1600-1860

The weights are called gold weights, opium weights, Burmese weights, or Asian weights. The animal weights are of Burmese origin but were used in the surrounding area. The weights were used in Burma, China, Persia, and India and were found as far away as Egypt due to trading to these areas at an early date. They were used with a balance scale. Until 1300 A.D. the *kyat* unit

Gold Weights

Alaungpaya (Alompra 1753-60) | Naungdoji (1760-63) | Bodowpaya (1781-1819)

Kongbaung paya oder Shwebo Min (1836-46) | Pagan Min (1846-52)

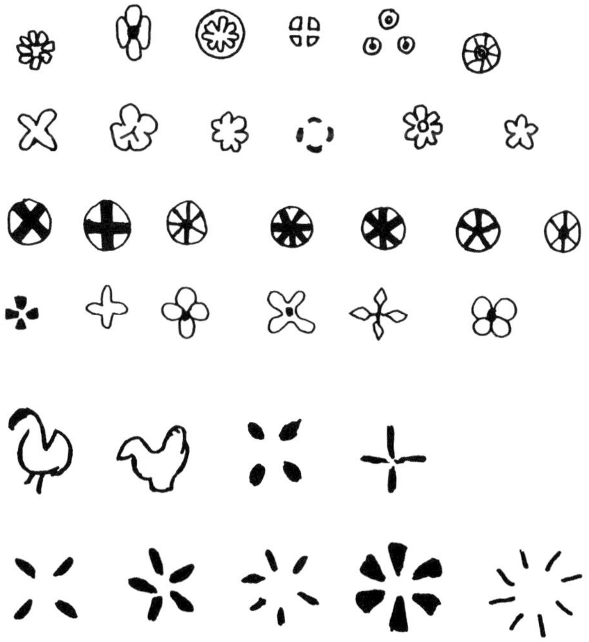

Gold Weights

weighed about 12.0 grams. By the 14th century the *kyat* weighed 14 grams and increased gradually until by 1908 it weighed 15 grams. It reached a high of 16.3 grams at the end of the 19th century.

The weights conform closely to the baht. Weights are one, two, three, four, five, six, eight, 10, 12, 16, 20, 50 or 100 baht. The largest weights weighed 1,600 grams, called one *viss*, 100 *kyat* or 100 *tikal*. Therefore one tical weighted about 16 grams, but that weight varied through the centuries. In the 19th century, weights of 2.5 and 5 viss were used but not at the present time. The most common size weight is 20 *kyat* with the majority of weights between two and 50 *kyats*. The bases are in the following shapes: hexagonal, octagonal, round, square, oval, rectangular, and pumpkin-shaped. On the bases are mounted any of a large variety of figures. The figures are the duck, lion, elephant, goose, Burmese crane, snake, chicken, stork, goat, bear, heron, bird of paradise, stag, Tibetan bull, horse, crested bull, cuckoo, mynah, hintha, monkey, frog, rat, buffalo, tiger, rabbit, dragon, horse, cock, dog, snail, turkey, worm, and squirrel. There are many varieties of many of the animals such as the ducks and lions. Some of the kinds of animals given may not exist at present because they have all been lost or remelted to form other weights. Most of the weights were made of a copper-tin alloy with variable amounts of zinc and lead, and during parts of the 15th and 16th centuries some of the weights had a stone core in the base. It is believed here were a few marble weights used during the 19th century. In about 700 B.C. in Persia and the surrounding area, duck and lion weights started to be used.

In the 16th and 17th centuries the weights were made of an alloy containing a large amount of copper, giving it a reddish color. In the 17th and 18th centuries the alloy contained more tin to give it a silvery color. In the 19th and early 20th centuries the weights were made of soft yellow bronze. Handles can be found on some of the 50, 100, and 250 *kyat* weights. Some of the square-based 10 *kyat* pieces also have handles. The larger weights of 100 **kyats** or greater have more elaborate decoration, and the weights of two *kyats* or less are missing some detail. Many counterfeit weights have been made from early times to the present. Signs or seals are mainly on the bases of the weights. Many of the weights of five *kyat* or less have the sign on the bottom of the base, or the sign is not present. During the 19th century, signs or marks in the form of star flowers were made on the base of the weights. Braun believes, but cannot confirm that the four petals were used in the early part of the century, five or six petals were used in the middle of the century, and eight or nine petals were used in the later part of the century. Some weights have more than one mark, while others do not have any marks. Seals were also used on some weights. The elephant weights primarily have these seals. The older weights are almost all black, dark brown, silvery bronze or bronze. Only modern weights are brassy in color. The actual materials can vary, but they mostly consist of copper, lead, and tin. In the 19th century, zinc also became important. The weights can also contain small amounts of nickel, iron, arsenic, and silver. Small bronze elephant weights were used in Burma to weigh silver bullion in the 20th century. They were also used to weigh opium during this period. Sometimes solder was added between the legs to increase the weight. In other cases, copper wire was wrapped around them to increase the weight. To reduce the weight part, the base would be removed. The elephant weight set normally consisted of seven different weights. There were many copies of weights made even at the time of their use. It is estimated that as many as one half of all weights seen are copies. Many were made to use when official weights were not available. Copies are also made today to sell to tourists and in a few cases deceive collectors. At present, modern sets are made in the form of frog, peacock and rhinoceros. These forms were never used in old days. Modern sets are also made of the elephant and *hintha*. Be cautious of sets that have an unnatural green or unpolished black patina, also pieces that have sharp edges or where identical examples of rare types are available. Complete sets of rare types can also indicate modern reproductions. (See Mitchiner p.365-366) (See Braun)

1 Baht (11.2 gram)
2 Baht (29-32 gram)
3 Baht (50 gram.)
4 Baht (69 gram)
5 Baht (79 gram)
6 Baht (94 gram)
8 Baht (126 gram)
10 Baht (163 gram)
12 Baht (183 gram)
16 Baht (252 gram)
20 Baht (312 gram)
50 Baht (794 gram)
100 Baht (1,616 gram)

WELA

Mumeng in Morobe Province, Papua New Guinea

This piece is similar to the *dangangtang* but has only eight egg cowries attached, and the central core is decorated with nassa shells to make four quarters colored alternately blue and red. It was used in bride price. See Barron, Colin, TMA November 1989.

WHALE TOOTH

Fiji

The tooth of the *cachalot*, or sperm whale, was called

Wela

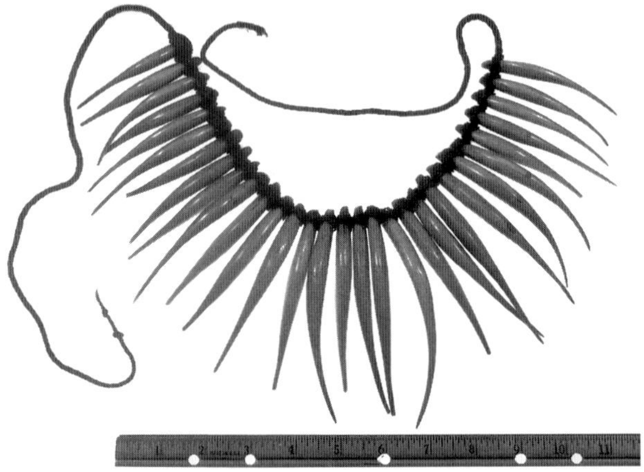

Whale Tooth Necklace

Whale Tooth

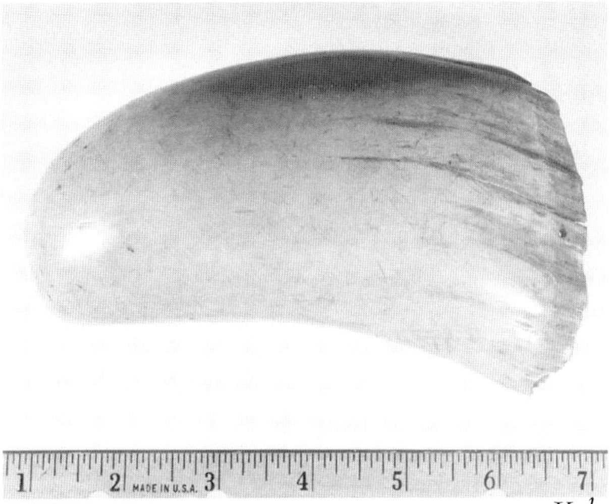

Kalo

tambua and was used as bride price and as a favorite medium of exchange. When a youth seeks a wife, the request must be accompanied by the presentation of a whale's tooth, and its acceptance constitutes a binding contract of marriage. It has a symbolic meaning similar to that of our engagement ring. In 1840, whale's teeth were only used for big transactions such as a canoe. "Such was the power of a whale's tooth that he who accepted it could not refuse the request it carried with it, whether it be for a mere gift or for an alliance, or for a human life." An old, polished, well-colored, red ivory tooth was worth about $25, while a white one was worth only about 25 cents. Some experts do not consider whale teeth to be money, but Brewster (p.17) relates a story which indicates they were used for compensation. To be presented with a tambua is a great honor. When Queen Elizabeth visited Fiji in the 1950s they presented her with a whale tooth. The necklace was made of thin shaved pieces of whale's teeth tied together in a chain at their base. The old original necklaces are very rare. (See Quiggin p. 130) (See Einzig p. 44) (See Mosher p. 30)

Solomon Islands

Sperm whale teeth, called *kalo*, were used as money in Marovo, New Georgia. It was considered an important currency. (See Hviding p. 93)

Yap Island

Whale teeth were attached to *gau* shell strings. See *Gau*

Willow Leaf Money

WHEAT - See Grain Currency

WHISKEY MONEY

America

A part of a workman's pay during the building of the railroad days was whiskey. It was also traded to the Indians for furs. (See Mosher p. 41) See Liquor

WHITE STAG NOTES

China, 118 B.C.

A small supply of notes were made from the skin of a white stag. Each piece was 1' square with a fringed border and was decorated. Each piece was valued at 40,000 copper coins. They were rare, as the Emperor Wu-Ti had only one white stag. Princes had to purchase a note to pay respect to the throne and present their gifts. (See Quiggin p. 248)

Wire Money

WILDCAT SKIN

Canada, early 1700s

The traders used many kinds of skins for trade. A blanket was at one time worth eight skins. (See Neufeld, p. 9)

WILLOW LEAF MONEY

Burma, 1600-1800

It is also called flower money or *ywetni* and was commonly used before and after 1287 A.D. in Burma in ingots of supposedly .900+ silver weighing 300 to 400 grams. The standard, however, was much smaller and was used from 1700 A.D. with reddish-yellow spots of *litharge* on one side and was 85 percent silver. An unusual pattern on one side resembled the pattern of frost on a window and was caused by the cooling silver. They were produced in the Shan provinces of the Upper Irrawaddy valley on the route to China. The thin flower money (9 - 16 gram) almost always has a hole for wearing, while the thick flower (13 - 311 gram) has no hole. There is also a flower tok that is thick with a crude concavity center reverse. (See Gear p.32) (See Semans p. 3.)

WIRE MONEY

Russia, 1547-1718

A short piece of silver wire was hammered flat and bent into a rough oval shape. A planchet was struck between two crude dies to form a coin. 1/2" - 3/4" (See Cheetem, Mitako)

WOTI SHELL - See Melo shell, Papua New Guinea, Kapauku tribe

WOOD - See Tukula

WOODEN BEAD MONEY

Nigeria

Small wood beads were used for small purchases.

WOODEN NICKELS

United States

The wood nickel originated in 1931 by the Tenino, Washington Chamber of Commerce as a fund raiser. It is an interesting item to collect, but it is not Odd & Curious Money. See Tally Sticks

WOODPECKER SCALPS

Yurok, Hupa, Shasta, Karuk tribes, United States

The *kokoneu* and *terer'it* species of woodpeckers were used as money. The *kokoneu* which were the larger and more brilliant were worth twice as much as the *terker'it* species. In 1872 the Karok Indians valued the scalps at five dollars and 2 1/2 dollars each respectively. At another time the *kokoneu* were worth $1 to $1.50 each, and the *terker'it* were worth 10 to 25 cents each. Among the Shasta the average bride price was 20-30 woodpecker scalps along with 15-20 full sized dentalium strings, 10 - 15 clam dish strings and possibly also a deer skin. The Yurok valued the scalps based on their size. The small ones were worth from $.50 to $1 each; the large ones from $1 to $5 each. Three large woodpecker scalps were worth a small boat. The scalps were used to decorate head dresses and other regalia. A headband called *sraisplcgok* made of 50 large woodpecker scalps was worth 10 strings of small dentalium shells. A large boat was worth 10 large or 60 small woodpecker scalps. A small boat was worth three large woodpecker scalps. (Kroeber p. 27) Woodpecker scalps were also used to purchase wives, pay for killing a man, adultery, and many other items. (See Quiggin p. 296) (See Sigler p. 36) (See Taxey p.80)

WOOL

1674, Rhode Island - colonial times

Wool was used as money and was valued at 1s. per pound in 1674. (See Taxay p. 58, 146)

WOSHELE

Africa, Zaire, Bankutu, Nkutshu, Zande, and Bushongo tribes.

It is a throwing knife that is also known as *shongo* or *oshele* (singular). It was made of a thick piece of iron. It was not a tool or weapon, but was the highest currency unit in the early 1900s. One *oshele* would purchase as many as five slaves. Two *woshele* would buy a wife. Two *woshele* were the normal bride price and also worth 1,250 *wudwe*, which was a slim iron hoe head. The oshele were normally broken up into small pieces because the value of the whole piece was too high for normal use. Only a wealthy chief could afford to keep one intact. The pieces are very rare. The handle was usually covered with a fiber net, animal skin, or copper bands. Those with wood or ivory handles are rare. (See Ballarini p.109) (See Spring p. 82) (See Quiggin p. 67-69)

Y-SHAPED - See Ogoja Penny

YAKARD - See Ogoja Penny

YAMS

Papua New Guinea

They are a source of food, currency, and a minor part of bride price.

Trobriand Islands

Yams were the principal currency with prices expressed in "standard yam baskets." They were also a store of value. Although unused yams were destroyed when the new harvest came in, the yams were readily accepted even when the native had a sufficient supply of yams on hand. (See Einzig p. 81-82)

Woshele

YAO STONES

Irian Jaya

The Dani tribe used these stones for bride price and for pigs. These smooth, flat green stones were also called *Je* stones. See *Je* stones.

YAP ISLAND STONE MONEY - See Stone Money

YAR - See Yar nu au.

YAR NU AU

Yap Island

A pearl shell (*pinctada margaritafera*) was bound on a sennit cord, and that cord was attached to another cord. That second cord had five-six pearl shells each bound on cords attached to it. The unit was called a *Botha A Yar*. Presentation strings may have 500 shells on them. They were used for local purchases and were considered women's money, while stone money was men's money. They were also called *yar nu valeu*. Small shells are found on Yap, but the larger, more valuable shells are imported from the Philippines or Palau. The shells from the Philippines have a yellowish tinge and are more valuable than the shells from Palau, which are dark blue at either end. A good imported *yar* is worth 50 or more local shells. The single shells are perforated at the hinge and have a tightly plaited handle made from attached sinnet. See *Lou tsu-k'uand.* 6-1/2" diameter (See Quiggin p. 143-144)

Yar Nu Au

YAR Nn VALEU

See yar nu au

YERAK

Dani Tribe, Irian Jaya

Plant fiber bands decorated with cowry shell down the center of the band and coix seeds and plaited orchid fiber at both edges of the band are called yerak. The bands are from 3/4 inch to two inches wide and six to nine feet long. Heider quotes an expedition which said the bands were used to set the price of pigs by measuring the distance around the pig directly behind the front legs. The pig was then valued at one cowry shell for each segment of the band it took to go around the pig. The bands were used as funeral gifts and were then distributed at the funeral. Matthiessen states, the belt was a form of currency that as an ornament was worn only at birth, at the time of initiation and in death. (See Traditional Money Association newsletter, Vol.12 Number 2, "Money of Men Who Eat Men", Col. Davidson) (See Heider)

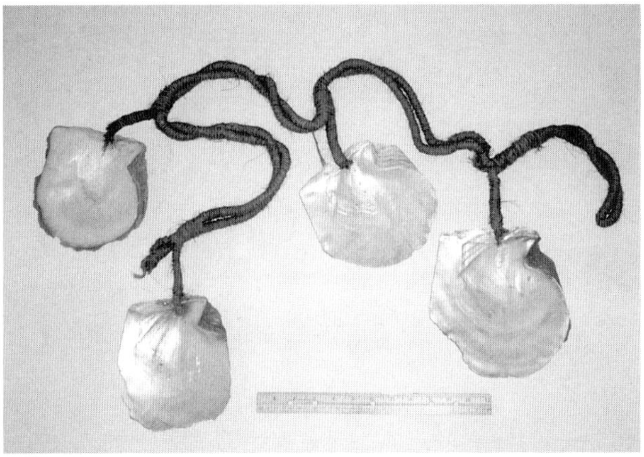

Yar Nu Au

YOKE - See Tingle Dangle Money

YELA
Rossel Island - See ndap and nko.

YUA - See ring money, Papua New Guinea

ZAPPOZAP
Lulua tribe and Nsapo people, Central Zaire, Africa

They were formerly known as a zappozap or *kasuyu* and now are called a Songe royal ritual axe from the Songe-Luba region. The axe has a worked iron head with a copper-covered handle of light material such as wood. On the spokes of the axehead, human heads are worked in the metal. They originally represented wealth but were not actual currency. The iron they were made from was actually bar money. They were an insignia of rank. At a later date they were used in native trading along with imported goods. At this time the axes acquired the status of currency. They were carried in parades and ceremonial displays by chiefs of the Songe people. The name zappozap originally comes from the name of a notorious brigand chief and slave raider of the Lulua who relocated his followers several times in the 1880s. He was succeeded by his son, also sometimes referred to as Zappo Zap. (See Quiggin p. 63.) Kriger suggests, "it was not that these hatchets themselves performed as currency in economic transactions, but rather they were made of money, that is, they were assemblages of bar iron currencies. These hatchets, which clearly were not built to be wielded as either tool or weapon, were instead made to serve as literal representations of wealth."

ZARU
Solomon Islands

A very old shell piece depicting two seated people facing away from each other over a ring. It was presented by a girl to the father of the boy she planned to marry to seal the marriage contract. *Zaru* were from the Roviana Lagoon and were used as money.

ZEBRA TAIL MONEY
Africa, Angola, Congo, Loango

The zebra tail was considered money and very valuable. One tail was worth two slaves. (See Mosher p. 27)

ZIKU
Choiseul Island, Solomon Islands

Arm rings were used as money with one *kesa* worth 10 *ziku*. They were considered only a substitute for *kesa*

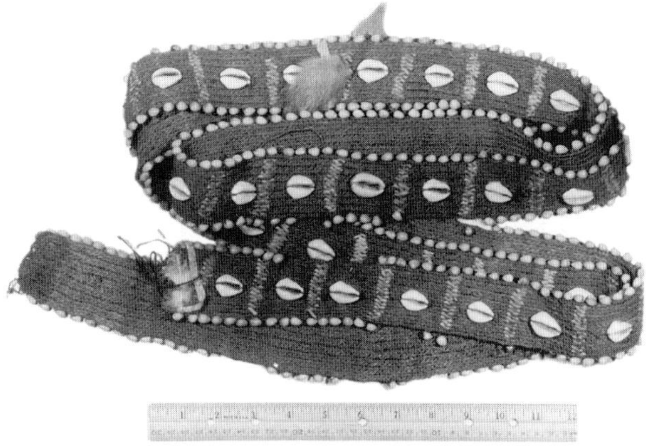

Yerak

Yerak

Zaru

and *kesa,* was always preferred. *Ziku* were used to pay fines in the same way *kesa* were used. (See Scheffler)

ZIMBABWE H CROSS - See Cross H Shaped

ZIMBU

This shell money was used in the kingdom of Congo before the arrival of the Portuguese. Later the shells were imported by the Portuguese from Bengela and Brazil. (Guyer p. 94.)

ZIMMER - See Fox Fur

ZONG

Africa

The *zong* is more a unit of account than a object of exchange by itself. *Mezong* is a packet of 10 *zong* held together by fiber. It is also a store of value. This iron spearhead was used as money. There is an old *zong* (plural *mezong*) used before the coming of whites and the new *zong* (*mandjong*) the whites brought. (See Schaedler p. 321) (See Guyer p. 85-93)

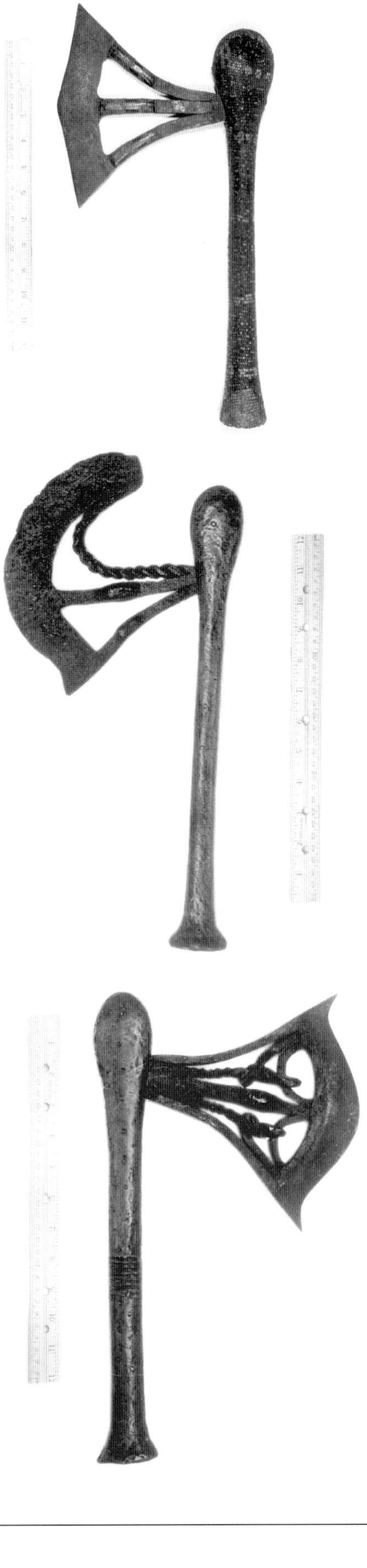

Zappozap

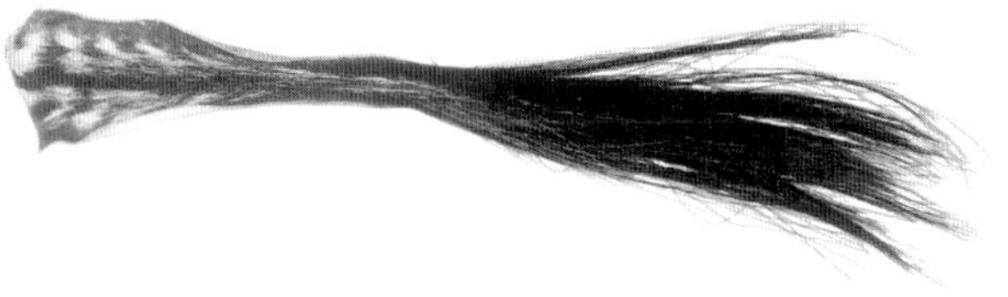

Zebra Tail Money

Zong

Bibliography

Adams, Monni. *Kuba Embroidered Cloth.* African Arts, November 1978.

Adhyatman, Sumarah. *Beads In Indonesia.* Jakarta, Penerbit Djambatan, 1993.

Akanbiemu, M.O. & Agili, Vickie. *Money In Nigeria: Past And Present.* Lagos, National Commission For Museums And Monuments, 1989.

Alexander, David T. *The Philippines, A Multi-cultered Numismatic Mosaic.* World Coins, October 1988.

Allen, Jamey. *Amber And Its Substitutes, Parts 1 & 2.* Bead Journal Winter, 1976.

Allen, Jamey. *Chevron-Star-Rosetta Beads, Parts 1 & 2.* Bead Journal Summer, 1983.

Alpers, Edward A. *Ivory And Slaves.* Berkeley, University Of California Press, 1975.

Althoff, Ralf. *Collection Kohler-Osbahr, Siamese Porcelain-Tokens.* Duisburg, Kohler-Osbahr Museum Part 2 Number 3, 1995.

Ambrose, W. R. *The Loneliness Of The Long Distance Trader In Melanesia.* Mankind, Vol. 11, 1978.

Ames, David W. *The Use Of A Transitional Cloth-Money Token Among The Wolof.* American Anthropologist, 1955.

Angell, Norman. *The Story of Money.* Garden City: Garden City Publishing, 1929.

Aring, Kenneth. Media Of Exchange In The Mongol Empire, 1990.

Armstrong, W. E. *Rossel Island Money: A Unique Monetary System.* The Economic Journal, Vol. 34, 1924.

Armstrong, W.E. *Shell-Money From Rossel Island.* Papua, Man # 119, November 1924.

Ashby, Gene. *Some Things Of Value, Micronesian Customs And Beliefs.* Eugene, Rainy Day Press, 1975.

Attenborough, David. *Journeys To The Past.* Guildford, Surrey, Lutterworth Press, 1981.

Attenborough, David. *The Tribal Eye.* New York, W.W. Norton & Company, 1976.

Baird, Donald. *The Indian Trade Gun And Gun-Flints From Burial 8 at The Pahaquarra Site.* Warren County, New Jersey, Bulletin Of The Archaeological Society Of New Jersey No. 42, 1987.

Balfour, Henry. *Note On The Use Of Elk Teeth For Money In North America.* The Journal Of The Anthropoligical Institute Of Great Britian And Ireland, 1890.

Ballarini, Roberto. *Black Africa's Traditional Arms.* Basiglio, Africa Curio, 1992.

Barlow, Kahleen. *The Role Of Women In Intertribal Trade Amoung The Murik Of Papua New Guinea.* Research In Economic Anthropology, Volume 7, Greenwich, Jai Press, 1985.

Barnett, H.G. *Palauan Society, A Study Of Contemporary Native Life In The Palau Islands.* Eugene, University Of Oregon Publications, 1949.

Barrett, S.A. *Marerial Aspects Of Pomo Culture, Part One.* Bulletin Of The Public Museum Of The City Of Milwaukee Volumn 20 #1, 1952.

Barnett, H.G. *The Nature of the Potlatch.* American Anthropologist Magazine, July - September 1938.

Bartle, J.F. *The Shell Money Of Auki Island.* Corona, October 1952.

Barton, R.F. *Ifugao Law.* University Of California Publications In American Archeology And Ethnology, Vol. 15 No. 1, February 15, 1919.

Bascom, William. *The Yoruba Of Southeastern Nigeria.* New York, Holt, Rinehart And Winston, 1969.

Battaglia, Debbora. *On The Bones Of The Serpent.* Chicago, University Of Chicago Press, 1990 .

Beauchamp, W.M. *Wampum Used In Council And As Currency.* The American Antiquarian, Volumn 20 #1, 1898.

Beauclair, Inez. *Ken-pai', A Glass Bracelet From Yap, Asian Perspectives.* Vol. v, 1., Hong Kong, Hong Kong University Press, 1962.

Beck, Horace. *Classification And Nomenclature Of Beads And Pendants.* York, George Shumway Publisher, 1981.

Beck, Horace. *Notes On Sundry Asiatic Beads.* Man No. 134, October 1930.

Beck, Horace. *The Magical Properties Of Beads.* Bead Journal, Spring, 1976.

Becker, Marshall Joseph. *Wampum: The Development Of An Early American Currency.* South Orange, Bulletin Of The Archaeological Society Of New Jersey # 36, 1981.

Belding, Barbara. *Ekipa Ornaments.* Ornament, Spring, 1997.

Belshaw, Cyril. *In Search Of Wealth.* American Anthropologist Vol. 57 # 1 Memoir # 80, February, 1955.

Belshaw, Cyril. *The Great Village.* London, Routledge & Kegan Paul, 1957.

Benedict, Burton. *Money: Tokens Of Value From Around The World.* Berkeley, The University Of California, 1991.

Benedict, Ruth. *Patterns of Culture.* Boston, Houghton Mifflin Company, 1934.

Bennett, Judith A. *Wealth Of The Solomons.* University Of Hawaii Press, Honolulu, 1987.

Beran, Harry. *Art Of The Massim Region Of Papua New Guinea*. Wollongong, Wollongong City Gallery, 1980.

Beresiner, Yasha. *An Introduction to Paper Money*. The Numismatist Magazine, Colorado Springs, !977, 1978.

Berg, M. L. *Yapese Politics, Yapese Money And The Sawei Tribute Network Before World War 1*. The Journal Of Pacific History Volume 27 Number 2, December 1992.

Berglund, Anders. *Some Observations On The Techniques Used For Striking Plate Money*. Journal Of The Russian Numismatic Society No. 32, Autumn, 1988.

Berglund, Anders And Talvia, Tuukka, And Zander, Randolph. *Russian American Company Scrip Notes Some Observations*. Journal Of The Russian Numismatic Society No. 28, Autumn, 1987.

Billings, Dorothy. *The Johnson Cult Of New Hanover*. Oceania Vol. 40, September 1969.

Blackmun, Barbara. *Blades of Beauty And Death*. Mesa College Art Gallery, 1990.

Blackwood, Beatrice. *Both Sides Of Buka Passage*. Oxford, At The Clarendon Press, 1935.

Blanchette, Jean-Francois. *Gunflints From Chicoutimi Indian Site (Quebec)*. Historical Archaeology Volume 9, 1975.

Blauer, Ettagale. *The Power Of Beads*. Lapidary Journal, October, 1994.

Blue, Martha. *A View From The Bullpen, Historic Trading Posts*. Flagstaff, Museum Of Northern Arizona, 1991.

Bohannan, Paul, and Dalton, George. *Markets in Africa*. Northwestern Press, Chicago, 1962.

Bohannan, Paul. *Some Principles Of Exchange And Investment Among The Tiv*. American Anthropologist, 1955.

Bolton, Reginald Pelman. *Indian Life Of Long Ago In The City Of New York*. Port Washington, Ira. J. Friedman, Inc., 1934.

Bolton, Reginald Pelham. *The Purchase Of Manhattan*. Bulletin Of The Archaeological Society Of New Jersey #32, 1975.

Bonnemaison, Joel. *Arts Of Vanuatu*. Honolulu, University Of Hawai'I Press, 1996.

Borel, Francis. *The Spendor Of Ethnic Jewelry*. New York, Harry N. Abrams, Inc., 1994.

Boston. J.S. *Ceremonial Iron Gongs Among The Ibo And The Igala*. Man # 52, March, 1964.

Boyer, Martha. *Mongol Jewellery*. Kobenhavn, Gyldendalske Boghandel, Nordisk Forlag, 1952.

Bragge, Laurence. *Habitat, Isolation And Subsistence Economy In The Central Range Of New Guinea*. Oceania, Vol. 44, September, 1973.

Brewster, A. B. *The Hill Tribes Of Fiji*. Philadelphia, J. B. Lippincott Company, 1922.

Briggs, L. Cabot. *The Living Races of the Sahara Desert*. Cambridge, The Peabody Museum, 1958.

Brincard, Marie-Therese. *The Art Of Metal In Africa*. Santa Ana, Charles W. Bowers Museum, 1983.

Brown, Delmer. *Money Economy In Medievel Japan*. New Haven, Institute Of Far Eastern Languages, 1951.

Brown, George. *Melanesians And Polynesians, Their Life-Histories Described And Compared*. New York, Benjamin Blom, Inc., 1972.

Brown, Paula. *Beyond A Mountain Valley*. Honolulu, University Of Hawai'i Press, .

Brown, Paula. *Highland Peoples Of New Guinea*. Cambridge, Cambridge University Press, 1975.

Brown, Paula. *Mingge-Money: Economic Changes In The New Guinea Highlands*. Southwestern Journal Of Anthropology Vol. 26 No. 3, 1970.

Brudin, J.A. *China: Coins Of Wang Mang And The Mantchu Dynasty*. Reprinted From The Numismatist, 1963.

Bulmer, Ralph. *Political Aspects Of The Moka Ceremonial Exchange System Among The Kyaka People Of The Western Highlands Of New Guinea*. Sidney, Oceania, Vol. 31 # 1, September, 1960.

Burridge, Kenelm, Mambu, London, Methuen & Co Ltd, 1960.

Burt, Ben. *Solomon Islanders, The Kwara'ae*. London, British Museum Publications, 1981.

Burt, Ben. *Tradition And Christianity. The Colonial Transformation Of A Solomon Islands Society*. Switzerland, Harwood Academic Publishers, 1994.

Bushnell, D.I. *The Origin Of Wampum*. Journal of the Anthropological Institute, Vol. XXXVI, 1906.

Busse, Mark; Turner, Susan; Araho, Nick. *The People Of Lake Kutubu And Kikori*. Port Moresby, Papua New Guinea National Museum, 1993.

Campbell, Shirley. *A Vakutan Mortuary Cycle, Death Rituals And Life In The Societies Of The Kula Ring*. Dekalb, Northern Illinois University Press, 1989.

Carey, Margaret. *Beads And Beadwork Of West And Central Africa*. Buckinghamshire, Shire Publications Ltd., 1991.

Carlton, R. Scott. *The International Encyclopedia Dictionary of Numismatics*. Iola, Krause Publications, 1996.

Carrier, James G. *History And Tradition In Melanesian Anthropology*. Berkeley, University Of California Press, 1992.

Carrier, James G. *Wages, Trade, And Exchange In Melanesa*. Berkeley, University Of California Press, 1989.

Carroll, Major Sheldon. *Major Carroll Deliveres Paper*

Money Talk At Central Coin Club Meeting. Sidney, Coin World article, April 5, 1967.

Carey, Margret. *Beads And Beadwork Of East And South Africa.* Aylesbury, Shire Publications Ltd., 1986.

Ceci, Lynn. *The Effect Of European Contact And Trade On The Settlement Pattern Of Indians In Coastal New York, 1524-1665: The Archeological And Documentary Evidence.* New York, City University of New York, 1977.

Ceci, Lynn. *The Value Of Wampum Among The New York Iroquois: A Case Study In Artifact Analysis.* Journal Of Anthropological Research Volumn 38 #1, Albuquerque, University Of New Mexico, 1982.

Cederlund, Ragnar. *The Siege Coins Of Landau, 1702 and 1713.* Numismatist, January, 1936.

Chaturabhand, Preecha. *People Of The Hills.* Bangkok, Editions Duang Kamol, 1987.

Chen, H.P. *1000 Varieties Of Chinese Sycees.* Hong Kong, 1988.

Chin, Lucas. *Beads Sarawak Museum.* Occasional Papers #2, Kuching, Lee Ming Press, 1984.

Chinnery, E. W. Pearson. *Notes On The Natives Of Certain Villages Of The Mandated Territory Of New Guinea.* Melbourne, H. J. Green, Government Printer, 1925.

Chowning, Ann. *Changes In West New Britian Trading Systerms In The Twentieth Century.* Mankind, Vol. 11, 1978.

Clark, Jeffrey. *Pearlshell Symbolism In Highlands Papua New Guinea, With Particular Reference To The Wiru People Of Southern Highlands Province.* Sydney, Oceania, June, 1991.

Clay, Brenda. *Mandak Realities.* New Brunswick, Rutgers University Press, 1986.

Clunie, Fergus. *Fijian Weapons & Warfare.* Suava, Bulletin of the Fiji Museum #2, 1985.

Cochrane, Glynn. *Big Men And Cargo Cults.* Oxford, Clarendon Press, 1970.

Codere, Helen. *Money-Exchange Systems And A Theory Of Money.* Man Vol.3 No. 4, December, 1968.

Codere, Helen. *Fighting With Property.* Monograph of the American Ethnological Society XVIII , New York, J.J. Augustin, 1950.

Codrington, R.H. *The Melanesians.* New York, Dover Publications, 1972 and Oxford, At The Clarendon Press, 1891.

Cole, Douglas and Chaikin, Ira. *An Iron Hand Upon The People, The Law Against The Potlach on the Northwest Coast.* Seattle, University of Washington Press, 1990.

Collins, June McCormick. *Valley of the Spirits.* Seattle, University of Washington Press, 1974.

Connell, John. *Melanesian Shell Money's New Economic Role.* South Pacific Bulletin, Fourth Quarter, 1978.

Connell, John. *The Bougainville Connection: Changes In The Economic Context Of Shell Money Production In Malaita.* Oceania, Vol. 48, December 1977.

Coole, Arthur Braddan. *Coins In China's History.* Mission, Kansas: Inter-Collegiate Press, 1965.

Coole, Arthur. *Ch'i Heavy Sword Coins And Debatable Pieces Of The Chou Era.* Lawrence, Quarterman Publications, Inc., 1976.

Cooper, Matthew. *Economic Context Of Shell Money Production In Malaita.* Oceania Vol. 41 # 4, June 1971.

Cotlow, Lewis. *In Search Of The Primitive.* Boston, Little, Brown and Company, 1966.

Counts, David and Dorothy. *The Vula of Kaliai: A Primitive Currency With Commercial Use.* Oceania Magazine Volume XLI No. 2, December, 1970.

Craig, Barry. *Children Of Afek, Tradition And Change Among The Mountain-Ok Of Central New Guinea.* Sydney, University Of Sidney, 1990.

Craig, William D. *Coins Of The World 1750-1850.* Racine, Western Publishing Company, Inc., 1976.

Cranstone, B.A.L. and Starzecka, Dorota Czarkowska. *The Solomon Islanders.* British Museum Publications Ltd., 1974.

Cranstone, B.A.L. *Melanesia - A Short Ethnography.* London, Charles Skilton Ltd., 1960.

Crawfor, John,. *The Silver Ringlets of Namibia.* Numismatist, April 1993.

Cresswell, Oliver D. *Early Coinage Of South East Asia.* Dallas, Numismatics International, 1974.

Cribb, Joe. *A Catalogue Of Sycee In The British Museum.* London, British Museum Publications, Ltd., 1992.

Cribb, Joe. *Money, From Cowrie Shells To Credit Cards.* London, British Museum Publications Ltd.,1986.

Crocombe, R. G. And Hogbin, G. R. *Land, Work And Productivity At Inonda.* New Guinea Research Unit Bulletin No. 2, Port Moresby, Australian National University, August 1963.

Crump, Thomas. *The Phenomen of Money.* London, Routledge & Kegan Paul.

Curtin, Philip D. *Africa Remembered, Narratives By West Africans From The Era Of The Slave Trade.* University Of Wisconsin Press, Madison, 1967.

Dalton, George. *Primitive Money.* American Anthropologist Vol. 67 #1, February, 1965.

Danks, Rev. Benjamin. *Shell-Money Of New Britian.* Journal Of The Anthropoligical Institute Vol. 18, 1888.

Darmody, Lynneeta. *Beads In Sarawak.* Ornament Vol. 11 # 2, 1987.

Davenport, William. *Red-Feather Money.* Scientific

American, March, 1962.

Davies, Glyn. *A History Of Money.* Cardiff, University Of Wales Press, 1994.

Deacon, A. Bernard. *Malekula, A Vanishing People In The New Herbrides.* London, George Routledge & Sons, Ltd., 1934.

De Boer. C., Die Tai Gandja Von Zentral-Sulawesi, Der Primitivgeld Sammler, EUCOPRIMO, Heft 1, 1994.

De Forest, John W. *History Of The Indians Of Connecticut From The Earliest Known Period To 1850.* Hartford, Wm. Jas. Hamersley, 1851.

Del Mar, Alexander. *Money And Civilization.* London, George Bell And Sons, 1886.

Del Mar, Alexander. *The History Of Money In America.* New York, The Cambridge Encyclopedia Company, 1899.

Delarozieere, Marie-Francoise. *Mauritanian Beads.* Ornament, (3), 1985.

Dentan, Robert. *The Semai- A Nonviolent People Of Malaya.* New York, Holt, Rinehart And Winston, 1968.

Dewey, William and Roberts, Allen. *Iron, Master of Them All.* The University of Iowa Museum of Art and The Project for Advanced Study of Art and Life in Africa, 1993.

Dillingham, Paul. A Series Of Articles Published By The Author At Various Times. Nashville.

Dodd, Agnes F. *History Of Money In The British Empire & The United States.* New York, Longmans, Green, And Co., 1911.

Dodson, O.H. *Money Tells The Story.* Racine, Whitman Publishing Company, 1962.

Donald, Leland. *The Slave Trade On The Northwest Coast Of North America.* Research In Economic Anthropology Volume 6, 1984.

Doty, Richard. *The Macmillan Encyclopedia Of Numismatics.* New York, Macmillan, 1982.

Douglas, Mary. *In The Active Voice.* London, Routledge & Kegan Paul, 1982.

Douglas, Mary. *Raffia Cloth Distribution In The Lele Economy.* Africa Vol. 28, London, Oxford Press, 1958.

Douglas, Mary. *The Lele Of The Kasai.* London, Oxford University Press, 1963.

Dubin,Lois Sherr. *The History Of Beads From 30,000 B.C. To The Present.* New York, Harry N. Abrams, Inc.,1987.

Dunn, E. J. *The Bushman.* London, Charles Griffin & Company, Limited, 1931.

Du Bois, Cora. *The People Of Alor.* Minneapolis, The University of Minnesota Press, 1944.

Du Toit, Brian M. *Akuna, A New Guinea Village Community.* Rotterdam, A. A. Balkema, 1975.

Dupre, Georges. *Geschichte Und "Abenteuer" Eines Geldobjektes Der Kwele (Volksrepublik Kongo): Mezong, Mondjos Und Mandjong.* EUCOMRIMO #3 1994.

Dutton, Tom. *Language And Trade In Central And South-East Papua.* Mankind, Vol. 11, 1978.

Ebbinghouse, David, and Winsten, Michael. *Tibetan DZi Beads.* Pt. 1, Ornament, (3), 1982.

Ederer, Rupert, J. *The Evolution Of Money.* Washington D. C., Public Affairs Press, 1964.

Edge-Partington, James. *An Album of the Weapons, Tools, Ornaments, Articles of Dress of the Natives of the Pacific Islands.* facisimile of the original work, London, The Holland Press, 1969.

Einzig, Paul. *Primitive Money.* London, Eyre & Spottiswoode, 1951.

Elkin, A.P. *Studies In Australian Totemism The Nature Of Australian Totemism.* Oceania Vol. 4, December, 1933.

Elmberg, John-Erik. *Balance And Circulation, The Ethnographical Museum.* Monograph Series No. 12, Stockholm, 1968.

Emmons, George. *The Chilkat Blanket.* Sitka, Friends Of The Sheldon Jackson Museum, 1993.

Emmons, George Thornton. *The Tlingit Indians.* Seattle, University of Washington Press, 1991.

Erickson, Joan Mowat. *The Universal Bead.* New York, W.W. Norton, 1969.

Ernst, T.M. *Aspects Of Meaning Of Exchanges And Exchange Items Among The Onabasulu Of The Great Papuan Plateau.* Mankind, Vol. 11, 1978.

Espinoza, Edgard And Mann, Mary-Jacque. *Identification Guide For Ivory And Ivory Substitutes.* Washington D.C., World Wildlife Fund, 1992.

Etienne, Mona and Leacock, Eleanor. *Women And Colonization.* A J. F. Bergin Publishers Book, 1980.

Eyo, Ekpo. *Nigeria And The Evolution Of Money.* Lagos, The Central Bank Of Nigeria, 1979.

Farr, Francine. *Pahouin Body Ornament.* Ornament Vol. 11 # 1, 1987.

Feil, Daryl. *From Pigs To Pearlshells: The Transformation Of A New Guinea Highlands Exchange Economy.* American Ethnologist Volume 9 Number 2, May, 1982.

Feil, Daryl Keith. *The Bride In Bridewealth: A Case From The New Guinea Highlands.* Ethnology,

Feil, D. K. *The Evolution Of Highland Papua New Guinea Societies.* Cambridge, Cambridge University Press, 1978.

Feil, D.K. *Ways Of Exchange.* Queensland, University Of Queensland Press, 1984.

Felix, Marc, Kipinga, Munchen, Verlag Fred Jahn, 1991.

Fenstermaker, G. B. *The Chinese Bead.* 1979.

Fenton, William. *The New York State Wampum*

Collection: The Case For The Integrity Of Cultural Treasures. Proceedings Of The American Philophical Society, Volumn 115 # 6, December, 1971.

Firth, Raymond. *Economics Of The New Zealand Maori*. Wellington, R.E. Owen, Government Printer, 1959.

Firth, Raymond. *Primitive Polynesian Economy*. New York, W.W. Norton & Company, Inc., 1965.

Firth, Raymond. *Themes In Economic Anthropology*. London, Tavistock Publications, 1967.

Fischer, Werner and Zirngibl, Manfred. *African Weapons*. Germany, Prinz-Verlag, 1978.

Fisher, Angela. *Africa Adorned*. New York, Abrams, 1984.

Forde, C. Daryll. *Habitat, Economy And Society*. London, Methuen & Co Ltd, 1961.

Fox, Sir Cyril. *The Distribution Of Currency Bars*. Antiquity, December, 1940.

Francis, Peter. Jr. *20 Easy Steps To Identifying Most Beads In Most Collections*. Lake Placid, Lapis Route Books, 1992.

Francis, Peter, Jr. *Another Bead Potpourri*. Ornament Vol. 10 # 3, 1987.

Francis, Peter, Jr. *The Asian Bead Study Tour 2, Thailand: Revolution And Ruin, Tradition And Change*. Ornament, Vol. 9 # 2, 1985.

Francis, Peter, Jr. *Beads And The Bead Trade In Southest Asia*. Lake Placid, Center for Bead Research, 1989.

Francis, Peter, Jr. *Beads At The Crossroads Of Continents*. Washington, Smithsonian Institution Press, .

Francis, Peter Jr. The Glass Trade Beads Of Europe, Lake Placid, New York, Lapis Route Books, 1988.

Francis, Peter, Jr. Beadmaking In Islam: The African Trade And The Rise Of Hebron, Beads, Volume 2, 1990.

Francis, Peter, Jr. Beads And The Discovery Of America, Ornament Vol. 8 (2), 1984.

Francis, Peter, Jr. Beads And The Discovery Of The New World, Occasional Papers No. 3, Lake Placid, The Center for Bead Research, 1986.

Francis, Peter, Jr. Beads Of The World, Atglen, Schiffer Publishing, Ltd., 1994.

Francis, Peter, Jr. The Glories Of Kedah, Ornament Vol. 15 # 1, 1991.

Francis, Peter, Jr. Heirlooms Of The Hills, Lake Placid, Lapis Route Books, 1992.

Francis, Peter, Jr. Ifugao Heirloom Beads, Ornament, Vol. 17 # 1, 1993.

Francis, Peter, Jr. Indian Agate Beads, Lake Placid, Lapis Route Books, 1982.

Francis, Peter, Jr. *Markets And The Alteration Of Beads In West Africa*. Ornament, Vol. 16 # 3, 1993.

Francis, Peter, Jr. *Mutisalah*. Ornament, Vol. 18 # 3, 1995.

Francis, Peter, Jr. *Peking Glass Beads*. Ornament, Vol. 14 # 2, 1990.

Francis, Peter, Jr. *Pumtek Beads*. Ornament, Vol. 18 # 4, 1995.

Francis, Peter, Jr. *West African Perspective The Early Bead Trade*. Ornament, Vol. 16 # 1, 1992.

Francis, Peter, Jr. *West African Perspective The Size Of The Bead Trade*. Ornament, Vol. 16 # 2, 1992.

Francis, Peter, Jr. *West African Powder Glass Beads*. Ornament, Vol. 16 # 4, 1993.

Francis, Peter, Jr. *Where Beads Are Loved*. Lake Placid, Lapis Route Books, 1993.

Frazier, Si & Ann. *The African Money Dictionary*. Lapidary Journal, April, 1994.

Freeman, Colin, And Holdsworth, David. *Arts & Crafts Of Papua & New Guinea*. Adelaide, Rigby Limited, 1971.

Friedburg, Arthur. *Money And Trade In New Netherland*. Colorado Springs, The Numismatist, June, 1993.

Furness, W. H. *The Island of Stone Money*. Lippincott, London, 1910.

Gabriel, Hannelore. *In Search Of The Shadow Soul*. Lapidary Journal, October, 1994.

Gabriel, Hannelore. *Shell Jewelry Of The Nagas*. Ornament, Vol. 9 # 1, 1985.

Garrard, Timothy. *Akan Weights And The Gold Trade*. New York, Longman Group Limited, 1980.

Garrard, Timothy. *Gold Of Africa*. New York, Prestel, 1989.

Garrard, Timothy. *Studies In Akan Goldweights*. Transaction Of The Historical Society Of Ghana, Vol. 13, Legon, June, 1972.

Gear, Donald And Joan. *Earth To Heaven, The Royal Animal-Shaped Weights Of The Burmese Empires*. Harrow, Twinstar, Ltd., 1992.

Gerber, Peter. *Indians of the Northwest Coast*. New York, Facts On File, Inc., 1989.

Gerlach, Martin. *Primitive And Folk Jewelry*. New York, Dover Publications, 1971.

Giay, Benny And Godschalk, Jan A. *Cargoism In Irian Jaya Today*. Oceania, 1993.

Gibbs, Howard D. *Quaint and Curious Moneys of Africa*. Numismatic Review, September, 1943, March, 1944, October, 1944, January - March, 1945.

Giday, Belai. *Currency and Banking Ethopia*. Addis Ababa, 1987.

Gill, Dennis. *The Coinage of Ethiopia, Eritrea, And Italian Somolia*. Mineola, Printing Mart, 1991.

Gilliland, Cora Lee. *The Stone Money Of Yap.* Washington, Smithsonian Institution Press, 1975.

Gillow, John. *Traditional Indonesian Textiles.* London, Thames And Hudson, 1992.

Gitlow, Abraham. *Economics Of The Mount Hagen Tribes.* New Guinea, New York, J.J. Augustin Publisher, 1947.

Glasse, Robert M. *Huli Of Papua.* Paris, Mouton & Co., 1968.

Glasse, R. M. *Pigs, Pearlshells, And Women.* Englewood Cliffs, Prentice-Hall, Inc., 1969.

Godelier, Maurice. *Salt Currency And The Circulation Of Commodities Among The Baruya Of New Guinea.* Studies In Economic Anthropology, Anthropological Studies # 7, 1971.

Godelier, Maurice. *The Making Of Great Men.* Cambridge, Cambridge University Press, 1986.

Goodale, Jane C. *To Sing With Pigs Is Human.* Seattle, University Of Washington Press, 1995.

Goodenough, Ward H. *Property, Kin, And Community On Truk.* New Haven, Yale University Oress, 1951.

Gordon, Albert F. *The Tribal Bead - A Handbook Of African Trade Beads.* New York, Tribal Arts Gallery, 1976.

Gowland, F.I.C. *Copper And Its Alloys In Prehistoric Times.* The Journal Of The Anthropolical Institute Of Great Britian And Ireland, Vol. 36, 1906.

Gray, Richard, and Birmingham, David. *Pre-Colonial African Trade.* Oxford, University Press, 1970.

Gray, Robert. *Sonjo Bride-Price And The Question Of African "Wife Purchase".* American Anthropologist, 1960.

Gregory, C. A. *Gifts To Men And Gifts To God: Gift Exchange And Capital Accumulation In Contemporary Papua.* Man Vol. 15, 1980.

Grierson, Philip. *The Origins Of Money.* London, The Athlone Press, 1977.

Grosz-Ngate. *Monetization Of Bridewealth And The Abandonment Of Kin Roads Tp Mattiage In Sana, Mali.* American Ethnologist, Volume 15 Number 3, August, 1988.

Guido, Margaret. *The Glass Beads Of The Prehistoric And Roman Periods In Britian And Ireland.* London, The Society Of Antiquaries Of London, 1978.

Guppy, H. B. *The Solomon Islands and Their Natives.* London, Swan Sonnenschein, Lowrey & Co., 1887.

Gustafsson, Berit. *Houses And Ancestors.* IASSA, 1992.

Guyer, Jane I. *The Iron Currenies of Southern Cameroon.* Symbols, A Publication of the Peabody Museum and the Department of Anthropology, Harvard University, Cambridge, December, 1985.

Guyer, Jane I. *Money Matters.* London, James Currey Ltd., 1995.

Haddon, A. C. *Copper Rod Currency From The Transvaal.* Man, Vol. 65, 1908.

Haddon, A. C. *Reports Of The Cambridge Anthropological Expedition To Torres Straits Vol. 4.* New York, Cambridge: At The University Press, 1912.

Haddon, A. C. *Reports Of The Cambridge Anthropological Expedition To Torres Straits Vol. 5.* New York, Cambridge: At The University Press, 1904, Reprinted Johnson Reprint Corporation, 1971.

Haddon, A. C. *Reports Of The Cambridge Anthropological Expedition To Torres Straits Vol. 6.* New York, Cambridge: At The University Press, 1908.

Haddon, A. C. *The Ethnolography Of The Western Tribes Of Torres Straits.* The Journal Of The Anthropological Instiute Of Great Britian And Ireland Vol. 19, 1890.

Hale, H. *Four Huron Wampum Records.* The Journal Of The Anthropological Institute Of Great Britian And Ireland, Vol. 26, 1897.

Hall, Martin. *Farmers, Kings, and Traders.* Chicago, University of Chicago Press, 1987.

Hamilton, Martha. *Silver In The Fur Trade.* Chelmsford, Martha Hamilton Publishing, 1995.

Hamilton, T. M. *Indian Trade Guns.*

Hammond, Peter, *Cultural And Social Anthropology.* London, The Macmillan Company, 1965.

Hanson, Charles E. *The Northwest Gun.* Lincoln, Nebraska State Historical Society, 1955.

Harding, J.R. *Conus Shell Disc Ornaments (Vibangwa) In Africa.* Journal Of Royal Institute Of Great Britian And Ireland Vol. 90, 1960.

Harding, Thomas. *A History Of Cargoism In Sio, North-East New Guinea.* Oceania, Vol. 38, September, 1967.

Harding, Thomas G. *Voyagers Of The Vitiaz Strait.* Seattle, University Of Washington Press, 1967.

Harms, Robert W. *River of Wealth, River of Sorrow.* New Haven, Yale University Press, !981.

Harrer, Heinrich. *I Come From The Stone Age.* New York, E. P. Dutton & Co., Inc., 1965.

Harris, Elizabeth. *The Russian Bead.* Northwest Colored Bead Chart No. 3, G. B. Fenstermaker, 1985.

Hart, C.M. And Pilling, Arnold. *The Tiwi Of North Australia.* New York, Holt, Rinehart And Winston, 1960.

Harter, Pierre. *The Beads Of Cameroon.* Beads, Volume 4, 1992.

Hasluck, Margaret. *Bride-Price In Albania.* Man # 203, December, 1933.

Hauser-Schaublin, Nabholz-Kartaschoff, Marie-Louise, and Ramseyer, Urs. *Textiles In Bali.* Berkley, Periplus Editions, 1991.

Havemeyer, Loomis. *Ethnography.* Boston, Ginn And

Company, 1929.

Healey, Christopher. *Maring Hunters And Traders.* Berkley, University Of California Press, 1990.

Hedges, Ken. *Money In Medieval Mexico.* World Coins Magazine, April, June, and July, 1970.

Heider, Karl. *Grand Valley Dani, Peaseful Warriors.* New York, Holt, Rinehart And Winston, 1979.

Heider, Karl. *The Dugum Dani.* Chicago, Aldine Publishing Company, 1970.

Heider, Karl. *The Grand Valley Dani Pig Feast: A Ritual Of Passage And Intensification.* Oceania Vol. 42, March, 1972.

Heizer, Robert. *Trade And Trails.* Northeast Vol. 15, Washington, 1978.

Henggeler, Joe. *Ivory Trumpets Of The Mende.* African Arts, February, 1981.

Herbert, Eugenia W. *Iron, Gender, And Power.* Bloomington, Indiana University Press, 1993.

Herbert, Eugenia W. *Red Gold Of Africa, Copper In Precolonial History And Culture.* Madison, The University Of Wisconsin Press, 1984.

Herdt, Gilbert H. *Guardians Of The Flutes.* New York, Columbia University Press, 1981.

Herle, Anita. *Naga Body Decoration.* Ornament Vol. 12 # 2, 1988.

Herskovits, Melville. *Economic Anthropology.* New York, Alfred A. Knopf, 1952.

Herskovits, Melville. *The Economic Life Of Primitive Peoples.* New York, Alfred A. Knopf, 1940.

Herskovits, Melville J. *Man And His Works.* New York, Alfred A. Knopf, 1956.

Hetzel, Francis X. *The First Taint Of Civilization.* Honolulu, University Of Hawaii Press, 1983.

Heusch, Lucde. *Objects, Signs of Africa.* Snoeck-Ducaju & Zoon.

Hodge, Frederick Webb. *Handbook Of American Indians North Of Mexico.* Smithsonian Institution Bureau of American Ethnology Bulletin 30 Parts 1 And 2, Washington, Government Printing Office, 1911.

Hodge, William. *The First Americans, Then And Now.* New York, Holt, Rinehart and Winston, 1932.

Hogbin, Ian. *Coconuts And Coral Islands.* National Geographic, March, 1934.

Hogbin, Ian. *A Guadalcanal Society, The Kaoka Speakers.* New York, Holt, Rinehart and Winston, 1964.

Hogbin, Ian. *Experiments In Civilization.* London, George Routledge & Sons, Ltd., 1939.

Hogbin, Ian. *Village.* London, The Athlone Press, 1963.

Hogbin, Ian. *Trading Expeditions In Northern New Guinea.* Oceania Vol. 5, June, 1935.

Hogbin, Ian. *Transformation Scene. The Changing Culture Of A New Guinea Village.* London, Routledge & Kegan Paul Limited, 1951.

Hogendorn, Jan, And Johnson, Marion. *The Shell Money Of The Slave Trade.* Cambridge, Cambridge University Press, 1986.

Hogg, Donald. *New Guinea.* Sydney, A.H. & A.W. Reed, 1969.

Holmberg, Berta. *Copper Coins Of Sweden.* Reprint From The Numismatist, 1962.

Horsh, Charles R. *The Maria Theresa Thaler: Austria's Famous Trade Coin.* NI Bulletin, Vol. 33 Number 3, March, 1988.

Hose, Charles. *The Pagan Tribes Of Borneo.* London, Macmillan And Co., Limited, 1912.

Hothem, Lar. *American Indian Axes And Related Stone Artifacts.* Paducah, Collector Books, 1989.

Howell, P.P. *On The Value Of Iron Among The Nuer, Man.* No. 144, October, 1947.

Huffman, Kirk W. *Trading, Cultural Exchange and Copyright: Important Aspects Of Vanuatu Arts.* Honolulu, University Of Hawaii Press, 1996.

Hughes, Ian. *Good Money And Bad: Inflation And Devaluation In The Colonial Process.* Mankind, Vol. 11, 1978.

Hugher, Ian. *New Guinea Stone Age Trade.* Terra Australis #3, Canberra, The Australian National University, 1977.

Hurst, Norman. *Ngola.* Cambridge, Hurst Gallery, 1997.

Hviding, Edvard. *Guardians Of Marovo Lagoon.* Pacific Islands Monograph Series 14, Honolulu, University of Hawai'i Press, 1996.

Ivens, W.G. *Melanesians of the South-east Solomon Islands.* London, Kegan, Paul, Trench, Trubner & Co., Ltd., 1927.

Ivens, Walter G. *The Island Builders Of The Pacific.* London, Seeley, Service & Co. Ltd., 1930.

Jablow, Joseph. *The Cheyenne in Plains Indian Trade Relations 1795-1840.* New York, Augustin, 1951.

Jacknis, Ira. *The Carver's Art Of The Indians Of Northwestern California.* American Indian Art Magazine, Autumn, 1995.

Jacobs, Julian. *The Nagas.* London, Thanes And Hudson, 1990.

Jain, Jyotindra & Aggarwala, Aarti. National Handicrafts And Handlooms Museum. New Delhi, Ahmedabad, Mapin Publishing Pvt. Ltd., 1989.

Jargstorf, Sibylle. *Glass Beads From Europe With Value Guide.* Atglen, Schiffer Publishing Ltd., 1995.

Jarvie, I.C. *Theories Of Cargo Cults: A Critical Analysis.* Oceania, Vol. 34, September, 1963.

Jarvie, I.C. *The Revolution In Anthropology.* New York, The Humanities Press, 1964.

Jen, David. *Chinese Cash.* Iola, Krause Publications, Inc., 2000.

Jenkins, Michael. *Glass Trade Beads In Alaska.* Bead Journal, Summer, 1975.

Jevons, W. Stanley. *Money and the Mechanism of Exchange.* New York, D. Appleton and Company, 1900.

Johansson, Sven-Olof. *Nigerian Currencies, Manillas, Cowries and Others.* Sweden: Alfa-Tryck, 1967.

Jolly, Margaret. *Banana Leaf Bundles And Skirts, History And Tradition In Melanesian Anthropology.* Berkley, University Of California Press.

Jones, G.I. *Native And Trade Currencies In Southern Nigeria During The Eighteenth And Nineteenth Centuries.* Africa, Vol. 28, 1958.

Johnson, Stephen. *Living Beads In Guatemala.* Bead Journal, Summer, 1975.

Jopling, Carol F. *The Coppers Of The Northwest Coast Indians: Their Origin, Development, And Possible Antecedents.* Philadelphia, The American Philosophical Society, 1989.

Kann, Edward. *The Currencies Of China.* New York, Durst Publications,,1978.

Kapferer, Bruce. *Transaction And Meaning.* Philadelphia, Institute For The Study Of Human Issues, 1976.

Karklins, Karlis. *Identifying Beads Used In The 19th Century Central East Africa Trade.* Beads, Volume 4, 1992.

Karkins, Karlis. *Trade Ornament Usage Among The Native Peoples Of Canada.* Ottawa, Minister Of The Environment, 1992.

Karys, Jonas K. *Ancient Lithuanian Currencies.* Bridgeport, 1959.

Kaschko, Michael. *An Archaeological Consideration Of The Ethnographic Fishook Set On Uki Island, Southeast Solomon Islands.* Wellington, The Royal Society Of New Zealand, Bulletin 11, 1976.

Keesing, Roger. *Custom And Confrontation, The Kwaio Struggle For Cultural Autonomy.* Chicago, The University Of Chicago Press, 1992.

Keller, Arnold. *Notgeld Handbook #1.* Manor Press

Kempers, A.J. Bernet. *The Kettledrums Of Southeast Asia.* Rotterdam, A.A. Balkema, 1988.

Kennedy, Carolee G. *Prestige Ornaments.* African Arts, July, 1991.

Kenyon, Ian & Thomas. *Comments On 17th Century Glass Trade Beads From Ontario.* Proceedings Of The 1982 Glass Trade Bead Conference, Rochester, Rochester Museum & Science Center, 1983.

King, Chester. *Protohistoric And Historic Archeology, Volumn 8.* Washington, Smithsonian Institution, 1978.

Kirk, Ruth. *Tradition & Change on the Northwest Coast.* Seattle, University of Washington Press, 1986.

Kjersmeier, Carl. *Ashanti Gold Weights In The National Museum.* Ethnographic Studies Ethnografisk Raekke 1, 1941.

Klima, George. *The Barabaig- East African Cattle-Herders.* New York, Holt, Rinehart And Winston, 1969.

Kneedler, H And Guehler. *Studies Of Old Siamese Coins.* London, Andrews Publishiing Company, 1977.

Kniffen,Gregory and Stokes. *The Historic Indian Tribes Of Louisiana.* Baton Rouge, Louisiana State University Press, 1987.

Konrad, Gunter and Ursula. *Asmat Life With The Ancestors.* Glashutten, Friedhelm Bruckner, 1981.

Kooijman, Simon. *Tapa In Polynesia.* Honolulu, Bishop Museum Press, 1972.

Korchnak, Lawrence. *Dutch Sieges Of The 16th And 17th Centuries.* Numismatist, December, 1990.

Krause, Chester, And Mishler, Clifford. *1990 Edition Standard Catalog Of World Coins.* Iola, Krause ublications, 1990.

Kriger, Colleen, E. *Price Of Men.* Heinemann, Portsmouth, 1999.

Kroeber, A. L. *Handbook Of The Indians Of California. Snithsonian Institution Bureau Of American Ethnology Bulletin 78,* Washington, Government Printing Office, 1925.

Kubary, J. *Ethnologische Beitrage zur Kenntnis des Karolinischen Inselgruppe und Nachbarschaft. Vol. 1* Berlin, 1885; *Die Palau-Inseln in der Sudsee* (Journal des Museums Godeffroy. Vol IV Hamburg, 1873; *Die Bewohner der Mortlock Inseln Mitteilungen der Geographischen Gesellschaft.* Hamburg, 1878-9.

Kuper, Adam. *Wives For Cattle.* London, Routledge & Kegan Paul, 1982.

Kuschel, Rolf. *Vengeance Is Their Reply.* Copenhagen, Dansk Psykologisk Forlag, 1988.

Laguna, Frederica. *Under Mount Saint Elias: The History And Culture Of The Yakutat Tlingit, Part 1.* Washington, D.C., Smithsonian Institution Press, 1972.

Larick, Roy. *The Circulation Of Spears Among Loikop Cattle Pastoralists Of Samburu District.* Kenya, Research In Economic Anthropology Volume 9, 1987.

LaViolette, Forrest E. *The Struggle For Survival.* Toronto, University of Toronto Press, 1973.

Lauer, Peter. *Changing Patterns Of Pottery Trade To The Trobriands Islands.* World Archaeology, Volume 3, No. 2, October, 1971.

Lawrence, Peter. *The Garia.* Manchester, Manchester University Press, 1984.

Lawrence, P. Gods, *Ghosts And Men In Melanesia.* Melborne, Oxford University Press, 1965.

Lawrence, Peter. *Road Belong Cargo.* Manchester, Manchester University Press, 1964.

Leach, Jerry and Edmund. *The Kula, New Perspectives On Massim Exchange*. Cambridge, Cambridge University Press, 1983.

Lederman, Rena. *What Gifts Engender*. Cambridge, Cambridge University Press, 1986.

Legros, Dominique. *Wealth, Poverty, And Slavery Among 19Th-Century Tutchone Athapaskans*. Research In Economic Anthropology Volume 7, 1985.

LeHunte, J. R. *Report of HMS Espiegle to Sir G. W. Des Voeux, Acting High Commissioner for the Western Pacific, October 10, 1883*. General Proceedings, nos. 1-83. Central Archives of Fiji and the Western Pacific, Suva, Fiji.

LeMay, Reginald. *Coinage Of Siam*. Bangkok, Bangkok Times Press, 1961.

Lewis, Albert. *Melanesian Shell Money In Field Museum Collections*. Chicago, Field Museum Press, 1929.

Lewis, Paul And Elaine. *Peoples Of The Golden Triangle*. London, Thames And Hudson Ltd., 1984.

Liep, John. *This Civilising Influence: The Colonial Transformation Of Rossel Island Society*. The Journal Of Pacific History, Volume 18 Number 1, January, 1983.

Lingenfelter, Sherwood G. *In The Court Or In The Village? Settling Disputes In Yap 1950-1979*. The Journal Of Pacific History, Volume 26 Number 1, June, !991.

Lincoln, Louise. *Assemblage Of Spirits*. New York, The Minneapolis Institute Of Arts, 1987.

Lips, Eva. *The Origin Of Things*. New York, A.A. Wyn, Inc., 1947.

Lipset, David M. *Seafaring Sepiks: Ecology, Warfare, And Prestige In Murik Trade*, Research In Economic Anthropology, Volume 7, 1985.

LiPuma,Edward. *Cosmology And Economy Among The Maring Of Highland* New Guinea, 1988.

LiPuma, Edward. *The Gift Of Kinship*, Cambridge, Cambridge University Press, 1988.

Liu, Robert. *African-Made Glass Ornaments*, Ornament, Vol. 8 # 2, 1984.

Liu, Robert. *Ancient Chinese Ornaments*, Ornament, Vol. 19 # 1, 1995.

Liu, Robert. *Conus Shell Ornaments*, Ornament, Vol. 14 # 4, 1991.

Liu, Robert. *Conus Shell Discs Revisited*, Bead Journal, Summer, 1975.

Liu, Robert. *Asiam Glass Ornaments Part 1*, Ornament, Vol. 8 # 4, 1985.

Liu, Robert K. *Collectible Beads*. Vists, Ornament, Inc., 1995.

Liu, Robert. *Granitic Beads And Their Simulations*. Ornament, Vol. 11 # 4, 1988.

Liu, Robert. *Himalayan Ornaments*. Ornament, Vol. 17 # 1, 1993.

Liu, Robert. *India, Idar-Oberstein And Czechoslovakia: Imitators And Competitors*. Ornament, Vol. 10 # 4, 1987.

Liu, Robert K. *Nueva Cadiz And Associated Beads*. Landcaster, G. B. Fenstermaker, 1982.

Liu, Robert. *Powder Glass Beads*. Ornament, Vol. 15 # 1, 1991

Liu, Robert K. *Tuareg Ornament: Its Origins, Derivatives, Copies, And Distribution*. Bead Journal.

Loeb, E.M. *The Distribution And Function Of Money In Early Societies, Essays In Anthropology*. Freeport, Books For Libraries Press, Inc., 1968.

Lowhaphandu, Viroj. *Coinage Of The Rattanakosin Era AD 1782-1982*. Bangkok, The Treasury Department, Ministry Of Finance, 1982.

Lutkehaus, Nancy. *Pigs, Politics, And Pleasure: Manam Perspectives On Trade And Regional Integration*. Research In Economic Anthropology, Volume 7, 1985.

Mack, John. *Ethnic Jewelry*. New York, Harry N. Abrams, Inc., 1994.

MacKenzie, Maureen Anne. *Androgynous Objects: String bags and gender in central New Guinea*. Paris, Harwood Academic Publishers, 1991.

Mair, Lucy. *African Societies*. London, Cambridge University Press, 1974.

Malinowski, Bronislaw. *Argonauts Of The Western Pacific*. New York, E.P. Dutton, 1961.

Malinowski, Bronislaw. *Kula: The Circulating Exchange Of Valuables In The Archipelagoes Of Eastern New Guinea*. Man, # 51, July, 1920.

Malinowski, Bronislaw. *Soil-Tilling And Agricultural Rites In The Trobriand Islands*. Bloomington, Indiana University Press, 1965.

Marshall, Rev. Harry Ignatius. *The Karen People Of Burma: A Study In Anthropology And Ethnology*. Columbus, The Ohio State University Bulletin, Vol. 26, Number 13, 1922.

Massey, J. Earl. *America's Money*. New York, Thomas Y. Crowell Company, 1934.

Matthiessen, Peter. *Under the Mountain Wall*. New York, Ballantine Books, 1962.

McCarthy, F.D. *"Trade " In Aboroiginal Australia, And "Trade" Relations With Torres Strait, New Guinea And Malaya*. Oceania, Vol. 10, September, 1939.

McKinnon, J.M. *Tomahawks, Turtles And Traders*. Oceania, Vol. 45, June, 1975.

McLachlan, R.W. *The Canadian Card Money, Montreal*. The Canadian Antiquarian And Numismatic Journal, Third Series, Vol. 7, 1910.

McNitt, Frank. *The Indian Traders*. Norman, University Of Oklahoma Press, 1962.

Mead, S.M. *The Last Initiation Ceremony At Gupuna Santa Ana. Eastern Solomon Islands: Extracted from Volume 10.* Records of the Auckland Institute and Museum, 1973.

Mead, Margaret. *The Mountain Arapesh, Vol. II.* Garden City, The Natural History Press, 1970.

Mead, Margaret And Calas, Nicolas. *Primitive Heritage.* New York, Random House, 1953.

Meggitt, Mervyn. *Blood Is Their Argument - Warfare Among The Mae Enga Tribesmen Of The New Guinea Highlands.* Mayfield Publishing Company, 1977.

Meggitt, M. J. *Pigs Are Our Hears, The Te Exchange Cycle Among The Mae Enga Of New Guinea.* Sidney, Oceania, Vol. 44 # 3, March, 1974.

Meggitt, Mervyn. *System And Subsystem: The Te Exchange Cycle Among The Mae Enga.* Human Ecology Volume 1, Number 2, 1972.

Meggitt, M. J. *The Lineage System Of The Mae-Enga Of New Guinea.* New York, Barnes & Noble, Inc., 1965.

Melitz, Jacques. *Primitive and Modern Money: an Interdisciplinary Approach.* Menlo Park, Addison-Wesley Publishing, 1974.

Meyer, Anthony JP. *Oceanic Art.* Koln, Konemann Verlagsgessellschaft mbH, 1995.

Merriam-Webster's Collegiate Dictionary, Tenth Edition. Springfield, Merriam-Webster, Incorporated, 1993.

Miller, Daniel. *An Organizational Approach To Exchange Media: An Example From The Western Solomons.* Mankind, Vol. 11, 1978.

Miller, Polly. *An Historical Explaination Of Alaskan Trade Beads.* Bead Journal, Fall, 1975.

Mira, William. *From Cowrie To Kina.* Sydney, Spink & Son Pty., 1986.

Mitchell, Donald. *Predatory Warfare, Social Status, and The North Pacific Slave Trade.* Ethnology Magazine, 1984.

Mitchiner, Michael. *Oriental Coins And Their Values-Non-Islamic States & Western Colonies.* London, Hawkins Publications, 1979.

Mitchiner, Michael. *Oriental Coins And Their Values-The Ancient & Classical World.* London, Hawkins Publications, 1978.

Moore, David R. & Turner, Charles. *Melanesian Art In The Australian Museum.* Sydney, Edwards & Shaw, 1968.

More, Phillip. *Doctorial Thesis On Primitive Money.* (Unpublished)

Mosher, Stuart. *The Story Of Money As Told By The Knox Collection Buffalo Museum Of Science.* Buffalo, Buffalo Museum of Science, 1952.

Muller, Kal. *New Guinea Journey Into The Stone Age.* Lincolnwood, Passport Books, 1993.

Munan, Heidi. *Lun Bawang Beads.* Beads, Volume 5, 1993.

Munn, Nancy D. *The Fame Of Gawa.* Cambridge, Cambridge University Press, 1986.

Munro, N.G. Coins Of Japan. 1904.

Martien, Jerry. *Shell Game.* Mercury House, San Francisco, 1996.

Murdock, George Peter. *Our Primitive Contemporaries.* New York, The Macmillan Company, 1934.

Murdock, George Peter. *Rank And Potlatch Among The Haida.* Yale University Publications In Anthropology Number 13, New Haven, Yale University Press, 1936.

Myers, Diana K. *Temple, Household, Horseback: Rugs Of The Tibetan Plateau.* The Textile Museum.

Newman, Thelma. *Contemporary Southeast Asian Arts And Crafts.* New York, Crown Publishers, Inc.,1977.

Newton, Douglas. *Crocodile and Cassowary.* New York, The Museum of Primitive Art, 1971.

Newton, Douglas. *New Guinea Art In The Collection Of The Museum Of Primitive Art.* Greenwich, Museum Of Primitive Art, 1967.

Neufeld, E.P. *Money and Banking in Canada.* Toronto, The Canadian Publishers, 1964.

Neuman, Klaus. *Not The Way It Really Was.* Honolulu, University of Hawaii Press, Pacific Islands Monograph Series, No. 10.

Nicolaisen, Johannes. *Ecology And Culture Of The Pastoral Tuareg.* Copenhagen, The National Museum of Copenhagen, 1963.

Nilles, J. *Natives Of The Bismarck, Mountains, New Guinea.* Oceania, Vol. 15, September, 1944.

Nitecki, Andre. *Equal Measure For Kings And Commoners, Goldweights Of The Akan.* Glenbow-Alberta Institute, 1982.

Northern, Tamara. *The Ornate Implement.* Hanover, Dartmouth College Museum and Galleries, 1981.

Northern, Tamara. *The Sign Of The Leopard Beaded Art Of Cameroon.* Storrs, The University Of Connecticut, 1975.

Nukunya, G.K. *Kinship And Marriage Among The Anlo Ewe.* New York, The Athlone Press, 1969.

Oberg, Kalervo. *The Social Economy of the Tlingit Indians.* Seattle, University of Washington Press, 1973.

O'Hanlon, Michael. *Paradise, Portraying The New Guinea Highlands.* London, British Museum Press, 1993.

O'Hear, Ann. *Ilorin Lantana Beads.* African Arts, August, 1986.

Oliver, Douglas. *A Solomon Islands Society, Kinship And Leadership Among The Siuai Of Bougainville.* Cambridge, Harvard University Press, 1955.

Oliver, Douglas. *Studies In The Anthropology Of Bougainville, Solomon Islands.* Papers Of The Peabody

Museum Of American Archaeology And Ethnology, Harvard University Vol. 29 # 1- 4, Cambridge, Published By The Museum, 1949.

Opitz, Charles J. *Odd & Curious Money, First Edition.* Ocala, First Impressions Printing, 1986.

Opitz, Charles J. *Odd & Curious Money, Second Edition.* Ocala, First Impressions Printing, 1991.

Opitz, Charles J. *Cowry Shells, Number One.* Ocala, First Impressions Printing, 1992.

Opitz, Charles J. *Yap Stone Money, Number Two.* Ocala, First Impressions Printing, 1993.

Opitz, Charles J. *Kula Ring, Number Three.* Ocala, First Impressions Printing, 1994.

Opitz, Charles J. *Potlatch, Number Four.* Ocala, First Impressions Printing, 1994.

Opitz, Charles J. *Wampum, Number Five.* Ocala, First Impressions Printing, 1995.

Opitz, Charles J. *Traditional Money From The Solomon Islands, Part 1.* Ocala, First Impressions Printing, 1996.

Opitz, Charles J. *Traditional Money From The Solomon Islands, Part 2.* Ocala, First Impressions Printing, 1997.

Opitz, Charles J. *Traditional Money Of The World, The Collection Of Charles And Karen Opitz.* Ocala, First Impressions Printing, 1998.

Opper, Marie-Jose And Howard. *Diakhite: A Study Of The Beads From An 18th &19th Century Burial Site In Senegal, West Africa.* Beads, Journal Of The Society Of Bead Researchers, Vol. 1, 1989.

Opper, Marie-Jose And Howard. *Kiffa Beads.* 1989.

Opper, Marie-Jose And Howard. *Powdered-Glass Beads And Bead Trade In Mauritania.* Beads, Volume 5, 1993.

Opper, Marie-Jose And Howard. *Rare Mauritanian Kiffa Beads.* Ornament Vol. 12 # 3, 1989.

Orchard, William C. *Beads & Beadwork of American Indians.* New York, Museum Of The American Indian Heye Foundation, 1929.

Orchard, William C. *The Technique Of Porcupine Quill Decoration Among The Indians Of North America.* New York, Museum Of The American Indian Heye Foundation, 1971.

Pankhurst, Richard. *Primitive Money: Money And Banking In Eithopia.* Commercial Bank Of Ethiopia, November, 1967.

Panoff, Michel. *Inter-Tribal Relations Of The Maenge People Of New Britian.* Port Moresby, New Guinea Research Bulletin Number 30, July, 1969.

Payne, Peter. *The Journal Of Primitive Money And Strange Media Of Exchange.* Series of Articles in Numismatic News, 1963-64.

Perczel, Csilla Fabo. *Ethiopian Crosses At The Portland Art Museum.* African Arts, May, 1981.

Picard, John And Ruth. *Chevron And Nueva Cadiz Beads, Volume 7.* Carmel, Picard African Imports, 1993.

Picard, John And Ruth. *Chevron Beads From The West African Trade, Volume 1.* Carmel, Picard African Imports, 1986.

Picard, John And Ruth. *Fancy Beads From The West African Trade, Volume 3.* Carmel, Picard African Imports, 1987.

Picard, John And Ruth. *Millefiori Beads From The West African Trade, Volume 6.* Carmel, Picard African Imports.

Picard, John And Ruth. *Russian Blues, Faceted And Fancy Beads From The West African Trade, Volume 5.* Carmel, Picard African Imports, 1989.

Picard, John And Ruth. *Tabular Beads From The West African Trade, Volume 2.* Carmel, Picard African Imports, 1986.

Picard, John And Ruth. *White Hears, Feather And Eye Beads From The West African Trade, Volume 4.* Carmel, Picard African Imports, 1988.

Pick, Albert. Briefmarkengeld, Munchen, Klinkhardt & Biermann, 1970.

Piddington, Ralph. *An Introduction To Social Anthropology.* London, Oliver And Boyd, 1950.

Poinar, George, Ph. D. *Older And Wiser. Lapidary Journal,* January, 1996.

Polanyi, Karl. *Trade and Market in the Early Empires. Glencoe,* The Free Press.

Pospisil, Leopold. *Kapauku Papuan Economy.* New Haven, Department Of Anthropology, Yale University, 1963.

Pospisil, Leopold. *The Kapauku Papuans Of West New Guinea.* New York, Holt, Rinehart And Winston, 1964.

Powdermaker, Hortense. *Life In Lesu.* London, Williams & Norgate Ltd., 1933.

Pratt, W.H. *Shell Money And Other Primitive Currencies.* Proceedings Of The Davenport Academy Of Natural Sciences, Vol. II, July, 1877.

Price, Christine. *Made In The South Pacific.* London, The Bodley Head, 1979.

Price, Willard. *Japan's Islands of Mystery.* London, 1944.

Pringle, Heather. *The Cradle of Cash.* Discovery Magazine, October, 1998.

Pryor, John. *Market Forces In The Creation Of Pomo Basketry Style And Pomo Ethnicity.* Research In Economic Anthropology, Volume 11, 1989.

Pryor, Frederic L. *The Origins Of The Economy.* New York, Academic Press, 1977.

Quennell, Marjorie & C. H. B. *Everyday Life in The New Stone, Bronze, & Early Iron Ages.* New York, B. T. Batsfoorn Ltd. 1945.

Quiggin, A. Hingston. *A Survey Of Primitive Money.*

London, Methuen & Co., 1949.

Quimby, George Irving. *Indian Culture And European Trade Goods.* Madison, The University Of Wisconsin Press, 1966.

Quimby, George Irving. *Indian Life In The Upper Great Lakes.* Chicago, The University Of Chicago Press, 1960.

Rabineau, Phyllis. *Feather Arts.* Chicago, Field Museum Of Natural History, 1978.

Rabus, B. *Yua, Muschelringe Aus Tridacna Gigas.* EUCOPRIMO # 2 1995.

Rabus, B. *Mamuli, Objects Of Value From Sumba.* EUCOPRIMO # 2 1990.

Radcliff-Brown, A.R. & Forde, Daryll. *African Systems Of Kinship And Marriage.* London, Oxford University Press, 1950.

Ramsden, H. A. *Chinese Early Barter And Uninscribed Money.* Yokohama, Jun Kobayagawa Co., 1912.

Ramsden, H.A. *Siamese Porcelain And Other Tokens.* London, Andrews Publishing Company, 1977.

Rappaport, Roy A. *Pigs For The Ancestors.* New Haven, Yale University Press, 1967.

Rattray, Capt. R. S. *Ashanti.* New York, Negro University Press, 1969.

Ratzel, Friedrich. *The History Of Mankind, Vol. 1 -3.* Translated from the second German edition by A. J. Butler, London, 1896.

Ray, Arthus J. *Indians in the Fur Trade: their role as trappers, hunters, and middlemen in the lands southwest of Hudson Bay 1660-1870.* Toronto, Universiity of Toronto Press, 1974.

Ray, Arthur and Freeman, Donald. *Give Us Good Measure: an economic analysis of relations between the Indians and the Hudson's Bay Company before 1763.* Toronto, University of Toronto Press, 1978.

Reed, Mort. *Odd and Curious.* U.S.A.: Fisher Printing Co., 1963.

Reichard, Gladys. *Melanesian Design A Study Of Style In Wood And Tortoiseshell Carvings, Vol. 1 & 2.* New York, Columbia Univeristy Press, 1933.

Reining, Conrad. *The Role Of Money In The Zande Economy.* American Anthropologist, !959.

Rickard, T.A. *The Knowledge And Use Of Iron Among The South Sea Islanders.* The Journal Of The Royal Anthropological Institute Of Great Britian And Ireland, Vol. 42, 1933.

Ridgeway, Sir William. *An Irish Decorated Socketed Bronze Axe.* Man # 84, November, 1919.

Ridgeway, William. *The Origin Of Metallic Currency And Weight Standards.* Cambridge, The University Press, 1892.

Ritzenthaler, Robert E. *Native Money Of Palau.* Milwaukee, North American Press, 1954.

Rivers, W. H. R. *The History Of Melanesian Society Vol. 1 & 2.* Oosterhout, Anthropological Publications, 1968.

Riviere, Peter. *Individual And Society In Guiana.* Cambridge, Cambridge University Press, 1984.

Rockefeller, Michael. *The Art Of New Guinea.* New York, Museum Of Primitive Art, 1967.

Rodman, William. *The Boars Of Bali Ha'i: Pigs In Paradise.* Honolulu, University Of Hawaii Press, 1996.

Rogers, E.S. *New Guinea: Big Man Island.* Toronto, The Royal Ontario Museum, 1970.

Rodgers, Susan. *Indonesian Power Jewelry.* Ornament, Vol. 10 # 1, 1986.

Rodgers, Susan. *Power And Gold.* Munich, Prestel-Verlag, 1990.

Rosenthal, David And Mussells, Jim. *An Introduction To Oceanic Fish Hooks.* Tribal Arts, Autumn, 1995.

Rosman, Abraham and Rubel, Paula. *Feasting With Mine Enemy: Rank And Exchange Among Northwest Coast Societies.* New York, Columbia University Press, 1971.

Ross, Harold. *Baegu Markets, Areal Ingegration, And Economic Efficiency In Malaita, Solomon Islands.* Urbana, University of Illinois, 1978.

Ross, Harold. *Baegu Social And Ecological Organization In Malaita, Solomon Islands.* Urbana, University Of Illinois Press, 1973.

Roth, H. Ling. *Great Benin.* New York, Barnes & Noble, Inc., 1968.

Rubel, Paula G. *Your Own Pigs You May Not Eat.* Chicago, The University Of Chicago Press, 1978.

Russell, T. *The Fataleka Of Malaita.* Oceania, Volume 21 Number 1, September, 1950.

Ryan, Dawn. *Christianity, Cargo Cults, And Politics Among The Toaripi Of Papua.* Oceania, December, 1969.

Safer, Jane, Fearer and Gill, Francis McLaaughlin. *Spirals From The Sea.* New York, Clarkson N Potter, Inc., 1982.

Sahlins, Marshall. *Stone Age Economics.* Chicago, Aldine-Atherston, Inc., 1972.

Salwen,Bert. *Indians of Southern New England And Long Island Period, Vol. 15.* Northeast, Smithsonian Institution, 1978.

Salisbury, R. F. *From Stone To Steel.* Melbourne, Melbourne University Press, 1962.

Saryan, L. A. *Ring Money In Prehistoric Armenia.* Armenian Numismatic Joournal, Vol. 16 # 4, December, 1990.

Saville, W.J.V. *In Unknown New Guinea.* Philadelphia, J.B. Lioppincott Company, 1926.

Schaedler, Karl-Ferdinand. *Earth And Ore.* Munchen, Panterra Verlag, 1997.

Scheffler, Harold. *The Genesis And Repression Of Conflict: Choiseul Island.* American Anthropolgist, Vol. 66, 1964.

Scheffler, Harold. *Choiseul Island Social Structure.* Berkley, University Of California Press, 1965.

Schjoth, Fredrik. *Revised By Virgil Hancock, Chinese Currency.* Iola, Krause Publications, 1965.

Schneider, Harold. *Livestock And Equality In East Africa.* Bloomington, Indiana University Press, 1979.

Schulman, Hans, and Gibbs, Howard. *Odd And Curious Money Of The World.* New York, Hans Schulman, 1956.

Schulman, Hans. P*rimitive Money At Fixed Prices.* New York, Hans M.F. Schulman, 1968.

Schulman, Hans, T. Becker And K. Seidl. *Collections Auction Catalogue.* New York, Schulman Coin & Mint, Inc., May 6, 1974.

Schuurkamp, Gerry. *The Min Of The Papua New Guinea Star Mountains.* Boroko, Gordon And Gotch, 1995.

Schwab, George. *Tribes Of The Liberian Hinterland.* Papers Of The Peabody Museum Of American Archaeology And Ethnology, Harvard University, Vol. 31, 1947.

Scurlock, William H. *The Book Of Buckskinning III,* Texarkana, Rebel Publishing Company, Inc., 1985.

Semans, Scott. African Bracelet Money. Seattle, Scott Seman, undated.

Semans, Scott. Bracelet Money & Manillas. Seattle, Scott Semans, undated.

Semans, Scott. Coinage Of Thailand. Seattle, Scott Semans, 1995.

Sexton, Jeanne. Crossroads Of Continents,. Washington D. C., Smithsonian Institution Press, 1988.

Shariffuddin, P. M. Brunei Cannon. The Brunei Museum Journal, Volume 1, Number 1, 1969.

Sharp, Lauriston. Steel Axes For Stone-Age Australians. Human Organizations, Summer, 1952.

Shaw and Ali. Tin 'Hat' And Animal Money. Kuala Lumpur, Museum Department States Of Malaya, 1970.

Sheppard, T. And Musham, J.F. Money Scales And Weights. London, Spink & Sons Ltd., 1975.

Shumway, George. English-Pattern Trade Rifles. Proceedings Of The 1984 Trade Gun Conference Part 2, Selected Papers, Research Records No. 18, 1985.

Siebert, Victor C. Mat Money. Extracted from Article in May 7, 1985 Issue of World Coin News.

Siers, James. Papua New Guinea. Wellington, Millwood Press, 1981.

Sigler, Col Phares. Strange Money Of The World. Reprint From The Numismatist, 1962.

Sillitoe, Paul. Give And Take. New York, St. Martin's Press, 1979.

Silverman, Eric Kline. *The Art Of Papua New Guinea Cultural Traditions Of The Sepik River.* Gainsville, University Presses Of Florida, 1988.

Simpson, Colin. *Plumes And Arrows Inside New Guinea.* Sydney, Angus and Robertson, 1971.

Singh, Saran. *The Enclclopedia Of The Coins Of Malaysa Singapore And Brunei.* Kuala Lumpur, Malaysa Numismatic Society, 1986.

Slotkin, J.S. & Schmitt, Karl. *Studies Of Wampum.* American Anthropologist, Vol. 51, 1949.

Smith, Bruce W. *An Introduction To Siam Gambling Tokens.* Journal Of East Asian Numismatics, Vol. 2 Number 5, 1995.

Smith, Marvin. *Chronology From Glass Beads: The Spanish Period In The Southeast, 1513-1670.* Proceedings Of The 1982 Glass Trade Bead Conference, Rochester, Rochester Museum & Science Center, 1983.

Smith, Marvin, & Good, Mary Elizabeth. *Early Sixteenth Century Glass Beads In The Spanish Colonial Trade.* Greenwood, Cottonlandia Museum Publications, 1982.

Smith, Marvin. *The Chevron Trade Bead In North America.* Bead Journal.

Smith, Timothy J. *Wampum As Primitive Valuables.* Research In Economic Anthropology Volume 5, Greenwich, Jai Press, 1983.

Sordinas, Augustus. *Modern Koli Beads In Ghana.* Man # 90, May, 1964.

Sorenson, E. Richard. *The Edge Of The Forest.* Washington, D.C., Smithsonian Institution Press.

Specht, Jim, and Fields, John. *Frank Hurley In Papua.* Bathurst, Robert Brown and Associates (Aust) Pty., 1984.

Speck, Frank G. *The Functions Of Wampum Among The Eastern Algonkian.* Memoirs Of The American Anthropological Association, Volume 5. Lancaster, The American Anthropolical Association, 1918.

Spring, Christopher. *African Arms And Armour.* London, British Museum Press, 1993.

Stanley, David. *Micronesia Handbook.* Chico, Moon Publications Inc., 1989.

Stanner, W. E. H. *Ceremonial Economics Of The Mulluk Mulluk and Madngella Tribes Of The Daly River, North Australia.* A Preliminary Paper, Oceania, December, 1933.

Stearns, Radford. *Tooth Money-A Great Way To Fill The Holes In Your Collection.* Colorado Springs, The Numismatist, Februaary, 1987.

Steiger-Hayley. *Wage Labour And The Desire For Wives Among The Lango.* Uganda Journal Vol. 8 #1, September, 1940.

Steiner, Christopher. *African Art In Transit.* Cambridge,

Cambridge Press, 1994.

Steiner, Christopher B. *The Trade In West African Art.* African Arts, January, 1991.

Steiner, Christopher. *West African Trade Beads.* Symbols Of Tradition, Ornament, Vol. 14 # 1, 1990.

Sternberg, Ilene. *Stalking The Nine.* Lapidary Journal, October, 1994.

Stewart, Gloria. *The Garrick Introduction To Sepik Art.* Melbourne, Garrick Publishers Pty, Ltd., 1972.

Stone, George Cameron. *Glossery Of The Construction, Decoration And Use Of Arms And Armor In All Countries And In All Times.* New York, Jack Brussel, Publisher, 1961.

Strathern, Andrew. *Finance And Production: Two Strategies In New Guinea Highlands Exchange Systems.* Oceania, September, 1969.

Strathern, Andrew And Marilyn. *Self-Decoration In Mount Hagen.* Toronto, University Of Toronto Press, 1971.

Strathern, Andrew. *Tambu And Kina: Profit, Exploitation And Reciprocity In Two New Guinea Exchange Systems.* Mankind, Vol. 11, 1978.

Strauss, Hermann. *The Mi-Culture Of The Mount Hagen People.* Ethnology Monographs # 13 Department Of Anthropology, University Of Pittsburgh, 1990.

Swadling, Pamela. *People Of The West Sepik Coast.* Port Moresby, National Museum And Art Gallery, 1979.

Swadling, Pamela. *Plumes From Paradise.* Queensland, Papua New Guinea National Museum, 1996.

Swanton, John R. *The Indians Of The Southeastern United States.* Smithsonian Institution Bureay Of American Ethnology Bulletin #137, Washington, Government Printing Office, 1946.

Taylor, Paul and Aragon, Lorraine. *Beyond The Java Sea.* Washington, D.C., The National Museum of Natural History, 1991.

Taxay, Don. *Money Of The American Indians And Other Primitive Currencies Of The Americas.* New York, Numismus Press, 1970.

Tehanetorens, Wampum Belts, Onchiota, Six Nations Indian Museum, 1983.

Temple, R.C. *Beginnings of Currency.* The Journal of the Anthropological Institute of Great Britian and Ireland Vol. 29, London, Kegan Paul, Trench, Trubner & Co., 1899.

Thomas, David. *Spanish Borderlands Sourcebooks.* New York, Garland Pub., 1992.

Thomas, Ernest S. *The African Throwing Knife.* The Journal Of The Royal Anthropological Institute Of Great Britian And Ireland, Vol. 60, 1930.

Thomas, Nicholas. *Oceanic Art.* London, Thames And Hudson, 1986.

Thurlow, Bradbury. *Italian Cast Coinage.* London, V.C. Vecchi & Sons, 1979.

Thurnwald, Richard. *Economics In Primitive Communities.* Oxford University Press, 1932.

Thurnwald, Richard. *Pigs And Currency In Buin.* Oceania, Vol. 5, December, 1934.

Tingstrom, Bertel. *Plate Money- The World's Largest Currency.* London, Royal Coin Cabinet of Sweden, 1986.

Tooker,Elisabeth. *The League Of The Iroquois: Its History, Politics, And Ritual.* Washington, Smithsonian Institution, 1978.

Tsu-k'uang, Lou. *Asian Folklore And Social Life Monographs, Volume 19.* Taiwan, The Orient Cultural Service, 1971.

Tuckson, Patricia May & Margaret. *The Traditional Pottery of Papua New Guinea.* Sydney, Bay Books, 1982.

Tumu, Akii, Munini, Pesone, Kyangali, Alome, Wiessner, Polly. *A View Of Enga Culture.* Madang, KPI Publishing, 1989.

Turle, Gillies. *The Art Of The Maasai.* New York, Alfred A. Knopf, 1992.

Uhl, Ted. *Walrus Skin Money.* Journal Of The Russian Numismatic Society, No. 7, June, 1982.

Ukers, William Hassison. *All About Tea.* The Tea and Coffee Trade Journal Co. ,1935.

Van Der Sleen. *A Handbook On Beads.* York, Pennsylvania, Liberty Cap Books, 1980.

Van Landewijk, J. E. J. M. *What Was The Original Aggrey Bead?* Legon, Ghana Journal Of Sociology, 1971.

VanStone, James W. *Indian Trade Ornaments In The Collections Of Field Museum Of Natural History.* Anthropolopy New Series No. 13, Chicago, Field Museum Of Natural History, 1989.

Vayda, Andrew. *Phases Of The Process Of War And Peace Among The Marings Of New Guinea.* Oceania Vol. 42, September, 1971.

Vecchi, Italo. *Italian Aes Rude, Signatum And The Aes Grave of Sicily.* London, V.C. Vecchi & Sons, 1979.

Vreeland, Nehemiah. *Wampum: The Native Substitute For Currency In North America.* The British Numismatic Journal And Proceedings Of The British Numismatic Society, First Series Volume 7, 1910.

Vial, L. G. *Stone Axes Of Mount Hagen.* New Guinea, Oceania, Vol. 11, September, 1940.

Vissering, W. *On Chinese Currency.* Taipei, Ch'eng-Wen Publishing Company, 1968.

Vogel, Susan. *African Art In Anthropology Collections,* New York, The Center For African Art, 1988.

Waite, Deborah. *Artefacts From The Solomon Islands In The Julius L. Brenchley Collection* London, British

Museum Publications Limited, 1986.

Waite, Deborah. *Art Of The Solomon Islands From the Collection Of The Barbier-Muller Museum.* Geneva, 1983.

Waite, Deborah. *Shell-Inlaid Shields From The Solomon Islands.* Art And Artists Of Oceania, The Dunmore Press, 1983.

Waite, Deborah. *Solomon Islands Sculpture.* Part of PhD.Theses with Colombia University, 1969.

Walton, James. *Iron Gongs From The Congo And Southern Rhodesia.* Man, # 30, February, 1955.

Wardwell, Allen. *Island Ancestors.* Oceanic Art From The Masco Collection, Detroit, University Of Washington Press, 1994.

Waung, Chi Zang. *The Ancient Coins And Currency Of China.* The Economic Journal, Vol. 23, 1913.

Weeden, William B. *Economic And Social History Of New England 1620-1789.* Boston, Houghton Mifflin Company, 1891.

Weeks, John H. *Among Congo Cannibals.* London, Seeley, Service & Co. Limited, 1913.

Weiner, Annette, and Schneider, Jane. *Cloth and Human Experience.* Washington, Smithsonian Press, 1989.

Weiner, Annette B. *Inalienable Possessions, The Paradox Of Keeping-While-Giving.* Berkeley, University Of California Press, 1992.

Weiner, Annette. *The Trobrianders Of Papua New Guinea.* New York, Holt, Rinehart And Winston, Inc., 1988.

Weiner, James. *Mountain Papuans.* Ann Arbor, The University Of Michigan Press, 1988.

Welsch, Robert L. *An American Anthropologist in Melanesia.* Honolulu, University of Hawaii Press, 1998.

Westerdijk. *The African Throwing Knife.* Netherlands, University of Utrecht, 1988.

Westervelt, Frances. *The Final Century Of The Wampum Industry In Bergan County.* New Jersey, Bergan County Historical Society, 1924.

White, J. Peter And Modjeska, N. *Acquirers, Users, Finders, Loser: The Use Axe Blades Make Of The Duna.* Mankind, Vol. 11, 1978.

Wicks, Robert S. *Money, Markets, And Trade In Early Southeast Asia.* Ithaca, Studies On Southeast Asia, 1992.

Widstrand, Carl Gosta. *African Axes.* Studa Ethnographica Upsaliensia, 15, 1958.

Wieschhoff, H.A. *Primitive Money.* Philadelphia, University Museum Bulletin, Vol 11 #3, December, 1945.

Wild, R.P. *Iron Disc Currency From Ashanti.* Man # 99, May, 1936.

Williams, F.E. *Orokaiva Society.* London, Oxford University Press, 1930.

Williams, Francis Edgar. *The Vailala Madness And Other Essays.* Honolulu, The University Press Of Hawaii, 1977.

Williams, Paul. *Wampum Of The Six Nations Confederacy At The Grand River Territory: 1784-1986.* Proceedings Of The 1986 Shell Bead Conference, Research Records #20, Rochester, Rochester Museum And Science Center, 1989.

Wilks, Ivor. *The Golden Stool And The Elephant Tail: An Essay On Wealth In Asante.* Research In Economic Anthropology Volume 2, 1979.

Wilson, R. Kent & Menzies, K. *Production And Marketing Of Artefacts In The Sepik District And The Trobriand Islands.* New Guinea Research Bulletin #20, The Australian National University, Canberra, 1967.

Wood, Howland. *The Gampola Larin Hoard.* New York, A.N.S., # 61, 1934.

Wood, Leona. *Tribes Of The Pacific Northwest Coast.* Ornament, Vol. 9 #4, 1986.

Woodford, Charles Morris. *A Naturalist Amoung The Head-Hunters.* London, George Philip & Son, 1890.

Woodford, C.M. *Notes On The Manufacture Of The Malaita Shell Bead Money Of The Solomon Group.* Man #43, 1908.

Woodward, Arthur. *Indian Trade Goods.* Portland, Binfords & Mort, 1967.

Worsley, Peter. *Cargo Cults.* Scientific American, May, 1959.

Xinwei, Peng. *A Monetary History of China, Volume 1 & 2.* Translated by Edward H. Kapkan, Center for East Asian Studies, Western Washington University, Bellingham. 1993.

Young, Michael. *Goodenough Island Cargo Cults.* Oceania, Vol. 42 #1, September, 1971.

Young, Michael. *Malinowski's Kiriwina.* Chicago, University of Chicago Press, 1998.

Yu-Ch'uan, Wang. *Early Chinese Coinage.* New York, Durst Numismatic Publications, 1980.

Zander, Randoph. *The Alaskan Parchment Scrip Of The Russian American Company 1816-1867.* Bellingham, Russian Numismatic Society, 1996.

Zirngibl, Manfred A. *Rare African Short Weapons.* Grafenau, Buch-und Offsetdruckerei Morsak, 1983.

Index

ABADA CLOTH - See - cloth - Nigeria 109
ABAQUARO 11
ABALONE (HALIOTIS) SHELL 11
ABO BEADS - see beads bauxite beads 40
ABOGWARO 11
ABRUS PRECATORIUS 11
ABUDJEDID CLOTH - See - cloth - abudjedid . . . 108
ABUTA - See Mauwai 219
ADJAGBA BEADS - See beads - adjagba 38
ADZE - See Axe Money 17
AES GRAVE 12
AES RUDE 12
AES SIGNATUM 12
AGATE BEADS - See beads - agate 38
AGATE BELT MONEY - See Belt Money 81
AGGREY BEADS - See Beads - aggrey 39
AGGRY BEADS - See Beads - aggry 39
AGUT - See Flying Fox Teeth 146
AKOSU BEADS - See akosu 39
AKWETE CLOTH - See - cloth - Nigeria 109
ALAS - See turtle shell 355
ALLEY BEADS - See beads alley 39
ALMONDS 12
ALUMINUM FOIL MONEY 13
ALUP - See Bagi 28
AMBASSADOR BEADS - See beads ambassador . . . 39
AMBER BEADS See Beads - amber 40
AMBUL - See mat - Yap 217
AM FAT - See shell money - Tanga 303
AMOLE - See Salt money 289
ANAHIDA BEADS - See beads - anahida 40
ANCHOR CURRENCY - See zong 383
ANCHOR CURRENCY - See mandjong 209
ANDANA 14
ANGOT - See Flying Fox Teeth 146
ANIMAL MONEY 14
ANKLET MONEY - See Ring Money 201
ANNULUS - See cowry 118
ANT NOSE - See Ghost's Head Money 149
ANTIMONY LUMPS 15
APRONS - BEADED 15
APUTA - See Mauwai 219
ARAGONITE - See Stone Money 316
ARANGIT 15
ARECA NUTS 15
ARINGIT 15
ARMBAND MONEY - See ABAQUARO 11
ARM RING MONEY 16
ARROW MONEY 16
ARROWHEAD MONEY 16
ASANTE BEADS - See beads - asante 40
ASHANTI WEIGHTS - See Weights 375
ATANA - See green snail shell 151
AUMAK - See Bamboo- Papua New Guinea 31
AXE MONEY 17
AXEHEAD - See Munshi Axe Head 231
BABYLONIAN CLAY TABLET - See Clay Tablet . . . 107
BAG MONEY - See Grivna, Bilum 152
BAGE - See salt - Africa, Ethiopia 289
BAGI SHELL MONEY 28
BAILER SHELL MONEY 29
BAKHIA 29
BAKONGA - See legband, Africa, Ekonda 201
BALA 29
BALL - See Musket Ball 232
BALL - See Quartz Balls 273
BALL - See Rubber 288
BALUBA CROSS - See Cross, Katanga 124
BAMBOO MONEY 31
BANANA BAR - See bar - Vietnam 33
BANGALA EXECUTION KNIFE - See Execution Knife - Bangala 141
BAGE - See Salt Money, Ethiopia 289
BANANA SEED MONEY 31
BANGALA SPEARHEAD MONEY - See Spearhead Money - Bangala 313
BANI'AU 32
BANNER STONE 32
BA'O - See Porpoise teeth 264
BAR MONEY 32
BAR MONEY - See Bean Money 77
BAR MONEY - See Calabar 99
BAR MONEY - See Chogin 105
BAR MONEY - See Lat 199
BAR MONEY - See Mukuba wa matwi 232
BAR MONEY - See Mint Bars 223
BAR MONEY - See Onganda 245
BAR MONEY - See Purr-Purr 273
BAR MONEY - See Rod Money 288
BANANA BAR 33
BARAFE 34
BARAVA 35
BARI 35
BARK CLOTH 35
BARLEY - Grain Currency 36
BARRAS - See cross, I-shaped 126
BARU'ILAA 36
BASKET 36
BASI - See Kula 189
BASIN 37
BAT BONE BELT 37
BAT HOE MONEY 37
BAT TEETH 37
BATA 37

BATAFALU . . . 37
BATAULIULI . . . 37
BATU CLOTH . . . 37
BAUXITE BEADS - See Beads - bauxite . . . 40
BEADS . . . 38
BEADS - See Borjookes . . . 89
BEADS - See Jacket . . . 166
BEADS - See Kudatama . . . 188
BEADS - See Ostrich Egg Shell Beads . . . 59
BEADS - See Turquoise . . . 66
BEAN MONEY . . . 77
BEARSKIN . . . 77
BEAR TEETH . . . 77
BEARD MONEY . . . 77
BEAVER PENDANT . . . 77
BEAVER SKIN . . . 77
BECKET . . . 79
BEDIL - See cannon . . . 100
BEEF . . . 79
BEER . . . 79
BEESWAX - See Wax . . . 375
BEETLE MONEY . . . 79
BEETLE LEG MONEY . . . 79
BEGGER BEADS - See beads - begger . . . 40
BEKU . . . 80
BEALONG - See Gambar . . . 148
BELA- See earrings, Flores . . . 135
BELL . . . 80
BELL CASH . . . 80
BELL- COPPER . . . 80
BELL-IRON . . . 81
BELT MONEY . . . 81
BELT PENDANT MONEY . . . 81
BENAM - See Beku . . . 80
BENE BIKIE - See bikie . . . 82
BENIN CLOTH - See cloth benin . . . 108
BERBER AGATE BELT MONEY . . . 81
BETEL NUTS . . . 82
BIKIE . . . 82
BILABA . . . 82
BILL- HOOK - See Knife Money . . . 180
BILLETS DE CONFIANCE - See playing card . . . 258
BILIUM . . . 82
BIPANE . . . 84
BIRD BEADS - See beads - bird . . . 40
BIRD OF PARADISE MONEY . . . 84
BIROK . . . 84
BIRU . . . 85
BIRUAN . . . 85
BITCHIE - See Mandjong . . . 209
BLADE - See Obsidian . . . 242
BLANKET MONEY . . . 85
BLOOM OF IRON . . . 87
BOAR TUSK . . . 87
BOAT - See Sycee . . . 322
BOAT MONEY - See Lat . . . 199
BODOM BEADS - See beads - bodom . . . 41
BOKONA . . . 89
BOLOKO . . . 89
BOMPATA . . . 89
BONE MONEY - See ivory money . . . 164
BONK - See - bar - Indonesia . . . 34
BOOKMARK MONEY - See Hansatsu . . . 155
BORJOOKES . . . 89
BOSU . . . 89
BOTHA A YAR - See Yar Nu Au . . . 381
BOTTLES . . . 90
BOW MONEY . . . 90
BOWLS - See - Pots . . . 90
BRACELET - See K'a K'im . . . 171
BRACELET - See Manilla . . . 209
BRACELET - See Ring Money . . . 275
BRAMBLES - See Tingle-Dangle money . . . 352
BRASS RING MONEY - See Ring money . . . 275
BRASS BEAD - See Bead - Brass . . . 41
BRASS FROG MONEY - See Animal Money . . . 14
BRICK TEA - See Tea Money . . . 337
BRIDE PRICE . . . 91
BRIDE PRICE BEADS - See beads - bride price . . . 41
BRIDGE MONEY - CHINA - See Tingle Dangle Money . . . 352
BRONZE DRUM - See Moko . . . 226
BROOCH . . . 91
BU MONEY - See PU money . . . 272
BUAYA - See Gambar . . . 148
BUAYA - See crocodile . . . 124
BUBI CURRENCY . . . 91
BUBU THROWING KNIFE - See Throwing Knife - Bubu . . . 344
BUFFALO . . . 91
BUFFALO BELL . . . 92
BUJI . . . 92
BULLET MONEY . . . 92
Kidney-shaped elephant series . . . 96
BUNDLES . . . 96
BUNG BEADS - See beads - bung . . . 41
BURIAL MONEY . . . 98
BURLAP MONEY . . . 99
BURNED MONEY - See burial money . . . 99
BUSHMAN'S BEADS - See Ostrich Egg Shell Beads 59
BUTTER . . . 99
BUTTONS . . . 99
BWANA . . . 99
CACAO - See Cocoa Bean Money . . . 114
CAKE - See Salt Money . . . 289
CAKE - See Soap Cakes . . . 311
CAKE - See Tukula . . . 358
CALABAR BAR . . . 99
CAMELS . . . 99
CAMPHOR . . . 99
CAMWOOD - See Tukula . . . 358
CANDY . . . 99
CANNON MONEY . . . 100
CANOE MONEY . . . 100

CANOE PROW 101
CANVAS MONEY 101
CARABAO 101
CARAPACE MONEY 101
CARD MONEY - See Playing Card Money 258
CARDBOARD COINS 101
CARGO CULT 102
CARIBOU SKIN MONEY 102
CARNELIAN BEADS - See beads - carnelian 41
CARTONES 102
CARTRIDGE MONEY 102
CASH 103
CASSOWARY BONE - See Dagger Money 127
CASSOWARY FEATHER 103
CAT EYE - See Abrus Precatorius 11
CATLINITE - See Peace Pipe 247
CATTLE 104
CELT - See Axe - Ireland 17
CH'ING BRIDGE - See Tingle Dangle Money . . . 352
CHAINS 104
CHABILI- See dao 128
CHALCHIHUITL - See Jade Money 52
CHAMOIS MONEY 104
CHAQUIRA 104
CHEESE MONEY 105
CHEETEM 105
CHESTNUT BURR 105
CHEVRON BEADS - See Beads - chevron beads . . . 42
CH'I TAO - See Knife Money 180
CHICKEN - See Egg Money 139
CHIEM GIM - See Money Sword 228
CHIEF BEADS - See beads - chief 43
CHILKAT BLANKET - See blanket 85
CH'ING MONEY - See Tingle - Dangle Money . . . 352
CHO GIN 105
CHOCOLATE DISK MONEY 106
CHOP MARKED COINS 106
CHUNG CH'IEN - See Bell Cash 80
CHUNG DZI - See - beads - dzi 48
C'IENG - See k'a kim 171
CICADA MONEY 106
CIGARETTES 106
CINNABAR 106
CLAM SHELL ARMBANDS 106
CLAMSHELL MONEY 106
CLAW MONEY - See Magatama 207
CLAY BEADS - See beads - clay 44
CLAY COINS - See Porcelain Money 44
CLAY TABLET 107
CLOAKS 107
COMB BEADS - See beads - feather 49
CLOTH MONEY 107
CLOVES 113
CLUBS 113
COAL MONEY 114
COAS - See Axe Money 17
COCK - See Crocodile Money, Gambar 124
COCOA BEAN MONEY 114
COCONUTS 115
COCONUT DISK - See Sek 295
COCONUT DISK - See - Tekaroro 343
COCONUT FIBER - See Belt Money 81
COCOS KEELING MONEY - See Ivory 164
CODFISH 115
COFFEE BEAN MONEY 115
COIL CURRENCY - See mitako 224
COIX SEED MONEY 115
COLLAR MONEY 116
COMB MONEY 116
COMPRESSED COAL - See Coal Money 114
CONCH SHELL MONEY 116
CONE SHELL 116
CONUS SHELL - See Biruan 84
CONUS SHELL - See Dibidibi 138
CONUS SHELL - See Mauwai 219
CONUS SHELL - See Som 311
CONUS SHELL - See To-Uba 355
CONUS SHELL - See Wauri 374
CONUS SHELL ARMBANDS - See Mwali 232
CONUS SHELL BEADS - See beads - conus 44
CONUS SHELL DISK MONEY - See Beads Conus shell 44
CONUS SHELL NECKLACES 117
CONUS SHELL RINGS - See rings 286
CONUS SHELL TIPS 117
COOKED BEADS - See - beads - koli 54
COON SKIN MONEY - See Raccoon Skin Money. 274
COPAL BEADS - See beads - copal 44
COPPER 117
COPPER BEADS - beads - copper 46
COPPERS - See Shield Money 303
COPRA 117
CORAL MONEY 117
CORAL SIMULATION BEADS - See beads - coral simulation 45
CORN 118
CORNALINE D'ALEPPO BEADS - See beads - cornaline d'Aleppo 46
COTTON 118
COWRY SHELLS 118
COWRY SHELL BAND - See Yerak 381
CRAB'S EYE - See Abrus Precatorius 11
CRESCENT - RIDGED 124
CROCODILE MONEY 124
CROSS, KATANGA 124
CROSS - "H" SHAPED 125
CROSS - I & DOUBLE T SHAPED 126
CROSS - SILVER 126
CRUMB BEADS - See beads - crumb 46
CRYSTAL 126
CUBS - GOLD 126
CUNEIFORM - See Clay Tablets 107
CUSCUS TEETH 127
CYPRAEA MONETA - See Cowry Shell Money . . . 118

DAFI. 127
DAGGER MONEY - See Kris 127
DALA 128
DAMBA - See abrus precatorius 11
DANGANGTANG 128
DANKI - See Bowls 90
DAO. 128
DAP - See ndap. 236
DAPI. 128
DAU BEADS - See beads - pagadua necklace 60
DAUYOYO - See Bagi 28
DAVE ALAVA 128
DAVERI. 128
DE 129
DEDEGE NECKLACE MONEY - See nassa shell. . . 235
DEER SKIN MONEY 129
DENTALIUM SHELL MONEY 130
DEOGANTA 131
DI - See Axe - Papua New Guinea, Mt Hagen 17
DI KURUGU - See Axe money - Papua New Guinea, Mt. Hagen 17
DIBANDA. 131
DIBIDIBI 131
DICE. 131
DIHUNGA - See liganda 202
DIMBO - See earrings central Sulawesi. 135
DISK - See Quartz Disk 273
DISK - See To-Uba. 355
DISK - See Tyere 361
DIWARRA. 131
DJIMBU 132
DOA - See liganda 202
DOBA 132
DOG TEETH MONEY 132
DOGA 133
DOGON BEADS - See beads - dogon 46
DOIT - See Rooster Money 288
DOLPHIN SHAPE - See Fish Coin 145
DOLPHIN TEETH - See Porpoise Teeth 264
DONGO - See bubi 91
DONKEY BEADS - See Beads donkey. 46
DONUT BEADS - See beads - donut 47
DOREI 134
DOUBLE SPIRAL 134
DOWEL MONEY. 134
DRIED SKIN - See Beaver Skin Money 77
DRIED SKIN - See Raccoon Skin Money 274
DRUM MONEY 134
Garamut drum. 135
DUBALIN - See Clam Shell Armbands 106
DUBIL 135
DUFFLES 135
DUGONG TEETH 135
DUPA - See Jembe. 169
DUTCH BEADS - See beads - dutch. 47
DZI BEADS - See Beads - dzi 48
EAGLE FEATHERS 135
EAR ORNAMENTS 135
EARRINGS 135
EBALE - See Ingonda 163
EBONY & SILVER BEADS - See beads - ebony & silver 64
EBUNI 136
EFUFY - See Ogoja Penny 244
EGG COWRY - See cowry - West New Guinea . . . 118
EGG MONEY - CHICKEN 139
EKIPA 139
ELEPHANT TAIL HAIR MONEY 140
ELK TEETH MONEY 140
EMPRESS BEADS - See beads - seed. 48
EMPUTE - See ibaka 161
ENSUBA - TRIANGULAR. 140
ENSUBA - POTATO MASHER TYPE 140
ERENGE 140
ERMINE 140
EVODIA SEED MONEY 140
EWUL. 141
EXCHANGE STONES. 141
EXECUTION KNIFE 141
EYE BEADS - See beads - eye. 49
FACE BEADS - See beads - face 49
FAE - See Pearl Shell Money 247
FAI - See Pearl Shell Money. 247
FALSE CHEVRON BEADS - See beads false chevrons 49
FANCY BEADS - See beads - fancy. 49
FANG AXES 141
FARAVEL - See Cloth - faravel 108
FE - See Pearl Shell Money, Stone Money - Yap . . 247
FEATHER BEADS - See beads - feather 49
FEATHER COIL 142
FEATHER MONEY 143
FEATHER STICK MONEY 144
FEATHERS - See Axe money 26
FELT MONEY 144
FERGHI CLOTH - See cloth - Ethiopia 108
FIANCE BEADS - See beads - fiance. 50
FIGURE 8 MONEY 144
FINGERS. 144
FIRAE 145
FISH 145
FISH COIN 145
FISH HOOK MONEY 145
FISH TEETH 146
FLINT 146
FLOWER MONEY - See Willow Leaf Money. 379
FLUSH EYE BEADS - See beads - flush eye 50
FLYING FOX FUR 146
FLYING FOX JAWS 146
FLYING FOX TEETH 146
FOX FUR 147
FRENCH AMBASSADOR BEADS - See beads - French ambassador 50
FRESHWATER PEARL BEADS - See beads - freshwater

pearl 50
FUNERAL MONEY - See Burial Money. 98
FUR 147
FURA 147
FUSIL - See gun money 153
GABAELA 147
GABAGA - See Cloth, Nigeria 108
GAIMA - See Axe - Papua New Ginea, Mt. Hagen . 17
GAJAH - See Gambar 148
GALIA 147
GAM - See Bailer Shell 29
GAMBAR 148
GANEKHE - See Je stone 168
GANFUR - See salt - Africa, Ethopia 289
GARNET BEADS - See beads - garnet 50
GAU 148
GAWAGAMBA - See ochre - Papua New Guinea . 243
GHISI - See Kissi Penny 179
GHOST BEADS - See beads - ghost 50
GHOST-FACE MONEY 149
GILE 149
GIN CURRENCY 149
GINIUBA - See Kula 189
GIN KWAN - See Ring Money - Japan 280
GIQUIPILLI - See Cocoa Bean Money 114
GIRAFFE'S HAIR AND TAIL MONEY 149
GIRAGIRA 149
GIRDLE MONEY - See Belt Money 81
GITZI - See Kissi Penny 179
GLASS BEADS - See beads - glass 50
GLASS WEIGHTS 150
GO MOMME - See Bar money 32
GOAT 150
GOBAELA 150
GOLD DUST MONEY 150
GOLD CUBS - See cubs - gold 126
GOLD-GLASS BEADS - See beads - gold-glass 50
GOLD LIP SHELL - See Kina Shell 176
GOLD WEIGHTS - See Weights 375
GONG 151
GOOSEBERRY BEADS - See - gooseberry 50
GOOSE QUILLS - See Quill Money 273
GRAIN CURRENCY 151
GRANITE BEADS - See beads - granite 51
GRATER MONEY - See Gridiron money 152
GREEN SNAIL SHELL 151
GREENSTONE - See Axe Money, Nephrite 17
GRIDIRON MONEY 152
GRIVNA 152
GRIWNA KUN - See Squirrel Skin 314
GUADALCANAL SHIELD - See Shield Money - Guadalcanal 303
GUBKAS CLOTH - See cloth - gubkas 108
GUBKAS - See Cloth money - gubkedi 108
GUM MONEY 152
GUNS 152
GUN MONEY 154
GUNPOWDER 154
H CROSS - See Cross "H" Shaped 125
HABO - See Je stone 168
HACIENDA TOKEN - See Leather 201
HAIR MONEY - See Human Hair Money 160
HAIRPIN MONEY - See Larin 199
HAKATA - See Shell Ring 296
HAKUNA - See Needle money, Ethiopia 238
HALBERD-HEAD MONEY 155
HALIOTIS - See abalone shell 155
HANDA 155
HANG - See bar money - (Vietnam) - banana bar . . 32
HANSATSU 155
HARISH BEADS - See beads - harish 51
HASHSHASH 155
HAT MONEY 156
HATO IME 156
HAWKBELL 156
HDE - See Kundja 196
HEAD - See Cowry Shell 118
HEAD MONEY - See Human Head Money 160
HEAD TAX TOKEN 156
HEADBAND MONEY 156
HEAVEN BANK NOTES - See burial money 98
HEBRON BEADS - See beads - Hebron 51
HELL BANK NOTES - See burial money 98
HIDES - See - Axe money 26
HINUILI 157
HIPPO BEADS - See - beads - hippo 51
HIPPOPOTAMUS TOOTH 157
HIRI TRADING SYSTEM 157
HO - See DE 129
HOBO NICKEL 157
HOE MONEY - See Axe Money 17
HOE MONEY - See Hashshash 155
HOE MONEY - See Jembe 169
HOE MONEY - See Khasu 176
HOE MONEY - See Sakania 289
HOE MONEY - See Shoka 306
HOE MONEY - See Spade Money 312
HOKATA 158
HOLLANDAIS CLOTH - See - cloth - hollandais . . 108
HONEY 158
HOOK - See Fish Hook money 145
HORIM 159
HORNBILL BEAK 159
HORSE 159
HORSESHOES 159
HUBBELL BEADS - See Beads - hubbell 51
HUDSON BAY BEADS - See Beads - Hudson Bay . 51
HUDSON BAY BLANKET - See Blanket Money - Hudson Bay 84
HUMAN HAIR 160
HUMAN HEAD MONEY 160
HUMAN TEETH 160
HUON GULF TRADE NETWORK 160
HUT TAX TOKEN 160

I'A'AFU - See Porpoise teeth 161
IBAKA. 161
IBOKA CLOTH - See cloth - Africa, Zaire 161
IHRIK 161
IKAKALAKA 161
IKAT CLOTH. 161
IKONGA. 161
IKUL KNIFE. 162
IKUMI. 162
IKUL IMBAANG 162
ILOON 163
IMPANDE SHELLS. 163
IMUN 163
INDIAN CORN - See Grain Currency. 151
INDO-PACIFIC BEADS - See - indo-pacific. 52
INGONDA 163
INGOTS - See Mint Bars 223
INK. 163
INSIGNIAS - See Axe money 26
INTERLOCKING BEADS - See - beads -
interlocking 52
IRON 163
IRON BULLET OR BALL - See antimony lump 15
IRON DISC CURRENCY 164
IRON STRIP MONEY 164
ISAGALIA 164
ITUMA 164
IVORY 164
IYAYAW - See Ogoja Penny 244
IWENGA - See Kundja. 196
JACKET. 166
JADE BEADS - See - beads - jade 52
JAD STONE - See Je Stone 168
JADE MONEY - See Nephrite. 238
JADEITE - See Beads - jadeite. 52
JALLA BEADS - See - jalla 53
JASPER BEADS - See - beads - jasper 53
JAM 167
JARS 167
JASPER 168
JATIM BEADS - See - beads - jatim. 53
JAWS - See Flying Fox Jaws 146
JAWBONES. 168
JE STONES 168
JE OAK - See - je stones. 168
JEMBE. 169
JETAK 169
JIBBU 169
JOB'S TEAR NECKLACE. 169
JOM 170
KAFA 170
KABADIR CLOTH - See Cloth - kabadir 112
KAIN TIMOR CLOTH 170
KAIPWESI 170
KALO - See Whale teeth 378
KALOMA - See Kula 189
KANDANGEI SHELL MONEY 171
KANO BEADS - See - beads - kano 54
KANOTAR 171
K'A K'IM. 171
KAPKAP 171
KAPA 174
KAPUT - See mis. 223
KARIBUTU - See Kula 189
KASUYU - See zappozap. 382
KATALU'M BUL - See Kula 174
KATANGA CROSS - See Cross - Katanga. 124
KATONGA RING - See Nsambu. 241
KATUDABABILE - See Samakupa 294
KEDEGE EGO DOPE - See marsupial tooth. 217
KEELING-COCOS MONEY - See ivory 164
KALUSAPE - See kesa 174
KENA - See Bosu. 89
KESA. 174
KETE KOME 175
KETTLEDRUM - See Kyee-Zee 197
KETTLEDRUM - See Moko. 226
KEY MONEY - See Knife money. 180
KEY MONEY - See Lotus root money. 206
KHASU. 176
KIBANGWA BEADS - See - beads - conus shell . . . 44
KIFFA BEADS - See - beads - kiffa. 54
KILINDI - See Ring Money 275
KILINDI - See Kissi penny 179
KILONDA. 176
KIN - See Ring Money 275
KINA MOKA. 176
KINA SHELL MONEY. 176
KING BEADS - See - beads - king. 54
KINGS BURIAL BEADS - See - beads - kings burial . 54
KING MANILLA - See Manilla - King. 209
KIRANA - See bubi 344
KIRINGI 179
KIRKUB 179
KIRKUP - See nose ornament - Torres Straits 241
KISSI PENNY. 179
KITOMA - See Kula 189
KLILT 180
KLUK BEADS - See - beads - udoud 66
KNIFE MONEY - Africa - China 180
KO - See nko 240
KOBAN - See Plate Money 251
KOFU 187
KOI KNGAL - See cassowary 127
KOI KUNDIL - See cassowary 127
KOKO - See Rice 274
KOKONON 187
KOKONON LULUAI 188
KOLA-NUT. 188
KOLI BEADS - See - beads - koli 54
KONGA - See Boloko. 89
KOPPERPLATMYNT - See Swedish plate. 252
KOSO. 188
KOTTA - See cowry 118

KPINGA - See throwing knife . . . 344
KRIS . . . 188
KROBO BEADS - See - beads - krobo . . . 54
KROO - See Palm Oil . . . 247
KUDATAMA . . . 188
KUNDUN - See Axe money - Papua New Guinea, Mt. Hagen . . . 17
KUE . . . 188
KUKUMALI - See KULA . . . 189
KUL . . . 189
KULA RING . . . 189
KUMAL . . . 196
KUNDJA . . . 196
KUNE TYPES I & 2 . . . 196
KUNEDAWESI - See Kula . . . 189
KUNGA - See Boloko . . . 89
KUNTU - See Cloth - Nigeria . . . 109
KURAKANIKANA . . . 196
KURIA . . . 196
KURIRI . . . 197
KURUGU - See Axe money - Papua New Guinea, Mt. Hagen . . . 17
KWA . . . 197
KWALOI'A . . . 197
KWARI'INARI . . . 197
KYEE-ZEE . . . 197
LALAI . . . 198
LAND - SNAILS - See Kuriri . . . 197
LANGTANG - See Cloth - langtang . . . 108
LANKAN BEADS - See - lankan . . . 60
LANTANA BEADS - See - beads lantana . . . 55
LA'ONIASI . . . 198
LAPLAP . . . 199
LARIN . . . 199
LAT . . . 199
LEACH MONEY - See lats . . . 199
LEAF MONEY . . . 200
LEATHER MONEY . . . 201
LEECH MONEY - See lat - smooth . . . 199
LEGBAND . . . 201
LELA - See cannon money, Irian Jaya . . . 100
LENDU . . . 202
LEOPARD TEETH . . . 202
LERALE . . . 202
LET BEADS - See beads - let . . . 55
LEWIS & CLARK BEADS - See - beads - Lewis & Clark . . . 55
LIDERAN . . . 202
LIGANDA . . . 202
LIGOMO . . . 203
LIKONGA BLADE MONEY . . . 203
LIMA ABALA . . . 203
LIME STICK - See Bosu . . . 89
LIMESTONE RING MONEY . . . 203
LINDERAN . . . 203
LINE MONEY - See Leaf Money . . . 200
LINEN MONEY . . . 204
LINGEME - See bokona . . . 89
LINOLEUM MONEY . . . 204
LILY ROOT MONEY - See lotus root money . . . 206
LIPSTICK . . . 204
LIQUOR . . . 204
LIRALE - See lerale . . . 202
LITLATLA . . . 204
LLAMITAS - See Axe money . . . 26
LOAF - See Sycee . . . 322
LOBOLO . . . 204
LODA . . . 205
LOGGOH KULLUT . . . 205
LOGWOOD - (See Tukula) . . . 358
LOIN-CLOTH . . . 205
LOKOLOKO - See lalai . . . 198
LOKONGO . . . 205
LOKULA' LOMBOLE - See throwing knife . . . 344
LOLOE AMAS - See Loda . . . 205
LOLOI - See Diwarra . . . 131
LONGO - See Lokongo . . . 198
LORAN EARRINGS . . . 206
LOSIL - See Sek . . . 295
LOSOL - See tajere . . . 332
LOST WAX - See Animal Money . . . 14
LOTUS ROOT HEART MONEY . . . 206
LUKASU . . . 206
LUMBER . . . 206
LUKUT SEKALA BEADS - See - beads - lukut sekala 56
LUN BAWANG BEADS - See beads - lun bawang . . 56
LUTUKU CLOTH - See cloth - Africa, Zaire . . . 111
MA - See mortar & pestle . . . 231
MACCA BEADS - See - beads - macca . . . 56
MACKINAW BLANKET - See blanket . . . 84
MADIBA - See Cloth - Africa, Zaire . . . 108
MAE EXCHANGE . . . 206
MAGATAMA . . . 207
MAGNESITE BEADS - see - beads - magnesite . . . 56
MAHEE . . . 207
MAHOGANY - See Logwood . . . 358
MAI . . . 207
MAIRI . . . 207
MAIZE . . . 207
MALAKI . . . 207
MAMEITAGIN - See Bean Money . . . 77
MAMULI . . . 207
MANCHESTER COTTON - See - cloth - manchester108
MANDJANG . . . 209
MANGANESE EARTH . . . 209
MANILLA . . . 209
MANILLA- KING . . . 214
MANILLA - QUEEN . . . 214
MANILLA - PRINCE . . . 214
MANTIS - See Gambar . . . 148
MANUM - See mis . . . 223
MAPLE SUGAR . . . 215
MARAHA - See mat - Penecost . . . 217
MARALI . . . 215

MARANGGA 215
MARBLE BEADS - See - beads - marble 39
MARIA THERESA THALER 216
MARTIN SKIN 216
MARSUPIAL FUR MONEY. 216
MARSUPIAL TOOTH NECKLACE 217
MASKS 217
MAT MONEY 217
MATA - See kesa 174
MATTY ISLAND BELT MONEY - See Belt Money - Matty Island. 81
MAUAI 219
MAULAVATA 219
MAUWAI 219
MBADI 219
MBARI - See mbadi 219
MBAKIHA - See Poata 220
MBARAKE - See Poata 220
MBI - See lalai. 198
MBIU - See pele strings 248
MBOKOMO 220
MBOLE. 221
MBOSSO 221
MBUL - See mat - Yap 217
MEJIT - See beads, jade 52
MELEGRINA - See Kina Shell 176
MELO SHELL 221
MELON BEADS - See - beads - melon 57
MELOTE 221
MERBOK 222
MEZONG - See Zong 383
MIDJOKO. 222
MIHEI - See cloth - Africa, Zaire 111
MIKAK 222
MILLEFIORI BEADS - See - beads - millefiori 57
MING BEADS - See - beads - ming. 57
MIMBOSS. 222
MING BANK NOTE. 222
MING TAO - See Knife Money. 180
MINKATA 223
MINT BARS. 223
MIS. 223
MITAKO 224
MIU 224
MLE - See Cloth - mle. 113
MMBUL 225
MOKA 225
MOKO 226
MOMOGO - See headband. 158
MON CLOTH - See cloth, Indonesia 112
MONDJO - See Mandjong. 209
MONDONO. 228
MONEY COWRY - See Cowry Shell 118
MONEY SWORD 228
MONEY TREE 228
MOON MONEY - See Tingle Dangle Money 352
MOON SHELL - See Bailer shell 29
MOOSE SKIN 231
MORFIA BEADS - See - beads - morfia. 58
MORTAR AND PESTLE 231
MOTHER OF PEARL - See Abalone Shell 11
MOTHER-OF-PEARL GAMBLING TOKEN 231
MUI - See pele strings 248
MUNSEIA. 231
MUNSHI AXEHEAD 231
MURUKAKALI - See Salt - Papua New Guinea . . . 289
MUSCAVADO - See Sugar 322
MUSKET BALL 231
MUKUBA WA MATWI. 232
MUSANGA. 232
MUSINA. 202
MUSKET. 232
MUSUKU 232
MUTAGA 232
MUTIBATA BEADS - beads mutisalah. 58
MUTIRAJA BEADS - See - beads - mutiraja. 58
MWALI. 232
NADJATA - See Trombash 357
NAGA 234
NAGATA - See Trombash. 357
NAILS. 234
NAIPE - See Axe money 26
NAMATAWUK 235
NANA BEADS - See - beads - pipe. 60
NASSA SHELL MONEY 235
NAVELA 235
NAVOI 235
NDALA. 236
NDAP. 236
NDOA - See Liganda 202
NDOVU 237
NECK RING MONEY. 237
NEEDLE MONEY. 238
NEGAM - See obsidian 242
NELO 238
NENENENE - See Porpoise teeth 264
NEPHRITE. 238
NEPTUNES - See Basins. 37
NEWSPAPER. 239
NET BAG - See Bilum 82
NFWAYA BEADS - See - beads - nfwaya. 58
NGALA. 239
NGBAKA 239
NGBELE - See Liganda. 202
NGERN RING - See Bar Money 32
NGIELE - See Mitako 224
NGINDZA - See throwing knife 344
NGKE - See bell money. 80
NGOLO - See Execution Knife. 141
NGON HOI - See Tok 354
NGON HOI - See Willow Leaf. 379
NGWOLO - See throwing knife 344
NICKELS - See Wooden Nickels. 380
NILA BEADS - See - beads - nila 58

NJA - See Manilla - coiled 209
NKALARI - See - beads - coral 45
NKO 240
NKWA - See bokona 89
NNABUO 240
NOMBA - See feather coil 142
NOSE ORNAMENT MONEY 241
NOTGELD 241
NOVEAPU 241
NSAMBU 241
NTA - See cloth - NTA 109
NTCHANG 241
NTET - See Fang Axe 141
NTUM IRON MONEY 242
NUEVA CADIZ BEADS - See - nueva cadiz 58
NUTMEG-GRATER MONEY 242
NUTS - See Almonds, Areca Nuts 12
NZIMBU SHELLS 242
O SHELL PENDANT 242
OAN KEK CLOTH - See cloth - Indonesia 112
OATS - See Grain Currency 151
OBAN - See Plate Money 251
OBSIDIAN 242
OCHRE 243
OGOJA PENNY 244
OGOSI - See je stones 168
OKPOHO OKUK 244
OLIVE OIL 244
OLIVE SHELLS 244
OMAK 245
ONGANDA 245
OPIUM WEIGHTS - See Weights 375
OPOSSUM TEETH - See Cuscus Teeth 127
ORANGE COWRY - See cowry 118
ORCHID BARK 245
ORMU STONE - See Axe - Irian Jaya 17
O-RINKA - See rhinoceros horn 274
OSHELE - See Woshele 380
OSTRICH EGG SHELL BEADS - See - beads - ostrich 246
OSTRICH FEATHERS 246
OTSJ 246
OTTER - See Sea Otter 295
OX EYE BEADS - See - beads - white heart 46
OXEN 246
PAAZONG - See Mandjong 209
PACK SADDLE SYCEE MONEY 246
PADRE BEADS - See Beads - padre 59
PAGADUA NECKLACE - See - beads - pagadua . . . 60
PAGE 247
PAGN - See - cloth - Africa, Wolof 109
PANG-O- See - beads - pang-o 60
PALAY - See Rice 274
PALM OIL 247
PANDANUS MAT - See mat 217
PANTS - See Pu Money 272
PATA - See -beads - lun bawang 56
PAWN - See Turquoise 359
PEAS 247
PEARL BUTTON MONEY - See Buttons 99
PEARL SHELL MONEY 247
PEACE PIPE 247
PEARL 247
PEARL SHELL 248
PEKING GLASS BEADS - See - beads - peking 60
PELANGI BEADS - See - beads - pelangi 60
PELE STRINGS 248
PENDANTS 248
PEPPER MONEY 248
PESTLE - See Mortar and Pestle 231
PHALANGER - See marsupial tooth 217
PIG MONEY 248
PIG MOUTH MONEY 250
PIG TEETH 251
PIG TUSK - See boar tusks 87
PINGA - See pingha 251
PINGHA 251
PINYON PINE NUTS 251
PIPE BEADS - See - beads - pipe 60
PIRR - See pele strings 248
PLATE MONEY - Japan, Russia 251
SWEDISH PLATE MONEY 252
PLAYING CARD MONEY 258
POATA 261
POLAR BEAR TEETH - See Bear Teeth 77
POLYCHROME BEADS - See Beads - polychrome . . 60
PONY BEADS - See Beads - pony 61
PORCELAIN BEADS - See - beads - porcelain 61
PORCELAIN COINS 262
PORCUPINE QUILLS 264
PORPOISE TEETH 264
POSTAGE STAMP MONEY - See Stamp Money . . . 315
POTATO MASHER - See Ensuba 140
POTLATCH SHIELD - See Shield Money 303
POTLATCH 265
POT BEADS - See - beads - sandcast 61
POTS 270
POTUMA - See Bosu 89
POUND BEADS - See Beads - pound 61
POWDER BEADS - See - beads - sandcast 62
PRAKAB 272
PRAYER BEADS - See - beads - prayer 61
PRAYER BOOK MONEY 272
PRIEST BEADS - See - beads - sandcast 62
PRINCE MANILLA - See Manilla - Prince 214
PROSSER BEADS - See - beads - prosser 61
PU MONEY (now BU) 272
PUMTEK - See Beads - pumtek 61
PURR-PURR 273
PWOMONDAP 273
QUARTZ BALLS 273
QUARTZ DISK 273
QUACHTLI 273
QUAQUA CLOTH - See - cloth - quaqua 108

QUEEN MANILLA - See Manilla - Queen 214
QUETZAL FEATHER MONEY 273
QUILL MONEY - See Gold Dust Money 273
QUIRANDA - See Bubi currency 92
RACCOON SKIN MONEY 274
RAFFIA CLOTH - See Cloth - raffia 109
RAGIDUP CLOTH - See Indonesia 316
RAI - See Stone Money - Yap 197
RAIN DRUM - See Kyee Zee. 197
RAPHIA CLOTH - See Cloth - Zaire 109
RAT MONEY 274
RATI SEEDS - See abrus precatorius 11
RAWHIDE TOKEN - See Leather 201
RAY 274
RAZOR - See Knife Money 180
REINDEER 274
RHINOCEROS HORN 274
RICE 274
RII - See Porpoise teeth 264
RING MONEY. 275
RING MONEY - See Mutaga 232
RING MONEY - See Legband 201
RING MONEY - See Limestone Ring 203
RING MONEY - See Litlatla 204
RING MONEY - See Manilla 209
RING MONEY - See Mbakiha 220
RING MONEY - See Mbarake 220
RING MONEY - See Minkata 223
RING MONEY - See Mitako 224
RING MONEY - See Navela 235
RING MONEY - See Neck Ring Money 237
RING MONEY - See Nsambu. 241
RING MONEY - See Poata 261
RING MONEY - See Shell Money. 296
RING MONEY - See Tridacna Arm Ring 357
RING MONEY - See Unus 361
ROANOKE - See wampum 287
ROD MONEY 288
ROKKE - See flying fox teeth 146
ROMAN BEADS - See - beads - roman. 62
RONGEI NA GAUNI 288
ROOSTER MONEY 288
ROTL 288
RUBBER 288
RUG MONEY 288
RUM MONEY 288
RUSSIAN TRADE BEADS - See Beads - Russian . . . 62
RYE - See Grain Currency 151
SABAGORAR 289
SABER MONEY - See knife money 180
SABLE 289
SADDLE SYCEE MONEY - See Pack Saddle
Money 246
SAGALI - See bundles 96
SAK - See Sek. 295
SAKANIA 289
SAMAKUPA - See Kula 189
SALAKA - See kesa 174
SALT MONEY 289
SAMAKUPA SHELL MONEY 294
SALT WATER SOAP CAKES - See Soap Cakes 311
SANDALWOOD 294
SANDCAST BEADS - See - beads - sandcast 62
SANTA CRUZ FEATHER COIL - See Feather Coil. . 141
SAPI-SAPI 294
SAUAD. 294
SAVI 295
SCARAB 295
SCHNAPPS 295
SEA OTTER 295
SEAL SKIN NOTE - See Walrus Skin Money 364
SEALING WAX - See Wax. 375
SEDABALA 295
SEED BEADS - See - beads - seed. 63
SEEDS - See Abrus precatorius. 11
SEEDS - See Banana Seeds. 31
SEEDS - See Evodia Seed Money 140
SEEDS - See Tamarind Seeds 334
SEK. 295
SEN BAR MONEY 296
SHAN SYCEE - See Sycee - Burma 322
SHARK VERTEBRAE. 296
SHEEP. 296
SHEEP SKIN TOKENS 296
SHELL BEADS - See - beads - shell 63
SHELL RINGS - See rings 275
SHELL MONEY 296
SHIELD MONEY 303
SHIRT - See Pu Money. 272
SHOKA. 306
SHONGO - See Woshele. 380
SIAM (BRASS OR COPPER) GAMBLING TOKENS. 306
SIAM (LEAD) GAMBLING TOKENS 306
SIAM (PORCELAIN) GAMBLING TOKENS - See
Porcelain coins 262
SIEGE MONEY 306
SILW'AE 307
SILK MONEY 307
SILVER 307
SILVER BAR - See Mint Bars 223
SILVER BEADS - See - beads - silver 64
SIMBOS OR SIMBU SHELLS - See Olive Shells. . . 244
SINNET. 308
SIRIPIYA 308
SITIM 308
SKIN - See Martin Skin Money 216
SKIN - See Moose Skin 231
SKIN - See Raccoon Skin Money 274
SKIN - See Sable Skin 289
SKIN - See Sea Otter 295
SKIN - See Squirrel Skin 314
SKIN - See Walrus Skin Money 364
SKIRTS 308
SKUNK BEADS - See - beads - skunk 64

SLAVES . . . 308
SNAIL SHELLS - See Musanga . . . 232
SNAIL SHELLS - See Ikumi . . . 162
SNAIL SHELLS - See Kiringi . . . 179
SNAKE BEADS - See - beads - snake . . . 64
SNAKE MONEY . . . 311
SOAP MONEY . . . 311
SOLEVU . . . 311
SOM . . . 311
SO-SO BEADS - See - beads - so-so . . . 64
SOSOROFA . . . 312
SOULAVA - See Bagi . . . 28
SOUNAVA - See Bagi . . . 28
SPADE MONEY . . . 312
SPEAR MONEY . . . 312
SPEARHEAD MONEY - See Ikonga . . . 161
SPEARHEAD MONEY - See Liganda . . . 202
SPEARHEAD MONEY - See Mahee . . . 207
SPEARHEAD MONEY - See Naga . . . 234
SPEARS - See Mimboss . . . 222
SPEAR THROWER . . . 314
SPERM WHALE - See Whale Tooth . . . 378
SPICES . . . 314
SPIKE - DUTSI . . . 314
SPIRAL CURRENCY . . . 314
SPONDYLUS SHELLS - See - beads - spondylus . . . 64
SQUIRREL SKIN . . . 314
STAMP MONEY . . . 315
STICKS - See Tally Sticks . . . 333
STOCKFISH . . . 316
STONE AXE - See Axe Money . . . 17
STONE BEADS - See - beads - stone . . . 65
STRIPED BEADS - See - beads - striped . . . 65
YAP STONE MONEY . . . 316
STONES . . . 321
STONE RING - See Navela . . . 235
STRAW TIN . . . 322
STRING MONEY . . . 322
SUGAR . . . 322
SWEDISH PLATE MONEY - See Plate Money . . . 252
SWORD - See Knife Money, Money Sword . . . 180
SWORD GUARD . . . 322
SYCEE . . . 322
TABU - see tambu . . . 335
T SHAPED AXE - See Axe Money . . . 17
TAFULIAE' . . . 330
TALHAKIMT PENDANTS - See - beads - talhakimt . 65
TAI GANDJA - See Earrings, Central Sulawesi, Indonesia . . . 135
TAIL - See Elephant Tail . . . 140
TAIL - See Giraffe Tail Hair . . . 149
TAIL - See Zebra Hair Money . . . 382
TAILPUN - See Turbo Shell . . . 359
TAIJANA . . . 332
TAI GANDJA - See earrings - central Sulawesi . . . 135
TAJADERAS - See Axe money - Mexico . . . 17
TAJERE . . . 332
TAKA . . . 332
TAKULAKOLA - See skirts . . . 308
TALARI - See Maria Theresa dollar . . . 216
TALENT . . . 333
TALI . . . 333
TALIBUM - See Green Snail Shell . . . 151
TALINA . . . 333
TALINA BARIONO . . . 333
TALLY STICKS . . . 333
TAIK . . . 334
TAMARIND SEEDS . . . 334
TAMBU . . . 335
TAMBUA - See Whale Tooth . . . 378
TAMLUNG - See K'a k'im . . . 171
TAMPANG . . . 336
TAN - See Feather Coil - Santa Cruz . . . 141
TAO - See knife, China . . . 180
TAPA CLOTH . . . 336
TAPSOKA . . . 336
TARKOLA . . . 337
TARNEIH . . . 351
TAU - See Feather Coil . . . 141
TAUS - See Shield, Canada . . . 303
TAUTAU . . . 337
TAVAU - See Feather Coil - Santa Cruz . . . 141
TEA MONEY . . . 337
TEE - CEREMONY . . . 340
TEETH - See Bat Teeth . . . 37
TEETH - See Boar Teeth . . . 84
TEETH - See Cuscus Teeth . . . 127
TEETH - See Dog Teeth . . . 132
TEETH - See Dugong Teeth . . . 135
TEETH - See Elephant Teeth . . . 164
TEETH - See Elk Teeth . . . 140
TEETH - See Fish Teeth . . . 146
TEETH - See Flying Fox Teeth . . . 146
TEETH - See Hippo Teeth . . . 157
TEETH - See Human Teeth . . . 160
TEETH - See Leopard Teeth . . . 202
TEETH - See Opossum Teeth . . . 127
TEETH - See Porpoise Teeth . . . 127
TEETH - See Sperm Whale Teeth . . . 378
TEETH - See Walrus Teeth . . . 364
TEETH - See WhaleTeeth . . . 378
TEKARORO . . . 343
TEKE NECKLACE . . . 343
TEKE - See mitako . . . 224
TELSUM BEADS - See - beads - telsum . . . 65
TEMA . . . 343
TEMO . . . 343
TEMOTU - See Feather Coil - Santa Cruz . . . 141
TER MAWON - See shell - New Caledonia . . . 296
TETITI SHELL BELT . . . 343
THIMBLES . . . 343
THROWING KNIFE . . . 344
TICTACTOE BEADS - See - beads - tictactoe . . . 65
TIGER COWRY - See cowry - Papua New Guinea. 118

TIGER TONGUE - See Lat 199
TILI - See salt - Papua New Guinea, Yandapu 289
TIN ANIMAL MONEY - See Gambar 148
TIN MONEY 351
TIN INGOT MONEY 351
TIN RING MONFY 351
TIN STRAW MONEY 351
TINALE COWRY - See cowry - West New Guinea. 118
TINETE 351
TINGALA COWRY - See cowry -
West New Guinea 118
TINTOL - See shell money - Tanga 303
TIN FOIL MONEY - See Aluminum Foil 13
TIN HAT MONEY - See Hat Money 156
TINGLE DANGLE MONEY 352
TINNAH - See Shield 303
TOBACCO 352
TOEA - Shell arm rings - See Mwali 232
TOGO STONE - See Quartz disk 273
TOK 354
TOKA - See porcelian coins 262
TOKEN - See Head tax token 157
TOKEN - See Hut tax token 160
TOKEN - See Leather 201
TOKEN - See Mother- of-Pearl 231
TOLUK 355
TOMENDA BEADS - See - beads - pipe 60
TO'ONILOBO 355
TORTOISE - See Crocodile Money 124
TORTOISE - See Gambar 148
TORTOISE - See Nose Ornament. 241
TORTOISE - See Turtle Shell 359
TORTOISE SHELL MONEY 359
TORTOISE SHELL ARMBANDS - See Navoi 359
TOSI BEADS - See - beads - tosi 65
TOUAU 355
TO-UBA 355
TOWEELAH - See Larin 199
TRADING AXE - See Axe Money 17
TRADE-WIND BEADS - See Beads - trade-wind . . . 65
TRADE GUN. 152
TRADE SILVER 355
TREE - See Money Tree 228
TRIDACNA CARVINGS 357
TRIDACNA RING 357
TRIODIA GUM - See Gum Money 152
TROMBASH 357
TSERA. 357
TUGUDU CLOTH - See Cloth - Nigeria, Tiv. 109
TUKULA 358
TULA 359
TURBO SHELL 359
TURKEDI - See Cloth - turkedi 108
TURMERIC POWDER 359
TURQUOISE 359
TURQUOISE BEADS - See - beads - turquoise 66
TURTLE SHELL MONEY 359
TUSK - See Dentalium Shell Money 130
TUSK - See Ivory 164
TUSK - See Walrus Tusk Money 364
TUSKER - See Pig Money 248
TYERE 361
U-shaped bar - See bar - Africa 32
U-shaped bar - See mbole 221
UDOUD - See Beads - udoud. 66
ULAWA SHELL MONEY 361
ULOS CLOTH 361
UMBU 361
UMUMU 361
UNABURU - See Porpoise teeth. 264
UNUS 361
URAKEMBAUM 362
USU USU 362
UTUTE 362
URUA CROSS - See Handa 155
UWAO - See dangangtang. 128
VASELINE BEADS - See - beads - vaseline 68
VAYGUA 362
VAYGUA - See Bagi. 28
VEGETABLE PEELER - See Kula 180
VENETIAN BEADS - See - beads - venetian. 68
VERTEBRAE - See Shark Vertebrae 296
VULA 362
VULA KASOKA - See vula 362
VULA MISI - See vula 362
WADMAL 363
WAKALA 189
WALRUS SKIN MONEY. 364
WALRUS TUSK MONEY 364
WAMPUM 365
WAPITI - See Elk Teeth Money 140
WARAZ 374
WAURI 374
WAX. 375
WEA WUNU WONA - See earrings 135
WEIGHTS - GOLD 375
WELA 378
WHALE TOOTH 378
WHEAT - See Grain Currency 151
WHISKEY MONEY 379
WHITE HEART BEADS - See - beads - white heart . 68
WHITE STAG NOTES 379
WILDCAT SKIN. 379
WILLOW LEAF MONEY 379
WIRE MONEY. 380
WOTI SHELL - See Melo shell 221
WOOD - See Tukula 358
WOOD BEADS - See - beads - wood 68
WOODEN BEAD MONEY. 380
WOODEN NICKELS 380
WOODPECKER SCALPS 380
WOOL 380
WOSHELE. 380
Y-SHAPED - See Ogoja Penny 244

YAKARD - See Ogoja Penny 244
YAMS 380
YAO STONES 380
YAP ISLAND STONE - See Stone Money. 316
YAR - See Yar nu au. 381
YAR NU AU 381
YAR Nn VALEU - See yar nu au 381
YAWOVAU - See bundles 96
YAPAGATU - See bundles 96
YERAK 381
YOKE - See Tingle Dangle Money 352
YELA - See ndap 236
YELA - See nko. 240
YUA - See ring - Papua New Guinea 275
ZAPPOZAP. 382
ZARU 382
ZEBRA TAIL MONEY 382
ZEN BEADS - See - beads - zen 68
ZIKU. 382
ZIMBABWE H CROSS - See Cross H Shaped 125
ZIMBU 382
ZIMMER - See Fox Fur. 147
ZONG 383